BASIC ANIMAL NUTRITION AND FEEDING
THIRD EDITION

D. C. Church, Ph.D.
Professor Emeritus
Department of Animal Science
Oregon State University
Corvallis, Oregon

W. G. Pond, Ph.D.
Nutrition Leader
US Meat Animal Research Center
Clay Center, Nebraska

WILLEY
John Wiley & Sons
New York · Chichester ·
Brisbane · Toronto · Singapore

Library of Congress Cataloging in Publication Data:

Church, D. C.
  Basic animal nutrition and feeding.

  Includes indexes.
  1. Animal nutrition.   2. Feeds.   I. Pond, Wilson G.,
1930–   .   II. Title.

SF95.C47   1988   636.08′52   87-29534

Printed in the United States of America

10 9 8 7 6 5 4

Preface

THIS BOOK, AS WITH the first two editions, is
intended for students or other readers interested
in the principles as well as the application of animal
nutrition. As such, it is assumed that the reader
will have a minimal knowledge of general
chemistry, preferably some exposure to organic
and biochemistry, and some understanding of
animal biology and husbandry.

Over the past 60 years there have been
tremendous advances made in animal nutrition and
related fields. We are at the point now where
essentially all of the essential nutrients have been
identified. It is still possible that some additional
mineral elements may be determined to be
essential, and it is also possible that one or more
vitamins may be added to the list. However, all of
the known nutrients appear to be adequate to
sustain animals on purified diets, therefore, any
unidentified nutrients surely are not too important
or are required in extremely small amounts. This
is not to say that all of the nutritionally-related
problems have been solved because much remains
to be learned about nutrition and infectious disease,
nutrition and many different stresses, and about
various nutritional interrelationships. One is
reminded of the comment by an anonymous person
"That meeting nutritional needs is like filling a
barrel to the nearest knothole. When the knothole
is plugged, you can then proceed to fill the barrel
up to the next knothole". Consistent with other
sciences, as the head of water builds up, it puts
more stresses on small unseen or unknown holes
which may then spring a leak. In the writers' view

we have the big knotholes plugged, but many small leaks remain to be plugged and new leaks may be expected to appear from time to time.

In any event, with a book of this type there is always a question of how much and what type of detail to present to the reader. The authors' preconception of the audience for the book may be correct and then it may not. Consequently, it is a matter of picking and choosing what to include or exclude. For this reason historical coverage has been omitted. More space could have been allotted on any of the subjects. For some readers there may be more information on nutrient metabolism than they might desire. Others will probably wish for more complete coverage in Part III on applied nutrition, especially with respect to more complete discussion of the various species and classes of animals. Regardless of the approach, some areas or subjects must be slighted in order to keep the size of the book within bounds and at a reasonable cost. Whatever the deficiencies of this book may be, it is hoped that it will serve a useful purpose by covering in broad scope a complicated and voluminous subject, and that it will serve to guide the student through the important areas of basic and applied animal nutrition.

D. C. Church and W. G. Pond

Table of Contents

PART I—INTRODUCTION

PART II—NUTRIENT METABOLISM

PART 1

INTRODUCTION

Nutrition and Its Importance in Modern Agriculture

NUTRITION IS A SUBJECT that interests many casual readers simply because they must eat to live and because, for most people, eating and drinking are pleasurable social experiences. If one needs added incentives to become familiar with the subject, there is the profit motive if one is dealing with domestic animals, or simply the desire to know more about the animal body, its functions, and its needs. In animal agriculture, adequate feeding of animals for production of meat, milk, eggs, or fiber is an essential component of the total enterprise. With regard to human nutrition it can be demonstrated very easily that nutrition may affect health and welfare, emotions, physical capabilities, and susceptibility to and recovery from disease; there is also the likelihood that the infirmities of old age may be delayed by adequate nutrition.

What is nutrition? A dictionary may define nutrition as "being nourished" or "the series of processes by which an organism takes in and assimilates food for promoting growth and replacing worn or injured tissue." These are, obviously, very simplified definitions. Nutrition today, as practiced by competent professionals, requires that the nutritionist be knowledgeable with respect not only to the nutrients, their function, occurrence, and to various interactions, but also with animal behavior and management, digestive physiology, and some aspects of biochemistry and analytical chemistry. In addition, knowledge is required in the fields of crop and soil science, endocrinology, bacteriology, genetics, and disease as related to nutrient needs and dietary requirements.

Although a very wide base of knowledge may be necessary for a thorough understanding of the subject, this is not to say that most people will not benefit from some knowledge of the fundamentals of animal nutrition. For example, one does not need to be a complete nutritionist to appreciate that vitamins are important to the animal body and that they may be required in different amounts during growth, maintenance, or lactation.

Animal nutritional science is partly the outgrowth of observations by animal husbandryists and livestock feeders over many centuries and, more recently, by teachers and scientists. Consulting nutritionists and veterinarians also provide input, particularly on aspects of applied nutrition. The quantitative aspects—the ability to describe nutrient requirements for different species in various situations, definition of deficiency signs and symptoms, and the metabolism of nutrients—are the result of countless experiments carried out by scientists throughout the world, primarily with domestic and laboratory animals, but also with various animal tissues or microorganisms and, to a lesser extent, with humans. For example, the laboratory rat has made a tremendous (but involuntary) contribution to our knowledge of vitamins, amino acids, minerals, and toxicants. The dog played an important part in the discovery of insulin and the discovery of the role of nicotinic acid in the prevention and cure of pellegra, and the guinea pig was the animal model used to elucidate the cause and prevention of scurvy.

Hamsters, monkeys, and other laboratory species have all played a role in expansion of the knowledge of nutrition.

Nutritional science has progressed at a rapid rate because of the availability of different types of models (tissue cultures, bacteria, laboratory animals, etc.) to substitute for various domestic species or humans. Such procedures have been used to collect and develop information that might be impossible to obtain with the target species. This may be so because of the cost or the inability to subject animals (humans, in particular) to a research regimen for a long enough time to get meaningful results.

Nutrition, as with other biological sciences, does not have the precision that is possible in a physical science. This is primarily because biological organisms are quite variable. In higher animals, geneticists say that no two are exactly alike; also, the environments that any two animals are exposed to are nearly always different, thus nutrient needs are apt to be different.

Animal nutrition, as practiced today, requires that the nutritionist be able to formulate diets, rations, or supplemental feeds that are sufficiently appetizing to ensure an intake adequate (but not necessarily maximal) for the purposes desired. He or she must nearly always take into account the cost of the supplemental or total mixture, and formulated rations should supply adequate nutrients without detrimental imbalances for the desired level of production. He or she must take into account the need for and required level of growth promotants, medicants, or other non-nutritive additives. In addition, the rations so formulated must have adequate milling, mixing, handling, and storage properties. A nutritionist may be called on to know or to do numerous other things, but these functions would seem to be the minimum that should be expected.

The great increase in the body of scientific nutritional information in the past 50 years has resulted in the specialization of nutritionists as with scientists in other fields. The first broad classification would be either human or animal nutrition. In human nutrition, clinical nutrition is an important field that deals with such subspecialities as weight reduction, dietetics, prenatal care, inborn diseases, diabetes, pediatrics, parenteral nutrition (given by means other than oral), and other similar topics. Community nutritionists are involved in such areas as nutrition education and school lunch programs, and those in commerce work in areas of marketing and nutritional evaluation of food products.

In the animal field, most nutritionists specialize in either nutrition or monogastric (simple-stomached) or ruminant (multicompartmented stomach) animals. Those dealing with monogastric species may be involved with poultry (chickens, turkeys, ducks, geese, etc.), swine, horses, pets (dogs, cats), fish and other aquatic species (relatively new), laboratory species (rats, mice, guinea pigs, monkeys, etc.) or captive animals in zoos. In the ruminant fields, specialities include sheep, goats, wild or captive species, dairy cattle, and beef cattle, the latter often being divided into cow–calf and feedlot specialities. As in other scientific areas, specialization allows the individual to become and stay more familiar with new literature and commercial practices than if one attempts to keep abreast of the total field of animal nutrition.

In addition to the previously mentioned specialities, it is rather common (particularly in the animal field) to find that one group of individuals tends to be highly oriented toward laboratory work and the biochemical metabolism of nutrients—often on a subcellular basis. Another group is more oriented toward animal production (whole animal or orientation toward organs rather than toward cellular or subcellular metabolism). Of course, different areas of expertise are required to do amino acid analyses of protein than are required to collect data on animal performance, egg quality, and so on. In practice, teams of individuals with different specialities often produce more complete and imaginative research results than the same people when working individually.

❑ CURRENT STATE OF THE ART

The great French chemist, Antoine Lavoisier (1743–1794), is often referred to as the founder of the science of nutrition. Following the early studies in the eighteenth century, progress was relatively slow in the nineteenth century. The need for protein, fat, and carbohydrates was recognized and most of the research emphasis was on these nutrients or energy utilization along with a gradual development of data for some of the mineral elements. The major portion of our knowledge of nutrition has been developed since the 1920s when some of the vitamins were first discovered. Since that time there has been a great accumulation of data on vitamins, the role of amino acids, essential fatty acids, macro- and microminerals, energy metabolism, and on nutrient requirements and nutrient deficiencies.

Today, we recognize more than 40 nutrients are needed in the animal diet (the number depends on the animal species) in contrast to the three nutrients that were recognized early in the nineteenth century. There is still some uncertainty on some of the mineral elements, and some nutritionists believe that additional vitamins will be discovered. Certainly, the unknown nutrients must not be highly important (or are needed in very small amounts) since domestic animals can be maintained through a complete reproduction cycle when fed purified diets made up of such ingredients as cellulose, starch, sugar, fat, purified proteins such as casein, mixtures of mineral salts, and purified vitamin sources.

Developments in nutrition have been facilitated greatly by improved analytical techniques (see Ch. 3) and a vastly greater knowledge of chemistry and biochemistry, animal physiology, and other related sciences. It has been only in recent years that data have been developed to show that some of the mineral elements may be required by animals. Information on mineral nutrition, in particular, has been greatly facilitated by instrumentation capable of detecting some of these elements in the parts per billion range.

Nutrient needs for chickens have been defined more precisely than for any other domestic species. The requirements of chickens for amino acids, essential fatty acids, fat- and water-soluble vitamins, energy, protein, and most of the minerals are known with reasonable certainty. Such information is less available for swine and even less so for horses and rabbits. Likewise, information for ruminant animals (cattle, sheep, goats) is less precise than that for chickens.

There are several explanations for these differences. One primary reason is that poultry are grown under much more uniform conditions than other domestic species. Broiler or layers are usually hybrids and many of the birds in a flock will be full sibs, both factors resulting in more uniform flocks. In addition, the age and weight of broilers that are marketed is relatively uniform and they usually are grown under rather similar conditions regardless of the geographical location. Furthermore, there is a tendency to feed them very similar diets, regardless of where the birds are grown. All of these factors make it less difficult to determine the nutrient needs of chickens (or turkeys) compared to other species.

There has been a gradual and continual improvement in commercial diets, resulting in more efficient animal production. One example of the effect of such changes is shown in Table 1.1, which compares performance of hens fed a diet typical of 1951 with a diet typical of 1977. This demonstration was done with 1977 birds fed 1951 and 1977 diets. Note that longevity, egg production, efficiency of feed utilization, and costs have been improved considerably during this period. Genetic improvements also have been made in the birds, but this example was not designed to show such changes. In general, the same trend in nutrient utilization and increased production is evident for the other domestic species, although the amount of improvement probably has been greater for poultry because of some of the reasons mentioned previously.

In the field of human nutrition, even with our relatively advanced knowledge on the topic, malnutrition remains a very important factor in the underdeveloped and developing countries and among the poor in other countries. Surveys that have been taken by world health organizations indicate that very important problems for the young include nutritional marasmus (deficiency of energy, protein and possibly other nutrients), kwasiorkior (deficiency of protein quality and/or quantity), and vitamin A deficiency. For all ages, iodine deficiency (goiter) and nutritional anemias (iron, vitamin B_{12}, folic acid, and other nutrients) remain severe problems.

TABLE 1.1 Egg production data on 1951 and 1977 formulas[a]

ITEM	FEED[b]		1977 AS % OF 1951
	1951	1977	
Mortality, %	10.6	7.5	70.8
Egg production, %	65.9	76.4	115.9
Egg production, av.	104.5	123.2	117.9
Feed/doz, eggs, lb	3.57	3.12	87.4
Egg wt, oz/doz	23.1	23.9	103.5
Pounds feed/lb eggs	2.47	2.08	84.6
Return over feed cost/hen, $	1.58	2.04	129.1

[a]From Sherwood (1).
[b]Hens were on test for 24 weeks.

❏ THE ROLE OF ANIMALS IN MEETING WORLD FOOD NEEDS

There have been marked improvements in crop production in the past 40–60 years. The development of hybrid corn and sorghums has resulted in almost universal use of hybrids in all areas of intensive production. At the same time, important crops such as corn and soybeans have been modified so that they are more adaptable to a wider range of environments. The so called "green revolution," which resulted in

the development of high yielding varieties of rice and wheat and their widespread use on a world-wide basis, has allowed substantial increases in foodgrain production. In addition, widespread use of higher levels of fertilizer, pesticides, herbicides, and other chemicals has added to the amount of food and feed that has been produced. The statistics and projections shown in Table 1.2 illustrate how world production has increased and how it must continue to increase if the human population is to be fed. These projections call for an increase of 188% for wheat

TABLE 1.2   World production and use of grains in relation to the world human population.

	YEAR			
ITEM	1960[a]	1980[a]	1985–86[b]	2000[a]
Population				
billions	3.038	4.415	4.845	6.098
Total Grains[c]				
Production	842	1,450	1,661	2,177
Food use	444	714		1,106
Food use per capita, kg	147	162		181
Other use	406	737		1,071
Total use	850	1,451	1,583	2,177
Coarse Grains				
Production	465	746	843	1,068
Food use	138	180		228
Food use per capita, kg	46	41		37
Other use	325	559		841
Total use	464	739	780	1,068
Wheat				
Production	237	442	503	682
Food use	175	292		486
Food use per capita, kg	58	66		80
Other use	70	157		197
Total use	245	449	490	682
Rice				
Production	140	263	315	427
Food use	130	243		393
Food use per capita, kg	43	55		65
Other use	11	21		34
Total use	141	263	313	427

[a]From ref. 2; data for 1960 and 1980 are averages of three years centered on 1960 or 1980. Values for 2000 are estimated on an standard rate of increase in population.
[b]Data from ref. 3. Projected production and consumption.
[c]Values expressed as millions of metric tons except for the per capita values on human use, which are in kg.

and 205% for rice production for a doubling of the human population.

Currently some countries such as India, Malaysia, and Indonesia, which were net importers of food grains for some time, are exporting surplus rice. At the same time there has been an increased consumption of animal products in many of the Asian countries.

Although increases in production of some cereal grains are probably higher percentagewise than those for animals, animal productivity has been improved considerably in the past three to four decades. Production of milk, meat, and eggs is markedly higher on a per animal basis, resulting in more efficient use of feed, labor, land, and capital. Aquaculture is becoming more important in a number of areas; where water is available, production of fish is more efficient than meats from our typical warm-blooded animals.

Even with the many marked improvements in crop and animal production, there is much concern that the population growth may outrun the world's capacity to produce food and feed because of limited arable land, usable water, and energy. Water for irrigation is in short supply in many areas. In some instances where ground water has been used for irrigation, the water level has been dropping, resulting in greater costs to get it to the surface. Increased energy costs, unless compensated for by comparable increases in product prices, will make it less feasible to use ground water for irrigation. Likewise, increasd prices for natural gas and other petroleum products directly affect fertilizer costs because some manufacturing processes use natural gas as a primary ingredient.

Many people feel the rising demand for food and feed can be met by continual technological devel-opments, improvements in marketing, and reduction in wastage. However, the critical shortage of water predicted by some individuals may, in itself, be a very big hurdle to overcome.

Animal products seem certain to have a major role in meeting increased demands in the future, although it is to be expected that animals will be fed less and less of the edible plant materials that are used in feeds currently, particularly in some of the developed countries. One reason for predicting less use of animal products in human diets in the future is that it is less efficient to pass food (edible for humans) through an animal and then feed the meat, eggs, or milk to a human. Furthermore, grains sold for human food bring a higher price than animal feeders can usually afford. These statements apply to items that can be considered edible by humans, but not to many of the feed ingredients consumed by domestic or wild animals. This premise is illustrated in Table 1.3, which shows that food edible to humans can be utilized efficiently by domestic animals, the reasons being that the bulk of the animal's diet can be made up of ingredients that are not edible for humans. In fact, in most areas of the world, the milk and meat produced by cattle, sheep, buffaloes, and goats is derived directly from grazing land not in cultivation and from crop residues, milling by-products, or wastes that normally never get into the food chain. On the other hand, a considerable amount of feed fed to animals in some countries is directly competitive for human use. It has been estimated that feed fed to pets in the USA could feed some 40 million people, although some pet food ingredients (animal offal of various types such as lungs, condemned livers, etc.) generally are not considered as edible in the USA.

Future developments in animal and human nutri-

TABLE 1.3 Inputs and returns of animal production.[a,b]

| PRODUCT | TOTAL ENERGY AND PROTEIN | | | | HUMAN EDIBLE ENERGY AND PROTEIN | | | |
| | ENERGY | | PROTEIN | | ENERGY | | PROTEIN | |
	INPUT, MCAL	RETURN, %	INPUT, KG	RETURN, %	INPUT, MCAL	RETURN, %	INPUT, KG	RETURN, %
Milk	19,960	23.1	702	28.8	4,555	101.1	111.5	181.4
Beef	20,560	5.2	823	5.3	1,869	57.1	39.9	108.8
Swine	1,471	23.2	66	37.8	588	58.0	29.0	86.0
Poultry	23.2	15.0	1.2	30.0	11.2	31.0	0.48	75.0

[a]Data from Bywater and Baldwin (4).
[b]Inputs are calculated as digestible energy and digestible protein and include cost of maintaining breeding herds and flocks.

tion are not highly predictable because many unknowns cannot be forseen. However, we can be certain that animals will be important to man for many years to come and it is important to continue to expand our knowledge of the subject of animal nutrition in order to be able to take advantage of any conditions that do develop in the future. As the reader progresses through this book, it will be evident there are many remaining gaps in our knowledge. Given time and resources, the deficiencies will be remedied gradually by the students of today who are the scientists and livestock producers of tomorrow.

❏ REFERENCES

1. Sherwood, D. H. 1979. *Feedstuffs* **51**(44):109.
2. Anon. 1983. *Long-term Grain Outlook*. Secretariat Paper No. 14, International Wheat Council, London, England.
3. USDA. 1986. *World Agricultural Supply and Demand Estimates*. ERS, USDA, April 10 issue.
4. Bywater, A. C. and R. L. Baldwin. 1979. Unpublished. Univ. of California, Davis, CA.

Introduction to Nutrition

THIS CHAPTER INTRODUCES THE names of various nutrients, and gives some information on components found in both plant and animal tissues, and on the differences in nutrient requirements of plants and animals.

At this point we define some terms used in nutrition. **Nourish** means to feed or sustain (an animal or plant) with substances necessary to life and growth. Thus, a **nutrient** may be defined as something that nourishes an animal or, more specifically, a chemical element or compound that is required in the diet of a given animal to permit normal functioning of the life processes. It is difficult to give a short, precise definition of a nutrient and still be accurate. Some compounds, such as starch, are utilized readily by most species as a source of energy (and thus provide nourishment), yet starch is not specifically required by an animal as a source of energy or for any other purpose. **Food** is an edible material that nourishes; **feed** means the same thing, but is more commonly applied to animal food than to human food. **Nutriment** is a word sometimes used to mean the same as food. A **foodstuff** or **feedstuff** is any material made into or used as food or feed, respectively. A **diet** is a mixture of feedstuffs used to supply nourishment to an animal. **Ration** is often used interchangeably with diet, but it may also mean a daily supply of food (or feed).

❑ NUTRIENTS REQUIRED BY PLANTS AND ANIMALS

Most readers know that animal feed and human food contain water, calories (energy), protein, carbohydrate, fat, vitamins, and minerals. If, for example, you look at a package of breakfast cereal, the box will list some components expressed in terms of amount per serving of items such as calories, protein, carbohydrate, fat, cholesterol, sodium, and potassium. Depending on animal age and species, animals require a source of nitrogen (N) in the form of *essential amino acids,* fat in the form of *essential fatty acids, essential mineral elements,* a source of *energy* that may vary from meat for carnivorous animals to coarse fibrous plant tissue for some herbivorous species, and some of the *fat-* and *water-soluble vitamins.* The amounts and proportions required are influenced by the type of gastrointestinal tract, the age of the animal, its level of productivity, what type of product is being produced (work, growth, milk, eggs, etc.), the dietary components available, and other poorly documented factors. If we return to the cereal box, we will see some of the required nutrients listed, showing what percentage of the recommended daily allowance is provided by one serving of the specific cereal. Because animals require some 40 odd nutrients, meeting dietary requirements may not always be a simple thing.

In contrast to animals, requirements for plants are relatively simple. In general, plants take up N in the form of nitrate or ammonia and they synthesize their complex proteins using these forms of N and other intermediate biochemicals (see Ch. 7). Plants, of course, require a number of the mineral elements (which cannot be synthesized except in an atomic reactor). The qualitative requirements for minerals appear to be essentially the same as for animals except that plants require boron (B); there is some evidence that plants may also require Al, Br, Cs, and Sr. Thus, the primary nutrient needs of plants are the required minerals and N, normally obtained from soil through the roots. Through the process of photosynthesis the plant takes in CO_2 and releases O_2 and synthesizes glucose, the basic biochemical required for plant growth. Using these basic components, the plant is capable of synthesizing all of the complex biochemicals that it requires for growth, protection, reproduction, and so on.

❑ COMPOSITION OF ANIMAL FOOD

The food an animal consumes may vary from very simple compounds such as salt (NaCl) or sugar to the extremely complex mixtures provided by some plant and most animal tissues. Not all components will be usable nutrients. Indeed, some of the material consumed may be insoluble and/or indigestible, and some may very well be toxic under certain conditions.

Table 2.1 contains an abbreviated listing of chemicals (and nutrients) that may be present in animal food. The names and terminology are introduced here to facilitate discussions in Chs. 2–5. Each category of nutrients will be discussed in considerably more detail in later chapters.

No attempt is made to give quantitative data in Table 2.1. Food composition varies so much that it would be meaningless. Of course, not all samples of any given food will contain all of the compounds shown in Table 2.1. For that matter, it is difficult to find published analytical data on all possible components of any food or feed; generally, this is so because of a more limited interest by the persons doing the analysis. For example, we might be primarily interested in proteins and have little or no interest in mineral content. The result is that tables of composition are usually pieced together from many different laboratories.

Water is a major item in most animal diets, although it is not listed in Table 2.1. The other ingredients make up the dry matter of the diet, which is further subdivided into organic compounds (organic matter) or inorganic (mineral) matter in the table.

Nearly all animal food will contain proteins, which are complex molecules containing various amino acids and other nonprotein components. Both animal and plant proteins may be very complex and will vary in their content of amino acids and the arrangement of the amino acids, resulting in differences in molecular size, solubility, and digestibility. In addition, plants contain many amino acids not found in proteins, and they may contain other N-containing compounds such as nitrates not classed as amino acids.

Lipids of many different types are found in both plant and animal tissues. Only two fatty acids, linoleic and linolenic, are thought to be specific dietary requirements for animals. However, other dietary lipids necessary for animal life include the fat-soluble vitamins not shown as lipids in the table.

Carbohydrates make up the majority of most plant tissues and may be quite complex in number and composition. In contrast, carbohydrates make up less than 1% of the tissue in animals. For the animal, carbohydrates serve as a source of energy and provide sufficient bulk to keep the digestive tract working smoothly. No specific carbohydrate is required

TABLE 2.1   A simplified schematic of elements and compounds that may be present in food.

Organic compounds

  Nitrogen containing

    Protein

      Essential amino acids—isoleucine, leucine, lysine, methionine, phenylalanine, threonine, tryptophan, valine

      Semi-essential—arginine, cystine, glycine, histidine, proline, tyrosine

      Non-essential—alanine, aspartic acid, glutamic acid, hydroxyproline, serine

    Nonprotein—peptides, amines, amides, nucleic acids, nitrates, urea, many non-protein amino acids, and hundreds of other compounds containing N

  Lipids

    Essential fatty-acids—linoleic, linolenic

    Sterols—cholesterol, vitamin D, many other related compounds

    Terpenoids—carotene, xanthophylls, and so on

    Waxes—cutin, etc.

    Phospholipids—lecithin

    Miscellaneous—free fatty acids, and so on

  Carbohydrates

    Monosaccharides—simple pentose or hexose sugars

    Disaccharides—sugars with two molecules of simple sugars

    Oligosaccharides—sugars with more than two simple sugars but still relatively small molecules

    Non-fibrous polysaccharides—dextrins, starches, pectins, etc.

    Fibrous polysaccharides—hemicelluloses, celluloses, xylans

  Vitamins

    Water-soluble—ascorbic acid, biotin, choline, cobalamin, folacin, niacin, pantothenic acid, pyridoxine, riboflavin, thiamin

    Fat-soluble—vitamins A, D, E, and K

  Miscellaneous—lignin; organic acids, compounds contributing to color, flavor and odor; toxins or inhibitors of various types; plant hormones

Inorganic

  Essential elements

    Macro—Ca, Cl, K, Mg, Na, P, S

    Micro—Co, Cr, Cu, F, Fe, I, Mn, Mo, Ni, Se, Si, Sn, V, Zn

  Possibly essential—As, Ba, Br, Cd, Sr

  Non-essential—Ag, Al, Au, B, Bi, Ge, Hg, Pb, Rb, Sb, Ti

  Often toxic—As, Cd, Cu, F, Hg, Mo, Pb, Se, Si

in the animal diet because those required by various organs or tissues can be synthesized in other tissues.

Vitamins account for only a very small amount of almost all food sources. Even so, feed and food sources vary widely in vitamin content, partly because most of the vitamins are subject to degradation by conditions promoting oxidation.

Minerals found in food and feed include the **macrominerals,** which are the essential elements required in relatively large amounts, and the **microminerals** or trace elements, which are required in much lesser amount. In addition, many other mineral elements may be taken up by plant tissues. The non-essential minerals are not believed to have any function in animal tissues at this time. Toxic minerals, which may include some of those that are essential, may be present in some plant tissues in sufficient amounts to cause problems.

Plant Composition

The chemical composition of whole plants is exceedingly diverse, being affected greatly by stage of growth and plant species. Generally, plants have the following relative composition: protein, moderate to low; fiber, moderate to high; seeds are high in starch, moderate to low in fiber, moderate to high in protein, moderate in lipids, low in minerals, and moderate to high in vitamins.

Data on a few animal feeds are shown in Table 2.2. Note that the water content of pasture grass and the whole corn plant is much higher than for the other feeds listed. Also the content of other components is generally lower. However, if we expressed all components on a water-free basis (dry matter basis), then the protein content of pasture grass would be about the same as the alfalfa hay (5.0 ÷ by dry matter content, or 0.321 = 15.57%). This illustrates a common practice that should be used when comparing feedstuffs, that is, to express nutrient content on a water-free basis. It is much easier to make comparisons when done in this manner.

With regard to other comparisons shown in Table 2.2, note that the protein content of alfalfa hay and pasture grass is relatively high for plant material. The whole corn plant is lower and the wheat straw is much lower. On the other hand, soybean meal and meat meal are concentrated sources of protein. Except for meat meal, none of these feeds contains much fat. With regard to carbohydrate content, meat meal is low, and that present is largely an artifact of the method of analysis used. Total carbohydrate data are not very meaningful except to show that plants contain large amounts. Feeding value is generally negatively related to the fiber content. Mineral content of feed sources may be quite variable. Generally, legumes are relatively high in Calcium (Ca); the soybean meal is moderate and the meat meal is quite high. Phosphorus (P) content is usually high in feeds high in protein; in this case, soybean meal is moderate and the meat meal is high. Many other examples of differences in plant composition and of animal feed sources are shown in other chapters and in the Appendix tables.

Composition of the Animal Body

The composition of animal body tissues tends to be relatively uniform. Typical body composition of an

TABLE 2.2   Percentage composition of selected animal feeds.[a]

FEED	WATER	PROTEIN	FAT	CRUDE FIBER	TOTAL CARBO-HYDRATE	ASH	CALCIUM	PHOSPHORUS
Pasture grass (young, leafy)	67.9	5.0	1.1	7.9	23.1	2.8	0.12	0.06
Corn plant, whole	75.7	2.0	0.6	5.8	20.4	1.3	0.07	0.05
Wheat straw	12.2	3.2	1.4	38.3	76.9	6.3	0.14	0.07
Alfalfa hay	8.6	15.5	1.7	28.0	65.1	9.0	1.29	0.21
Corn grain	14.6	8.9	3.9	2.1	71.3	1.3	0.02	0.27
Soybean meal	10.9	46.7	1.2	5.2	35.3	5.9	0.30	0.65
Meat meal	5.8	54.9	9.4	2.5	5.0	24.9	8.49	4.18

[a]Data taken from various NRC publications.

TABLE 2.3 Composition of the animal body.[a]

SPECIES	COMPONENTS, %			
	WATER	PROTEIN	FAT	MINERALS
Calf, newborn	74	19	3	4
Steer, thin	64	19	12	5
Pig, 100 kg	49	12	36	2–3
Hen	57	21	19	3
Horse	60	18	18	4
Rabbit	69	18	8	5
Human	60	18	18	4

[a]Values do not include contents of the gastrointestinal tract.

adult mammal is about 60% water, 16% protein, 20% fat, and 4% mineral matter. Carbohydrates (blood and tissue glucose, liver and muscle glycogen) usually are not listed, but amount to less than 1% of body tissue.

Differences among species in body composition are not as large as illustrated in Table 2.3. In the limited data shown, age (and changing fat content) causes more differences than species. Humans tend to vary more in fat content than most domestic or wild species. Wild terrestrial species, except for those that hibernate, do not accumulate nearly as much fat as do domestic species. The aquatic species (such as seals, whales, etc.) that accumulate large amounts

of subcutaneous fat do so to improve body insulation as an aid in maintaining their body temperature above that of the environment.

The changes in body composition with increasing weight, fatness, and age are illustrated in Table 2.4. Although these data are rather old, they are based on the analysis of the complete bodies of 60 head of cattle, something that is unheard of in modern laboratories. Note that the water content of the empty body gradually decreases as the dry matter and fat content increase. Protein and ash decrease only slightly while fat content increases from 4% in the very young calf to 31.1% in an animal weighing 545 kg. If these data were expressed on a fat-free basis, changes in

TABLE 2.4 Composition of steers at increasing body weights.[a]

NORMAL BODY WEIGHT, LB/KG	COMPONENTS, %[b]				
	WATER	DRY MATTER	PROTEIN	FAT	ASH
100/45	71.8	28.2	19.9	4.0	4.3
200/91	69.5	30.5	19.6	6.3	4.6
300/136	66.3	33.7	19.4	9.8	4.5
400/182	65.8	34.2	19.3	10.6	4.4
500/227	62.9	37.1	19.2	13.7	4.2
600/273	62.2	37.8	19.2	14.0	4.6
700/318	60.8	39.2	18.8	15.9	4.5
800/364	57.9	42.1	18.7	19.2	4.2
900/409	54.1	45.9	17.7	25.5	3.8
1000/454	53.1	46.9	17.6	25.5	3.8
1100/500	48.0	52.0	16.2	31.9	3.9
1200/545	48.6	51.4	15.7	31.1	3.7

[a]Taken from Armsby (1).
[b]Analyses are shown on the basis of empty body weight (without the contents of the gastrointestinal tract), and are the result of analyzing the entire bodies of 60 "well-fed animals."

TABLE 2.5　Change in body composition of cattle with increasing body size.[a]

ITEM[b]	EMPTY BODY WEIGHT, KG		
	300	400	500
Protein	163	157	152
Fat	299	431	573
Energy	15.6	20.6	26.1
Calcium	14.9	14.2	13.7
Phosphorus	8.1	7.8	7.5

[a]After ARC (2).
[b]Expressed as g/kg or, for energy, as Mj/kg.

composition from 45 to 545 kg would be: ash, 4.44 to 5.33%; protein, 20.73 to 24.08%; dry matter, 25.17 to 29.41%; water, 74.8 to 70.6%—all very nominal changes for cattle increasing 1,200% in weight.

A more recent example of changes in empty body composition of cattle is shown in Table 2.5 for Holstein cattle increasing in weight from 300 to 500 kg. When expressed as g/kg of weight, protein content decreased slightly as did the Ca and P contents. Fat increased 192% and the energetic value of the tissues increased by 167%. It is clear from the data presented in Tables 2.4 and 2.5 that the two major variables in animal body composition are the concentrations of water and fat, and that these two components vary inversely.

Mineral composition of the whole body will vary with age, fatness, and to some extent with species. Mineral content of the bones increases as the young animal matures and bone salts replace much of the cartilage in the skeleton. For cattle, average quoted values for the whole body are (%): Ca, 1.33; P, 0.74; K, 1.19; Na, 0.16; S, 0.15; Cl, 0.11; and Mg, 0.04.

❏ REFERENCES

1.　Armsby, H. P. 1922. *The Nutrition of Farm Animals*. The Macmillan Co., N.Y.
2.　ARC. 1980. *The Nutrient Requirements of Ruminant Livestock*. Agr. Res. Council and the Commonwealth Agr. Bureaux, England.

3

Common Methods of Analysis for Nutrients and Feedstuffs

THE SCIENCE OF NUTRITION has progressed rapidly in recent decades, partly because of the extensive research effort that has been expended to learn more about nutrition. Expansion of knowledge and an improved understanding of nutritional needs and nutrient metabolism are possible, in part, because methods are continually being developed and improved to quantitatively evaluate the nutrient content of foods, feeds, and animal tissues. Thus, to have a moderately good understanding of nutrition, the reader should have at least a minimal acquaintance with laboratory analyses that are commonly utilized and at least a limited knowledge of chemistry. Although a detailed knowledge is not required, some understanding of analytical procedures will make for easier reading and some familiarity with organic structures will facilitate learning when studying those chapters dealing with specific nutrients.

❏ SAMPLING FOR ANALYSIS

In the early days of nutrition research, it was not uncommon to analyze the whole animal body. Today, such practices are less feasible because equipment is not adapted to such methods and the cost would be tremendous. It is seldom feasible today to analyze the whole bodies even of small animals such as rats or chicks. Modern chemical methods are geared to procedures that require small amounts of material that must be collected and prepared in a manner that gives the best reasonable estimate of the total batch. For example, if we are interested in the protein content of hay produced from a field, where do we begin? We certainly cannot grind up all of the hay produced; even one bale would tax the facilities of most laboratories. Consequently, we resort to the use of core samples taken from as many different bales as is reasonable. Perhaps as many as 25–50 core samples may be taken from one stack of bales which represents the hay from the field in question. The assumption is that each core will correspond reasonably well to the total composition of the bale from which it came and that, if we sample enough bales, our composite sample will be representative of the total hay crop. This is an assumption that may not always work out in practice, but it is the appropriate statistical approach.

The core samples are brought to the laboratory, ground, mixed well, and small subsamples taken for analyses. For the common Kjeldahl analysis which is used for crude protein (see the section on proximate analyses), a typical sample size is 2 g of material. A micro-Kjeldahl procedure now in use allows the use of a sample that contains about 1 mg of N, or a sample of about 100 mg of the hay in question. Thus, we may base our estimate of protein content of the total field on a very small amount of material. Consequently, the material being analyzed must be representative if results are to be meaningful.

Similar procedures are used for other commodities. One small sample of grain may be used to evaluate a carload. Liquids are assumed to be more homogeneous than solids, but this is not always true and errors may creep in if care is not taken in sampling. With respect to the beef carcass, the 9-10-11 rib cut has been shown to give a relatively accurate estimate of the total carcass for fat, protein, water, and ash (minerals). As a result, we can obtain this cut from one side of the carcass, bone it, grind it up, and analyze it for the constituents of interest.

❏ ANALYTICAL METHODS

Most of the analytical methods in common use depend on various chemical procedures which are specific for a given element, compound or group of compounds. Quantitative data may be obtained by gravimetric procedures, but more often are obtained by other methods which involve the use of acid or base titration, colorimetry, chromatography, and so on. A relatively common characteristic of chemical methods is that they often involve drastic degradation of feeds with reagents such as concentrated solvents or other treatments that are biologically harsh. As a result, one of the big problems in nutrient analysis is that a chemical procedure may be quantitative in terms of finding out how much of a given nutrient or compound is in the feed, but such analyses are often more difficult to relate to animal utilization. For example, a forage might be analyzed for its Ca content, but the data provide no information on how much of the Ca is available to the animal.

Because chemical methods often leave questions regarding the availability of nutrients from feeds, biological procedures are used sometimes, although they are usually more tedious and expensive. However, such methods may give a much more accurate estimate of animal utilization; in other words, biological methods tell us how much of a nutrient the animal uses from the feed. Chicks or rats are often used in tests of this type. If, for example, it was desired to determine the effect of heating on utilization of proteins from soybean meal, one or more groups of chicks can be fed unheated meal along with other necessary nutrients. Other chicks would be fed meal that had been heated to different temperatures or for different lengths of time. Such comparisons will provide a reasonably good biological estimate of the effect of heat treatments on the soy proteins.

Microbiological methods may be used in a manner similar to the biological procedures just described for chicks. Bacteria have been isolated that have specific requirements for one or more of the essential amino acids or for specific water-soluble vitamins. These organisms can be used to determine how much of a given amino acid or vitamin is available in a given product or mixture. The information may or may not be applicable to rats, chicks or swine, but it is more likely to be applicable than that from a chemical method.

❑ SPECIFIC METHODS OF ANALYSIS

Dry Matter

The determination of dry matter is probably the most common procedure carried out in nutrition laboratories. The reason for this is that natural feedstuffs, animal tissues or other samples of interest may be quite variable in water content, and we must know the amount of water if analytical data are to be compared for different feeds. When grain is bought or fed, obviously its value with 14% moisture is not the same as that with 10% moisture. After analysis, nutrient composition can be expressed on a dry basis or a normal "as fed" basis, which would be about 90% dry matter for most grains.

The simplest means of determining dry matter is to place the test material in an oven and leave it until all of the free water has evaporated. Temperatures used are usually 100–105°C. Moisture also can be estimated with moisture meters, devices that give immediate results by means of a probe inserted into the test material (Fig. 3.1). Some of these devices depend on electrical conductivity; they are very useful for quick answers, such as at a grain buying station, when buying hay, and so on, but results are not so precise as those obtained by actually drying the test material in an oven. Newer equipment includes microwave ovens adapted for obtaining weights before and after drying (also shown in Fig. 3.1).

Figure 3.1 *Examples of equipment used to determine moisture, which can give rapid information on water content. Left. A simple meter depending on electrical conductivity. Courtesy of Epic, Inc. Right. A more elaborate instrument, useful in the laboratory, which depends on microwave energy for moisture analysis. Courtesy of Photovolt Co.*

The determination of dry matter, as with most procedures, is not always as simple as the previous discussion implied. This statement applies to any material that has a relatively high content of volatile compounds. Most fresh plant tissues contain some volatile compounds, but the amount is low enough that the volatiles usually can be ignored with little error. However, some plants contain large amounts of essential oils, terpenes, and so on, that may be lost in drying and, thus, give an erroneous answer with the usual procedures. Of the common feedstuffs, silages or other fermented products may have large amounts of easily vaporized compounds such as volatile fatty acids (acetic, propionic, butyric) and ammonia. Furthermore, some sugars may decompose and many proteins become partially insoluble at temperatures above 70°C.

There are several means of avoiding excessive losses of volatiles. Drying in vacuum ovens, freeze drying, oven drying at 70°C or less, and distillation with toluene have been used. One example of the effect of these different procedures on different silages is shown (1): oven drying at 100°C, 44.4% dry matter; oven drying at 70°C, 46.8%; freeze drying, 47.2%; toluene distillation, 47.7%; and toluene distillation corrected for total acids, ethanol and ammonia, 48.2%. These data show that very substantial losses may occur if silage is dried in the usual manner.

Proximate Analysis

The proximate analysis is a combination of analytical procedures developed in Germany well over a century ago. It is intended for the routine description of feedstuffs and, although from a nutritional point of view it has many faults, it is still used widely. In some instances its use has been encouraged and prolonged because of laws that require listing of minimum and maximum amounts of components that may be present in commercial feed mixtures. The different fractions that result from the proximate analysis include: water, crude protein, ether extract, ash, crude fiber, and nitrogen-free extract. We have already discussed water (or dry matter); more detailed discussion of the other components follows.

Crude Protein.   The procedure used to determine crude protein is known as the Kjeldahl method. Material to be analyzed first is digested in concentrated H_2SO_4 which converts the N to $(NH_4)_2SO_4$. This mixture is then cooled, diluted with water and neutralized with NaOH, which changes the N into the form of ionized ammonium. The sample then is distilled, and the distillate containing the ammonium is titrated with acid. This analysis is accurate and repeatable, but it is relatively time consuming and involves the use of hazardous chemicals. A micro apparatus is shown in Fig. 3.2.

From a nutritional point of view, the data are applicable to ruminant species which can efficiently utilize almost all forms of N, but the information may be of little value for monogastric species (such as humans, swine, poultry). Monogastric species have specific requirements for various amino acids (see Ch. 7) and do not efficiently utilize non-protein N compounds such as amides, ammonium salts, and urea. The crude protein analysis does not distinguish one form of N from another, thus it is not possible to determine if a feed mixture has urea or the highest quality of protein such as casein (from milk). In addition, nitrate N is not converted to ammonium salts by this procedure so N in this form is not included.

Ether Extract.   This procedure requires that ground samples be extracted with diethyl ether for a period of 4 h or more. Ether-soluble materials include quite a variety of organic compounds (see Ch. 9), only a few of which have much nutritional significance. Those of quantitative importance include the true fats and fatty acid esters, some of the compound lipids, and fat-soluble vitamins or provitamins such as the carotenoids. The primary reason for obtaining ether extract data is an attempt to iso-

Figure 3.2 *A micro-Kjeldahl apparatus which is designed for nitrogen analyses of small samples. The digestion apparatus is shown on the left and the distillation equipment immediately to the right.*

late a fraction of feedstuffs that has a high caloric value. Provided the ether extract is made up primarily of fats and fatty acid esters, this may be a valid approach. If the extract contains large percentages of plant waxes, essential oils, resins, or similar compounds, it has little meaning because compounds such as these are of little value to animals.

Ash.   Ash is the residue remaining after all the combustible material has been burned off (oxidized completely) in a furnace heated to 500–600°C. Nutritionally, ash values have little importance, although excessively high values may indicate contamination with soil or dilution of feedstuffs with such substances as salt and limestone. In the proximate analysis, data on ash are required to obtain other values. It should be noted that some mineral elements, such as iodine and selenium, may be volatile and are lost on ashing. Normally, these elements represent only very small percentages of the total, so little error is involved.

Crude Fiber.   Crude fiber is determined by using an ether-extracted sample, boiling in dilute acid, boiling in dilute base, filtering, drying, and burning in a furnace. The difference in weight before and after burning is the crude fiber fraction. This is a tedious laboratory procedure that is not highly repeatable. It is an attempt to simulate digestion that occurs first in the gastric stomach and then in the small intestine of animals. Crude fiber is made up primarily of plant structural carbohydrates such as cellulose and hemicellulose (see Ch. 8), but it also contains some lignin, a highly indigestible material associated with the fibrous portion of plant tissues. For the monogastric animal, crude fiber is of a variable but low value; for ruminants, it is of variable value, but it is much more highly utilized than by monogastrics.

Nitrogen-Free-Extract [*NFE*].   This term is a misnomer in that no extract is involved. It is determined by difference; that is, NFE is the difference between the original sample weight and the sum of weights of water, ether extract, crude protein, crude fiber, and ash. It is called N-free because ordinarily it would contain no N. NFE is made up primarily of readily available carbohydrates, such as the sugars and starches (see Ch. 8), but it may also contain some hemicellulose and lignin, particularly in such feedstuffs as forages. A more appropriate analysis would be one specifically for readily available carbohydrates—one in which starches are hydrolyzed to sugars and the mixture analyzed for all sugars

present. Nutritionally, the NFE fraction of grains is utilized to a high degree by nearly all species, but NFE from forages and other roughages is less well utilized.

A diagram of the proximate analysis scheme illustrating the sequence of procedures as well as the major fractions that are isolated is shown in Fig. 3.3.

Detergent Extraction Methods

Analytical methods, primarily intended for forages, have been developed by Van Soest (2), co-workers, and other scientists interested in in this topic. Micro methods also have been developed. Use of these methods allows plant components to be divided as shown:

Neutral-Detergent Extraction.   Samples are boiled for 1 h in a solution containing primarily sodium laural sulfate. This detergent extracts lipids, sugars, organic acids, and other water-soluble material, pectin (usually classified as a fibrous carbohydrate), non-protein N compounds, soluble protein, and some of the silica and tannin. The non-soluble material is referred to as neutral-detergent residue or, more commonly, neutral-detergent fiber (NDF). The NDF contains the major cell wall components such as cellulose, hemicellulose, and lignin. It may also contain

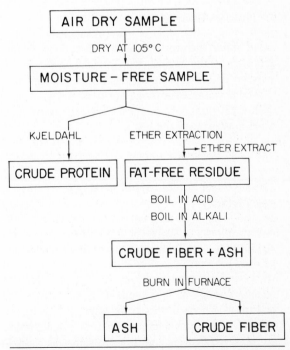

Figure 3.3 Flow diagram for the proximate analysis.

minor cell wall components including some protein, bound N, minerals, and cuticle. The soluble material, often referred to as cell wall contents (CWC) is highly digestible by all species, with the possible exception of the pectins, and any silica and tannin. The NDF is only partially digestible by any species, but can be used to a greater extent by animals such as ruminants, which depend on microbial digestion for utilization of most fibrous plant components.

Acid-Detergent Extraction.   Samples are boiled for 1 h in a solution containing cetyl trimethylammonium bromide in H_2SO_4. Components soluble in acid-detergent include primarily hemicelluloses and cell wall proteins, and the residue includes cellulose, lignin and lignified N (indigestible N), cutin, silica, and some pectins. It is usually referred to as acid-detergent fiber (ADF).

These detergent methods are often used alone, but may be used together, or the ADF method may be substituted for the crude fiber method partly because it is more repeatable and faster. The ADF fraction can be further extracted with sulfuric acid to isolate lignin. The pros and cons of the methods have been discussed in detail by Van Soest (2).

pH of Feedstuffs

The pH of feedstuffs is rarely used to evaluate materials except for fermented products such as silage, cannery residues, or other similar mixtures. It should be pointed out that pH of mineral supplements may be of importance with respect to palatability or metabolism by the animal. With respect to silage, pH may be determined by mixing 100 g of silage with 100 ml of water, expressing the juice, and measuring with a pH meter. Good quality silages should have a pH between 3.8 and 5.0.

❑ SPECIALIZED ANALYTICAL METHODS

A wide variety of analytical methods find some use in nutrition from time to time. Such methods may be used for feedstuffs and rations, animal tissues, or with urine and fecal samples, depending on the situation. The list of such methods is far too long to discuss in a book of this type; however, there are several methods involving specialized equipment that are used extensively and deserve some discussion.

Bomb Calorimetry

The oxygen bomb calorimeter (Fig. 3.4) is an instrument used to determine energy values of solids, liquids or gases. The energy value of a given sample is determined by burning it in a pressurized oxygen atmosphere. When the sample is burned, the heat produced raises the temperature of water surrounding the container in which the sample is enclosed, and the temperature increase provides the basis for calculating the energy value. Bomb calorimetry finds extensive use for evaluating fuels such as natural gas and coal. In nutrition its most useful application is in determining the digestible energy of feedstuffs or rations. The gross energy value (that obtained by burning) of feedstuffs has little or no direct application, as it is almost impossible to distinguish between constituents that are well utilized by animals and those that are poorly utilized (see Ch. 10).

Amino Acid Analysis

Chemical methods for amino acid analysis have been available for a good many years, but it is only in the last 15–20 years that semiautomated equipment, such as that shown in Fig. 3.5, has been available. This

Figure 3.4 *A modern oxygen bomb calorimeter used for energy determinations of feed and other combustible materials.*

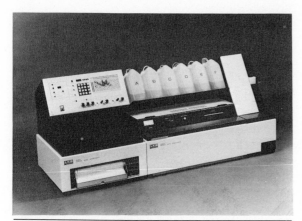

Figure 3.5 *One example of several amino acid alalzers used for quantitatively determining individual amino acids. Courtesy of LKB Instruments.*

Figure 3.6 *A modern atomic absorption spectrophotometer. Courtesy of the Instrumentation Laboratory.*

type of equipment is capable of fractionating protein preparations that have been hydrolyzed into the constituent amino acids. The preparations are placed on chromatographic columns, and various solutions are passed through the columns, resulting in separation and evolution of the individual amino acids in a relatively short time (a few hours). This type of equipment has greatly facilitated collection of data on amino acid composition of foods and feeds as well as on metabolism and requirements of amino acids.

Atomic Absorption Spectrophotometry

Atomic absorption spectrophotometric instruments (Fig. 3.6) have greatly facilitated analyses for most mineral elements (cations). In the operation of these instruments, liquid or solid materials are ashed and resuspended in liquid which may be put directly into the instrument. Body fluids such as blood plasma and urine may be used directly. The solution passes through a flame that serves to disperse the molecules into individual atoms. Radiation from a cathode lamp is passed through the flame, and the atoms absorb some of this radiation at specific wavelengths. With instruments such as this, vast numbers of samples can be analyzed in a short time.

Gas-Liquid Chromatography

The forerunner of the gas-liquid chromatograph (GLC) was developed to analyze rumen volatile fatty acids. Since that time (early 1950s), tremendous improvements have occurred in this technique and in the available instrumentation (Fig. 3.7). Such instruments are capable of handling almost any compound that can be vaporized or those that are in gas form.

The sample to be analyzed is placed in the instrument and is moved through a heated chromatographic column by means of gas. This process allows the quantitative separation of closely related chemical compounds (such as acetic and propionic acid) quite rapidly. This process requires only very small samples. In

Figure 3.7 *One example of many gas-liquid chromatographs on the market. Courtesy of GOW-MAC Instrument Co.*

nutrition, GLC's have been particularly useful for fatty acid analyses, but are capable of handling many other organic compounds.

Automated Analytical Equipment

The gradually increasing cost of labor has stimulated the development of instrumentation designed to do a number of simultaneous repetitive analyses (Fig. 3.8). Such equipment has found widespread use in the medical field, particularly, but has application as well in the nutrition laboratory. For example, it is possible to obtain simultaneous data on blood serum for glucose, total lipids, cholesterol, Ca, P, Mg, urea, and total protein as well as other compounds. This is just an example of the type of information that may be obtained on one tissue. Increased availability of more complete data on animals would greatly improve our knowledge of nutrient metabolism of healthy as well as sick animals. The speed of analysis and the fact that such equipment is highly automated have increased greatly the volume of information that may be obtained at a given cost, even though the equipment itself is expensive.

Infrared.   Use of infrared light rays for feed analyses is of recent origin. Instruments have been available for less than 10 years and in some respects are still in the developmental stages. Analyses are obtained by placing a sample in a receptacle and im-

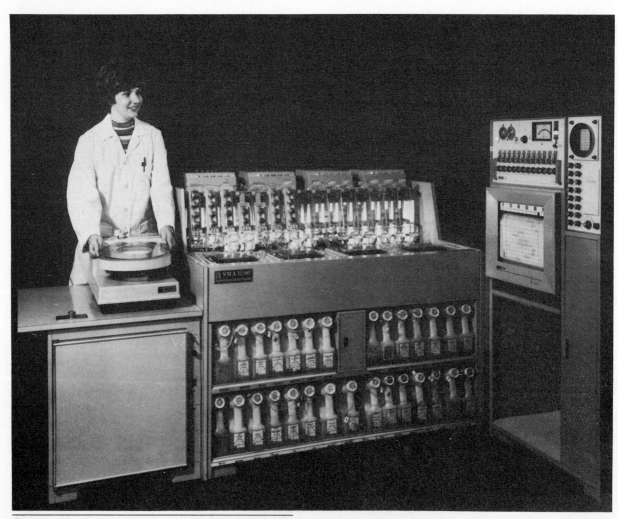

Figure 3.8 *One example of a multichannel analyzer. Some of these instruments can do simultaneous analyses on 12–15 chemical components (or more) from tissues such as blood serum. Courtesy of Technicon Instruments Corporation.*

pinging infrared light on the sample. The reflected light goes back into the instrument and the changes caused by the sample can be detected and related to composition of the sample by a built-in computer. Analyses are usually restricted to lipids, protein, fiber, and moisture, although some instruments have been used for Ca, P, salt, and occasionally for other ingredients. These instruments were developed initially for use with grains, but are being used currently with other feedstuffs including mixed feeds and ground forages. The major advantage is time since it takes only about 20 seconds per sample. Obviously, in the grain or feed trade, this would be a tremendous asset as compared to most analytical methods which may require one to several days to get data back from the laboratory. By that time the feed may be gone or have been consumed. These instruments have at least two disadvantages. One is that a range of samples must be available in order to calibrate the machine. Consequently, samples with at least as much variation as the test samples must be available for this purpose. In addition, calibration samples must be available for every type of feed to be used. A second major disadvantage is the cost. Currently, instruments may cost from $20,000–80,000. Thus, a relatively high rate of use would be required to justify such an expense.

Other Instrumentation. There are a number of other types of instrumentation that have been developed in recent years that may, at times, be used for nutritionally related research. Some of the instruments, or methods available include: automated instruments for measuring blood flow; blood cell counters; high pressure liquid chromatography, nuclear magnetic resonance, and DNA synthesizers; inductively coupled plasma emission spectrophotometers; flow cytometers, and so on. When available, such instrumentation and methods allow the collection of much more data than would otherwise be possible or, in some instances, the collection of data that could not otherwise be obtained.

❏ SUMMARY

Analytical methods used for nutrients, feeds, animal tissues, and so on, have become quite complex and sophisticated in recent years. When such complicated devices work as designed, they allow very rapid accumulation of much more data, which can be very useful for increasing our knowledge of animal biology and nutrition. However, the rapid generation of reams of data is not a guarantee that it is accurate, and it is this latter fact that must be given due consideration when using such equipment.

❏ REFERENCES

1. Brahmakshatriya, R. D. and J. D. Donker. 1971. *J. Dairy Sci.* **54**:1470.
2. Van Soest, P. J. 1982. *Nutritional Ecology of the Ruminant.* O & B Books, Inc., Corvallis, OR.

4

The Gastrointestinal Tract and Nutrition

Some knowledge of the gastrointestinal tract (GI tract) is important to those who study nutrition because it is concerned so intimately with the utilization of food and nutrients. The various organs, glands, and other structures involved are concerned with procuring, chewing, and swallowing food and with the digestion and absorption of nutrients as well as with some excretory functions.

Digestion and absorption are terms that will be used frequently in this chapter. **Digestion** has been defined simply as the preparation of food for absorption. As such, it may include mechanical forces (chewing or mastication; muscular contractions of the GI tract), chemical action (HCl in the stomach; bile in the small intestine), or enzymic activity from enzymes produced in the GI tract or from microorganisms in various sites in the tract. The overall function of the various digestive processes is to reduce food to a molecular size or solubility that will allow for absorption.
Absorption includes various processes that allow small molecules to pass through the membranes of the GI tract into the blood or lymph systems.

☐ ANATOMY AND FUNCTION OF THE GASTROINTESTINAL TRACT

The GI tract of simple-stomached mammalian species includes the mouth and associated structures and glands, esophagus, stomach, small and large intestines, pancreas, and liver. The tract itself is essentially a modified tubular structure used for ingestion and digestion of food and the elimination of some of the wastes of metabolic activity produced by the animal body. Its ultimate purpose is to provide for the efficient assimilation of nutrients necessary for life and to reject dietary constituents unnecessary for or potentially harmful to the animal.

Types of GI Tracts

Among the many species of mammals and birds there are many differences in the GI tract. The animal does not, of course, exist in a sterile environment, and in many instances the GI tract has been modified to take advantage of symbiotic relationships with various microorganisms. Concentrated microbial populations are found in the lower part of the small intestine and in the large intestine of all species; other species have developed modifications of the upper GI tract that allow microbes to thrive and produce products that are beneficial to the animal in the process of partially digesting some of the ingested food. Mammals with an uncomplicated stomach are sometimes referred to as monogastrics* or as non-ruminants. They may also be classified in other ways (see subsequent discussion) according to the interest of the writer.

Existing animal species have evolved many variations in their digestive tracts that allow them to utilize diets of varying composition or quality ranging from nectar (hummingbird and other nectar-eating birds) to coarse fibrous plant material (elephant and other large herbivorous species, horse, some ruminants). Some of these differences are characterized in schematic drawings shown in Fig. 4.1 or listed in Table 4.1.

Carnivores are animals whose diet is composed primarily of non-plant material—that is, meat, fish, insects, and so on. They are represented in Fig. 4.1 by the dog and the mink. In general, the diet of a

*Note: Some writers prefer to use terms such as ruminant and non-ruminant to designate the type of GI tract. Monogastric is a term that has been used for many years, and the writer sees no objection to continued usage. Those who object do so because ruminants have only one glandular stomach compartment.

carnivore is relatively concentrated and highly digestible—except for hair, feathers, and other types of resistant proteins and bones. The GI tract of carnivores is represented by a gastric stomach and a relatively short and uncomplicated intestine. The large intestine is uncomplicated in that it is not sacculated. Carnivores fall in one type of classification described as hindgut fermentors, which is further subdivided into cecal or colonic digesters (see Table 4.1). They have the capability of digesting limited amounts of fibrous foods, but fermentation of fiber is quite limited compared to any other species listed in Table 4.1. It is believed that the fiber consumed by most omnivores (plant and animal eaters) and by all carnivores has little importance as a source of nutrients, although the fiber may serve a useful function in providing bulk in the GI tract. Although dogs and cats have little or no cecal capacity and an unsacculated colon (not typical of fiber digesters), they are known to eat grass, presumably because they have some specific need for it.

Omnivores and herbivores (plant eaters) generally have more complicated GI tracts that have been modified in some manner to improve utilization of plant tissues. The pig and rat are two examples of omnivorous species shown in Fig. 4.1. Note that the pig has a long but simple small intestine, a moderate-sized cecum, and a sacculated large intestine. In Table 4.1, the pig (and man) are classified as colonic digesters. In comparison, the rat has a shorter but simple small intestine, an enlarged cecum, and an unsacculated large intestine (classed as a cecal fermentor). Both of these species depend on hind gut fermentation to varying degrees, the pig having fermentation in both the cecum and colon, while most of the fermentation in the rabbit GI tract occurs in the cecum.

The sheep, pony, and rabbit are three examples of herbivorous species with quite different adaptations to handle fibrous diets. In the sheep's case, because it is a ruminant, there is a complex large stomach with extensive fermentation followed by a long but simple small intestine, a relatively large cecum, and a rather short large gut—allowing both pregastric and hind gut fermentation (although not listed in this manner in Table 4.1). The horse has a small, simple stomach with a relatively short small intestine, but with a large cecum and a very large sacculated hind gut. On the other hand, the rabbit has a medium-sized stomach with a relatively short and simple small gut, but with a large sacculated

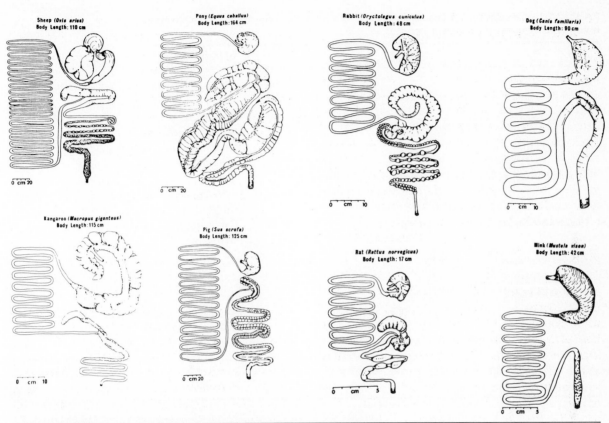

Figure 4.1   *Some examples of mammalian digestive tracts drawn to illustrate major
anatomical differences. The sheep and kangaroo represent pregastric digesters. Note that there is
some similarity between the sacculated stomach of the kangaroo and the cecum of the pony and,
to a lesser extent, the pig (both hind gut fermentors). Sacculation is a distinguishing
characteristic of herbivores whether in the stomach, cecum, or large gut. The cecum of the dog is
small and is absent in mink. Reprinted by permission from* Dukes' Physiology of Domestic
Animals, *9th ed. (1).*

cecum and a medium-sized unsacculated hind gut.
Both the horse and rabbit have a substantial amount
of hind gut fermentation.

Within these groups the ruminants represent a
highly specialized class because of their ability to
digest fiber and other carbohydrates more completely than the other groups. Some pregastric fermentation occurs in other species of non-ruminants
that have sacculated stomachs (Table 4.1), but it has
not been described as well in the literature as that
of ruminants. Among the hind gut fermentors, the
large herbivores (horse, rhinoceros, elephant) depend on fermentation of fiber in the large gut. Their
diet may be equally as fibrous as that of some ruminants, but such animals tend to eat more per unit
of metabolic size (body weight$^{0.75}$) while digesting

less of low quality feeds. Another example is the
Chinese panda (*Ailuropoda melanoleuca*). This bear-
like animal exists almost exclusively on bamboo
shoots. It is said that captive pandas weighing less
than 90 kg may consume almost 20% of their body
weight of bamboo leaves per day (2). In man, the
cecum is reduced to a point of little if any function,
but the colon is sacculated and fermentation occurs
there.

When animals depend heavily on cecal fermentation, there is often an association with coprophagy
(feces eating) as in rabbits. Such adaptations often
result in two kinds of feces. Only the finer material
is selected for recycling through coprophagy. This
practice allows these small herbivores to consume
fibrous diets that would otherwise be inadequate in

TABLE 4.1 Classification of some animal species according to areas in the gastrointestinal tract where extensive fermentation occurs.

CLASS	SPECIES	DIETARY HABIT
Hind gut fermentors		
Cecal fermentors	*Various rodents*	
	Capybara	Grazer
	Rabbit	Selective herbivore
	Rat	Omnivore
Colonic digesters with Sacculated colon		
	Horse, Donkey, Zebra	Grazer
	New World monkey	Selective herbivore
	Pig, Man	Omnivores
Unsacculated colon	Dog, Cat	Carnivores
	Fruit-eating bats	Herbivores
Pregastric fermentors		
Ruminants and pseudo-ruminants	All species	Herbivores
Non-ruminants	Colobine monkey	Selective herbivore
	Hamster, Vole	Selective herbivores
	Kangaroo, Wallaby, Quokka	Herbivores
	Hippopotamus and possibly other suisformes	Herbivores
	Three-toed tree sloth	Herbivore

some of the essential nutrients such as essential amino acids or vitamins (see a later section). Microbial activity in the gut provides a more complete supply of some vitamins and amino acids which, when coprophagy is practiced, is beneficial to the animal. Further detail on non-ruminant species may be found in books such as Swenson (1), and for ruminants in Hofmann (3) or Church (4). More specific information follows on monogastric, avian, and ruminant species.

Monogastric Species

The mouth and associated structures—tongue, lips, teeth—are used for grasping and masticating food; however, the degree of use of any organ depends on the species of animal and the nature of its food. In omnivorous species, such as humans or swine, the incisor teeth are used primarily to bite off pieces of the food and the molar teeth are adapted to mastication of nonfibrous materials. The tongue is used relatively little. In carnivorous species the canine teeth are adapted to tearing and rending, while the molars are pointed and adapted to only partial mastication and the crushing of bones. Herbivorous species, such as the horse, have incisor teeth adapted

to nipping off plant material, and the molars have relatively flat surfaces that are used to grind plant fibers. The jaws are used in both vertical and lateral movements, which shred plant fibers efficiently. Rodents have incisor teeth that continue to grow during the animal's lifetime, allowing the animal to use its teeth extensively for gnawing on hard material such as nut shells. Their incisor teeth would not withstand such rugged use without the continual growth and would be worn down greatly.

In the process of mastication, saliva is added, primarily from three bilateral pairs of glands—submaxillary, at the base of the tongue; sublingual, underneath the tongue; and the parotids, below the ear. Other small salivary glands are present in some species. Saliva aids in forming food into a bolus, which may be swallowed easily, and has other functions such as keeping the mouth moist, aiding in the taste mechanisms, and providing a source of enzymes (see a later section) for initiating enzymic digestive processes.

Photographs of portions of the GI tract of the rabbit and pig are shown in Fig. 4.2. These pictures illustrate the relative differences in size of the stom-

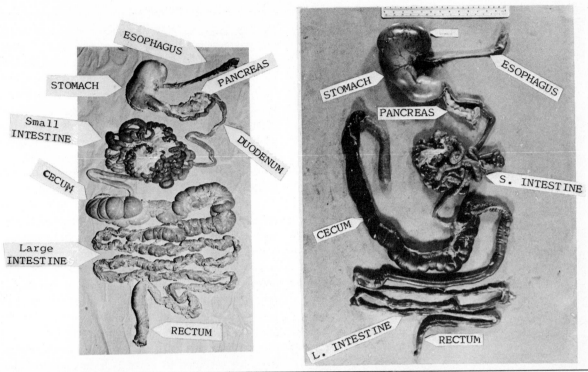

Figure 4.2   *Photographs of dissected tissues showing the principal parts of the gastrointestinal tract (GI tract) of the pig (left) and the rabbit (right). Note the differences in relative size of the various parts and the much more apparent sacculation in the large intestine of the pig. Approximate weights of the donors were: pig, 100 kg; rabbit, 2 kg. Photos by D. C. Church.*

ach compared to the intestines. The pig, for example, has a relatively large stomach, with the capacity in the adult said to be 6–8 liters. The shape of the stomach of different species varies as does the relative size. Mucosal tissues lining the interior of the stomach are divided into different areas which are

supplied with different types of glands as illustrated in Fig. 4.3. In the cardiac region the cells produce primarily mucus, probably as a means of protecting the stomach lining from gastric secretions. In the peptic gland region the lining is covered with gastric pits (Fig. 4.4), which open into gastric glands. These produce a mixed secretion of acid, enzymes, and mucus. The glands consist of two main types of cells, the body chief or peptic cells, which produce proteolytic enzymes, and the parietal or oxyntic cells, which secrete HCl. In the pyloric region, mucus-producing cells again are found. The enzymes produced and their function are discussed in a later section.

The relative length of the small intestine of various animal species varies greatly. In the pig it is comparatively long (15–20 m), but in the dog it is rather short (about 4 m). The duodenum, the first short section, is the site of production of various digestive juices. Furthermore, a variety of digestive juices from the pancreas as well as bile come into the duodenum within a short distance of the pylorus of the

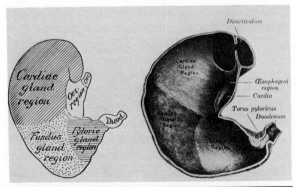

Figure 4.3   *Diagrams of the stomach of the pig illustrating the various zones and types of mucosal areas found in the stomach lining.*

Figure 4.4 *Surface of human stomach's inner lining (glandular mucosa) is seen enlarged some 260 diameters in this scanning electron micrograph. The view shows the tops of epithelial cells, the gastric pits, and characteristic folds of a normal stomach. Courtesy of Jeanne M. Riddle, Wayne State Univ. School of Medicine.*

considerably in different animal species. In the adult pig, the large intestine is about 4–4.5 m in length and is appreciably larger in diameter than the small intestine. The length and diameter of the cecum varies considerably, generally being much larger in herbivorous species than in omnivorous or carnivorous species. Note the very large size (Fig. 4.2) of the cecum of the rabbit compared to the pig. The horse also has a very large cecum and large bowel relative to other segments of its GI tract. In general, the large intestine acts as an area for absorption of water and secretion of some mineral elements such as Ca. An appreciable amount of bacterial fermentation takes place in the cecum and colon. Data on horses indicate that the volatile fatty acids (acetic, propionic, butyric) may be absorbed from the cecum as are some peptides and other small molecules. This area may be vital for synthesis of some of the water-soluble vitamins and, perhaps, proteins in species such as the horse and rabbit. Because proteins and other large molecules originating in the cecum and colon are not subject to action of the digestive juices, they are assumed to be of little use to the host. Further data are required to understand overall function of the cecum and large intestine.

The pancreas and liver are vital to digestive processes because of the digestive secretions produced (see a later section). Bile, from the liver, has many important functions, and the liver is an extremely active site of synthesis and detoxification. The liver also is an important storage site for many vitamins and trace minerals.

Avian Species

The GI tract of avian species (Fig. 4.5) differs considerably in anatomy from typical monogastric species. Birds have no teeth, for example, although some prehistoric forms did have teeth. Thus, the beak and/or claws serve to partially reduce food to a size that may be swallowed. Although some insect-eating species have no crops, other types have crops of variable sizes. Ingested food goes directly to the crop where fermentation probably occurs in some species. The proventriculus of birds is the site of production of gastric juices and the gizzard serves some of the functions of teeth in mammalian species, acting to physically reduce particle size of food. Current data indicate little proteolytic digestion occurs in either the proventriculus or gizzard and that removal of the gizzard has little effect on digestion if the food is ground. In the small intestine most of the

stomach. Ducts from the liver and pancreas join to form a common bile duct that empties into the duodenum in some species, while other species have separate ducts. An appreciable amount of absorption may occur in the duodenum (see later section on absorption). The small intestine, in general, accounts for most of the absorption in the GI tract, and it is lined with a series of finger-like projections, the villi, which serve to increase the absorption area. Each villus contains an arteriole and venule, together with a drainage tube of the lymphatic system, a lacteal. The venules drain ultimately into the portal blood system which goes directly to the liver; the lymph system empties via the thoracic duct into the vena cava, a large vein.

The large intestine is made up of the cecum, colon, and rectum. Relative sizes of these organs vary

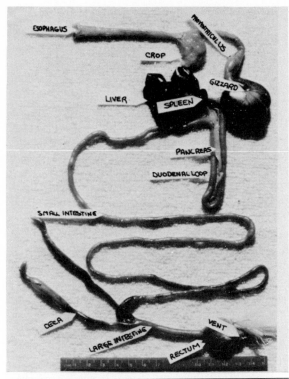

Figure 4.5 *Digestive tract of the chicken. Note the rather uncomplicated and unsacculated small and large intestines and the presence of two ceca. Photo by Don Helfer, Oregon State University.*

enzymes found in mammalian species are present, with the exception of lactase. The pH of the small intestine is slightly acid, and protein digestion is assumed to result from a combination of the common proteolytic enzymes. Data on absorption indicate that it is similar to mammalian species. The ceca and large intestines are sites for water resorption. Some fiber digestion occurs in the ceca because of bacterial fermentation, but at much lower levels than in most mammals. Removal has very little effect on digestion. Total digestibility by birds is similar to that in mammals for non-fibrous diets. Further information on avian species may be found in Swenson (1).

Ruminants

The mouths of ruminants differ from other mammalian species in that they have no upper incisor teeth, and only a few species have canine teeth. Thus, they depend on an upper dental pad and lower incisors in conjunction with lips and tongue for prehension of food. Ruminant species may be divided

into roughage eaters, selective eaters, and transitional types (3), and these various types utilize differences in tongue mobility and in lip structure, particularly, to facilitate selection and consumption of feedstuffs. With respect to mastication, ruminant species have molar teeth so shaped and spaced that the animal can chew only on one side of the jaw at one time. Lateral jaw movements aid in shredding tough plant fibers.

Saliva production in ruminants is very copious, reaching amounts of $150+$ l/day in adult cows and 10 l or more in sheep. Production of saliva is relatively continuous, although greater quantities are produced when eating and ruminating than when resting. Saliva provides a source of N (urea and mucoproteins), P and Na, which are utilized by rumen microorganisms. It is also highly buffered and aids in maintaining an appropriate pH in the rumen, in addition to other functions common to monogastric species.

The stomach of the ruminant (Fig. 4.6) is divided into four compartments—**reticulum, rumen, omasum,** and **abomasum.** The reticulum and rumen are not separated completely, by any means, but have different functional purposes. The reticulum functions in moving ingested food into the rumen or into the omasum and in regurgitation of ingesta during rumination. The rumen acts as a larger fermentation vat and has a very high population of microorganisms (see a later section). Function of the omasum is not clearly understood although it appears

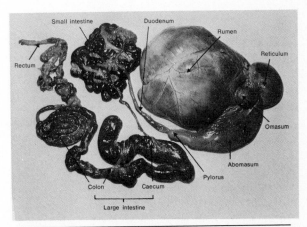

Figure 4.6. *The stomach and intestines of the sheep dissected out to illustrate the relative volumes of the various parts. Note the very large size of the stomach as compared to that of other non-ruminant species. Courtesy of CSIRO. From Anonymous (5)*

to aid in reducing particle size of ingested food, and it obviously has some effect on controlling passage of ingesta into the lower tract. Some absorption occurs in the omasum. The abomasum is believed to be comparable in function to the glandular stomach of monogastric species.

The stomach of ruminant species makes up a greater percentage of the total GI tract than is the case for other species. In adults the stomach may contain 65–80% of total digesta in the entire GI tract. The intestinal tract is relatively long, typical values for cattle and sheep, respectively, are: small intestine, 40 and 24–25 m; cecum, 0.7 and 0.25 m; and colon, 10 and 4–5 m.

In the young ruminant the reticulum, rumen, and omasum are relatively underdeveloped because the suckling animal primarily depends on the abomasum and intestine for digestive functions. As soon as the animal starts to consume solid food, the other compartments develop rapidly, reaching relative mature size by about 8 wk in lambs and goats, 3–4 mo. in black-tailed deer and 6–9 mo. or more in domestic bovines.

Another anatomical preculiarity of ruminant species is that they have a structure called the **reticular groove** (sometimes erroneously called the esophageal groove). This structure begins at the lower end of the esophagus and, when closed, forms a tube from the esophagus into the omasum. Its function is to allow milk from the suckling animal to bypass the reticulo-rumen and escape bacterial fermentation. Closure of this groove is stimulated by the normal

sucking reflexes, by certain ions and by solids in suspension in liquid. It does not appear to remain functional in older animals unless they continue to suckle liquid diets.

There is a well-developed pattern of rhythmic contractions of the various stomach compartments that act to circulate ingesta into and throughout the rumen, into and through the omasum, and on to the abomasum. Of importance also are contractions that aid in regurgitation during **rumination.** This is a phenomenon peculiar to ruminants. In effect, it is a controlled form of vomiting, allowing semiliquid materials to be regurgitated up the esophagus, swallowing of the liquids and a deliberate remastication of and swallowing of the solids. Ruminants may spend 8 h/day or more in rumination, depending on the nature of their diet. Coarse, fibrous diets result in more time ruminating. Inhibition of rumination results in a marked reduction in feed consumption. The origin of ruminating is not clear; perhaps it was an evolutionary development allowing animals to consume feed hastily and then retire in relative safety from predators to rechew their food at leisure.

Eructation (belching of gas) is another mechanism which is quite important to ruminants. Microbial fermentation in the rumen results in production of large amounts of gases which must be eliminated. This is accomplished by contractions of the upper sacs of the rumen which force the gas forward and down; the esophagus then dilates and allows the gas to escape. During this process much of the gas penetrates into the trachea and lungs. A common prob-

TABLE 4.2   Comparative capacity of the gastrointestinal tract of different species.[a]

	RELATIVE CAPACITY, %				RATIOS	
ANIMAL	STOMACH	SMALL INTESTINE	CECUM	COLON AND RECTUM	INTESTINAL TO BODY LENGTH	GASTROINTESTINAL SURFACE TO BODY SURFACE AREA
Cattle	71	18	3	8	20:1	3.0:1
Sheep, goat	67	21	2	10	27:1	
Horse	9	30	16	45	12:1	2.2:1
Pig	29	33	6	32	14:1	
Dog	63	23	1	13	6:1	0.6:1
Cat	69	15		16	4:1	0.6:1
Man	17	67		17		

[a]Values are based on old European data obtained on organs after autopsy. It should be noted that the volume of an organ after removal from the body may be quite different than the relative capacity in the live, functioning animal. Nevertheless, these data probably provide a reasonable relative comparison for differences in capacities of the different parts of the GI tract.

lem in ruminants is bloat, a condition that develops for the most part, as a result of formation of froth in the rumen. Froth, if found in the area where the esophagus enters the rumen, inhibits eructation, a safety mechanism preventing inhalation of froth into the lungs.

❑ COMPARATIVE CAPACITY OF THE GASTROINTESTINAL TRACT

The relative capacities of the GI tract from different species varies greatly as shown in Table 4.2. Assuming that these values are truly representative of these animal species, it is evident that there are tremendous differences. Humans have a very small GI tract compared to any of the other species. The pig has a very large stomach capacity for a simple stomach animal, and the horse shows the adaptation of a herbivorous animal to handle the large amounts of roughage naturally consumed. Ruminant species have, by far, the largest stomach. It might be pointed out that volume is subject to change, depending upon the amount of bulkiness of the diet and with time after feeding, so these values are not fixed.

Note, also, that the intestinal length (expressed as a ratio of intestinal to body length) is much greater in the ruminant species, and that the values for the horse and pig are much greater than those for the dog and cat. This gives a crude estimate of the relative difference in absorptive surface in the gut of these different species. Also, the ratio of intestinal surface to body surface is much greater for the cow and horse than for the dog and cat.

❑ THE ROLE OF DIGESTIVE JUICES IN DIGESTION

Digestive juices have very important roles in the overall digestive processes. In monogastric and avian species the digestive juices attack the food before it is subjected to microbial action in the cecum and large gut. In ruminant species the digestive juices are supplementary to the digestion that occurs first in the rumen as a result of microbial fermentation.

Digestive enzymes are found in saliva in small amounts. The glandular stomach (or abomasum or proventriculus) is a major source of proteolytic enzymes and HCl. The pancreas is an important source of enzymes which act on proteins, starches, and fats, and glands in the wall of the duodenum produce a variety of enzymes which act on sugars, protein fragments, or lipids. In areas of the GI tract where microorganisms grow, enzymes of microbial origin can be found. The enzymes from the glandular stomach are produced in the peptic gland region and are given off into the lumen of the organ. Pancreatic secretions enter the duodenum via a duct which joins the bile duct from the gall bladder (if present) or liver.

A list of the various enzymes involved is shown in Table 4.3 together with information on origin, substrate acted on and end-products produced. The enzymes are listed according to the general type of compound hydrolyzed—amylolytic (carbohydrates), lipolytic (lipids), or proteolytic (proteins).

With regard to the amylolytic enzymes, a number of species produce small amounts of salivary amylase, but it is not believed to be of major importance because of the relatively short time it might act in the mouth and because the usual stomach pH is too low for continued activity, provided food is mixed well with stomach juices and that pH drops rapidly. Numerous saccharidases are produced by the pancreas and intestinal mucosa. Pancreatic amylase is of major importance in hydrolyzing starch, glycogen, or dextrins to maltose. The various enzymes that act on oligosaccharides or disaccharides are produced by the small intestine mucosa. These include maltase, isomaltase, lactase, and sucrase. However, not all enzymes are found in all animals. For example, little if any lactase is found in species other than mammals. This is logical, of course, because lactose is found only in milk. In young mammals, lactase levels are high while they are consuming milk, but production of the enzyme tapers off after milk consumption ceases. Likewise, sucrase is not found in ruminant (and some other) species. With a natural diet, sucrose normally entering the stomach of a ruminant animal would be fermented in the rumen and would never reach the small intestine in any quantity. If young animals are fed sucrose in milk replacers, any digestion that takes place occurs in the lower gut as a result of microbial activity, often resulting in diarrhea if much sucrose is fed. Also, in ruminants the pancreatic production of amylase is low, presumably a result of the fact that natural diets do not contain much starch and because most of that entering the stomach would be fermented there. Some starch-like compounds (microbial storage polysaccharides) do enter the gut in these situations, but much less than would occur in animals fed high-grain diets. The overall result is that ruminant animals have a more limited capability to digest starch

36

TABLE 4.3 Principal digestive enzymes secreted by the gastrointestinal tract, substrates attacked and end-products produced.

TYPE, NAME	ORIGIN	SUBSTRATE, ACTION	END PRODUCTS	COMMENTS
Amylolytic				
Salivary amylase	saliva	starch, dextrins	dextrins, maltose	None in ruminants; of minor importance in other species
Pancreatic amylase	pancreas	starch, dextrins	maltose, isomaltose	Low in ruminants
Maltase, Isomaltase	s. intestine	maltose, isomaltose	glucose	Low in ruminants
Lactase	s. intestine	lactose	glucose, galactose	High in young mammals
Sucrase	s. intestine	sucrose	glucose, fructose	None in ruminants
Oligoglucosidase	s. intestine	oligosaccharides	misc. monosaccharides	
Lipolytic				
Salivary lipase	saliva	triglycerides	diglyceride + 1 fatty acid (FA)	Of minor importance in young mammals
Pancreatic lipase	pancreas	triglycerides	monoglyceride + 2 FA	
Intestinal lipase	s. intestine	triglycerides	glycerol + 3 FA	
Lecithinase	pancreas, s. intestine	lecithin	lysolecithin, free FA	
Proteolytic				
Pepsin[a]	gastric juice	native protein	proteoses, peptones, polypeptides	Clots milk; hydrolyzes native proteins in acid pH

Enzyme	Source	Substrate	End products	Remarks
Rennin[a]	abomasum	clots milk (casein)	Ca caseinate	Important in young mammals
Trypsin[a]	pancreas	native proteins or products of pepsin and rennin digestion	peptides with terminal arginine or lysine group	
Chymotrypsin	pancreas	}	peptides with terminal aromatic amino acid	
Elastase	pancreas	}	peptide with terminal alphatic amino acid	
Carboxypeptidase A	pancreas	peptides with aromatic or alphatic amino acid	small peptides, neutral amino acids, acidic amino acids	
Carboxypeptidase B	pancreas	peptides with terminal arginine or lysine	basic amino acids	
Aminopeptidases	s. intestine	peptides	amino acids	
Dipeptidases	s. intestine	dipeptides	amino acids	
Nucleases (several types)	pancreas, s. intestine	nucleic acids	nucleotides	
Nucleotidases	s. intestine	nucleotides	purine and pyrimidine bases, phosphoric acid, pentose sugars	

[a]These enzymes are given off in inactive forms, probably as a means of protecting the body tissues. Pepsinogen is activated by HCl to the active form, pepsin; rennin is activated by HCl; trypsinogen by an intestinal enzyme, enterokinase, and by trypsin. The proforms of chymotrypsin, carboxypeptidases, and amino peptidases are activated by trypsin.

192

in the gut than species such as the pig or humans.

Animals do not produce enzymes that will hydrolyze complex carbohydrates such as xylan, cellulose, and hemicellulose. Consequently, any activity that takes place on such compounds is a result of microbial enzymatic activity. This appears to be an illogical evolutionary development for herbivorous species which consume relatively large amounts of these carbohydrates. Perhaps, with increasing knowledge of digestive physiology, we will one day have a logical explanation for the absence of such enzymes.

With respect to the proteolytic enzymes, the proenzymes are converted to active enzymes by the activation of trypsinogen by enterokinase, an enzyme produced by the intestinal mucosa. Trypsin, in turn, activates chymotrypsinogen and procarboxypeptidase. Pepsin is relatively inactive except at a rather low pH. Thus, in the young suckling animal where stomach pH is apt to be on the order of 4–4.5, pepsin is relatively inactive. In fact, some information indicates very little pepsin secretion in calves until they start to consume solid food. Rennin is an important enzyme in young suckling mammals. Its major action is to coagulate milk into a clot (also produced by HCl and pepsin), which allows a continuous and prolonged flow of milk into the small intestine, thus avoiding an excessive overload of the duodenum immediately following a meal. Rennin production is reduced considerably after milk feeding ceases.

The activity of the various proteolytic enzymes is quite specific, as is true for most enzymes. Pepsin, for example, tends to attack peptide bonds involving an aromatic amino acid (phenylalanine, tryptophan, or tyrosine), and it also has significant action on peptide bonds involving leucine and acidic residues. However, it liberates only a few free amino acids. Trypsin acts on peptide linkages involving the carboxyl group of arginine and lysine, and chymotrypsin is most active on peptide bonds involving phenylalanine, tyrosine, and tryptophan. The action of trypsin and chymotrypsin is additive, resulting in more complete degradation of proteins to small peptides. These enzymes are termed endopeptidases because they hydrolyze interior bonds. Those that act on terminal amino acids are called exopeptidases.

Carboxypeptidase A rapidly liberates carboxyl terminal amino acids, but the other type (B) acts only on peptides with terminal arginine or lysine residues. Similar comments apply to the other peptidases.

Young mammals are capable of absorbing relatively large protein molecules from colostrum which provides them with a source of antibodies (immunoglobulin). These proteins apparently avoid digestion because of some delay in enzyme production and because, in some species, of the presence of trypsin inhibitors which protect the immunoglobulins without completely inhibiting the digestion of other milk proteins.

In addition to gastric enzymes, HCl has an important effect on gastric digestion. It activates both pepsin and rennin and provides a pH that is more or less optimal for pepsin activity. HCl, as well as pepsin and rennin, also has the property of coagulating milk proteins and has some hydrolytic activity in addition.

In the small intestine, bile from the liver has several important roles. Note that not all species have gall bladders, examples being the rat, horse, deer, elk, moose, and camel. In other species including humans, swine, chickens, cattle, and sheep, the gall bladder serves as a reservoir for temporary storage of bile. Bile contains various bile salts (glycocholates and taurocholates), which are important in providing an alkaline pH in the small intestine and in emulsifying fats. The bile salts are absorbed easily in the small intestine and are recirculated back to the liver rapidly. In addition to bile salts, bile pigments present are responsible for its color and, ultimately, for most of the color in feces and urine. Bilirubin or its oxidation products account for much of the pigment. These pigments are waste products, being derived from the porphyrin nucleus of hemoglobin, which is metabolized in the liver. Bile also serves as a route of excretion for many different metallic elements, inactivated hormones, and various harmful substances.

Fat digestion is a result of the emulsifying action of bile salts and enzymatic action of pancreatic lipase. Pancreatic lipase preferentially hydrolyzes fatty acids in the 1 and 3 positions of triglycerides to produce two free fatty acids and a 2-monoglyceride. The bile salts and hydrolyzed fats form micelles which increases greatly the surface area of fat droplets (up to 10^4 increase). The micelles are absorbed by the intestinal epithelium and a major portion passes into the lymph system which empties into the vena cava vein.

❑ RUMEN METABOLISM

Rumen Microorganisms

In the GI tract of the ruminant, as opposed to other types of animals that have no pregastric fermentation, ingested food is exposed to very extensive pregastric fermentation. Most of the ingesta is fermented by microbes before it is exposed to typical gastric and enteric digestive enzymes and chemicals.

The reticulo-rumen provides a very favorable environment for microbial survival and activity—it is moist and warm and there is an irregular introduction of new digesta and a more or less continual removal of fermented digesta and end-products of digestion. The overall fermentation is anaerobic in nature. A vast number of bacterial types may be found in the rumen, typical counts approaching numbers of 25–50 billion/ml. Characteristics of species that have been studied are too detailed to discuss here, except to note that a wide variety exists in cell size, shape, structure, and in metabolism. In addition to bacteria, some 35 species of ciliate protozoa have been identified from the rumens of animals in different situations, although the variety that may be found in any one animal is considerably less. Protozoal counts vary widely, but typical values to be expected are on the order of 20,000–500,000/ml. Most, if not all, protozoal species ingest rumen bacteria and many also ingest food particles. Considerably lower concentrations of flagellated protozoa are sometimes found, particularly in young animals. In addition, relatively large counts of phages (bacterial viruses) have been noted in recent years, and almost any organism found on feed or in water may be recovered from the rumen, although many of them may not be natural inhabitants of the rumen. Yeasts sometimes occur in large numbers, but not with great regularity. The fate of rumen microorganisms is that, eventually, they will pass into the abomasum and intestines where they are digested by and provide nutrients for the host animal.

Rumen Fermentation

Carbohydrates. Carbohydrates of various types make up the major portion of the diet of herbivorous animals. There may be many different types (see Ch. 8), but for our discussion here they can be classed as fibrous (hemicellulose, cellulose, xylans) or readily available (primarily sugars, starches). In the rumen of an animal fed at a low level (i.e., maintenance), essentially 100% of the readily available carbohydrates (RAC) will be fermented by the rumen microorganisms. The principal end-products of fermentation are the volatile fatty acids (primarily acetic, propionic and butyric), carbon dioxide, methane, and heat. The animal, in turn, uses the volatile fatty acids as a source of energy for its life processes

in contrast to most species that use glucose as the principal energy source. The fibrous carbohydrates also are fermented by rumen microorganisms and the end-products are the same, although less propionic acid is produced normally than from RAC. Because animal tissues do not produce cellulase or hemicellulase enzymes, microbial fermentation is the only means by which animals can indirectly use these complex carbohydrates. The ruminant animal is unusual in that it is capable of utilizing a larger proportion of fibrous carbohydrates than other herbivorous animals such as the horse or rabbit, which depend on microbial digestion in the cecum and large intestine for the digestion that occurs.

If ruminant animals are fed large amounts of grain or pelleted roughage, then moderate amounts of RAC or cellulose may pass out of the rumen before fermentation can be completed. In this case, the RAC is exposed to pancreatic and intestinal enzymes that may digest some part of it. However, the capability of the animal to digest large amounts of sugars (especially sucrose) or starches is limited because of limited production of the appropriate enzymes. In such cases microbial digestion of RAC also may occur in the lower gut.

Feeding unadapted animals large amounts of grains, particularly wheat, may result in abnormal rumen fermentation, which results in high production of lactic acid and a very acid rumen. This condition may cause morbidity or death if severe enough.

Proteins. Although some rumen bacteria may require amino acids or peptides, and it is believed that most ciliate protozoa must ingest bacteria for survival, the overall mixtures of rumen microorganisms generally do not respond in this manner. There are many proteolytic organisms that attack dietary protein with the result that a considerable amount of it is degraded to ammonia and organic acids, which may, in turn, be utilized by other microbial species to synthesize amino acids and bacterial proteins. Most cellulose-digesting bacteria require ammonia. The net result of feeding plant (or animal) protein is that a considerable portion of it is degraded and resynthesized into different microbial proteins. If the quality of the dietary protein is low, this is an advantage to the host animal. However, if a high quality protein, such as soybean meal, is fed, then it is a disadvantage because the overall quality of microbial protein normally is lower than that of soybean meal.

Rumen microorganisms also are capable of utilizing simple N sources such as urea (a normal mammalian excretory product), amino acids, nitrates, amides, amines, and so on. Thus, this allows use of urea, an economical source of N, in ruminant diets in many, although not all, instances. The net effect of normal rumen metabolism of protein is that it allows the animal to exist on a wide variety of diets, but overall efficiency of protein utilization is low because it is biologically inefficient to degrade and resynthesize complex molecules such as proteins.

Recent research data suggest that solubility and degradability of protein sources are quite important to ruminants expected to perform at a high level. There is some evidence that high producing dairy cows require larger amounts of some amino acids, particularly methionine, lysine, and leucine, than they can obtain from microbial protein. If a protein is fed that is either not soluble or only partially degraded in the rumen, but which can be digested in the gut, then it is sometimes possible to provide the animal with the needed amino acids. This type of protein, called by-pass protein, is present to some degree in many feed sources. However, all of the answers on this topic are not in, and a considerable amount of additional research will be required to utilize this information on a routine basis in formulating diets for ruminants.

Lipids.   Lipid consumption by herbivorous animals is low because most forage contains only limited amounts. Of that present, a considerable portion is in the form of galactosyl diglycerides, compounds in which galactose (a simple sugar) has replaced one of the fatty acids normally found in a common triglyceride. Another characteristic of herbage lipids is that a high percentage of the fatty acids are unsaturated (see Ch. 9).

In the rumen, the microbes do not alter greatly the fat fraction, although some may be synthesized. When fed low to moderate levels of dietary fat, the rumen microorganisms hydrolyze fat, producing free fatty acids and glycerol. Rumen microbes modify the unsaturated fatty acids by either saturating them or causing changes in the location of double bonds or altering the normal *cis* bond to a *trans* double bond. These are two of the characteristics that are common to ruminant milk or body fat. In addition, some of the fat synthesis that takes place results in the production of odd-length and branched-chain fatty acids. For example, butterfat may have fatty acids with 9, 11, 13, 15, 17, and 19 carbon atoms, numbers not at all characteristic of plant fatty acids, which usually have even numbers of carbon atoms.

The rumen population is intolerant to high dietary levels of fat. When added fat is used, it is fed normally at no more than 5 to 7% of the total diet. Higher levels are apt to result in abnormal rumen fermentation unless the fat is protected from the organisms by coating fat droplets with casein, which is then treated with formaldehyde.

Gas production.   Anaerobic fermentations such as those that occur in the rumen result in the production of copious amounts of gases. A fairly typical composition of the gases would be: 65% CO_2, 25–27% CH_4, 7% N, and trace amounts of O_2, H_2, and H_2S. Calorimetry data indicate that cattle may produce up to 600 l of gases/day (3). Methane, which has a high heat equivalent, represents a direct loss of energy to the animal (see Ch. 10). It is produced in anaerobic fermentations as a means of getting rid of excess hydrogen. If eructation (see earlier section) is inhibited, bloat may result; bloat can be chronic or acute, and the latter can cause death very rapidly.

Vitamin synthesis.   Rumen microorganisms have the capability of synthesizing essentially all of the B-complex vitamins (see Ch. 15) required by the host animal. Although some synthesis may occur in the intestines or cecum of other species, the amount synthesized in the rumen is probably greater than that in the lower gut. Normally, deficiencies of only two B-complex vitamins ever cause any problem for ruminant species. Cobalamin (B_{12}) may be deficient at times because of a shortage of cobalt, an essential component of the vitamin. This, of course, can be remedied by supplying more cobalt in the diet. Thiamin (B_1) may also be a problem. Data suggest that synthesis is reduced in the rumens of animals fed high-RAC diets. Also, some information shows that some loss of thiamin (and other vitamins) may occur in instances where the diet is quite high in these vitamins. Problems associated with thiamin deficiency are discussed in Ch. 15. There is also some evidence that insufficient niacin may be involved in ketosis of lactating dairy cows.

Some evidence also shows that rumen activity may result in a decrease in vitamin A or carotene content of diets. Although not proven by research, it appears likely that these unsaturated compounds may be saturated partially, resulting in loss of vitamin A activity. However, the consumption of carotene is usually at sufficiently high levels that this effect of the rumen is not a problem for the animal.

❏ CONTROL OF GASTROINTESTINAL ACTIVITY

The gastrointestinal system of an animal is a very complex system controlled by a combination of nerve stimulation and inhibition and by a number of gastrointestinal peptide hormones. Cranial parasympathetic neurons provide innervation via the vagus nerve to the esophagus, stomach, small intestine, and proximal portions of the large intestine. The sacral segment of the spinal cord provides parasympathetic innervation to the distal portion of the colon, rectum, and the internal anal sphincter. Controls are also provided by gastrointestinal peptide hormones acting alone or in conjunction with neural controls.

A gastrointestinal hormone has been defined as a peptide that is biosynthesized, although not exclusively, in cells of some part of the wall of the digestive tract and that, whatever else it may do, influences in either an endocrine, paracrine, neurocrine, or neuroendocrine manner the physiological activity of some organ or organs of digestion. More simply, the actions of gastrointestinal peptide hormones and hormone-like peptides include stimulation and reduction of secretions, motility, and absorption. Some may have other functions (6).

The major gastrointestinal peptide hormones that have been characterized at this time are listed in Table 4.4. Note that most of them are produced in the stomach or in duodenal tissues. The exceptions

TABLE 4.4 Gastrointestinal peptide hormones and functions related to activity of the gastrointestinal tract.

HORMONE	ORIGIN	RELEASING MECHANISM	FUNCTION
Gastrin	Pyloric antrum of the stomach or abomasum of ruminants	Vagal nerve stimulation; food in the stomach; stomach distension	Stimulation of acid secretion by gastric glands
Gastric-inhibitory Polypeptide (GIP)	Gastric antrum, duodenum, jejunum	Fats and fatty acids plus bile in the duodenum	Inhibition of gastric secretion and motility
Secretin	Duodenal mucosa	Acidification of the duodenum, peptones in duodenum	Stimulation of volume and bicarbonate outputs of pancreatic secretion and, in some species, of bile
Cholecystokinin (CCK)	Duodenal mucosa, brain	Long-chain fatty acids, amino acids, peptones	Contraction of gallbladder and pancreas; stimulates synthesis of pancreatic enzymes; inhibits gastric acid secretion; enhances insulin release, may induce satiety
Somatostatin	Abomasal antrum and duodenum, nerve cells in GI tract	Vagal stimulation and changes in the composition of intestinal chyme	Inhibits release of gastrin, secretin, and CCK; inhibits ion transport in intestines
Pancreatic Polypeptide	Pancreas	Nerve stimulation; entry of food into the duodenum; insulin hypoglycemia	Reduction or inhibition of pancreatic secretions
Vasoactive Intestinal Peptide (VIP)	Many neural tissues throughout body	Neural stimulation, prolonged exercise, fasting	Stimulates pancreatic exocrine secretions; potent vasodilator

are pancreatic polypeptide, which is produced in the pancreas, and vasoactive intestinal peptide (VIP), which is produced primarily by nervous tissues in many locations in the body.

The major point to be made here is that the neural and neuroendocrine controls result in a coordinated series of secretory and motor activities that provide for an orderly sequence of action. The coordinated muscle activity serves to mix and transport digesta through the total GI tract. In addition, the intestinal hormones stimulate or inhibit secretions of various glands necessary for digestion and absorption of nutrients. Other hormones may also be involved; that is, various adrenal hormones and parathormone have marked effects on absorption and excretion of some mineral elements. Several hormones—insulin and glucagon from the pancreas, adrenocortical hormones, thyroid hormone, and others from the pituitary—have effects on glucose utilization. Other examples could be given, but this topic is too complicated to present in detail in this text.

❑ ROLE OF THE INTESTINAL TRACT IN TRANSPORT OF NUTRIENTS

Most of the absorption of nutrients takes place in the upper intestinal tract, including the duodenum and the jejunum—and to a lesser extent, the ileum.

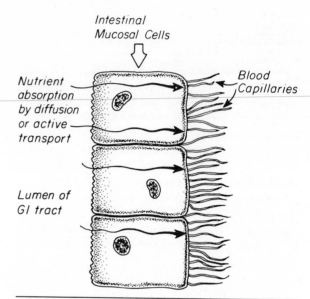

Figure 4.8 *Diagram of arrangement of intestinal mucosal cells.*

The rate of passage of nutrients through the digestive tract is only a matter of a few hours in most species, so it is clear that opportunity for processing and absorption of nutrients is limited. The degree of absorption of nutrients from the intestinal tract is increased enormously by an increase in the absorptive surface. For example, in the human adult, if the surface area of the intestine were in the form of a simple cylinder, it would be approximately 3,300 cm². However, it is increased to about 2 million cm² by virtue of folds, villi and microvilli, each of which increases surface area by several times. A diagram of nutrient absorption from the GI tract showing epithelial cells along the surface of the villi and the microvilli associated with each individual cell is shown in Fig. 4.7. Fig. 4.8 shows a diagram of a small segment of the GI tract illustrating the arrangement of the single layer of epithelial cells lining the intestine and the villi which increase the absorptive surface. In Fig. 4.9 are photographs of a jejunal intestinal epithelial cell from newborn and 4-day-old pigs. The microvilli and subcellular components of a single cell are visible at a magnification of 1,800X (7).

The rate of metabolism of the intestinal mucosa (the intestinal epithelium) is one of the fastest of any tissue in the body. In the human adult, there is a turn-over of about 250 g of dry matter/day, an amount that contributes significantly to the maintenance requirements of the individual.

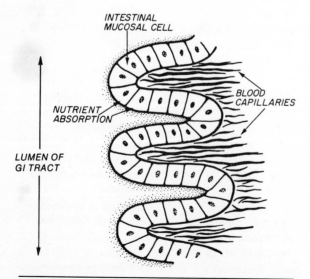

Figure 4.7 *Diagram of epithelial cells lining the intestinal tract and villi which increase the absorptive surface.*

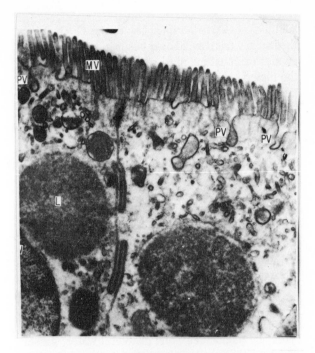

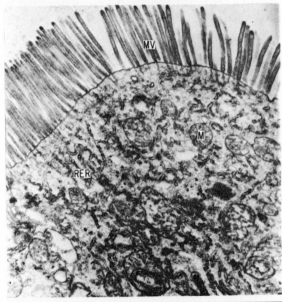

Figure 4.9 *Top: Electronmicrographs of jejunal intestinal epithelium 1.5 h after feeding cow's colostrum (open). Bottom: same except specimen came from a 4-day-old piglet (closed). Note: indentations and vesiculation of plasmalemma in open piglet and lack of activity in closed piglet. PV = pinocytotic vesicle; MV = microvilli; L = lysosome; N = nucleus; RFR = rough endoplasmic reticulum; M = mitochondria. From Broughton and Lecce (7). Courtesy of J. C. Lecce.*

The passage of individual nutrients from the intestinal lumen into the intestinal epithelial cell and then into the blood or lymph may occur by passive diffusion (pore size of cells in jejunum is 7.5 angstroms or 0.0000075 mm), by active transport or by pinocytosis (phagocytosis). Pinocytosis involves engulfment of large particles or large ions in a manner similar to the way an amoeba surrounds its food. This occurs in newborn animals to allow absorption of immune globulins from colostrum.

The passage of a nutrient across the intestinal mucosal cell membrane and into the blood or lymph, whether by diffusion or by active transport, involves (a) penetration of the microvillus and of plasma membrane, which encapsulates the epithelial cell, (b) migration through the cell interior, (c) possible metabolism within the cell, (d) extrusion from lateral and basal aspects of the cell, (e) passage through the basement membrane, and (f) penetration through the vascular or lymphatic epithelium into blood or lymph. The exact means of transfer of each individual nutrient will be discussed in subsequent chapters on individual nutrient requirements and metabolism.

❑ ROLE OF BLOOD AND LYMPH IN NUTRIENT TRANSPORT

A broad concept of nutrient flow through the body is illustrated in Fig. 4.10 (lymph system not shown). Briefly, a nutrient passes across the epithelial cell and enters either blood capillaries or the lymph system and is carried through the portal vein to the liver or, when materials enter the lymph, through the thoracic duct to the heart. The liver acts as a central organ in metabolism because many complex and vital reactions occur there. After traversing the liver, venous blood reaches the right atrium of the heart and passes into the right ventricle, from which it is pumped through the lung for oxygenation. From the lung it returns to the left atrium of the heart and passes into the left ventricle, the largest and most muscular chamber of the heart. From the left ventricle it is pumped through the aorta to enter all tissues of the body, carrying oxygenated blood and nutrients from the GI tract and those synthesized in other tissues, including the liver. The nutrients enter the capillaries in all tissues of the body and, in this way, nourish every cell. The same capillary system carries waste products from the cell into veins for transport to sites of further metabolism or for excretion. The kidney plays an important role in acting

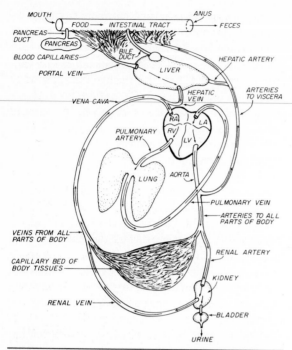

Figure 4.10 *Diagram of routes of nutrient absorption, flow of nutrients and fluids in the body, and routes of excretion. The lymph system is not shown.*

as a filter to dispose of waste materials. In addition to waste product excretion through the kidney, other waste products can be disposed of by re-excretion back into the intestinal lumen. This takes place by accumulation in the liver and excretion via the bile. In addition, excretory products pass through the blood capillaries into the intestinal epithelium. Thus, two-way traffic moves across the epithelial cells—both absorption of nutrients from the intestinal lumen and excretion of metabolites and waste materials across the intestinal wall—but in opposite directions. In addition to excretory products, there is considerable loss from the body of nutrients that have already served a productive function. For example, the loss via feces of cells sloughed off from the intestinal mucosa represents an obligatory loss of protein, minerals, and other nutrients, even though they have been utilized in normal body function.

The GI tract provides the most readily accessible route for non-gaseous substances to enter the body. Consequently, it must carefully select those substances through a variety of mechanisms, including rapid rejection of toxic compounds (vomiting or increased rate of passage) and gastric digestion, before they reach the more permeable intestinal tract. In

addition, selective permeability of the GI tract epithelium is vital to avoid over absorption of toxic compounds or of natural nutrients—particularly some of the mineral elements—or reabsorption of toxic metabolites such as ammonia.

❑ BLOOD AND NUTRITION

There is a great body of information relating normal blood components to pathology, both animal and human, but considerably less information on mild (subclinical) nutritional problems with animals. Regardless of this deficiency, some discussion on this topic is justified in a book on animal nutrition. Further and more detailed information can be found in many reference books on the topic.

Very briefly, blood is composed of the formed elements—erythrocytes or red blood cells, leukocytes (neutrophils, eosinophils, basophils, lymphocytes and monocytes), and platelets; water, gasses (O_2, CO_2, N_2), and various chemicals dissolved or suspended in the blood. If blood is allowed to clot, the remaining fluid is called serum. If unclotted blood is centrifuged, the cells are spun down and the fluid is called plasma.

Typical values for some blood components for some of the domestic animal species are shown in Table 4.5. Of course, many other components are found in blood in small amounts because blood will contain any chemical transported to or from the various body tissues. In addition, many different enzymes are found in blood, some of which have useful diagnostic values in nutrition.

Blood Evaluation in Nutrition

Anemia is a fairly common problem in animals; in most lower animals nutritional anemias are due to a reduction in red cell production as distinguished from a reduction in hemoglobin synthesis. Anemia may develop as a result of deficiencies of Fe, Cu, Co (indirectly to Co, directly to vitamin B_{12}), and folic acid or a general malnutrition from inadequate protein or energy. Anemia can be confirmed by a low packed cell volume (percentage of space of blood occupied by red cells after centrifugation), by a low hemoglobin content in blood or by a microscopic examination of red cells. Red cells may be smaller than normal (microcytic), normal (normocytic), or larger than normal (macrocytic) and have normal (normochromic) amounts, more (hyperchromic), or less (hypochromic) hemoglobin in the cells.

TABLE 4.5 Typical amounts or ranges of some blood components in domestic animals.

	ANIMAL SPECIES				
BLOOD CHEMICAL	CATTLE	SHEEP	SWINE	HORSE	CHICKEN, LAYER
Serum proteins, g/dl					
Total serum protein	7.7	5.4	6.3	6.5	5.4
Albumin	3.6	3.1	2.0	3.25	2.5
Globulin	3.9	2.3	4.3	3.25	2.9
Other whole blood components, mg/dl					
Total non-protein N	20–40	20–38	20–45	20–40	20–35
Urea N	6–27	8–20	8–25	10–20	0.4–1
Uric acid		0.05–2		0.05–1	0.8–5.0
Amino acid N	4–8	5–8	6–8	5–7	4–9
Lactic acid	5–20	9–12		10–16	20–100
Glucose	40–70	30–50	80–120	60–110	130–290
Serum components					
Total cholesterol, mg/dl	50–230	100–150	100–250	75–150	125–200
Calcium, mg/dl	8–12	8–12	8–12	8–12	10–30
Phosphorus, inorganic, mg/dl	4–8	4–8	4–8	3–6	3–8
Magnesium, mg/dl			2–5		3–4
Potassium, meq/l.			3.5–5.5		3.8–6.0
Chloride, meq/l.	130–150	150–160	140–160	145–150	

Groups of blood chemistries now are done routinely on humans on instruments such as shown in Fig. 3.8. Such packages are often referred to as blood or metabolic profiles. They are less commonly done on domestic animals, but a fair amount of research has been done on this topic, particularly on dairy cattle. The blood values often included in profiles are: packed cell volume, hemoglobin, glucose, serum urea, inorganic P, Ca, Mg, Na, K, total protein, albumin, and globulin. Recognizing that there may be substantial differences caused by breeds, seasons (diet and environment), age, stage and level of production, and other factors, this approach appears to have a useful place in nutritional evaluation of herds, but a series of analyses may be needed to establish the trends for a particular herd. Payne's work (8) in England showed that 57% of 30 "normal" dairy herds had abnormal profiles. In another report from the same laboratory, only 13% of 191 herds had completely normal profiles, 61% had one or two abnormal components, and 11% had four or more abnormal components. Other workers (7) have concluded that such profiles have almost no practical use for individual cows because of extreme abnormal concentrations in blood metabolites. Based on data obtained in the English studies with lactating dairy cows, the following conclusions were made: PCV has been related to milk yield (not surprising that anemia could be indirectly related to milk production). Blood glucose (low) may be indicative of inadequate energy intake or incipient problems with ketosis. Blood Mg has been shown to be useful in predicting problems, particularly to indicate herds that may be susceptible to future problems with Mg tetany. Blood albumin has been proven to be a useful item to include. Low blood albumins are indicative of low protein intake and are indicative of poor fertility in dairy cows. Animals that grow at a faster rate than others sometimes have high serum albumin, hemoglobin and glucose and low concentrations of K. Other workers feel that serum urea is also indicative of protein consumption (sheep or cattle) and that some of the same inferences can be made as with albumin. Other work also indicates a rather low correlation between blood glucose and energy consumption and that plasma free fatty acids are more highly related (negatively) to energy consumption.

For the mineral elements, blood data may be difficult to relate to dietary status for any element stored in appreciable amounts in body tissues. For example, blood P is somewhat more sensitive to dietary status than Ca, but neither are particularly accurate, because of hormonally controlled homeostasis, and a series of analyses may be required to detect any change in mineral status of either of these elements unless the animal is grossly deficient. With Mg, blood or urine levels are reasonably good evaluators. For Na, K, and Cl, saliva would be preferred to blood. With the trace minerals, blood values are less informative than tissue levels.

☐ DIGESTIBILITY AND PARTIAL DIGESTION

Digestion, as indicated previously, is defined as the preparation of food for absorption by the GI tract. However, most authors tend to use an implied definition meaning disappearance of food from the GI tract. This broad definition would include absorption as well as digestion.

Digestibility data are used extensively in animal nutrition to evaluate feedstuffs or study nutrient utilization (see Ch. 5 for more detail). The reader should be aware that digestibility is variable; in other words, the same feedstuff given to the same animal is not always digested to the same extent. Several

factors may alter the extent of digestion. These include level of feed intake, digestive disturbances, nutrient deficiencies, frequency of feeding, feed processing, and associative effects of feedstuffs (nonadditive effects of combining different feedstuffs). Marked differences also exist in the ability of different animal species to digest a particular feedstuff, particularly roughages. Note in Table 4.6 where seven different species have been fed the same alfalfa hay, that there are appreciable differences in digestion of the different fractions listed. This information reflects the ability of the GI tract to utilize fibrous feeds, clearly indicating an advantage of ruminant species and the horse over swine, rabbits, and guinea pigs.

The term **partial digestion** implies that total digestion in the GI tract can be subdivided into fractions that are digested in different parts of the tract. In ruminant species enough research has been done in recent years to provide a considerable amount of information on this subject. Less information is available on other domestic animals. Data on sheep and cattle (see Ch. 9) indicate that about two-thirds of digestible organic matter and energy disappear from the forestomach (reticulo-rumen, omasum), the remainder being digested in the intestines. The more fibrous portions (crude fiber, cell walls), as well as readily available carbohydrates, are digested to a somewhat greater extent (65–90% of total digestion) in the forestomach. Digestibility of N is quite variable, but is relatively more important in the small intestine; this is a reflection of passage of large amounts of microbial proteins into the small intestine.

TABLE 4.6 Digestibility of alfalfa hay by different species.[a]

| SPECIES | DIGESTION COEFFICIENTS, % | | | | | |
	ORGANIC MATTER	CRUDE PROTEIN	ETHER EXTRACT	CRUDE FIBER	NFE	TDN
Cattle	61	70	35	44	71	48.3
Sheep	61	72	31	45	69	48.1
Goat	59	74	19	41	69	46.9
Horse	59	75	10	41	68	46.0
Pig	37	47	14	22	49	30.5
Rabbit	39	57	21	14	51	30.9
Guinea pig	52	58	12	33	65	40.5

[a]From Maynard and Loosli (9). The alfalfa hay in question contained 86.1% dry matter, 16.2% crude protein, 1.6% ether extract, and 26.9% crude fiber.

❏ FECAL AND URINARY EXCRETION

Fecal material excreted by animals is comprised of undigested residues of food material; residues of gastric juices, bile, pancreatic, and enteric juices; cellular debris from the mucosa of the gut; excretory products excreted into the gut; and cellular debris and metabolites of microorganisms that grow in the large intestine or, in the case of ruminants, in the forestomach.

Undigested food residues are largely dependent upon the type of food consumed and the type of GI tract; thus, in roughage eaters, undigested residues will usually account for more of the total than would be the case with monogastric species consuming a diet low in fiber. Sloughed cellular debris may reach substantial amounts. Using data from rats, it has been estimated that the dairy cow may slough about 2,500 g of cells daily from the interior of the gut wall.

The color of feces is from plant pigments and stercobilinogen produced by bacterial reduction of bile pigments. The odor is from aromatic substances, primarily indole and skatole, which are derived from deamination and decarboxylation of tryptophan in the large intestine.

Urine represents the main route of excretion of nitrogenous and sulfurous metabolites of body tissues. In addition, usually it is the principal route for excretion of some of the mineral elements, particularly Cl, K, Na, and P. Urine is, essentially, an aqueous solution of these various components with minor amounts of pigments and sloughed cells from the urogenital tract.

The color of urine is due primarily to urochrome, a metabolite of bile pigments complexed with a peptide. The urine from ruminants (other than suckling animals and those on high-grain feed) usually is basic, being in the pH range of 7.4 to 8.4. The basic reaction is characteristic of herbivorous animals because of the relatively large amounts of Na and K ions found in vegetation. Urine usually is in the acidic range in monogastric species. In mammals, urea is the principal N-containing compound excreted with lesser amounts of other compounds such as ammonia, allantoin, creatine and creatinine. In birds the major N-containing compound in urine is uric acid.

Only traces of protein normally are found in urine. The presence in quantity of proteins such as albumin and globulins is indicative of kidney disease in adults, although it may occur in young animals under normal conditions, particularly within a few days after normal consumption of colostrum. Carbohydrates such as glucose or fructose sometimes may be found in mammalian urine following ingestion of a meal high in soluble carbohydrates. However, carbohydrates in the urine are usually indicative of disease. Ketones are found at times, particularly in animals suffering from starvation or ketosis.

❏ SUMMARY

The gastrointestinal tract of higher animals is a very complicated system with complex nervous and hormonal controls. Although the anatomy of the GI tract varies among species or groups such as ruminants and non-ruminants or between mammals and birds, the essential digestive functions are similar—that is, the GI tract will break the food down to a molecular size and solubility which can be absorbed. Animals eat foods their GI tract can accommodate in terms of bulk and nutrient content and indigestible components. Domestic animals, however, do not have such specific food requirements as many wild species, some of which may exist only on nectar or only one plant species.

Nutrient requirements for ruminants are simplified by rumen synthesis of microbial proteins and B-vitamins. Likewise, vitamin requirements for species that have extensive fermentation in the large gut are also simplified. In addition, amino acid requirements are less complex for species that practice coprophagy as a result of bacteria protein synthesis in the gut.

❏ REFERENCES

1. Swenson, M. J. (ed.). 1977. *Dukes' Physiology of Domestic Animals,* 9th ed. Comstock Publ. Associates, Ithaca, N.Y.
2. Schaller, G. B. 1981. *National Geographic* **160**(6): 735.
3. Hofmann, R. R. 1973. *The Ruminant Stomach.* East African Literature Bureau, Nairobi, Kenya.
4. Church, D. C. (ed.) 1987. *The Ruminant Animal.* Prentice-Hall, Inc., Englewood Cliffs, N.J.
5. Anonymous. 1972. Rural Research in CSIRO, p. 4, June issue.
6. Titchen, D. A. 1986. In *Control of Digestion and Metabolism of Ruminants,* p. 227. Prentice-Hall, Inc., Englewood Cliffs, N.J.
7. Broughton, C. W. and J. C. Lecce. 1970. *J. Nutr.* **100**:445.
8. Payne, J. M., et al. 1973. *Brit. Vet. J.* **129**:370; 1974, **130**:34.
9. Maynard, L. A. and J. K. Loosli. 1969. *Animal Nutrition,* 6th ed. McGraw-Hill Book Co., N.Y.

5

Measurement of Feed and Nutrient Utilization and Requirements by Animals

$\mathbf{A}$ knowledge and understanding of nutrient utilization is a necessary step in evaluating feedstuffs or for defining nutrient requirements for development of feeding standards for animals (a compilation of nutrient requirements for various situations). Nutrient utilization from a given feedstuff may be affected by the type of GI tract, species, age, level of consumption (plane of nutrition), feed processing, nutrient requirement, disease, parasites, and stresses of various types. Consequently, if we calculate the utilization of protein from alfalfa for a young, growing pig, the values most likely will be quite different than for a mature sow, not to mention the differences likely to be found for other species.

Methods that are applicable for evaluation of nutrient utilization are more or less common to all animal species. In this chapter we will discuss some of the more common methods that are utilized. Information on specific nutrients will often be presented in more detail in chapters on those nutrients.

❑ METHODS

Growth Trials

Growth, as defined by Brody (1), is "the constructive or assimilatory synthesis of one substance at the expense of another (nutrient) which undergoes dissimilation." In the broadest sense, growth of an animal consists of an increase in body weight resulting from assimilation by body tissues of ingested nutrients. This is usually accompanied by an increase in height or other measures of skeletal size. The increase in weight is composed of the sum of the increases in weight of individual components making up the body, namely: water, fat, protein, carbohydrate, and minerals (ash). It can be expressed as absolute gain in a given period of time or as relative gain (usually expressed as a percentage). Growth trials usually include the measurement of absolute gain in body weight during a period of feeding a test diet. Rate of gain is then expressed as average daily or weekly gain (absolute gain) or in terms of final weight as a percentage of initial weight (relative gain).

Animals used in a growth experiment usually are fed the test diet concurrently with similar animals fed a standard (or basal) diet of known nutritive quality which allows normal growth. In this way direct comparisons can be made among various feed or nutrient sources, and they can be ranked in order of their ability to promote weight gain or efficiency of feed utilization. Growth is often used interchangeably with weight gain; strictly speaking, the two terms are different because an equal increase in body weight between animals does not necessarily indicate equal growth of body tissues. One animal may deposit more lean muscle mass while its penmate may deposit more fat which has a much higher energy content (see Ch. 10). If this occurs, it gives a misleading estimate of diet utilization.

Normally, a growth trial involves ad libitum feeding of a diet. Knowing the rate of gain and the total feed consumption, feed efficiency (feed required per unit of gain or units of gain per unit of feed) can be computed. Feed efficiency also is a very useful estimate of nutrient adequacy of a test diet. Diets that promote a high rate of gain will usually result in a greater efficiency than diets that do not allow such rapid gain. This is illustrated in Table 5.1. The simple explanation for this response is that the rapidly gaining animal utilizes less of the total feed consumption for maintenance and more is available for gain (see Ch. 10).

TABLE 5.1 Inverse relationship between daily gain and feed required per unit of gain.

DIET	DAILY GAIN	FEED TO GAIN RATIO
Pigs[a]		
Diet 1	717 g	3.19
Diet 2	702 g	3.49
Diet 3	695 g	3.57
Diet 4	689 g	3.74
Cattle[b]		
Diet 1	1.54 kg	6.76
Diet 2	1.31 kg	7.14

[a]Taken from Lindemann *et al.* (3).
[b]Taken from Zobell (2).

Physical characteristics, nutrient content, or palatability factors may affect total feed intake (see Ch. 19). To rule out this type of variation, paired feeding experiments can be conducted. In such studies, test diets are fed to animals of comparable size and at equalized intake based on the voluntary consumption by the member of the pair eating the least. Paired feeding eliminates differences in animal performance related to palatability of the feed, but it penalizes the animal consuming the more adequate diet and tends to reduce the magnitude of difference in growth of animals fed the test diets.

In studies with large animals, where costs per animal are much greater than for small animals, it is desirable, if feasible, to have data on individual animals rather than on groups. For example, if one animal in a group does poorly for some unknown reason or if it dies, the data on feed utilization are much less valid than if all animals perform about the same. Consequently, when feasible, it is desirable to obtain feed consumption on individual animals. With some of our modern technology, individual data on feed consumption can be obtained, at a price, with electronically controlled feeding apparatus such as that illustrated in Fig. 5.1. With apparatus of this type the animal wears a "key" in its ear (or around its neck) that triggers the feeder to open; only this animal can gain access to the feed. Feeders of this type allow the animal to eat at any time it desires. In addition, animals can be penned in groups where their performance will be more nearly normal than if they were kept in individual pens or were tied or confined for every feeding.

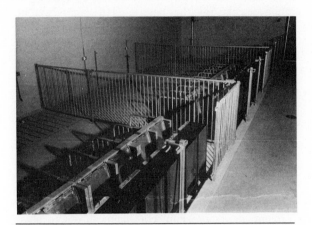

Figure 5.1 *An electronic feeder used for obtaining data on feed consumption for individual pigs maintained in pens. Courtesy of American Calan, Inc.*

Growth trials have a number of advantages and disadvantages. They allow the accumulation of relatively large amounts of data at rather reasonable costs. In addition, the animals usually can be maintained under conditions that are at least similar to normal environmental situations, whether it be hot, cold, wet, windy, and so on. One of the principal disadvantages is that growth is one of the more variable biological parameters that can be measured. If we put 10 animals in a pen, it is unlikely that all 10 will gain at the same rate. Their rate of gain (and feed efficiency) will be affected by so many different factors for which we cannot usually account that, from a statistical point of view, rather large numbers of animals are required for a valid estimate of a dietary effect. Such variation frequently requires that 12 to 15 or more animals are needed per treatment to detect statistical differences between dietary treatments. If working with chicks or layers, this may not be such a problem because many more can be used for the same cost as for one pig. In addition, most of the genetic variation in chicks can be ruled out since many, if not all, could be full sibs (full brothers or sisters). In a similar manner with larger species, some of the genetic variations can be ruled out if use is made of litter mates (swine), full or half sibs (sheep) and half sibs or identical twins (cattle) when they are available.

Another problem is the simple matter of getting an accurate weight. If 10 animals are weighed three days in a row, some variation will be evident among the weights for each animal. This may be caused by

some increase (decrease) due to gain (or loss) of body tissues, more (or less) water in the gut resulting from a recent drink, variation in gut and stomach fill resulting from a change in feed consumption or time of defecation; perhaps an animal is sick on one of the days and has consumed very little feed. Human error in reading and recording weights also is a factor. The net result is that such a simple thing as measuring body weight is not as simple as it first seems, and any errors that result make it more difficult to evaluate differences in animal performance.

Other Types of Feeding Trials

There are many other types of feeding trials that do not involve young, growing animals. For example, a lactation trial could be conducted with any mammalian species in which it was desired to measure the quantity and/or quality of milk produced. In some instances it might be desired to measure milk production indirectly by measuring gain of the young or weighing them before and after suckling. This is a common practice for laboratory animals or pigs; certainly, it is not a common practice to milk mice routinely, though it can be done. For birds, egg production trials are used commonly to test differences in feedstuffs, diets, and so on. With horses, the effect of diet on endurance or speed might be of interest, although difficult to measure.

In the previously mentioned types of studies, there was some measurement of a quantitative trait for animals producing at a level sufficiently high so that production could be measured with some confidence. However, there are many instances where we might want to assess nutrient utilization or requirements of animals that might essentially be near maintenance. The animals might not be gaining enough weight or producing enough milk or eggs to give a valid test. It might be desirable to determine the effect of a nutrient level in the diet on some other productive function or the toxic effects of a feedstuff. For example, we might want to determine the effect of an iodine deficiency on goiter incidence in young lambs, the likelihood of a urea toxicity when fed to wintering cows eating poor quality hay, or the vitamin A requirements of male roosters for adequate sperm production. These are just examples of the many different types of feeding trials that may be used where some common measure of production (gain, milk, eggs) is not the criterion for evaluation.

Digestion Trials

Conventional Methods. Digestion trials are used to determine the proportion of the nutrients in a feed or diet that can be absorbed from the GI tract. Animals are fed a diet of known composition over a time period of several days during which the feces are collected and analyzed (at some later time) for the components of interest. Maintaining a constant daily feed intake is advisable to minimize day-to-day variation in fecal excretion. Time required for feed residues to traverse the GI tract is 1 to 2 days or less for most monogastrics and longer for ruminants. Therefore, a preliminary period of 4 to 10 days is needed to void the GI tract of residues of pre-test feed and to allow adaptation of the animal to the test diet. A collection period of 4 to 10 days follows the preliminary adjustment period. Since diets and animals are controlled more closely because the time span is less than for a typical feeding trial and between-animal variability tends to be lower than for growth, usually 4 to 6 animals per treatment will be sufficient for statistical purposes.

Values can be obtained for apparent digestibility of any desired nutrient, but data may be rather meaningless for some nutrients such as vitamins and some minerals that are either present in extremely small amounts or that are excreted via the feces. It is because of the latter reason that the coefficients are termed "apparent." Feces are an important route of excretion for some mineral elements and for nitrogenous and lipid compounds (and for small amounts of some non-fibrous carbohydrates) derived from the body as well as from food residues. Digestibility is calculated as shown:

Apparent digestibility (%)

$$= \frac{\text{Nutrient intake } - \text{ Nutrient in feces}}{\text{Nutrient intake}} \times 100$$

Indicator Methods. A second method, involving indicators, is often the one of choice when it is impossible or inconvenient to measure total feed intake or to collect total feces. This method depends on the use of a reference substance, which should be indigestible, nonabsorbable, nontoxic, and easily analyzable in feed and feces. *Internal indicators* or markers are those such as lignin that are present in the feed but that are digested to a negligible degree, if at all. Lignin is plagued with problems of incomplete recovery and difficulty in analysis, but even so has

been used extensively with herbivorous species of range animals. Silica has been used to a limited extent but recovery is a problem, presumably because of contamination with soil. Acid-insoluble ash (ash in the feed insoluble in boiling HCl) has been used with a reasonable degree of success, but it is not without some problems. *External indicators* or markers are chemicals, such as chromic oxide, that either are added to the feed or given to the animals in capsules or by drenching or introduction into the rumen or through a cannula of some type. External markers that have been used with success in various situations include use of stained feeds; chromic oxide; rare-earth elements such as lanthanum, cerium, ytterbium, or dysprosium; chromium affixed to fiber in a "mordanting" process; and various water-soluble markers. Chromic oxide has been used extensively, but it presents problems of administration to range animals, usually via a capsule given orally or mixed in a supplemental feed. Irregular excretion and incomplete recovery are common problems. With stained particles, it is necessary to recover them from the feces by the tedious process of washing and sieving. Some of the rare-earths show promise for less effort in analysis, particularly if the compound is radioactive and can be counted in an automated counter. Water-soluble markers are usually used to measure flow of fluids in the GI tract. A common marker is polyethylene glycol. Further information of a recent nature on use of these markers has been presented by Merchen (4).

A formula for calculating the digestibility of a nutrient using the indicator method is shown:

Apparent digestibility (%)

$$= 100 - \left(100 \times \frac{\% \text{ indicator in feed}}{\% \text{ indicator in feces}} \right.$$
$$\left. \times \frac{\% \text{ nutrient in feces}}{\% \text{ nutrient in feed}} \right)$$

This method provides an estimate of digestibility of any or all nutrients without knowing either the total feed consumption or the total excretion of feces. Indicators lend themselves to use with group-fed animals in pens by "grab sampling" of feces from the rectum (or pen floor) and in pasture and range studies where measurement of both feed consumption and fecal output may be difficult if not impossible. Consumption of feed on pasture may be estimated by the following equation, where dry matter (DM) is used as an illustration:

DM intake (units/day)

$$= \frac{(\text{units of DM in feces/day}) \times (\text{amount of indicator per unit of dry feces})}{\text{amount of indicator/unit of DM in feed}}$$

In this situation total fecal collection is required. A bag attached to the animal (Fig. 5.2) can be used for this purpose.

In pasture studies it is difficult to estimate actual consumption accurately because grazing animals graze selectively, especially when there is a wide variety of plant species available. Apparent digestibility and total feed intake from pasture can be estimated with the simultaneous use of two indicators. The external indicator (such as chromic oxide) can be administered to the animal in known amounts and the internal indicator (such as lignin), since it is essentially undigestible, can be measured as a percentage of the diet and used as described previously to calculate apparent digestibility.

Digestibility by Difference

In many instances it is desirable to evaluate the digestibility of a feedstuff when fed in a mixture with one or more other feeds. Examples would include protein supplements, tallow, or a single feed grain—feedstuffs that would normally never make up a complete diet by themselves. In this situation it is necessary to determine digestibility by difference. With this method a basal diet is fed and the basal diet plus the test feed are fed at one or more levels. If time and numbers of animals permit, more valid estimates can be obtained if all animals are fed alternately the basal and basal + test feeds, although this is often not the practice. After digestibility of the complete diets has been determined, the digestibility of the test feed can be calculated as shown:

Digestibility of test feed (%)

$$= \frac{\substack{\text{Dig. (\%) for basal} \\ \text{+ test feed}} - \left(\substack{\text{dig. (\%) of basal} \\ \times \text{ fraction of nutrient} \\ \text{in basal + test feed}} \right)}{\substack{\text{Fraction of nutrient from test} \\ \text{feed in basal + test feed}}}$$

An example of data from a trial with lambs is shown in Table 5.2. When using this formula, values for a specific nutrient must be used in each instance.

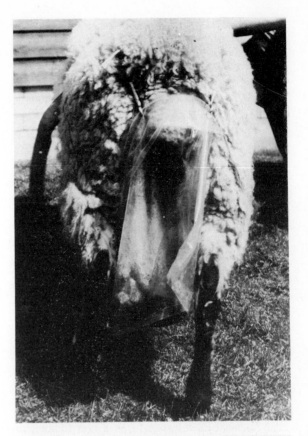

Figure 5.2 *One example of a harness and plastic bag used for fecal collections with sheep. Courtesy of G. Fishwick, Glasgow University Vet School.*

Associative Effects

A common phenomenon observed with digestibility data is that mixtures of feedstuffs do not always give results that would be characteristic if digestibility of

TABLE 5.2   An illustration of digestion coefficients calculated for the total diet and by difference and of an associative effect of feeds.

		DIGESTIBILITY, %		
			EXPERIMENTAL N SOURCES	
ITEM	BASAL DIET	#1	#2	#3
Complete diet				
Crude protein	57.3	71.5	72.8	72.9
Organic matter	76.9	78.7	79.5	78.5
By difference				
Crude protein[a]	—	85.8	88.2	89.0
Organic matter	—	87.3	104.7	95.1

[a]Use of the formula (see text) requires fewer computations. The formula for N source #1 is:

$$\frac{71.5 - (57.3 \times 0.5_a)}{0.5_b} = 85.8,$$ where 0.5_a is the fraction of crude protein in the basal feed in the basal + test diet and 0.5_b is the fraction of crude protein in the test feed in the same diet.

the mixture was the mean of the individual feedstuffs. This response is referred to as a non-additive or **associative effect.** This is illustrated in Table 5.2 with data on organic matter digestibility. Note that digestibility, calculated by difference, of the organic matter for N source #2 is >100%. Obviously, this is not possible. What has happened is that the addition of the N source to the diet stimulated digestion of the basal diet so that the mixture was more digestible than when the basal diet was fed alone. This response is often observed, particularly for herbivorous animals that depend to a great extent on microbial fermentation. The apparent reason is that dietary components in the test diet which stimulate fermentative activity are usually responsible for the increased digestibility.

Apparent vs. True Digestibility

Except for fibrous carbohydrates, there is some excretion of all major classes of nutrients via the feces that were not part of the immediate dietary intake. Sloughed intestinal cells and digestive enzymes make a substantial contribution to the total body excretion. Apparent digestibility is simply a measurement of the proportion of the diet that does not appear in the feces. The true digestibility of a nutrient is that proportion of the dietary intake which is absorbed from

the GI tract, excluding any contributions from body sources. With regard to N, fecal N derived directly from ingested food is called **exogenous N** (not from body tissues); that derived from body tissues is termed **fecal metabolic N** (endogenous). Thus, for protein, true digestibility can be estimated by subtracting the amount of N appearing in the feces of an animal fed a low-protein diet from the amount of N appearing in the feces of animal fed a test diet as illustrated in Table 5.3.

The apparent digestibility of protein in a feed is influenced by the level of protein in the feed. This is so because the amount of endogenous protein will be a smaller percentage of the total. This is illustrated in Table 5.3. Note that true digestibility remains the same for animals fed both a low and high level of protein.

Determination of true digestibility is easier said than done in most instances. With some monogastric or avian species that have a very short digesta retention time, it may be feasible to feed a protein-free diet. However, this is not the case for herbivorous species that depend upon microorganisms for some of their digestion. If rumen bacteria do not have a source of N, they do not sustain normal function for long. In some cases simple-stomached animals may be fed milk or egg protein and the assumption is made that 100% of it will be absorbed, an assumption that may or may not be true. The

TABLE 5.3   Steps in calculating true digestibility of a protein.

LINE #	ITEM	PROTEIN INTAKE	
		HIGH	LOW
1	Daily N intake, g	20	10
2	Daily fecal N, g	5	3
3	Apparent N absorption, g (1-2)	15	7
4	Apparent dig., % (3 ÷ 1 × 100)	75	70
5	Metabolic fecal N, g	1	1
6	Unabsorbed dietary N, g (2-5)	4	2
7	True N absorption, g (1-6)	16	8
8	True N dig., % (7 ÷ 1 × 100)	80	80

usual method for farm animals other than birds is to
feed graded levels of protein, determine excretion,
and then construct a regression line and extrapolate
the regression line back to a zero protein intake and
calculate the fecal excretion (see Fig. 5.3). This procedure gives reasonably good estimates and is the
method used commonly in most nutrition studies that
require this type of information.

Balance Trials

Balance trials are conducted in a similar manner to
digestion trials except that more information is required. The intent is to get an accurate measure of
total intake and total excretion in order to determine
if there is a net retention (positive balance) or loss
(negative balance) of the nutrient in question. This
type of study usually is applicable to N, energy, and
some of the major minerals. With N, for example,
we would certainly need to collect information on
urinary excretion because urine is an important route
of N excretion. If we wanted to be more precise,

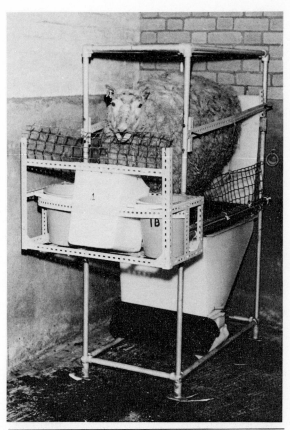

Figure 5.4 *One type of a metabolism cage, primarily of
plastic, which is easy to maintain and keep clean.
Courtesy of A. R. Michell, Univ. of London.*

we might also collect body hair (or wool or feathers),
sloughed cells from skin, and, possibly, any dermal
excretions such as sweat. If we were dealing with a
lactating animal, certainly we would need data on
milk. For complete information on energy (see Ch.
10), other data are required. One type of metabolism
cage useful for such trials with sheep or goats is
shown in Fig. 5.4.

Although balance trials are somewhat more tedious to carry out than digestion trials, the added
data (particularly for N, energy and some mineral
elements) provide more complete information on animal requirements or nutrient utilization of feedstuffs. This is true particularly if we are dealing with
a young, growing animal or an animal producing at a
relatively high level (milk, eggs, work). However, it
should be pointed out that short-term studies can
lead to exaggerated retention values (either positive
or negative) that would not be typical of animal response over a period of weeks or months.

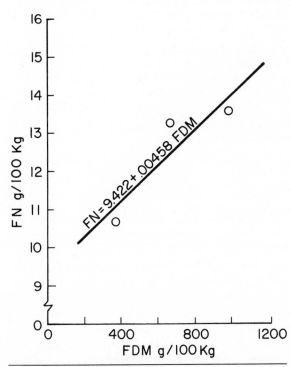

Figure 5.3 *This graph illustrates the type of regression
line that can be calculated to estimate metabolic fecal N in
relation to fecal dry matter (FDM). The same type of line
could be constructed in relationship to N consumption.
From Strozinski and Chandler (5).*

TABLE 5.4   An example of semipurified diets used with swine.[a,b]

INGREDIENT	DIET FOR WEANLING PIGS, %	DIETS FOR LACTATING SOWS OR BOARS, %	
		1	2
Glucose monohydrate	40.4	24.78	51.6
Dextrin	25.0		
Corn starch		40.00	
Protein source	25.0		
Isolated soybean protein			36.0
Alfalfa meal		1.00	3.0
Corn oil	3.0		
Lard (or corn oil)		8.00	3.0
Mineral premix	5.6[c]	0.22[d]	0.22[d]
Dicalcium phosphate		2.00	2.0
Limestone		1.50	1.5
KH_2PO_4		1.50	0.5
Iodized salt		0.50	0.50
Vitamin premix	1.0[e]	0.50[f]	0.50[f]
Total	100.0	100.0	100.0

[a]From Pond and Houpt (8).

[b]Substitution of crystalline amino acids for the protein sources would create a more nearly purified diet.

[c]Supplies the following (in g/kg diet): $CaHPO_4 \cdot 2H_2O$, 20; $CaCO_3$, 15; KH_2PO_4, 15; NaCl, 5; $FeSO_4 \cdot 7H_2O$, 0.55; $CuSO_4 \cdot 5H_2O$, 0.05; $MnSO_4 \cdot H_2O$, 0.15; $ZnSO_4 \cdot 7H_2O$, 0.30; MgO, 0.80; $CoCl_2 \cdot 6H_2O$, 0.005; KI, 0.0003; $NaSeO_3$, 0.0005.

[d]Contains the following mineral salts in glucose monohydrate, in units/kg of diet: MgO, 0.8 g; $FeSO_4 \cdot 7H_2O$, 0.55 g; $MnSO_4 \cdot 4H_2O$, 0.15 g; ZnO, 0.10 g; $CoCl_2 \cdot 6H_2O$, 5 mg; Na_2SeO_3, 0.10 mg.

[e]Supplies the following (in mg or IU per kg diet): thiamin, 3.0; folic acid, 2.0; menadione, 5.0; cobalamine, 0.01; choline dihydrogen citrate, 2,500; riboflavin, 6.6; niacin, 50.0; calcium pantothenate, 30.0; pryidoxine, 3.0 mg; α-tocopheryl acetate, 100 IU; retinyl palmitate, 10,000 IU; vitamin D_3, 1,200 IU.

[f]Contains the following vitamins in glucose monohydrate, in units/kg of diet: thiamin, 2.8 mg; riboflavin, 8.2 mg; niacin, 44 mg; calcium pantothenate, 33 mg; pyridoxine, 3 mg; folic acid, 4 mg; menadione, 2 mg; vitamin B_{12}, 27.5 μg; choline dihydrogen citrate, 2.5 g; vitamin A, 8,200 IU; vitamin D_3, 550 IU; vitamin E, 50 IU; biotin, 0.2 mg; inositol, 220 mg; para-aminobenzoic acid, 200 mg.

Purified Diets

Because of the many different compounds or undesirable (and/or unknown) proportions of compounds that may be present in natural feeds, purified diets have been developed to allow more precise nutritional studies. They may sometimes be referred to as synthetic, purified, semipurified, and so on. Examples of diets for swine are shown in Table 5.4. Depending on the species of animal involved, its age, and other factors, such diets usually are based on ingredients with a sugar source such as glucose, some starch, and various amounts of cellulose. N may be supplied by a purified protein source such as casein (from milk) or isolated soybean protein or by crystalline amino acids. Mineral requirements can be met by using various mineral salts that are soluble and digestible. Vitamins may be supplied by a rich source such as yeast, liver concentrates, or synthetic sources. Essential fatty acids can be added by themselves or supplied by a product such as purified corn oil, and so on. In some instances only a portion of the ingredients might be highly purified.

Such diets as described and shown in Table 5.4, obviously, may not be very palatable because of the texture and lack of normal flavors and odors associated with natural feeds. They can be quite expensive, especially when used with large animals. However, the big advantage is that the nutritionist has a much better control of exactly what the animal is consuming.

Use of purified diets has allowed us to more completely understand requirements for most of the essential nutrients. It should be pointed out that it still may be difficult to determine if some elements are required when the amount needed is extremely small. Even some of the more purified mineral sources still may contain trace amounts of other elements. This is one reason that there is some uncertainty about the needs for some mineral elements.

❑ RUMEN DIGESTION TECHNIQUES

The high cost of digestion trials, especially with cattle, has prompted the development of in vitro techniques that allow simulation of rumen fermentation under controlled conditions. Quite a variety of methods has been developed. Some are more suitable than others for a specific purpose. For batch trials, a small amount of rumen fluid is obtained from a rumen-fistulated animal (Fig. 5.5). After most of the feed particles have been removed, the fluid is placed

in a container along with some buffer (to simulate saliva) and the test sample. The combination then is fermented at rumen temperature (39°C) for a period of time, usually 24 to 48 h. Where the object is to predict (or correlate) live animal digestion from in vitro digestion, adequate methods have been developed that give a more valid estimate of animal digestion of roughage and forage than can be obtained by using chemical analyses. These methods are not as useful for evaluating animal utilization of grains and other concentrates.

Continuous fermenters have also been developed (4, 6, 7). If designed and maintained properly, it is possible to simulate feed input and rumen outflow (and/or absorption) for a period of days or weeks. It is, therefore, possible to simulate rumen conditions more closely than can be done with batch cultures where conditions would be more representative of feeding an animal one time per day.

Rumen fermentation procedures have proved to be useful for screening feedstuffs or generally characterizing them for use by ruminants, especially when only small samples are available (as, for example, from a plant breeding trial in the greenhouse). These methods also are useful for studying rumen function and metabolism of specific compounds. For example, determination of what types of non-protein N can be used by rumen microorganisms, production of volatile fatty acids from a diet processed in different ways, and so on.

The nylon bag technique (14) also is an efficient means of evaluating rumen digestion. In this procedure the feedstuff in question is placed in a nylon (or other undigestible cloth) bag suspended in the rumen of an animal with a rumen fistula. The bags then are removed after a period of time and loss of material (from fermentation) in the bag is determined. Such methods are useful in evaluating relative differences between feedstuffs, but do not give values similar to those from live animal digestion trials. This method is, perhaps, more useful for studying rumen digestion of concentrates (grains) than the in vitro method where relative digestion is of interest.

❑ BIOLOGICAL VARIATION IN DIGESTION AND ABSORPTION OF NUTRIENTS

Biological availability of nutrients is not fixed at a given level, but is affected by a number of factors. Increased feed intake above maintenance tends to

Figure 5.5 *An animal with a rumen cannula in place.*

TABLE 5.5 An example of typical variation in digestibility encountered with sheep.

ANIMAL NO.	DIGESTIBILITY, %		
	DRY MATTER	CRUDE PROTEIN	ENERGY
1	76.9	77.1	80.8
2	73.1	73.0	77.3
3	72.3	77.2	80.1
4	78.7	77.3	73.1
5	76.0	67.4	74.6
Overall mean	76.5	73.6	77.2

depress digestibility, especially in ruminants (9). Part of this variation results from more rapid passage through the GI tract and, thus, there is less time for microbial or enzymatic activity on the digesta. Studies with sheep have demonstrated, even in animals of the same breed, sex, and age, that there may be a considerable difference in size of the stomach capacity, which in turn affects eating rate, amount eaten, and passage rate through the GI tract. Undoubtedly, there are other unrecognized factors that alter digestibility, but the point to be made here is that all animals do not digest a given diet to the same extent. An example with sheep is shown in Table 5.5. Data are shown on digestibility of crude protein, energy, and dry matter. In this instance, digestibility of dry matter was less variable than the others, but there was still a range of 4.6 units. The ranges shown in this table are not extreme values by any means.

Aside from differences related to source of feedstuffs, variation exists in absorptive capacity based on the specificity of a wide variety of specialized transport systems present in the intestinal epithelium. This specialization is illustrated by comparing the maximum absorptive capacity of humans for vitamin B_{12}, which has been estimated at 1 mcg/day, with that for glucose which is 3,600 g/day. The recognition of existence of such specific absorption pathways of widely differing capacities has resulted in the development of a number of research techniques for absorption studies. These include various surgical preparations (see a later section), cannulation of the portal vein or thoracic duct, whole-body counting of radioactivity after administration of radio-isotopes, and a variety of other techniques, many of which will

be discussed in more detail in later chapters in conjunction with metabolism of individual nutrients.

☐ SURGICAL PROCEDURES FOR STUDYING NUTRIENT ABSORPTION AND UTILIZATION

A wide variety of surgical techniques has been developed to aid in study of nutrient absorption. Fistulation of the rumen of cattle, sheep, or goats is quite a common procedure that allows sampling of contents and infusion of known quantities of substances at known rates directly into the rumen. Stomach fistulation of simple-stomached animals and abomasal cannulations (Fig. 5.6) are common procedures. Cannulas can be inserted in various parts of the intestinal tract. Most of these procedures have

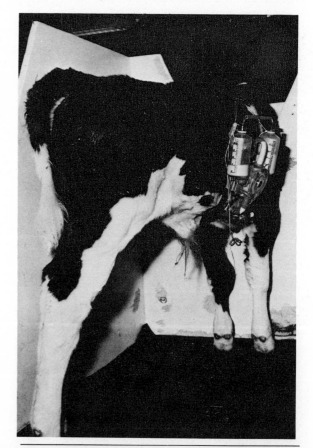

Figure 5.6 *An animal with one type of abomasal-intestinal cannula which allows volumetric measurements to be made of digesta. Courtesy of C. Noël, Univ. of Laval, Quebec, Canada.*

been done on sheep or cattle (less common in cattle than sheep because of the expense). However, it is now a more common practice to establish cecal and ileal cannulas in swine or horses.

In addition to these methods, several procedures have been perfected that allow catheters to be implanted in specific veins or arteries. Thus, blood going into or out of specific organs can be sampled or chemicals can be injected at the same site. With calves, the catheters are frequently exteriorized in the lumbar area where they are accessible to the researcher but not damaged easily by the animal.

Rates of absorption of individual radioisotopes can be measured effectively by surgical techniques that consist of tying off a segment of the intestinal tract and measuring disappearance over a short time span of known amounts of a substance injected directly into the lumen of the gut between the two ligatures. This is done in the live (anesthetized) animal. An extension of this in vivo procedure involves a related in vitro technique whereby a segment of intestinal tract is removed, everted so that the mucosal side is exterior and the ends ligated as above. The substance whose transport across the intestinal lining is being studied is then injected into the lumen of the everted intestinal segment which has been placed in a beaker containing physiological saline solution. The appearance of the injected substance in the beaker contents or its disappearance from the everted intestinal segment is then used to estimate its absorption. Such in vivo and in vitro techniques based on surgical procedures add another dimension to the study of nutrient absorption and utilization and, although they do not substitute for more conventional methods, frequently they can add significant knowledge.

☐ ESTIMATION OF NUTRIENT REQUIREMENTS OF ANIMALS

The establishment of a substance as an essential nutrient for any animal depends on the demonstration of adverse effects on the animal in the absence of that substance from the diet. The array of such nutrients depends on the animal species and, in some instances, on the stage of the life cycle. In contrast, we may have substances that may stimulate production, especially growth, which may not be required in the diet. In this instance, the determination of optimum levels is dependent upon demonstrating a growth response in a given situation (see Ch. 16).

Sequence of Events in Nutrient Deficiency

The discovery of most of the nutrients as essential dietary constituents has been accomplished largely with farm and laboratory animals. Regardless of the nutrient deficiency, the same sequence of events prevails:

Nutrient deficiency
↓
Biochemical defect
↓
Functional defect
↓
Microscopic anatomical defect
↓
Macroscopic (grossly visible) defect
↓
Morbidity, Death

The above sequence of events is well illustrated in the deficiency of the B-vitamin, thiamin. The biochemical defect is a failure to produce the coenzyme, cocarboxylase (thiamin pyrophosphate), which is responsible for removing one carbon from pyruvic acid in the formation of acetyl coenzyme A. Thus, pyruvic acid accumulates in the tissues, resulting in poor appetite and reduced growth (functional defect). Microscopic lesions of nervous tissue follow and, later, grossly visible signs of deficiency develop, including emaciation and tremors (polyneuritis in birds). Morbid signs may occur during this period of time; death is the final result if the deficiency is not alleviated.

The point at which symptoms of a deficiency are reversible varies with different tissues and species of animals. Damage to the animal may vary from essentially none to permanent effects on specific tissues or just an overall stunting of growth and reduced final liveweight. For example with cattle, one of the early symptoms of vitamin A deficiency in young animals is night blindness in which the animal can see normally in daylight but vision is very poor in the dark. If the deficiency continues a step further, the optic foramen partially closes off, pinching the optic nerve, and permanent blindness occurs. Further progression results in constriction of the blood vessels to the eye to the extent that the eye ruptures. The animal may still survive at this point (with appropriate surgery in some cases), but the damage cannot be reversed.

The biochemical, functional, and structural defects associated with nutrient deficiencies usually are specific for each nutrient and may vary somewhat from animal species to species. Details of these changes are given in subsequent chapters dealing with each class of nutrient. For some nutrients, biochemical changes in blood and tissues are the best indices of dietary adequacy, but for others growth or balance trials provide the best information.

Establishing Specific Nutrient Requirements

There are numerous factors that affect nutrient requirements of individual animals, some of which are discussed in more detail in Chs. 17 and 18. There is a considerable amount of qualitative information on humans indicating that acute or chronic infections or other disease may either alter absorption or normal metabolism of nutrients in some tissues, increase catabolism of some nutrients, or depress appetite (10, 11). In addition, it has been shown with experimental animals that genetic lines may have different requirements for some of the B-vitamins (rats), higher or lower than normal arginine requirements (chickens), or high Zn requirements (cattle). Thus, it is difficult to determine precisely requirements for a broad population of animals.

Figure 5.7 depicts a theoretical range of nutrient consumption that might be observed under production conditions if nutritional management is not sound or if unknown factors affect nutrient requirements.

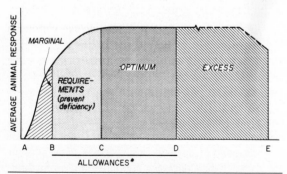

Figure 5.7   *A theoretical presentation of nutrient requirements for an animal under production conditions. Zone A to B, intake is less than requirements and may predispose the animal to deficiency symptoms. B to C represents the minimum intake needed to prevent deficiency symptoms but it may lead to suboptimum performance. C to D represents an optimum performance and maximum return for the producer. D to E represents a zone ranging from levels where increasing intake is excessive and uneconomical to levels that may be toxic and reduce performance.*

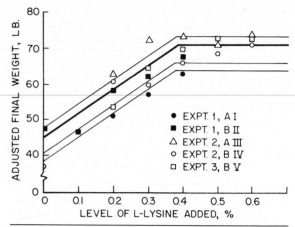

Figure 5.8   *Relationship of final weight (adjusted to equal initial weight) to lysine level fed. From Miller et al. (12).*

It illustrates the point that nutrient requirements cannot be fixed at some specific level for a variable population subjected to many different environmental factors.

Examples of Experimental Data Obtained with Growth Trials

The requirements of structural nutrients such as protein, individual amino acids, Ca and P can be determined effectively by growth and balance experiments. An example of the type of experimental data from a growth trial used to estimate nutrient requirements is shown in Fig. 5.8. The quantitative lysine requirement of the weanling pig was determined in a series of three different growth experiments. Ad libitum feeding was used throughout. Precautions in experimental work are important to minimize the variability from factors other than the dietary variable of interest, in this instance, lysine. Thus, standardized environmental conditions (pen size, temperature, number of animals/pen, and so on) are important, and animals should be assigned to experimental diets with minimum bias introduced by differences in sex, breeding, body weight, disease level, and other similar potential sources of variation. Increments of the nutrient in question then are added to the basal diet, and body weight gain and feed consumption over the experimental period are recorded. Thus, Fig. 5.8 clearly shows that in experiment 1 the weight gain was related directly to level of lysine added to the diet up to and including the highest level (0.4% L-lysine added to the basal diet which contained 0.33% lysine). From this single experiment, the minimum lysine requirement for growth could not be judged because a plateau was not reached. In subsequent experiments, higher levels of lysine were added to the basal diet and a plateau in weight gain could be demonstrated beyond which no further gain was achieved by an additional increment of L-lysine. By applying appropriate statistical procedures, the quantitative lysine requirement of the weanling pig could be stated with reasonable assurance under the conditions of the experiment (0.71% lysine at 12.8% protein; 9.05% lysine at 21.7% protein. Simply by observing the shape of the curve formed by connecting points within experiments, a reasonable estimate of the requirement can be made even without resorting to mathematical procedures more complex than calculating the mean for each group. In Fig. 5.8, experiments 1 and 2 each employed two protein levels, 12.8% (A) and 21.7% (B). Thus, the data show further that the response to increments of lysine is similar at both protein levels, although weight gain is higher at the 21.7% level. Clearly, by careful attention to experimental design, much valuable information can be obtained on nutrient requirements using only the growth trial, as illustrated here.

❑ LABORATORY ANIMALS AS MODELS FOR FARM ANIMALS AND HUMANS

Laboratory animals play an important role in contributing to knowledge of nutritional requirements and interrelationships of farm animals and humans. The numbers of animals and housing facilities necessary to obtain meaningful data with farm animals are often so large as to be economically prohibitive. Also, the life cycle of small animal species generally is shorter than that of farm animals, so data can be obtained over several generations/year. Each year thousands of mice, rats, hamsters, guinea pigs, rabbits, and other mammalian species—as well as avian species, such as Japanese quail, and a variety of reptiles and fishes—are used in nutritional research. Of course, the results obtained provide information applicable directly to the species used, but often the information can be extrapolated to farm animals or to humans. Among the farm animals, the pig is especially useful as a model for human nutrition studies because its digestive system is similar anatomically

and functionally to that of humans. The National Research Council has published a series on the nutrient requirements of laboratory and farm animals and of humans. One of these (13) provides both narrative and tabular data on the nutrient requirements of cats, guinea pigs, hamsters, monkeys, mice, and rats. Similar publications are available for other individual species of larger animals including dogs, rabbits, horses, swine, sheep, mink and foxes, beef cattle, dairy cattle, and poultry. The science of nutrition knows no limits in terms of the kind of animal life selected for obtaining new information of use in the feeding of humans and animals, as numerous microorganisms are utilized in addition to the various animals mentioned.

❑ SUMMARY

A number of methods have been discussed that are commonly used for either evaluating feedstuffs or for measuring nutrient utilization by animals. The most commonly used include growth-fattening trials or other feeding trials designed to quantitate some particular factor related to feed or nutrient utilization. Digestion and balance trials normally are carried out with fewer animals under more precise conditions. Data from digestion trials are used widely for evaluating feedstuffs and, subsequently, for diet formulation or for refining information on nutrient requirements and establishing more accurate feeding standards for animals.

Other methods used frequently include various in vitro rumen procedures intended to simulate in vivo rumen fermentation. Surgical procedures also are useful in order to obtain data, such as information on absorption from the gut, flow of blood to the liver, and so on, that cannot be obtained with intact animals. Laboratory animals (and microorganisms) also often find use in studying nutrition.

❑ REFERENCES

1. Brody, S. 1945. *Bioenergetics and Growth.* Reinhold Pub. Corp., N.Y.

2. Zobell, D. R. 1986. Proc. West. Sec. Amer. Soc., *Animal Sci.* **37**:96.

3. Lindemann, M. D., E. T. Kornegay, and R. J. Moore. 1986. *J. Animal Sci.* **62**:412.

4. Merchen, N. R. 1987. In *The Ruminant Animal,* p. 172, D. C. Church (ed.). Prentice-Hall, Inc., Englewood Cliffs, N.J.

5. Strozinski, L. L. and P. T. Chandler. 1972. *J. Dairy Sci.* **55**:1281.

6. Czerkawski, J. W. and G. Breckenridge. 1977. *Brit. J. Nutr.* **38**:371.

7. Hoover, W. H., et al. 1976. *J. Animal Sci.* **43**:528, 535.

8. Pond, W. G. and K. A. Houpt. 1978. *Biology of the Pig.* Cornell Univ. Press, Ithaca, N.Y.

9. Grovum, W. L. 1987. In *The Ruminant Animal,* p. 202, D. C. Church (ed.). Prentice-Hall, Inc., Englewood Cliffs, N.J.

10. Barnes, L. A., Y. D. Coble, Jr., D. I. Macdonald, and G. Christakis (eds.). 1981. *Nutrition and Medical Practice.* AVI Pub. Co., Inc., Westport, CT.

11. Schrimshaw, N. W. and V. R. Young. 1976. *Sci. Amer.* **234**(3):51.

12. Miller, E. R. et al. 1964. *J. Nutr.* **82**:64.

13. NRC. 1978. *Nutrient Requirements of Laboratory Animals.* Nat. Acad. Sci., Washington, D.C.

PART 2

NUTRIENT
METABOLISM

6

Water

WATER IS NOT OFTEN classed as a nutrient even though it makes up about one-half to two-thirds of the body mass of adult animals, up to 90% of that of newborn animals, and accounts for more than 99% of the molecules in the body (the latter is possible because water molecules are smaller than most others). However, the importance of an adequate supply of potable water for livestock is well recognized, and it currently is receiving more emphasis in the quest to clean up polluted environments by improving the quality and dependability of water supplies.

❏ FUNCTIONS

Water serves two basic functions for all terrestrial animals: namely, as a major component in body metabolism and as a major factor in body temperature control. These functions are discussed in the following sections.

Water and Body Metabolism

From a functional view point, water is extremely important to any biological organism, a fact easily substantiated by the sudden termination of productive functions and life when insufficient water is available, as contrasted to relatively long-term life when the supply of other nutrients is restricted. All of the biochemical reactions that take place in an animal require water. Many of the biological functions of water are dependent on the property of water acting as a solvent for an extremely wide variety of compounds and because many compounds ionize readily in water. Solvent properties are extremely important because most protoplasm is a mixture of colloids and crystalloids in water. In addition, water serves as a medium for transportation of slurries and semi-solid digesta in the GI tract, for various solutes in blood and tissue fluids and cells, and in excretions such as urine and sweat. Water provides for dilution of cell contents and body fluids so that relatively free movement of chemicals may occur within the cells and in the fluids and GI tract. Thus, water serves to transport absorbed substances, conveying them to and from their sites of metabolism.

In addition to functions just mentioned, water is involved in many chemical reactions. In hydrolysis, water is a substrate in the reaction, and in oxidation, water is a product of the reaction.

Metabolic water or water of oxidation, results from the oxidation of organic components in the cells of the body. Oxidation of one mole of glucose re-quires six moles of O_2 and produces six moles of CO_2 and six moles of water. The amount of O_2 required for oxidation of starch, fat, and protein is shown in Table 6.1. Note that much more O_2 is required to oxidize fat, 2.02 l/g of fat versus 0.83/g of starch or 0.97/g of protein. If expressed as O_2/g of water formed, protein requires 2.44 l of O_2. The metabolic water produced/per gram of food is much higher for fat (1.07) than for the other two nutrients.

Ingestion and metabolism of fat, carbohydrate, and protein results in increased respiration and heat dissipation and, for protein, increased urinary excretion of urea, the principal excretory product of N metabolism in mammals. Large amounts of water are required for dilution and excretion via the kidney of the urea, and the amount of water derived from oxidation is not sufficient to meet the excretory demands as well as that from increased respiration.

It has been calculated that in a hot, dry environment (ambient temperature 26°C, relative humidity 10%) an animal loses 23.5 g of respiratory water in the process of producing 12.3 g of metabolic water. The heat generated amounts to about 100 Kcal. Part of the heat (13.6%) is offset by the heat of vaporization of the expired water. If the remainder (86 Kcal) had to be dissipated by sweating, it would cost 149 ml of water. Because of the added needs for excretion, protein results in a negative effect on conservation of water—and should be avoided in a situation of water stress. With respect to fats, Schmidt-Nielsen (1) has shown, in dry climates at least, that ingestion of fat results in less net metabolic water than ingestion of carbohydrates (because of the added respiration required). The overall result is that carbohydrates supply more net metabolic water than either proteins or fats.

In hibernating animals, metabolic and preformed water (that associated with body tissues catabolized during a period of negative energy balance) apparently are adequate to supply total body needs for the

TABLE 6.1   Metabolic water production from nutrients.

| NUTRIENT | OXYGEN (l) PER GRAM OF | | METABOLIC WATER PRODUCED PER GRAM OF FOOD, G |
	FOOD	WATER FORMED	
Starch	0.83	1.49	0.56
Fat	2.02	1.88	1.07
Protein	0.97	2.44	0.40

time periods required. Studies with domestic cattle and horses indicate that metabolic water may account for about 5–10% of total water intake, but some desert ruminants apparently get as much as 16–26% of their total water requirement from metabolic water. This compares to 10–13% of the total water requirement of humans (sedentary, non-heat stressed) from metabolic water.

Water and Body Temperature Regulation

Water has a number of physiochemical properties that allow it to have a marked effect on temperature regulation. Its high specific heat, high thermal conductivity, and high latent heat of vaporization are properties that allow accumulation of heat, ready transfer of heat, and loss of large amounts of heat on vaporization. These physical properties of water are enhanced by physiological characteristics of animals. The mobility of the blood and the rapidity with which it may be redistributed quickly in the body, large evaporative surfaces in the lungs and the body surface for sweating, the ability to constrict blood flow to body surfaces during cold stress, as well as other factors, allow animals to control body temperatures within desired ranges in most instances.

The specific heat of water is considerably higher than that of any other liquid (or solid). Many animals rely on the cooling capacity of water as it gives up its latent heat during evaporation by panting or sweating. As 1 g of water changes from liquid to vapor, whether by panting or sweating, it takes up about 580 Cal of heat. In terms of heat exchange, this is a very efficient use of water when it is realized that to heat 1 g of water from freezing to boiling requires only 117 Cal. Because of this great capacity to store heat, any sudden change in body temperature is avoided. Water has greater thermal conductivity than any other liquid, and this is important for the dissipation of heat from deeply situated regions in the body. Many animals dissipate internal and absorbed heat by evaporation of body water. For example, in one study sweating accounted for 21%, conduction and convection from the skin 16%, and respiratory evaporation 5% of the net loss of heat in a *Bos indicus* steer.

❏ WATER ABSORPTION

Water is absorbed readily from most sections of the GI tract. In ruminant species usually there is a net absorption from the rumen and omasum. In the abomasum of ruminants or the glandular stomach in other species, usually there is a marked net outflow of fluids (which accompany gastric secretions), although undoubtedly some fluids may be absorbed. The same is true for the duodenum where fluids from the pancreas, bile, and intestinal glands cause a net inflow of water. In all species, there is a net absorption from the ileum, jejunum, cecum, and large gut, but the amount absorbed (and moisture in the feces) varies considerably from species to species and from diet to diet within species.

Osmotic relationships within the particular organ have a marked effect on absorption. Following a meal, normally there will be more solutes in the digesta; this will increase the osmotic pressure, which may result in an inflow of water into the organ (rumen, small gut), depending on the amount of fluid consumed prior to, during and after the meal. This is a mechanism that allows the body to maintain optimum consistency of the digesta throughout the GI tract. If fluids are ingested without food, absorption is more rapid and complete because of the osmotic relationships mentioned above.

Other factors also affect absorption. For example, polysaccharides such as pectin tend to form gels in the GI tract. Such gels hold water and reduce absorption from the gut and, as a result, are usually laxative. For some species the ingestion of undigestible fiber also tends to reduce water absorption somewhat. In addition, any factor promoting diarrhea, whether from the diet ingested, microbial toxins, altered osmotic relationships, or because of other physiological reactions (stresses of various types which may stimulate intestinal motility), will result in reduced water absorption from the gut.

❏ BODY WATER

Water content of the animal body varies considerably; it is influenced over the long term by age of the animal and the amount of fat in the tissues. Water content is highest in fetuses and in newborn animals, declines rapidly at first, and then slowly declines to adult levels. This has been illustrated previously in Fig. 2.1. When body water is expressed on the basis of the fat-free body, the water content is relatively constant for many different animal species, ranging from 70–75% of fat-free weight, with an average of about 73%. As a result of this constant relationship, the composition of the animal body can be estimated with reasonable accuracy if either the fat or water content is known. Body water can be estimated with various dyes, deuterium oxide, or tritium by administering them intravenously and determining the amount of dilution of the test compound; fat content of the tissues may be calculated by the formula:

$$\text{percent fat} = 100 - \frac{\text{percent water}}{0.732}$$

The greatest amount of water in the body tissues will be found as intracellular fluids, which may account for 40% or more of total body weight. Most of the intracellular water is found in muscle and skin with lesser amounts in other tissues. Extracellular water is found in interstitial fluids, which occupy spaces between cells, blood plasma, and other miscellaneous fluids such as lymph, synovial, and cerebrospinal fluids. Extracellular water accounts for the second largest water "compartment," or roughly one-third of the total body water of which about 6% is blood plasma water.

Most of the remaining body water will be found in the contents of the GI tract and urinary tract. The amount present in the GI tract is quite variable, even within species, and is greatly affected by type and amount of feed consumed. As indicated, body water tends to decrease with age and has an inverse relationship with body fat. Body water is apt to be higher in lactating cows that in dry cows (usually less body fat also), and extracellular water is greater in young male calves than in female calves of the same age.

It might be noted that water easily passes through most cell membranes and from one fluid compartment to another. Passage from compartment to compartment is controlled primarily by differences in osmotic or hydrostatic pressure gradients, and it is a passive reaction in that energy is not required (or only in extremely small amounts) for this movement.

Water absorbed from the GI tract enters the extracellular fluid in the blood and lymph. Blood volume is largely regulated by body Na, the major cation in blood plasma. The volume and osmotic pressure of the extracellular fluid are also regulated by thirst and by antidiuretic hormone. This hormone, which is produced by the pituitary, promotes tubular reabsorption of water by the kidney, thereby reducing water loss. Thus, variations in water intake and excretion largely control osmoconcentration. Flow of water between the extracellular and intracellular fluids also is important in maintaining osmoconcentration.

Physiological abnormalities or disease (fever, diarrhea) may result in body dehydration or in retention of excess water in the tissues (faulty blood circulation or adrenal gland activity). The result is, of course, that normal values for body water may not be applicable to these situations.

❏ WATER TURNOVER

Water turnover is a term used to express the rate at which body water is excreted and replaced in the tissues. Tritium-labeled water has been used to estimate turnover time in a variety of different species. In cattle, a typical half-life value (time for half of tritium to be lost) is about 3.5 days. Non-ruminant species probably have a more rapid turnover because they have less water in the GI tract. Those species that tolerate greater water restriction (camel, sheep) also have lower turnover rates than species which are less tolerant to water restriction (horse, European cattle). Water turnover is affected greatly by climatic factors such as temperature and humidity or by ingestion of material, such as NaCl, which increases urinary or fecal excretion.

❏ WATER SOURCES

Water available to an animal's tissues is derived from (a) drinking water, (b) water contained in or on feed, (c) metabolic water, (d) water liberated from polymerization reactions such as condensation of amino acids to peptides, and (e) preformed water associated with body tissues catabolized during a period of negative energy balance. The importance of these different sources differs among animal species, depending on diet, habitat, and ability to conserve body water. Some species of desert rodents and antelopes are said not to require drinking water except in rare situations, but this condition does not apply to domestic farm animals, which all require copious amounts of water when producing at a high level, particularly when they are heat-stressed (illustrated later).

The water content of feedstuffs consumed by animals is highly variable. For example, in forage it may range from a low of 5–7% in mature plants and hays to as high as 90% or more in lush young vegetation. Likewise, precipitation and dew on ingested feed may, at times, account for a very substantial amount of water consumption.

One example of water consumption is given in Table 6.2. In this case sheep were maintained indoors at a stable temperature and were fed diets collected with the aid of esophageal-fistulated steers. The samples were collected at various times in the growing season and were dried after collection. Although the amount of diet fed was rather constant, the diet varied in protein content and in energy utilization (metabolizable energy). In this example water in the feed amounted to only about 50 g/day and the sheep drank about 88% of their total water. Metabolic water (calculated values) contributed 9–10% of the total. Total water input amounted to 2.95 g/g of dry matter for the June diet and 2.31 g/g of dry matter for the September diet.

TABLE 6.2 Water metabolism of sheep maintained indoors at 20–26°C.[a]

ITEM	MONTH OF COLLECTION OF RATIONS	
	JUNE	SEPT.
Feed Consumption		
Dry matter consumed, g/day	795	789
Crude protein, g/day	122	50
Metabolizable energy, Mcal/day	2.00	1.39
Water input,		
Water drunk, g/day	2,093	1,613
% of total	87.8	88.1
Water in feed, g/day	51	50
% of total	2.1	2.7
Metabolic water,[b] g/day	240	167
% of total	10.1	9.1
Total input, g/day	2,384	1,830
Water output		
Fecal water, g/day	328	440
% of total	13.8	24.0
Urinary water, g/day	788	551
% of total	33.0	30.1
Vaporized water,[c] g/day	1,268	839
% of total	53.2	45.9
Total output	2,384	1,830

[a]From Wallace et al. (2); diets were dried samples collected during June or September from steers with esophageal fistulas.
[b]Calculated to be produced at rate of 120 g/Mcal of ME.
[c]Equal to insensible water.

TABLE 6.3 Relationship between water drunk and moisture content of forage.[a]

WATER INTAKE, *l*/KG OF DM	MOISTURE CONTENT OF FORAGE, %
3.7	10
3.6	20
3.3	30
3.1	40
2.9	50
2.3	60
2.0	65
1.5	70
0.9	75

[a]From Hyder *et al.* (3).

The amount of water provided by green forage can be very substantial. Data in Table 6.3 show the relationship between moisture content of the forage and the amount of free water drunk by sheep. Observations generally indicate that sheep will seldom drink water when the forage moisture content is 65–70% or higher.

❑ WATER LOSSES

Loss of water from the animal body occurs by way of urine, feces, so-called insensible water—that lost via vaporization from the lungs and dissipation through the skin, and sweat from the sweat glands in the skin during warm or hot weather. Loss from the lungs, skin, and kidney occurs continuously, although at variable rates. Loss via urine and feces occurs at periodic intervals.

Water excreted via urine acts as a solvent for products excreted from the kidney. Some species have greater ability to concentrate urine than others. Sometimes this is related to the type of compound excreted. For example, avian species excrete primarily uric acid rather than urea as an end product of protein metabolism. These species excrete urine in semi-solid form with only small amounts of water. However, mammalian species cannot concentrate urine to nearly such an extent. Birds also have another slight advantage in that production of uric acid results in production of more metabolic water than does urea.

The kidney of most species has great flexibility in the amount of water that may be excreted. Minimal amounts required for excretion (called obligatory water) usually are exceeded greatly except when water intake is restricted. Consumption of excess water during periods of heat stress or consumption of diuretics such as caffeine and alcohol may increase kidney excretion of water considerably. Within a given species the amount of kidney concentration of urine depends on the type of compound being excreted. The amount required to excrete chlorides and carbonates is similar and appears to be additive. That required for urea is somewhat less than for these salts, but the sum of that for urea and these salts is not additive.

Examples of loss via the urine are shown in Tables 6.2 and 6.6. In Table 6.2 where sheep were on dry feed and not heat-stressed, urine accounted for 30–33% of water losses. In Table 6.6, where dairy cows were given ad lib or restricted water and some were heat-stressed, urine volume ranged from 10–30 l/day and from 24–43% of water excreted.

Fecal losses of water in man are usually about 7–10% of urinary water. In ruminant species such as cattle, fecal water loss usually exceeds urinary losses, although not when heat-stressed. Other species tend to be intermediate. Animals that consume fibrous diets usually excrete a higher percentage of total water via feces, and those that form fecal pellets usually excrete drier feces and, presumably, are more adapted to drier climates and more severe water restriction than is the case for species that do not form fecal pellets. Note in Table 6.2 that fecal water represented 13–24% of total excretion with sheep, but with normal dairy cows (Table 6.8) it was 30–32% of total and 17–20% when the cows were heat-stressed.

Insensible water losses account for a relatively large amount of total loss, particularly at temperatures that do not induce sweating or in species that do not sweat—that is, 45–55% of total losses for sheep in a metabolism chamber versus about 30–35% for humans under somewhat similar conditions.

Air inhaled into the lungs may be very dry, but is about 90% saturated with water when exhaled. During periods of hyperventilation that occur with hot temperatures, loss from the lungs is increased greatly and will increase to 50% or more of the total excretion in sweating cows that are heat-stressed. Insensible water loss through the skin is relatively low.

Loss of water via sweat may be very large in species such as man and horses whose sweat glands are distributed over a large portion of the body surface. Sweating is used as a means of dissipating body heat and is said to have an efficiency of about 400% compared to respiratory heat loss. Heat-tolerant species generally have well-developed sweat glands. This is one explanation why *Bos indicus* cattle are more heat tolerant than *Bos taurus* breeds. Species that have poorly developed sweat glands must keep cool either by panting (e.g., dog, chicken) or by finding shade or water (e.g., swine) to cool the body.

❏ REGULATION OF DRINKING

The regulation of drinking is a highly complex physiological process. At times, it is induced as a result of dehydration of body tissues. However, drinking may also occur when there is no apparent need to rehydrate tissues. When an animal is thirsty, salivary flow usually is reduced and dryness of the mouth and throat may stimulate drinking—a relationship that may, indirectly, be traced to a decrease in plasma volume. Other information indicates salivary flow is not a critical factor in initiation of drinking. Oral sensations apparently are involved that may be influenced by osmotic receptors in the mouth. For example, dogs with esophageal fistulas (which can prevent water from entering the stomach) will stop drinking after shamdrinking a more or less normal amount of water. However, the shamdrinking will be repeated again in a few minutes. There is ample evidence to indicate that passage of water through the mouth is required for a feeling of satiety, because placing water in the stomach by a tube leaves animals restless and unsatisfied.

Most domestic animals generally drink during eating periods if water is close at hand or soon afterwards when they can. Frequency of drinking is increased in hot weather as is the amount consumed. Under herded conditions in some of the dry areas of Africa and India, cattle, sheep, and goats may be watered on a three-day cycle. This frequency is undoubtedly inadequate for maximum production, but maximum production is not the objective under such adverse conditions.

❏ WATER REQUIREMENTS

Water requirements for any class or species of healthy animals are difficult to delimit except in very specific situations. This is so because numerous dietary and environmental factors affect water absorption and excretion and because water is so important in reg-

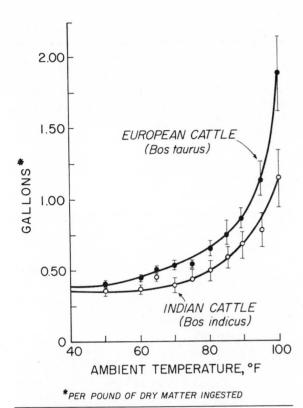

Figure 6.1 *Water requirements of European and Indian cattle as affected by increasing temperatures. From Winchester and Morris (4).*

ulation of body temperature. Other factors, such as ability to conserve water, differences in activity, gestation, lactation, and so on, compound the problem when different classes or species of animals are compared. As a result of these different factors, relatively little effort has been made to quantify water needs, except in a few specific situations.

It is well recognized that water consumption is related to heat production and, sometimes, to energy consumption. Also, water requirements can be related to body surface area in non-stressing situations. At environmental temperatures that do not result in heat stress, there is a good linear relationship between dry matter consumption and water consumption. However, when the temperature reaches stressing levels, feed consumption is apt to decrease while water consumption is increased greatly. One example of this is shown in Fig. 6.1. Note in the figure that water consumption/unit of feed consumption by cattle goes from about 0.35 gal (3.0 lb)/lb of dry matter consumed at 40°F to about 1.9 gal (16.3 lb) at 100°F for *Bos taurus* cattle. When ex-

pressed as a percentage of body weight, non-heat stressed non-lactating cattle may drink on the order of 5–6% of body weight per day. Water consumption may increase to 12 + % of body weight per day when they are heat stressed. Seasonal differences in confined cattle primarily reflect temperature stress. Data on feedlot steers (5) show average daily winter consumption to be 19 liters of water as opposed to 31 liters in the summer.

Dietary Factors

As mentioned, dry matter intake is highly correlated to water intake at moderate temperatures. There is evidence also to show that water content of feed consumed affects total water intake. However, this is primarily a factor in consumption of excess water when forage is very lush with a high water content. Other dietary factors affecting water intake include consumption of high levels of protein, but here the effect is because of greater required urinary excretion. When urea has been used as the major source of N in ruminant diets, some evidence shows that it resulted in greater urine volume than an equivalent amount of N in the form of purified soy protein. It should be pointed out also that young mammals consuming only milk need additional water, especially in warm or hot weather. Although milk of most species is about 85–88% water, the high content of protein results in high obligatory urinary water loss and without additional water, performance is likely to be reduced.

An increased intake of fats also may increase water intake. Consumption of feeds such as silages tends to increase intake and urinary excretion as illustrated in Table 6.4. In this instance note that total water consumed per kilogram of dry matter was appreciably higher in animals on the silage diet. Perhaps excess water was consumed because the silage-fed cattle also excreted more urine.

There is ample evidence that consumption of NaCl or other salts will increase consumption and excretion of water greatly by different animal species. Some salts may cause diarrhea and greater fecal excretion of water, but those, such as NaCl, that are absorbed almost completely, result in much greater urinary excretion and tissue dehydration occurs if water is not available.

Environmental Factors

High temperature, as mentioned previously, is the major factor causing increased consumption of water.

TABLE 6.4 Effect of rations and level of feeding on water intake of Holstein heifers.[a]

ITEM[b]	HAY		SILAGE	
	AD LIB.	MAINTENANCE	AD LIB.	MAINTENANCE
Dry matter intake, kg/100 kg BW	2.06	1.24	1.70	1.15
Feed water, kg/kg feed DM	0.11	0.12	3.38	3.38
Water drunk, kg/kg feed DM	3.36	3.66	1.55	1.38
Total water, kg/kg feed DM	3.48	3.79	4.93	4.76
Urine, kg/kg feed DM	0.93	1.14	1.85	1.68

[a]From Waldo et al. (6).
[b]BW = body weight; DM = dry matter

Associated with heat stress is high humidity, which also increases the need for water because heat losses—resulting from evaporation of water from the body surface and lungs—are reduced with high humidity.

In confined animals, design and accessibility of watering containers influences intake as does cleanness of the containers. In range animals the distance that must be traveled between water and forage affects the frequency of drinking and the amount consumed—that is, the greater the distance the less frequently the animal drinks and the less it consumes in a 24 h period.

Volume of Water Required

In very general terms animals will consume 3–4 g of water for every gram of dry feed consumed when they are not heat-stressed. This is an over simplification, of course. Those species that have the capability to conserve water require less and those adapted to a wet environment consume more. For example, sheep generally do not consume at the 4:1 ratio, but are more apt to be between 2.5:1 and 3:1. Cattle require more water than sheep because they are not as efficient at conserving water. Birds generally require less than mammalian species. Young animals generally require more water per unit of body weight than adult animals. Activity, of course, will increase requirements, but nervous, highly strung animals also will likely consume more water than less active animals. Other variables affecting absorption

and excretion as well as dietary factors discussed will alter water requirements.

Swine generally consume 2–2.5 kg of water/kg of dry feed at moderate temperatures and horses and poultry consume 2–3 kg/kg of dry feed (7). Cattle appear to need 3–5 kg of water/kg of dry feed and young calves appear to need 6–8 kg/kg of feed. In addition to these general values, water consumption will be increased by milk production; the additional requirement for cattle has been estimated at 1–1.8 kg of water/kg of feed over that required for a comparable animal not in lactation. Pregnancy also increases the need for water and ewes bearing multiple fetuses require more water than those bearing singles. The expected water consumption of adult farm animals and poultry in temperate environments as recommended by the NRC (7) has been summarized in Table 6.5.

TABLE 6.5 Expected water consumption of various classes and species of adult livestock in a temperate climate.[a]

ANIMAL	LITERS/DAY
Beef cattle	22–66
Dairy cattle	38–110
Sheep and goats	4–15
Horses	30–45
Swine	11–19
Chickens	0.2–0.4
Turkeys	0.4–0.6

[a]From NRC (7).

Water Restriction

There are many areas in the world where water supplies are more restrictive than feed supplies, either because of a lack of surface water or well water or because the available water is brackish and not suitable for consumption in adequate amounts to sustain the animals. Consequently, a relatively high percentage of animals, both domestic and wild, are faced with water shortages at some time during the year.

Fluid intake by animals is intermittent, even more so than food intake for most species, but the loss of water from the body is continuous, although variable. Thus, the body must be able to compensate in order to maintain its physiological functions. The most noticeable effect of moderate water restriction is reduced feed intake and reduced productivity. Urine and fecal water excretions drop markedly. With more severe restriction, weight loss is rapid as the body dehydrates. These changes are illustrated in Table 6.6. The dehydration is accompanied by increased renal excretion of N and electrolytes such as Na^+ and K^+. Water restriction causes more severe or quicker responses when temperatures are stressing. In addition to the dehydration that occurs, pulse rate and rectal temperatures usually increase, especially at hot temperatures, because the animal no longer has sufficient water to evaporate to maintain normal body temperatures. Respiration rate also will increase in these conditions. Eventually, there is a relatively marked increase in blood concentration, loss of intra- and extracellular and total body water, nausea, difficulty in muscular movements, and (in humans) loss of emotional stability. Animals tend to become highly irritable and bad tempered. Eventually, prostration and death will follow if severe water deprivation continues long enough.

Animals vary greatly in the amount of dehydration they can withstand; the camel is an example of one that can withstand weight loss of about 30% or more. Most mammals cannot survive such severe dehydration as this. With moderate restriction most species show some adaptation and can compensate partially for it by reducing excretion.

Water intoxication may occur in some species (humans, calves) as a result of sudden ingestion of large amounts after a short time period of deprivation. In calves, death may result because of a slow adaptation of the kidney to the sudden high water load.

❑ WATER QUALITY

Generally, it has been assumed that water safe for human consumption may be used safely by stock, but it appears that animals can tolerate higher salinity than humans; thus, it is probable that tolerances for other substances may be different, also. An NRC (7) report on this topic is recommended for additional reading.

TABLE 6.6　Effect of 50% water restriction at 18° or 32°C in dairy cows.[a]

MEASUREMENT	18°C AD LIB	18°C 50% AD LIB	32°C AD LIB	32°C 50% AD LIB
Body weight, kg	641	623	622	596
Feed consumption, kg/day	36.3	24.9	25.2	19.1
Urine vol., l/day	17.5	10.1	30.3	9.9
Fecal water, kg/day	21.3	10.5	11.7	8.2
Total vaporization, g/h	1133	583	1174	958
Total body water, %	64.5	50.9	67.9	52.6
Extravascular fluids, %	59.0	45.5	61.5	46.9
Plasma volume, %	3.9	3.9	4.4	3.9
Metabolism, Kcal/day	798	694	672	557
Metabolic water, kg/day	2.5	2.0	2.1	1.9
Rectal temperature, °C	38.5	38.5	39.2	39.5

[a]Data from Seif et al. (9).

Water quality may affect feed consumption directly because low quality water normally will result in reduced water consumption and, hence, lower feed consumption and production. Substances that may reduce palatability of water include various saline salts. At "high" rates of consumption, these salts may be toxic. Substances that may be toxic without much affect, if any, on palatability include nitrates and flourine as well as salts of some heavy metals. Other materials that may affect palatability or be toxic include pathogenic microorganisms of a wide variety, algae and/or protozoa, hydrocarbons, and other oily substances, pesticides of various types, and many industrial chemicals that sometimes pollute water supplies.

With regard to the mineral salts found in water, those apt to be present in high amounts include carbonates and bicarbonates, sulfates and chlorides of Ca, Mg, Na, and K. At a given concentration the sulfates generally are more detrimental to the animal than the carbonates or chlorides. An example of the effect of a moderate amount of NaCl on high producing dairy cows is shown in Table 6.7. Note that added NaCl resulted in increased water consumption and a slight reduction in feed consumption and milk production. Higher levels of NaCl would produce more drastic effects.

Most domestic animals can tolerate a total dissolved solid concentration of 15,000–17,000 mg/l, but production is apt to be reduced at this concentration. Water classified as good should have less than 2,500 mg/l of dissolved solids. According to NRC (7), water containing less than 1,000 mg/l of total soluble salts is safe for any class of livestock or poultry. Water containing 1,000–5,000 mg/l is safe, but may cause temporary mild diarrhea in animals not accustomed to it. Concentrations between 3,000 and 5,000 mg/l may cause watery feces and increased mortality in poultry and that with 5,000–7,000 mg/l is acceptable to all domestic animals except poultry. Concentrations greater than 7,000 mg/l are unfit for poultry and swine and should not be used for pregnant or lactating cattle, horses or sheep or for young growing animals of any species. Water containing more than 10,000 mg/l (1%) of soluble salts is unfit for use as drinking water under any conditions. In the writers view the NRC recommendations are on the conservative side, but they do provide guidelines for evaluating water quality for animals.

It should be pointed out that all of the dietary essential mineral elements are usually found in most water supplies, particularly in surface waters such as lakes. A substantial portion of the Na, Ca, and S requirement may be supplied in this manner. Consequently, water supplies should not be overlooked as a source of some of the needed mineral elements.

❑ SUMMARY

Water is required by animals in larger amounts than any other material ingested, and it serves many different functions of utmost importance to the animal body. Body tissues on a fat-free basis are about 73% water. The content generally decreases with age and with fatness. Water is absorbed rapidly from the stomach and gut and passes freely into most tissues and organs, depending on osmotic pressure gradients. The turnover time for water is rapid, often with a half-life value of about three days or less. Water is supplied primarily by free water obtained by drinking, but metabolic water from oxidative and other reactions may supply a substantial amount for some species adapted to dry environments. The ability to reduce water losses via feces, kidney, lungs, or body surface is related to adaptation to dry climates. Water requirements are directly related to dry feed consumption. As a rule of thumb we could say that about three units of water will be consumed per unit of dry feed, but this will be affected by animal species, type of diet, and particularly by hot environmental temperatures. Water restriction reduces feed consumption and may be very stressing to animals in hot environments. Water quality is of considerable importance to animals because water sup-

TABLE 6.7   Effect on high producing dairy cows of consuming tap water or tap water + 2,500 ppm of NaCl.[a]

ITEM	TAP	SALINE
Consumption, kg/day		
Hay	12.2	11.4
Grain	8.1	8.0
Water	136	145
Milk yield, kg	34.8	32.9
Respiration/min	78.4	78.6
Rectal temp, C	39.2	39.1

[a]Data from Jaster et al. (8).

plies in many parts of the world are saline or have excess salts of other kinds. Many species can tolerate at least 1% of total dissolved solids, but the amount that can be tolerated will depend on the specific chemical compounds present.

❏ REFERENCES

1. Schmidt-Neilsen, K. 1964. *Desert Animals, Physiological Problems of Heat and Water.* Oxford Univ. Press, Oxford, England.

2. Wallace, J. D., D. N. Hyder, and K. L. Knox. 1972. *Amer. J. Vet. Res.* **33**:921.

3. Hyder, D. N., R. E. Benent, and J. L. Norris. 1968. *J. Range Mgmt.* **21**:392.

4. Winchester, C. F. and M. J. Morris. 1956. *J. Animal Sci.* **15**:722.

5. Hoffman, M. P. and H. L. Self. 1972. *J. Animal Sci.* **35**:871.

6. Waldo, D. R., et al. 1965. *J Dairy Sci.* **48**:1473.

7. NRC. 1974. *Nutrients and Toxic Substances in Water for Livestock and Poultry.* Nat. Acad. Sci., Washington, D.C.

8. Jaster, E. H., J. D. Schuh, and T. N. Wegner. 1978. *J. Dairy Sci.* **61**:66.

9. Seif, S. M., H. D. Johnson, and L. Han. 1973. *J. Dairy Sci.* **56**:581.

7

Proteins and
Amino Acids

PROTEINS ARE ESSENTIAL ORGANIC constituents of living organisms, and are the class of nutrients in highest concentration in muscle tissues of animals. All cells synthesize proteins for part or all of their life cycle, and without protein synthesis, life could not exist. Except in animals whose intestinal microflora can synthesize protein from non-protein N sources, protein or its constituent amino acids must be provided in the diet to allow normal growth and other productive functions. All cells contain protein and cell turnover is very rapid in some tissues such as epithelial cells of the intestinal tract. The percentage of protein required in the diet is highest for young growing animals and declines gradually to maturity when only enough protein is required to maintain body tissues. Productive functions such as pregnancy and lactation increase the protein requirement because of increased output of protein in the products of conception and in milk, and because of an increased metabolic rate.

Proteins vary widely in chemical composition, physical properties, size, shape, solubility, and biological functions. All proteins are composed of simple units, amino acids. Although there are more than 200 naturally occurring amino acids, only about 20 are commonly found in most proteins and up to 10 are required in the diet of animals because tissue synthesis is not adequate to meet metabolic needs. The basic structure of an amino acid is illustrated by glycine, the simplest amino acid:

GLYCINE

The essential components are a carboxyl group (—C$\underset{OH}{\overset{O}{<}}$) and an amino group (NH$_2$) on the C atom adjacent to the carboxyl group. This NH$_2$ group is designated the α-amino group.

The general structure representing all amino acids can be designated as follows:

GENERAL STRUCTURE
FOR AMINO ACIDS

where R is the remainder of the molecule attached to the C atom associated with the α-amino group of the amino acid. The chemical structure of 20 of the amino acids is given in Fig. 7.1.

Amino acids not synthesized in animal tissues of most species in sufficient amounts to meet metabolic needs are termed **essential** or **indispensable,** while those generally not needed in the diet because of adequate tissue synthesis are termed **non-essential** or **dispensable.** The array of amino acids that cannot be synthesized in sufficient amounts in the tissues of some animal species or at certain stages of the life cycle varies slightly from the original classification of Rose (1), but this list of dietary essential amino acids still serves as a good guide. Dietary

essential amino acids for growth of rats as suggested by Rose (1) are as follows:

ESSENTIAL (INDISPENSABLE)	NON-ESSENTIAL
Arginine	Alanine
Histidine	Aspartic acid
Isoleucine	Citrulline
Leucine	Cystine
Lysine	Glutamic acid
Methionine (can be replaced partially by cystine)	Glycine
	Hydroxyproline
Phenylalanine (can be replaced partially by tyrosine)	Proline
	Serine
Threonine	Tyrosine
Tryptophan	
Valine	

Arginine is required in the diet of some species for maximum growth. In most species, adults do not require dietary arginine for maintenance. However, mature dogs and cats fed arginine-deficient diets show severe signs of deficiency, including hyperammonemia, tremors, and high levels of urinary orotic acid (2).

Citrulline can completely replace arginine in the diet of the cat and other species (3). The cat has a high sulfur amino acid requirement and is the only species known to require taurine. Taurine is a beta-amino sulfonic acid and is not present in protein, but occurs as a free amino acid in the diet. Cats fed taurine-deficient diets develop degeneration of the retina of the eye (4), which appears at a higher frequency when dietary sulfur-containing amino acids are also low.

Recent evidence (Visek (2)) indicates that dietary histidine is needed for adult humans, contrary to the earlier assumption that synthesis is sufficient in adults.

Asparagine is required for maximum growth during the first few days of consumption of a crystalline amino acid diet; certain other dispensable amino acids also may be required for maximum growth under some conditions.

In animals whose gastrointestinal microflora synthesize protein from non-protein N sources (ruminants and other herbivores), the amino acid balance of the diet is of little nutritional consequence except for high producing animals; mainly, the quantities of N and readily available carbohydrate are important.

ALIPHATIC

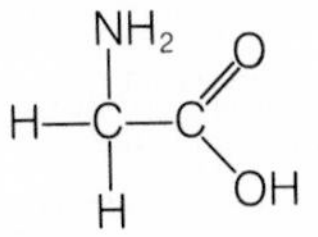

GLYCINE
(amino acetic acid)

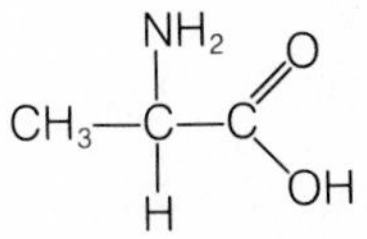

ALANINE
(α-amino propionic acid)

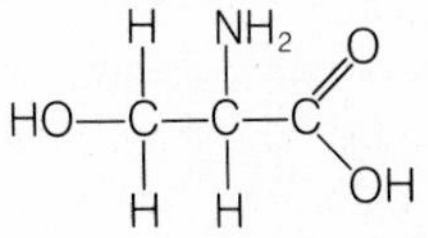

SERINE
(β-hydroxy α-amino propionic acid)

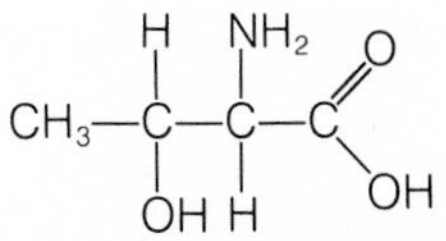

THREONINE
(α-amino β-hydroxy-N-butyric acid)

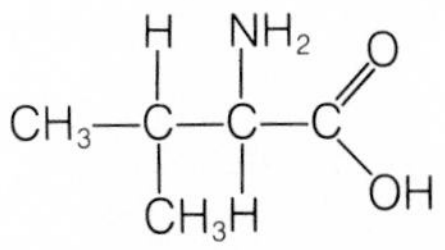

VALINE
(α-amino isovaleric acid)

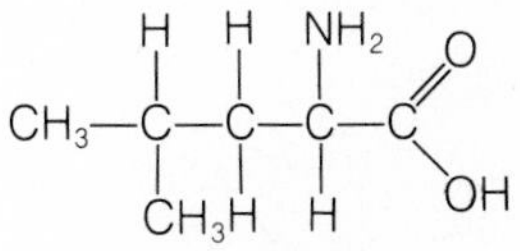

LEUCINE
(α-amino isocaproic acid)

AROMATIC

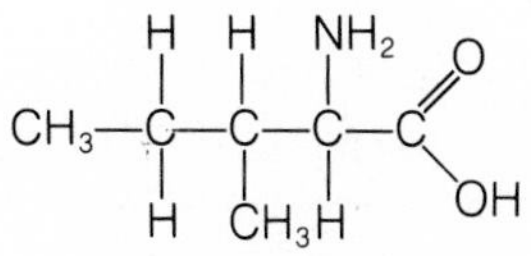

ISOLEUCINE
(β-methyl α-amino valeric acid)

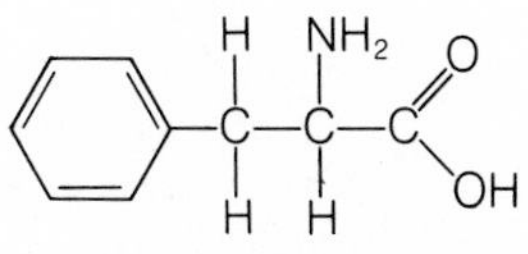

PHENYLALANINE
(β-phenyl α-amino propionic acid)

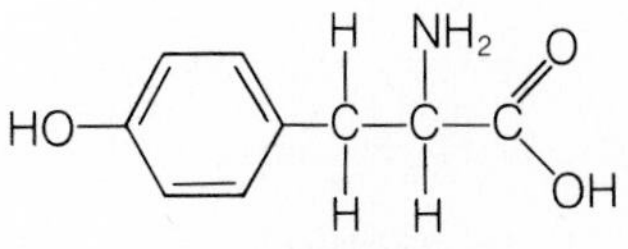

TYROSINE
(β-para hydroxy phenyl α-amino
propionic acid)

SULFUR-CONTAINING

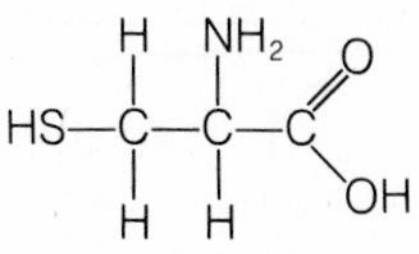

CYSTEINE
(β-thiol α-amino propionic acid)

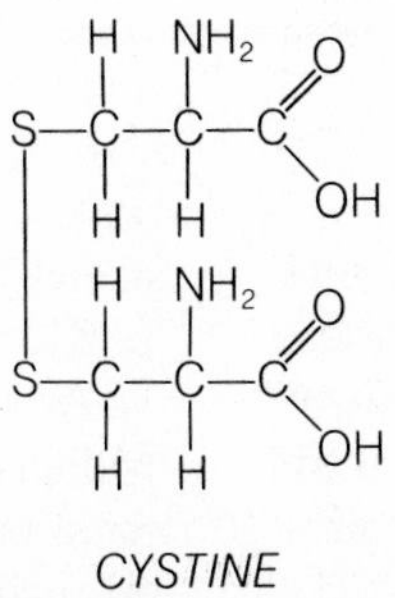

CYSTINE
di-(β-thiol α-amino propionic acid)

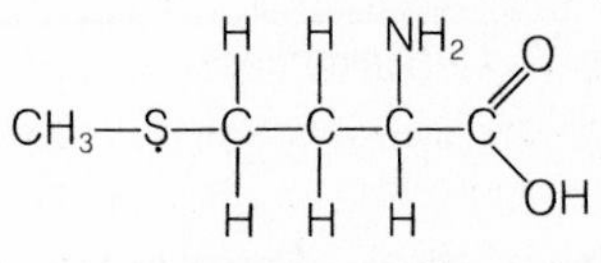

METHIONINE
(gamma methyl thiol α-amino-
N-butyric acid)

Figure 7.1 *Chemical structure of amino acids.*

HETEROCYCLIC

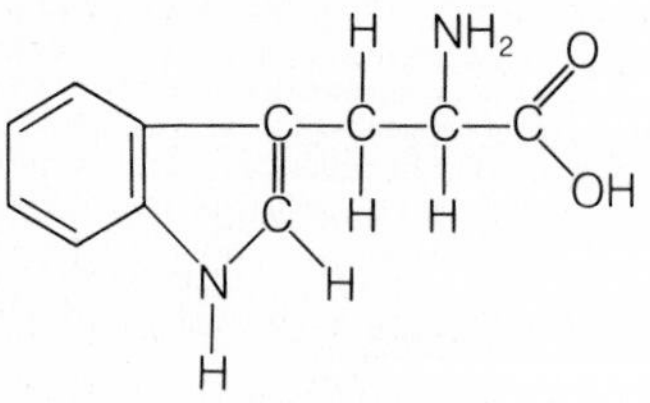

TRYPTOPHAN
(β-3-indole-α-amino propionic acid)

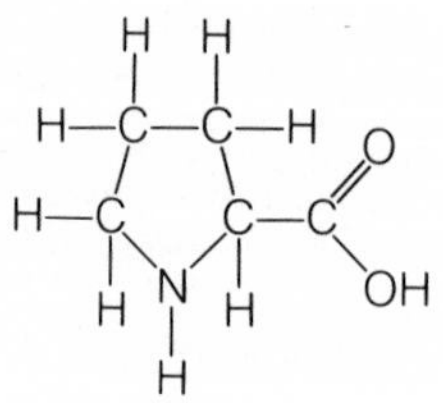

PROLINE
(pyrolidine-2-carboxylic acid)

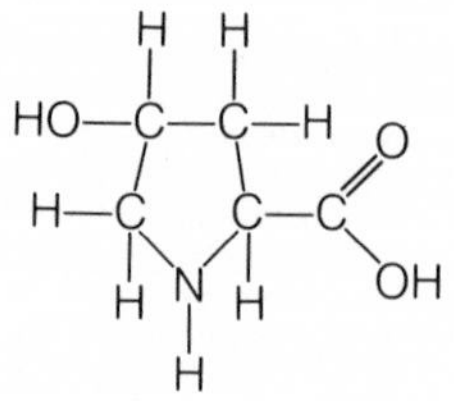

HYDROXY PROLINE
(4-hydroxy pyrolidine-2-carboxylic acid)

ACIDIC

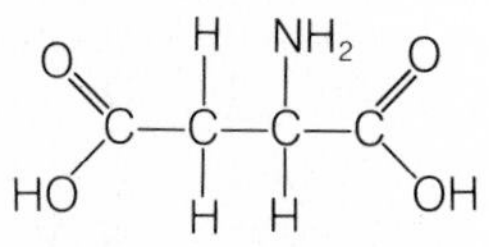

ASPARTIC ACID
(α-amino succinic acid)

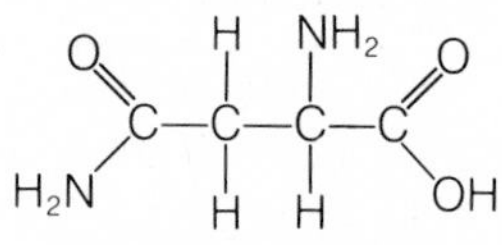

ASPARAGINE
(α-amino succinamic acid)

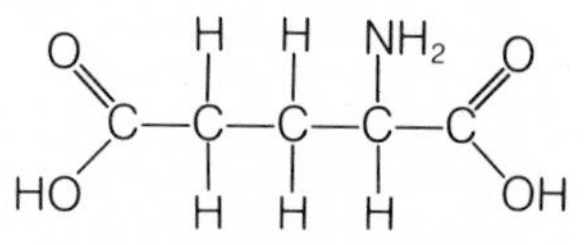

GLUTAMIC ACID
(α-amino glutaric acid)

BASIC

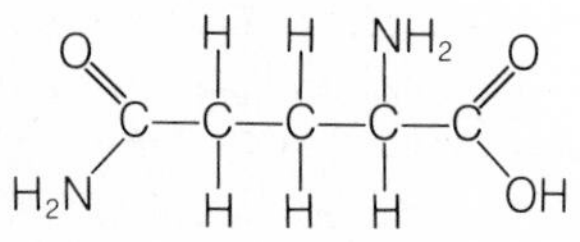

GLUTAMINE
(α-amino glutaramic acid)

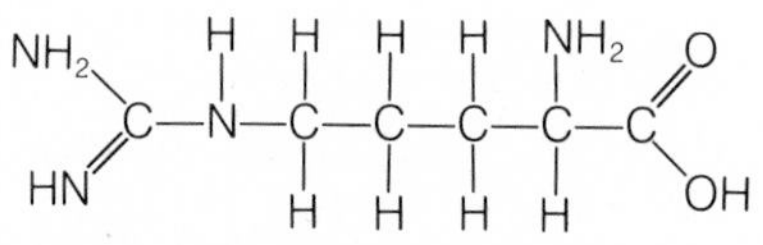

ARGININE
(β-guanidino α-amino valeric acid)

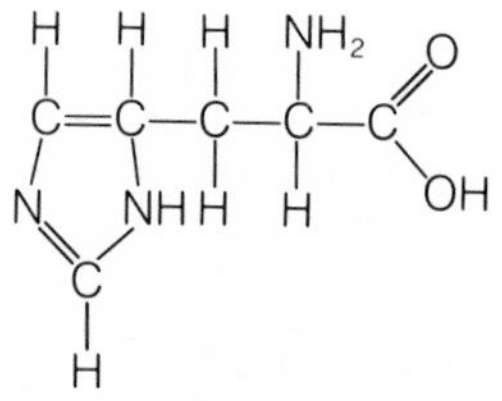

HISTIDINE
(β-imidazol α-amino propionic acid)

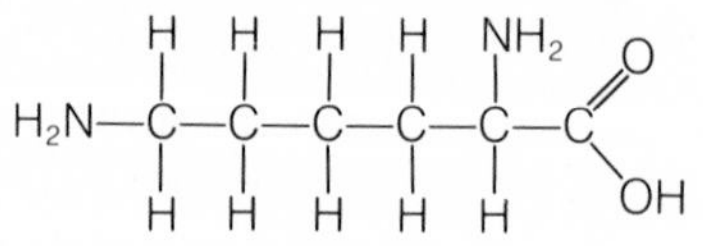

LYSINE
(α, epsilon diamino caproic acid)

Figure 7.1   (*Continued*).

The synthesis of protein from amino acids occurs by joining of individual amino acids to form long chains. The length of the chain and the order of arrangement of amino acids within the chain are two of the main factors determining the characteristics of the protein.

The linkage between one amino acid and another is called a peptide bond (A, on p. 81). The dipeptide alanyl-glycine would be formed as shown in B on p. 81.

All naturally occurring amino acids are in the L-configuration, which is, with a few exceptions, the most biologically active form. Synthetic amino acids are usually found as the racemic mixture of L- and D-isomers. The schematic representation of L- and D-amino acids is shown in C on p. 81.

A

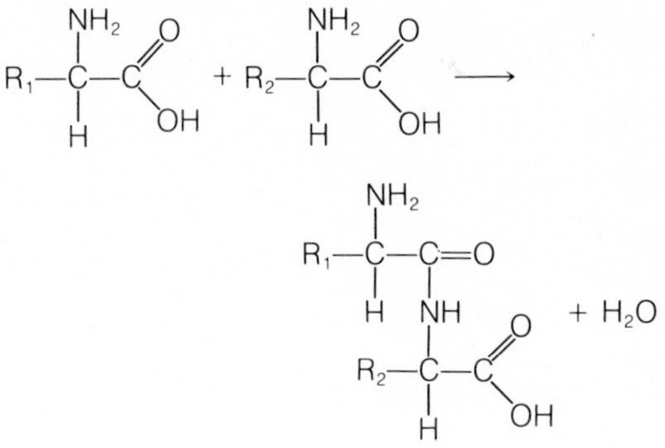

B

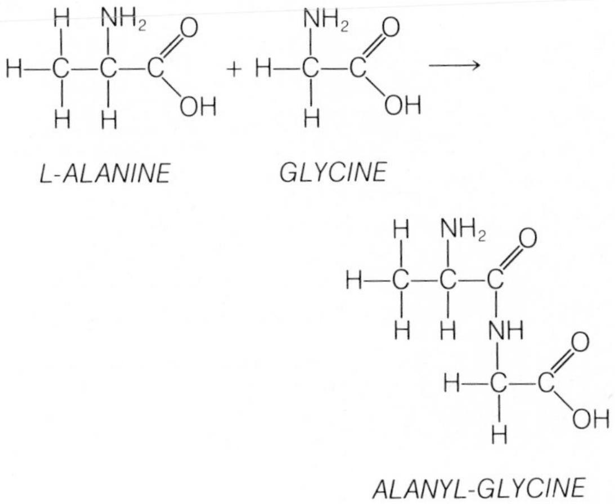

L-ALANINE   GLYCINE

ALANYL-GLYCINE

C

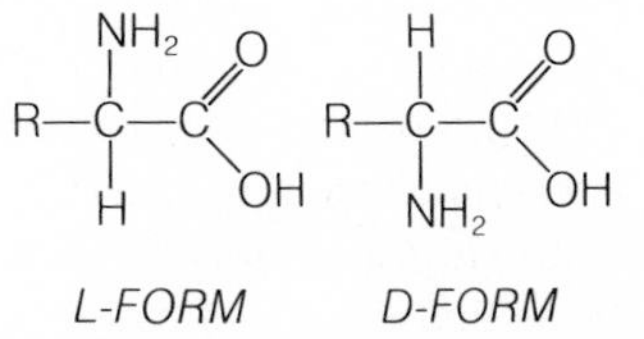

L-FORM   D-FORM

Elongation of the chain by additional amino acids proceeds from tripeptides to polypeptides and eventually to a complete protein molecule of specific amino acid content and sequence. The amino-acid composition of hundreds of proteins has been determined and in many cases the exact structure of the protein is known. The amino acid sequences of wheat germ cytochrome c and human cytochrome c are shown in Fig. 7.2 (5). These two enzymes, one of plant origin and one of animal origin, are remarkably similar in their structure, illustrating the commonality associated with evolutionary processes. This molecule is very small compared with most proteins. The molecular weight of most proteins is 35,000 to 500,000 with 350 to 5,000 amino acid residues.

The amino acid compositions of some common proteins of plant and animal origin are shown in Table 7.1. Egg albumin is considered the most nearly perfect protein for meeting animal needs because of its nearly ideal amino acid composition and its high digestibility. A single feedstuff may be composed of several distinct proteins and the adequacy of its protein will depend on the composite amino acid mixture supplied by the individual protein fractions. This is illustrated in Table 7.1 (6–8) by the wide differences in the amino acid composition of four protein fractions from corn (maize) endosperm. Zein is notably low in lysine and tryptophan. A genetic mutation discovered by Purdue University scientists (9) involves a gene for high lysine and tryptophan (referred to as the "opaque-2" gene). The proportion of zein in opaque-2 corn is lower and that of glutelin and other protein fractions is higher than in common corn, resulting in a grain with a more favorable balance of amino acids when used as a dietary component for most species.

Similar genetic mutations in barley and other cereal grains have resulted in seeds with an altered amino acid composition. Some amino acids are present in animal tissues in higher quantities than in plant tissues. For example, hydroxyproline is absent from the plant proteins in Table 7.1, but is abundant in animal connective tissue, especially collagen. A sensitive measure of the nutritive value of protein is the balance among its essential amino acids. The essential amino acid composition of proteins is as variable as the number of proteins present in nature; no two proteins have an identical amino acid composition.

All proteins can be classified on the basis of their shape, their solubilities in water, salt, acids, bases and alcohol, and on the basis of other special characteristics. Such a broad classification includes the following:

A. Globular proteins—soluble in water or in dilute acids or bases or in alcohol
    Albumins—soluble in water
    Globulins—soluble in dilute neutral solutions of salts of bases and acids
    Glutelins—soluble in dilute acids or bases
    Prolamines (gliadins)—soluble in 70–80% ethanol
    Histones—soluble in water
    Protamines—soluble in water

B. Fibrous proteins—insoluble in water, resistant to digestive enzymes
    Collagens—can be converted to gelatin
    Elastins—similar to collagens but cannot be converted to gelatin

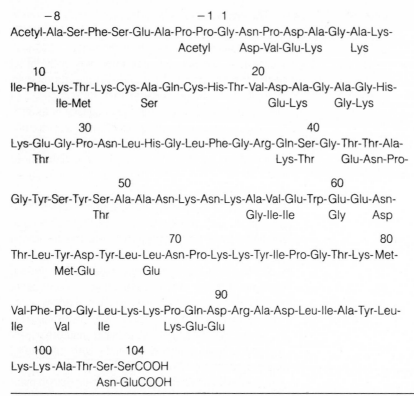

```
         -8                           -1  1
Acetyl-Ala-Ser-Phe-Ser-Glu-Ala-Pro-Pro-Gly-Asn-Pro-Asp-Ala-Gly-Ala-Lys-
                        Acetyl      Asp-Val-Glu-Lys      Lys

        10                            20
Ile-Phe-Lys-Thr-Lys-Cys-Ala-Gln-Cys-His-Thr-Val-Asp-Ala-Gly-Ala-Gly-His-
        Ile-Met         Ser                   Glu-Lys        Gly-Lys

        30                            40
Lys-Glu-Gly-Pro-Asn-Leu-His-Gly-Leu-Phe-Gly-Arg-Gln-Ser-Gly-Thr-Thr-Ala-
        Thr                                   Lys-Thr        Glu-Asn-Pro-

        50                            60
Gly-Tyr-Ser-Tyr-Ser-Ala-Ala-Asn-Lys-Asn-Lys-Ala-Val-Glu-Trp-Glu-Glu-Asn-
                Thr                     Gly-Ile-Ile        Gly      Asp

        70                            80
Thr-Leu-Tyr-Asp-Tyr-Leu-Leu-Asn-Pro-Lys-Lys-Tyr-Ile-Pro-Gly-Thr-Lys-Met-
        Met-Glu         Glu

        90
Val-Phe-Pro-Gly-Leu-Lys-Lys-Pro-Gln-Asp-Arg-Ala-Asp-Leu-Ile-Ala-Tyr-Leu-
Ile      Val      Ile            Lys-Glu-Glu

        100       104
Lys-Lys-Ala-Thr-Ser-SerCOOH
                Asn-GluCOOH
```

Figure 7.2 *The amino acid sequence of wheat germ cytochrome* c *and for comparison below this sequence, the residues that differ in human cytochrome C. Residues indicated by negative numbers are absent in all cytochromes C. From: Smith (8).*

Keratins—insoluble in water, resistant to digestive enzymes, contain up to 15% cystine

C. Conjugated proteins—proteins which contain a wide array of compounds of a non-protein nature. Some examples of protein-lipid and protein-carbohydrate complexes should help to clarify their importance in animal tissues.

Protein-lipid Complexes

An egg yolk phospholipid-protein complex was recognized more than a century ago; now hundreds of lipid-protein complexes are known. Electrostatic, hydrophobic, and hydrogen bonds as well as other forces contribute to the stability of lipoproteins. A few protein-lipid complexes of importance in animal production are discussed here.

A very important type of protein-lipid complex is represented by the membrane proteins of animal cells. Biological membranes act as a permeability barrier, transport substances across the boundary between the interior and exterior of the cell, act as supports for catalytic functions, and probably perform other important, though less well-defined functions (10). These membranes are composed of proteins, lipids, and carbohydrates in various proportions. The chemical composition of some important cell membranes is summarized in Table 7.2.

Myelin is a lipoprotein abundant in the nervous system as a sheath around nerve fibers. Peripheral and central nervous tissues contain about 80% and 35% myelin, respectively. Erythrocyte membranes contain mucolipids, phospholipids, and loosely bound proteins. Mitochondria contain structural protein, matrix protein, and about 30% lipids, mainly phospholipids. Fatty acids and other lipids are adsorbed to the surface of blood serum proteins to form lipoproteins. The protein content of plasma lipoproteins ranges from 2% in chylomicrons to about 50% in high density lipoproteins. The structure and function of serum lipoproteins has been described in detail (11).

TABLE 7.1 Amino acid composition of some plant and animal products.

| | EGG ALBUMIN | CORN ENDOSPERM[a] | | | | | | | | BEEF[d] | PORK[d] | LAMB[d] | BOVINE INTRA-MUSCULAR COLLAGEN[e] |
| | | ALBUMIN | | GLOBULIN | | ZEIN | | GLUTELIN | | | | | |
		N[b]	O[c]	N	O	N	O	N	O				
Alanine	5.7	9.8	7.9	8.4	7.3	10.9	10.5	4.5	4.7	6.4	6.3	6.3	10.4
Arginine	5.9	11.6	11.7	9.6	8.9	2.1	2.3	5.8	5.3	6.6	6.4	6.9	4.5
Aspartic acid	9.2	11.1	10.8	8.2	8.0	5.9	5.7	6.8	6.9	8.8	8.9	8.5	3.8
Cystine/2	3.0		5.3	1.8	1.8	1.0	1.4			1.4	1.3	1.3	
Glutamic acid	15.7	16.5	13.2	19.2	18.2	27.4	24.9	12.9	14.6	14.4	14.5	14.4	7.7
Glycine	3.2	8.8	7.9	5.3	5.5	1.6	2.0	3.3	3.8	7.1	6.1	6.7	32.8
Histidine	2.4	3.2	2.6	3.4	3.8	1.4	1.4	3.8	4.2	2.9	3.2	2.7	0.6
Hydroxyproline	0	0	0	0	0	0	0	0	0				10.5
Isoleucine	7.1	4.6	3.9	4.2	4.3	4.2	4.6	3.4	3.4	5.1	4.9	4.8	1.3
Leucine	9.9	6.3	6.3	13.2	10.7	22.4	21.2	8.1	8.6	8.4	7.5	7.4	2.5
Lysine	6.4	6.4	5.5	4.4	4.6	0.1	0.2	3.7	3.6	8.4	7.8	7.6	2.3
Methionine	5.4		1.6	2.0	1.9	1.7	1.3	1.4	1.1	2.3	2.5	2.3	0.6
Phenylalanine	7.5	2.9	4.6	5.8	6.3	7.6	8.0	3.8	3.8	4.0	4.1	3.9	1.4
Proline	3.8	6.6	5.7	7.2	7.6	10.7	10.5	8.7	10.1	5.4	4.6	4.8	11.8
Serine	8.5	7.0	5.4	5.9	5.4	6.2	5.6	3.7	3.7	3.8	4.0	3.9	4.0
Threonine	4.0	5.4	4.7	4.0	4.1	3.2	2.9	3.3	3.4	4.0	5.1	4.9	1.8
Tryptophan	1.2	1.1	3.0	0.3	1.3		0.2		0.5	1.1	1.4	1.3	
Tyrosine	3.8	3.2	5.0	4.7	4.9	5.6	6.0	2.9	3.1	3.2	3.0	3.2	0.4
Valine	8.8	12.6	6.0	5.8	7.1	4.5	3.4	5.4	5.6	5.7	5.0	5.0	2.3

[a]From: Concon, J. M. (ref. 5). Expressed as g/100 g protein.
[b]Normal maize.
[c]Opaque-2 maize.
[d]From: Schweigert and Payne (ref. 6). Expressed as % of crude protein (6.25).
[e]From McClain et al. (ref. 7). Expressed as residues/1000 residues.

TABLE 7.2 Chemical composition of some cell membranes.[a]

MEMBRANE	PROTEIN %	LIPID %	CARBOHYDRATE %	RATIO OF PROTEIN TO LIPID
Myelin	18	79	3	0.23
Blood platelets	33–42	51–58	7.5	0.7
Human red blood cell	49	43	8	1.1
Rat liver cells	58	42	5–10	1.4
Nuclear membrane, rat liver cell	59	35	2.9	1.6
Mitochondrial outer membrane	52	48	2.4	1.1
Mitochondrial inner membrane	76	24	2–3	3.2
Retinal rods, cattle	51	49	4	1.0

[a]From Guidotti (10).

Protein-carbohydrate Complexes (Glycoproteins)

Proteins can complex with carbohydrate to form glycoproteins. These complexes arise from the acceptance of sugars by amino aid residues in the polypeptide chain. Protein complexes of sulfated polysaccharides occur in three types designated chondroitin sulfate A, B, and C. Cartilage, tendon, and skin are high in chondroitin sulfates complexed with protein. Mucoproteins are complexes of protein with the amino-sugars, glucosamine, and galactosamine; the hexoses, mannose, and galactose; the pentose, fucose, and sialic acid. The enzyme, serum cholinesterase, is a mucoprotein, as is the hormone, gonadotrophin. Mucous secretions contain abundant amounts of mucoproteins. The mucoproteins of submaxillary salivary gland secretions are potent inhibitors of agglutination of red blood cells by influenza viruses. Ovalbumin is a mucoprotein containing glucosamine and mannose. Ovomucoid, the trypsin inhibitor in egg white, is a glycoprotein distinguished by its high heat stability and high carbohydrate content. It contains about 14% hexosamine and 7% hexose. Aspartic acid is apparently the amino acid immediately concerned in linkage of the protein to the carbohydrate part of the complex.

❏ FUNCTIONS

Proteins perform many different functions in the animal body. Most body proteins are present as components of cell membranes, in muscle and in other supportive capacities such as in skin, hair, and hooves. In addition, blood plasma proteins, enzymes, hormones, and immune antibodies all serve important specialized functions in the body even though they do not contribute greatly to the total protein content of the body.

Tissue Proteins

Collagen.   The molecule consists of a triple-helix (2,800 Å long and 15 Å diameter) arranged in parallel and quarter-staggered to give the characteristic banded appearance of collagen. It has a compact structure and great strength. Collagen content increases with aging of the animal and, due to its characteristic shrinkage on heating as a result of its high proline and hydroxyproline content, the toughness of cooked meat from older animals is a well-known

phenomenon. It is insoluble in water and resistant to digestive enzymes.

Elastin.   The molecule resembles denatured collagen and consists of long, randomly ordered polypeptide chains. It is rubber-like in its response to stretching and, when stretched to the elastic limit, it breaks more easily than collagen. It is always found in combination with a large proportion of collagen even in ligaments and artery walls where it is most effective in restoring the tissue to its original shape or position. It is only a minor component of musculature but, like collagen, is insoluble in water and resistant to digestive enzymes.

Myofibrilar Proteins.   These are the proteins of sarcoplasm, which is the material extracted from finely homogenized muscle with dilute salts. Most of the protein in this extract is in solution and contains more than 20 enzymes involved in muscle metabolism as well as mitochondrial fragments and particles of sarcoplasmic reticulum.

Contractile Proteins.   Three proteins—actin, tropomyosin B, and myosin—take part in muscle contraction. Myosin is the major component of the thick filaments of striated muscle. Its most important feature is its enzyme activity in an ATPase. Actin, when extracted from myosin, is in the globular form when ATP is present. The globular form polymerizes on the addition of neutral salts to give chain-like molecules of fibrous actin with the simultaneous change of the bound ATP to ADP and liberation of a molecule of inorganic P. The reverse process occurs in the absence of ATP. Tropomyosin B has no enzyme properties and does not combine in solution with either actin or myosin. The complicated interactions between the contractile proteins and their unique chemical structure are vital to normal muscle metabolism.

Keratins.   Proteins of hair, wool, feathers, hooves, horns, claws, and beaks are similar in composition in that they are resistant to acid, alkali, and heat treatment and especially resistant to breakdown by digestive enzymes. Therefore, their value as protein supplements for animals is understandably limited unless they are processed adequately.

Blood Proteins.   The chief proteins of the blood are albumin and a series of globulins (α, β, γ) along with thromboplastin, fibrinogen, and the conjugated protein, hemoglobin. The composition of the serum proteins of the normal pig at various ages is shown

TABLE 7.3 Approximate serum protein concentrations of pigs at various ages.

	NEWBORN	6 WEEKS	3 MONTHS	1 YEAR
Total serum protein, g/dl serum	2 to 3	4 to 5	5 to 6	7 to 8
Albumin, g/100 g serum protein	18	47	45	52
α-globulin, g/100 g serum protein	60	25	29	18
β-globulin, g/100 g serum protein	16	19	16	13
γ-globulin, g/100 g serum protein	6[a]	9	10	16
Albumin:Globulin ratio	0.2	0.90	0.82	1.1

[a]At 24 h (after sucking) the value is 45–48 g/100 g serum protein because of colostrum ingestion.

in Table 7.3. Blood contains a large array of conjugated proteins, including lipoproteins, enzymes and protein-hormones whose distinct composition and structure and specific physico-chemical properties allow separation and isolation by electrophoresis, centrifugation, extractions, and other means.

Enzymes. Enzymes, sometimes referred to as organic catalysts, are all protein in nature and are all relatively specific in their reactions. Some are hydrolytic (as the digestive enzymes), some are involved in other degradative metabolic reactions and others are involved in synthetic processes. Animal cells contain hundreds of enzymes each with a specific structure and distinct reactive group.

Hormones. Hormones, like enzymes, are produced by cells in minute quantities and have profound effects on metabolism. The action of enzymes is restricted usually within the same cell or in close proximity to the site of elaboration; in contrast, hormones are carried by the blood from the site of release to the target organ often far removed from site of release. Not all hormones are proteins. Some important protein hormones are insulin, growth hormone, gonadotrophic hormone, parathyroid hormone, and calcitonin.

Immune Antibodies. Like enzymes and hormones, antibodies constitute only a minute proportion of total body protein, but they perform a vital role in protecting the animal against specific infections. Antibodies against specific infections can be acquired (passive immunity) by placental transfer to the fetus from the blood of the dam, by ingestion and absorption of antibody-rich colostrum by the newborn, or by injection into the susceptible animal of purified sources of antibodies from other animals. Exposure of a susceptible animal to an antigen (pathogen) stimulates antibody production against the pathogen, resulting in active immunity.

❏ METABOLISM

Protein metabolism will be considered in two phases: catabolism (degradation) and anabolism (synthesis); both processes proceed simultaneously in animal tissues. Individual amino acids, which are the basic units required in metabolism by the animal, normally are present in the diet as constituents of intact proteins which must be hydrolyzed to allow their component amino acids to be absorbed into the body. Thus, the conversion of dietary protein to tissue protein (or egg or milk protein) involves the following:

Intact dietary protein
↓　　hydrolysis in GI tract (catabolism)
Amino acids in intestinal lumen
↓　　absorption from GI tract
Amino acids in blood
↓　　synthesis in tissues (anabolism)
Intact tissue proteins

Hydrolysis of dietary proteins is accomplished by proteolytic enzymes elaborated by epithelial cells lining the lumen of the GI tract and by the pancreas (see Ch. 4). The efficiency with which hydrolysis occurs determines the degree of absorption of individual amino acids and contributes to the nutritional value of the dietary protein. The other important factor contributing to nutritional value is the balance of absorbable essential amino acids. Proteins can be characterized nutritionally on the basis of digestibility and absorbability (protein hydrolysis in the GI tract and subsequent absorption of amino acids) as well as on the degree of utilization of amino acids after absorption. Dietary proteins not containing the correct proportion of essential amino acids to meet the animal's needs cannot be used efficiently for tissue protein synthesis. Even proteins hydrolyzed easily in the GI tract do not have a high nutritional value if they have a deficiency or an imbalance of one or more amino acids. This is exemplified by the growth failure observed in young animals fed a diet deficient in one of the essential amino acids.

Digestible protein refers to that disappearing from the ingesta as it passes down the GI tract. Apparent protein digestibility of feed represents the difference between what is in the feed and in the feces which includes both unabsorbed and metabolic (endogenous) fecal N. Metabolic fecal N arises from normal metabolism of tissue protein and includes N from cells sloughed from the intestinal lining and residues of digestive enzymes and other substances secreted into the lumen of the GI tract. After absorption, amino acids are subject to further losses in utilization through metabolism in the liver and other tissues. These losses of N occur in the mammal mainly as urinary urea N and in birds as uric acid. Because the degree of utilization of a feed protein depends not only on its digestibility and absorbability but also on utilization of its component amino acids after absorption, protein sources can be ranked in a quantitative way as to their nutritive value. Measures of nutritive value of proteins and their application to feeding practice are described later in this chapter.

Absorption of Amino Acids

The intestinal epithelium is an effective barrier to diffusion of a variety of substances. There is very limited transfer of proteins, polypeptides or even dipeptides across the intestinal epithelium except in early postnatal life (in most species during the first 24 h), when intact protein is absorbed by pinocytosis. Certain dipeptides and tripeptides are absorbed, but the biological importance of the phenomenon is unclear. However, it is likely that absorption of some protein molecules or molecular fragments may be related to the development of food allergies.

Absorption of amino acids takes place by active transport. The brush border membrane of the small intestine contains at least two active transport systems, one for neutral amino acids and one for basic amino acids. The amino acid moves across the intestinal cell membrane against a concentration gradient requiring energy supplied by cellular metabolism. The naturally occurring L-forms of amino acids

are absorbed preferentially to the D-forms, probably as a result of specificity of active transport systems. Removal of the carboxyl group by formation of an ester, removal of the charge on the amino group by acetylation, or introduction of a charge into the side chain of a variety of amino acids prevents active transport, emphasizing the highly specific nature of the carrier system. Some amino acids may compete with each other for transport. For example, a high concentration of leucine in the diet increases the requirement for isoleucine. Arginine, cystine, and ornithine inhibit lysine transport, and arginine, lysine, and ornithine inhibit cystine transport. Some neutral amino acids inhibit basic amino acid transport; for example, methionine inhibits lysine transport. Apparently, basic amino acids do not inhibit neutral amino acid transport. Other amino acids—for example the three basic amino acids, ornithine, arginine, lysine—share a common transport system with cystine. Proline and hydroxyproline apparently share a common transport system along with sarcosine and betaine, and have a high affinity for the neutral amino acid transport system as well as for their own. Whether a common transport system for glycine, alanine, and serine exists in intestinal epithelium as it does in some microorganisms is unknown.

Fate of Amino Acids after Absorption

The fate of amino acids after absorption can be divided broadly into three categories: (a) tissue protein synthesis; (b) synthesis of enzymes, hormones, and other metabolites; and (c) deamination or transamination and use of the carbon skeleton for energy. The first two of the above will be discussed together as their synthesis involves similar metabolic processes.

Synthesis of Protein

Protein synthesis in animal tissues requires the presence of nucleic acids. All living cells contain many different nucleic acids that play a number of vital roles. Deoxyribonucleic acid (DNA), a chromosomal component of cells, carries the genetic information in the cell and transmits inherited characteristics from one generation to the next. It is the blueprint of protein synthesis. DNA controls the development of the cell and the organism by controlling the formation of ribonucleic acid (RNA). There are three different kinds of RNA in cells; ribosomal RNA, transfer RNA, and messenger RNA. All three types are involved in the synthesis of proteins. Ribosomal RNA is part of the structure of the ribosome which is the site of formation of proteins in the cell. Transfer RNA carries specific amino acids to the ribosome where they interact with messenger RNA. Messenger RNA determines the sequence of amino acids in the protein being formed. Thus, synthesis of each protein is controlled by a different messenger RNA. This basic information in protein synthesis is needed for appreciation of the overall role of proteins in normal growth and development of animals.

DNA is composed of phosphate-linked deoxyribose and four nitrogenous bases, adenine, cytosine, guanine, and thymine. Their two- and three-dimensional structures and the structure of DNA are shown in Fig. 7.3. The molecule is in the form of a long double helix chain of nucleotides composed of phosphate-linked deoxyribose sugar groups to each of which is attached one of the four bases. The bases always are paired, adenine with thymine and guanine with cytosine. The sequence of pairs can vary infinitely, and this sequence determines the exact protein to be synthesized by the cell. The paired arrangement is illustrated diagrammatically in Fig. 7.3 (12). Changes in DNA occur in mutation and subsequent selection.

The transfer of information from DNA in the nucleus to the site of protein synthesis in the cytoplasm is accomplished by RNA. The composition of RNA is similar to that of DNA, except that ribose replaces deoxyribose, and uracil replaces thymine. The nucleotides of RNA are linked through their phosphate groups to form long chains as in DNA.

Protein synthesis occurs by transfer of amino acids to ribosomes, particles attached to membrane surfaces and to which amino acids are linked in sequence predetermined by the sequence of nitrogenous bases in DNA and, in turn, in RNA. Ribosomes have molecular weights approximating 4 million, 40% of which is RNA, with the remainder being protein. The ribosomes act as templates for the orderly array of amino acid linkage during protein synthesis. The addition of amino acids to a growing polypeptide chain in this way occurs very rapidly. For example, a molecule of hemoglobin is synthesized in about 1.5 min.

Figures 7.4 (13) and 7.5 (14) illustrate symbolically how the amino acids are positioned in forming the polypeptide chain during protein synthesis. All of the information needed to determine the three-dimensional structure of a protein is associated with the amino acid sequence. Figure 7.4 shows the amino acids joined head to tail to form a ring of a fictitious

protein. Amino acids are classified on the basis of the size of the side chain and the degree to which the amino acid is polarized (separated regions of plus and minus electric charge). Translation of messenger RNA into protein at a ribosome is illustrated in Fig. 7.5 (14). Each nucleotide triplet (codon) on the messenger RNA chain encodes a specific amino acid. Each molecule of transfer RNA in turn binds only the amino acid corresponding to a particular codon. Through all of the differences in functions of proteins (antibodies, hormones, enzymes, structural proteins) there is a commonality: they work by selectively binding to molecules.

Exciting new research with pig and cattle muscle cells grown in tissue culture promises to provide insight into the control mechanisms governing rate of muscle growth in animals. These isolated cell culture techniques allow testing the effects of individual components such as growth hormone and other serum factors singly and in combination on rate of protein synthesis.

Other evidence suggests that protein degradation in muscle tissue is controlled by cathepsins and that calcium activating factors (CAF) may be an important determinant of net rate of muscle growth in animals. Present knowledge of protein turnover and the function of cellular organelles is growing rapidly.

Such basic research on control of protein synthesis and degradation in living animals is important for developing a more complete understanding of the growth process and in controlling it for efficient meat production. The relative importance of changes in rate of muscle protein synthesis versus muscle protein degradation in contributing to net protein accretion during growth is not fully understood, but is an area of active research. Knowledge of the mechanisms of muscle protein synthesis and degradation generated from basic research in animals used for meat production also may find application to humans.

The growth process is fundamental to all living organisms and is not restricted to young growing animals, but is characteristic of maintenance of tissues whose cellular turnover continues throughout life, such as skin and intestinal lining. During the past few years, a series of polypeptide growth factors (PFG) have been discovered and characterized with respect to their role in cellular metabolism (15). These substances take part in growth regulatory processes and probably far outnumber the classical polypeptide hormones such as growth hormone and insulin, whose structures and general functions have been known for years. PFG's, which have been characterized in

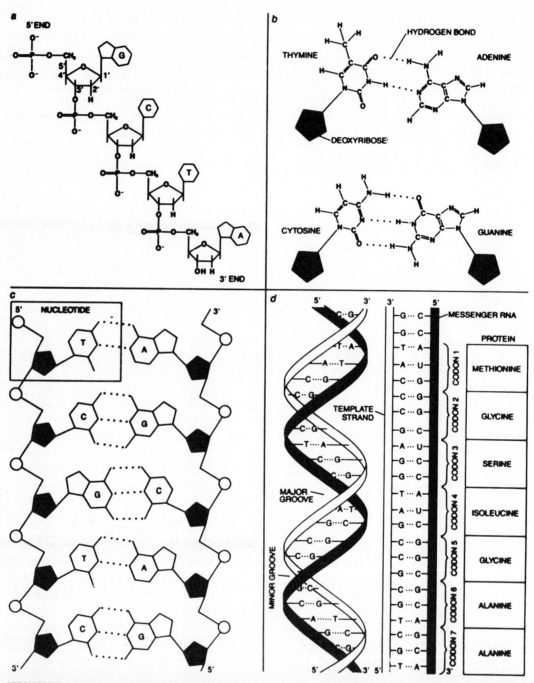

STRUCTURE OF DNA has a backbone (*a*) made up of bonded sugar and phosphate groups, to each of which is attached one of four bases: guanine (*G*), cytosine (*C*), thymine (*T*) or adenine (*A*). The phosphate group is represented by the structures with the *P* at the center, the sugar by the pentagon with an oxygen atom (*O*) at the top. A phosphate group connects the 5′ carbon atom of one sugar to the 3′ carbon atom of the next. The combination of sugar-phosphate group and base constitutes a nucleotide (*b*). (The distan-ces between atoms are not to scale.) The nature of the hydrogen bonding of the bases is such that thymine always pairs with adenine and cytosine always pairs with guanine. The structure that results is shown in two dimensions (*c*) and in three: the double helix (*d*). In conveying the genetic message of DNA the sequence of the cod-ing strand (*color*) is transcribed into a strand of messenger RNA, which serves to make a variety of proteins. The *U* in the strand of messenger RNA stands for uracil, the RNA counterpart of thymine.

Figure 7.3   *Structure of DNA. Reproduced with permission from Scientific American 253(4):58–67 (page 60), Oct. 1985.*

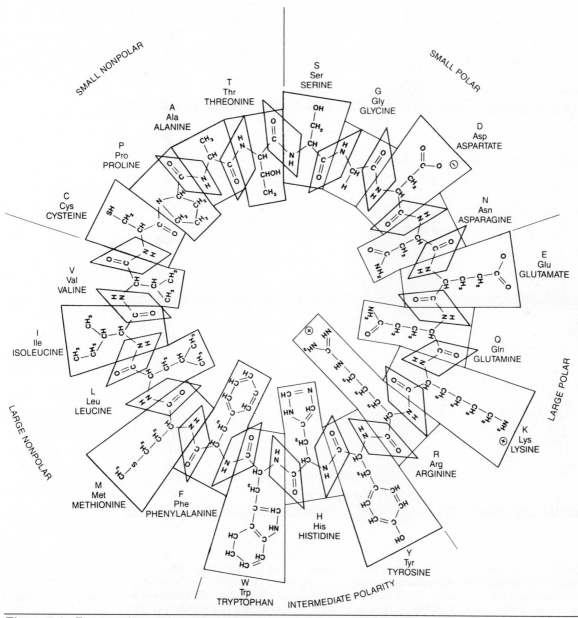

Figure 7.4 *Twenty amino acids specified in the genetic code are the basic components of all proteins. Here the amino acids are shown joined head to tail to form a ring (which is not the structure of any real protein); their three-letter and one-letter abbreviations are indicated. The arrangement places amino acids that have similar chemical properties near one another in the ring. An approximate classification in five groups is based on the size of the amino acid's side chain and on the degree to which it is polarized. (A polar molecule has separated regions of positive and negative electric charge.) These factors have a major influence on the folding of a protein. In the evolution of a protein a mutant form is more likely to be accepted if an amino acid is replaced by one that has similar properties—by one found nearby in the ring. The ring is similar to one proposed by Rosemarie M. Swanson of Texas A&M University. From R.F. Doolittle, (13). By permission of Sci. Am. and the author.*

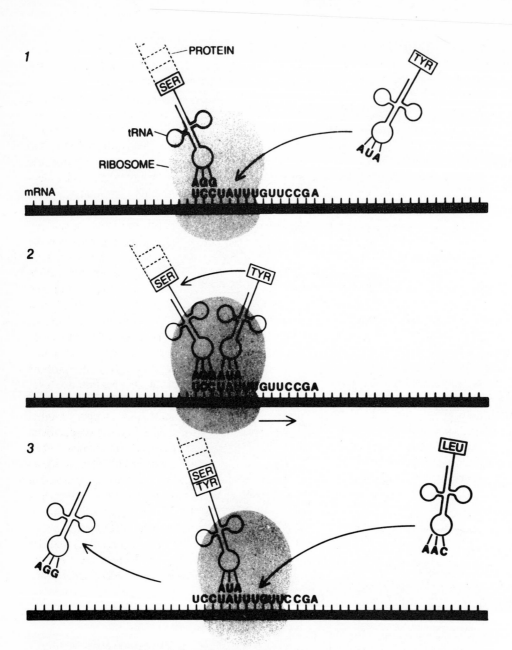

TRANSLATION of mRNA into protein at a ribosome follows the same steps in both eukaryotes and prokaryotes. Each nucleotide triplet, or codon, on the mRNA chain encodes a specific amino acid. Each molecule of tRNA in turn binds only the amino acid corresponding to a particular codon. A tRNA recognizes a codon by means of a complementary nucleotide sequence called an anticodon. Here the addition of one amino acid to a protein chain is shown. An incoming tRNA molecule carrying the amino acid tyrosine binds to the codon exposed at a binding site on the ribosome (*1*). The tyrosine forms a peptide bond with serine, the last amino acid on the protein chain (*2*). As the ribosome advances one codon (*3*), exposing the binding site to the next incoming tRNA, the serine tRNA is released.

Figure 7.5   *Translation of mRNA into protein. Reproduced with permission from Scientific American 253(4):68–78 (page 72), Oct. 1985, and the author (Darnell, 14).*

detail with regard to amino acid sequence, include epidermal growth factor (EGF), insulin-like growth factors I and II (IGF I and IGF II) (also known as somatomedins C and B, respectively), nerve growth factor (NGF), and platelet-derived growth factor (PDGF), among others. At least 20 other PGFs have been partially or initially characterized. A full appreciation and knowledge of the role of this broad array of PGF's in animal growth and biology awaits further research; it does seem clear that protein metabolism and animal development and maintenance at the cellular, tissue, and organ levels are influenced greatly by these PGF's. Actions vary from endocrine (elaborated in a specific cell type and transported to target cells by the blood), to paracrine (elaborated in a specific cell type and transported to target cells in close proximity by diffusion), to autocrine (elaborated in a specific cell type and active in the same cell in which produced). In food animal production, considerable attention has been devoted by scientists recently to determining the role of IGF I (somatomedin C) in muscle growth and lean tissue accretion. The role of nutrition in affecting PGF metabolism and the overall effects of such actions on animal growth and productivity is almost completely unknown. It is known that plasma levels of IGF I are depressed in human infants suffering from protein-calorie malnutrition, but the real biological significance of this relationship is unclear.

Deamination and Transamination

Deamination involves removal of the amino group from the carbon skeleton of the amino acid and entrance of the amino group into the urea (ornithine) cycle. The process is illustrated below.

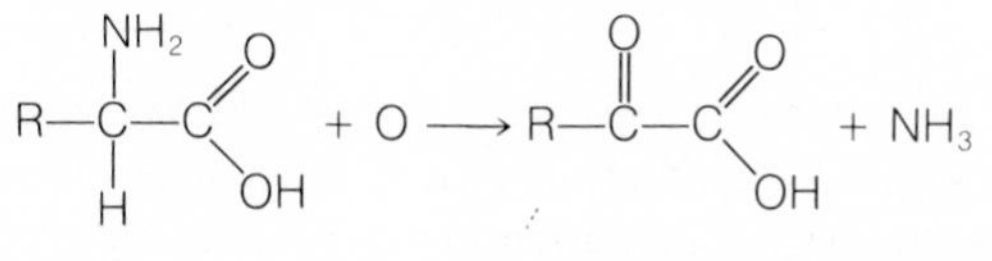

Transamination involves the transfer of an amino group from one amino acid to the carbon skeleton of a keto acid. The process is illustrated below.

Amino acids available for protein synthesis at the tissue level arise either from absorption from the GI tract or from synthesis within the animal tissues by transamination. The ability of animal tissues to synthesize amino acids from other compounds is the basis for their classification as essential or non-essential. Of the ten amino acids listed as essential for most simple-stomached animals, several can be replaced by their corresponding α-hydroxy or α-keto analogs, illustrating that it is the carbon skeleton that the animal is unable to synthesize. For example, the α-keto analogs of arginine, histidine, isoleucine, leucine, methionine, phenylalanine, tryptophan, or valine promote normal growth of rats fed diets devoid of the corresponding amino acid but adequate in amino group donors. The α-hydroxy analogs of isoleucine and tryptophan partially can replace the amino acid, while those of threonine and lysine are not utilized for growth by rats. Several amino acids, though not themselves dietary essentials, are synthesized from essential amino acids. Cystine is produced from methionine and can replace approximately half the dietary methionine; tyrosine is produced from phenylalanine and can replace approximately one-third the dietary phenylalanine. Many amino acids are precursors or supply part of the structure of other metabolites. For example, methionine supplies methyl groups for creatine and choline and is a precursor of homocysteine, cystine, and cysteine; arginine, when urea is removed, yields ornithine; histidine is decarboxylated to form histamine; tyrosine is iodinated in the thyroid gland to form the hormone, thyroxine and is used in the formation of adrenaline, noradrenaline, and melanin pigments; tryptophan is a precursor of serotonin (5-hydroxy-tryptamine) and the vitamin, niacin; lysine and methionine are the precursors of carnitine [β-hydroxy-(γ-N-trimethylammonia)-butyrate].

Urea Cycle

Ammonia resulting from deamination is joined by carbon dioxide and a phosphate group from ATP to form carbamyl phosphate which in turn combines with ornithine to form citrulline. Through a series of reactions involving formation successively of citrulline, arginosuccinate and arginine, the formation of urea takes place (Fig. 7.6). The "urea" or "ornithine" cycle is a key metabolic phenomenon in protein metabolism. The breakdown of arginine produces urea and ornithine, making ornithine available to repeat

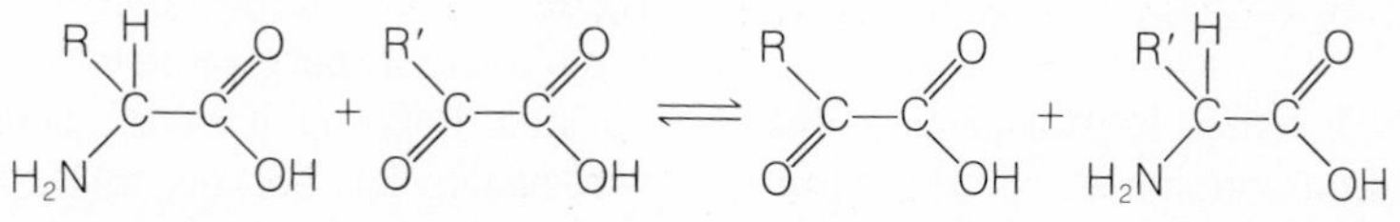

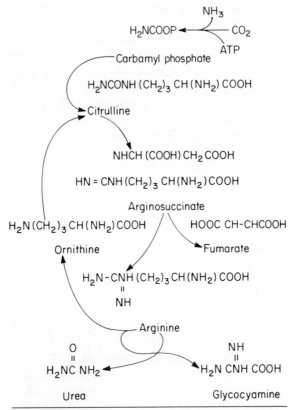

Figure 7.6 *Diagram of the urea (ornithine) cycle that occurs in mammals.*

the cycle. Urea is excreted in urine and is the chief route of N excretion in mammals. In birds, ornithine synthesis does not occur and the main route of N excretion is as uric acid. Uric acid is the principal end product of purine metabolism in humans and other primates, but in other mammals it is the oxidation product of uric acid, allantoin. The structural formulas of urea and uric acid are:

The N in position 1 comes from aspartate, that in positions 3 and 9 from glutamine, and that in po-

sition 7 from glycine. This high metabolic requirement for glycine, which is used for synthesis of uric acid, probably accounts for the fact that during periods of rapid growth the chick may require dietary glycine even though some tissue synthesis occurs.

Hippuric acid is a common constituent of the urine of herbivorous animals, where it acts as a detoxification product of benzoic acid which often is present in high quantities in plant diets. Its structural formula is:

❑ PROTEIN AND AMINO ACID REQUIREMENTS AND DEFICIENCIES

There is no evidence of a metabolic requirement for dietary protein per se, but only for amino acids. Simple stomached omnivores such as the pig, chicken, and human require specific dietary amino acids (essential amino acids) while some non-ruminant herbivores such as horses and rabbits are able to utilize non-protein N for microbial amino acid synthesis in the lower part of the GI tract. Adult ruminants, such as cattle and sheep, can depend entirely on nonprotein N in the diet by virtue of their rumen microbes which can synthesize amino acids and protein from nonprotein N and which are themselves subsequently utilized as a source of protein by the host animal. Quantitative requirements for N and amino acids for different species performing various productive functions are discussed in more detail in Ch. 18.

Inadequate protein (N or amino acids) probably is the most common of all nutrient deficiencies because most energy sources are low in protein and protein supplements are expensive. The quantitative protein requirement is greater for growth than for maintenance, is affected by sex (males tend to have a higher requirement) and by species, and probably by genetic makeup within species.

The ratio of calories to protein in the diet is important. Most animals tend to eat to satisfy energy requirements. Growing pigs and chickens fed a diet containing a marginal level of protein can be made protein deficient if caloric density of the diet is increased by fat. This occurs because the reduced daily intake of a high calorie diet provides insufficient protein intake if the percentage of protein is marginal. Protein is diverted to energy only when it is provided in excess of the metabolic requirement or calorie intake is insufficient.

Signs of protein deficiency include: anorexia, reduced growth rate, reduced or negative N balance, reduced efficiency of feed utilization, reduced serum protein concentration, anemia, fat accumulation in the liver, edema (in severe cases), reduced birth weight of young, reduced milk production, and reduced synthesis of certain enzymes and hormones. A young pig fed a diet deficient in lysine and tryptophan is shown in Fig. 7.7 alongside a littermate fed an adequate diet.

The small stature, low serum protein concentration, anemia, and edema ("pot-belly" appearance) of infants suffering from kwashiorkor are typical manifestations of protein deficiency in humans. In severe protein or amino acid deficiency, growth is arrested completely.

Deficiencies of individual essential amino acids generally produce the same signs listed above, because a single amino acid deficiency prevents protein synthesis in the same way that a shortage of a particular link in a chain prevents elongation of the chain (Fig. 7.8). Thus, individual amino acid deficiencies result in deamination of the remaining amino acids, loss of the ammonia as urea and use of the carbon chain for energy. Certain amino acid deficiencies produce specific lesions. For example, tryptophan de-

Figure 7.8 *Amino acid deficiencies in pigs. Top. A lysine-deficient pig which lost 2 lb in 28 days. Its littermate gained 25 lb in the same period when fed the same diet supplemented with 2% dl-lysine. Bottom. A tryptophan-deficient pig which lost 8 lb in 21 days. Its littermate gained 25.5 lb in the same period when fed the basal diet supplemented with 0.4% dl-tryptophan. Courtesy of W.M. Beeson, Purdue University.*

ficiency produces eye cataracts; threonine or methionine deficiency produces fatty liver; lysine deficiency in birds produces abnormal feathering (Fig. 7.9).

Most individual feedstuffs are inadequate in one or more amino acids for growing animals. For example, corn is especially deficient in lysine and tryptophan (Fig. 7.7) and supports very slow growth. However, by providing soybean meal rich in lysine and tryptophan, an adequate balance of amino acids is provided. Thus, although soybean meal is deficient in methionine-cystine and will not support normal growth by itself, when combined with corn, the two feedstuffs complement each other by compensating for their individual amino acid deficiencies. The same

Figure 7.7 *Amino acid deficiency in pigs. Littermates fed an adequate diet containing opaque-2 corn (pig B) as compared to a pig fed inadequate amounts of lysine and tryptophan. Photo by J.H. Maner.*

Figure 7.9 *Lysine deficient turkey poult. Note white barring of the flight feathers of the deficient bird on the right. Both birds are the same age. By permission of S.J. Slinger, Univ. of Guelph, Ontario, Canada.*

dramatic complementary effect of two proteins is seen at the breakfast table when milk is mixed with corn flakes or another cereal to provide a balanced protein meal. The amounts of essential amino acids provided by a diet containing 95% corn are shown in Fig. 7.10 along with the amino acid requirements for the 10 to 20 kg pig. Of the 10 amino acids required in the diet, only arginine, leucine, and phenylalanine-tyrosine are present in excess of the requirement. When a protein supplement such as soybean meal is provided to make a mixed diet containing 18% protein, the requirement for all of the essential amino acids is met (Fig. 7.11). In contrast, sesame meal, which contains approximately the same amount of protein as soybean meal, cannot be used as the sole source of supplementary protein because of its in-

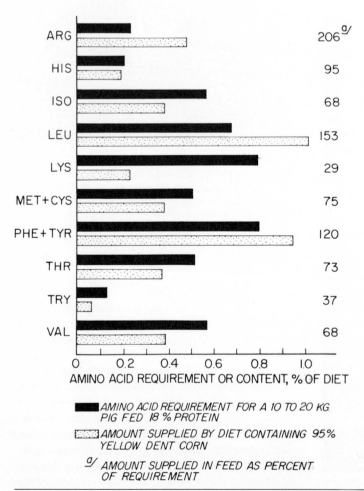

Amino Acid	Amount supplied in feed as percent of requirement
ARG	206
HIS	95
ISO	68
LEU	153
LYS	29
MET+CYS	75
PHE+TYR	120
THR	73
TRY	37
VAL	68

AMINO ACID REQUIREMENT OR CONTENT, % OF DIET

◼ AMINO ACID REQUIREMENT FOR A 10 TO 20 KG PIG FED 18% PROTEIN

▨ AMOUNT SUPPLIED BY DIET CONTAINING 95% YELLOW DENT CORN

a/ AMOUNT SUPPLIED IN FEED AS PERCENT OF REQUIREMENT

Figure 7.10 *Amino acid requirements for a 10 to 20 kg pig and the amounts supplied by 95% yellow corn.*

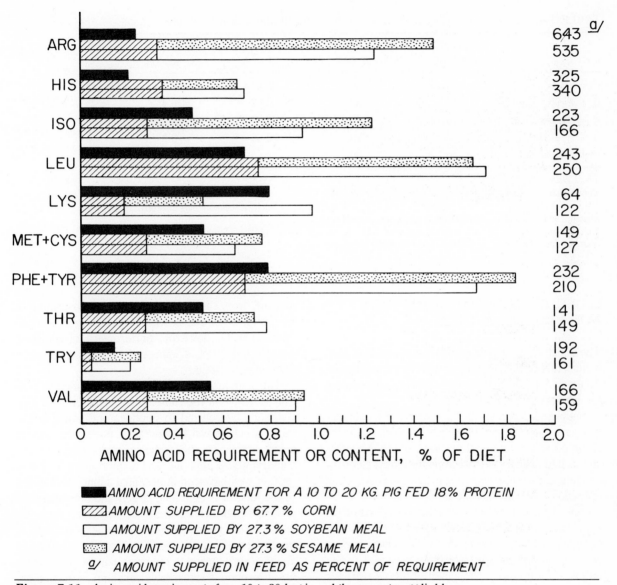

Figure 7.11 *Amino acid requirements for a 10 to 20 kg pig and the amounts supplied by a diet containing corn and soybean meal or sesame meal.*

adequate lysine content for the growing pig. An 18% protein corn-sesame meal diet would be a poor choice; thus, one must be concerned not only with meeting total protein needs, but also individual amino acid needs. Crystalline amino acids may be used to balance amino acid deficiencies in practical diets, but the high cost of synthetic amino acids often precludes their use in this manner.

Commercial production of amino acids using microorganisms whose genetic makeup is changed by newly developed recombinant DNA techniques (16)

may have important impacts on the feed and food industries.

The delicate balance among amino acids in promoting growth is shown in Table 7.4 in which the importance of the level of limiting amino acids on growth of pigs is illustrated. The addition of the first limiting amino acid, lysine, does not produce a maximum growth response unless the second and third amino acids, threonine and tryptophan, are supplemented. Such relationships must be taken into account in formulating diets for non-ruminant animals.

TABLE 7.4.   Importance of amino acid balance in promoting growth of pigs.[a]

DIET	NUMBER OF PIGS[b]	DAILY BODY WEIGHT GAIN, G	FEED PER GAIN, G	SERUM UREA N, MG/DL
Basal (B)[c]	16	490	3.21	12.1
B + tryptophan (tr)	16	530	3.02	10.4
B + threonine (th)	16	440	3.29	10.2
B + tr + th	16	610	2.69	8.9
High protein diet[d]	16	690	2.66	14.6

[a]From Wahlstrom *et al.* (ref. 17).
[b]Pigs weighed 24 kg initially and were fed the diets for 28 days.
[c]Diet contained 86.7% corn, 10.2% sunflower meal, 0.52% added L-lysine monohydrochloride plus minerals, vitamins, and an antibiotic supplement; total protein content was 12%.
[d]Diet contained 74.7% corn, 22.7% sunflower meal, 0.31% added L-lysine monohydrochloride, plus minerals, vitamins, and an antibiotic supplement; total protein content was 16%.

❑ USE OF D-AMINO ACIDS AND NON-PROTEIN N (NPN)

The unnatural D-isomer of most amino acids is used inefficiently or not at all for growth by most animals. An exception is D-methionine, which can be used by the chick as a methionine source.

Supplementation of the diet with the D-isomers of amino acids can serve as a source of non-specific N for growth of rats and, perhaps, of other simple-stomached animals. NPN compounds such as diammonium citrate also can serve this purpose. Urea utilization by simple-stomached animals for non-essential amino acid synthesis depends on its hydrolysis to ammonia. Current evidence indicates that urease is not produced by mammalian cells. Thus, any incorporation of N of urea into body tissues depends on microbial urease in the lumen of the GI tract for hydrolysis of urea. Microorganisms can use ammonia for synthesis of amino acids and proteins, but the restriction of ureolytic activity to the area of the GI tract beyond the site of maximal amino acid absorption by the host would limit the availability of amino acids which the microbes synthesize, unless coprophagy occurs. Therefore, in simple-stomached animals a response to urea can be possible only if the basal diet meets essential amino acid requirements, but not total N requirement, and the ammonia released by bacterial urease is incorporated into non-essential amino acids by body tissues. Reports of such an effect in humans and other species suggest that some urea N is incorporated into body tissues if the above conditions are met. In ruminants, where the rumen microbial activity is anatomically "up-

stream" from the sites of most active absorption of nutrients, NPN can be the main dietary N component. Usually, however, performance of ruminant animals fed NPN is improved by supplementation with intact protein.

Nitrogenous compounds can be classified as protein or NPN. In the rumen most ingested food proteins are hydrolyzed to peptides and amino acids, most of which will be degraded further to organic acids, ammonia, and carbon dioxide. Most rumen bacteria utilize ammonia and many require it. When protein well balanced in essential amino acids is fed to the host, it is degraded largely and new microbial protein is synthesized from dietary amino acids, as well as from ammonia and organic acids present in the rumen. The net result is that the mixture of amino acids supplied to the lower part of the GI tract for absorption is remarkably constant. Some protein sources, such as those in certain processed plant by-products and in some animal protein products, are incompletely digested in the rumen and pass into the small intestine partially intact, where they are subjected to further hydrolysis by the proteolytic enzymes of the host animal. Such proteins are called "bypass" proteins. It has been proposed that some bypass protein is necessary for maximum growth and milk production. Proteins can be protected from rumen degradation by lipid encapsulation, chemical derivitization such as by formaldehyde treatment, or use of inhibitors of microbial amino acid deamination. Protective coating can be used as a means of preserving proteins of high biological value by inhibiting their hydrolysis by rumen microorganisms. Supplements of free amino acids in ruminant diets do not.

survive ruminal degradation. Furthermore, specific amino acids are degraded in the rumen at different rates. Microbial protein synthesis in the lower part of the GI tract of horses and rabbits also may result in improved protein nutrition to the host through absorption of amino acids from the lower GI tract or through coprophagy.

The ammonia released from deamination of amino acids or from hydrolysis of dietary urea may be absorbed through the rumen or lower part of the GI tract wall for use at the tissue level in amino acid synthesis or for urea synthesis in the liver. An appreciable amount of urea formed by the liver is excreted into the rumen via saliva or through the rumen wall and thereby made available to the rumen microflora for amino acid synthesis.

Urea is only one of many NPN compounds that may be ingested. Many forages have large amounts of NPN in the form of amino acids, peptides, amines, amides, and nucleic acids. Such NPN compounds (with the possible exception of nucleic acids) are all readily available to rumen microorganisms. The efficiency of utilization of NPN compounds by the animal depends on the solubility of the NPN and on the availability to the microflora of readily available carbohydrates.

Microbial protein formed from NPN compounds has a high nutritive value. Lambs and calves fed NPN and little or no protein grow well (18). Cows fed NPN and no protein or amino acids can lactate (19) and reproduce normally (20). However, at present it is not possible to achieve maximum production with animals fed diets with only NPN as an N source because microbial synthesis of limiting amino acids is insufficient to meet the needs for production of muscle protein and milk in genetically superior animals.

❑ AMINO ACID ANTAGONISM, TOXICITY AND IMBALANCE

Amino acid antagonism refers to growth depression that can be overcome by supplementation with an amino acid structurally similar to the antagonist. Excess lysine, for example, causes a growth depression which, in chicks, can be reversed by additional arginine. Antagonism differs from imbalance in that the supplemented amino acids need not be limiting (21).

The term, amino acid toxicity, is used when the adverse effect of an amino acid in excess cannot be overcome by supplementation with another amino acid. Methionine, if added to the diet in excess, produces growth depression not overcome by supplementation with other amino acids.

Amino acid imbalance has been defined as any change in the proportion of dietary amino acids that has an adverse effect preventable by a relatively small amount of the most limiting amino acid or acids. A simple method for detecting amino acid imbalances is to offer a choice of an amino acid imbalanced diet and a protein-free diet. Rats and pigs will reject a diet that is imbalanced but will support life, and consume largely the protein-free diet that will not support life. The rejection of the imbalanced diet is due probably to some biochemical or physiological disturbance. It may be related to the change in plasma-free amino acid pattern that, in turn, alters the satiety center in the hypothalamus or the release or metabolism of one or more peptides associated with food intake behavior.

Adverse effects of excess consumption of individual amino acids have been reviewed (24). Interest in this subject has arisen partly because of the existence of inherited disorders such as phenylketonuria, in which affected individuals lack the necessary enzymes to metabolize phenylalanine properly, and tyrosinemia II, in which tyrosine aminotransferase is lacking. In each of these diseases special diets low in the respective amino acid must be provided to allow normal development. Tryptophan, histidine, and methionine toxicity have been studied extensively in animals. Feed intake and growth are severely depressed by excesses of any of these three amino acids and to a lesser degree by excesses of other amino acids. Adverse effects of excess consumption can vary from a slight suppression of food intake, followed by a return to normal intake, to marked suppression of intake, tissue damage, and death (21). The D-isomers of amino acids are also toxic when consumed in excess, and in some cases may be more toxic than the natural L-forms (24).

Excessive Protein Intake

It is important to be aware of any adverse effects of feeding excesses of any nutrients, and protein is no exception. Sugahara *et al.* (25) fed growing pigs 16, 32, or 48% protein and observed a linear depression in weight gain with increasing protein. Feed intake was depressed and hair became dull and coarse. High protein diets produced changes in liver water and protein content. Other work has shown that a high protein diet reduces activity of several adipose tissue enzymes associated with fatty acid synthesis in swine. The extent to which the reduced feed intake and weight gain associated with high protein intake is due to increased blood and tissue ammonia concentration or to other metabolic changes is unknown.

Ammonia toxicity is a practical problem in ruminants fed urea as a NPN source. Ammonia is absorbed from the rumen as well as from the omasum, small intestine and cecum of ruminants. Absorption is increased at higher pH, probably as a result of an increase in the proportion of ammonia in relation to ammonium ion, the former passing freely across membranes, the latter not. Bartley *et al.* (26) found that high rumen ammonia concentration may exist without producing toxicity if the diet is readily fermentable and lowers rumen pH into the acid range. Toxic symptoms in ruminants include uneasiness, labored breathing, excessive salivation, muscle and skin tremors, incoordination, tetany, and death within 1 or 2 h of onset of symptoms. Emptying the rumen of animals showing toxic signs results in a rapid decrease in blood ammonia concentration and quick recovery of the animal (26). Similar signs have been reported in ammonia intoxicated pigs (27). Peripheral blood contains 1 to 4 mg ammonia/dl at the height of toxic symptoms. Much higher levels would be found in portal blood before reaching the liver for metabolism.

Blood glucose, lactate, pyruvate, pentoses, and ketones all rise during ammonia toxicity, suggesting a drastic effect on energy metabolism, perhaps by inhibition of the citric acid cycle. Visek (28) has provided evidence that ammonia causes cell death and has suggested that excessive protein intake of humans and animals may increase the incidence of cancer of the GI tract by increasing cell turnover rate due to greater exposure to ammonia and thereby increasing the probability of mutations resulting in neoplastic cell formation. Negative effects of ammonia on tissue metabolism may go unrecognized when peripheral blood ammonia concentrations are in the normal range. Under such conditions, urinary orotic acid excretion has been suggested as a reliable index of ammonia load in relation to urea cycle capacity in some animal species (Visek, 29).

Some or all of the above effects of ammonia may affect the animal as a result of excessive protein intake. The growth depression associated with excessive levels of protein in the diet is the most visible sign of protein toxicity, whether the effects are produced through its catabolism to ammonia or by other means.

❑ MEASURES OF NUTRITIVE VALUE OF PROTEINS

The degree of utilization of a feed protein depends not only on its absorbability, but also on its utilization after absorption. Protein sources often are evaluated on the basis of their biological value (BV). BV is defined as that percentage of N absorbed from the GI tract which is available for productive body functions. BV is determined experimentally by measurement of total N intake and N losses in urine and feces. A formula for calculating BV is shown:

$$\frac{N \text{ intake } - [\text{fecal N } - \text{ urinary N}]}{N \text{ intake } - \text{ fecal N}} \times 100$$

Some N is lost in the feces as a result of endogenous losses (metabolic fecal N) and the urinary loss of N involves both excess dietary N and end-products of metabolism, such as urea involving obligatory losses (endogenous N). The Thomas Mitchell method of determining BV takes these metabolic and endogenous N losses into account. It provides an estimate of the efficiency of use of the absorbed protein for combined maintenance and growth. The BV of several plant and animal proteins for growing and adult rats are shown in Table 7.5 (30).

Among the natural sources of protein, egg protein is considered to have the highest BV. Single protein sources that have very poor BV when fed alone may yield a BV similar to that of a single high quality protein when combined with other proteins. Thus, a complementary effect is exemplified in the use of a mixture of corn and soybean meal to supply the total amino acid requirement of growing pigs; corn alone or soybean alone would not promote maximum growth.

TABLE 7.5   Biological value of proteins for growing and adult rats.[a]

	STATE OF LIFE	
PROTEIN	GROWING	ADULT
Egg albumin	97	94
Beef muscle	76	69
Meat meal	72–79	—
Casein	69	51
Peanut meal	54	46
Wheat gluten	40	65

[a]From Mitchell and Beadles (30).

Other measures of protein adequacy are the protein efficiency ratio (PER) and net protein utilization (NPU) or net protein value (NPV). PER is by definition the number of grams of body weight gain of an animal per unit of protein consumed. Conventionally, this index is obtained by feeding laboratory rats, but the same calculations could be made for any animal species fed a particular protein mixture (or a specific diet). It is important in any measure of protein utilization to maintain a low or marginal level of dietary protein because even poor quality protein may allow reasonable growth and productive performance when fed at a higher level of total N than required by the animal. Also, an unrealistically low PER may be obtained with a good protein source if fed at a level above the amount needed for maximum weight gain.

NPU measures efficiency of growth by comparing body N resulting from feeding a test protein with that resulting from feeding a comparable group of animals a protein-free diet for the same length of time (31). Thus,

$$NPU = \frac{\text{Body N with test protein} - (\text{body N with protein-free diet})}{\text{Total N intake}}$$

A large number of values can be obtained over a brief test period of 1–2 weeks. The NPU of several plant and animal protein sources are shown in Table 7.6. NPU values are correlated highly with values obtained by PER and also agree closely with results using other methods of protein quality assay, including chemical score, relative nutritive value (RNV), dye binding capacity, and pepsin digestible N. Each of these methods has merit, but the details of the procedures used for each are beyond the scope of this discussion.

When utilizing digestibility as well as BV data, it is possible to compute a net protein value (NPV) which is simply the product of the two values. Thus, NPV = BV × digestion coefficient.

With the development of automated methods for assay of free amino acid concentrations of blood plasma (column chromatography and gas-liquid chromatography), it is possible to explore the possibility of using changes in amino acid patterns following ingestion of the test protein to assess protein quality. Identification and standardization of such factors as optimum fasting interval and level and duration of feeding eventually may provide a more useful predictive tool. Changes in ratio of non-essential to essential amino

TABLE 7.6 Net protein utilization (NPU) of plant and animal protein sources.[a]

	NPU
Animal protein sources	
Whole egg	91.0
Fish (cod)	83.0
Egg albumin	82.5
Whey, dried	82.0
Milk, dried	75.0
Beef muscle	71.5
Beef heart	66.6
Beef liver	65.0
Casein	60.0
Meat meal	35.5–48.3[b]
Fish meal	44.5–54.6[b]
Feather meal	21.2–35.6[b]
Hair meal	11.4–33.4[b]
Blood	3.8
Blood + .8% isoleucine	30.5
Gelatin	2.0
Plant protein sources	
Wheat germ	67.0
Cottonseed meal	58.8
Soybean meal	56.0
Linseed meal	55.8
Bran	55.3
Corn (maize)	55.0
Peanut meal	42.8
Dried yeast	42.3
Seaweed	42.0
Wheat gluten	37.0
Rice gluten	36.0

[a]From Miller and Bender (31) with rats.
[b]From Johnston and Coon (32) with chicks.

acids in the plasma in protein deficiency also offer encouragement for further refinements in this concept of protein evaluation. Blood plasma concentrations of a specific amino acid in animals fed increments of that amino acid provide a useful aid in establishing the requirement for that amino acid (Fig. 7.12), or in determining its bioavailability as a simple and useful index of protein adequacy and amino acid balance. At levels of dietary protein either above or below the requirement or with diets deficient or imbalanced in one or more amino acids, blood urea-N

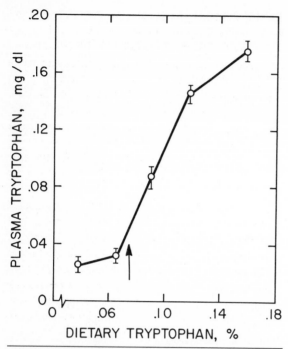

Figure 7.12   *Relationship of plasma tryptophan to dietary protein and tryptophan adequacy.*

In the microbiological assay the test material is digested by enzymatic or by acid or alkaline hydrolysis and the amino acid composition of the hydrolysate is determined by microbiological assay. The rate and degree of release of amino acids from the protein is taken as an index of the availability to the animal.

The fecal analysis method is a balance trial in which percentage amino acid availability is estimated by the following formula (37):

Amino acid (AA) availability, %

$$= \text{Total AA intake} \\ \frac{- \left[\begin{array}{c} \text{Total fecal AA} \\ \text{protein diet} \end{array} - \begin{array}{c} \text{Total fecal AA} \\ \text{protein-free diet} \end{array} \right]}{\text{Total AA intake}}$$

The extent of absorption of amino acids from the large intestine and the degree of their degradation in the lower intestinal tract are not defined well. Therefore, estimates of amino acid absorption in the small intestine can be made only with animals fitted

is elevated (33). Animals fed diets providing optimum levels of protein and essential amino acids have a minimum blood urea-N concentration. Figures 7.12 and 7.13 depict the changes in plasma amino acid and blood urea-N concentration, respectively, in relation to dietary protein and amino acid adequacy. Note that the serum urea values of pigs fed amino acid supplements (Table 7.4) fit well with this concept.

All of the estimates of protein utilization described have their limitations and no one estimate is superior to all others under all conditions. If one is interested in simplicity and a minimum of facilities and analytical work, perhaps PER provides the best estimate of protein value for growth, since only weight gain and protein consumed in a particular time period of 2–3 weeks are needed.

Biological Availability of Amino Acids

Several methods exist for the estimation of amino acid availability to the animal from a variety of feedstuffs. These methods include: microbiological assay, fecal analysis, analysis of terminal ileum contents, growth assay, and plasma free amino acids (34–36).

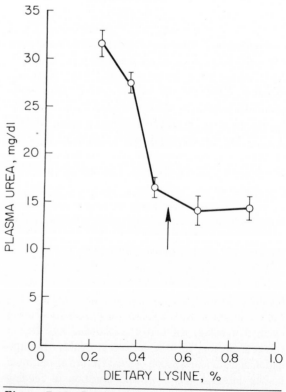

Figure 7.13   *Relationship of plasma urea to dietary protein or lysine adequacy.*

surgically with a cannula at the terminal end of the ileum. The amino acid content of ileal contents collected in this way can be used to calculate the availability of individual amino acids from the small intestine (ileal analysis) using the same formula as for fecal analysis. Estimates of quantitative amino acid absorption also can be made with a surgical preparation allowing the collection of blood from the hepatic portal vein and vena cava coupled with simultaneous determination of rate of flow through the portal vessel.

In the chick, in which urinary and fecal N are excreted together, the method combines urinary and fecal losses. However, the same formula can be applied to mammals by collecting feces if the assumption is made that urinary loss of free amino acids is negligible. This method allows calculation of availability of individual amino acids. Values greater than 90% availability are obtained commonly. Bioavailability of amino acids from several feedstuffs as es-

timated by ileal or fecal analysis by Tanksley and Knabe (38) is shown in Table 7.7. The growth assay can be used to study the availability of one or a series of amino acids from a test protein. The procedure is to feed the test diet alongside diets of known amino acid availability such as a crystalline amino acid diet. By comparing the growth curve of animals fed the test protein with that of animals fed the amino acid diet containing the amino acid of concern at several incremental levels, it is possible to estimate the proportion of amino acid in the test protein utilized for growth.

Measurement of free amino acids in the plasma of animals at intervals following a meal of the test protein allows a means of estimating the availability of one or more amino acids. Stockland and Meade (39) found differences in the availability to the rat of isoleucine, threonine, and phenylalanine from several sources of meat and bone meal. Using the same method, they found isoleucine, methionine, and thre-

TABLE 7.7 Apparent absorbability of essential amino acids in several protein sources estimated by ileal versus fecal analysis.[a]

	SBM[b]		MBM[c]		PM[d]		CSM[e] GLANDLESS		SOLVENT		SCREW PRESS	
COMPONENT	I[f]	F[g]	I	F	I	F	I	F	I	F	I	F
Nitrogen, %	81	89	59	72	78	85	86	92	72	73	75	78
Amino acid, %												
Arg	92	94	74	76	93	95	96	97	87	87	90	90
His	89	93	65	72	80	88	92	96	79	80	81	83
Iso	83	87	59	66	79	80	85	88	66	65	70	69
Leu	83	88	62	69	79	83	85	89	69	68	73	72
Lys	89	89	61	68	69	78	87	89	62	58	64	61
Met	77	81	72	67	88	77	83	85	65	65	66	66
Phe	88	89	66	70	89	88	91	93	77	78	82	81
Thr	77	85	50	66	61	75	79	87	62	64	65	67
Try	82	91	55	67	70	82	83	91	69	71	68	74
Val	81	86	61	70	76	80	85	90	68	68	71	72
Average, %	85	88	62	69	78	83	86	90	70	70	73	73

[a]From Tanksley and Knabe (38).
[b]Soybean meal, solvent 44% protein.
[c]Meat and bone meal, 50% protein.
[d]Peanut meal, mechanically extracted, 50% protein.
[e]Cottonseed meal; glandless 55% protein, solvent 41% protein, screw press 41% protein.
[f]Ileal.
[g]Fecal.

onine to vary in availability from different samples of meat and bone meal for the pig. The basis for judging availability is the change in relative concentrations of amino acids in the plasma following a meal of the test protein. The duration of fasting and the selection of appropriate intervals for blood sampling are of importance and must be established for each species used and for the conditions of a particular experiment.

Processing methods including grinding, pelleting, drying, oil extraction, and heating have been developed by the feed industry to improve the value of a large number of feedstuffs. Probably the greatest single factor affecting amino acid availability from feedstuffs is proper heating of feedstuffs during processing. The application of heat must be a balance between beneficial and destructive effects. Reductions in amino acid availability can result from their destruction or their delayed release during digestion owing to change in linkages between amino acids and other diet components.

A chemical method for estimating lysine availability in animal protein feeds was developed by Carpenter (40) utilizing the reaction of 1-fluoro-2:4-dinitrobenzene with the epsilon amino group of lysine. The method suffers because of destruction during prolonged hydrolysis of the protein and because of the reaction of lysine with the carbohydrate of many commonly fed feedstuffs. A modified method (41) is available by which the need for correction factors to account for lysine destruction or the influence of carbohydrate is eliminated, and modified procedures for estimating available lysine in milk products are available (42). Chemical estimation of bioavailable methionine has been proposed.

Biosynthesis, metabolism, and functions of carnitine, derived from lysine and methionine and present in large amounts in animal products are under extensive study in premature infants and in individuals fed parenterally. It appears that carnitine biosynthesis may be insufficient to meet metabolic needs under some conditions (43).

❏ SUMMARY

Proteins and their constituent amino acids are present in all living organisms. About 20 amino acids are found in most proteins and up to 10 are required in the diet (commonly called essential or indispensable) because tissue synthesis is not adequate to meet metabolic needs. The essential components of amino acids are a carboxyl group and an amino group on the carbon atom adjacent to the carboxyl group. The 10 essential amino acids for most non-ruminant animal species are: arginine, histidine, isoleucine, leucine, lysine, methionine (can be replaced partially by cystine), phenylalanine (can be replaced partially by tyrosine), threonine, tryptophan, and valine. Arginine and histidine are required by adults of some species.

All proteins can be classified on the basis of their shape and solubilities in water, salt, acids, bases and alcohol. Many protein-lipid (lipoproteins) and protein-carbohydrate (glycoproteins) complexes exist in biological systems. Proteins and their complexes serve many body functions. They are constituents of cell membranes, muscle, skin, hair, hooves, blood plasma, enzymes, hormones, and immune antibodies.

Ingested proteins are hydrolyzed to their constituent amino acids before absorption into the body from the gastrointestinal tract. In ruminant animals, microorganisms inhabiting the rumen can synthesize amino acids and protein from non-protein N and carbohydrates and this microbial protein provides the amino acids needed by the host animal.

After absorption, amino aids are used for tissue protein synthesis, synthesis of enzymes, hormones, and other metabolites or are deaminated and the carbon skeleton used for energy by the animal. Tissue protein synthesis requires the presence of nucleic acids; deoxynucleic acid (DNA) is the blueprint of protein synthesis and controls the development of the cell and the organism by controlling the formation of ribonucleic acids (RNA's). Three kinds of RNA, ribosomal, transfer and messenger, are involved in the sequence of events in tissue protein synthesis. Net rate of muscle protein synthesis in animals is controlled by synthetic and degradative factors whose nature and control currently are under intensive investigation. Polypeptide growth factors are receiving attention as factors associated with growth in animals.

N released from protein and amino acid degradation in the body is excreted mainly in the form of urea in mammals and uric acid in birds. Blood urea rises in animals fed protein in excess of needs or in animals fed diets deficient in total protein or in one or more essential amino acids. Signs of protein deficiency include anorexia, reduced growth rate, reduced blood serum protein concentration, anemia, fat accumulation in the liver, edema (in severe cases), reduced birth weight of young, reduced milk production, and reduced synthesis of certain enzymes and hormones. Deficiencies of individual essential amino acids generally produce the same signs, because a single amino acid deficiency prevents protein synthesis just as a shortage of a particular link in a chain prevents elongation of the chain.

❑ REFERENCES

1. Rose, W.C. 1984. *J. Biol. Chem.* **178**:753.
2. Visek, W.J. 1984. *Ann. Rev. Nutr.* **4**:137.
3. MacDonald, M.L., Q.R. Rogers, and J.G. Morris. 1984. *Ann. Rev. Nutr.* **4**:521.
4. NRC. 1981. *Taurine Requirement of the Cat.* National Academy Press, Washington, D.C.
5. Concon, J.M. 1966. In *Proc. High Lysine Corn Conf.*, Purdue Univ., West Lafayette, Ind., p. 67.
6. Schweigert, B. and B. Payne. 1956. Amer. Meat Inst. Found Bull. No. 30, Chicago, IL.
7. McClain, et al. 1965. *Proc. Sci. Exp. Biol Med.* **119**:493.
8. Smith, E.L. 1970. Ch. 6 in *The Enzymes*, P.D. Boyer (ed.). Academic Press, N.Y., p. 276.
9. Mertz, E.T., L.S. Bates, and O.E. Nelson. 1964. *Science* 145:279.
10. Guidotti, G. 1972. *Ann. Rev. Biochem.* **41**:731.
11. Scanu, A.M. and C. Wisdom. 1972. *Ann. Rev. Biochem.* **41**:703.
12. Felsenfeld, G. 1985. *Sci. Amer.* **253**:58.
13. Doolittle, R.F. 1985. *Sci. Amer.* **253**:88.
14. Darnell, J.E., Jr. 1985. *Sci. Amer.* **253**:68.
15. James, R. and R.A. Bradshaw. 1984. *Ann. Rev. Biochem.* **52**:259.
16. Watson, J.D., J. Tooze, and D.T. Kurtz. 1983. *Recombinant DNA: A Short Course.* W.H. Freeman and Co., N.Y., pp. 1–260.
17. Wahlstrom, R.C., G.W. Libal, and R.C. Thaler. 1985. *J. Animal Sci.* **60**:720.
18. Loosli, J.K., et al. 1949. *Science* 110:144.
19. Virtanen, A.I. 1966. *Science* **153**:1603.
20. Oltjen, R.R. 1969. *J. Animal Sci.* **28**:673.
21. Harper, A.E., N.J. Benevenga, and R.M. Wohlhueter. 1970. *Physiol. Rev.* **50**:428.
22. Rogers, Q.R., R.I. Thomas, and A.E. Harper. 1967. *J. Nutr.* **91**:561.
23. Devilat, J., W.G. Pond, and P.D. Miller. 1970. *J. Animal Sci.* **30**:536.
24. Benevenga, N.J. and R.D. Steele. 1984. *Ann. Rev. Nutr.* **4**:157.
25. Sugahara, M., D.H. Baker, B.G. Harmon, and A.H. Jensen. 1969. *J Animal Sci.* **29**:598.
26. Bartley, E.E., et al. 1976. *J. Animal Sci.* **43**:835.
27. Chow, Kye-Wing, W.G. Pond, and E.F. Walker. 1970. *Proc. Soc. Exp. Biol. Med.* **134**:122.
28. Visek, W.J. 1978. *J. Animal Sci.* **46**:1447.
29. Visek, W.J. 1979. *Nutr. Rev.* **37**:273.
30. Mitchell, H.H. and J.R. Beadles. 1950. *J. Nutr.* **40**:25.
31. Miller, D.S. and A.E. Bender. 1955. *Brit. J. Nutr.* **9**:382.
32. Johnston, J. and C.N. Coon. 1979. *Poult. Sci.* **58**:919.
33. Eggum, B.O. 1972. *Brit. J. Nutr.* **24**:983.
34. Meade, R.J. 1972. *J. Animal Sci.* **35**:713.
35. Rerat, A. 1978. *J. Animal Sci.* **46**:1808.
36. Zebrouska, T. 1978. *Feedstuffs* **50**(53):15.
37. Bragg, D.B., C.A. Ivy, and E.L. Stephenson. 1969. *Poult. Sci.* **48**:2135.
38. Tanksley, T.D. and K. Knabe. 1980. Proc. Georgia Nutr. Conf., p. 157.
39. Stockland, W.L. and R.J. Meade. 1970. *J. Animal Sci.* **31**:1156.
40. Carpenter, K.J. 1960. *Biochem. J.* **77**:604.
41. Roach, A.G., P. Sanderson, and D.R. Williams. 1967. *J. Sci. Food Agr.* **18**:724.
42. Holsinger, V.H. and L.P. Posate. 1975. In *Protein Nutritional Quality of Foods and Feeds*, Vol. 1, Part 1, M. Friedman (ed.). Marcel Dekker, Inc., NY., pp. 479–502.
43. Rebouche, C.J. and D.J. Paulson. 1968. *Ann Rev. Nutr.* **6**:41.

8

Carbohydrates

CARBOHYDRATES ARE THE MAJOR components in plant tissues and they comprise up to 50% of the dry matter of forages, although higher concentrations (up to 80%) may be found in some seeds, especially cereal grains. The chloroplasts in plant leaves synthesize their carbohydrates, using solar energy, carbon dioxide, and water, and give off oxygen. This is a vital process for animals because they could not exist without this transformation of energy and the free oxygen produced as a byproduct of the photosynthetic reaction.

❑ CLASSIFICATION AND STRUCTURE

One method of classifying carbohydrates is shown in Table 8.1. Classification, as done in this manner, is strictly on the basis of the number of carbon atoms per molecule of carbohydrate and on the basis of the number of molecules of sugar in the compound.

Thus, a monosaccharide has only one molecule of sugar, a disaccharide has two molecules, an oligosaccharide (not shown) may have 3–10 sugar units, and a polysaccharide >10 sugar units. Most plant tissues contain many different types of carbohydrates; only sources with relatively high concentrations are shown in Table 8.1.

TABLE 8.1 Classification of carbohydrates and their occurrences.

COMPOUND	MONOSACCHARIDE CONTENT	OCCURRENCE
Monosaccharides (*simple sugars*)		
Pentoses (5-C sugars) ($C_5H_{10}O_5$)		
Arabinose		pectin; polysaccharide, araban
Xylose		corn cobs, wood; polysaccharides
Ribose		nucleic acids
Hexoses (6-C sugars) ($C_6H_{12}O_6$)		
Glucose		disaccharides; polysaccharides
Fructose		disaccharides (sucrose)
Galactose		milk (lactose)
Mannose		polysaccharides
Disaccharides ($C_{12}H_{22}O_{11}$)		
Sucrose	glucose-fructose	sugar cane, sugar beets
Maltose	glucose-glucose (glucose-4-α-glucoside)	starchy plants and roots
Lactose	glucose-galactose	milk
Cellobiose	glucose-glucose (glucose-4-β-glucoside)	fibrous portion of plants
Trisaccharides ($C_{18}H_{32}O_{16}$)		
Raffinose	glucose-fructose-galactose	certain varieties of eucalyptus, cottonseed, sugar beets
Polysaccharides		
Pentosans ($C_5H_8O_4$)$_n$		
Araban	ababinose	pectins
Xylan	xylose	corn cobs, wood
Hexosans ($C_6H_{10}O_5$)$_n$		
Starch (a polyglucose glucoside)	glucose	grains, seeds, tubers
Dextrin	glucose	partial hydrolytic product of starch
Cellulose	glucose	cell wall of plants
Glycogen	glucose	liver and muscle of animals
Insulin (a polyfructose fructoside)	fructose	potatoes, tubers, artichokes
Mixed polysaccharides		
Hemicellulose	mixtures of pentoses and hexoses	fibrous plants
Pectins	pentoses and hexoses mixed with salts of complex acids	citrus fruits, apples
Gums (partly oxidized to acids)	pentoses and hexoses	acacia trees and certain plants

Many different carbohydrate compounds or carbohydrate-containing compounds are found in plant and animal tissues. However, from a nutritional point of view, the list of important compounds is rather short. Some compounds, such as glycerol, may be intermediate between a carbohydrate and a lipid. Structurally, glycerol is an alcohol and it is partially soluble in water. However, it is a component of triglycerides (fats) and it is also soluble in ether, a characteristic of most lipids. In addition, one or more molecules of different monosaccharides (simple sugars) may be found in complex compounds. For example, ribose, a simple 5-carbon sugar, is an essential component of adenosine triphosphate (ATP), which is important in the transfer of energy at the cellular level.

Simple carbohydrates have the empirical structure of $C_nH_{2n}O_n$, while most complex compounds have a structure corresponding to $C_nH_{2n-2}O_{n-1}$, or essentially with carbon combined with hydrogen and oxygen in the same ratio as water. When two or more molecules are joined together, the formula represents the loss of one or more molecules of water. Chemically, carbohydrates are polyhydroxyl aldehydes and ketones, with an aldehyde (—C=O) or

$$H$$

ketone (C—C—C) group in their structure. Structures of some of the common monosaccharides or disaccharides are illustrated in Fig. 8.1. Although the chain-type structure shown in Fig. 8.1 is a common way to depict sugar formulas, the biologically-active structures of these compounds are more aptly shown in the Haworth or chain-like forms shown below on p. 108.

❏ FUNCTIONS

The primary function of carbohydrates in animal nutrition is to serve as a source of energy for normal life processes. However, in plants some of the simple sugars, especially glucose and ribose, are involved in energy transformations and tissue synthesis. Less soluble forms, such as starch, serve as energy reserves in roots, tubers, and seeds. The rather insoluble fractions (cellulose, hemicellulose) are most important in providing structural support for the living plants. The broad array of simple carbohydrates found in a variety of foods and feeds is illustrated in Fig. 8.1.

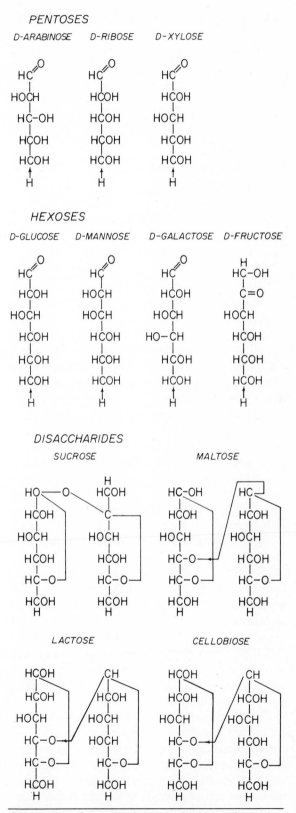

Figure 8.1 *Structure of monosaccharides and disaccharides.*

*OPEN-CHAIN
FORM*

TWO WAYS OF DEPICTING THE PYRANOSE FORM

Carbohydrates and lipids are the two major sources of energy for the animal body. The lipid content of most diets of food-producing animals is <5%, so that the greatest proportion of energy comes from carbohydrates. In human diets, in which a greater amount of food of animal origin is consumed, the proportion of energy coming from carbohydrate is considerably less than in diets of domestic farm animals. The total energy intake coming from fat in human diets in the USA is usually >30% and may often be as high as 50% or more.

Although carbohydrates serve as a significant source of energy for body tissues, only limited evidence shows a dietary requirement for any specific carbohydrate by higher animals and man, even though certain insects may have a requirement (6). This point is academic, however, because virtually all natural food sources contain some carbohydrate. Brambila and Hill (4) showed that chicks can grow normally on carbohydrate-free diets if the calorie to protein ratio is optimum and if triglycerides are included in the diet. The use of free fatty acids as the sole non-protein energy source resulted in growth depression as a result of failure of the body to produce glucose from amino acids in the absence of the glycerol from triglycerides.

The ultimate source of energy for most cells (plant and animal) is glucose. This basic unit is made available to animal cells either by ingestion of glucose or its precursors by the animal, or by conversion from other metabolites. The carbon skeletons of these substances and of products of fat metabolism (Ch. 9) provide the energy for maintaining normal life processes.

❑ METABOLISM

Preparation for Absorption

Only monosaccharides can be absorbed from the GI tract, except in newborn animals capable of absorbing larger molecules. Thus, for absorption to occur, poly-, tri-, and disaccharides must be hydrolyzed by digestive enzymes elaborated by the host or by microflora inhabiting the GI tract of the host. Principal digestive enzymes elaborated by animals were discussed and listed in Ch. 4. The carbohydrate-splitting enzymes (carbohydrases) are effective in hydrolyzing most complex carbohydrates to monosaccharides except for those with a glucose-4-β-glucoside linkage (see Table 8.1), such as in cellulose. Microflora of the rumen of ruminants and the cecum and colon of some non-ruminants, such as the horse and rabbit, produce cellulase, so that these species can utilize large quantities of cellulose. Other non-ruminant species, including humans and swine, also utilize cellulose by anaerobic fermentation in the large intestine. The hydrolysis of cellulose is dependent on cellulase, an enzyme that is not produced by mammalian cells. Cellulose is a major component of plant cell walls and, together with hemicelluloses, often is present in combination with lignin, a highly insoluble and biologically unavailable mixture of polymers of phenolic acid. Lignification increases with plant age and, in mature trees, lignin is the chief structural component. Vegetables and cereals are low in lignin while grasses are intermediate and legumes are higher in lignin. The amount of lignin present affects the bioavailability of the cellulose and hemicellulose for microbial use and in this way affects the nutritive value of a plant material for animals.

The importance of plant fiber in animal and human nutrition is of increasing interest. There is evidence for a protective effect of dietary fiber against atherosclerosis in humans through a reduction in blood lipids and against colon cancer, possibly through an increased rate of passage of food residues through the GI tract.

In ruminants and other species with large microbial populations in the GI tract, anaerobic fermentation of carbohydrates results in the production of large quantities of volatile fatty acids (VFA), mainly acetic, propionic and butyric acids, and provides a large proportion of the total energy supply. Even in pigs, whose ability to utilize cellulose is less than that of ruminants, some of the energy required for maintenance can be provided by VFA produced by microbial action on fiber in the large intestine. The role of VFA in nutrition will be discussed later in this chapter.

Absorption

The upper or cranial section of the small intestine, the duodenum and jejunum, has the greatest capacity to absorb monosaccharides. The lower small intestine (lower ileum) absorbs less, and the stomach and large intestine absorb little if any sugars. Cori (5) observed in 1925 that selective absorption of monosaccharides occurs from the GI tract of the rat. He showed that galactose and glucose are absorbed very efficiently, but that mannose, which differs from glucose only in the configuration of the hydroxyl group at carbon 2 (see Fig. 8.1), is absorbed at only about 20% of the efficiency of glucose. Wilson (18) compiled a table showing the selective absorption of six different monosaccharides by a variety of animal species (Table 8.2). In general, glucose and galactose are absorbed at the highest rate and arabinose at the lowest rate among the six monosaccharides compared, regardless of the species tested. Active (energy-dependent) transport is established for glucose and galactose, but probably it does not operate for other sugars. Glucose and galactose appear unchanged in the portal vein after absorption. Failure to discover specific chemical alterations in the molecule during absorption suggests that, perhaps, transport involves adsorption of the sugar to some type of membrane carrier located in the plasma membrane on the luminal border of the cell. Conversion of some monosaccharides to glucose occurs within the intestinal mucosal cell; conversion of fructose to glucose remains relatively constant over a wide range of fructose concentrations, but the rate of movement of fructose into the cell is proportional roughly to the luminal concentration.

Fructose is converted to lactic acid by the intestine of some animal species; the rat converts up to 50% of fructose to lactic acid, as measured by mesenteric vein cannulation, but the guinea pig produces very little. Fructose in blood of mature animals is very low, but in fetal and newborn lambs and pigs it is high. Aherne et al. (1) found that fructose was absorbed with little or no intestinal conversion to glucose in 3-, 6-, or 9-day-old pigs and suggested that fructokinase activity (enzyme needed for conversion of fructose to glucose) of the liver but not the intestine increases with age in the pig. Intravenous administration of sucrose, fructose, or lactose to hypoglycemic baby pigs fails to alleviate the hypoglycemia, and intravenous administration of di-

TABLE 8.2 Selective absorption of sugars by different animals.[a]

| | RATE OF SUGAR ABSORPTION (GLUCOSE TAKEN AS 100) | | | | | |
ANIMAL	GALACTOSE	GLUCOSE	FRUCTOSE	MANNOSE	XYLOSE	ARABINOSE
Rat	109	100	42	21	20	12
Cat	90	100	35	—	—	—
Rabbit	82	100	—	—	—	60
Hamster	88	100	16	12	28	10
Man	122	100	67	—	—	—
Pigeon	115	100	55	33	37	16
Frog	107	100	46	51	29	
Fish	97	100	62	—	57	49

saccharides to animals generally results in their excretion in the urine.

Sugars apparently share a common pathway of transport across the intestinal mucosal cell. This being true, competitive inhibition between glucose and galactose as well as between glucose and several derivatives of glucose is no surprise. Based on relationships of this kind, Wilson (18) proposed the minimal structural requirements for intestinal transport of sugars as in the Haworth or chain-like structure shown previously. Xylose is not transported actively against a concentration gradient and does not inhibit galactose transport appreciably, yet evidence suggests a common carrier even for such widely different sugars as glucose and xylose. Further details of the mechanism of transport of sugars across the mucosal cell to the blood are beyond the scope of this discussion.

Several important factors affect the absorption of glucose. It is reduced by short-term (24- or 48-h) fasting, but increased by chronically restricted food intake. The basis for this apparent difference in functional capacity of the small intestine in fasting vs underfed animals is not understood well. Diabetic animals absorb glucose more rapidly than normal; adrenalectomy results in a reduction in glucose absorption but has no effect on xylose absorption; thyroidectomy and ovariectomy reduce glucose absorption. Thus, a variety of endocrine factors affect absorption of sugars.

Intravenous administration of glucose is a common means of reversing hypoglycemia. It results in a rise in blood glucose concentration followed by a gradual decline to normal concentration as uptake by tissues for energy occurs and as liver and muscle store glycogen, which is synthesized from surplus glucose. No glucose appears in the urine of normal animals given a glucose load because the kidney functions to retain it in the body. Glucose is found in the urine of animals only with kidney damage or diabetes, a metabolic disease associated with faulty glucose utilization. In each instance, blood glucose concentration exceeds the kidney threshold, the level at which the kidney is no longer capable of preventing urinary loss.

Deficiency of specific disaccharidases (enzymes) in the GI tract results in serious gastrointestinal upsets. Young mammals fed large amounts of sucrose develop severe diarrhea, and death may occur from an insufficiency of sucrase during the first few weeks of life. Ruminant species apparently produce no sucrase. Feeding appreciable amounts of sucrose to liquid-fed young animals results in severe diarrhea. In addition, these species have low levels of starch-splitting enzymes. Adult pigs fed lactose may develop diarrhea and gas discomfort because of a deficiency of lactase, and lactase deficiency is prevalent also in some human population groups and appears to have a genetic basis. Affected individuals are unable to tolerate milk products containing lactose.

Xylose feeding of young pigs results in depressed appetite and growth and causes eye cataracts. The mechanism whereby xylose causes these abnormalities in young animals is not known.

In the absence of diseases such as infectious diarrhea or of other pathological conditions affecting absorption, the absorption of soluble carbohydrates often exceeds 90%. Endogenous (fecal metabolic) losses result in a net (apparent) absorbability approximating 80% or more in non-ruminant animals. Thus, except in abnormal situations such as those noted previously, the available energy is similar for a wide variety of carbohydrate sources.

The rate of digestion of starch is affected by many factors, including particle size, nature of the starch (amylase and amylopectin content), interactions of starch with protein and fat, and the presence of antinutrients such as phytate, tannins, saponins, and enzyme inhibitors (10).

Metabolic Conversions

Monosaccharides not converted to glucose in the intestinal mucosal cell during absorption may be converted to glucose by reactions in the liver. The animal body stores very little energy as carbohydrate, but some glucose is converted to glycogen, which is stored in liver and muscle tissues. Glycogen is a starch-like compound and can be converted rapidly back to glucose. Thus, the level of blood sugar is maintained within a rather narrow range in normal animals by conversion of circulating blood glucose to glycogen and by reconversion to glucose by the process of glycogenolysis when the blood level declines. The blood glucose concentration increases after a meal, but returns to the fasting level within a few hours. This homeostasis is under endocrine control with insulin and glucagon from the pancreas playing an important role in maintaining the blood glucose concentration within normal limits for the species. Storage of glycogen after a carbohydrate meal prevents marked elevation in blood sugar (hyperglycemia), and release of glucose by breakdown of glycogen during fasting prevents low blood sugar

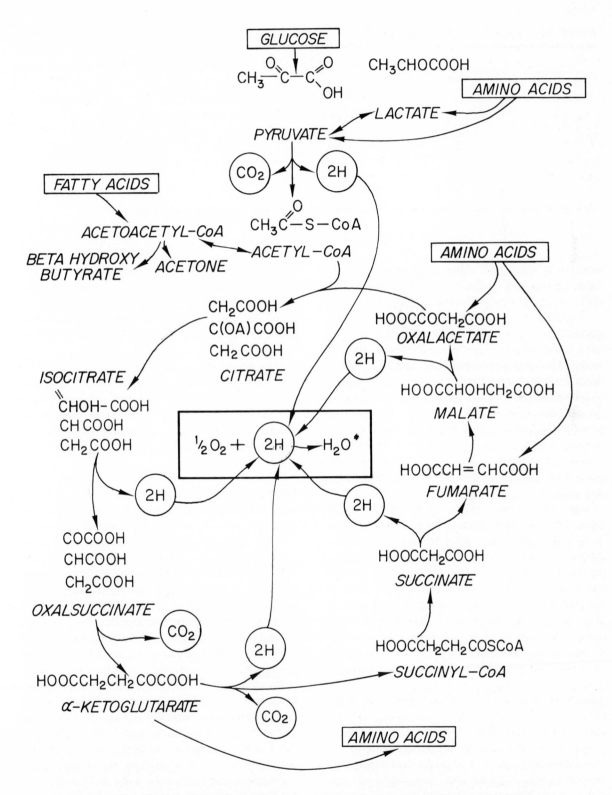

*HEAT PRODUCTION = 57,000 calories per molecule of water formed (represents wasted energy and is the amount of energy that must be ingested and absorbed for the animal to stay in energy balance).

Figure 8.2 *The citric acid (Krebs) cycle through which carbohydrates are oxidized to produce energy.*

TABLE 8.3 Metabolism of the carbon chain of amino acids.

| citric acid cycle | | | NICOTINIC ACID AND SEROTONIN |
ACETATE	PYRUVATE	α-KETOGLUTARATE	
isoleucine	alanine	arginine	tryptophan
leucine	cystine	glutamic acid	
phenylalanine	glycine	hydroxy proline	
treonine	methionine	histidine	
tyrosine	serine	lysine	
valine		proline	

levels (hypoglycemia), although some variation occurs. In diabetes mellitus, hyperglycemia occurs, and, with excess insulin release, hypoglycemia.

The formation of glycogen from glucose (glycogenesis) requires two molecules of adenosine triphosphate (ATP) for every molecule of glucose. Glucose molecules are added, one unit at a time, to form the long chain of glycogen. Uridine triphosphate (UTP) also is involved in the conversion of glucose to glycogen. ATP is a high-energy compound supplied to the cell mainly by biological oxidations, involving the transfer of electrons from specific substrates to oxygen. Free energy produced with this transfer is captured in the form of the energy-rich ATP. Phosphorus uptake by adenosine diphosphate (ADP) to form ATP is called oxidative phosphorylation. The process is a driving force for many biochemical processes including absorption of nutrients from the GI tract and synthesis of proteins, nucleic acids, fats, and carbohydrates. ATP-dependent reactions include those in which ATP provides the energy for enzyme catalyzed processes such as nutrient synthesis (for example, glycogen from glucose), and those in which part of the ATP molecule (a high-energy phosphate) is transferred to an appropriate receptor such as glucose in the reaction:

$$\text{Glucose} + \text{ATP} \xrightarrow{\text{glucokinase}} \text{glucose-6-PO}_4 + \text{ADP}.$$

The breakdown of glycogen to form glucose is, in essence, the reverse process (glycogenolysis).

Glucose also can be formed by body tissues from non-carbohydrate metabolites, including lipids and amino acids. This process is called gluconeogenesis. All of the non-essential amino acids along with several of the essential ones (arginine, methionine, cystine, histidine, threonine, tryptophan, and valine) are glu-

cogenic. That is, when metabolized they can give rise to a net increase in glucose. Some (isoleucine, lysine, phenylalanine, and tyrosine) are both glucogenic and ketogenic; they can give rise to glucose and acetone or other ketones. Leucine is strictly ketogenic.

The amino acids used for gluconeogenesis or for energy enter the citric acid cycle (Fig. 8.2) as acetate, pyruvate, or α-ketoglutarate as listed in Table 8.3. Amino acids not used for protein synthesis enter the general pool of metabolites that provide energy for normal body maintenance and productive functions.

Glycogen storage is limited. Therefore, when ingestion of carbohydrate exceeds current needs for glycogen formation, glucose is converted to fat. This is accomplished by the breakdown of glucose to pyruvate, which then is available for fat synthesis.

The conversion of glycogen to glucose-6-phosphate and finally to pyruvate and to lactate under anaerobic conditions in muscle (glycolysis) occurs through a series of transformations (Fig. 8.3). A fraction of the glucose-6-phosphate produced from glycogenolysis can enter the hexose-monophosphate pathway (pentose shunt) under the influence of the coenzyme NADP, ultimately to form ribose-5-phosphate, a source of ribose for nucleic acids (DNA, RNA) and nucleotide coenzymes (ATP), and to form hexose and trios phosphates. However, most of the glucose-6-phosphate metabolism is by the glycolytic (or Embden-Meyerhof) pathway. Here, glucose-6-phosphate is rearranged to form fructose-6-phosphate and phosphorylated by ATP to fructose 1,6-diphosphate, which is, in turn, cleaved to glyceraldehyde-3-phosphate and dihydroxyacetone phosphate. Glyceraldehyde-3-phosphate is used for glyceride synthesis and undergoes a series of trans-

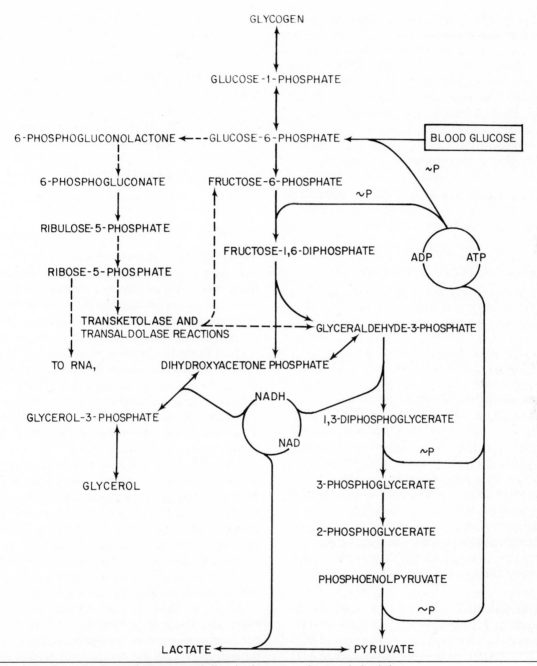

Figure 8.3 *General scheme of glucose metabolism in the pentose shunt and glycolytic pathways. Courtesy of Lloyd, McDonald, and Crampton (1978),* Fundamentals of Nutrition, *2nd ed., W. H. Freeman and Co., San Francisco, CA, p. 67.*

formations ultimately to form pyruvate. Pyruvate is an important metabolite in glucose metabolism because it can be converted to acetyl CoA in the mitochondria or it can be reduced to lactate in the cytoplasm by oxidation of NADH. Mitochondrial pyruvate metabolism includes removal of one carbon

(decarboxylation) by thiamin decarboxylase and the ultimate formation of acetyl CoA. Further metabolism of acetyl CoA occurs in the citric acid (Krebs) cycle (Fig. 8.2), the final common energy pathway for carbohydrate, fat, and carbon skeletons of amino acids. Lactate accumulates in the cytoplasm by oxidation of NADH to NAD, and is related to muscle fatigue following strenuous exercise. These two important metabolic cycles, the Krebs citric acid cycle and the Embden-Meyerhof glycolytic pathway, form the basis for understanding energy metabolism in animals. The importance of vitamins, including thiamin, riboflavin, niacin, and pantothenic acid, as cofactors in catalyzing these reactions, is discussed in more detail in Ch. 14. The complex, yet systematic, interplay of the nutrients in controlling and coordinating the living animal through cellular and subcellular activities is an exciting and fascinating picture, only the generalities of which are within the realm of discussion for this book.

Energetics of Glucose Catabolism

The total energy released in the conversion of glucose to CO_2 and H_2O is 673 Kcal/mole. This can be illustrated as follows:

$$C_6H_{12}O_6 \longrightarrow 6\ CO_2 + 6\ H_2O + 673\ Kcal$$

The molecular weight of glucose is 180.2. Thus, the gross energy value of glucose is $673/180.2 = 3.74$ Kcal/g. In the oxidation of metabolites via the citric acid cycle (Fig. 8.2), 57 Kcal/mole of water formed (total of $6 \times 57 = 342$ Kcal) represents heat production and is wasted energy, equivalent to the amount of energy that must be ingested and absorbed for the animal to stay in energy balance.

Catabolism of one mole of glucose by the glycolytic pathway is associated with the following amounts of adenosine triphosphate (ATP) trapped at each stage of oxidation to CO_2 and H_2O:

Glycolytic pathway	8 moles of ATP
2 pyruvate to 2 acetyl CoA	6 moles of ATP
2 acetate to CO_2 and H_2O	24 moles of ATP
Total	38 moles of ATP

ATP serves as a major form of high-energy phosphate bonds. One mole of ATP has a value of about 8 Kcal/mole. That is,

$$ATP \longrightarrow ADP + 8\ Kcal/mole$$

The conversion of the free energy of the oxidation of glucose has an efficiency of 40 to 65%, depending on the assumptions and calculations made.

❏ ABNORMAL CARBOHYDRATE METABOLISM

Of the many problems in abnormal metabolism that occur in animals, diabetes and ketosis are concerned primarily with faulty carbohydrate metabolism. Although diabetes does occur in lower animals, adequate information is not at hand to evaluate its importance. In humans it is an important disease, affecting people of all ages. Ketosis, on the other hand, appears to be more of a problem with domestic animals.

Ketosis

This syndrome involves an excess of ketones (acetone, acetoacetate, and β-hydroxybutyrate) accumulating in body tissues due to a disorder in carbohydrate or lipid metabolism. Increased concentration in blood is termed ketonemia or acetonemia; if levels are high enough to spill into the urine, the condition is called ketonuria. The disease is common in cattle at the peak of lactation and in sheep in late pregnancy; it is characterized by hypoglycemia, depleted liver glycogen, elevated mobilization of adipose tissue lipids, increased production of ketones and lipemia. These changes in energy metabolism resemble diabetes mellitus of man and animals. The impaired utilization of energy results in increased breakdown of tissue proteins for energy, loss of body weight, decreased milk production in lactating animals, and abortion in pregnant animals. Water consumption is increased due to excessive loss of body fluids in the urine in response to ketonuria. The ketones in urine are accompanied by excessive losses of electrolytes (K, Na); this triggers tissue dehydration and induces increased water intake. In ruminants, propionic acid is the major volatile fatty acid (VFA) used for glucogenesis. The only pathway for fatty acids to be converted to glucose, except for propionic, is through acetyl CoA and the tricarboxylic acid cycle, and there is no net increase in glucose synthesis by these reactions.

Because limited glucose is absorbed from the GI tract in ruminants, liver synthesis of glucose is a major source for maintenance of blood glucose and tissue glycogen levels. Thus, during periods of great physiologic demand for glucose, such as in lactation or pregnancy, ketosis becomes a serious practical problem in ruminants. Metabolic vitamin B_{12} deficiency has been implicated in ketosis in dairy cattle; this possible relationship needs further study. There is also evidence that supplementary niacin may prevent or alleviate ketosis in cows. In pregnant ewes, ketosis is partly precipitated by reduced feed intake caused by reduced stomach capacity as a result of increased uterine size, especially when multiple fetuses are present.

Ketosis also occurs in swine and other nonruminants during starvation or chronic underfeeding, often at the onset of a sudden new energy demand such as at the beginning of lactation. Treatment of ketosis generally has centered on the restoration of normal blood glucose concentration. Thus, intravenous glucose injections are common. Hormones, such as ACTH and adrenal corticoid hormones, also have been used, but the mechanism of their action is outside the realm of this discussion.

❑ DIABETES MELLITUS

Diabetes mellitus is relatively common in humans, but occurs with apparently less frequency in other animals. The disease is diagnosed partly on the basis of higher than normal fasting levels of blood glucose. The disease is not a single entity; instead, it is a spectrum of clinical disorders of which excessive blood glucose (hyperglycemia) is a common denominator (3). The three basic types are: insulin-dependent diabetes mellitus (IDDM), also called juvenile onset or Type I diabetes; non-insulin dependent diabetes (NIDDM), also called adult onset or Type II diabetes; and gestational diabetes. The common metabolic defect in each of these three forms is improper production and/or utilization of the hormone, insulin, which is produced by the pancreas. Insulin acts on cells throughout the body to promote glucose utilization.

IDDM occurs as a result of destruction of the beta cells of the Islets of Langerhans in the pancreas. The disease usually occurs early in life, but can appear at any age. IDDM has a genetic component, but environmental factors also play a role. A number of compounds, such as alloxan and streptozotocin, as well as viruses such as Coxsackie B-4, rubella, and mumps, attack the beta cells and destroy insulin production. Affected individuals require insulin administration one or more times daily to keep blood glucose in the normal range.

NIDDM generally appears first in adult life and is associated with a defect in utilization of insulin by the liver and other tissues. Insulin production and blood plasma levels of insulin are normal but defective cellular uptake of glucose and impaired release of glucose from liver results in hyperglycemia. The concept of insulin receptors present on cell surfaces has led to the knowledge that NIDDM is associated with a relative deficiency of cell-surface binding sites for normal glucose uptake and utilization. This deficiency is partially under genetic control and accounts for the greater tendency to develop NIDDM in some families than in others. NIDDM is aggravated in obesity; thus, weight reduction often alleviates the symptoms and maintenance of ideal body weight may delay or prevent onset of NIDDM in genetically prone individuals. Thus, although diet appears to be unrelated to onset of IDDM, it is of great importance in the management of NIDDM in humans.

Gestation pregnancy diabetes is induced by increased tissue resistance to the action of insulin and involves an increase in blood glucose and blood ketones. Many women who develop gestation diabetes recover after delivery. Gestation diabetes is probably the most common form of the disease in domestic animals.

Because insulin is required for normal glucose utilization, its absence or cellular resistance to it results in hyperglycemia, urinary loss of glucose (glucosuria), and other changes as described for ketosis. Humans and animals with a tendency toward diabetes show an impaired glucose tolerance (an abnormally long time for clearance of oral or injected doses of glucose from the blood). Glucose tolerance curves in the normal, diabetic and hyper insulin human are shown in Fig. 8.4. A glucose tolerance test indicates not only the ability of the pancreas to secrete insulin, but also the ability of the liver to utilize glucose. Mild diabetes mellitus can be controlled by feeding low-carbohydrate, high-protein diets.

Diabetes can be induced artificially by administration of alloxan, a drug that selectively destroys pancreatic cells that produce insulin. Protein and amino acid metabolism as well as carbohydrate and lipid metabolism are affected by insulin deficiency. Insulin deficiency results in severe negative N balance, glucose loss in urine (glycosuria), excessive urine volume (polyuria), and electrolyte loss associated with the hyperglycemia and ketonemia. The interference with glucose utilization in insulin deficiency is related to the membrane transfer system whereby extracellular glucose is transported into the cell for metabolism. The action of insulin on the membrane transport system appears to be the means by which glucose utilization is controlled by insulin. Insulin also

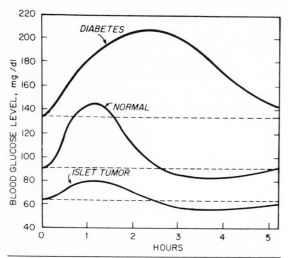

Figure 8.4 *Glucose tolerance curve in the normal person, in a diabetic person, and in a person with an islet tumor (hyperinsulinism). From A. C. Guyton (1968),* Textbook of Medical Physiology, *W. B. Sanders Co., Philadelphia, PA.*

promotes protein synthesis apart from its effects on glucose metabolism.

Insulin-like Growth Factors

Before we leave the subject of the role of insulin in diabetes, we introduce briefly the present concepts of its relationship to insulin-like growth factors present in blood serum and other body tissues. Insulin-like growth factor I (IGF-I) has a structure very similar to that of insulin. First designated somatomedin C, this substance was found to be related to bone growth. In fact, the early assays for its activity, which was believed to be controlled by the growth hormone somatotropin, consisted of measuring its uptake by chondrocytes in long bone growth plates of animals. Since then, a second insulin-like growth factor (IGF-II) has been discovered that has been postulated to be related to fetal growth (7). Human IGF-I and IGF-II have been isolated and their amino acid sequence determined (14) and bovine IGF-I and II have been isolated and characterized (9). The exact role of these peptide growth factors in animal growth and how they interrelate with insulin, growth hormone and other hormones in controlling cellular metabolism is unknown.

Details of this rapidly growing field of biology are beyond the scope of this discussion, but it seems certain that unfolding secrets of growth will reveal important links between insulin, insulin-like growth factors, and carbohydrate, protein, and energy metabolism. The exact role of carbohydrate nutrition in this exciting arena remains to be elucidated.

❑ PLANT FIBERS AS ENERGY SOURCES

The energy from most plants is available largely as carbohydrate, with only a small fraction except in the case of certain oil-bearing seeds such as soybeans of the calories provided as fat. The carbohydrates are present as mono- and disaccharides, starches, and a mixture of other complex carbohydrates, including cellulose and lignin, which resist hydrolysis by digestive enzymes elaborated by the host animal. In the ruminant animal, the large microbial population residing in the rumen contains species that elaborate enzymes capable of hydrolyzing cellulose present in plant cell walls, particularly those associated with the leaf and stem portion of the plant and the outer bran layer of seeds. Nonruminant animals, including the horse, pig, and human, are able to utilize some of these fibrous feeds by virtue of the presence of similar microbial populations residing in the colon and cecum. Van Soest (15) described a method for partitioning plant tissue into two fractions based on nutritional availability: cell wall constituents and cell contents. Cell walls contain large amounts of lignin and cellulose, whereas cell contents consist of simple sugars and starches and are easily hydrolyzed to glucose by the enzymes secreted by the host. Fibrous portions of plants (stems, leaves, seed coats) are high in cellulose; therefore, their energy is unlocked by anaerobic microbial fermentation in the rumen or cecum-colon to yield volatile fatty acids (VFA). Recent advances (8) in measurements of fibrous material following enzymic removal of starch can be used along with the acid and neutral detergent methods of Van Soest (16) and Van Soest and Wine (17) to characterize energy sources.

Ruminants consuming all-forage diets obtain most of their energy as VFA produced by anaerobic microbial fermentation of fiber in the rumen. VFAs are readily absorbed from the rumen; the amounts absorbed from the large intestine of nonruminant are less certain, but may be as much as 30% of the digestible energy intake in swine (13).

Recombinant DNA (gene splicing) techniques may

be applied soon in carbohydrate nutrition by cloning cellulase genes from microorganisms. Changing the microbial activities in the gastrointestinal tract of animals may be applied in this way to enhance the breakdown of the holocellulose-lignin bond to increase the utilization of cellulose. Cloning procedures could also provide the basis for production in monoculture of superior cellulolytic microbes for degradation of fibrous feedstuffs. The extent to which such biotechnology will be applied in animal feeding will depend ultimately on economic incentive for developmental effort as well as on constraints imposed by biological limits on the host animal and its gastrointestinal microbial ecosystem.

❏ CARBOHYDRATE COMPOSITION OF FOOD AND FEED

Detailed carbohydrate composition of feed is not given in the Appendix tables. For readers interested in such information, a fairly detailed presentation is given in Table 8.4. Further information may be found in many other reference books.

❏ SUMMARY

Carbohydrates are the major constituents of plant tissues. Plants synthesize carbohydrate (glucose) using solar energy, carbon dioxide, and water, and give off oxygen. This process, photosynthesis, is vital for animals; they could not exist without this transformation of energy and the free oxygen released. Carbohydrates contain C, H, and O in approximately a ratio of 1 to 2 to 1. The most simple carbohydrate is a monosaccharide such as glucose. A disaccharide has two molecules of a simple sugar (for example common table sugar is sucrose, composed of glucose and fructose); an oligosaccharide may have 3–10 sugar units, a polysaccharide >10 sugar units. Animal tissues contain glucose and its polymer, glycogen, the storage form of carbohydrate energy with only trace amounts of other carbohydrates. Plant tissues may contain mono-, di-, oligo-, and polysaccharides, including starches, which are hydrolyzed by digestive enzymes of animals, and cellulose, which is not. Cellulose is a major component of plant cell walls, and together with hemicellulose, is often present in combination with lignin, a biologically unavailable mixture of polymers of phenolic acid.

Lignification increases with plant age; lignin is a major structural component of mature plants and of trees. Vegetables and cereals are low, grasses are intermediate, and legumes high in lignin. The amount of lignin present affects cellulose and hemicellulose bioavailability for microbes and in this way affects the nutritive value of plant materials for animals.

In ruminants and animals such as the horse and rabbit with large microbial populations in the lower gastrointestinal tract, anaerobic fermentation of starch and cellulose produces large quantities of volatile fatty acids (acetic, propionic, butyric), which are used to provide a large part of the total energy supply to the host animal.

Soluble carbohydrates ingested by non-ruminants are hydrolyzed in the small intestine and absorbed by active transport as monosaccharides largely from the duodenum and jejunum. Glucose can be formed in body tissues from lipids and amino acids (gluconeogenesis); absorbed glucose and that resulting from gluconeogenesis can be stored in limited amounts in liver and muscle as glycogen or converted to body fat by breakdown first to pyruvate. The complex system of reactions by which glucose and its metabolites are oxidized to provide energy is called the Krebs (citric acid) cycle. Glucose metabolism to pyruvate and lactate for entrance into the citric acid cycle proceeds through the pentose shunt and glycolytic pathways. The total energy released in the conversion of glucose to carbon dioxide and water is 673 Kcal/mole (the molecular weight of glucose is 180.2; thus, the gross energy value of glucose is $673/180.2 = 3.74$ Kcal/g).

Abnormal carbohydrate metabolism in animals is associated with diabetes and ketosis. Diabetes is common in humans and has been produced in farm animals, dogs, and cats. It results from an insufficiency of insulin from the pancreas or defective cellular utilization; insulin insufficiency results in severe negative N balance, glucose loss in urine, excessive urine volume, and electrolyte loss. The action of insulin on transport of glucose into the cell for metabolism appears to be the means by which glucose utilization is controlled by insulin. Ketosis is the presence of excess ketones (acetone, acetoacetate and β-hydroxybutyrate) in blood and body tissues; it is common in cattle at the peak of lactation and in sheep in late pregnancy, which represent periods of great physiological demand for glucose. Ketosis treatment centers on the restoration of normal blood glucose concentration.

TABLE 8.4 Carbohydrates in various foods and feeds, % as fed.[a,b]

FOOD OR FEED	MONOSACCHARIDES		DISACCHARIDES		POLYSACCHARIDES				FIBER[c]	NITROGEN-FREE EXTRACT
	GLUCOSE	FRUCTOSE	SUCROSE	LACTOSE	STARCH	DEXTRANS	CELLULOSE	LIGNIN		
Alfalfa hay, early bloom	—[d]	—	—	—	—	—	24	6	19	36
Apple	1.7	5.0	3.1	0	0.6	0	0.4	—	1.8	8.6
Asparagus	0	—	0	—	—	—	—	—	29	32
Beans, navy	0	—	0	—	35.2	3.7	3.1	—	—	—
Barley, grain	—	—	—	—	—	—	—	3	5	67
Bermuda grass hay	—	—	—	0	—	—	25	8–12	25–30	40–60
Corn, sweet, fresh	0.5	0	0.3	0	14.5	0.1	0.6	—	—	—
Corn syrup	21.2 plus 26.4% maltose	0	0	0	0	34.7	0	0	—	—
Corn grain	—	—	—	0	62	—	—	—	2	69
Corn silage, dough stage	—	—	—	0	—	—	10	—	7	17
Corn silage, mature	—	—	—	0	—	—	26	—	7	15
Grapes (Concord)	4.8	4.3	0.2	0	0	0	0	—	0	—
Honey	34.2	40.5	1.9	0	0	1.5	0	0	0	—
Jellies	0	0	40–65	0	0	0	0	0	0	—
Maple syrup	0	0	62.9	0	0	0	0	0	0	—
Milk, cow, whole	0	0	0	4.9	0	0	0	0	0	—
Molasses	8.8	8.0	53.6	0	0	0	0	0	0	—

Oat, mill byproduct	—	—	0	—	—	—	13.5	54.5
Oats, grain	—	—	0	—	—	—	10–12	60–65
Oat hay, early bloom	—	—	0	—	—	23	24 (cell walls 49%)	43
Orange	1.8	4.6	0	—	—	—	—	—
Peas								
immature	0	5.5	0	4.1	0	1.1	—	—
mature, dry	0	6.7	0	4.1	0	5.0	—	—
Potatoes (white)	0.1	0.1	—	17.0	—	0.4	0.6	19
Rice, with hull	—	—	—	—	—	—	0.4	66
Rice, polished	2.0	0.4	—	72.9	0.9	0.3	0.4	80
Wheat flour	—	0.2	—	68.8	5.5	—	2–3	65–70
Wheat bran	—	—	—	—	—	3	10–11	50–55
Sunflower seeds, w/hull	—	—	—	—	—	—	29	19
Sunflower seeds, w/o hull	—	—	—	—	—	—	10–13	25
Timothy hay, early bloom	—	—	—	—	—	26–34	30–36 (cell walls, 66%)	40–43

The values listed in this table do not represent the total information available on carbohydrate composition of individual feedstuffs. The primary purpose of the table is to provide the basis for an appreciation of the wide variation that exists among food and feed sources in carbohydrate composition.

From: M. G. Hardinge, J. G. Swarnes and H. Crooks (1965), *J. Am. Diet. Assoc.* **46**:198–201, and Atlas of Nutritional Data on U.S. and Canadian Feeds, NAS-NRC and Canad. Dept. Agr. (1975), Washington, D.C.

The newer analytical procedure for describing fiber components in terms of neutral detergent fiber (NDF) (cell walls) and acid detergent fiber (ADF) eventually will provide more meaningful information on biologically available energy of fibrous feedstuffs. The NDF, ADF, and lignin content of some unusual feedstuffs (plant residues, wood products, manures) has been reported by Van Soest and Robertson (Proc. Cornell Nutr. Conf., 1976, p. 102, Cornell Univ., Ithaca, N.Y. 14853).

No value indicated.

❏ REFERENCES

1. Aherne, F. X., V. W. Hays, R. C. Ewan, and V. C. Speer. 1969. *J. Animal Sci.* **29**:444.

2. Allen, R. S. 1977. Ch. 27 in *Duke's Physiology of Domestic Animals,* 9th ed., M. J. Swenson (ed.). Cornell Univ. Press, Ithaca, N.Y.

3. Arky, R. A. 1983. Prevention and therapy of diabetes mellitus. *Nutr. Rev.* **41**:165.

4. Brambila, S. and F. W. Hill. 1966. *J. Nutr.* **88**:84; 1967, **91**:261.

5. Cori, C. F. 1925. *J. Biol. Chem.* **66**:691.

6. Dadd, R. H. 1963. *Advances in Insect Physiology* **1**:447. Academic Press, N.Y.

7. Daughaday, W. H., K. A. Parker, S. Borowsky, B. Trivedi, and M. Rapadia. 1982. *Endocrinol.* **110**:575.

8. Englyst, H. N. and J. H. Cummings. 1984. *Analyst* **109**:937.

9. Honegger, A. and R. E. Humbel. 1986. *J. Biol. Chem.* **261**:569.

10. Jenkins, D. J. A., A. J. Jenkings, T. M. S. Wolever, L. K. Thomspon, and A. K. Rao. 1986. *Nutr. Rev.* **44**:44.

11. Montencourt, B. S. 1983. *Biotechnology* **1**:166.

12. Prior, R. L. and S. B. Smith. 1983. *J. Nutr.* **113**:1016.

13. Rerat, A., M. Fiszlewies, P. Herpen, P. Vaugelade, and M. Durand. 1985. *C. R. Acad. Sci. Paris 300 Series* III:467.

14. Rinderknecht, E. and R. E. Humbel. 1978. *J. Biol. Chem.* **253**:2769.

15. Van Soest, P. J. 1967. *J. Animal Sci.* **26**:119.

16. Van Soest, P. J. 1963. *J. Assoc. Official Agric. Chem.* **46**:829.

17. Van Soest, P. J. and R. H. Wine. 1967. *J. Assoc. Official Agric. Chem.* **50**:50.

18. Wilson, T. H. 1962. *Intestinal Absorption.* W. B. Sanders Co., Philadelphia, PA.

9

Lipids

LIPIDS ARE ORGANIC COMPOUNDS that are insoluble in water but soluble in organic solvents and serve important biochemical and physiological functions in plant and animal tissues. The lipids of importance in nutrition of humans and animals can be classified as follows:

Simple lipids are esters of fatty acids with various alcohols. Fats and oils and waxes are simple lipids. Fats and oils are esters of fatty acids with glycerol, and waxes are esters of fatty acids with alcohols other than glycerol.

Compound lipids are esters of fatty acids containing groups in addition to an alcohol and fatty acid. They include phospholipids, glycolipids, and lipoproteins. Phospholipids (phosphatides) are fats containing phosphoric acid and N. Glycolipids are fats containing carbohydrate and, often, N, and lipoproteins are lipids bound to proteins in blood and other tissues.

Derived lipids include substances derived from the previous groups by hydrolysis—that is, fatty acids, glycerol, and other alcohols.

Sterols are lipids with complex phenanthrene-type ring structures (see a later section), whereas **terpenes** are compounds that usually have isoprene-type structures.

Fats and oils quantitatively make up the largest fraction of lipids in most food materials and are characterized by their high energy value. One gram of a typical fat yields about 9.45 Kcal of heat when completely combusted, compared with about 4.1 Kcal (see Ch. 10) for a typical carbohydrate.

121

❑ STRUCTURE

The most important lipid constituents in animal nutrition include: fatty acids; glycerol; mono-, di-, and triglycerides; and phospholipids. Glycolipids, lipoproteins, and sterols may be imporant in metabolism, but these lipids as well as waxes and terpenes are quantitatively unimportant, nutritionally, or are poorly utilized.

Fatty Acids

The fatty acids consist of chains of C atoms ranging from 2 to 24 or more C's in length that have a carboxyl group on the end of each chain. The general structure is RCOOH, where R is a C chain of variable length. Acetic acid, a major product of microbial fermentation of glucose in ruminants, has 2 C's. Its formula is: CH_3COOH.

Myristic acid, a constituent of milk fat, has 14 C's. Its formula is: $CH_3(CH_2)_{12}COOH$.

These fatty acids are saturated. That is, each C atom in the chain (except the carboxyl group) has 2 H atoms attached to it (3 H's at the terminal C). Some fatty acids are unsaturated; one or more pairs of C atoms in their chain are attached by a double bond and H has been removed. Linoleic acid, a constituent of corn oil and other plant oils high in polyunsaturated fatty acids, has 18 C's and two double bonds. Its formula is:

$$CH_3(CH_2)_4CH{=}CHCH_2CH{=}CH(CH_2)_7COOH$$

LINOLEIC ACID

Most fatty acids commonly found in animal tissues are straight chained and contain an even number of C's. Branched-chain fatty acids and those with an odd number of C's are more common in microorganisms; however, tissues of ruminant animals, particularly, contain relatively large amounts of these acids as a result of rumen fermentation.

Fatty acids containing double bonds can occur as the *cis* or the *trans* isomer as illustrated below:

$$\begin{array}{l} H{-}\overset{\|}{C}{-}(CH_2)_7{-}CH_3 \\ H{-}C{-}(CH_2)_7{-}COOH \end{array}$$

OLEIC ACID (cis)

$$\begin{array}{l} CH_3{-}(CH_2)_7{-}\overset{\|}{C}{-}H \\ \quad H{-}C{-}(CH_2)_7{-}COOH \end{array}$$

ELAIDIC ACID (trans)

The names, number of C's and number of double bonds for fatty acids most common in plant and animal tissues are given in Table 9.1. It is generally believed that linoleic, linolenic, and arachidonic acids cannot be synthesized by animals, although some work (1) suggests the pig may synthesize some linoleic and arachidonic. The position of the double bond in the C chain is critical to biological activity. Table 9.2 shows the position of the double bonds in each of the common unsaturated fatty acids.

Glycerol

The formula for glycerol is:

$$\begin{array}{l} HOCH_2 \\ | \\ HOCH \\ | \\ HOCH_2 \end{array}$$

GLYCEROL

It is the alcohol component of all triglycerides common in animal and plant tissues and is a component of the phosphatides—lecithin, cephalin, and sphingomyelin.

Mono-, Di-, and Triglycerides

Monoglycerides, diglycerides, and triglycerides are esters of glycerol and fatty acids. An ester is formed by reaction of an alcohol with an organic acid; the structure of an ester and the linkage between glycerol and fatty acids in glycerides is illustrated:

$$R{-}\overset{O}{\overset{\|}{C}}{-}OH + HOR' \rightleftharpoons R{-}\overset{O}{\overset{\|}{C}}{-}OR' + H_2O$$

A monoglyceride, diglyceride and triglyceride would have the following general structures, where R, R', and R'' represent three different fatty acids:

$$\begin{array}{llll} \alpha & H_2COH & H_2COH & H_2COOCR \\ \beta & H{-}COH & H{-}COOCR' & H{-}COOCR' \\ \alpha' & H_2COOCR'' & H_2COOCR'' & H_2COOCR'' \end{array}$$

The fatty acid composition of triglycerides is variable. The same or different fatty acids may be in all three positions; for example, if stearic acid occupied all three positions, the compound would be termed tristearin (a simple triglyceride), whereas if butyric, lauric, and palmitic acid each occupied one position, the compound would be called butyrolauropalmitin (glyceryl butyrolauropalmitate), a mixed triglyceride.

TABLE 9.1   Fatty acids most common in plant and animal tissues.

ACID	NO. CARBONS	NO. DOUBLE BONDS	ABBREVIATED DESIGNATION
Butyric (butanoic)	4	0	C 4:0
Caproic (hexanoic)	6	0	C 6:0
Caprylic (octanoic)	8	0	C 8:0
Capric (decanoic)	10	0	C10:0
Lauric (dodecanoic)	12	0	C12:0
Myristic (tetradecanoic)	14	0	C14:0
Palmitic (hexadecanoic)	16	0	C16:0
Palmitoleic (hexadecenoic)	16	1	C16:1
Stearic (octadecanoic)	18	0	C18:1
Oleic (octadecenoic)	18	1	C18:1
Linoleic (octadecadienoic)	18	2	C18:2
Linolenic (octadecatrienoic)	18	3	C18:3
Arachidic (eicosanoic)	20	0	C20:0
Arachidonic (eicosatetraenoic)	20	4	C20:4
Lignoceric (tetracosanoic)	24	0	C24:0

The chain length and degree of unsaturation of the individual fatty acids making up the triglyceride determines its physical and chemical properties. Simple triglycerides of saturated fatty acids containing ten or more carbons are solid at room temperature, whereas those with less than ten carbons usually are liquid. Triglycerides containing only long-chain saturated fatty acids are solids, whereas those containing a preponderance of unsaturated fatty acids are liquids.

Several constants are used commonly to characterize the chemical properties of fats. Constants of some common fats are given in Table 9.3. Each of these has some application in nutrition. **Saponification number** is the number of mg of KOH required for the saponification (hydrolysis) of 1 g of fat. The saponification number of a low molecular-weight fat (short-chain fatty acids) is large and becomes smaller as the molecular weight of the fat increases. Thus, the saponification number gives a measure of the average chain length of the three fatty acids in the fat. **Reichert-Meissl [RM] number** is the number of ml of 0.1N KOH solution required to neutralize the volatile water-soluble fatty acids (short-chain) obtained by hydrolysis of 5 g of fat. Beef tallow and other high molecular-weight fats contain practically no volatile acids and therefore have RM numbers of near zero, but butter contains a higher proportion of volatile acids and has a RM number of 17–35. **Iodine number** is the number of g of iodine that can be added to the unsaturated bonds in 100 g of fat. Iodine number is a measure of the degree of hydrogenation (saturation) of the fatty acids in the fat. A completely saturated fat such as tristearin has an iodine number of zero, whereas a liquid fat such as linseed oil has an iodine number of 175 to 202.

TABLE 9.2   Position of double bonds in unsaturated fatty acids.

ACID	POSITION OF DOUBLE BONDS[a]	PRECURSOR
Palmitoleic	9	Palmitic
Oleic	9	Stearic
Linoleic	9,12	None
Linolenic	9,12,15	None
Arachidonic	5,8,11,14	Linoleic

[a]C atoms are numbered from carboxyl end.

Phospholipids (phosphatides)

Phospholipids on hydrolysis yield fatty acids, phosphoric acid, and usually glycerol and a nitrogenous base. The general formula for lecithin is shown on

TABLE 9.3 Constants of some common fats.[a]

FAT	SAPONIFICATION NO.	REICHERT-MEISSL NO.	IODINE NO.
Beef	196–200	1	35–40
Butter	210–130	17–35	26–38
Coconut	253–262	6–8	6–10
Corn	187–193	4–5	111–128
Cottonseed	194–196	1	103–111
Lard	195–203	1	47–67
Linseed	188–195	1	175–202
Peanut	186–194	1	88–98
Soybean	189–194	0–3	122–134
Sunflower	188–193	0–5	129–136

[a]The constants for animal fats may vary outside the range of values listed because of unusual composition of dietary fats.

page 124. Cephalins are similar to lecithins except that choline is replaced by hydroxyethyl amine in the molecule. Sphingomyelins do not contain glycerol, but contain fatty acids, choline, phosphoric acid, and the nitrogenous base, sphingosine.

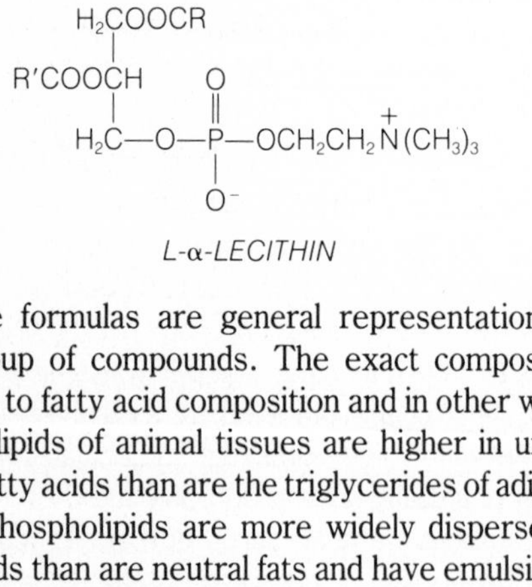

L-α-LECITHIN

These formulas are general representations of each group of compounds. The exact composition varies as to fatty acid composition and in other ways. Phospholipids of animal tissues are higher in unsaturated fatty acids than are the triglycerides of adipose tissue; phospholipids are more widely dispersed in body fluids than are neutral fats and have emulsifying properties that allow them to serve important functions in lipid transport.

Sterols

The most abundant sterol in animal tissue is cholesterol, shown below:

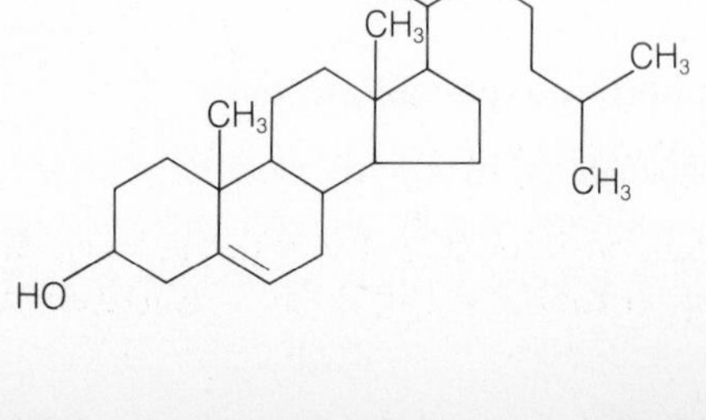

Other important sterols in animals are ergosterol (yields vitamin D_2 when irradiated); 7-dehydrocholesterol (yields vitamin D_3 when irradiated); bile acids; androgens (male sex hormones); and estrogens and progesterones (female sex hormones).

❏ FUNCTIONS

The functions of the lipids can be listed broadly as follows: to supply energy for normal maintenance and productive functions; to serve as a source of essential fatty acids; to serve as a carrier of the fat-soluble vitamins.

Energy Supply

The hydrolysis of triglycerides yields glycerol and fatty acids, which serve as concentrated sources of energy. Most of the variation among fat sources in the amount of utilizable energy they contain is related to their digestibility, but except in abnormal or special conditions of malabsorption, the true digestibility of fats exceeds 80%. When the total lipid content of the diet is low (<10%), as often occurs when animals are fed all-plant diets, apparent digestibility may be much less than this due to the higher proportion of metabolic fecal lipids on a low-fat diet. Also, a high proportion of waxes or sterols in the diet tends to reduce absorbability of the lipid, as these components are usually poorly digested and absorbed.

All of the energy in the diet except that present in essential fatty acids (see next section) may be provided by carbohydrate. Thus, no requirement exists for lipids as an energy source in the diet. Animals fed fat-free diets often develop fat-soluble vitamin deficiencies, however.

Essential Fatty Acids (EFA)

Linoleic acid (C18:2) and linolenic acid (C18:3) apparently cannot be synthesized by animal tissues, or at least not in sufficient amounts to prevent pathological changes, and so must be supplied in the diet. Arachidonic acid (C20:4) can be synthesized from C18:2, and, therefore, is required in the diet only if C18:2 is not available.

The exact mechanisms by which EFA function in maintaining normal body functions are not known, but two probable vital areas are: they are an integral part of the lipid-protein structure of cell membranes, and they appear to play an important part in the structure of prostaglandins, hormone-like compounds widely distributed in reproductive organs and other tissues of humans and animals. The functions and metabolism of prostaglandins are active areas of research. Prostaglandins are biosynthesized from arachidonic acid and have a wide variety of metabolic effects including the following: lower blood pressure, stimulate smooth muscle contraction, inhibit norepinephrine-induced release of fatty acids from adipose tissue, and a variety of other tissue and species-specific effects.

Skin lesions and other abnormalities have been traced to deficiencies of certain fatty acids in non-ruminant species. The skin lesions that develop in pigs fed a fat-free diet are illustrated in Fig. 9.1. The following effects of a deficiency of EFA have been reported: scaly skin and necrosis of the tail; growth failure; reproductive failure; elevation of trienoic-tetraenoic ratio of tissue fatty acids; edema, subcutaneous hemorrhage, and poor feathering in chicks.

Holman (2) suggests that in the rat a ratio of trienoic acids to tetraenoic acids of more than 0.4 in tissue lipids indicates a deficiency of EFA and that a level of linoleic acid at or exceeding 1% of the calories in the diet is sufficient to maintain a ratio of less than 0.4. Babatunde et al (1) found increased triene-tetraene ratios in heart, liver, and adipose tissues of pigs fed diets containing no fat or 3% hydrogenated coconut oil compared to values obtained with 3% safflower oil, but found no skin lesions and no reduction in weight gain of pigs fed coconut oil, which aggravates EFA deficiency in the rat. Their work and that of Kass et al. (3) suggested the possibility that some linoleic acid synthesis occurs in the pig. Young ruminants (calves, kids, lambs) apparently require EFA in their diet, but no reports have ap-

Figure 9.1 *A fat-deficient pig that was fed a diet with 0.06% ether extract. Note loss of hair, scaly, dandruff-like dermatitis, especially on feet and tail. Courtesy of W. M. Beeson, Purdue University.*

peared of EFA deficiency in adult ruminants. This is somewhat puzzling because rumen microflora hydrogenate most unsaturated fatty acids so that one would expect EFA deficiency to be more likely than in other animals. Arachidonic acid has been found in high concentration in reproductive tissue of cattle and presumably is synthesized there as a precursor of prostaglandins. Additional studies clearly are needed to determine the degree of importance of linoleic and other fatty acids in the diet of pigs, cattle and other species, including man.

Carrier of the Fat-Soluble Vitamins

Absorption of the fat-soluble vitamins (A, D, E, and K) is a function of digestion and absorption of fats. Fat-soluble vitamins are dispersed in micelles similar or identical to those formed in the absorption of fatty acids (see a later section). Mixed micelles containing monoglycerides and free fatty acids take up fat-soluble vitamins more efficiently than micelles not containing them. A bile acid sequestrant, cholestyramine, has been shown to reduce absorption of vitamin K when added to the diet, supporting the concept of an obligatory formation of bile salt-containing micelle formation. Because only a low level of dietary fat is needed for micelle formation, frank deficiencies of vitamin A, D, E, or K are unlikely to occur under normal dietary conditions.

☐ ABSORPTION

The preparation of lipids for absorption and the absorption process itself have been described (4, 5).

Digestion and absorption of lipids are illustrated schematically in Fig. 9.2.

The upper small intestine is the site of the major processes of preparation for absorption. Dietary lipids, mainly triglycerides, are discharged slowly from the stomach and are mixed with bile and pancreatic and intestinal secretions. Emulsification occurs here due to the detergent action of the bile salts and the churning action of the intestine, and the lipid particle size is reduced to spheres of 500–1000 mμ in diameter. This smaller particle size allows for greater surface exposure to pancreatic and intestinal lipases which adsorb on the particle surface and attack fatty acids in the 1 and 3 (α) positions, resulting in hydrolysis of triglycerides to β-monoglycerides and free fatty acids (FFA). The β-monoglycerides and FFA then combine with salt-phospholipid-cholesterol micelles (in about a 12.5:2.5:1 molar ratio) to form mixed micelles; these are essential for efficient absorption. Bile salts are detergent-like compounds that facilitate digestion and absorption of lipids. The presence of bile is necessary for efficient fat and fat-soluble vitamin absorption; in its absence, cholesterol absorption is reduced to near zero. Pancreatic lipase activity and resynthesis of triglycerides in the intestinal mucosal cells are promoted by bile salts.

The mixed micelles join with cholesterol and fat-soluble vitamins to form larger and more complex mixed micelles, each containing hundreds of molecules and having a diameter of 5–10 mμ. These mixed micelles form microemulsions that then render the lipid ready for absorption as hydrolysis proceeds.

Bile salts are secreted in copious quantities (30 g/day in adult man). Bile salts are reabsorbed readily from the GI tract in the lower jejunum and recycled to the liver; thus, the amount of daily secretion exceeds by several fold the amount present in the body at any one time as well as the amount of daily synthesis by the liver.

Several bile acids are common in animals, differing only in minor changes in the steroid portion of the molecule. Common bile acids are: cholic, deoxycholic, taurocholic, and glycocholic acid. In the last two, the amino acids, taurine and glycine, respectively, are part of the molecule. The structure of cholic acid is shown:

CHOLIC ACID

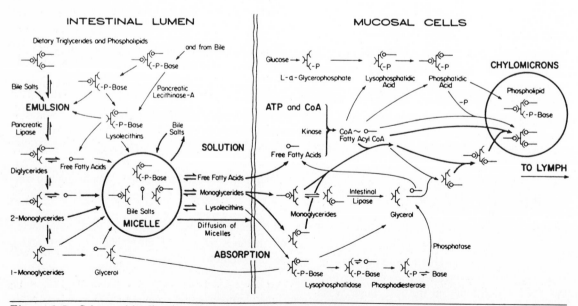

Figure 9.2 *Scheme of fat digestion, absorption, and resynthesis. The* heavy arrows *indicate the more important pathways. From Davenport, H. W. (1982).* Physiology of the Digestive Tract, *5th Ed., Yearbook Medical Publishers, Inc., p. 220.*

The main site of absorption of lipids is the proximal (upper) jejunum, but some absorption occurs along the intestinal tract from the distal (lower) duodenum to the distal small intestine. Glycerol and short-chain FA (C2-C10) are absorbed by passive transport into the mesenteric veinous blood and then to the portal blood. Monoglycerides and long-chain FA enter the brush border (microvilli) and the apical core of the absorptive intestinal mucosal cells by diffusion. To a limited extent, some triglycerides may be absorbed intact as a fine emulsion of particles averaging 500 Å in diameter.

Most of the phospholipids in the intestinal lumen are hydrolyzed partially by pancreatic and intestinal lipases to yield FFA. The remainder of the molecule (lysophospholipid) is absorbed intact along with a small proportion of unhydrolyzed phospholipid. Although free cholesterol is absorbed readily, most other dietary sterols except vitamin D are absorbed poorly. Cholesterol esters must be hydrolyzed by pancreatic and intestinal lipases to form free cholesterol for absorption by displacement of the endogenous cholesterol of the microvilli lipoprotein. After entering the mucosal cell, free cholesterol is again esterified before transfer to the lymph system via the lacteals.

After entering the epithelial cell, long-chain FA are converted to derivatives of coenzyme A in the presence of ATP. This fatty acid-coenzyme A complex (termed fatty acyl coenzyme A) reacts with monoglyceride within the cell to form di- and then triglycerides. The triglycerides thus formed contain only FA of C12 or greater chain length because shorter chain FA are absorbed directly into the portal system.

Before leaving the mucosal cell, the mixed lipid droplets become coated with a thin layer of protein adsorbed to the surface. These protein-coated lipid droplets are called chylomicrons and consist mainly of triglycerides with small quantities of phospholipids, cholesterol esters, and protein. The chylomicrons leave the mucosal cell by reverse pinocytosis and enter the lacteals via the intercellular spaces. Lacteals lead to the lymphatic system, which carries the chylomicrons to the blood via the thoracic duct. A summary of the major conversions that occur in transport of long-chain FA, phospholipids, cholesterol, and monoglycerides by the intestinal mucosal cell is diagrammed in Fig. 9.3.

Although mammals absorb most of these long-chain FA into the lymphatic system, the chicken apparently absorbs its dietary lipids directly into the portal blood, which carries them directly to the liver. Nevertheless, the process of re-esterification of FA to triglycerides in the mucosal cell is similar in birds and mammals.

❏ TRANSPORT AND DEPOSITION

Absorption of fat after a meal is associated with a large increase in lipid concentration of the blood referred to as lipemia. Blood lipids consist of chylomicrons formed within the intestinal mucosal cell during absorption, as well as lipids arising from mobilized depot stores and from synthesis in body tissues, especially the liver and adipose tissues. Blood lipids are transported as lipoproteins ranging from very low density (such as chylomicrons) to high density. The density is increased as the proportion of protein in the complex increases and the lipid decreases. Density, composition, and electrophoretic mobility have been used to divide lipoproteins into four major classes: chylomicrons (lowest density; that is, high ratio of lipids to protein), very low-density lipoproteins (VLDL), low-density lipoproteins (LDL), and high-density lipoproteins (HDL) (6). The composition of each of these four classes is summarized in Table 9.4.

Chylomicrons are made by the body in the small intestine from dietary fat, and VLDL, IDL, LDL, and HDL are synthesizd in the liver and small intestine. Free fatty acids (FA) are transported as a complex with albumin. Very rapid removal of chylomicrons occurs from the blood by the liver, fat depots, and other tissues. For example, half of an injected dose of ^{14}C-labeled tripalmitin is removed from the blood plasma of dogs within 10 min.

The type and quantity of dietary lipid and the time after a meal are major determinants of the composition and concentration of lipids in blood at a particular time. In addition, such factors as species, age, and endocrine status of the individual have an influence. Levels of cholesterol in the blood are affected by diet as well as by hepatic synthesis, but the ratio of free cholesterol to cholesterol esters and free cholesterol to phospholipid are rather constant in normal animals within a given species.

All tissues of the body store triglycerides. Adipose tissues (fat depots) are the most notable storage sites. Adipose tissue is capable of synthesizing fat from carbohydrate and of oxidation of fatty acids. Because stored triglycerides are a ready source of energy, continuous deposition and mobilization clearly

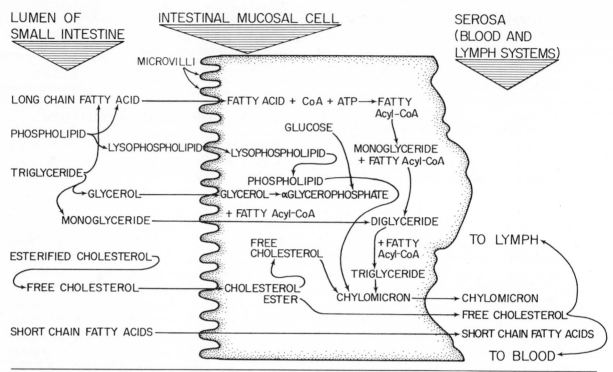

Figure 9.3 *Schematic diagram of the major conversions that occur in transport of lipids across the intestinal mucosal cell during absorption.*

occurs in adipose tissue. Energy intake in excess of current needs results in a net deposition of triglycerides (fattening) and energy intake less than current needs (as in fasting) results in a net loss of triglycerides.

Triglycerides of depot fat tend to have a fatty acid composition characteristic for each animal species. In non-ruminants, however, the fatty acid composition of the depot fat resembles that of the diet. This is illustrated in Table 9.5 for the pig fed semi-purified diets containing various sources of fat. The depot fat of ruminant animals is less responsive to

TABLE 9.4   Composition of lipoprotein isolated from normal subjects.

LIPOPROTEIN CLASS[a]	DENSITY RANGE (G/ML)	ELECTRO-PHORETIC MOBILITY	COMPOSITION (WEIGHT %)				
					CHOLESTEROL		
			PROTEIN	TRIGLYCERIDE	FREE	ESTER	PHOSPHOLIPID
Chylomicrons	<0.94	Origin	1–2	85–95	1–3	2–4	3–6
VLDL (Beta lipoprotein)	0.94–1.006	Prebeta	6–10	50–65	4–8	16–22	15–20
LDL (Beta lipoprotein)	1.006–1.063	Beta	18–22	4–8	6–8	45–50	18–24
HDL (alpha lipoprotein)	1.063–1.21	Alpha	45–55	2–7	3–5	15–20	26–32

[a]VLDL denotes very-low-density lipoprotein, LDL low-density lipoprotein, and HDL high-density lipoprotein.
From Schaefer and Levy (1985) (ref. 6).

TABLE 9.5   Effect of dietary fatty acid composition on fatty acid composition of the depot fat of growing pigs.[a]

FATTY ACID DESIGNATION	DIETARY FAT		PIG DEPOT FAT	
	SAFFLOWER[b]	HYDRO-GENATED COCONUT[b]	SAFFLOWER[b]	HYDRO-GENATED COCONUT[b]
8:0		7.8		
10:0		5.7	0.2	0.2
12:0		44.5	0.2	0.6
14:0	trace	17.2	2.0	3.9
16:0	8.8	9.2	15.6	21.0
16:1			13.0	16.5
18:0	1.5	10.4	50.7	55.9
18:1	9.3	5.0		
18:2	80.4	0.2	17.2	0.9
18:3	trace		0.1	0.1

[a]From Babatunde et al. (1).
[b]Percent of total fatty acids.

dietary fatty acid composition due to the action of the rumen microflora in metabolizing dietary fatty acids, although minor changes can be produced by dietary changes. Depot fat of ruminants can be changed to resemble dietary fat if the action of the rumen microflora is circumvented. Ogilvie et al. (7) accomplished this by duodenal feeding of sheep, and others have been able to obtain softer depot fat in cattle and sheep by feeding very high levels of unsaturated FA, a portion of which presumably traverses the rumen without being metabolized by rumen microflora. Other workers showed that fatty acid composition of body fat can be modified by protecting dietary fat from rumen metabolism by coating with formaldehyde-treated casein. The depot fat composition of ruminants also can be changed by altering the proportion of readily fermentable carbohydrates fed. Ruminant fats are also characterized by odd-length and branched-chain fatty acids, which are derived from volatile fatty acids, and by the presence of *trans* isomers, which result from microbial metabolism of dietary unsaturated fatty acids.

Body lipids clearly are in a dynamic state of metabolism. The turnover rate of triglycerides in adipose tissue is extremely rapid. For example, the half-life in mice is five days; in rats, eight days. The turnover rate of phospholipids and cholesterol also is rapid and may vary from one day for liver in some species to 200 days for brain in other species.

❑ FATTY ACID AND TRIGLYCERIDE METABOLISM

Liver, mammary gland, and adipose tissue are the three major sites of biosynthesis of fatty acids and triglycerides. The liver is the central organ for lipid interconversion and metabolism and its role can be summarized as follows: synthesis of fatty acids from carbohydrates; synthesis of fatty acids from lipogenic amino acids; synthesis of cholesterol from acetyl CoA; synthesis of phospholipids; synthesis of lipoproteins; synthesis of ketone bodies (acetone, β-hydroxybutyric and acetoacetic acid); degradation of fatty acids; degradation of phospholipids; removal of phospholipids and cholesterol from blood; lengthening and shortening fatty acids; saturating and desaturating fatty acids; control of depot lipid storage; and storage of liver lipids.

Synthesis of fatty acids by liver and adipose tissue follows similar pathways, but the relative contribution made by each tissue differs greatly among the species studied. For example, in the mouse and rat about half of the synthesis occurs in the liver, but in the chicken (8) and pigeon (9) nearly all occurs in the liver; in the pig (8) nearly all occurs in adipose tissue and in the cow and sheep (10) both liver and adipose tissue are important, although the latter predominates.

Factors controlling fat synthesis in ruminant animals are not elucidated fully. A major portion of the energy absorbed from the GI tract for lipid synthesis is in the form of volatile FA (VFA) (acetic, propionic, and butyric acids). Although it has been believed that acetate is the primary substrate for fatty acid synthesis in ruminants, recent work indicates that lactate may be an important substitute. Prior and Scott (11) ranked relative potency of substrates in inducing lipogenesis in ruminant adipose tissue as follows: glucose > propionate > lactate > acetate.

Fatty Acid Biosynthesis

Synthesis begins with acetyl CoA (2 carbons) derived from carbohydrates, from certain amino acids, or from degraded fats (see tricarboxylic acid cycle, Fig. 8.2). The fatty acid chain is assembled in 2-carbon units by joining of the carboxyl head of one fragment to the methyl tail of another. Fatty acids build up from acetic acid units that are made reactive by com-

bining first with coenzyme A to form acetyl-CoA and then with carbon dioxide to form the CoA ester of malonic acid. Malonyl-CoA and acetyl-CoA can condense into an intermediate compound. Further reactions then reduce the intermediate to the CoA ester of a four-carbon fatty acid, butyryl-CoA. This, like acetyl-CoA, can condense with a molecule of malonyl-CoA, ultimately giving the ester of the 6-carbon fatty acid; the chain thus lengthens by successive steps. Animal tissues synthesize carbon chains up to C16 in this way. Malonyl-CoA is, in effect, the source of the 2-C units. It combines with the even-numbered fatty acid-CoA esters. The details of fatty acid biosynthesis are illustrated in Fig. 9.4. The biosynthesis of fatty acids occurs primarily in the microsomes of cells, but fatty acid oxidation and synthesis of triglycerides occurs mainly in the endoplasmic reticulum. Enzymes can use acetyl CoA to add C2 units to existing long-chain FA (C12, C14, C16), but formation of FA longer than C18 in this way is re-

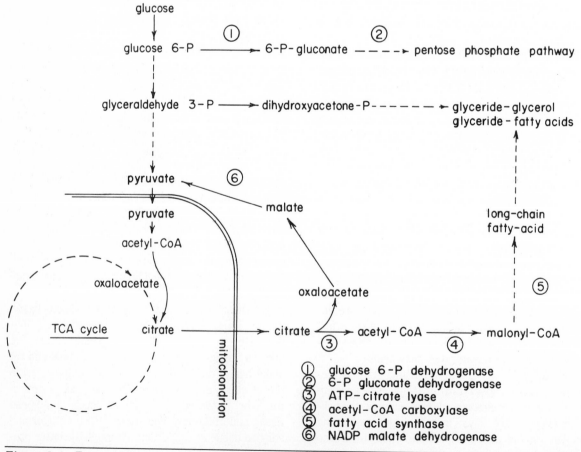

Figure 9.4 *Fatty acid biosynthesis. Note the enzymes involved at various stages. From Mersmann, 1986.*

stricted to conversion of C18:2 to C20:4 and smaller amounts of other longer chain FA.

Desaturation of FA occurs in animal tissues, but the extent is limited, as evidenced by the inability of most animals to synthesize C18:1, C18:3 and C20:4 from saturated FA of the same chain lengths. Desaturation of C18:0 to C18:1 and of C16:0 to C16:1 occurs at the 9, 10 position and subsequently moves 3 carbons toward the carboxyl end of the chain after elongation of the chain by 2 carbons at the carboxyl end. The mechanisms of desaturation of fatty acids in animal tissues are incompletely understood.

Triglyceride Biosynthesis

Synthesis occurs by fatty acid acyl CoA reacting with α-glycerol phosphate to form a phospholipid which is then converted to a diglyceride and thence to a triacylglycerol (triglyceride), or by fatty acyl CoA reacting with a monoglyceride to form a diglyceride and thence a triglyceride. The details of triglyceride biosynthesis are illustrated in Fig. 9.5.

Triglyceride Catabolism

Adipose tissue, composed primarily of triacylglycerol (triglyceride), is in a dynamic state with triglycerides undergoing continuous synthesis and degradation (lipolysis). The lipolytic process is under endocrine control. Initiation of the process is controlled by formation of a complex between the hormone and its

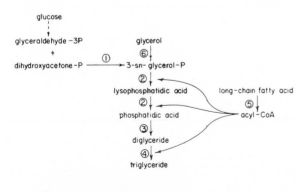

①   α-glycerolphosphate dehydrogenase
②   glycerolphosphate acyltransferase
③   phosphatidate phosphohydrolase
④   diglyceride acyltransferase
⑤   acyl-CoA synthase
⑥   glycerol kinase

Figure 9.5 *Triglyceride biosynthesis. Note the enzymes involved at various stages. From Mersmann, 1986.*

receptor located on the adipocyte (fat cell) surface, followed by intracellular generation of cyclic adenine monophosphate (cAMP), and a cascade of other enzymatic steps to yield fatty acids and glycerol. Lipolysis is stimulated by a number of hormones, including epinephrine, synthetic beta adrenergic agonists such as isoproterenol, adrenocorticotropin, and somatotropin (growth hormone). Lipolysis is inhibited in some mammals by receptors on the adipocyte surface called alpha adrenergic receptors. In swine, no such receptors have been demonstrated (12). Inhibition of lipolysis also occurs in the presence of adenosine and in response to prostaglandins and insulin in most species. It appears that each animal species has mechanisms of physiological control of lipolysis which are unique to that species. It seems clear that physiological factors that control net fat accretion in animals involve complex regulatory systems that include lipogenesis as well as lipolysis. The ultimate fat content of the animal body depends on the net balance of these two opposing processes at the cellular and subcellular level.

Fatty Acid Catabolism

Fatty acids released from hydrolysis of triglycerides are transported via the blood to various body tissues to be used as an oxidative energy source. Oxidation occurs in the mitochondria of skeletal muscle, liver, cardiac muscle, adipose tissue, and other tissues to yield CO_2 and ketones as products. Breakdown of long-chain FA proceeds by stepwise removal of two carbons at a time beginning at the carboxyl end (β-oxidation). The process is not exactly the reverse of synthesis, although acetyl CoA is the form in which the C2 fragments are removed. Before oxidation begins, the fatty acid is activated by esterification with CoA to form acyl CoA. At least three different enzymes are involved in oxidation of FA, one specific for short-chain (C2 and C3) and one for long-chain (C12 to C18) fatty acids. These enzymes (dehydrogenases) remove hydrogens and C2 units as acetyl CoA, as illustrated in Fig. 9.6. The acetyl CoA released in oxidation is available for resynthesis of fatty acids, for synthesis of steroids or ketones or for entry into the tricarboxylic acid cycle. The total energy produced by complete degradation of long-chain fatty acids comes partly from the β-oxidation sequence and partly from the oxidation of acetyl CoA in the tricarboxylic acid (TCA) cycle.

Although even-numbered carbon FA are by far the most prevalent in animal tissues, some odd-num-

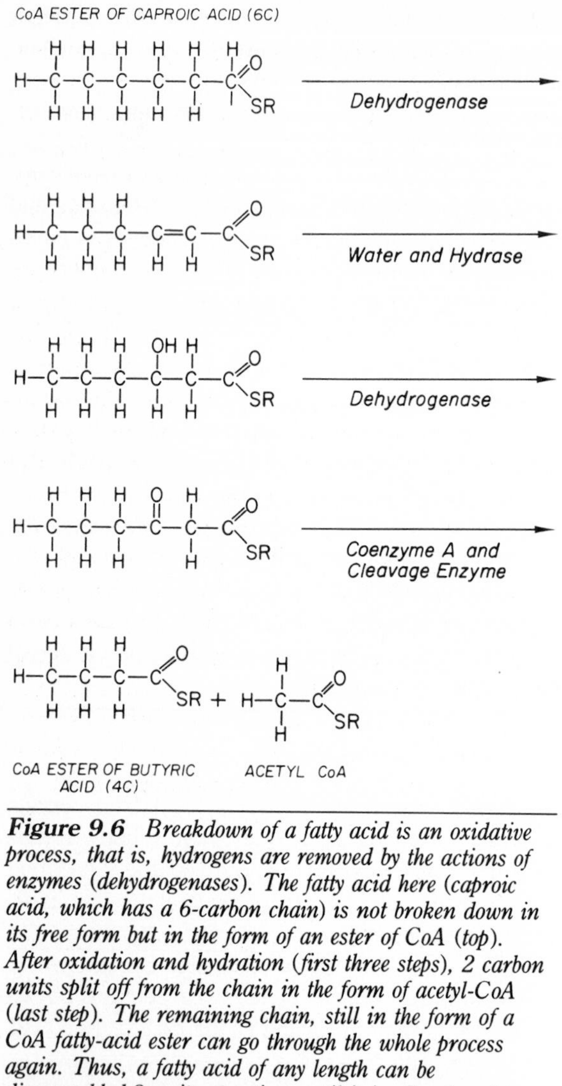

CoA ESTER OF CAPROIC ACID (6C)

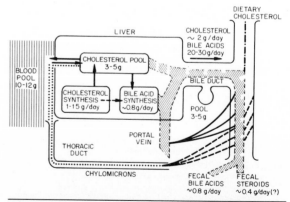

Figure 9.6 *Breakdown of a fatty acid is an oxidative process, that is, hydrogens are removed by the actions of enzymes (dehydrogenases). The fatty acid here (caproic acid, which has a 6-carbon chain) is not broken down in its free form but in the form of an ester of CoA (top). After oxidation and hydration (first three steps), 2 carbon units split off from the chain in the form of acetyl-CoA (last step). The remaining chain, still in the form of a CoA fatty-acid ester can go through the whole process again. Thus, a fatty acid of any length can be disassembled 2 units at a time until it is all reduced to acetyl-CoA or, of an odd-length acid, to propionyl-CoA. Adapted from Green (13).*

5 g and the blood pool is 10–12 g. Daily synthesis is 1–1.5 g, of which about half is converted to bile acids. Secretion of cholesterol and bile acids into the intestinal lumen via the bile duct approximates 2 and 20–30 g/day, respectively, but due to reabsorption by the enterohepatic circulation, less than 1 g of each is lost in the feces. Thus, compounds that reduce absorption of cholesterol and bile acids may have a profound effect on the body pool of cholesterol and on its biosynthesis. One such compound is cholestyramine, a non-absorbable resin which has been used to control hypercholesterolemia (10).

In addition to excretion of cholesterol in the bile and its conversion to bile acids, it can be used for steroid hormone synthesis (progesterone, adrenal cortical hormones, testosterone, and estrogen) or stored as a component of pathologic deposits in bile ducts (gall stones) and in arteries (atherosclerotic plaques). Conjugation of bile acids with taurine or glycine results in the excretion of these conjugated bile acids in the bile as taurocholic and glycocholic acid, respectively.

Phospholipid Metabolism

The most abundant phospholipid in animal tissues is lecithin (phosphatidyl choline). It can be synthesized by two pathways, either by making use of choline directly or by methylation of phosphatidyl ethanolamine. The latter conversion occurs only in the liver, but the former can occur also in other tissues.

Degradation of phospholipids occurs in most mammalian tissues by hydrolysis of carboxyl-esters and phosphate esters. Fatty acids and other metabolites

bered carbon FA are present which are oxidized by a slightly different route.

Steroid Metabolism

Cholesterol is the most abundant steroid in the diet and the precursor of most other animal steroids. Biosynthesis is from acetyl CoA. Regulation of biosynthesis is partly by dietary intake; a high intake depresses synthesis by the liver, and low intake or reduced absorption results in increased synthesis. The turnover of cholesterol in humans is summarized in Fig. 9.7. The liver of adult man contains about 3–

Figure 9.7 *Summary of the turnover of cholesterol in man. From Bergstrom in Ciba Foundation Symposium on the Biosynthesis of Terpenes and Sterols, Little, Brown and Co., 1959.*

released by hydrolysis can enter the tricarboxylic acid cycle. Glycerol can enter the glycolysis pathway or be used in triglyceride or phospholipid synthesis.

Ketones

Formation of ketones (ketogenesis) is a continuous process, but may be excessive in certain disorders described in more detail later. The ketones are acetone, acetoacetic acid, and β-hydroxybutyric acid. The ketones are removed rapidly from the blood by skeletal muscle and other peripheral tissues and provide a substantial supply of energy for use by these tissues. Their synthesis originates with acetyl CoA:

Acetyl CoA $\longrightarrow$ Acetoacetyl CoA

Acetoacetic acid $\begin{array}{l}\nearrow \text{Acetone} \\ \searrow \text{β-hydroxybutyric acid}\end{array}$

❏ EFFECTS OF FREQUENCY OF FEEDING ON METABOLISM

It has been assumed generally that the composition of the diet and the level of dietary intake were the two factors responsible for controlling body composition and metabolism of energy. Now it is clear that the distribution of intake during a fixed period of time has an important effect on lipogenesis and body composition in some species. Such terms as meal eater vs. nibbler, single feeder vs. multiple feeder, and others have been used to describe the phenomenon of feeding frequency. Bodies of meal-eating rats (those trained to consume the entire 24-h ration in 2 h) contain more fat and less protein and water than nibblers. Leveille (15) found that adipose tissue accounted for only 50–90% of total fatty acids synthesized in nibbling rats, but at least 95% in meal-

fed rats. Meal-eating alters activities of enzymes involved in both carbohydrate and fat metabolism. Metabolic adaptations developed in the rat by meal-eating persist for several weeks after feed is provided ad libitum. Meal-fed chickens have been shown to have elevated plasma cholesterol and much higher incidence of atherosclerosis than ad libitum-fed chickens (both groups on a high-cholesterol diet), even though daily feed intake was less in meal-fed chickens. Livers of meal-fed chickens incorporate more acetate into fatty acids than those of controls, and apparently are similar to the rat in their response to feeding frequency. In the pig, meal-eating also appears to influence weight gain and efficiency of feed utilization, but longer time of fasting (one 2-h feeding every 48 h) is needed than in the rat or bird to achieve increased adipose tissue lipogenesis associated with a longer post-absorptive state. The rise in malic enzyme, plasma FFA, increased FA synthesis, and oxidation are illustrated in Table 9.6. The capacity of the GI tract also increases in meal-fed as compared with nibbling animals. Ruminants, whose rumen provides a reservoir of nutrients for absorption on a comparatively continuous basis, have not been shown to respond to frequency of feeding changes with appreciable changes in body composition.

Cohn (16) suggested, on the basis of data obtained with non-ruminants, that humans should increase frequency of food intake as a means of minimizing obesity, reducing serum lipid and cholesterol levels, and decreasing susceptibility to atherosclerosis and diabetes mellitus. More research with humans is needed to evaluate this suggestion. Although data with humans are limited, other evidence suggests that infrequent meals predispose humans to obesity, increase serum cholesterol, and impair glucose tolerance.

TABLE 9.6 Effect of frequency of feeding on pig adipose tissue enzymes, fatty acid synthesis, and oxidation of plasma free fatty acids. (FFA).[a]

FEEDING PATTERN	MALIC ENZYME[b]	CITRATE CLEAVAGE[b] ENZYME	PLASMA FFA[c]	FA SYNTHESIS	FA OXIDATION[d]
Nibbler	118 + 10	33 + 5	190 + 15	188 + 36	89 + 16
Meal-fed (2 h/24)	106 + 14	39 + 5	296 + 23	218 + 38	106 + 21
Meal-fed (4 h/48)	219 + 15	36 + 4	628 + 94	248 + 26	118 + 18

[a]From Allee et al. (14).
[b]Nanomoles substrates converted to product/min/mg protein. Meq/ℓ.
[c]Nanomoles glucose-5-^{14}C converted to fatty acid/100 mg tissue/2 h.
[d]Nanomoles glucose-5-^{14}C converted to CO_2/100 mg tissue/2 h.

Long-term fasting results first in depletion of liver and muscle glycogen and then oxidation of tissue lipids to meet energy requirements. Increased lipogenesis occurs in liver and less so in adipose tissue after refeeding of fasted animals. The rates of fatty acid and cholesterol synthesis are affected by prefasting diet (high fat diets inhibit the increase in lipogenesis), prefasting body weight (restricted-fed animals have greater fatty acid incorporation into depot fats than controls, but less turnover of cholesterol) and post-fasting diet (high fat diets inhibit lipogenesis).

❏ OBESITY IN HUMANS AND ANIMALS AS RELATED TO LIPID METABOLISM

Mounting evidence shows that obesity has a strong genetic basis involving differences between lean and obese individuals in activities of tissue enzymes associated with lipid synthesis and oxidation. Fat cells (adipocytes) from genetically obese rats convert more pyruvate or glucose to glyceride-glycerol than those from rats made obese by hypothalamic lesions which cause excessive feed intake. Adipose tissue enzymes associated with lipogenesis are higher in obese than in lean strains of swine, and adipose tissue lipolysis in response to administration of epinephrine is less in obese than in lean swine. Gluconeogenic enzymes are higher in obese swine; the enzyme response to fasting and refeeding is greater in the lean pig. The net deposition of fat in the body is a balance between lipogenesis and lipolysis processes that occur simultaneously at varying rates. The degree of saturation of body fat varies among and within animal species. Ruminants tend to have more highly saturated fat than nonruminents and the body fat composition of ruminants is less responsive to diet. Pigs vary in degree of saturation of body fat according to genetic background via unknown mechanisms, possibly associated with their selection for altered lipid metabolism or for degree of obesity. Obese pigs tend to have more highly saturated body fat than do lean pigs.

Lipid deposition in the body is related both to number of adipose cells and to their individual size. There is a close spatial and temporal relationship between formation of adipocytes and the blood vessel formation required to supply nutrients to the adipocyte; it seems reasonable to assume that blood vessels would precede the formation of adipocytes at a particular site. The histologic origin of the adipocyte still is uncertain, but now it appears that preadipocytes (cells that ultimately accumulate lipids to become adipocytes) can proliferate postnatally, even during adulthood. This postnatal increase in adipocyte number probably varies among species. In swine, there is a different distribution of small and large adipocytes in obese and lean swine; obese swine

TABLE 9.7 Types of familial hyperlipidemia.

| TYPE | CHARACTER OF LIPOPROTEIN ELEVATION | LEVEL OF PLASMA | | APPEARANCE OF PLASMA |
		CHOLESTEROL	TRIGLYCERIDES	
I	Chylomicrons very high	normal to moderately high	very high	cream layer at top, clear below
IIA	LDL very high	very high	normal	clear, often with yellow-orange tint
IIB	LDL very high VLDL moderately high	very high	moderately	moderately turbid
III	VLDL and LDL of abnormal composition	very high	very high	turbid to opaque
IV	VLDL very high	normal to moderately high	high to very high	turbid to opaque
V	Chylomicrons high VLDL very high	moderately high	very high	"cream layer" at top, turbid to opaque below

have more small adipocytes (20 to 30 microns diameter) than lean swine, although maximum cell diameter is greater in obese (190 microns) than in lean (140 microns) swine. The appearance of biphasic distribution of cell diameter both in lean and obese swine one-year old has been interpreted as evidence that adipocyte hyperplasia continues into adulthood in swine.

Body fat deposition in humans and animals clearly is a dynamic phenomenon, encompassing both anatomic (adipocyte size and number) and biochemical (lipogenesis and lipolysis) variables. The role of nutrition in affecting adipocyte size and number and in controlling lipid synthesis and oxidation is not understood fully. Nutritionists must be aware of and concerned about the importance of obesity in health and must continue to identify interactions between genetics and nutrition with respect to body composition and metabolism.

❏ EFFECT OF DIETARY CARBOHYDRATE SOURCE ON LIPID METABOLISM

Considerable recent interest has focused on the effects of dietary carbohydrate on lipid metabolism, especially since reports linking high sucrose intake with atherosclerosis. Epidemiological studies with humans implicating such a relationship stimulated research activity in this area. Plasma triglyceride and cholesterol tend to be elevated in animals fed high levels of sucrose, and these plasma components have been implicated in human atherosclerosis. The effect of sucrose is assumed to be related to the metabolism of the fructose moiety, but no proof exists for that. It does seem clear that refined glucose or starch does not induce increased plasma triglycerides. Much more research is needed before the exact role of dietary carbohydrate source on lipid metabolism is understood.

❏ ABNORMALITIES IN METABOLISM OF LIPIDS

Abnormal metabolism of lipids may occur in animals and humans as a result of genetic factors or in response to alterations in environment, including diet. Persons whose genetic makeup results in high levels of lipoproteins circulating in the blood (familial hyperlipoproteinemia) have been categorized according to the type of lipoprotein patterns associated with their high blood-lipid levels. Table 9.7 shows the types of familial hyperlipidemia that have been identified, the character of the lipoprotein elevation, the degree of elevation of plasma cholesterol and triglycerides, and the appearance of the blood plasma.

Patients with homozygous familial Type II hypercholesterolemia have 6 to 8 times the level of cholesterol in their blood and always develop heart disease, often by 20 years of age. Those who are heterozygous (carry one normal gene along with the one for hypercholesterolemia) also have predictable heart disease problems, but their cholesterol levels are only 2 to 3 times higher than normal. Although such people number only about 1 in 500 in the total population, they have about 5% of all heart attacks among people under 60 years of age. Such patients lack cell surface receptors for LDL in the liver, a defect that blocks removal of these lipoproteins from the blood. These patients not only cannot remove LDL from blood efficiently, they produce more LDL than normal. LDL's are released from the liver in the form of VLDL, which carries triglycerides as well as some cholesterol. The VLDL are carried to body fat tissues that remove the triglycerides. In the normal liver, the LDL receptors bind the VLDL remnants and degrade them. A small fraction escapes this degradation and is converted to LDL. In the Type II hypercholesterolemia patient, the VLDL remnants cannot be removed from the plasma and are converted to LDL, accounting for the abnormally high levels of this lipoprotein in the blood of these patients. Thus, a double burden plagues the person with this LDL receptor genetic defect: LDL is oversynthesized from VLDL remnants and the LDL produced cannot be removed from the plasma. The use of drugs such as cholestyramine to lower blood cholesterol in Type II patients acts by reducing cholesterol absorption from the intestine, thus depriving the liver of this source of cholesterol.

Fatty Livers

Because the liver is a key organ in metabolism, it is not surprising that factors affecting liver function have far-reaching effects on the overall well-being of the animal. A common manifestation of abnormal liver function is accumulation of lipids in the liver. Normally, fat constitutes about 5% of the wet weight of the liver, but the value may be 30% or more in pathologic conditions. Fatty liver may arise from: high fat or high cholesterol diet; increased liver lipogenesis due to excessive carbohydrate intake or excessive intake of certain B-vitamins (biotin, riboflavin, thiamin); increased mobilization of lipids from adipose tissue due to diabetes mellitus, starvation, hypoglycemia, increased hormone output (growth hormone, adrenal corticotrophic hormone, adrenal corticosteroids); decreased transport of lipids from liver to other tissues due to deficiencies of choline, pantothenic acid, inositol, protein, or certain amino acids (methionine, threonine); cellular damage to the liver (cirrhosis, necrosis) because of infections, vitamin E-Se deficiency, or liver poisons such as chloroform and carbon tetrachloride.

Atherosclerosis

This is the name used to describe a disease characterized by progressive degenerative changes occurring in the blood vessels and heart of humans and animals, and that ultimately is responsible for more deaths among humans in the USA than any other single cause. More than half (54%) of all deaths in the USA result from cardiovascular disease and about two-thirds of these are due to atherosclerotic heart disease and one-eighth to cerebral accidents (strokes) resulting from atherosclerosis. Among the factors responsible for development of atherosclerosis, nutrition has received perhaps the most attention. The observation that serum cholesterol concentration seems to be correlated with incidence of atherosclerosis has led to numerous studies of the influence of diet on serum cholesterol. The cholesterol of blood is transported in association with other lipids and with proteins. Each species of animals has its own peculiar serum lipoprotein composition, but the profile for normal humans provides a useful guide. β-lipoproteins are highest in cholesterol, and it is this fraction that is elevated in atherosclerosis (Table 9.4).

The effect of saturated animal fats (such as butter, tallow, lard) and eggs (high in cholesterol) on serum cholesterol of man has received much attention and publicity. Saturated fats tend to raise serum cholesterol and, of course, consumption of products high in cholesterol such as eggs add to the body burden of cholesterol in addition to that synthesized by liver. Despite the wide public attention to animal products as possible culprits in contributing to the prevalence of atherosclerosis in humans, scientists still disagree as to their role. Some consider elevated serum triglycerides as a possible factor in the atherosclerotic process (dietary sucrose elevates serum triglycerides), but others believe other nutritional and met-

abolic factors are important. A series of genetic lipoprotein disorders associated with early development of atherosclerosis was described earlier in this chapter. The five genetically determined causes of hyperlipidemia in humans (hypercholesterolemia and/or elevated triglycerides) require dietary modifications to give partial control. Individuals affected with any of these types of hyperlipidemia are treated by changing the dietary polyunsaturated to saturated fatty acid ratio to 2:1. Saturated fat should not exceed 10% and total fat 35% of total diet calories. Such drastic dietary changes as these have not been recommended for the general population whose mean fasting plasma cholesterol in adults is about 215 mg per deciliter compared with >300 mg per deciliter in most cases of familial hyperlipidemia.

The National Heart and Lung Institute Task Force on Atherosclerosis has identified the following factors as increasing the risk from coronary heart disease: age; male sex; elevated serum lipids (hypercholesterolemia, hyperlipidemia); hypertension; cigarette smoking; impaired glucose tolerance (diabetes mellitus); and obesity. In addition, psychological stress and heredity are often mentioned as possible contributing factors.

Considerably more research is needed to clarify the role of diet in cardiovascular disease and, although the ultimate work must be done in humans, experimental animal models provide much useful data. The pig is a superior model because the morphology and biochemistry of the atherosclerotic lesion resembles that observed in humans, and severe lesions can be inducd by diet. There is a close resemblance of swine and human serum lipoprotein fractions (8). The hypercholesterolemia induced in swine by feeding a high cholesterol diet is distinguished by an increase in low density lipoprotein concentration. Current evidence indicates that low density lipoproteinemia is associated with increased atherogenesis in humans while an increase in high density lipoproteins in the serum (associated with increased physical exercise) may be protective. The Food and Agriculture Organization (FAO) of the United Nations has recommended for population groups with a high incidence of atherosclerosis, obesity and maturity-onset diabetes that for body weight maintenance the diet should contain 10 to 15% of the energy from protein and 30 to 35% of the energy from fat, and that the fat should have a linoleic acid content amounting to at least one-third of the total fatty acids. The diet should provide less than 300 mg of cholesterol daily. The total role of diet and other environ-

TABLE 9.8 Lipid composition of selected foods (mg/100 grams).

FOOD	CHOLES-TEROL	TOTAL FAT	FATTY ACIDS					
			SATURATED	MONO-SATURATED	POLYUN-SATURATED	18:3	20:5	22:6
Beef steak, choice grade	71	26.1	11.2	11.7	1.0	.3	—	—
Wheat, hard red winter	0	2.5	.4	.3	1.2	.1	—	—
Cheese, cheddar	105	33.1	21.1	9.0	0.9	0.4	—	—
Soybean oil	0	100.0	14.4	23.3	57.9	6.8	—	—
Chicken, skin only	109	32.4	9.1	13.5	6.8	0.3	—	—
Tallow	102	100.0	47.3	40.6	7.8	2.3	—	—
Pork leaf fat	110	94.2	45.2	37.2	7.3	0.9	—	—
Wheat germ oil	0	100.0	18.8	15.1	61.7	6.9	—	—
Avocados	0	17.3	2.6	11.2	2.0	0.1	—	—
Raspberries	0	.4	trace	trace	0.3	0.1	—	—
Lamb Loin	71	27.4	12.8	11.2	1.6	0.5	—	—
Beans	0	1.5	0.2	0.1	0.9	0.6	—	—
Peas	0	2.4	0.4	0.1	0.4	0.2	—	—
Walnuts, black	0	56.6	3.6	12.7	37.5	3.3	—	—
Pork, ham	74	20.8	7.5	9.7	2.2	0.2	—	—
Chicken, dark w/o skin	80	4.3	1.1	1.3	1.0	trace	—	—
Chicken, white w/o skin	58	1.7	0.4	0.4	0.4	trace	—	—
Broccoli	0	0.4	trace	trace	0.2	0.1	—	—
Herring, Pacific	77	13.9	3.3	6.9	2.4	0.1	1.0	0.7
Herring, Atlantic	60	9.0	2.0	3.7	2.1	0.1	0.7	0.9
Perch, white	80	2.5	0.6	0.9	0.7	0.1	0.2	0.1
Pike, walleye	86	1.2	0.2	0.3	0.4	trace	0.1	0.2
Salmon chum	74	6.6	1.5	2.9	1.5	0.1	0.4	0.6
Smelt, rainbow	70	2.6	0.5	0.7	0.9	0.1	0.3	0.4
Smelt, sweet	25	4.6	1.6	1.2	1.0	0.3	0.2	0.1
Snapper, red	—	1.2	0.2	0.2	0.4	trace	trace	0.2
Sunfish	67	0.7	0.1	0.1	0.2	trace	trace	0.1
Swordfish	39	2.1	0.6	0.8	0.2	—	0.1	0.1
Trout, brook	68	2.7	0.7	0.8	0.9	0.2	0.2	0.2
Trout, lake	48	9.7	1.7	3.6	3.4	0.4	0.5	1.1
Trout, rainbow	57	3.4	0.6	1.0	1.2	0.1	0.1	0.4
Tuna, bluefin	38	6.6	1.7	2.2	2.0	—	0.4	1.2
Whitefish, lake	60	6.0	0.9	2.0	2.2	0.2	0.3	1.0
Crab, blue	78	1.3	0.2	2.2	0.5	trace	0.2	0.2
Crayfish	158	1.4	0.3	0.4	0.3	trace	0.1	trace
Lobster, northern	95	0.9	0.2	0.2	0.2	—	0.1	0.1
Shrimp, Atlantic white	182	1.5	0.2	0.2	0.6	trace	0.2	0.2
Shrimp, Atlantic brown	142	1.5	0.3	0.3	0.5	trace	0.2	0.1
Oyster, eastern	47	2.5	0.6	0.2	0.7	trace	0.2	0.2
Scallop, unspecified	45	0.8	0.1	0.1	0.3	trace	0.1	0.1

mental factors, compared with genetic factors, in the development of cardiovascular disease (atherosclerosis) in humans and animals is incompletely understood, but such knowledge is of great concern to animal and human nutritionists in charting the course of future efforts in altering the chemical composition of animal products for optimum use by humans (19).

During the period 1950 through 1987, the proportion of animal fat has decreased and that of plant oils (high in PUFA) has increased in the food consumed by the US population. The effects of this shift on health and longevity remain to be seen, although deaths due to cardiovascular disease have declined steadily since the 1960s. The total lipid and cholesterol content and saturated and unsaturated fatty acid content of a variety of animal and plant products are listed in Table 9.8. Current typical diets in the USA contain 40% of the calorie intake from fat, of which saturated fatty acid contributes more than one-half of the calories. Average cholesterol intake is about 450 to 500 mg daily. One can get an estimate of the relative amounts of saturated and polyunsaturated fatty acids in the diet by expressing the values as a ratio of one to the other. The average American diet has a P/S (polyunsaturated to saturated) ratio of about 0.5/1.0. Most clinical studies show significant reductions in plasma cholesterol when this ratio is changed to 1.0/1.0 or greater by increasing the amount of plant oils such as soybean and corn oil and decreasing animal fat. These decreases in cholesterol are observed even when total calories from fat remain at 40% of the diet, but even greater decreases are obtained in most individuals by reducing the amount of fat as well as the proportion of saturated fat in the diet. The Council of Agricultural Science and Technology, in a more conservative stance, concluded that, except for the obese, there is limited evidence that dietary changes will have an important effect on the incidence of coronary heart disease.

Recent evidence shows an apparent special protective effect of fish oils against the atherogenic process. The unique fatty acids in fish oils that set them apart from other fats containing high amounts of polyunsaturated fatty acids are the so-called omega-3 fatty acids, consisting of linolenic acid (C18:3), eicosapentaenoic acid (EPA) (20 Carbons, 5 double bonds), and docosahexaenoic acid (DHA) (22 Carbons, 6 double bonds).

These acids contribute to the "fishy odor" of most seafish. At least one role of these omega-3 acids appears to be to increase the clotting time of blood. Marine fish have a higher content of omega-3 fatty acid than freshwater fish. The content varies with species, season of the year, water temperature, and the food eaten by the fish.

❑ SUMMARY

Lipids are organic compounds containing C, H, and O, but differ from carbohydrates in being insoluble in water. They serve important biochemical and physiological functions in plant and animal tissues. Simple lipids are esters of fatty acids with alcohols; compound lipids are esters of fatty acids containing groups in addition to an alcohol and fatty acid. Compound lipids include phospholipids (lipids containing phosphoric acid and N), glycolipids (lipids containing carbohydrates and often N) and lipoproteins (lipids bound to proteins). The most important lipid constituents in nutrition include fatty acids, glycerol, mono-, di-, and triglycerides and phospholipids. Fatty acids consist of chains of carbon atoms (2 to 24 or more carbons) and are characterized by a carboxyl group on one end of the carbon chain. Most fatty acids in animal tissues are straight chained and have an even number of carbons and are esterified to glycerol to form triglycerides. The fatty acid composition of triglycerides in tissues of non-ruminant animals resembles that of the dietary fat; that in tissues of ruminants is less variable and contains mostly saturated fatty acids owing to the action of rumen microflora. Degree of softness of triglycerides depends on number of double bonds (degree of unsaturation) of the constituent fatty acids and on chain length. Simple triglycerides of saturated fatty acids containing 10 or more carbons are solid at room temperature, those with less are usually liquid; triglycerides containing a preponderance of unsaturated fatty acids (linoleic, 18 carbons, 2 double bonds; linolenic, 18 carbons, 3 double bonds; arachidonic, 20 carbons, 4 double bonds) are liquids.

The functions of lipids are to supply energy for normal maintenance and production (one gram of fat yields about 9.45 Kcal of heat compared with about 4.1 Kcal for carbohydrate), to serve as a source of essential fatty acids (linoleic, linolenic) and to serve as a carrier of the fat-soluble vitamins. The exact mechanisms by which essential acids act in maintaining normal body functions probably include their presence in the lipid-protein structure of cell membranes and in prostaglandins.

Absorption of lipids from the gastrointestinal tract depends on emulsification and formation of micelles containing bile salts, phospholipids, and other lipids that render the lipid ready for absorption as hydrolysis proceeds by lipases elaborated into the intestinal lumen by the host animal. Absorption of long-chain fatty acids occurs mainly via the lymphatic system while short-chain fatty acids may enter the portal vein. There is a large increase in lipid concentration of the blood (lipemia) following a meal; absorbed lipids are carried in the blood as chylomicrons. Lipids mobilized from depot storage sites and those synthesized in body tissues are transported as lipoproteins ranging from very low density to high density. Liver, mammary gland, and adipose tissue are the three major sites of fatty acid biosynthesis from carbohydrates and amino acids. Synthesis progresses from acetyl CoA (2 carbons) to longer chain fatty acids by successive additions of 2-carbon fragments. Fatty acid catabolism proceeds by stepwise removal of two carbons at a time. Steroids such as cholesterol are synthesized from acetyl CoA. Synthesis is partially controlled by dietary intake of cholesterol; a high intake depresses liver synthesis.

Animals in positive energy balance are depositing energy largely as depot fat triglycerides (glycogen storage also occurs, but in much smaller amounts). Evidence indicates that obesity has a strong genetic basis. Lipid deposition is related both to number and size of individual adipose cells and is clearly a dynamic phenomenon, encompassing both anatomic (cell size and number) and biochemical (lipogenesis and lipolysis) variables.

Abnormalities in lipid metabolism may result in liver fat accumulation, due to high fat or high cholesterol intake, to increased mobilization of depot fat as in diabetes mellitus, starvation or increased output of hormones (growth hormone, adrenal corticosteroids), or to decreased transport of lipids from the liver as in deficiencies of choline, pantothenic acid, or protein. Atherosclerosis, in humans and animals, is associated with elevated blood levels of low-density lipoprotein cholesterol. The role of diet in atherosclerosis is still unclear, although some evidence indicates a protective effect of reduced intake of total fat, cholesterol and saturated fatty acids.

❏ REFERENCES

1. Babatunde, G. M., et al. 1967. *J. Nutr.* **92**:293.
2. Holman, R. T. 1960. *J. Nutr.* **70**:405.
3. Kass, M. L., W. G. Pond, and E. F. Walker, Jr. 1975. *J. Animal Sci.* **41**:804.
4. Allen, R. S. 1977. In *Duke's Physiology of Domestic Animals,* 9th ed., M. J. Swenson (ed.). Cornell Univ. Press, Ithaca, N.Y.
5. Masoro, E. J. 1968. *The Physiological Chemistry of Lipids in Mammals.* W. B. Saunders Co., Philadelphia; PA.
6. Schaefer, E. J. and R. I. Levy. 1985. *New Eng. J. Med.* **312**:1300.
7. Ogilvie, B. M., G. L. McClymont, and F. B. Shorland. 1961. *Nature* **190**:725.
8. O'Hea, E. K. and G. A. Leveille. 1969. *J. Nutr.* **99**:338.
9. Goodridge, A. G. and F. G. Ball. 1967. *Amer. J. Physiol.* **213**:245.
10. Ballard, F. J., R. W. Hanson, and D. S. Kronfeld. 1969. *Fed. Proc.* **28**:218.
11. Prior, R. L. and R. A. Scott. 1980. *J. Nutr.* **110**:2011.
12. Mersmann, H. J. 1986. Lipid Metabolism in Swine. In *Swine in Cardiovascular Research.* CRC Press, Boca Raton, Fl., pp. 76–97.
13. Green, D. E. 1960 *Sci. Amer.,* Feb.
14. Allee, G. L., D. R. Romsos, G. A. Leveille, and D. H. Baker. 1972. *J. Nutr.* **102**:1115.
15. Leveille, G. A. 1972. *Nutr. Rev.* **30**:151.
16. Cohn, C. 1964. *Fed. Proc.* **23**:76.
17. Scott, R. A., S. G. Cornelius, and H. J. Mersmann. 1981. *J. Animal Sci.* **53**:977.
18. Chapman, M. J. and S. Goldstein. 1976. *Atherosclerosis* **24**:141.
19. Davenport, H. W. 1982. *Physiology of the Digestive Tract,* 5th ed. Yearbook Medical Publishers, Inc., Chicago, IL., p. 220.

10

Energy Metabolism

$\mathbf{T}$HE TOPIC OF ENERGY and its metabolism is known as bioenergetics. In the overall subject of animal nutrition, it is very important because energy is, quantitatively, the most important item in an animal's diet and all animal feeding standards (Ch. 18) are based on energy needs. As such, an appreciable amount of effort has been expended to study the metabolism of energy by animals. The reader may feel that non-ruminant animals are slighted unduly in this chapter; however, considerably more work, particularly on net energy, has been done on ruminant species than on non-ruminant species. Very little information is available on wild species. Those readers interested in more detail than is presented here are referred to Brody (1), Kleiber (2), Mitchell (3), and Blaxter (4). These books are outdated in some respects, but comprehensive texts on this topic otherwise are not available. Other sources of interest include NRC (5) and ARC (6) publications.

With all other nutrients, modern laboratory procedures allow us to fractionate feedstuffs, animal tissues and so forth into their component parts, and we can isolate proteins, lipids, different minerals, and vitamins, which we can weigh, see, smell, or taste. However, study of energy metabolism requires a different approach because energy may be derived from most organic compounds ingested by an animal. The animal derives energy by partial or complete oxidation of organic molecules ingested and absorbed from the

141

diet or from metabolism of energy stored in the form of fat or protein and to a slight extent from carbohydrates.

The mechanisms by which biological organisms cope with energy transfer and oxidation are outside the scope of this chapter. Biochemists have, in general, defined the different compounds and enzyme systems that accomplish these reactions (see Ch. 8). Energy transfer from one chemical reaction to another occurs primarily by means of high energy bonds found in compounds such as ATP (adenosine triphosphate) and other related compounds. It is sufficient for our purposes here to say that all animal functions and biochemical processes require a source of energy to drive the various processes to completion. This applies to all life processes and animal activity such as chewing, digestion,

maintenance of body temperature, liver metabolism of glucose, absorption from the GI tract, storage of glycogen or fat, or protein synthesis.

In normal body metabolism there is a tremendous transfer of energy from one type to another. For example, from chemical to heat (oxidation of fat, glucose, or amino acids); from chemical to mechanical (any muscular activity), or from chemical to electrical (glucose oxidation to electrical activity of the brain). Based on biochemical laboratory data, the energy cost of many of these reactions can be estimated with reasonable precision, but other animal functions such as excretion and digestion have an energy input from so many different tissues and chemical reactions that it is difficult to evaluate their cost to the animal.

❑ ENERGY TERMINOLOGY

Energy may be defined as the potential to perform work where work is the product of a given force acting through a given distance. However, a broad definition such as this is not applicable directly to animals because we usually are more concerned with the utilization of chemical energy. Chemical energy may be measured in terms of heat and expressed as calories (or BTU's), although, according to physicists, the joule is a more precise means of expression. In international usage a calorie (cal) is the amount of heat required to raise the temperature of 1 g of water from 14.5° to 15.5°C and is equivalent to 4.1855 joules. A kilocalorie (Kcal) is equal to 1,000 cal and a megacalorie (Mcal), or therm, is equal to 1,000 Kcal or 10^6 cal. The joule has been adopted as the standard unit of measurement by several European countries, but the unit of measurement really is of no consequence.

    The manner in which energy is partitioned into various fractions in terms of animal utilization is

shown schematically in Fig. 10.1. Detailed discussion on each of these fractions follows.

Gross Energy (GE)

Gross energy (GE) is the quantity of heat resulting from the complete oxidation of food, feed, or other substances. The term, "heat of combustion," which is used in chemical terminology, means the same thing. GE is measured in an apparatus called an oxygen bomb calorimeter (see Fig. 3.4). GE values often are obtained on feedstuffs or diets in the process of arriving at energy utilization. Energy values of different feedstuffs or nutrients vary, but typical values are (Kcal/g): carbohydrates, 4.10; proteins, 5.65; and fats, 9.45. The differences between these nutrients primarily reflect the state of oxidation of the initial compound. The chemical energy varies inversely with the C:H ratio and the O and N content. For example, a typical monosaccharide such as glucose has an empirical formula of $C_6H_{12}O_6$, or one atom of oxygen/atom of C; whereas in a fat molecule

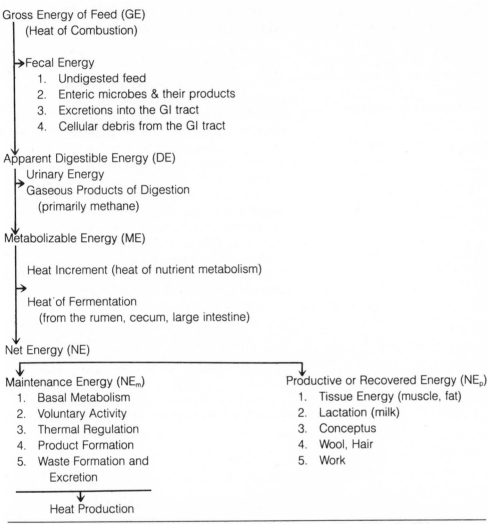

Figure 10.1 *Schematic diagram of energy utilization by animals. The reader should be aware that some publications (5, 6) have chosen to use different abbreviations and some added terminology. Those used in this figure have been in use many years and, thus, the authors see no reason to change. Losses of energy by way of the feces, urine, and gaseous products cannot be utilized or recovered by the animal (unless it practices coprophagy). Heat produced in the animal body—such as those items listed under ME or NE maintenance—can be useful in maintaining a stable body temperature unless the animal is in a heat-stressing situation. Recovered energy may range from almost nil, (hair, wool) to more than 30% of GE for high-producing dairy cows.*

such as tristearin, there are 6 atoms of O and 57 atoms of C; thus the fat requires more oxygen for oxidation and gives off more heat in the process.

Examples of GE values of some selected tissues, nutrients or compounds are shown in Table 10.1. Note, for example, that a poor quality feed such as oat straw has the same GE value as corn grain, which is an excellent source of energy for animals. This comparison clearly points out the fact that GE values,

by themselves, are of little practical value in evaluating feeds for animal usage because animals cannot digest some feed components, especially fibrous types, as completely as the heat of combustion might indicate. Of course, increases in fat or protein will result in higher energy values and an increase in ash will reduce the values. In human nutrition, GE is used to report caloric values of food. This is somewhat more reasonable than for domestic animals be-

TABLE 10.1   Gross energy values (dry basis) of various tissues, nutrients or feedstuffs.

ITEM	GE, KCAL/G
Carbohydrates	
Glucose	3.74
Sucrose	3.94
Starch	4.18
Cellulose	4.18
Glycerol	4.31
Fats, fatty acids	
Average fat	9.45
Butterfat	9.1
Beef fat (ash-free)	9.4
Corn oil	9.4
Coconut oil	8.9
Acetic acid	3.49
Propionic acid	4.96
Butyric acid	5.95
Palmitic acid	9.35
Stearic acid	9.53
Oleic acid	9.50
Nitrogenous compounds	
Average protein source	5.65
Beef muscle (ash-free)	5.3
Casein	5.9
Egg albumin	5.7
Gluten	6.0
Alanine	4.35
Glycine	3.11
Tyrosine	5.91
Urea	2.52
Uric acid	2.74
Ethyl alcohol	7.11
Methane	13.3
Feeds	
Corn grain	4.4
Wheat bran	4.5
Grass hay	4.5
Oat straw	4.5
Soybean meal	5.5
Linseed oil meal	5.1

cause humans do not eat the quantities of indigestible material that most lower animals do.

Digestible Energy (DE)

The GE of food consumed minus fecal energy is called apparent DE. In practice the GE intake of an animal is carefully measured over a period of time accompanied by collection of fecal excretion for a representative period. Both feed and feces are analyzed for energy content and this, then, allows for calculation of DE. It might be noted (see Fig. 10.2) that energy lost in the feces accounts for the *single largest loss* of ingested nutrients. Depending upon the species of animal and the diet, fecal losses may range from 10% or less in milk-fed animals to 60% or more in animals consuming poor quality roughage.

Apparent DE is not a true measure of the digestibility of a given diet or nutrient because the GI tract of an animal is an active site for excretion of various products that end up in feces, and because there may be considerable sloughing of cellular debris from cells lining the GI tract. In addition, undigested microbes and their metabolic by-products may constitute a large portion of the feces of some species. Although some of these microbes might be digestible if passed through the stomach and small intestines, much of the growth occurs in the cecum and large intestine

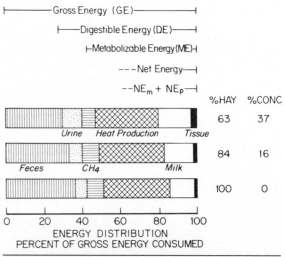

Figure 10.2   A graphic illustration of energy terminology and the different systems of expressing energy value of feeds. The bar chart shows relative energy losses when a mixed diet is fed to a lactating dairy cow. Reproduced by permission of P. W. Moe, USDA, ARS, Beltsville, MD.

where there are no enteric enzymes and where much less absorption occurs than in the small intestine. Only in the case of fibrous plant components such as cellulose and xylan, which are foreign to the animal body, are values a measure of true digestibility.

True digestible energy is determined by measuring, in addition, the energy in fecal excretions (metabolic fecal energy) of an animal that is fasting or being fed a diet presumed to be completely absorbed, such as milk or eggs (refer to Ch. 5), or in some cases, where the animal is fed intravenously. This amount is then subtracted from total fecal excretion of the fed animal. This determination is not feasible with most herbivorous species and is done only in practice with poultry.

Note also (Fig. 10.1) that some heat production occurs in conjunction with fecal production. It is not measured when determining fecal energy but would include items 4 and 5 listed under Maintenance Energy.

Total Digestible Nutrients (TDN)

TDN is not shown in the scheme in Fig. 10.1, but it is a measure of energy still used to some extent in diet formulation in the USA for ruminants and swine. TDN is roughly comparable to DE, but is expressed in units of weight or percent. When conversion of TDN to DE is desired, the values used usually are 2,000 Kcal of DE/lb of TDN or 4.4 Kcal/g. TDN is determined by carrying out a digestion trial and summing the digestible protein and carbohydrates (NFE and crude fiber) plus 2.25 times digestible ether extract (crude fat). Fat is multiplied by 2.25 in an attempt to account for its higher caloric value which is about 2.25X that of digestible carbohydrates.

As compared to DE, TDN undervalues protein because protein is not oxidized completely by the body whereas it is in a bomb calorimeter. Multiplication of digestible protein by 1.25 would put TDN on a more comparable basis with DE. The formula for TDN is: TDN = DCP + DNFE + DCF + 2.25(DEE).

Although most nutritionists recognize that TDN or DE tend to overvalue roughages as compared to some version of NE, the popularity of TDN is partially because of the relative ease of obtaining the necessary information and also because of the better understanding of its use by non-professionals. Current NRC publications tend to emphasize other energy values, but it should be pointed out that most of these values for ME or NE were derived from TDN values.

Metabolizable Energy (ME)

ME is defined as the GE of feed minus energy in feces, urine, and gaseous products of digestion. Values so obtained account for further losses as a result of digestion or metabolism of the ingested feed. Losses of combustible gases are negligible and are normally ignored in many monogastric species, although some losses occur as a result of fermentation in the cecum and large gut. ME is used commonly to evaluate feedstuffs for poultry and in establishing feeding standards, because feces and urine are excreted together. Thus, it is convenient to use ME values for these species. An appropriate formula for calculating ME for swine where DE is known is:

$$ME \text{ (in Kcal/kg)} = \frac{DE \text{ (in Kcal/kg)} \times 0.96 - (0.202 \times protein \%)}{100}$$

Methane usually accounts for most of the combustible gases in ruminant species, and may range from 3 to 10% of GE, depending on the nature of the diet and level of feed intake. Low quality diets result in larger proportions of methane and, generally, the percentage of GE lost as methane declines as feed intake increases. Several formulas exist for calculating gaseous energy losses in ruminants. One given by Blaxter and Clapperton (7) is: methane = 1.30 + 0.112D − L (2.37 − 0.050D), where methane is expressed as Kcal/100 Kcal of GE of feed, D = digestibility of energy at a maintenance level of feeding, and L = the level of feeding as a multiple of maintenance. A second formula developed by Swift et al. (8) is: methane = 2.41X + 9.80, where methane is in grams and X represents hundreds of grams of carbohydrate digested. On the average, methane production is about 8% of GE at maintenance and it falls to 6–7% at higher levels of feeding.

Urinary energy losses usually are relatively stable in a given animal species, although they reflect differences in diet, particularly when excess protein is fed or when forages are consumed that may contain essential oils or detoxification products such as hippuric acid. For ruminants a correction factor of 7.45 Kcal/g of N has been used to account for energy excreted from amino acids metabolized, and a factor of 8.22 has been used for poultry. Actual urinary energy losses run on the order of 3% of GE in ruminants, or 12–35 Kcal/g of N excreted.

ME for ruminants often is calculated by the formula: $ME = DE \times 0.82$. Many of the NRC values given for ME of ruminant feeds are so calculated. However, this is only an approximation as the ME/DE ratio may vary considerably, being affected by the nature of the diet and the level of feeding. ME values seldom are determined in practice, unless animals are used in calorimetric studies where apparatus is available to collect respiratory gases. There are very few such installations available. However, it is generally agreed by energy workers that ME is the most descriptive and reproducible measurement of feeds, especially when fed at the maintenance level.

"True" Metabolizable Energy

Sibbald (9) has developed a procedure for estimating the actual ME of diets for poultry. Birds, of course, excrete a mixture of feces and urine, thus simplifying the determination of energy of excreta as compared to other species. In this procedure a chicken (generally a rooster) is fasted for 21 h. The bird then is weighed and either force-fed a weighed amount (20–25 g) of the diet or feedstuff in question or it is fasted. The bird is returned to its cage and droppings for the next 24 h are collected and analyzed for components of interest. This method appears to give an accurate measure of the ME. The formula for calculation is: $ME \text{ (Kcal/g feed)} = (GE \times X) - (Y_{ef} - Y_{ec})/X$, where GE is the gross energy of the feed in Kcal/g, Y_{ef} is the energy voided as excreta by the fed bird, Y_{ec} is the energy voided as excreta by the fasted bird, and X is the weight of feedstuff in grams.

Net Energy (NE)

As indicated in Fig. 10.1, NE is equal to ME minus the heat increment (HI) and the heat of fermentation (HF). Many writers combine the HI and HF as it is very difficult to arrive at precise estimates of each in ruminants or some of the herbivores, such as horses, in which a considerable amount of fermentation may take place in the cecum and large intestine.

The NE of food is that portion which is available to the animal for maintenance or various productive purposes. The portion used for maintenance is used for muscular work, maintenance and repair of tissues, for maintaining a stable body temperature, and

for other body functions; most of it will leave the animal body as heat. That used for productive purposes may be recovered as energy in the tissues or in some product such as milk, or be used to perform work.

The HI (also called specific dynamic effect when referring to a specific nutrient) may be defined as the heat production associated with nutrient digestion and metabolism over and above that produced prior to food ingestion. The resulting heat is produced by oxidative reactions that are (a) not coupled with energy transfer mechanisms (high energy bonds) or (b) the result of incomplete transfer of energy; (c) partly due to heat production resulting from work of excretion by the kidney and (d) increased muscular activity of the GI tract, respiratory, and circulatory systems resulting from nutrient metabolism.

Estimates made many years ago indicate that 80 + % of the HI originates in the viscera. Short-term experiments with animals which have had their livers removed show very little additional heat production after food ingestion, indicating that metabolism in the liver accounts for most of the HI. When individual products are fed to rats or dogs, feeding lean meat results in a prolonged period of heat production that amounts to 30–40% of GE. The HI (dog) from other foodstuffs are: fat, 15%; sucrose, 6%; starch, 20–22%. In cattle, according to Blaxter (4), the HI of a complete diet is about 3% of GE at half maintenance and increases to 20 + % at 2X maintenance and to higher levels in high producing animals (Fig. 10.2). Examples of values for different species are shown in Table 10.2. Note that some of the values in the table are expressed as a percentage of ME rather than GE; using ME increases the percentage values relative to those mentioned above. For example, the values on sheep fed chopped hay and fresh grass (Table 10.2) would be about 24 and 27%, respectively, if expressed on the basis of GE.

It should be pointed out that the HI is not a constant for a given animal and a given foodstuff, but depends on how the nutrient is utilized. For example, if most of the material is absorbed and deposited in the tissues, the HI is very low. Incomplete proteins or amino acid mixtures fed to monogastric species result in oxidation of most of the amino acids and a high HI; a deficiency of an essential nutrient required in metabolic reactions, such as Mg or P, will result in a high HI. Frequent feeding results in a lower HI than infrequent feeding, and an increased feed intake results in a larger HI. The reader should note that

TABLE 10.2 Heat increment of feeding for some dietary components or diets for different species.

| NUTRIENT | SPECIES | | | | |
	RAT	SWINE	SHEEP	CATTLE	RABBIT
ME basis, % at maintenance[a]					
Fat	17	9	29	35	
Carbohydrate	23	17	32	37	
Protein	31	26	54	52	
Mixed rations	31	10–40	35–70	35–70	
ME basis, % ~ 2X maintenance[b]					
Chopped hay			45		
Fresh grass			47		
GE basis, % at 2X maintenance[c]					
Mixed diet				16–19	
Mixed diet					26

[a]Data from Armstrong and Blaxter (10).
[b]Webster (11).
[c]Data from Brody (1).

the HI is not the same as total body heat production (see Fig. 10.2) because the body will produce heat regardless of whether the animal is fasting or fed. With lactating dairy cows, Tyrrell and Moe (12) found that heat production accounted for 35–39% of GE intake.

The HF is, as mentioned, poorly quantified. A non-growing yeast culture comparable in size to that of an adult man has been estimated to produce 100X the heat production of the man. However, Blaxter (4) estimates the HF in ruminant animals to be 5–10% of GE, and Webster (11) has determined that it is about 65 Kcal/Mcal of fermented energy. In monogastric species some HF would originate from fermentation in the lower small intestine, cecum, and large gut, but quantitative information is not available.

Both the HI and HF may serve useful purposes to the animal in a cold environment. The heat resulting from the HI and HF may be used to warm the body just as well as that produced by more controlled metabolism of nutrients (thermogenesis). However, at temperatures that result in heat stress to the animal, the HI is detrimental, requiring additional expenditure of energy to dissipate it by various means. In ruminant species, limited data indicate that feeding of urea in place of protein tends to reduce

heat production, and that heat production is less when minimal amounts of protein are fed. Increasing the fat content of a ration appears to be helpful because fat has a low HI, and reducing the fiber content may also be helpful in hot climates.

NE accounts for more of the losses in metabolism of feed (or by the animal) than other measures described, thus, it should be the method of choice for feed evaluation or establishment of animal requirements. However, because it varies with environmental temperatures outside the comfort zone and because of the limited amount of data on feeds and animals (because of cost and limited facilities), the improvement over DE, TDN, or ME is not as great as would be anticipated.

Other Methods of Measuring Feed Value

A method called Starch Equivalents (SE) is in use in some areas of Europe at the present time, although it has largely been replaced by ME. The SE system was devised in Germany by Kellner many years ago. In effect, energy retention of fattening animals is measured by the C-N balance methods and feed values are expressed in relation to the value of starch, rather than in Kcal as with the NE method.

The Scandinavian Food Unit System is used also

in Europe. With this method, feedstuffs are evaluated in feeding trials by replacing barley with the feed in question, and feed value is expressed relative to barley. There are fodder units, fattening feed units, and milk production units. Thus, this method essentially is the same as the SE method.

❑ METHODS OF MEASURING HEAT PRODUCTION AND ENERGY RETENTION

If one wishes to study the utilization of ME, it is necessary to measure either (a) the animal's heat production or (b) energy retained in the tissues, that used for productive work, or in a product such as milk. If one of these quantities (a or b) is known, then the other can be determined by subtracting the known one from ME. Heat production may be measured in various ways. Some of these methods are discussed briefly. For more detail see the references cited at the beginning of this chapter.

Direct Calorimetry

Animals lose heat from the body by radiation, convection, and conduction from the body surface, by evaporation of water from the skin and lungs, and by excretion of urine and feces. In direct calorimetry the animal is enclosed in a well-insulated chamber that is equipped to measure these heat losses by the use of thermocouples or by circulation of water in pipes in the chamber. Newer types, called gradient-layer calorimeters, measure heat loss electrically as it passes through the wall of the chamber. The HI may be measured by feeding first at a low level and then at a higher level, or by fasting the animal and then feeding. These types of calorimeters are quite expensive to build and to operate and seldom are used where large animals are the main item of interest.

Indirect Calorimetry

In indirect calorimetry, heat production of the animal is estimated by determining O_2 consumption and, usually, CO_2 production. Some of the pioneer work-

TABLE 10.3 Thermal equivalents of oxygen and carbon dioxide and the corresponding percentage of fat and carbohydrates oxidized for different respiratory quotients in mammals.

RQ	O_2, KCAL/L	CO_2 KCAL/L	CO_2 KCAL/G	O_2 CONSUMED (%) BY CARBOHYDRATES	FAT	HEAT PRODUCED (%) BY OXIDATION OF CARBOHYDRATES	FAT
0.70	4.684	6.694	3.408	0	100	0	100
0.72	4.702	6.531	3.325	4.4	95.6	4.8	95.2
0.74	4.727	6.388	3.252	11.3	88.7	12.0	88.0
0.76	4.752	6.253	3.183	18.1	81.9	19.2	80.8
0.78	4.776	6.123	3.117	24.9	65.1	26.3	73.7
0.80	4.801	6.001	3.055	31.7	68.3	33.4	66.6
0.82	4.825	5.884	2.996	38.6	61.4	40.3	59.7
0.84	4.850	5.774	2.939	45.4	54.6	47.2	52.8
0.86	4.875	5.669	2.886	52.2	47.8	54.1	45.9
0.88	4.900	5.568	2.835	59.0	41.0	60.8	39.2
0.90	4.924	5.471	2.785	65.9	34.1	67.5	32.5
0.92	4.948	5.378	2.738	72.7	27.3	74.1	25.9
0.94	4.973	5.290	2.693	79.5	20.5	80.7	19.3
0.96	4.997	5.205	2.650	86.3	13.7	87.2	12.8
0.98	5.022	5.124	2.609	93.2	6.8	93.6	6.4
1.00	5.047	5.047	2.569	100	0	100	0

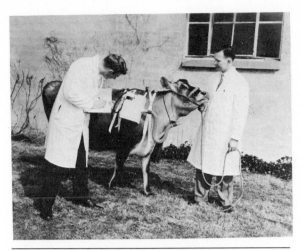

Figure 10.3 *This photograph illustrates the use of portable equipment to measure CO_2 production by a cow with a cannulated trachea. Similar equipment can be used to measure oxygen consumption when a face musk can be used. Courtesy of P. W. Moe, USDA, ARS, Beltsville, MD.*

ers in animal nutrition (see Brody, 1) demonstrated that O_2 consumption and CO_2 production are correlated closely to heat production. It is well known that one mole of glucose requires six moles of O_2 for oxidation, produces six moles of CO_2 and yields 673 Kcal or 5.007 Kcal/l of O_2 used or/l of CO_2 produced. Average values for carbohydrates are 5.047 Kcal/l. With respect to fats, relatively more O_2 is required for oxidation and the caloric equivalent of a mixed fat is 4.69 Kcal/l of O_2 consumed, or 6.6 Kcal/l of CO_2 produced. Similar values for mixed proteins are 4.82 Kcal/l of O_2 and 5.88 Kcal/l of CO_2.

The ratio of the volume of CO_2 produced to the volume of O_2 consumed is known as the **respiratory quotient** (RQ). Thus, typical RQ's for carbohydrate are 1.0; for mixed fats, 0.7; and for mixed protein, 0.81. Note that each specific carbohydrate, fatty acid, or protein may have an RQ distinctive for that particular compound. For example, the RQ of fats with short-chain fatty acids is about 0.8, but that for long-chain fatty acids is about 0.7.

Because animals cannot completely oxidize the N in protein, the RQ usually is corrected by deducting an appropriate amount of energy to account for this. Methane production in the rumen also is a product of incomplete oxidation. A formula adopted by energy workers for heat production is: Heat (Kcal) = 3.866

O_2 + 1.200 CO_2 − 0.518 CH_4 − 1.431 N, where O_2 = l of oxygen consumed; CO_2 = l of carbon dioxide produced; CH_4 = l of methane produced; and N = g of N excreted in the urine. Thus, with information on these various items, we can calculate how much protein was oxidized and estimate what percentage of the total heat was derived from carbohydrate or fat. For example, if we have an RQ of 0.78 that has been corrected for protein, we can look in an appropriate table (Table 10.3) and see that this is equivalent to oxidation by body tissues of 26.3% carbohydrate and 73.7% fat.

As indicated, the RQ usually will be between 0.7 and 1.0. Two exceptions are worthy of note. RQ values in excess of 1.0 may result when carbohydrates are used for the synthesis of body fats, or where excess CO_2 is produced in animals with acidosis (ketosis). The RQ for protein metabolism is different for birds (0.72) and mammals (0.81). This is a reflection of differences in composition of the major end products of excretion (uric acid, urea).

Apparatus for Measuring Respiratory Gases

The most simple means of measuring O_2 consumption is with a face mask and a spirometer, a simple device into which the animal breathes for a short period of time. O_2 consumption is measured in the process. This apparatus has the disadvantage that it only can be used for short periods while an animal is confined. With modifications, spirometers can be used to measure O_2 consumption in active animals, or the same type of information may be obtained in animals with a cannulated trachea as shown in Fig. 10.3.

Most equipment for measuring respiratory gases involves the use of chambers in which the animal is maintained (Fig. 10.4). Provision is made for introducing feed and water and for collection of excreta. There are two types. The closed circuit type is designed so that air and respiratory gases are recirculated through the chamber. However, if the animal is kept in the chamber for more than a few hours, provision must be made to remove vaporized water, CO_2, and CH_4, and O_2 must be added to it. The expense of operation is relatively great. The other type, an open circuit, differs in that outside air is passed through the chamber continuously. This requires that careful measurements be made of the amount of air of known composition going through, and the outgoing air also must be sampled carefully

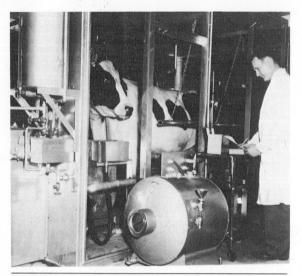

Figure 10.4   *An example of an open circuit respiration chamber used at the USDA Experiment Station at Beltsville, MD. Courtesy of P. W. Moe.*

for analyses for O_2, CO_2, and CH_4. This is the most common type in use with large animals at the present time. Automated sampling and analyzing instrumentation, which may be hooked up to a computer, are available so that collection of data is relatively convenient, although relatively expensive.

❑ OTHER METHODS OF MEASURING ENERGY RETENTION

Comparative Slaughter Technique

An accurate measurement of energy value of feeds requires the measurement of the actual amount of energy retained by the animal or produced as a useful product, or the measurement of all forms of energy loss. In growing and fattening animals the measurement of energy retention has proven to be useful for broilers, cattle, and swine. In work with broilers, the energy value of carcasses of day-old chicks after they are ground and dried is measured by bomb calorimetry. Similar chicks are then fed for a specified period of time and the energy values of their carcasses are then determined. Thus, the amount of energy deposited can be calculated. In the work with cattle (13), body energy retention is measured as the difference in energy of the carcass of groups of animals slaughtered before and after a feeding pe-

riod. In practice, one group is fed at maintenance and the other group at some higher level. Energy retention is estimated based on carcass specific gravity, from which the amount of fat and protein in the tissues may be estimated. This type of procedure, although dependent upon several indirect measures, has merit in that it is measuring energy retention of the animal in a relatively normal environment as opposed to an animal enclosed in a respiration chamber where temperatures usually are in a thermoneutral zone and animals are inhibited from much physical activity.

Carbon-Nitrogen Balance

The principal forms in which energy is stored in the growing and fattening animal are as protein and fat; carbohydrate reserves are very low. If the C and N intake and excretion are known, then deposition in the tissues may be calculated. One must measure the amounts consumed and excreted and CO_2 and CH_4 in respiratory gases. Body protein is assumed to contain 16% N and 51.2% C; thus, the amount of protein storage can be computed when C and N retention are known. The remainder of the C is fat which contains an average of 74.6% C, so the amount of fat storage then is computed. The amount of protein stored is multiplied by 5.32 Kcal/g and fat by 9.37 Kcal/g (for cattle) to give an estimate of caloric storage.

❑ SOME IMPORTANT CONCEPTS IN ENERGY METABOLISM

Heat Production and Body Size

Most mammals and birds are called homeotherms; that is, they maintain a stable body temperature, although minor fluctuations of relatively short duration may occur as a result of extensive chilling, heat stress, fevers, or vigorous exercise. With a constant body temperature, heat production over a period of time is equal to heat loss. In the nutritional physiology of animals, we are concerned with heat production (or loss) if we wish to relate information obtained with calorimetric studies (see later section) to more normal environmental conditions. Calorimetric data are obtained under very specific conditions, and it is not feasible to attempt to duplicate all of the situations—diet, temperature, humidity,

TABLE 10.4 Typical values for heat production of fasting adult animals of different species.

ANIMAL	BODY WEIGHT, KG	HEAT PRODUCTION, KCAL/DAY			
		PER ANIMAL	PER KG OF BODY WEIGHT	PER SQUARE METER OF SURFACE AREA	PER KG WEIGHT$^{0.73}$
Rat	0.29	28	97	840	69
Hen	2.1	115	55	701	67
Dog	14.0	485	35	745	71
Sheep	50	1060	21	890	61
Man	70	1700	24	950	77
Pig	122	2400	20	974	72
Cow	500	7470	15	1530	80

activity, and disease—which are encountered by animals in their normal environment or to account for differences in age, size, species, and breed.

The early nutrition research showed clearly that heat production was not well correlated to body weight of animals (see Table 10.4), and much research effort was expended to develop means of predicting heat production and establish some overall 'law' that applies to animals in general. With inanimate objects, it is known that rate of cooling is proportional to surface area. Furthermore, surface area varies with the square of linear size or to the 2/3 power of weight if specific gravity is constant; thus, surface area varies with the square of linear size or the 2/3 power of volume, so heat production can be related to body surface or volume.

The body surface of a living animal is quite difficult to measure. A variety of different methods have been attempted, but repeatibility of such measurements is low, even that of such methods as measuring the surface of the skin after it is removed. This is due partly to the fact that surface area of a living animal is not constant. It may change with environmental temperature when the animal stretches out, rolls up in a ball, by fluffing up of feathers or otherwise changes its posture. Furthermore, the ability of most animals to constrict or dilate blood vessels in the skin effectively alters the normal skin temperature and heat loss. Insulation of the body by subcutaneous fat, thick skin, hair, wool, or feathers has a marked effect on heat loss, as well. For example, at 16–17°C shearing increased the feed requirement 18% for housed sheep and 24% for exposed sheep and requirements were increased considerably more at colder temperatures (14). In addition, heat loss has been shown

to be related to the profile of the animal; thus, a long-legged, long-necked animal, such as a giraffe, would have a markedly different exposed area as compared to an animal with a short, compact body, such as a pig.

Even though these various factors are involved in heat loss, it can be related reasonably well to surface area estimated by multiplying body weight by a fractional power (and thus to body heat production). Body weight (BW) multiplied by a fractional power is referrred to as **metabolic weight** or **metabolic size**. Although there has been extensive controversy on this subject in the past, all current feeding standards in the USA and Europe now use BW multiplied to the 0.73 or 0.75 power to estimate heat production. Note in Table 10.4 that heat production of different species ranges from 97 Kcal/kg of BW down to 15 for animals ranging from the rat to the cow. However, when heat production is expressed on the basis of surface area (estimated from BW), the heat production/kg of $BW^{0.73}$ is much more uniform, ranging from 61 to 80 Kcal/day. Obviously, these values are not identical, but expression on this basis gives a reasonably good means of comparing markedly different animals. Brody's (1) book presents data indicating similar estimates of heat production when expressed in this manner for animals ranging in size and diversity from the canary to the elephant.

The preceding comments apply to adult animals in a quiet state. Other factors that may affect heat production are discussed in a later section. The point to remember is that energy metabolism may be similar in widely diverse animals, but it is not identical and may be altered by many different factors.

Heat Expenditure and the Environment

Animals lose heat by conduction, convection and radiation from the body surface, and by evaporation of water from the body surface and the lungs and oral surfaces. The rate at which heat is lost depends on the difference in temperature between the body surface and its environment. In addition, by constriction or dilation of blood vessels in the skin and extremities, the body surface may be cooled or warmed to some extent as compared to interior body temperature, thus increasing or decreasing surface temperature in relation to the environment. The effective surface temperature of the body is influenced greatly by insulation of subcutaneous fat, thickness of skin, and skin covering. On the other hand, insulation is reduced greatly by air movement or when the body surface is wet (i.e., conductivity of water is 24X that of air at body temperature).

Important concepts in energy metabolism are those of a thermoneutral environment and critical temperature. A **thermoneutral environment** is defined as one in which the animal does not need to increase energy expenditure to either warm or cool

the body. This temperature range is also called the comfort zone. The **critical temperature** (see Fig. 10.5) is usually defined as the point at which an animal must increase its heat production to prevent body temperature from falling, or (according to some writers) increase the rate of heat dissipation to prevent body temperature from rising. This upper point is sometimes called the point of hyperthermal rise.

The critical temperature for fasting animals in a cold environment is relatively high, being about 18–20°C for steers with a normal hair coat and about 30°C for sheep with a fleece of 5 mm in length. This is opposed to a critical temperature in steers of about 7°C when fed at maintenance and −1°C when fed to gain 500 g/day. The critical temperature of sheep fed at maintenance decreases from about 28°C with fleece of 1 mm in length to −3°C with fleece of 100 mm in length (4). Thus, the HI is being used to warm the body and reduces greatly the effective critical temperature as does added skin insulation (wool).

Shivering is a means of increasing heat production by an involuntary contraction of muscles. Further heat production occurs by oxidation of fats or proteins from the tissues or diets. Heat loss may be reduced in cold climates as the animal adapts to it, probably by reducing loss from the body surface more efficiently by constriction of blood vessels near the surface, particularly in the extremities. In addition, some animals, such as the sheep and eland, are more efficient in taking up O_2 from the air, with the result that less cold air must be inspired. Studies with arctic animals suggest that heat generated by activity, such as searching for food, may substitute completely for that which otherwise would be generated in the body of an inactive animal.

Most animals have much better means of protecting themselves from a cold than a hot climate. For arctic animals, temperature gradients between the animal and its environment may reach 100°C for short periods of time. Such extremes in hot environments do not allow animals to survive.

In a hot climate the animal must cool itself by increasing evaporation from the body surface, by more rapid respiration and panting, finding shade, or by immersing itself in water. The point at which heat stress occurs in animals varies with species and numerous environmental factors. The actual temperature that may cause heat stress is reduced by high humidity (which reduces evaporative cooling rate), by a high level of feeding, by feeding any ration that produces a high HI (high protein or high fiber for ruminants), or by restriction of water consump-

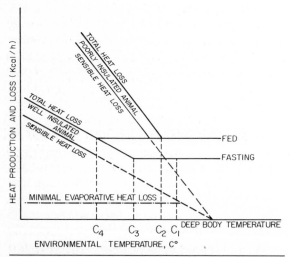

Figure 10.5 *A schematic representation of the relation between environmental temperature and the energy exchanges of homeotherms in cold environments. The heavy lines show the total heat loss of animals well and poorly insulated, fasting and fed. The horizontal part of this line defines the zone of thermal neutrality in which range heat loss is unaffected by environmental temperature. The lower limit of the thermoneutral zone is the critical temperature, C_1, C_2, C_3, or C_4, below which more heat must be produced to maintain body temperature. Reproduced by permission from Hafez and Dyer (15).*

tion. Note that evaporation is the only way that an animal can cool itself (other than immersion in cooler water) **if** environmental temperature exceeds body temperature.

❏ BASAL METABOLISM

Basal metabolism may be defined as the condition in which a minimal amount of energy is expended to sustain the body. Determinations are carried out under standardized conditions, and such information provides comparative base values where energy requirements are not confounded by other factors. In order to meet the requirements for basal metabolism, the animal should be in (a) a post-absorptive state, (b) a state of muscular repose but not asleep, and (c) in a thermoneutral environment. The post-absorptive state is used so that the HI and HF do not add to the body heat production. Only a few hours (overnight for man) of fasting are required in most monogastric species for the GI tract to approach this condition. However, in ruminants food requires many hours to pass out of the GI tract and a true state of post-absorption is obtained rarely, although it may be approached as indicated by a very low methane production. A state of muscular repose is needed so that an unknown amount of activity does not increase heat production. This may be difficult to obtain in animals, particularly those that have not had extensive training for such measurements.

Although perhaps not very precise, estimates of the needs for basal metabolism are that about 25% of the energy needs are required for circulation, respiration, secretion, and muscle tonus, and that the remaining portion represents the cost of maintaining electrochemical gradients across cell membranes and synthetic processes involved in replacing proteins and other macromolecules (16). Note that these values would not apply in many situations where energy expenditure is required for thermoregulation, metabolism of food, and so on. The values are not necessarily minimal because sleeping, prolonged fasting or starvation, torpidity, or hibernation can reduce energy expenditure.

Factors Affecting Basal Metabolism

Age. Age has a pronounced effect on basal metabolism in species that have been studied. For example, heat production in humans is about 31 Kcal per square meter of body surface at birth; this increases to about 50–55 at about 1 year of age and then declines gradually to 35–37 during the early to middle 20s. Further declines occur in older people.

The effect of age on heat production in sheep is shown in Table 10.5. Note the marked decline in heat production, particularly between 9 and 15 weeks of age, during which period the lambs were weaned. Other data presented by Moe (17) suggest that fasting heat production of cattle declines from 140 Kcal at one month of age to 80 Kcal ($BW^{0.73}$) at 48 months of age. Part of the change with age may be related to differential development of tissues which have different O_2 requirements.

Neuro-endocrine Factors. It is well known that energy expenditure may be different in the two sexes. In humans, basal metabolism of the male typically is 6–7% higher than that of the female, a difference which shows up at 2–3 years of age. In domestic animals, castration results in a 5–10% depression in basal metabolism. Thyroid activity has a pronounced effect as hypothyroid individuals may have a very low basal metabolism. Nervous, hyperactive animals have a high heat production, as might be expected. Related to hormonal changes are marked seasonal differences in basal energy metabolism of some species of wild animals.

Species and Breed Differences. A basal metabolism value of 70 Kcal $BW^{0.73}$ is considered to be an average value where BW is in kg. Note, however, in Table 10.4 that sheep tend to be about 15% below this and cattle about 15% above. Furthermore, data

TABLE 10.5 Fasting metabolism of lambs and sheep as affected by age.[a]

AGE	BODY WT, KG	KCAL/KG$^{0.73}$
1 wk	5.8	132
3 wk	9.1	111
6 wk	13.0	119
9 wk	18.0	116
15 wk	24.3	68
6 mo.	28.2	63
9 mo.	33.9	62
1–2 yr		63[b]
2–4 yr		58[b]
4–6 yr		55[b]
Over 6 yr		52[b]

[a]From Blaxter (10).
[b]Wether sheep.

from the Rowett Research Institute indicate that average values for Ayrshire steers were about 100 Kcal/$BW^{0.73}$ as compared to 81 Kcal for Angus steers; similar differences also have been observed between breeds of sheep and dairy cows. Thus, breed differences may be almost as marked as species differences. With respect to the differences between sheep and cattle, Blaxter (4) argues that cattle originated and developed in cold northern climates where heat production was a critical factor for survival, while sheep probably originated in subtropical areas where low heat production has survival value.

Marked exceptions to the general interspecies value of 0.73 include marsupials and primitive echidna which are much lower; also a number of animal species apparently have elevated metabolic rates. Some of the differences may be artifacts because it is quite difficult to have identical conditions when measuring heat production for all animals.

Miscellaneous Factors.   Other factors that have been shown to have some effect on basal metabolism include adaptation to fasting, where heat production/unit of surface area decreases with length of fast; muscular training (hypertrophy of muscles), which results in increased heat production; and mental effort, which causes a slight increase.

❏ MAINTENANCE

Maintenance may be defined as a condition in which a non-productive animal neither gains nor loses body energy reserves. In modern day agriculture, we are interested only rarely in just maintaining animals, as we are usually interested in keeping animals for some productive purposes. In practice, the term maintenance has been used frequently to apply to productive animals that are growing, pregnant, and/or lactating animals, as well as non-productive adults. If we are to establish the maintenance needs of an animal, several factors must be considered. In addition to needs for basal metabolism, we must account for energy losses occurring during nutrient metabolism; we must, in some manner, account for increased physical activity by the animal associated with normal functions such as grazing, and for environmental factors that may alter energy needs. Studies with beef cattle suggest that 65–70% of the ME needed for normal production is utilized to meet the needs of maintenance (18).

In biochemical terminology, energy required for maintenance is primarily for the production of ATP.

This energy, along with wasted energy (that not converted to ATP), is eventually lost as heat.

Energy for maintenance is used to carry out service functions that are performed by tissues and organs for the benefit of the entire organism. Included are such things as the work of circulation and respiration, liver and kidney work, and nervous functions. These account for 35–50% of the energy needed for maintenance. Cell maintenance is the other major need. Such functions as ion transport (particularly Na and Ca), and protein and lipid turnover account for 30–50% of maintenance energy requirements. Other metabolic processes such as glycogen turnover, gluconeogenesis, ketogenesis, urea synthesis, RNA and DNA synthesis, among many others, require the expenditure of energy and, thus, contribute to the animal's maintenance energy expenditures.

Maintenance energy expenditures may vary with age, body weight, breed or species, sex, physiological state, season, temperature, and previous nutrition. A complete explanation is not available at this time for all variations known, but part of this variation may be explained by differences in rates of substrate cycles. For example, energy expenditure for ion transport varies among tissues and is apparently greater in lactating than in non-lactating animals, is higher in young than in mature animals, and is greater in cold-adapted animals than in those not cold-adapted (19). Similarly, protein turnover rates vary tremendously among tissues, are higher in young than in mature animals, and decrease in response to lower planes of nutrition.

Some variation in ME needs may be explained by variations in proportions of various body tissues or organs. A change in the proportions of these tissues may have a large impact as illustrated in Table 10.6. In this example, nutritional treatment has influenced body weights and weights of the GI tract, liver, kidney, heart, and fasting heat production.

In calorimetric experiments the maintenance requirements of non-productive animals may be measured with precision. However, in such situations the animal is much less active than under more normal conditions, and it has proved to be quite difficult to put precise estimates on maintenance requirements that are reliable under different environmental conditions. Information on sheep (20) indicates that maintenance requirements of wethers are about 60–70% greater for grazing animals than for those housed in inside pens primarily because of additional activity associated with grazing. The exact amount

TABLE 10.6 Effect of nutritional treatment on organ weight and fasting heat production of lambs.[a]

NUTRITIONAL TREATMENT	BODY WEIGHT, KG	DIGESTIVE TRACT, G	LIVER, G	KIDNEY, G	HEART, G	FASTING HEAT PRODUCTION, KCAL/DAY
High	44.0	1,889	668	121	155	1,674
Medium	47.2	1,653	625	114	143	1,549
Low	39.9	1,304	428	93	126	1,143
Very low	34.4	1,162	350	83	130	966

[a]Adapted from Ferrell and Jenkins (18).

depended on condition of the sheep, the environment, and availability of herbage. If one assumes that heat production of maintenance for sheep in pens is about 70 Kcal/kg $BW^{0.73}$ (6), then this would indicate heat production when grazing of about 115 Kcal/kg $BW^{0.73}$. Work with Holstein dairy cows in calorimeters (20) indicates a maintenance requirement in the order of 114–122 Kcal of ME/kg $BW^{0.75}$, a value about equal to heat production of 100 Kcal/kg $BW^{0.75}$.

Frequently, energy requirements are estimated by feeding trials with animals under normal farm conditions. Although data of this type are less precise in that less information is available on actual tissue gain or loss of energy, such information may have more practical value than calorimetric data. Most feeding standards are based on the assumption that maintenance requirements under normal conditions are appreciably higher than basal or fasting metabolism rates, and the basal rate × 2 is used frequently, or 1.25–1.35 × fasting metabolism values when calculating maintenance requirements. Current NRC nutrient recommendations for cattle are based on maintenance estimates which were estimated by the comparative slaughter technique (13). In this work the maintenance requirement was estimated to be 77 Kcal/kg $BW^{0.75}$, a value that would seem to be too low as compared to calorimetric experiments on cattle. If this is the case, then NE of maintenance values given for feedstuffs (see Appendix tables) would over-estimate the relative value as compared to NE of gain.

☐ EFFICIENCY OF ENERGY UTILIZATION

Efficiency of energy utilization is of practical as well as academic concern to people involved in animal production because efficiency is a vital factor in profitable production. The most common means of expressing efficiency is in terms of units of production/unit of feed required (weight of gain, eggs or milk/unit weight of feed consumed). Where diets and type of production are similar, this gives a satisfactory comparison of gross efficiency. However, if we compare gain produced by a high concentrate ration to that produced on a high roughage ration, the comparison is poor in terms of utilization of available energy (DE, ME, or NE), because the roughage is apt to be much lower in available energy than a concentrate.

Another factor must be considered when efficiency is measured in terms of units of production, particularly when dealing with body gain or loss in weight. Although the energy value of milk can be calculated easily if fat percentage is known or that of eggs can be estimated with reasonable precision, the energy content of body gain may vary widely. In studies with dairy cows, Reid and Robb (20) point out that caloric value of body gain ranged from 4.8 to 9.4 Mcal/kg and that for body loss from 6.3 to 7.9 Mcal/kg; they suggested that body tissue gain or loss could range from as much as 100% water to about 90% fat. In growing animals most of the tissue gain in early post-natal growth is proteinaceous (lean tissues contain about 75% water), but during fattening, added tissue may contain 90% fat. For these extremes, the combustion values of 1 g of added tissue would range from 1.4 to 8.5 Kcal, or a ratio of about 1:6, indicating clearly that weight gain may be of little value in estimating caloric efficiency. If gain resulted only from water retention, the spread would be considerably greater.

Information from a variety of sources indicates that caloric efficiency is greatest for maintenance, followed by milk production and then by growth and fattening. The relative efficiency of maintenance may be due, largely, to the more efficient utilization of the HI and HF in maintaining body temperature. The less efficient use of energy for production as compared to maintenance is due in part to a decline in digestibility of a given diet as feed intake increases (particularly so in ruminants).

Early post-natal growth is quite efficient because it approaches that of maintenance, but the efficiency declines with age, partly because of gradually increased fat deposition. Nevertheless, research on swine, sheep, and cattle suggests that the energy cost of protein deposition is greater than that for fat deposition; partial efficiencies (estimates which may be arbitrary to some degree) indicate an energetic efficiency of 35% for protein and 70 + % for fat deposition. The reason for the lower efficiency of protein may be because of its dynamic state and more rapid turnover in the body than for lipid tissues. Examples of the range in efficiency that might be expected in ruminants and swine are shown in Table 10.7.

Gross efficiency (caloric value of product/caloric intake) is affected greatly by age, as indicated, and level of production. Young animals generally eat considerably more per unit of metabolic size than older animals, so that maintenance requirements represent a smaller percentage of dietary intake. The same comment applies to thin animals as opposed to fat animals, or to any situation where animals are fed at appreciably less than maximum intake. Because of this, in many production situations it is economically feasible to feed for maximum intake and rate of production.

Net efficiency (caloric value of product/caloric intake **above** maintenance) is less affected by level of intake and, perhaps, more by genetic capability of

the animal. In high producing animals, size is not a factor.

Examples of the range in efficiency that might be expected in swine and ruminants as suggested by Reid (21) are shown in Table 10.7. Relative efficiencies for utilization of NE suggested by Kleiber (2) are: fat production in adult steers, 100; maintenance in cattle, 120; milk production by cow; 119; maintenance in swine, 145; growth and fattening in swine, 125; and fattening in swine, 130. Reid (21) has made interesting calculations on efficiency of production of food energy by different domestic species of animals. In these calculations, he has considered the cost of maintenance of the dam and has included credit for the carcass of the dam towards total food production. His calculated values in terms of percentage of DE recovered in food are: pork, 18; eggs, 12; broilers, 12; milk (3,600 kg/year), 22; milk (5,400 kg/year), 27; and beef, 6. One reason for the low overall efficiency of beef production is that a beef cow produces at a very low level compared to a dairy cow; thus, maintenance is a much greater proportion of total feed intake and gross efficiency drops considerably.

A graphic illustration of changes in energy utilization with increasing feed consumption is shown in Fig. 10.6. The changes in energy losses from a consumption of 8 lb (maintenance) to 20 lb/day were: feces, 20 to 27; methane, 10 to 7; urine, 2–3 to 3; heat production, 13 to 18 (as a % of gross energy consumption). Thus, although losses increased from 45 to 55% of GE intake, maintenance becomes a smaller proportion of the total (from about 55 to 21%), with the net result that the gross and net efficiency improve at the higher rate of feeding.

The data shown in Fig. 10.6 are more applicable to ruminants than to non-ruminants because there is, generally, less depression in digestibility as feed consumption increases in non-ruminant animals. Calculations by the ARC (6) indicate that the change in digestibility of a diet, expressed as a multiple of maintenance can be described by the equation:

$$\text{Change in digestibility} = 0.107 - 0.113 \times \text{DE}$$

This equation implies that a diet having a digestibility of 70% DE at maintenance would have a digestibility of 67.2% at twice maintenance [0.70 − (0.107 − 0.113 × 0.70)] and 56.1% at five times maintenance. Although DE values may decrease, the increased energy lost in feces tends to be compensated for by decreased methane and urinary energy losses.

TABLE 10.7   Efficiency of energy utilization by pigs and ruminants ingesting diets of the usual range of quality fed in practice.[a]

ITEM	PIGS	RUMINANTS
Digestible energy, %	75–90	50–87
Utilization of ME above maintenance, %		
Body gain	75–80	30–62
Milk production	75–85	40–75
Fattening during lactation[b]		73

[a]From Reid (21). Data from a variety of sources. That for ruminants include diets ranging from fair quality forages to high-concentrate rations.
[b]Data from Moe et al. (22).

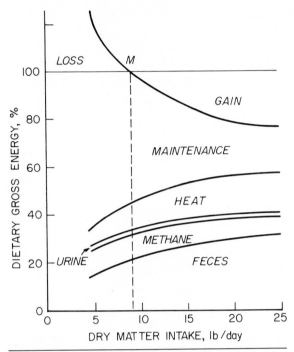

Figure 10.6 *A theoretical example of the proportional changes in energy balance with increasing intake by a ruminant. The proportion of energy lost in methane declines somewhat with increasing intake. Fecal losses increase because of reduction of digestibility with increased consumption. From Reid (23).*

This occurs, in part, due to an increased production in the rumen of propionic acid (used more efficiently than acetic or butyric acids) and a reduction in methane production without having any appreciable effect on digestibility.

❑ ENERGY TERMINOLOGY USED IN RATION FORMULATION AND FEEDING STANDARDS

As pointed out in previous discussions on the different categories of energy, GE has no value in itself for evaluation of feedstuffs or animal requirements. DE is often used in the USA, as is TDN, and these require no further explanation at this point. For poultry the NRC recommends the use of ME for chickens and turkeys, and an appreciable amount of information is available on feedstuffs and animal requirements for these species. For swine, DE, TDN, or ME values are used in practice.

In Great Britain, the ARC (Agricultural Research Council) has supported the suggestions of Blaxter and has adopted ME as the preferred base for energy. In the USA, three versions of NE are used in varying degrees for ruminants. These are discussed in succeeding paragraphs.

Estimated Net Energy [ENE]

Based on some calorimetric work, Moore et al. (24) developed a formula which allows NE to be estimated from TDN; the resulting value is called ENE. The formula is:

$$ENE \text{ (as Mcal/100 lb)} = 1.39 \times \%TDN - 34.63$$

or

$$ENE \text{ (as Mcal/kg dry matter)} = 0.307 \times \%TDN - 0.764.$$

Morrison (25) adopted this formula in the last edition of his book, and it has been used relatively widely as a result. Some dairy nutritionist still favor use of these values, partly because relatively few data are available on NE values of feedstuffs as compared to TDN values.

Net Energy for Lactation [NE$_l$]

Calorimetric experiments have been carried out at the USDA Experiment Station at Beltsville in which

The net effect is that ME is less affected than DE by intake. For example, the ME of a diet having a DE of 70% is expected to be 57% at maintenance. At two and five times maintenance, the ME is expected to be about 56% and 53%, respectively. Thus, an increase in feed consumption of a diet of this type from maintenance to five times maintenance is expected to result in a decrease in ME of less than 7% but a decrease in digestibility of 20% in DE.

Efficiency also may be affected by other factors that may alter digestibility and metabolizability of diets. For example, in a number of instances it has been demonstrated clearly that there are associative effects of different dietary components; that is, that there is a non-additive effect on digestibility when the components are combined in one diet. This type of normal phenomenon has not been well defined with regard to when and how often it occurs.

Efficiency may also be altered by various feed additives. For example, two antibiotic feed additives, monensin and lasalocid, generally result in reduced feed consumption with little if any effect on daily gain.

the NE requirements for milk production have been studied in high-producing dairy cows, primarily Holsteins, and results have been summarized (17, 22). NE_l is, in effect, a measure of the total energy requirement of the non-pregnant cow for milk production. The average NE requirement for maintenance was calculated to be 73 Kcal/kg $BW^{0.75}$, which is roughly equivalent to 118 Kcal for $ME/kg^{0.75}$. The amount of NE required for milk production was calculated to be 0.74 Mcal NE_l/kg of 4% fat-corrected milk. To calculate NE_l values from DE or TDN, the authors suggest the equations:

$$NE_l \text{ (as Mcal/kg dry matter)}$$
$$= 0.68 \text{ DE (as Mcal/kg DM)} - 0.36$$
$$NE_l \text{ (as M cal/kg dry matter)}$$
$$= 0.037 \times \%TDN - 0.77$$

Adjustments can be made in requirements for tissue gain or loss of cows, for excess N intake, and for pregnancy. The authors agree that further refinement is needed, but the reader might note that the NRC has adopted this terminology for their publication on dairy cows.

Net Energy of Maintenance and Gain [NE_m, NE_g]

This system, also called the California system (see the section on comparative slaughter technique), has come into use and has also been adopted by the NRC for growing beef and dairy cattle. In this scheme (13), the NE for maintenance, NE_m, is calculated separately from the NE_g, primarily because maintenance is a more efficient process, energetically, than is grain. However, this causes some complications in formulation of diets (see Ch. 22). Relatively few feedstuffs have been evaluated with this procedure at this time, although NRC publications give calculated values that were derived with the following formulas. Where DE or TDN are known, ME is first calculated:

$$ME \text{ (as Mcal/kg of feed)}$$
$$= DE \text{ (as Mcal/kg)} \times 0.82$$

or $$ME = 3.615 \text{ TDN}$$

For NE,

$$\text{Log F} = 2.2577 - 0.2213 \text{ ME}$$
$$\text{(where F} = \text{g dry matter/kg } BW^{0.75})$$
$$NE_m = 77/F$$
$$NE_g = 2.54 - 0.0314F$$

or

$$NE_m \text{ (as Mcal/kg dry matter)}$$
$$= 0.029 \times \%TDN - 0.29$$
$$NE_g \text{ (as Mcal/kg dry matter)}$$
$$= 0.029 \times \%TDN - 1.01$$

❏ SUMMARY

Qualitatively, energy is the most important component of the diet (other than water) needed by animals. Various methods such as total digestible nutrients, digestible, metabolizable, and net energy have been devised to describe and quantify animal utilization of feed energy. All have some faults that do not allow highly precise application of these methods except in rather specific environmental situations. Information collected on many different species shows that heat production (or loss) can be equated with reasonable accuracy to body surface area which can, in turn, be estimated by multiplying body weight by the 0.73 or 0.75 power. There are, however, variations from this interspecies value, but it serves as a reasonable means for comparative purposes. Body heat production usually is estimated under standard conditions such as fasting (post-absorptive), at maintenance or some higher level of activity. Heat production measurements for active free-ranging animals are frought with many uncertainties, especially in animals that are difficult to train in the use of equipment or in species that fly or swim. Nevertheless, even with some of the problems that have been mentioned, energy requirements for the domestic species are reasonably well quantified and are satisfactory guides for practical livestock production in most situations.

❏ REFERENCES

1. Brody, S. 1945. *Bioenergetics and Growth.* Hafner Pub. Co., N.Y.

2. Kleiber, M. 1961. *The Fire of Life.* John Wiley & Sons, N.Y.

3. Mitchell, H. H. 1962. *Comparative Nutrition of Man and Domestic Animals,* Vol. 1; 1964, Vol. 2. Academic Press, N.Y.

4. Blaxter, K. L. 1967. *The Energy Metabolism of Ruminants,* 2nd ed. Hutchinson & Co., London, England.

5. NRC. 1981. *Nutritional Energetics of Domestic Animals and Glossary of Energy Terms.* Nat. Acad. Sci., Washington, D.C.

6. ARC. 1980. *The Nutrient Requirements of Ruminant Livestock.* Agr. Res. Council, Commonwealth Agr. Bureaux, London, England.

7. Blaxter, K. L. and J. L. Clapperton. 1965. *Brit. J. Nutr.* **19:**511.

8. Swift, R. W., et al. 1948. *J. Animal Sci.* **7:**475.

9. Sibbald, I. R. 1976. *Poultry Sci.* **55:**303.

10. Armstrong, D. G. and K. L. Blaxter. 1957. *Brit. J. Nutr.* **11:**247.

11. Webster, A. J. F. 1979. In *Digestive Physiology and Nutrition of Ruminants,* Vol. 2, 2nd ed., D. C. Church (ed.). O & B Books, Inc., Corvallis, OR.

12. Tyrrell, H. F. and P. W. Moe. 1972. *J. Dairy Sci.* **55:**1106.

13. Lofgreen, G. P. and W. N. Garrett. 1968. *J. Animal Sci.* **27:**793.

14. Elvidge, D. G. and I. E. Coop. 1974. *N. Zealand J. Expt. Agr.* **2:**397.

15. Hafez, E. S. E. and I. A. Dyer (eds.). 1969. *Animal Nutrition and Growth.* Lea & Febiger Pub. Co., Philadelphia, PA.

16. Passmore, R. 1971. *Proc. Nutr. Soc.* **30:**122.

17. Moe, P. W. and H. F. Tyrrell. 1975. *J. Dairy Sci.* **54:**548.

18. Ferrell, C. L. 1988. In *The Ruminant Animal.* Prentice-Hall, Inc., Englewood Cliffs, N.J.

19. Milligan, L. P. and B. W. McBride. 1985. *J. Nutr.* **115:**1374.

20. Young, B. A. and J. L. Corbett. 1972. *Austral. J. Agr. Res.* **23:**77.

21. Reid, J. T. 1970. In *Physiology of Digestion and Metabolism in the Ruminant.* Oriel Press, Newcastle-Upon-Tyne, England.

22. Moe, P. W., H. F. Tyrrell, and W. P. Flatt. 1971. *J. Dairy Sci.* **54:**548.

23. Reid, J. T. 1962. In *Animal Nutrition's Contributions to Modern Animal Agriculture.* Cornell University Spec. Publ.

24. Moore, L. A., H. M. Irvin, and J. C. Shaw. 1953. *J. Dairy Sci.* **36:**93.

25. Morrison, F. B. 1956. *Feeds and Feeding,* 22nd ed. Morrison Pub. Co., Ithaca, N.Y.

| 11 |

Macrominerals

AT LEAST 21 MINERAL elements have been shown to be required by at least some animals species and an additional five may be essential metabolically based on indirect or limited data. The required mineral elements can be divided into two groups based on the relative amounts needed in the diet, namely, macrominerals and micro or trace minerals. The macrominerals are: calcium (Ca); phosphorus (P); sodium (Na); chlorine (Cl); potassium (K); magnesium (Mg); and sulfur (S).

Some mineral elements—such as Ca and P—are required as structural components of the skeleton and others—such as Na, K, and Cl—function in acid-base balance; still others—such as Zn and Cu—are contained in enzyme systems. Many minerals have more than one function.

Animal tissues contain many minerals in addition to those recognized as dietary essentials. Some of these may have a metabolic function not yet recognized, but others may be present as inocuous contaminants. Still others are toxic to the animal at relatively low concentrations. Even the required minerals may be toxic if present in the diet in excess.

The subcommittee on Mineral Toxicity in Animals (1) reviewed the literature on maximum tolerable levels of minerals in the diets of domestic animals and emphasized that "all mineral elements, whether essential or non-essential, can affect an animal adversely if included in the diet at

161

excessively high levels." Toxicity of minerals not known to be required by animals is covered in Ch. 13, while toxic signs of required macrominerals are described later in this chapter and those of required trace minerals are covered in Ch. 12.

Each of the minerals known to be required is discussed with respect to distribution in body tissues, functions, metabolism, deficiency signs, and toxicity. The amounts of each of the macrominerals (except S) present in newborn and adult mammals of several species are shown in Table 11.1 (2). The proportions of each mineral, expressed as amount/kg of fat-free body tissue are similar among species in adults. Newborn animals also have similar composition, but differences in the degree of physiological maturity are reflected in the amounts of Ca, P, and Mg present among the species. Guinea pigs, humans, and pigs are more mature physiologically at birth than rabbits, rats and mice and have higher concentrations of bone minerals. The Ca:P:Mg ratios of both newborn and adults are remarkably similar among species. One can infer from such data that macromineral metabolism and nutrition, with some exceptions, is similar among animal species and therefore that observations on one species may be extrapolated to others.

❏ CALCIUM (Ca)

Tissue Distribution

About 99% of the Ca stored in the animal body is in the skeleton as a constituent of bones and teeth (3). It occurs in about a 2:1 ratio with P in bone, primarily as hydroxyapatite crystals:

$$Ca_{10-x}^{++}(PO_4^{\equiv})_6(OH^-)_2(H_3O^+)_{2x}$$

where x may vary from 0 to 2. When $x = 0$, the compound is called octacalcium phosphate; when $x = 2$ it is called hydroxyapatite. Ca is present in blood mostly in the plasma (extracellular) at a concentration of about 10 mg/dℓ and exists in three states (4): as the free ion (60%), bound to protein (35%), or complexed with organic acids such as citrate or with inorganic acids such as phosphate (5–7%).

Functions

The most obvious function of Ca is as a structural component of the skeleton. A brief description of normal bone metabolism is needed to develop a full appreciation of the function of Ca as a major skeletal component. Bone is a metabolically active tissue with continuous turnover and remodeling both in growing and mature animals. The physiological control of bone metabolism is related to both endocrine and nutritional factors. Blood is the transport medium by which Ca is moved from the GI tract to other tissues for utilization. Elaborate controls exist to maintain a relatively constant Ca concentration in the plasma. A decline in plasma Ca concentration triggers the parathyroid gland to increase secretion of parathyroid hormone (PTH) which stimulates the biosynthesis of the metabolically active form of vitamin D (1,25-dihydroxy cholecalciferol or 1,25-$(OH)_2D_3$) by the kidney (see vitamin D, Ch. 14), which, in turn, causes increased Ca absorption from the GI tract and increased resorption of Ca from bone. An increase in plasma Ca concentration triggers "C cells" in the thyroid gland to release calcitonin, a hormone that depresses plasma Ca by inhibiting bone resorption. Thus, dietary factors that affect Ca absorption have an effect on the endocrine system in direct response to the amount of Ca reaching the blood from the GI tract (6). The amount of Ca absorbed from the GI tract depends on amount ingested and proportion absorbed. As the percentage of Ca in the diet increases, the proportion absorbed tends to decline. This is related to the fact that Ca absorption is an active process under the control of a Ca-binding protein (CaBP; see vitamin D, Ch. 14) which, at least in most species, is vitamin-D dependent. The ab-

TABLE 11.1   Ca, P, Mg, Na, K, and Cl content of newborn and adult animals (amounts/kg of fat free body tissue).[a]

	MAN	PIG	DOG	CAT	RABBIT	GUINEA PIG	RAT	MOUSE
Newborn								
Body wt, g	3560	1250	328	118	54	80	5.9	1.6
Water, g	823	820	845	822	865	775	862	850
Ca, g	9.6	10.0	4.9	6.6	4.6	12.3	3.1	3.4
P, g	5.6	5.8	3.9	4.4	3.6	7.5	3.6	3.4
Mg, g	0.56	0.32	0.17	0.26	0.23	0.46	0.25	0.34
Na, meq	82	93	81	92	78	71	84	—
K, meq	53	50	58	60	53	69	65	70
Cl, meq	55	52	60	66	56	—	67	—
Adult								
Body wt, g	65	125	6.0	4.0	2.6	—	0.35	0.027
Water, g	720	750	740	740	730	—	720	780
Ca, g	22.4	12.0	—	13.0	13.0	—	12.4	11.4
P, g	12.0	7.0	—	8.0	7.0	—	7.5	7.4
Mg, g	0.47	0.45	—	0.45	0.50	—	0.40	0.43
Na, meq	80	65	69	65	58	—	59	63
K, meq	69	74	65	77	72	—	81	80
Cl, meq	50	—	43	—	32	—	40	—

[a]Source: Widdowson and Dickerson (2). To convert meq (milliequivalents) to mg, multiply by 23 for Na, 39 for K, and 35.5 for Cl; to convert g to meq, divide by 20,000 for Ca, 31,000 for P, and 12,000 for Mg.

solute amount absorbed generally is greater in animals fed high-Ca diets, despite the lower percentage absorption. In vitamin-D deficiency, Ca absorption is reduced, because of impaired CaBP formation, so that skeletal abnormalities can occur even in the presence of adequate dietary Ca.

Bone apposition occurs by activity of osteoblasts (bone-forming cells) at growth plates and in other areas of rapid bone growth. Bone resorption occurs concomitantly by two processes, one by resorption of bone surfaces by activity of osteoclasts (bone-resorbing cells) and the other by resorption deep within formed bone (osteocytic resorption). The latter process now generally is believed to be the major process of bone resorption. The continuous apposition and resorption of bone is the basis for bone growth and for changes in its shape and density.

Ca controls the excitability of nerve and muscle. Reduced Ca^{++} concentration produces increased excitability of pre- and postganglionic nerve fibers. Higher than normal Ca^{++} concentrations have the opposite effect on nerves and muscles, causing them to be hypoexcitable. It has been postulated (7) that Ca imposes constraints on the ionic movements of Na and K by interacting with surface structures of the cell.

Ca is required for normal blood coagulation.

The great importance of Ca in cellular metabolism has become appreciated recently through new knowledge of its role in sarcoplasmic reticular function in skeletal and cardiac muscle and in the physiological functions of the nervous system. In cardiac and skeletal muscle, Ca release from the sarcoplasmic reticulum is controlled by a series of relationships beyond the scope of this discussion. Suffice it to say that Ca sequestration by a Ca-stimulated ATPase is functionally important for muscle relaxation and Ca release provides a source of Ca for myofilament activation, the importance of which is still uncertain (8). Furthermore, skeletal muscle protein synthesis appears to be closely associated with a Ca-activated factor whose nature and physiological importance is currently under study.

Recent work has demonstrated that Ca^{++} regulates the level of phosphorylation of a number of endogenous proteins in the nervous system, especially through the activation of calmodulin-dependent protein kinases (9). The total significance of Ca as the key ion in this rapidly growing field of calmodulin metabolism with respect to neurotransmitter synthesis in the overall function of the nervous system is still unclear. However, the explosive growth of this field of investigation has revealed that the Ca^{++} ion serves vital functions never before appreciated. The implications of these newly discovered functions in applied nutrition are still unclear but provide for an exciting future for research in Ca metabolism.

Metabolism

The overall movement of Ca in metabolism is diagrammed schematically in Fig. 11.1. In the growing animal, net retention of Ca occurs in the body; that is, the amount stored in bone and other tissues exceeds that lost in feces, urine, and sweat. In nonpregnant, nonlactating adults, the amount of Ca ingested equals the amounts lost if the metabolic requirement is met.

Absorption.   Dietary Ca is absorbed largely from the duodenum and jejunum of most animals. An exception appears to be the hamster in which most absorption is from the ileum. Absorption occurs both by active (energy-dependent) and passive (diffusion) transport. In rats and man, and presumably in other species, about half of the dietary Ca is absorbed by active transport. The importance of a vitamin D-dependent protein carrier of Ca in active transport has been elucidated as described in Ch. 14. Other factors in addition to vitamin D affect efficiency of Ca absorption. Increased dietary Ca concentration decreases the percentage of Ca absorbed, although the absolute amount absorbed tends to remain relatively constant within the normal range of Ca concentration of the diet. Lactose as well as lysine and, to a lesser extent, several other amino acids have been shown to enhance Ca absorption in rats, but phytic and oxalic acids decrease its absorption by forming insoluble complexes of Ca oxalate and Ca phytate. Such factors as high pH of the intestinal contents, high levels of dietary fat, which might be expected to form insoluble fatty acid-Ca soaps, and high fiber levels in the diet, probably are not of great significance (7).

Ossification of the skeleton to form hydroxyapatite crystals requires that the product of Ca ions and P ions in the fluid surrounding the bone matrix ex-

ceed a critical minimum level. Thus, if the product $(Ca^{++})(PO_4^{=})$ falls below the concentration required to precipitate Ca phosphate in the crystal lattice structure, ossification fails to occur and rickets or osteomalacia results, whether the deficiency is one of Ca or P, or both. Calcification is an active process, specifically requiring ATP.

Excretion.   The three major routes of Ca excretion are feces, urine, and sweat. Fecal output includes both an unabsorbed fraction and an endogenous fraction, largely arising from secretions of the intestinal mucosa; the latter probably is reabsorbed partially, as illustrated in Fig. 11.1. Therefore, that appearing in the feces is termed fecal endogenous Ca and represents about 20–30% of total fecal Ca. The apparent Ca absorbability (feed Ca minus fecal Ca) generally approximates 50%, although the percentage tends to decline as intake increases.

Urinary output of Ca generally is considerably less than that of fecal output in most species (Table 11.2). About half of the plasma Ca, mainly ionized Ca, is filtered in the kidney; more than 99% of this is reabsorbed under normal conditions. Diuretics generally do not affect Ca excretion, but Ca chelators, such as large intravenous doses of Na-citrate, Na-EDTA or Ca-EDTA, increase greatly Ca excretion. Data obtained from human studies show clearly that increasing dietary protein intake above the metabolic requirement causes a striking increase in urinary Ca excretion.

Loss of Ca in sweat is of only minor significance in most species, but in man, horses, and other species in which sweating is prominent, large amounts of Ca can be lost by this route. Consolazio *et al.* (10)

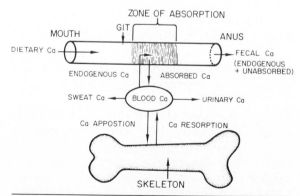

Figure 11.1   *Schematic diagram of overall metabolism of Ca.*

TABLE 11.2 Distribution of fecal and urinary Ca excretion in humans, cattle, and rats.[a]

SPECIES	AGE	Ca INTAKE	FECAL Ca	URINE Ca
			(mg/day)	
Man				
Male	11–16 yr	1,866	1,018	127
	23	1,461	1,229	72
Female	14–16 yr	874	655	194
	55–63	713	586	500
Cattle	young adult	29,000	27,000	500
Rats	12 wk	44.1	20.8	0.9

[a]Source: Bronner (7).

estimated sweat loss of more than 1 g of Ca/day in adult men doing heavy physical work at high environmental temperatures. Sweat losses equalled or exceeded fecal and urinary losses in these men.

Figure 11.2 Top. Bowed legs in a pig with Ca-deficiency rickets. Courtesy of L. Krook, Cornell University. Bottom. An advanced stage of rickets in a calf. Courtesy of J. W. Thomas, Michigan State University.

Signs of Deficiency

The main effect of Ca deficiency is on the skeleton. In young, growing animals a simple Ca deficiency results in rickets and, in adults, the disease is called osteomalacia. In each case the bones become soft and often deformed due to failure in calcification of the cartilage matrix. The familiar skeletal changes associated with rickets are illustrated in Fig. 11.2. Simple Ca deficiency or vitamin D deficiency, which results in poor utilization of dietary Ca, even when the Ca level of the diet is adequate, may produce such abnormal bone development. The histological picture in rickets is one of the reduced calcification. The degree of change is related to the growth rate of the animal. In species such as the pig, dog, and chick, in which body weight may be doubled in a few days and the skeletal mineral turnover rate is therefore very rapid, a Ca deficiency may produce profound changes in bone after only a few days. In other species, such as sheep and cattle, a longer period is required to show deficiency signs.

A deficiency of Ca (or even normal amounts) in the presence of excess P also causes abnormal bone, but, in this instance, excess bone resorption by osteocytic osteolysis (resorption deep within bone) results in osteodystrophy fibrosa. This condition is characterized histologically by replacement of osseous tissue with fibrous connective tissue. The parathyroid gland is hyperactive in an attempt to maintain normal blood serum Ca. The disease is called nutritional secondary hyperparathyroidism. There is a generalized effect on the entire skeleton. "Big head" disease of horses (Fig. 11.3), simian bone disease of monkeys and twisted snouts of pigs (Fig. 11.4) may result from feeding excess P. High P diets depress intestinal absorption of Ca in horses.

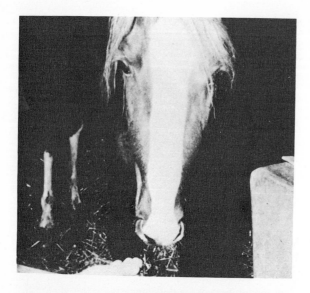

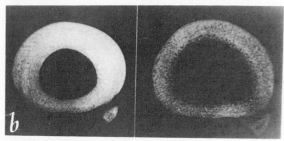

Figure 11.3 *Top, Nutritional secondary hyperparathyroidism (NSHP) in a horse; "big head," a spontaneous case. The facial bones are enlarged and the facial crest is no longer visible. Bottom. Radiographs of a section of the metacarpus of a horse (left) fed normal Ca:P diet; right, horse fed excess P. In HSHP the cortex is thinner and the radiographic density is markedly decreased. Courtesy of L. Krook, Cornell University.*

The histological picture of the nasal turbinate is similar to that often observed in growing pigs with atrophic rhinitis (AR). Although AR is considered by many to be strictly of infectious origin, apparently dietary Ca-P imbalance is responsible partially in many instances (11).

Lameness and spontaneous bone fractures often, but not necessarily, accompany both osteomalacia and nutritional secondary hyperparathyroidism in adult animals. Reproduction and lactation are affected adversely in rats fed Ca deficient diets. The demands of the fetus for Ca are tremendous during late gestation. In rats, fetal uptake of Ca/h in late gestation is equal to the total maternal Ca blood content. Thus, inadequate dietary intake necessitates re-

sorption of Ca from the maternal skeleton to meet fetal needs.

Although blood serum Ca concentration may decline slightly during the early weeks of dietary Ca deficiency, control by parathyroid hormone (increases bone resorption) and calcitonin (inhibits bone resorption) renders this a relatively useless index of Ca nutrition. Only by frequent serial blood sampling over an extended period of weeks or months is monitoring of serum Ca meaningful.

A reduction in bone ash content occurs in all forms of dietary Ca deficiency or Ca-P imbalance. All bones of the skeleton are affected, although the magnitude of change may vary. The proportion of Ca and P remains constant (about a 2:1 Ca-P ratio). The bone ash may be determined directly by ashing the fat-free bone or indirectly by determining specific gravity or by expressing density as g ash/unit volume. This latter method eliminates the need to ether-extract the bone before ashing. Changes in bone density of large magnitude can be identified by radiography, but this method is too insensitive to perceive differences not exceeding about 30%.

In humans there is increasing concern about the high incidence of osteoporosis in the elderly. It is estimated that at least 10% of women over 50 years

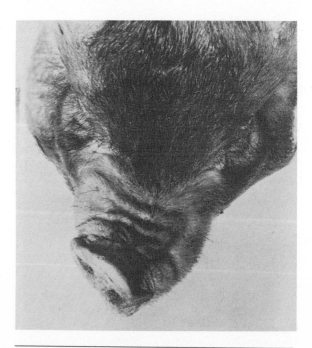

Figure 11.4 *A pig with a distorted snout caused by NSHP which was induced by a dietary Ca-P imbalance.*

of age in the USA have bone loss severe enough to cause hip, vertebrae, and long-bone fractures (12). At least part of this high frequency is believed to be due to suboptimum dietary Ca intake during an extended period of time. Surveys of daily Ca intake in the USA indicate that the value declines gradually in both men and women to levels well below recommended levels after age 35. Osteoporosis is characterized by reduction in bone mass with resulting tendency to fracture. The failure in production of estrogen in postmenopausal females is undoubtedly partially responsible for the higher incidence of osteoporosis in women than in men, but dietary Ca level also appears to play an important part.

Recently, interest has been shown in the effects of physical inactivity on Ca excretion. Striking increases in Ca losses in urine and feces were noted in astronauts confined to small space capsules in the early space flights. Salton *et al.* (13) observed a two-fold increase in Ca excretion by healthy human subjects after three weeks of bed rest. The possible implications for animal production in close confinement systems are under study. Available evidence indicates that degree of exercise may have important effects on Ca utilization.

Severe Ca deficiency may produce hypocalcemia which results in tetany and convulsions. Follis (14) outlined the pathogenesis of Ca tetany in animals as follows. Ca deficiency: deficient intake; disturbance in absorption, with vitamin D deficiency or diarrhea; excessive kidney excretion; formation of complexes; and parathyroid effects, either hypofunction (maldevelopment) or removal. Ca tetany is related to the requirement of Ca in normal transmission of nerve impulses and in muscle contraction. Ca tetany may be transient or may culminate in sudden death. Presumably, death results from failure in normal heart muscle contractions. Ca is needed in association with Na and K in normal heart muscle contraction. A causal relationship appears to exist between low dietary Ca intake and a higher risk of hypertension in humans. The physiological mechanisms of this effect are unknown (15).

The classical example of Ca tetany is the "milk fever" or parturient paresis syndrome of dairy cattle. The condition occurs usually early in lactation during the period of large drains on body Ca reserves for milk production. The etiology probably is related to endocrine function. Both the parathyroid gland and calcitonin-secreting cells of the thyroid may be involved. Dietary Ca intake prior to and during early lactation is important in influencing the capability of these glands to respond appropriately to the sudden change in metabolic demands for Ca imposed by lactation. Ca tetany in dairy cattle and other species responds dramatically to intravenous injection of $CaCl_2$, Ca lactate, or other Ca salts to elevate serum Ca above the concentration of 5 or 6 mg/dℓ that is associated with onset of tetany.

Blood-clotting time is influenced by Ca. The clotting process consists of a complicated series of reactions as outlined in Ch. 14. Such substances as oxalate, citrate, and EDTA are commonly used to prevent blood coagulation in vitro and these same compounds, if administered in large quantities, may also form salts with Ca in vivo and interfere with blood clotting. A reduction in ionized Ca in blood of sufficient magnitude to become a limiting factor in blood clotting is not always seen in simple dietary Ca deficiency. Widespread hemorrhage has been observed in tissues of rats and dogs fed diets severely deficient in Ca.

Particle size and rate of reactivity of limestones have been shown to vary widely, but the effect of these differences on animal performance is unclear; growing pigs apparently utilize with similar efficiency the Ca in limestones differing in particle size and rate of reactivity.

Toxicity

Acute Ca toxicity has not been reported but chronic ingestion of Ca in excess of metabolic requirements results in abnormalities in bone which can be regarded as manifestations of toxicity. The tendency toward hypercalcemia resulting from continued absorption of excess Ca stimulates calcitonin production by the thyroid. The inhibitory effect of calcitonin on bone resorption is a homeostatic mechanism aimed at minimizing the sources of serum Ca of other than dietary origin. Calcitonin has a stimulatory effect on $1,25(OH)_2D_3$ accumulation in kidney tubules; whether the action is a direct effect is unclear (16). Sustained calcitonin secretion leads to excess bone mass in response to inadequate bone resorption relative to bone apposition. This abnormal thickening of bone cortex is termed osteopetrosis. It has been produced in growing dogs (Fig. 11.5) by feeding 2.0% Ca-1.4% P diets from weaning to young adulthood, and in mature dairy bulls by prolonged feeding of high Ca diets designed for lactating dairy cows. Tumors of the ultimobranchial (calcitonin-producing requires about 3.3 g Ca/day for maximal egg production. The amount in relation to body size would be considered toxic to mammals, but is required by the caged hen to prevent cage fatique, a condition resulting in excess removal of Ca phosphate from medullary bone and proneness to fracture. Thus, clearly the level of a mineral required to produce toxicity is dependent on species as well as on physiological (productive) state of the animal. This principle generally applies to most minerals.

Urinary calculi (kidney stones) which block the kidney tubules or ureters may occur in animals. The calculi are not believed to be formed by high Ca alone, but rather to require imbalances of other minerals or formation of abnormal complexes with cholesterol or other steroids. In ruminants, excess P in relation to Ca is more likely to cause calculi.

Excess Ca in the diet reduces the absorption and utilization of other minerals. The classical example of a nutritional disease precipitated by high dietary Ca in pigs is the Zn deficiency disease, parakeratosis. The Zn deficiency may not appear in animals fed a normal level of Ca but can become a serious problem when dietary Ca is increased without changing Zn intake. Similar reductions in mineral utilization induced by excess Ca have been reported for Mg, Fe, I, Mn, and Cu.

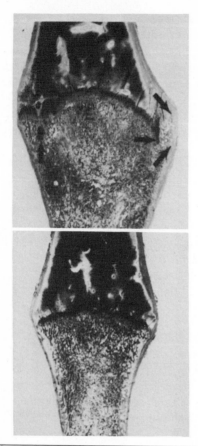

Figure 11.5 *Excess bone mass (osteopetrosis) in the dog fed excess Ca (top) or normal (bottom) level showing costochondral junction with irregular growth of cartilage at horizontal arrow, cartilage cells island at vertical arrow, and thick perichondral ring at oblique arrows. Courtesy of L. Krook and Cornell Veterinarian.*

cells) tissue of the thyroid of these bulls were observed, presumably in response to the sustained hyperactivity resulting from continued hypercalcemia.

Calcification of soft tissues may occur in high Ca feeding, but such calcification only occurs in sites of cellular damage such as in atherosclerosis or inflammation. Tissue damage from Mg deficiency is associated with soft tissue calcification, but high Ca in itself usually does not induce it. A diet containing 2.5% Ca and 0.4% available P has been shown to produce nephrosis, visceral gout, and Ca urate deposits in the ureters of growing pullets. Increasing the P level to achieve a more nearly optimum Ca-P ratio in such high Ca diets prevented the kidney lesions. The Ca requirement of laying hens is much higher than in most animals and birds because the egg shell is composed mostly of $CaCO_3$. The hen

❑ PHOSPHORUS (P)

Tissue Distribution

The P content of adult humans approximates 1.1% of the fat-free body, of which about 80% is in the skeleton. Bone ash contains about 18% P. The percentage of P in the body and the proportion of total P in the skeleton increases throughout prenatal and postnatal life as ossification of the skeleton progresses to maturity. The P in the skeleton is present as part of the hydroxyapatite crystal (see Ca section) while that in the soft tissues is present mostly in organic forms. Table 11.3 gives the P content of an array of organs and tissues of adult man (17). In blood serum, P exists in both inorganic and organic form, the latter as a constituent of lipids. Of the inorganic P, about 10% is bound to serum proteins and 50–60% is ionized. The P in red blood cells is present as inorganic P, organic acid-soluble P, lipid P, and RNA P, the proportions varying with age and species (18). Total serum P concentration under normal conditions in most species is 6–9 mg/dℓ. The transfer

TABLE 11.3 Calcium, phosphorus, and magnesium content of organs and tissues of adult humans[a]

TISSUE OR ORGAN	Ca	P	Mg
	(% OF FRESH TISSUE)		
Skin	0.015	0.083	0.0102
Skeleton	11.51	5.19	0.191
Teeth	25.46	13.24	0.618
Striated muscle	0.014	0.116	0.0198
Nerve tissue	0.015	0.224	0.0107
Liver	0.012	0.127	0.0081
Heart	0.018	0.123	0.0168
Lungs	0.017	0.228	0.0069
Spleen	0.010	0.169	0.0124
Kidney	0.019	0.124	0.0169
Alimentary tract	0.009	0.111	0.131
Adipose tissue	0.009	0.055	0.0060
Remaining tissue (solid)	0.047	0.163	0.0170
Remaining tissue (liquid)	0.008	0.088	0.0084
Total composition			
Whole body	1.98	1.06	0.045
Fat-free	2.07	1.11	0.047
Bone ash	39.44	17.80	0.654

[a]Source: Forbes et al. (17).

rates of P among spatially distinct compartments of the body have been calculated by Lax *et al.* (19), using the assumption that each compartment exchanges P with others through a central compartment (blood). The exchange rate of P among several of the important organs was highest for the skeleton, followed in descending order by muscle and heart. The average time spent by a single P atom in each compartment also was calculated (2.8 h for blood cells vs. 393 h for brain); the length of time in a compartment was found to be related to the metabolic activity of the tissue. Thus, P movement within the body clearly is in a dynamic state.

Functions

As with Ca, the most obvious function of P is as a component of the skeleton. In this role, it provides structural support for the body. Because Ca and P occur together in bone, the discussion of the function of Ca (see Ca section) in bone also applies to P. P is a component of phospholipids which are important in lipid transport and metabolism and cell-membrane structure. As such, P is present in virtually all cells (see Ch. 9). P functions in energy metabolism as a component of AMP, ADP, and ATP and of creatine phosphate. The importance of high-energy phosphate bonds in normal life processes was discussed in Ch. 9. P is a component as phosphate of RNA and DNA, the vital cellular constituents required for protein synthesis (see Ch. 7). It is a constituent of several enzyme systems (cocarboxylase, flavoproteins, NAD).

Metabolism

The metabolism of P can be discussed in terms of bone metabolism, the metabolism of phospholipids, and of high-energy phosphate compounds such as ATP, ADP, and creatine phosphate. Bone metabolism was discussed earlier and phospholipid metabolism and metabolism of high-energy phosphate compounds are discussed in Ch. 9 (Lipids) and in other sections relating to energy utilization.

Absorption of P from the GI tract occurs by active transport (16) and passive diffusion. Vitamin D apparently has an effect on P absorption. In vitro work has shown that P may traverse the intestinal cell membrane against a concentration gradient in the presence of Ca and requires Na. P absorption is related directly to dietary P concentration. An excess of dietary P in relation to Ca depresses Ca absorption. This may be because of formation of insoluble Ca phosphate salts and/or to Ca being bound by phytic acid (the hexaphosphoric acid ester of inositol). Many plant seeds are high in P, much of which is present as phytic acid, decreasing the bioavailability of P for non-ruminants. Bioavailability of phytate-P for swine and poultry is influenced by phytase present in plant materials, by the pH of the GI tract, and the ratio of Ca to P in the diet. Estimates of bioavailability of total plant P range from 20 to 60%.

P absorption from the GI tract is rapid as demonstrated by radioisotope studies with ^{32}P. Much of the labeled P is incorporated into phospholipids in the intestinal mucosal cells.

Secretion of P into the intestinal lumen (endogenous fecal P) occurs, but this loss does not represent as high a proportion of the daily loss as for Ca. Most of the P excretion occurs through the kidneys and renal excretion appears to be the main regulator of blood P concentration. When intestinal absorption of P is low, urinary P falls to a low level with reabsorption by the kidney tubules approaching 99%. Kidney excretion of P is under control of para-

Figure 11.6   P-deficient cow. Note stiffness and thin condition. Bones were depleted to such an extent that one rib was broken in a casual examination. Courtesy of R. B. Becker, Florida Agr. Expt. Sta.

thyroid hormone and 1,25-dihydroxy vitamin D as a part of the overall blood homeostatic mechanism for Ca and P.

Signs of Deficiency

The most common sign of P deficiency in growing animals is rickets (refer to Fig. 11.2). The gross and histological changes in rickets have been described earlier (see Ca section and Ch. 14). Fecal output of P tends to remain relatively unchanged while urinary excretion is reduced, but the total excretion may still exceed intake when Ca intake is relatively high. Ca excretion in both urine and feces is increased in P deficiency as a manifestation of reduced calcification of bone. As the deficiency progresses, appetite fails and growth is retarded. Deficient animals (Fig. 11.6) often have a depraved appetite and may chew on wood and other inappropriate objects. This abnormal behavior of eating or chewing is termed pica (Fig. 11.7). Adults fed low P diets may exhibit pica, and bone density is decreased as in rickets (Fig. 11.8). Impaired fertility has been reported in P-deficient cattle. Blood-serum Ca is increased and serum P is decreased by P deficiency.

Blood P homeostasis is more complicated than that for blood Ca because blood P is in equilibrium not only with bone P but also with several organic P compounds. Nevertheless, kidney excretion of P is sufficiently controlled by parathyroid hormone secretion and 1,25-dihydroxy vitamin D to result in relatively stable serum P concentration even with severe dietary P deficiency. P, as well as Ca, metabolism was thoroughly reviewed by Borsle (20).

Toxicity

An excess of dietary P results in nutritional secondary hyperparathyroidism manifested in excessive bone resorption (fibrous osteodystrophy) which may result in lameness and spontaneous fractures of long bones. Growing pigs with severe bone resorption produced by low Ca-high P diets may suffocate be-

Figure 11.7   Pica. A P deficiency, as well as deficiencies of other nutrients, may result in a depraved appetite (pica). This example shows some of the material recovered from the stomach of a deficient cow. It includes oyster shells, porcelain, teeth, a section of cannon bone, inner tube, tire casing, pieces of metal, and pebbles. Courtesy of R. B. Becker, Florida Agr. Expt. Sta.

Figure 11.8   A P-deficient pig. Note enlarged joints and crooked hind legs. This pig was fed a diet with 0.3% P. Courtesy of W. M. Beeson, Purdue University.

cause of softening of the ribs to the extent that normal respiratory movements are inhibited. High phosphate diets depress intestinal absorption of Ca, plasma Ca, and Ca retention in horses.

Ca-P ratios greater than 1:2 may produce fibrous osteodystrophy in growing or adult animals. Lean meat and many cereal grain by-products (notably wheat bran) contain several times as much P as Ca (see section on Ca deficiency).

High P has a laxative effect so that dietary excesses result in diarrhea and high fecal loss of P as well as other nutrients.

❏ MAGNESIUM (Mg)

Mg is distributed widely in the body and, except for Ca and P, is present in larger amounts in the body (see Table 11.1) than any other mineral. About half of body Mg is in bone at a concentration of 0.5–0.7% of the bone ash (21). Mg in soft tissues is concentrated within cells; highest concentration is in liver and skeletal muscle. Blood Mg is distributed about 75% in red blood cells (6 meq/ℓ) and 25% in serum (1.1 to 2.0 meq/ℓ). The concentration in serum seems to vary among species as shown in Table 11.4. Of the serum Mg, about 35% is protein-bound in mammals and birds, even though total Mg is variable among species.

TABLE 11.4　Serum Mg concentration of man and animals.[a]

SPECIES	Mg CONCENTRATION (meq/ℓ)
Cow	1.6
Dog	1.6
Goat	1.9
Horse	1.5
Hen	1.6
Human	2.0
Mouse	1.1
Pig	1.3
Rabbit	2.1
Rat	1.6
Sheep	1.7

[a]Source: Wacker and Vallee (21).

Functions

Mg is required for normal skeletal development as a constituent of bone; it is required for oxidative phosphorylation by mitochondria of heart muscle and probably by mitochondria of other tissues. Mg is required for activation of enzymes which split and transfer phosphatases and the many enzymes concerned in the reactions involving ATP. As discussed elsewhere (see Chs. 8, 9, 10), ATP is required in such diverse functions as muscle contraction, protein, nucleic acid, fat, and coenzyme synthesis; glucose utilization; methyl-group transfer; sulfate, acetate, and formate activation; and oxidative phosphorylation, to name but a few. By inference, the activation action of Mg extends to all of these functions. Mg is a cofactor in decarboxylation and is required to activate certain peptidases. Specific examples of enzyme systems requiring Mg for activity have been described by Wacker and Vallee (21). Current knowledge of Mg in nutrition has been reviewed (22).

Metabolism

Examination of the functions of Mg shows clearly that its metabolism is complex and varied (21–23). Absorption from the GI tract occurs mostly from the ileum. No carrier is known for Mg absorption nor has vitamin D been shown to enhance its absorption. Although some have suggested a common pathway for Ca and Mg absorption, the fact that Ca is absorbed mainly from the upper small intestine and is associated with a vitamin D-dependent binding protein, suggests no common pathway.

Homeostatic control of blood and tissue Mg is not understood clearly. Hyperparathyroidism is associated with increased urinary excretion and reduced serum Mg, but a specific effect on Mg aside from the concomitant release of Mg from bone when Ca is released in response to parathyroid hormone has not been shown. Some evidence suggests an effect of plasma Mg on parathyroid activity.

Mg excretion occurs via the feces and urine. About 55 to 60% of ingested Mg is absorbed, and the absolute amount absorbed is proportional to dietary intake. Urinary excretion accounts for about 95% of losses of absorbed Mg, and fecal excretion accounts for most of the remainder. Endogenous fecal excretion is largely into the proximal small intestine, so that, as with Ca, probably some reabsorption occurs as it traverses the GI tract.

Signs of Deficiency

Mg deficiency in growing rats results in anorexia, reduced weight gain, reduced serum Mg, hypomagnesemic tetany and, within 3–5 days, characteristic hyperemia of the ears and extremities (24). Repka (25) found a close association between occurrence and severity of cutaneous hyperemia and plasma Mg concentration. Continued and severe hypomagnesemia was accompanied by slight hypercalcemia after 3 weeks and depression of some of the liver enzyme systems requiring Mg. Kidney Ca elevation in Mg deficiency is accompanied by a decrease in total serum Mg, but an increase in the ratio of free to total Mg (26). Concentration of Mg in liver was not depressed. Severe leukocytosis develops concurrently with hyperemia of extremities. Mg deficiency in pigs results in weak and crooked legs, hyperirritability, muscular twitching, reluctance to stand, tetany, and death. Plasma and urinary histamine are elevated in Mg deficiency, and serum and liver glutamic oxalacetic transaminase activity are increased.

Tufts and Greenberg (27) demonstrated the calcification and necrosis of the kidney that occur in Mg deficiency. High dietary Ca and P appear to aggravate the Mg deficiency, probably due to depressed Mg absorption, and accentuate the calcification of soft tissues associated with inadequate Mg.

Red blood-cell Mg concentration is reduced as well as plasma Mg concentration, but the decline is more gradual and reaches 50% of control values by the 10th day as compared to the 4th or 5th day for plasma Mg concentration. Although liver Mg concentration is unaffected, skeletal muscle concentration is reduced by 25% or more. Bone Mg content is reduced in Mg deficiency when expressed either as percentage of Mg in whole bone or in the bone ash and skeletal deformities are apparent (Fig. 11.9).

A decline in tissue K and a rise in tissue Ca and Na occur in Mg-deficient animals. Activities of several Mg-dependent enzymes, including plasma alkaline phosphatase, muscle enolase and pyruvate phosphokinase, are depressed in Mg deficiency, but many others are not. Mitochondria of kidney tubule cells are swollen in Mg deficiency as shown by electron microscopy. Chow and Pond (28) showed mitochondrial swelling in liver from ammonia-intoxicated rats and observed loss of intramitochondrial Mg and PO_4 ions. Head and Rook (29) proposed that high ammonia interferes with Mg absorption by forming the insoluble Mg ammonium phosphate (struvite) at alkaline pH.

Figure 11.9   *Mg deficiency in the pig. The normal pig on the left was fed 413 ppm of Mg for 3 weeks and the pig on the right (deficient) was fed 70 ppm of Mg for the same period. Note extreme leg weakness, arched back, and general unthriftiness of the deficient pig. Courtesy of W. M. Beeson, Purdue University.*

A common problem of grazing cattle is a syndrome called grass tetany, Mg tetany, or wheat-pasture poisoning. It occurs most frequently in cattle grazing cereal forages or native pastures in periods of lush growth (usually in spring months), but it is also a problem at times in cattle fed conventional wintering ration, Sjollema (30) first described the symptoms of tetany which have been ascribed to hypomagnesemia (low blood Mg). The etiology of Mg tetany is not understood completely, although it is agreed generally that hypomagnesemia, whatever its underlying cause, is the triggering factor. Phytic acid P decreases Mg absorption in non-ruminants, but no difference between organic and inorganic P was observed in affecting Mg absorption in sheep (31). The high level of K and protein usually present in lush pastures has suggested the possibility of an antagonism with Mg. Newton et al. (32) found that sheep fed high K tended to excrete more [28]Mg in urine and feces, and that high K interfered with Mg absorption, but not its re-excretion into the GI tract. Elevated urinary Mg excretion has been reported in sheep fed high N (urea) diets and an increased severity of Mg deficiency occurs in rats fed high Ca, K, or protein diets.

High concentrations of *trans*-aconitate, an intermediate in the citric acid cycle, have been observed in early season forages and have been suggested as having a role in Mg tetany (33, 34). Intravenous administration of either *trans*-aconitic or citric acid into cattle produces tetany resembling clinical Mg tetany (35). The implications of these findings in relation to grass tetany are not realized fully, but the syndrome apparently is more complicated than a simple dietary Mg deficiency. Recent evidence implicates high Al levels (2,000–6,000 ppm) in some samples of rapidly growing forage which may alter solubility and affect the incidence of Mg tetany. In practice, supplemental Mg from a variety of inorganic sources is effective in preventing Mg tetany. The problem is one of the practical difficulties in administering Mg to free-ranging cattle and sheep on pasture.

Evidence from rats and monkeys suggests that submarginal Mg intake increases susceptibility to atherosclerosis in the presence of high cholesterol intake. The significance of this relationship in the incidence of atherosclerosis in humans and animals is unknown.

Toxicity

Mg toxicosis in animals includes depressed feed intake, diarrhea, loss of reflexes, and cardiorespiratory depression (1). Severe diarrhea and reduced feed intake and growth have been observed in calves fed 2.3% or more Mg (36) and accidental feeding of high-Mg diets to sheep results in diarrhea and anorexia. Intravenous injection of $MgSO_4$ was shown in 1869 to result in peripheral muscle paralysis of dogs. Subsequent early work confirmed this and led to the use of Mg as an anesthetic for surgery. Mg decreases the release of acetylcholine at the neuromuscular junction and sympathetic ganglia.

Mg induces a drop in blood pressure and high serum concentrations (greater than 5 meq/ℓ) affect the electrocardiogram and may cause the heart to stop in diastole (37).

❑ POTASSIUM, SODIUM, AND CHLORINE (K, Na, Cl)

These three minerals are considered together because they are all electrolytes that play a vital role in maintaining osmotic pressure in the extracellular and intracellular fluids, and in maintaining acid-base balance. Each has its own special functions, in addition, which will be discussed separately.

Distribution in Body Tissues

The total body contents of K, Na, and Cl in newborn and adults of several mammals including man are shown in Table 11.1. Normal ratios among electrolytes are remarkably constant among species. Houpt

(38) has described the tissue distribution and interrelationship of K, Na, and Cl in maintaining acid-base balance. K is present mainly within cells (about 90% of body K is intracellular) and is exchangeable readily with the extracellular fluid. On the other hand, Na is present largely in extracellular fluid with less than 10% within cells. Of the other 90%, about half is adsorbed to the hydroxyapatite crystal of bone and half is present in plasma and interstitial fluids. Cl acts with bicarbonate (HCO_3) to balance electrically the Na of the extracellular fluid. Excess excretion of Na by the kidney is accompanied by Cl excretion. Cl is present almost exclusively in the extracellular fluid. Gamble (39) diagrammed the concentrations of K^+, Na^+, Cl^-, HCO_3^-, and organic constituents of blood plasma, interstitial fluid, and intracellular fluid (Fig. 11.10). The meq of cations/ℓ within each compartment exactly equals the meq of anions/ℓ to ensure electrical neutrality. The composition depicted for cell fluids is only an approximation, because some individual tissues have cell electrolyte composition considerably different than the mean.

Functions

K is located mostly within cells and, by means of an energy-requiring system related to Na movement, it influences osmotic equilibrium; K functions in maintenance of acid-base balance in the body; it is required in enzyme reactions involving phosphorylation of creatine and is required for activity of pyruvate kinase. K facilitates uptake of neutral amino acids by cells, and influences carbohydrate metabolism by affecting uptake of glucose into cells. It is required for normal tissue protein synthesis in protein-depleted animals and is required for normal integrity of the heart and kidney muscle and for a normal electrocardiogram.

Na functions as the extracellular component through an energy dependent Na "pump," along with K and Mg and intracellular components, in maintaining osmotic pressure. It functions in maintaining acid-base balance in the body and in nerve impulse transmission by virtue of the potential energy associated with its separation from K by the cell membrane.

Cl functions in regulation of extracellular osmotic pressure and in maintaining acid-base balance in the body. It is the chief anion of gastric juice where it unites with H ions to form HCl.

Metabolism

K, Na, and Cl ions are not absorbed in appreciable amounts from the stomach, but considerable ab-

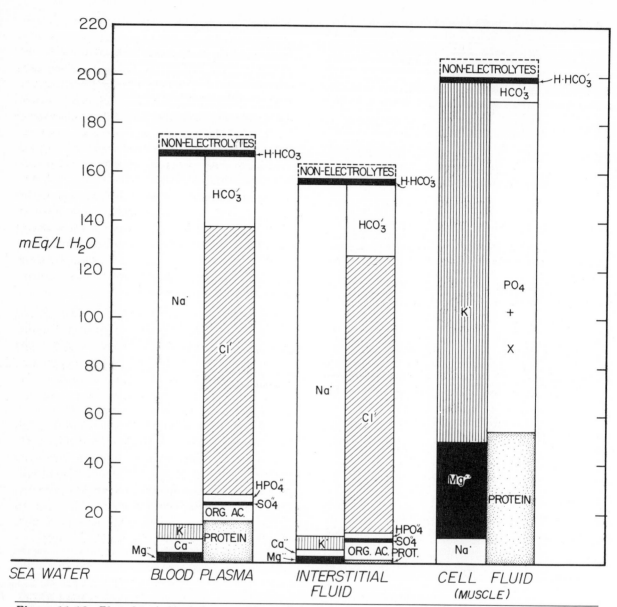

Figure 11.10 *Electrolytes in blood plasma and intracellular fluid. From Gamble (39).*

sorption takes place from the upper small intestine and lesser amounts from the lower small intestine and large intestine. The daily secretion of fluids into the GI tract from saliva, gastric juice, bile and pancreatic juice contributes 4–5 times the daily oral intake of these ions. Thus, large variation in intake has a relatively small effect on the total load of fluids and electrolytes entering the GI tract. About 80% of the NaCl load and 50% of the K load on the GI tract is from secretions. Cl is secreted in large quantities in the stomach, Na is secreted into the upper

small intestine, and K mainly into the ileum and large intestine (40). All three ions are absorbed both by passive and active processes; Na and K cross the mucosa by active transport in the intestine but largely by diffusion in the stomach, whereas Cl is transferred by active processes in the stomach and upper intestine, but by passive diffusion in the large intestine (40).

The regulation of K, Na, and Cl ion concentrations within rather narrow limits in extra- and intracellular compartments of the body is not completely understood. Ingestion of more of each mineral than needed results in ready excretion by the kidneys. Thus, toxicity is not likely unless water intake is restricted, which impedes urine output. Na is excreted by the kidney and partial, but not complete, reabsorption occurs from the kidney tubules. That not reabsorbed is lost in the urine. The plasma level of the Na tends to be controlled by the action of the hormone, aldosterone, secreted by the adrenal cortex. Its action is to increase Na reabsorption from the kidney tubule. A fall in plasma Na, as a result of reduced intake, results in increased aldosterone release. Aldosterone production is, in turn, under the control of the adrenocorticotrophic hormone of the anterior pituitary gland, and its secretion is impaired in hypophysectomized animals.

The antidiuretic hormone of the posterior pituitary also plays a part in Na excretion through its response to changes in osmotic pressure of the extracellular fluid induced by water deprivation. Osmoconcentration results in increased antidiuretic-hormone release as a means of conserving water. Thus, the complex relationships between body Na content, aldosterone secretion, and antidiuretic hormone secretion, although incompletely understood are of utmost importance in maintaining fluid electrolyte homeostasis. In animals that perspire extensively, such as the human and the horse, large amounts of Na are lost from the body by this route. K intake usually exceeds by several times the metabolic requirements for it, yet K toxicity does not occur ordinarily because of the ability of the kidney to regulate its excretion. Aldosterone also affects K excretion; high K in extracellular fluid stimulates aldosterone secretion in the same way that low Na does. A rather constant ratio of Na to K in the extracellular fluid is maintained. In K deficiency some Na is transferred inside the cell to replace K, and in that way preserves osmotic and acid-base equilibrium. When intake of either Na or K is inadequate, the deficiency is aggravated by increasing the intake of the other. Cl concentration in the extracellular fluid tends to be controlled in relation to Na. Excess kidney excretion is also affected by bicarbonate ion (HCO_3^-) concentration. If plasma bicarbonate rises, an equal amount of Cl is excreted in the urine to maintain an equal concentration of cations and anions in the plasma.

K and Cl homeostasis are closely related. A deficiency of one leads to a metabolic deficiency of the other. K reabsorption by the kidney tubule requires the presence of Cl. Thus, KCl is more effective than other K salts in repletion from K deficiency.

Deficiency Signs

K.   Deficiency of K results in abnormal electrocardiograms in calves, chicks, and pigs as well as in other species. Postmortem examination may not always reveal pathological changes in heart muscle, but in rats tiny gray opacities on the ventricles of the heart and loss in striations have been observed. Kidney lesions also have been observed. Growth retardation, unsteady gait, general overall muscle weakness, pica (Fig. 11.11), and emaciation followed by death are the symptoms of K deficiency in animals and birds. Mg deficiency results in failure to retain K and, in this way, may lead to K deficiency in animals and man. Diarrhea is associated with loss of electrolytes, notably K, in abnormally high quantities in the feces, thereby upsetting osmotic pressure relationships and acid-base balance.

Na.   The main signs of Na deficiency are reduced growth rate and efficiency of feed utilization in growing animals and reduced milk production and weight loss in adults (Fig. 11.12). Na deficiency in growing pigs is associated with an immediate decline in Na urinary excretion, hemoconcentration, and decreased plasma volume.

A cloudy appearance of the cornea of the eye has been reported in rats (14). Smith and Aines (41) studied salt (NaCl) deficiency in lactating dairy cows and found that Na, K, and Cl concentration of milk remained unchanged as did the plasma Na concentration. Urinary excretion of Na declined to near zero within a month and appetite and milk production dropped sharply. Animals deprived of Na display a

Figure 11.11 *A K-deficient lamb. This picture illustrates the wool biting and pulling that may occur in deficient animals, although it has not been observed in other experiments. Courtesy of W. K. Roberts.*

Figure 11.12 *A salt-deficient cow. Note the dehydrated appearance of the animal. From Smith and Aines (41).*

great craving for it and have been observed to drink urine in an effort to satisfy their craving. The Na ion appears to be the critical mineral in NaCl deficiency (41).

Cl.   Depressed growth rate seems to be the major sign of Cl deficiency. Low dietary Cl results in a decline in urinary Cl concentration to near zero, and Cl concentration of skin, muscle, liver, kidney, brain, viscera, and total carcass is reduced. Kidney lesions develop within one month of feeding on a Cl-deficient diet. Leach and Nesheim (42) described a syndrome in chicks fed Cl-deficient diets. They show a characteristic nervous reaction induced by sudden noise; they fall forward with their legs extended backward.

In practice, Na and Cl are supplied in the diet together as common salt and it appears that the metabolic requirement for each is proportional to the amounts contributed by NaCl.

Toxicity

Because the kidney normally regulates its excretion of K, Na, and Cl in accord with variations in dietary intake, a toxicity of any of the three electrolytes is unlikely except when water intake is restricted, drinking water is saline, or as a result of renal malfunction. Chronic K excess induced by one of the above means results in hypertrophy of the adrenal cortex with accompanying changes in aldosterone output. A high level of dietary K reduces the apparent absorption of Mg in ruminants (1,43). Studies with goats indicated that supplementary K may in-

crease the cellular uptake and retention of Mg because of increased cellular K levels. Lentz *et al.* (44) suggested that prolonged elevation of K in blood plasma of ruminants may lead to a series of metabolic disturbances, including elevated insulin secretion, that play an important role in the etiology of grass tetany. The complex metabolic relationships between dietary K and Mg in ruminant nutrition remain incompletely understood.

Chronic, excess Na ingestion results in hypertension associated with degenerative vascular disease. The glomeruli of the kidney are affected. Excess salt ingestion has been implicated in the etiology of hypertension in humans (45). There is evidence that average salt intake among humans in the USA is higher than desirable. Continued high intakes of salt increase total extracellular fluid volume; this is the basis for the use of low salt diets in hypertension and congestive heart failure.

Acute salt toxicity has been produced experimentally in growing pigs (46) by severely restricting water intake while simultaneously providing feed containing 2% NaCl for 1 or 2 days. Symptoms included staggering, marked weakness, paralysis of hind limbs or general paralysis, violent convulsions, and death. Postmortem examination revealed no lesions except a slight increase in volume of fluid in the pericardium and small hemorrhages in the liver.

Excess Cl is not likely, but the use of purified diets containing amino acids and other salts added in the hydrochloride form may increase the total acidity of the diet. Scott *et al.* (47) recommended that extra K and Na be added to such diets to assure maintenance of acid-base balance.

❏ SULFUR(S)

Tissue Distribution

S is required by animals mainly as a component of organic compounds. These include the amino acids methionine, cystine, cysteine; the vitamins biotin and thiamin; certain mucopolysaccharides, including the chondroitin sulfate and mucoitin sulfates; heparin; glutathione; coenzyme A. Because proteins are present in every cell of the body, and S-containing amino acids are components of virtually all proteins (usually 0.6 to 0.8% of the protein), S is distributed widely throughout the body and in every cell and makes up about 0.15% of body weight.

Functions

S functions mainly through its presence in organic metabolites. Inorganic sulfate from exogenous dietary sources and from endogenous release from S-containing amino acids are used in synthesizing the chondroitin matrix of cartilage, in biosynthesis of taurine, heparin, cystine and other organic constituents in the animal body (48). In birds, sulfate is incorporated into feathers, gizzard lining and muscle. Its functions in organic compounds will be listed in terms of the metabolic function of the compounds containing it.

Inorganic SO_4 functions in acid-base balance as a constituent of intracellular, and to a lesser extent, extracellular fluid; as a component of S-containing amino acids, it is required for protein synthesis (see Ch. 7); as a component of biotin, it is important in lipid metabolism (see Ch. 15); and as a component of thiamin, it is important in carbohydrate metabolism (see Ch. 15); as a component of coenzyme A, it is important in energy metabolism (see Chs. 8, 9, 15); as a component of mucopolysaccharides, it is important in collagen and connective tissue metabolism; and as a component of heparin, it is required for blood clotting; S is a component of ergothioneine of red blood cells and of glutathione, a universal cell constituent; and S is a component of certain hormones as a constituent of amino acids.

Metabolism

Absorption of inorganic sulfate from the GI tract is inefficient. Active transport of $SO_4^=$ takes place from the upper small intestine. Inorganic S is needed in the diet to prevent an increase in the S-amino acid requirement (48). Both inorganic and organic forms of S are used for sulfation of cartilage mucopolysaccharides.

Organic forms of S are absorbed readily, as discussed elsewhere (Chs. 7, 8, 9, 15) in relation to the compounds that contain S. Inorganic S is excreted via the feces and urine. Unabsorbed S is reduced probably in the lower GI tract and excreted as sulfate (49). Endogenous fecal S enters the GI tract largely through the bile as a component of taurocholic acid. Urinary S is present mainly as inorganic $SO_4^=$, but also as a component of thiosulfate, taurine, cystine, and other organic compounds. Because the bulk of body S is present in amino acids, that urinary S excretion tends to parallel urinary N excretion is

not surprising. High protein diets are associated with large amounts of urinary S and N.

In ruminants fed non-protein N, a growth response may be obtained by inorganic S supplementation. Rumen microflora incorporate N into cellular protein, but synthesis is limited if S is not available in sufficient quantities for formation of S-amino acids. Thus, inorganic S may be important in ruminant nutrition, but only in terms of its need by microflora of the rumen for protein synthesis. Sheep, which produce wool high in S-containing amino acids, need a higher S : N ratio than non-wool-producing ruminants. Birds, whose feathers are high in S-amino acids, likewise have a higher S requirement than mammals.

Deficiency Signs

Inorganic S has not been shown to be essential for animals for normal maintenance or productive functions. Deficiency of methionine, thiamin, or biotin, however, each of which contains S, certainly produces functional and morphological lesions as discussed elsewhere (Chs. 7 and 15). Also, the absence of inorganic S from the diet may increase the requirement for S-containing amino acids, implying that S from these sources is used for synthesis of other organic forms of S in the absence of inorganic S.

Sheep fed non-protein N to replace protein without concomitant supplementation with S show reduced wool growth, and weight gain of sheep and cattle is depressed in S deficiency. These effects on animal performance are manifestations of inadequate microbial nutrition on which the host depends for synthesis of organic metabolites and therefore cannot be considered as direct S deficiency.

Toxicity

Because the intestinal absorption of inorganic S compounds is low, S toxicity is not a practical problem. Excesses of S-amino acids cause anorexia and growth depression, but such effects are observed with excesses of amino acids in general, not specifically the S-amino acids. The toxicity of S is determined, to a large extent, by the enzyme systems of the exposed animal, and by whether the animal has the capacity to form H_2S from the inorganic sulfate sources presented (1). Ultimately, the toxicity of S depends on its form; while elemental S is considered one of the least toxic elements, H_2S rivals cyanide in toxicity (1).

❏ SUMMARY

The mineral elements required in the diet of animals for normal body functions can be divided into two groups according to the relative amounts needed in the diet, macrominerals and micro or trace minerals. The required macrominerals are calcium (Ca), phosphorus (P), sodium (Na), chlorine (Cl), potassium (K), magnesium (Mg), and sulfur (S). Some minerals such as Ca and P are required as structural components of the skeleton and others such as Na, K, and Cl function in acid-base balance; many have more than one function. All minerals, whether essential or not, can affect an animal adversely if included in the diet at excessively high levels.

Metabolism of Ca is under delicate endocrine control; parathyroid hormone (from the parathyroid gland), calcitonin (from the thyroid), and the metabolically active form of vitamin D (1,25 dihydroxy cholecalciferol from the kidney) work in concert to maintain Ca homeostasis when dietary Ca is varied. Ca deficiency results in reduced bone calcification (rickets in growing animals, osteomalacia in adults). P, like Ca, is a major constituent of the skeleton; also, it is a component of phospholipids, which are important in lipid transport and cell membrane structure, and is a constituent of several enzyme systems. P deficiency results in rickets. Mg is widely distributed in the body and is third to Ca and P in total body mineral content. About half is in bone; Mg in soft tissues is concentrated within cells. Mg is required for a normal skeleton, for oxidative phosphorylation by mitochondria and for activation of many enzyme systems. Deficiency results in anorexia, reduced serum Mg, and tetany. K, Na, and Cl are all electrolytes vital in maintaining osmotic pressure in the extracellular and intracellular fluids and in maintaining acid-base balance. K is present mainly within cells; Na is present mainly, and Cl almost exclusively, in extracellular body fluids. Cl acts with bicarbonate (HCO_3^-) to balance electrically the Na of the extracellular fluid. Na functions in transfer of nerve impulses by virtue of the potential energy associated with its separation from K by the cell membrane. K deficiency results in an abnormal electrocardiogram, general muscle weakness, and emaciation. The main sign of Na deficiency is reduced feed intake and weight loss. Depressed growth and kidney lesions are the major signs of Cl deficiency. S is required mainly as a constituent of organic compounds, including the amino acids methionine, cysteine, and cystine; the vitamins biotin and thiamin; certain mucopolysaccharides; coenzyme A. Inorganic sulfate from exogenous dietary sources and from endogenous release from organic substances such as S-containing amino acids is used in synthesizing other organic constituents, including heparin, mucopolysaccharides, and other compounds that contain S. Deficiency signs of S are related to the signs observed for nutrients which contain S.

Interactions between and among macrominerals and between individual macrominerals and trace minerals are increasingly recognized as important in nutrition. For example, a dietary Ca to P ratio of greater than 2 to 1 or less than 1 to 2 may produce adverse responses in some animals; ratio of K to Mg in the diet may be of importance in the etiology of Mg tetany in ruminants; high dietary Ca may precipitate a Zn deficiency in non-ruminants.

❏ REFERENCES

1. NRC. 1980. *Mineral Tolerances of Domestic Animals.* Natl. Acad. Sci. Washington, D.C.

2. Widdowson, E. M. and J. W. T. Dickerson. 1964. In *Mineral Metabolism,* Vol. 2, Part A. Academic Press, N.Y.

3. Schuette, S. A. and H. M. Linkswiler. 1984. In *Present Knowledge in Nutrition,* 5th Edition, The Nutrition Foundation, Inc., Washington, D.C.

4. D'Souza, A. and M. N. Flock. 1973. *Amer. J. Clin. Nutr.* **26**:352.

5. Wasserman, R. H. 1977. Ch. 34 In *Duke's Physiology of Domestic Animals,* pp 413–432, edited by M. J. Swendson. Cornell Univ. Press, Ithaca, N.Y.; Anghileri, L. J. 1982. *Role of Calcium in Biological Systems,* Vols. I, II, III. CRC Press, Inc., Boca Raton, FL.; Wassweman, R. H. 1982. Metabolism of Calcium. In *Ann. Rev. Nutr.,* Vol. 2. Annual Reviews, Inc., Palo Alto, CA.

6. Tanaka, Y., H. Frank and H. F. DeLuca. 1973. *J. Nutr.* **102**:1569; Kenny, A. D. 1981. *Intestinal Calcium Absorption and Its Regulation.* CRC Press, Inc., Boca Raton, FL.

7. Bronner, F. 1964. In *Mineral Metabolism,* Vol. 2, Part A. Academic Press, N.Y.

8. Sutko, J. L. 1985. *Fed. Proc.* **44**:2959.

9. Fujisawa, H., T. Yamauchi, H. Nakata, and S. Okano. 1984. *Fed Proc.* **43**:3011.

10. Consolazio, C. F., et al. 1964. *J. Nutr.* **78**:78.

11. Brown, W. R., L. Krook and W. G. Pond. 1966. *Cornell Vet.* **56**:supplement 1, p. 108.

12. Alvioli, L. V. 1984. *Ann. Rev. Nutr.* **4**:471.

13. Salton, B. 1968. *Circulation* **38,** Suppl. VII.

14. Follis, R. H., Jr. 1958. *Deficiency Disease.* C. C. Thomas, Springfield, IL.

15. Karanja, N. and D. A. McCarron. 1986. *Ann. Rev. Nutr.* **6**:475.

16. Henry, H. L. and A. W. Norman. 1984. *Ann. Rev. Nutr.* **4**:493.

17. Forbes, R. M., A. R. Cooper, and H. H. Mitchell. 1956. *J. Biol. Chem.* **223**:969.

18. Widdowson, E. M. and J. W. T. Dickerson. 1964. In *Mineral Metabolism,* Vol. 2, Part 2. Academic Press, N.Y.

19. Lax, L. C., S. Sidlofsky, and G. A. Wrenshall. 1956. *J. Physiol.* **132**:1.

20. Borsle, A. B. 1974. *Ann. Rev. Physiol.* Vol. 36, p. 361.

21. Wacker, W. E. C. and B. L. Vallee. 1964. In *Mineral Metabolism.* Academic Press, N.Y.

22. Aikawa, J. K. 1981. *Magnesium: Its Biological Significance.* CRC Press, Inc., Boca Raton, FL.

23. Walser, M. 1967. In *Rev. Physiol. Biochem. and Exptl. Pharmacol.* Springer-Verlag, N.Y.

24. Follis, R. H. 1958. *Deficiency Disease.* C. C. Thomas Pub., Springfield, IL.

25. Repka, F. J. 1972. Ph. D. Thesis, Cornell Univ., Ithaca, N.Y.

26. Bunce, B. E. and J. E. Bloomer. 1972. *J. Nutr.* **102**:863.

27. Tufts, E. V. and D. M. Greenberg. 1938. *J. Biol. Chem.* **122**:693; **122**:715.

28. Chow, Kye-Wing and W. G. Pond. 1972. *Proc. Soc. Exptl. Biol. Med.* **139**:150.

29. Head, M. J., and J. F. Rook. 1955. *Nature* **176**:262.

30. Sjollema, B. 1932. *Nutr. Abst. and Rev.* **1**:621.

31. Dutton, J. E. and J. P. Fontenot. 1967. *J. Animal Sci.* **26**:1409.

32. Newton, G. L., J. P. Fontenot, R. E. Tucker, and C. E. Polan. 1972. *J. Animal Sci.* **35**:440.

33. Burau, R. and P. R. Stout. 1965. *Science* **150**:766.

34. Stout, R. R., J. Brownell, and R. C. Burau. 1967. *Agron. J.* **59**:21.

35. Bohman, V. R., et al. 1969. *J. Animal Sci.* **29**:29.

36. Gentry, R. P., et al. 1978. *J. Dairy Sci.* **61**:1750.

37. Standbury, J. B. and A. Farah. 1950. *J. Pharmacol. Exptl. Therap.* **100**:445.

38. Houpt, T. R. 1977. In *Duke's Physiology of Domestic Animals,* 9th ed., p. 443. Cornell Univ. Press, Ithaca, N.Y.

39. Gamble, J. L. 1954. *Chemical Anatomy, Physiology and Pathology of Extracellular Fluid.* Harvard Univ. Press, Cambridge, MA.

40. Wilson, T. H. 1962. *Intestinal Absorption.* W. B. Sanders, Philadelphia, PA.

41. Smith, S. E. and P. D. Aines. 1959. Cornell Agr. Expts. Sta. Bul. 938.

42. Leach, R. M. and M. C. Nesheim. 1963. *J. Nutr.* **81**:193.

43. Fontenot, J. P., M. B. Wise and K. E. Webb, Jr. 1973. *Fed. Proc.* **32**:1925

44. Lentz, D. E., F. C. Madsen, J. K. Miller, and S. L. Hansard. 1976. *J. Animal Sci.* **43**:1082.

45. Papper, S. 1982. *Sodium: Its Biological Significance.* CRC Press, Inc., Boca Raton, FL.

46. Bohstedt, G. and R. H. Grummer. 1954. *J. Animal Sci.* **13**:933.

47. Scott, M. L., M. C. Nesheim, and R. J. Young. 1969. *Nutrition of the Chicken.* M. L. Scott and Assoc. Pub., Ithaca, N.Y.

48. Baker, D. H. 1977. *Sulfur in Nonruminant Nutrition,* pp. 1–122. Natl. Feed Ingredients Assoc., Des Moines, IA.

49. Hays, V. W. 1972. In *The Searching Seventies.* Natl. Feed Ingred. Assoc. Proc., Moorman Mfg. Co., Quincy, IL.

12

Micro (Trace)
Minerals

THE DISTINCTION BETWEEN MACROMINERALS and micro or trace minerals is based on the relative amounts required in the diet for normal body function. The role of trace elements in animal and human health is of interest and importance from the standpoint of distinguishing between beneficial and harmful effects. Modern analytical techniques permit detection of minute traces of elements in animal tissues. For example, 25 different trace elements have been reported in human blood serum and kidney tissue, some of them in concentrations lower than those which could be detected by previous methods (1). Of these elements, only about half are required in the diets of humans. Fox and Tao (2) have tabulated responses in mineral content of animal tissues in relation to low or high dietary intake. Elements shown to be required in the diet as well as those for which no metabolic or dietary requirement has been established tend to concentrate in certain tissues in direct proportion to the amount supplied in the diet. Excessive accumulation even of required elements can produce toxic signs. This principle will be illustrated often in this chapter.

The list of trace minerals required by animals continues to grow. The latest mineral added to the list is Si, which was shown in 1972 (3) to be required for growth of chicks. The following are known now to be required by one or more animal species for normal life processes: Co (cobalt); I (iodine); Fe (iron); Cu (copper); Zn (zinc); Mn (manganese); Se (selenium); Cr (chromium); F (fluorine); Mo (molybdenum); and Si (silicon). In addition, the following are possibly required elements, based on limited evidence obtained with one or more animal species: Al (aluminum) (4); As (arsenic) (5); Cd (cadmium) (6); Ni (nickel) (7–9); V (vanadium) (10, 11); Sn (tin) (12); B (boron) (13); Br (bromine) (13); Pb (lead) (13); Li (lithium) (13).

The trace minerals function as activators of enzyme systems or as components of organic compounds and, as such, are required in small amounts. A vast array of enzyme systems require trace elements for activation.

Examples of enzymes requiring specific trace minerals are given for each mineral. Note that Mg, a macromineral, functions in many respects like the trace elements.

Each of the trace elements whose essentiality is established firmly is discussed in terms of tissue distribution, functions, metabolism, deficiency signs, and toxicity. Numerous reviews are available (14–18). Kubota (19) has described the regional distribution of trace element problems in North America and has developed Co, Se, and Mo soil maps of the USA (see Fig. 12.1) that are useful in identifying problem areas for trace element deficiencies and toxicities in animals and humans.

❏ COBALT (Co)

The only known animal requirement for Co is as a constituent of vitamin B_{12} (see Ch. 15). Co was recognized first as an important diet constituent as early as 1929 when large amounts were shown to be capable of stimulating red blood cell synthesis in rats. Later, Underwood and Filmer (20) showed that "wasting disease" of sheep and cattle in Australia could be cured or prevented by Co, and Smith *et al.* (21) showed that vitamin B_{12} injections brought about dramatic improvement in sheep showing Co deficiency.

Tissue Distribution

Liver, kidney, adrenal, and bone tissue contain Co in the highest concentration in all species studied. The forms in which it exists in tissues other than as a constituent of vitamin B_{12} are not known completely, although other bound forms do exist. Askew and Watson (22) reported 150 ppb of Co in dry liver from normal sheep compared with 20 ppb in liver of Co-deficient sheep; dried spleen, kidney, and heart of normal sheep also contained more Co.

Co supplementation of gestation diets of cows results in a higher concentration of Co in the tissues

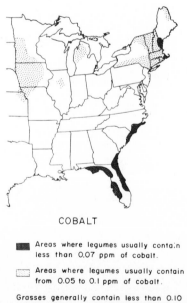

COBALT

▣ Areas where legumes usually contain less than 0.07 ppm of cobalt.

▢ Areas where legumes usually contain from 0.05 to 0.1 ppm of cobalt.

Grasses generally contain less than 0.10 ppm of cobalt throughout most of the U.S.

Figure 12.1a *Geographic distribution of Co-deficient areas in the eastern United States.*

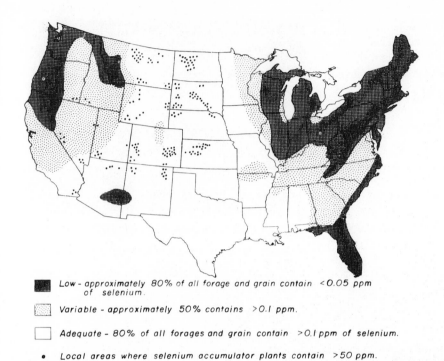

■ Low - approximately 80% of all forage and grain contain <0.05 ppm
    of selenium.

▨ Variable - approximately 50% contains >0.1 ppm.

☐ Adequate - 80% of all forages and grain contain >0.1 ppm of selenium.

• Local areas where selenium accumulator plants contain >50 ppm.

Figure 12.1b *Geographic distribution of low-, variable-, and adequate-Se areas in the United States.*

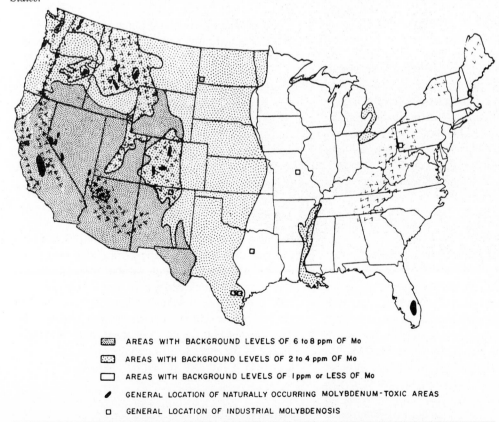

▨ AREAS WITH BACKGROUND LEVELS OF 6 to 8 ppm OF Mo

▨ AREAS WITH BACKGROUND LEVELS OF 2 to 4 ppm OF Mo

☐ AREAS WITH BACKGROUND LEVELS OF 1 ppm or LESS OF Mo

▰ GENERAL LOCATION OF NATURALLY OCCURRING MOLYBDENUM-TOXIC AREAS

☐ GENERAL LOCATION OF INDUSTRIAL MOLYBDENOSIS

Figure 12.1c *Generalized regional pattern of Mo concentration in legumes and its relation to Mo-toxic areas in the United States. Figure 12.1a, b and c courtesy of J. Kubota, USDA.*

of calves; similarly, Co content of milk is increased by supplementation of the lactation diet. This extra Co apparently is not present as a constituent of vitamin B_{12}, as it is not utilized until the young animal has developed a functioning rumen.

Functions

All evidence indicates that Co functions only as a constituent of vitamin B_{12}. Co deficiency, in the presence of adequate vitamin B_{12} intake, has never been produced in non-ruminants. Likewise, ruminants with normal rumen function apparently do not require dietary Co greater than that needed for microbial vitamin B_{12} synthesis. Although Co can activate certain enzymes, there is no evidence that it is required for this purpose because the enzymes will function in the presence of other divalent metals.

Metabolism

Inorganic Co is absorbed poorly from the GI tract in animals, although adult humans may be an exception. About 80% of an orally administered dose of radioactive Co appears in the feces of rats and cattle. Most of the parenterally administered Co is excreted through the kidney. Although some loss occurs via the GI tract, the amount is small and probably via the bile and intestinal wall, but not from the pancreas. Tissue Co appears to be eliminated slowly. No synthesis of vitamin B_{12} in animal tissues from inorganic Co is known, even though tissue levels are high.

Large oral doses of Co induce polycythemia (increased RBC concentration) in several species. The mechanism apparently is by production of anoxia, possibly by binding SH compounds, with increased RBC synthesis as a compensatory response.

Deficiency Signs

Because Co functions as a constituent of vitamin B_{12}, the deficiency signs described for vitamin B_{12} (see Ch. 15) apply for Co. Ruminants grazing in Co-deficient areas show loss of appetite, reduced growth or loss in body weight followed by emaciation (Fig. 12.2), normocytic normochromic anemia, and eventually death. Fatty degeneration of the liver and hemosiderosis of the spleen occur. Microbial synthesis of B_{12} in the rumen of deficient ruminants is depressed greatly. The first notable response to Co feeding is an improved appetite followed by increased blood hemoglobin concentration. Critical levels of Co in diets for ruminants below which Co deficiency signs appear are 0.07 to 0.11 ppm of dry matter.

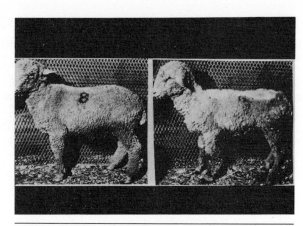

Figure 12.2   *Co-deficient sheep. Note the severe emaciation and wool chewing that has occurred. The lamb on the left received an adequate diet. By permission of S. E. Smith, Cornell University.*

Soil maps (14, 19) show large areas in the USA, Australia and other parts of the world where soil is deficient in Co, resulting in low Co content of plant tissues and deficiencies in animals consuming the plants.

Co deficiency in grazing ruminants is treated by orally administering small dense pellets of Co oxide and Fe. The pellets lodge in the rumen and are dissolved gradually over a period of months, yielding a constant supply of Co for vitamin B_{12} synthesis. Such a technique eliminates the need for a mineral supplement which may not be voluntarily consumed in appropriate amounts by free-ranging animals. Australian work indicates that two pellets offer enough abrasion to provide a steady supply of Co for vitamin B_{12} synthesis for more than 5 years in sheep.

Toxicity

Because of its low absorption rate, Co toxicity is not likely. A daily intake of 3 mg Co/kg body weight for 8 wk is tolerated by sheep without harmful effects. Higher doses result in appetite depression and anemia. Co given as a soluble salt to provide 300 mg Co/kg body weight is lethal to sheep. Cattle may be less tolerant than sheep. A concentration of about 2 mg/kg in the diet of growing pigs produced no toxicity over a 100-day feeding period (23).

❑ IODINE (I)

It was suggested nearly 150 years ago that I deficiency caused goiter in humans, but the theory was rejected until about 1900 when it was observed that I was concentrated in the thyroid gland and the concentration was reduced in persons with goiter (18). Tragically, endemic goiter continues today as a widespread problem in the developing countries as it was 50 years ago (24), and may be as high as 45% to 50% in some areas. Thyroxin was isolated in 1919 and synthesized in 1927. The structure of thyroxin ($3,3',5,5'$-tetraiodothyronine or T_4) is shown below.

THYROXIN

Of the several compounds showing thyroid activity, thyroxin is present in blood in the highest concentration (25). The thyronine nucleus (structure shown above, minus I's) is essential for activity. Other compounds with thyroid activity include: T_3 or $3,5$-$3'$-triodothyronine (similar to thyroxin in activity); $3,5$-diiodo-$3'$-$5'$-dibromothyronine (nearly as active); and $3,5,3'$-triiodothyropropionic acid (300 times as active as thyroxin).

Tissue Distribution

The thyroid gland contains the highest concentration of I (0.2–5% of dry weight) and in the largest amount (70–80% of total body I). I also is preferentially concentrated in the stomach (or abomasum), small intestine, salivary glands, skin, mammary gland, ovary, and placenta. Species differences exist in this capacity. The total I content of the adult human is 10–20 mg. The concentration of inorganic I in most tissues in 1–2 mcg/100 g, and that of organically bound I is about 5 mcg/100 g for muscle with higher concentration in tissues that concentrate I.

The only known function of I is as a constituent of thyroxin and other thyroid-active compounds. Thus, it is intimately associated with basal metabolic rate.

Metabolism

Inorganic I is absorbed from the GI tract by two processes, one in common with other halides (Cl, Br) and one specific for I. The specific I transport system is present in the stomach as well as the small intestine. The stomach and a midsection of the small intestine secrete I from the serosal to the mucosal surface. In fact, the gastric juice reaches an I concentration up to 40 times that of the plasma in humans. The I-specific transport mechanism is saturated by high I concentrations. This is in common with the similar system in the thyroid gland, but differs in that GI tract absorption is not affected by thyroid stimulating hormone (TSH) from the anterior pituitary gland, although thyroid tissue is affected profoundly.

Salivary secretion of I is an active process in most species, as evidenced by the 40-fold concentration of radioactive I in the saliva as compared to plasma of animals given radioiodine. The rat apparently is an exception.

The I supply to the developing embryo is enhanced by at least two mechanisms. The ovary and placenta both concentrate I by an active process. The role of the ovary is best illustrated in birds. Radioiodine injected into the hen is taken up by the yolk of eggs laid afterward, indicating that the yolk is an I store for the developing chick embryo. Similarly, placental tissue of mammals concentrates I in late pregnancy. A second mechanism favoring fetal I uptake is the presence in fetal serum of a specific thyroxin-binding protein which increases in concentration in late fetal development and has a higher affinity for thyroxin than the thyroxin-binding protein of the maternal plasma. This favors the fetus receiving an adequate I supply if the combined thyroxin content of the maternal and fetal plasma is low. The mammary gland also concentrates I, and the transfer of inorganic I is by an active process resulting in a 40-fold concentration of I in milk as compared to plasma. Although some T_4 and T_3 are found in milk, the amounts are small under normal conditions.

The key organ for I metabolism is the thyroid gland. It concentrates I by an active process which is enhanced by thyroid stimulating hormone (TSH) secreted by the anterior pituitary gland. The I-concentrating ability of the thyroid is expressed as a ratio of the I concentration of the thyroid to the I concentration of the serum (T/S value). Normal animals have a T/S value of 20. The T/S value is decreased by hypophysectomy and increased by stimulating TSH release.

I reaching the thyroid from the plasma is concentrated in the lumen of follicles of the thyroid, each of which is composed of a single layer of cells arranged as a sphere. The I so stored is contained in a colloid protein, thyrogiobulin. Inorganic radioiodine given intravenously appears largely as protein-bound I (thyroproteins) in the thyroid gland shortly after injection. The iodinated proteins of the thyroid include mainly thyroglobulins (the thyroactive fraction), but also small amounts of others.

I is oxidized by peroxidase to a reactive form for thyroglobulin formation. Gross (25) outlined the steps in biosynthesis of the thyroid active compounds, thyroxin (T_4), 3,5,3'-triiodothyronine (T_3), 3-monoiodotyrosine (MIT), and 3,5-diiodotyrosine (DIT). Tyrosine present in the thyroglobulin molecule can be iodinated to form MIT, which is in turn used to form 3,3'-diiodothyronine or MIT can be iodinated further to form DIT, which is in turn used to form T_3 or T_4. The amount of I in thyroglobulin, therefore, is dependent on the proportions of these tyrosine derivatives present.

Thyroglobulin does not appear in the plasma but is hydrolyzed by thyroid proteases in the thyroid follicle. On hydrolysis only the iodothyronines are detected in the plasma. Free iodothyronines are deiodinated by enzymes in the thyroid, and the free I is available for recycling through thyroglobulin.

Iodothyronines are transported in the plasma bound to a globulin (thyroxin-binding globulin or TBG) or to a thyroxin-binding prealbumin. Some binding of thyroxin by plasma albumin occurs also. TBG, however, binds most of the iodothyronines at normal plasma concentrations. No evidence has shown that thyroxin and its derivatives leave the plasma, except for entrance into lymph. Thus, the concentration of free iodothyronines in the blood plasma and extracellular fluids probably controls the rate of transfer to sites of action. Only about 0.05% of total plasma thyroxin is present in the free state.

The protein bound I (PBI) level of the serum varies with level of thyroid activity, as well as with species and age. Plasma PBI levels are increased with hyperthyroid activity and generally are higher in young animals and in pregnancy. Although plasma PBI levels provide a general assessment of thyroid activity, consistent results have not been obtained in attempts to relate them to growth rate or milk production.

About 80% of thyroid hormones entering the tissue are broken down by de-iodinization by liver, kidney and other tissues with the liberated I recycled for further use and the tyrosine residues catabolized or used for tissue protein synthesis. The remaining 20% is lost to the body through excretion via the bile, by conjugation to form glucuronides or sulfate esters, or by oxidative deamination (25). Inorganic I is excreted mainly via the kidneys. Smaller amounts are lost to sweat and in feces. The salivary gland secretes large amounts, but most of this is reabsorbed from the GI tract.

Deficiency Signs

Because I functions as a constituent of thyroid-active compounds which, in turn, play a major role in controlling the rate of cellular oxidation, it is not surprising that a dietary deficiency of I has profound effects on the animal. Dietary I deficiency reduces basal metabolic rate (BMR). I deficiency in young animals is called cretinism, and in adults, myxedema. Tissues of I-deficient animals consume less oxygen and the reduced BMR is associated with reduced growth rate and reduced gonadal activity. Skin becomes dry and hair brittle. Reproductive problems associated with I deficiency include resorbed fetuses, abortions, stillbirths, irregular or suppressed estrus in females, and a decreased libido and deterioration of semen quality in males. Pigs and calves produced by I-deficient dams may be hairless with dry, thick skin (Fig. 12.3) or, if hair is present, the coat is harsh and sparse, or in sheep the wool is scanty. The fleece of adult sheep recovered from I deficiency in early life may be of poor quality because of interference with normal development of the wool producing cells.

Thyroid enlargement (goiter) is induced by an attempt of the thyroid gland to secrete more thyroxin in response to TSH stimulation. TSH is released in response to a reduced thyroxin production. Thyroid hormones, in a negative feedback arrangement, inhibit release of thyrotropic hormone releasing factor (TRF) by the hypothalamus and thyroid stimulating hormone (TSH) by the anterior pituitary. In the absence of adequate thyroxin for inhibiting TSH release, the thyroid gland becomes hyperactive and

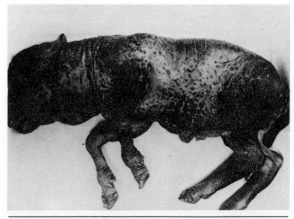

Figure 12.3 *An iodine-deficient lamb showing hairlessness, thick wrinkled skin, and a marked enlargement of the thyroid gland. Photo courtesy of W. M. Hawkins, Montana State University.*

enlarged. Goiter is a common problem in human and animal populations living in inland areas in many parts of the world. The use of iodized salt has reduced the problem, but endemic goiter still remains as a major nutritional disease in many areas (24).

In addition to simple I deficiency, several goitrogenic substances are present in common foods. These antithyroid compounds act by interfering with the iodinization of tyrosine, thus blocking iodothyronine synthesis.

Natural goitrogens present in plants consumed by animals and humans include thiocyanite in cassava; glucosinolates, which on hydrolysis release thiocyanate, in cabbage, rape and mustard; a glucopeptide in soybeans; metabolites of anthocyanin pigments in peanuts (24). Synthetic compounds with goitrogenic properties include polychlorinated biphenyls (PCBs) used as plasticizers, polybrominated biphenyls (PBB's) used as fire retardants, organochlorine compounds (DDT, DDD, and Dieldren) used as insecticides, and various antifungal and antibacterial agents such as ethylene carbamates (EBDC), sulfanamides, and tetracyclines (24). The mechanisms of action of natural and synthetic goitrogenic agents have as a common basis the inhibition of uptake of inorganic I by the tyrosine skeleton to form iodothyronines.

Toxicity

Long-term chronic intake of large amounts of I reduced thyroid uptake of I, but marked species differences exist in tolerance of high intakes of I. Fertility of male rats fed 2,400 ppm I for 200 days is unaffected (26); reproduction of female swine is unaffected by the same intake during gestation, but rabbits show increased prenatal mortality. Egg production of hens was reduced markedly by feeding 312 ppm and terminated with 5,000 ppm I, and hatchability was reduced (27). An effect on thyroxin production seems unlikely, as egg production was resumed within 1 week after withdrawal of the I from the diet.

Instances of goiter resulting from consumption of large amounts of high-iodine plants such as kelp have been reported in humans in Japan (28) and in horses in Florida (29). Excess iodine disturbs all thyroid functions, including transport of I, synthesis of thyroxin, and release of the hormone (30).

Apparently, the levels of I normally encountered in nutrition are far less than levels necessary to cause toxic symptoms. Single oral massive doses of I are toxic and may be lethal, but such toxicity must be categorized as poisoning in the general sense.

❏ ZINC (Zn)

Zn was shown to be an essential nutrient for animals in 1934 when Todd *et al.* (31) produced a deficiency in the rat. In farm animal nutrition the disease of swine termed parakeratosis was shown later to result from Zn deficiency (32). Subsequently, Zn deficiency has been produced experimentally in other farm animals, and Zn deficiency in humans has been reported as a practical problem. The nutrition, physiology, and metabolism of Zn has been reviewed in detail (14, 33–36).

Tissue Distribution

Zn is distributed widely in body tissues, but is in highest concentration in liver, bone, kidney, muscle, pancreas, eye, prostrate gland, skin, hair, and wool. Radioactive Zn given orally or intravenously to normal or Zn-deficient cattle reaches a peak concentration in the liver within a few days, but concentrations in red blood cells, muscle, bone, and hair do not peak until several weeks later. Deficient animals retain more ^{65}Zn in skin, testes, scrotum, kidney, muscle, heart, lung, and spleen than normal animals, suggesting tissue specificity in meeting needs when Zn supply is short. Zn is a constituent of a large number of enzymes and the tissue distribution of Zn is associated roughly with the tissue distribution of enzyme systems to which it is related. For example, when bone Zn is high, alkaline phosphatase of bone is high. The high concentration of Zn in the pancreas probably is related both to its presence in digestive enzymes and to its association with the hormone, insulin, which is secreted by the pancreas.

The Zn concentration in blood is divided between the cells and plasma in a 9:1 ratio. Plasma Zn is bound loosely to albumins (1/3) and more firmly to globulins (2/3) and is responsive to dietary levels. Most of the Zn in RBCs is present as a component of carbonic anhydrase.

Amounts of Zn in heart, kidney, liver, and muscle of normal cattle, chickens, sheep, and swine have been summarized (37). Tables summarizing the Zn content of foods of animal and plant origin have been prepared (38).

Functions

Zn is a constituent of numerous metalloenzymes, including carbonic anhydrase, carboxypeptidases A and B, several dehydrogenases, alkaline phosphatase, ribonuclease, and DNA polymerase. Zn activates some enzymes and plays a role in the configuration of DNA and RNA. Its biochemical functions have been reviewed by Chesters (39).

The biochemical functions of Zn are related to the functions of the enzymes of which it is a constituent. Zn also is an activator of several metalloenzyme systems and probably shares with other metal ions, which it can replace, the function of binding reactants to the active site of the enzyme. Zn is required for normal protein synthesis and metabolism, and is a component of insulin and, in this way, functions in carbohydrate metabolism.

Metabolism

Absorption of Zn from the GI tract occurs throughout the small intestine and amounts to 5–40% of the intake. Regulation of Zn absorption occurs in the intestinal cell (54, 55). Isolated intestines from rats deficient or adequate in Zn nutrition absorb greater or lesser amounts of Zn, thereby contributing to Zn homeostasis (36). Transfer of Zn out of the intestinal mucosal cells to the plasma is controlled closely by metallothionein, a low molecular weight binding protein which is synthesized in response to a rise in plasma Zn concentration. Thus, the overall process of Zn absorption appears to be regulated by intracellular compartmentalization as well as by endogenous secretion of Zn in excess of immediate meta-

bolic needs from the intestinal cells into the intestinal tract lumen. The regulatory pathway of Zn movement across the intestinal cell is depicted in Fig. 12.4. Details of the biochemical and physiological aspects of zinc absorption have been reviewed (40, 41).

The absorption of Zn is affected adversely by high dietary Ca concentration, and the presence of phytate further aggravates it. The complexing of Zn by phytate forms an insoluble and unabsorbable compound and is one mechanism whereby Zn availability to animals is reduced. A chelating agent, ethylene diamine tetra acetate or EDTA, improves Zn availability by competing with phytate to form an EDTA-Zn complex that allows absorption of Zn either as free Zn ion or as the EDTA-Zn complex. The presence of low molecular weight binding ligands such as histidine and cystine in feedstuffs such as soybean meal and corn decrease it. Although some research suggests a role for picolinic acid in enhancing Zn absorption, the reports have not been corroborated by others. Diets containing similar amounts of Zn may produce a variable incidence of parakeratosis in swine and variable weight gain in chicks and rats. Phosphate also binds Zn and may be a factor in the observed difference among protein sources in Zn availability.

Zn metabolism and movement in tissues has been

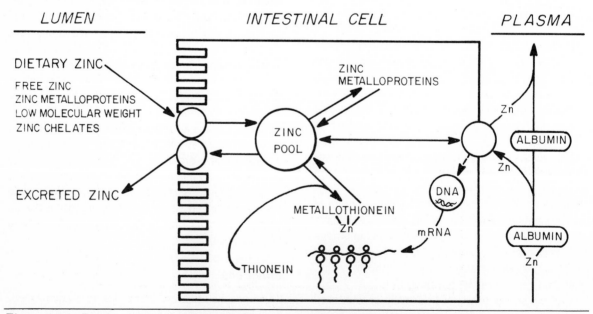

Figure 12.4 *Regulatory pathway of dietary zinc processing by intestinal cells. (Dashed line denotes induction of metallothionein mRNA; thionein is metal-free metallothionein) (34). Courtesy R. J. Cousins.*

studied by Pekas (42) who used ^{65}Zn infusion to follow Zn movement in the body. He reported that Zn is removed from the blood rapidly by the tissues and that tissues saturated with Zn (muscle) translocate Zn to unsaturated tissues (liver, pancreas and kidney). Saturated tissues were characterized by no net change in Zn content, and unsaturated tissues showed a marked increase in Zn content. Injected Zn is excreted largely in the feces. Thus, fecal Zn in animals on an adequate Zn intake includes both unabsorbed and endogenously secreted Zn. The pancreatic juice appears to be the main route of excretion of endogenous Zn. Endogenous losses are reduced during dietary Zn deficiency, serving to conserve body stores. Except in abnormal conditions such as nephrosis or hypertension, urinary losses of Zn are very low. Excretion can be increased 10-fold by administration of EDTA. Placental transfer of Zn is related directly to maternal dietary intake (14, 43).

In animals that sweat freely, Zn loss by this route can be extensive in hot environments. Prasad *et al.* (44) showed that humans may lose 5 mg Zn/day on a diet adequate in Zn; Zn-deficient individuals lose less than half than under the same environmental conditions, again illustrating the homeostatic control of body Zn stores.

Marked fluctuations in liver Zn content may occur in response to varied Zn intake. Zn in excess of current needs is bound in the liver to metallothonein, which, as in the intestinal cell, is synthesized in response to a rise in plasma Zn. Glucocorticoids cause liver to accumulate Zn with a concomitant decrease in plasma Zn. The role of the liver cell in processing Zn is depicted in Fig. 12.5. While the biological significance of this hormone-induced shift in tissue Zn is not understood fully, it has been suggested that

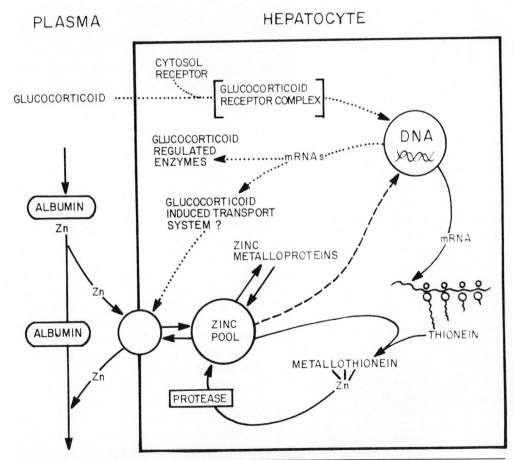

Figure 12.5 *Pathway of zinc processing by hepatocytes: role of plasma zinc and glucocorticoids. (Dashed line denotes induction of metallothionein mRNA by zinc; dotted lines denote glucocorticoid-related events; thionein is metal-free matallothionein) (34). Courtesy R. J. Cousins.*

any stress involving an increase in glucocorticoid activity may lead to an increase in liver metallothionein synthesis. The role of Zn in this stress related response undoubtedly will receive further study.

Deficiency Signs

The most conspicuous sign of Zn deficiency is growth retardation (Fig. 12.6) and anorexia in all species studied and a reduction in plasma alkaline phosphatase activity and in plasma Zn concentration. Thickening or hyperkeratinization of the epithelial cells is common (parakeratosis in swine, see Fig. 12.7). Rats show scaling and cracking of the paws, rough hair coat and alopecia (loss of hair); sheep show abnormal changes in wool and horns; poor feathering and dermatitis occur in poultry.

Zn deficiency retards bone formation and is associated with reduced division and proliferation of cartilage cells in the epiphyseal growth plate (18, 70). Bone alkaline phosphatase is reduced, bone density is depressed and Zn content of bone and of liver are reduced. Apgar (43) has reviewed the effects of Zn deficiency on reproduction in animals and Prasad (44) described the clinical manifestations of Zn deficiency.

Hens fed Zn-deficient diets for several months show no abnormalities, but chicks produced show poor livability and a high incidence of malformations. Chicks from hens fed adequate levels of Zn develop a perosis-like leg abnormality when fed Zn-deficient diets. This defect has been prevented by feeding histidine or histamine. The mechanism of this protective effect is unknown. Feeding female rats Zn-deficient diets during gestation results in high early

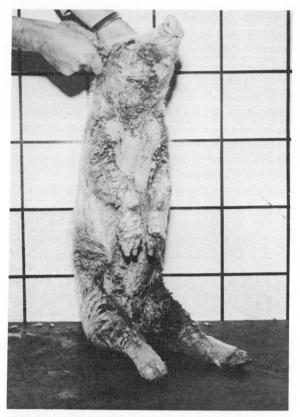

Figure 12.7 *A pig with severe Zn deficiency (parakeratosis). This pig received 10 ppm Zn, 1.06% Ca and 0.66% P in its diet. It lost 2.0 lb in 14 days. Courtesy of J. H. Conrad, Purdue University.*

mortality as well as difficulty in parturition and abnormal changes in maternal behavior of the dams. The effects of Zn deficiency are aggravated by intraperitoneal injection of EDTA (a chelating agent) in late pregnancy. EDTA increases Zn excretion and is itself excreted rapidly. Sheep fed a Zn-deficient diet during pregnancy and lactation show reduced plasma and wool Zn and their lambs are affected likewise at 6 weeks of age. Pups from Zn-deficient dams show lower liver and total body Zn concentrations than controls and have a smaller birth weight.

Zn deficiency has drastic effects on the male reproductive organs. Hypogonadism is observed in Zn-deficient males of all species studied. In humans, hypogonadism, suppressed development of secondary sex characteristics and dwarfism have been observed in Iranian and Egyptian young men (44). Recovery of testes size and sperm production are achieved in young animals repleted with Zn.

Figure 12.6 *Effect of inadequate Zn on growth of pigs. From left to right, pigs received 46, 36 and 24 ppm of Zn. Note the severe parakeratosis in pig on the far right. Courtesy of W. M. Beeson, Purdue University.*

Wound healing of Zn-deficient animals is delayed severely. The exact mode of action of Zn in tissue repair is unknown, but the role of Zn in normal protein synthesis probably provides a clue to the relationship. Decreased activity of hepatic enzymes, leucine aminopeptidase, and ornithine transcarbamylase has been noted in Zn deficient swine.

Zn deficiency causes impairment of glucose tolerance in rats, supporting the known relationship between Zn and insulin. The glucose intolerance is not related to blood insulin concentration, but to peripheral resistance to insulin action (45).

A striking feature of Zn deficiency is the dramatic remission of clinical signs when Zn is administered. This is illustrated in parakeratosis in Zn-deficient pigs. The skin of animals with severe lesions shows marked improvement after a few days of Zn refeeding and complete disappearance of the lesion within 2–3 weeks; feed intake improves immediately after Zn is added to the diet.

Toxicity

A wide margin of safety exists between the required intake of Zn and the amount that will produce toxic effects. Although the requirement for most species is less than 50 mg/kg of diet, levels of 1–2.5 g/kg have been fed to rats with no deleterious effects. Smith and Larson (46) observed anemia, growth failure and death in rats fed 1% Zn, although lower levels (0.7%) allowed life but induced anemia and reduced growth. Zn fed at 1 g/kg showed no ill-effects in pigs, but levels of 4 and 8 g/kg produced depressed growth, stiffness, hemorrhages around bone joints and excessive bone resorption (47). Birds are similar to swine in their tolerance to Zn, but sheep and cattle are less tolerant. Levels of 0.9–1.7 g/kg of Zn depress appetite and induce depraved appetite manifested by wood-chewing and excessive consumption of mineral supplements by sheep. The lower tolerance of ruminants to high dietary Zn may be related to changes in rumen metabolism brought about by a toxic effect of Zn on the rumen microflora.

Because the anemia produced by excess Zn can be prevented by extra Cu and Fe, it has been suggested that the anemia is an induced Cu and Fe deficiency as a result of interference with their absorption from the GI tract in the presence of high Zn. This adverse effect of excess Zn on Cu, Fe, and Mn level of liver has been substantiated with Japanese quail (48).

In most studies reviewed (16), no adverse effects occurred when dietary Zn concentration was below 600 ppm. Many factors influence Zn toxicity; dietary Pb (46), Cu deficiency, marginal Se intake, and low Ca intake exacerbate it, while soybean protein appears to protect against excess Zn compared with casein, perhaps due to its phytate content (16). Details of the toxic effects of Zn have been reviewed (16, 49).

❏ IRON (Fe)

Iron has been recognized as a required nutrient for animals for more than 100 years. Despite this fact, Fe deficiency remains a common disease affecting nearly half of the human population in some areas of the world and persisting as a major problem in livestock production. Reviews of Fe metabolism and nutrition are numerous (14, 16, 50–52).

Tissue Distribution and Function

Sixty to 70% of body Fe is present in hemoglobin in red blood cells and myoglobin in muscle; 20% is stored in labile forms in liver, spleen, and other tissues and is available for hemoglobin formation; the remaining 10–20% is fixed firmly in unavailable forms in tissues as a component of muscle myosin and actomyosin and as a constituent of enzymes and associated with metalloenzymes (50). The absolute amounts of Fe present in various forms in several species are summarized in Table 12.1 (51). Fe is present in hemoglobin, myoglobin, and heme enzymes, cytochromes, catalases, and peroxidases as heme, an organic compound consisting of Fe in the center of a porphyrin ring. In hemoglobin, which contains 0.34% Fe, an atom of ferrous Fe in the center of the porphyrin ring connects heme, the prosthetic group with globin, the protein. Hemoglobin contains four porphyrin rings and combines reversibly with atmospheric oxygen brought into the blood via the lungs. Hemoglobin is found within the red blood cell. Myoglobin, which has one-fourth the molecular weight of hemoglobin (16,500), is present in muscle and has an affinity for oxygen greater than that of hemoglobin. The heme enzymes—catalases and peroxidases—contain Fe in the ferric state (Fe^{+++}). Each of these classes of enzyme liberates oxygen from peroxides. Cytochrome enzymes are heme enzymes of the cell mitochondria and act in electron transfer by virtue of the reversible oxidation of Fe ($Fe^{++} \rightleftharpoons Fe^{+++}$). Cytochromes a, b, and c, cytochrome ox-

TABLE 12.1   Amounts and distribution of Fe in the rat, dog, calf, horse, and man.[a]

SPECIES	BODY WT.	IRON CONTENT, G				
		TOTAL BODY	HEMOGLOBIN	MYOGLOBIN	CYTOCHROMIC	STORAGE
Calf	182.0	11.13	7.55	1.060	0.0053	2.517
Dog	6.35	0.44	0.300	0.040	0.00059	0.100
Horse	500.0	33.0	19.85	6.45	0.0715	6.617
Man	70.0	4.26	3.10	0.120	0.00336	1.03
Rat	0.25	0.015	0.011	0.0003	0.00006	0.0036

[a]Adapted from Moore (51).

idase, and others have been identified, but only cytochrome c is readily extractable from tissues. Other enzymes containing Fe include xanthine oxidase, succinic dehydrogenase and NADH-cytochrome reductase.

Fe in blood plasma is bound in the ferric state (Fe^{+++}) to a specific protein, transferrin, a β_1-globulin. Transferrin is the carrier of Fe in the blood and is saturated normally only to the extent of 30–60% of its total Fe-binding capacity.

Fe is stored in liver, spleen and bone marrow as an Fe-protein complex, ferritin, and as a component of hemosiderin. Fe makes up 20% of the ferritin-Fe complex and is present in the ferric state. Hemosiderin contains 35% Fe as ferric hydroxide. It is present in tissues as a brown, granular pigment. Ferritin can be considered the soluble and hemosiderin the insoluble form of storage Fe. Under normal conditions, and in Fe deficiency, Fe is stored in about equal amounts in each form, but in Fe excess, hemosiderin Fe predominates.

Metabolism

Absorption.   Fe is absorbed mainly from the duodenum in the ferrous state (Fe^{++}), and usually only to the extent of 5–10%. The body holds absorbed Fe tenaciously for reuse. Thus, the Fe released from hemoglobin breakdown associated with RBC destruction (RBC life is 60 to 120 days in most species) is recycled for resynthesis of hemoglobin. This conservation of Fe is illustrated in the diagrammatic outline of Fe metabolism in Fig. 12.8. Absorption is more efficient under acid conditions; thus, the amount of Fe absorbed from the stomach and duodenum, where HCl from stomach secretion results in a low pH, is greater than from the ileum. In rats there is a gradient from the upper to lower end of the small

intestine in absorption of Fe, with Fe uptake more than 10 times greater in the proximal duodenum than in the distal ileum. Iron absorption is increased by certain amino acids (valine, histidine); ascorbic acid; organic acids (lactic, pyruvic, citric); and certain sugars (fructose, sorbitol), probably by forming soluble chelates with Fe.

Tophan *et al.* (53) have shown that xanthine oxidase in intestinal mucosa promotes incorporation of iron into transferrin for transport in blood. Thus, the oxidation of Fe^{++} to Fe^{+++} for transport in blood (which is associated with ceruloplasmin for Fe mobilization from liver) is accomplished by xanthine oxidase in the intestinal mucosa. Maximum absorption occurs at pH 2 to 3.5. Fe absorption is greater in Fe-depleted animals than in animals receiving adequate Fe, and the absolute amount of Fe absorbed is increased as the size of an oral dose increases, but the percentage absorption decreases. Fe present in hemoglobin and myoglobin is absorbed readily as heme Fe. High levels of inorganic phosphates reduce Fe absorption by forming insoluble salts; phytate also has been reported to reduce Fe absorption, but the practical importance in normal diets is unknown. High levels of other trace elements, including Zn, Mn, Cu, and Cd, also reduce Fe absorption, presumably by competing at protein binding sites in the intestinal mucosa. Neonatal pig intestinal cell membranes and cytoplasm contain Fe-binding substances (54). Other data from the same laboratory indicate that the serosal as well as the mucosal epithelium regulate Fe transfer from the intestinal lumen of the pig.

The ultimate regulation of Fe absorption is dependent apparently on the Fe concentration of the intestinal mucosal cells; that is, of the Fe taken up by the mucosal cells, only a small part is transferred from the cell to the blood; the bulk is retained in the cell and lost in the intestinal lumen when the cell is sloughed off in the normal process of regeneration of intestinal epithelium. In deficient animals Fe is transferred more readily from the mucosal cell to blood until saturation of the tissues results in a return to normal retention of Fe in the mucosal cell. Parenterally administered Fe decreases Fe absorption in some species by transfer into the intestinal epithelial cell from the serosal side (from the blood). Thus, the "mucosal block" theory of Fe absorption, which was advanced by Hahn *et al.* in 1943 (55) remains as an important general concept, even though the mechanisms may not be exactly as envisioned originally.

Excretion.   Body Fe is retained tenaciously (see Fig. 12.8). Fecal Fe mainly is unabsorbed dietary Fe, but a small amount (0.3–0.5 mg/kg in humans) is lost through bile and sloughed intestinal mucosal cells. Even when Fe is injected, very little of it is excreted in either feces or urine, although urinary Fe loss does occur when parenteral Fe is given in excess of the plasma Fe-binding capacity or when chelating agents are given. Small amounts of Fe are lost in sweat in humans.

Placental and Mammary Transfer.   Considerable species variability exists in the efficiency of transfer of Fe to the fetus across the placenta. Fe is transported to the fetus by an active process and concentration in the fetal circulation exceeds that in maternal plasma. Transferrin does not cross the placenta; rather, Fe is dissociated from transferrin on the maternal side of the placenta and reassociated with transferrin on the fetal side. As gestation progresses, more and more Fe is transferred to the fetus. Although the newborn of some species have a relatively high liver Fe concentration, the newborn pig is not supplied well with Fe and is prone especially to Fe deficiency. The low placental transfer of Fe is

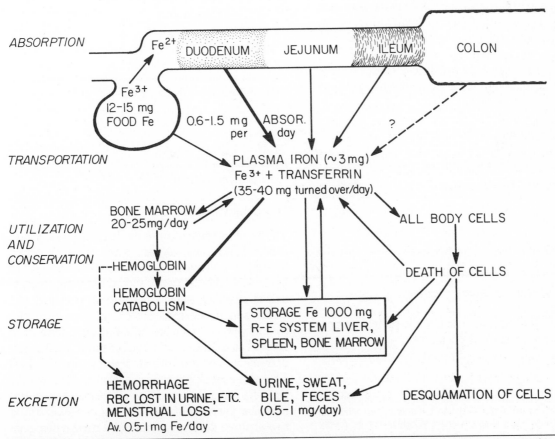

Figure 12.8   *Schematic representation of iron metabolism in man. RBC = red blood cells; R-E system = reticuloendothelial system. From Moore and Dubach (50).*

not increased appreciably even by high levels of supplementation of the maternal diet or by parenteral administration to the sow.

Milk of all species is low in Fe. Attempts to increase the Fe concentration of sow milk by parenteral Fe or by feeding extra Fe to the sow during lactation have not resulted in appreciable increases in milk Fe content.

Storage and Mobilization.   Fe is stored within the cells of the liver, spleen, bone marrow, and other tissues as ferritin and hemosiderin in roughly equal proportions. Incorporation of plasma Fe (transferrin) into ferritin in liver cells is energy-dependent (ATP) and is related to the reduction of Fe^{+++} of transferrin to Fe^{++}, making it available for ferritin formation. Release of Fe^{++} in liver ferritin to plasma is catalyzed by xanthine oxidase. Similar reactions are presumed to occur in other Fe-storage tissues. The corresponding mechanisms for release and uptake of hemosiderin between transferrin and storage tissues are not known.

The turnover rate of Fe in the plasma is very rapid; about $10\times$ the amount of Fe in the plasma at any one time is transported each day. Most of this is used for hemoglobin synthesis. Inorganic radioiron appears almost entirely as a component of hemoglobin in 7 to 14 days in humans. The continuous redistribution of body Fe can be summarized (14) as follows:

Quantitatively most important:

plasma $\longrightarrow$ erythroid marrow $\longrightarrow$

red cell $\longrightarrow$ senescent red cell $\longrightarrow$ plasma

Less important:

plasma $\longrightarrow$ ferritin and hemosiderin $\longrightarrow$ plasma

plasma $\longrightarrow$ myoglobin and

Fe-containing enzymes $\longrightarrow$ plasma

Enzymes contain Fe bound to the protein, to porphyrin, or to flavins (metalloenzymes)* or as a loosely bound activator (metal activated enzymes).* A par-

*Metalloenzymes have the active metal firmly bound in a constant stoichiometric ratio to the protein of the enzyme; in metal-activated enzymes, the activating metal is loosely bound and readily lost on processing. Often metals loosely bound in this way can be replaced by other metal ions without loss of the activity of the enzyme.

TABLE 12.2   Fe-containing enzymes and proteins in animals.[a]

Metalloporphyrin enzymes
Cytochrome oxidase
Cytochrome C
Other cytochromes (P-450, b_5)
Peroxidase
Catalase
Aldehyde oxidase
Metalloflavin enzymes
NAdH cytochrome C reductase
Succinic dehydrogenase
Lactic dehydrogenase
α-glycerophosphate dehydrogenase
Choline dehydrogenase
Aldehyde dehydrogenase
Xanthine oxidase
Metalloproteins other than enzymes
Hemoglobin (>10% of body iron)
Myoglobin (10% of body iron)
Transferrin
Ovotransferrin
Lactotransferrin
Ferritin

[a]Adapted from Bowen (56) and Dallman (52).

tial list of Fe-containing enzymes in mammals and birds, along with some important Fe-containing proteins is given in Table 12.2.

Deficiency Signs

The most common sign of Fe deficiency is a microcytic, hypochromic anemia, which is characterized by smaller than normal red cells and less than normal hemoglobin. Fe-deficiency anemia is a common problem in newborn animals because of inefficient placental and mammary transfer. In pigs unsupplemented with Fe, blood hemoglobin declines from about 10 g/dℓ at birth to 3 or 4 g/dℓ at three weeks. The extremely rapid growth rate of young pigs (5X birth wt at three weeks) results in a dilution effect of total body Fe stores unless Fe is fed or injected. Intramuscular injection of 150–200 mg of Fe-dextrin at two or three days of age maintains normal hemoglobin level at three weeks of age at which time consumption of dry feed provides ample Fe. Anemic pigs show pallor, labored breathing, rough hair coats, poor appetite, reduced growth rate (Fig. 12.9) and increased susceptibility to stresses and infectious agents. Heavy infestation with internal parasites of the blood-sucking type leads to an induced Fe-deficiency anemia in many animal species, including sheep, pigs, cattle, and humans.

Suckling lambs and calves also become anemic if fed exclusively on milk. Veal calves have light-colored muscle because of low myoglobin content and low blood hemoglobin. This is a desired characteristic of veal in most markets and has led to the practice of feeding low-Fe milk replacers.

Fe deficiency anemia in humans is most common in children and among women of child-bearing age because of large losses of Fe during menstruation. Menstrual loss accounts for 16–32 mg of Fe during the cycle or 0.5–1.0 mg/day in addition to the 0.5–1.0 mg excretion by other routes. Thus, the Fe loss in adult women may be twice that of adult men. Most surveys indicate that Fe deficiency anemia in humans is a major disease problem worldwide; in some countries 30–50% of the population may be affected. Fe deficiency in humans is associated with pallor, chronic fatigue, and general lack of the sense of well-being. The fact that the response to Fe supplementation includes a rapid return to a sense of well-being, which occurs before increased hemoglobin synthesis can occur, suggests that Fe-containing enzymes are affected (50). Although changes in activities of Fe-containing enzymes in Fe deficiency in humans are

not well documented, reduced liver catalase in Fe-deficient swine has been recorded.

Fe is involved at several steps in the synthesis and degradation of brogenic amines, which are involved in behavior. The relationship between iron deficiency anemia and behavioral changes that may accompany it is of interest in humans (52) and could have implications in animals.

Toxicity

Fe overload has been produced in animals by injection or by long periods of excessive intake and in humans by repeated blood transfusions or after prolonged oral administration of Fe. Chronic Fe toxicity causes diarrhea, reduced growth and efficiency of feed utilization and may produce signs of P deficiency. Acute toxicity, including vascular congestion of tissues and organs, metabolic acidosis, and death, has been produced in pigs and rabbits given oral doses of ferric ammonium citrate or ferrous sulfate. Excess Fe is found in the tissues as hemosiderin. Transferrin concentration is normal and plasma Fe is increased only until transferrin is saturated. The reticuloendothelial cells rather than the parenchyma accumulate the excess Fe. Liver fibrosis is common in some cases of human Fe toxicity because of a genetic defect in control of Fe absorption and excretion (idiopathic hemochromatosis), but it is not associated normally with Fe toxicity in animals. In the genetic defect, Fe accumulates in the parenchyma, but in excess Fe intake in humans and animals it accumulates in reticuloendothelial cells.

Baby pigs have been administered ten times the amount of Fe normally injected for prevention of anemia with no ill effects. Hemoglobin tended to be elevated, but growth rate was not affected. However, some forms of organic Fe, such as ferric ammonium citrate, may cause death of newborn pigs when administered orally to supply 200 mg of Fe. Generally, when metabolic Fe demand is high as in rapidly growing suckling animals, a wide margin of safety exists between adequate and toxic dosages.

Fe toxicity may be reduced by dietary Cu, P, and vitamin E, while certain amino acids (valine and histidine), ascorbic acid, simple carbohydrates, and several organic acids (lactic, pyruvic, citric) increase Fe absorption. The enhancement of Fe absorption is believed to be due to formation of complexes with Fe that render it soluble during its transit down the GI tract. It follows that precipitation as the insoluble hydroxide would decrease Fe toxicity; this is the

Figure 12.9 *Fe deficiency in pigs. Pig on the left received 115 ppm Fe and the pig on the right received 15 ppm of Fe. Pig on the left weighed 65 lb and the pig on the right 22.5 lb at 74 days of age. Courtesy of W. M. Beeson, Purdue University.*

basis on which milk of magnesia is used in treatment of Fe toxicosis.

❑ COPPER (Cu)

Cu was first shown to be a dietary essential in 1928 (56). A number of reviews are available on the role of Cu in nutrition (14, 16, 17, 36, 57, 58).

Tissue Distribution

The liver, brain, kidneys, heart, pigmented part of the eye, and hair or wool are highest in Cu concentration in most species; pancreas, spleen, muscles, skin and bone are intermediate; and thyroid, pituitary, prostate, and thymus are lowest. The concentration of Cu in tissues is highly variable within and among species. Young animals have higher concentrations of Cu in their tissues than adults, and dietary intake has an important effect on the Cu content of liver and blood. Cu in blood is 90% associated with the α_2-globulin, ceruloplasmin, and 10% in the red blood cells as erythrocuprein. Pregnancy is associated with increased plasma Cu in the form of ceruloplasmin, apparently in response to elevated blood estrogens.

Functions

Cu is required for the activity of enzymes associated with Fe metabolism, elastin and collagen formation, melanin production, and integrity of the central nervous system. It is required for normal red blood cell formation (hematopoiesis), apparently by allowing normal Fe absorption from the GI tract and release of Fe from the reticuloendothelial system and the liver parenchymal cells to the blood plasma (Fig. 12.10). This function appears to be related to the required oxidation of Fe from the ferrous to ferric state for transfer from tissue to plasma. Ceruloplasmin is the Cu-containing enzyme required for this oxidation. Cu is required for normal bone formation by promoting structural integrity of bone collagen and for normal elastin formation in the aorta and the remainder of the cardiovascular system. This appears to be related to the presence of Cu in lysyl oxidase, the enzymes required for removal of the epsilon amino group of lysine in the normal formation of desmosine and isodesmosine, key cross-linkage groups in elastin. Cu is required for normal myelination of the brain cells and spinal cord as a component of the enzyme cytochrome oxidase which is essential for myelin formation. Numerous enzymes,

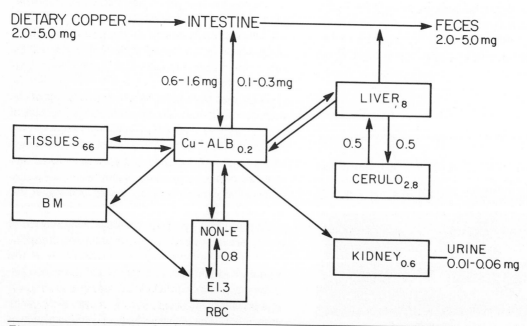

Figure 12.10   *Schematic representation of some metabolic pathways of copper in humans. Numbers in the boxes refer to mg of Cu in the pool. The numbers next to the arrows refer to mg of Cu transversing the pathway each day. Cu-Alb = direct-reading fraction; CERULO = ceruloplasmin; NON-E = nonerythrocuprein; BM = bone marrow; RBC = red blood cell. From Cartwright and Wintrobe (59).*

including lysyl oxidase, cytochrome C oxidase, ferroxidase, and tyrosinase are Cu dependent.

Cu is required for normal hair and wool pigmentation, presumably as a component of polyphenyl oxidases which catalyze the conversion of tyrosine to melanin and for incorporation of disulfide groups into keratin in wool and hair.

Metabolism

Absorption. Site of Cu absorption from the GI tract varies among species; in the dog, it is absorbed mainly from the jejunum, in humans from the duodenum, in the rat from the small intestine and colon. Degree of absorption is also variable, exceeding 30% in humans, but less in other species studied. A Cu-binding protein has been found in the duodenal epithelial cells of the chick, which presumably plays a part in Cu absorption. The pH of the intestinal contents affects absorption; Ca salts reduce Cu absorption by raising pH. Absorption is also affected by other elements; ferrous sulfide reduces Cu absorption by forming insoluble CuS; Hg, Mo, Cd, and Zn all reduce Cu absorption. The last two have been shown to displace Cu from a Cu-binding protein in the intestinal mucosa of chicks; the mode of action of Hg and Mo is not clear, although the formation of insoluble $CuMoO_4$ has been suggested as the explanation for the effect of Mo.

Some forms of Cu are absorbed more readily than others; cupric sulfate is more readily absorbed than cupric sulfide; cupric nitrate, chloride, and carbonate are more readily absorbed than cuprous oxide. Metallic copper is very poorly absorbed (14, 16).

Transport and Tissue Utilization. Absorbed Cu is loosely bound to plasma albumin and is distributed to the tissues and taken up by the bone marrow in red blood cell formation where it is present partly as erythrocuprein. Cu reaching the liver is taken up by parenchymal cells and stored or released to the plasma as Cu-albumin and in larger quantities as a component of ceruloplasmin or is used for synthesis of a large array of Cu-containing enzymes (see Table 12.3) and other Cu-containing proteins.

Excretion. Bile is the major pathway of Cu excretion (see Fig. 12.10). Smaller amounts are lost in intestinal cell and pancreatic secretions, in urine, and negligible amounts in sweat. Radiocopper studies indicate the main source of urinary Cu is that loosely bound to albumin in the plasma.

TABLE 12.3 Metalloprotein enzymes, metalloporphyrin enzymes and non-enzyme metalloproteins containing Cu in animals.[a]

Metalloprotein enzymes
Tyrosinase
Monoamine oxidase
Ascorbic acid oxidase
Ceruloplasmin
Galactose oxidase
Metalloporphyrin enzymes
Cytochrome oxidase
Metalloproteins other than enzymes
Erythrocuprein
Hepatocuprein
Cerebrocuprein
Milk copper protein

[a]From Bowen (56).

Deficiency Signs

Dietary Cu deficiency is associated with a gradual decline in tissue and blood Cu concentration. Blood Cu levels below 0.2 μg/ml result in interference with normal hematopoiesis and anemia. The anemia is hypochromic microcytic in some species (rat, rabbit, pig) but in some it is hypochromic macrocytic (cattle, sheep) or normochromic (chicks, dogs). Cu deficiency shortens RBC life span and reduces Fe absorption and utilization. Thus, the anemia appears to be related in part to a direct effect on RBC formation arising from the need for Cu as a component of RBCs and in part to an indirect effect related to the reduced ceruloplasmin concentration of plasma which in this way reduces Fe absorption and utilization. Apparently no interference with heme biosynthesis occurs in Cu deficiency.

A widespread problem in lambs that has been traced to a Cu deficiency results in incoordination and ataxia. Low levels of Cu in pastures used for grazing, coupled with high intakes of Mo and S, precipitate the condition which is known as swayback or enzootic neonatal ataxia. Newborn lambs most often are affected, but a similar condition also can be produced in the young of goats, guinea pigs, pigs, and rats. Degeneration and failure in myelination of the nerve cells of the brain and spinal cord are the basis for the observed nervous disorder. The Cu content of the brain is reduced, leading to a reduction in cytochrome oxidase activity which is necessary for phospholipid synthesis. Intramuscular injection of Cu-glycine, Cu-EDTA, or Cu-methionine complexes into pregnant ewes has been used successfully to prevent swayback in lambs. Genetic diseases of mice and human infants associated with abnormal Cu metabolism and resembling dietary Cu deficiency have been described (60).

Cu deficiency results in bone abnormalities in many species—pigs, chicks, dogs, horses, and rabbits. A marked failure of mineralization of the cartilage matrix occurs. The cortex of long bones is thin, although the Cu, P, and Mg concentrations of the ash remain normal. The defect appears to be related to a change in the cross-link structure of collagen, rendering it more soluble than collagen from normal bones. The lysyl oxidase activity of bones from Cu-deficient chicks is reduced 30–40%.

The hair and wool of Cu-deficient animals fail to develop normally, resulting in alopecia and slow growth of fibers (Fig. 12.11). Wool growth in sheep is sparse and normal crimping is impeded, leading to straight, hair-like fibers termed steely wool. The change in wool texture is related to a decrease in disulfide groups and increase in sulfhydryl groups and an interference with arrangement of the polypeptide chains. The pigmentation process is extremely sensitive to Cu. Levels of dietary Cu that fail to produce anemia, nerve damage, or bone changes can produce

pigmentation failure in the wool of black sheep or in the hair of pigmented cattle. Achromotrichia (loss of hair pigmentation) can be produced in wool in alternating bands by feeding a Cu-deficient or Cu-adequate diet to sheep in alternating intervals. Blockage of the pigmentation process is achieved within two days by feeding Mo and inorganic sulfate to sheep in the presence of marginal Cu. Presumably, the effect of Cu deprivation on pigmentation is related to its role in conversion of tyrosine to melanin.

Cu-deficient chicks, pigs and cattle show cardiovascular lesions and hemorrhages. Cu deficiency causes aortic rupture in turkey poults. More than 30 years ago, falling disease in cattle in Australia was found to be related to a progressive degeneration of the myocardium of animals grazing on Cu deficient plants. Later, the histological changes in blood vessels of chicks and pigs were found to be related to a derangement of the elastic tissue of the aorta and other blood vessels. The role of Cu in cardiovascular lesions associated with coronary heart disease in humans is not known but merits study.

Fetal death and resorption in rats and reduced egg production and hemorrhage and death of the embryos in poultry have been shown to be produced by Cu deficiency. Reproduction failure of cattle in Cu-deficient locations has also been reported, but a specific effect of Cu in contributing to the syndrome has not been established. In poultry, the primary lesion appears to be a defect in RBC and connective tissue formation in the embryo, possibly induced by a reduction in monoamine oxidase activity.

In ruminants there appears to be a larger problem of Cu deficiency than of Cu toxicity worldwide (61). There is wide variation in Cu content in plants (legumes have higher concentrations than grasses) and in the bioavailability of their Cu. Therefore, Cu concentration alone may be of little nutritional significance (61).

Toxicity

Sheep and calves appear to be more susceptible to Cu toxicity than other species. Hemoglobinuria, jaundice and tissue necrosis have been observed in calves fed a milk substitute containing 115 ppm Cu. Death of sheep, with accompanying hemoglobinuria from excess Cu, has been reported on pasture because of continued free-choice consumption with a trace-mineral salt mixture containing the recommended Cu level. Underwood (14) points out that Cu toxicity occurs in sheep when the Cu content of soil and

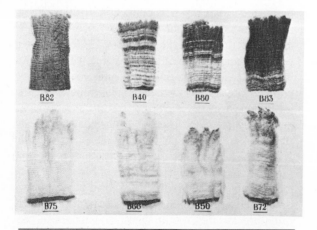

Figure 12.11 *Wool from Cu-deficient (or excess Mo) sheep. Normal wool on the left. The other samples show banding of black wool, loss of definition of crimp, and, in some, secondary waves. By permission of G. L. McClymont.*

pasture is high, when Mo of plant is low, or when liver damage from consumption of certain poisonous plants predisposes to Cu poisoning by decreasing the ability of the liver to dispose of Cu. Plants such as lupin and *Heliotropium europium,* which contain toxic alkaloids, produce Cu toxicity in ruminants by impairing hepatic capacity to metabolize ingested Cu (14, 16).

Much research has been done on supplementation of growing swine diets with high levels of Cu since the report by Braude of improved growth rate with 250 ppm Cu added to practical diets (62). The mode of action of Cu in producing this growth response still is not known, and the occasional toxicity associated with its use at this level has resulted in concern about the use of levels above 250 ppm. Signs of toxicity vary from a slight growth depression and mild anemia to sudden death accompanied by liver damage and hemorrhage. Death losses with 250 ppm Cu are believed not to be the result of inadequate feed mixing, as only isolated cases of such toxicity have been reported. Levels of 425+ ppm Cu produce marked anemia, jaundice and liver damage. When a level of 250 ppm of Cu has resulted in depressed weight gain, there is a microcytic hypochromic anemia associated with it, but usually no liver damage. Gipp *et al.* (63) reported reduced liver Fe and mean corpuscular volume and hemoglobin concentration in growing pigs fed a semipurified diet containing 250 ppm of Cu. These changes were prevented by feeding extra Fe, indicating an induced Fe deficiency. Source of protein is an important factor in the response to added Cu; milk protein is associated with more severe anemia and growth depression than soybean protein. Presumably, the interaction between Cu and Fe and the effect of protein source on Cu toxicity both are related to effects on absorption of Cu and Fe from the GI tract. Variations among animals in Cu toxicity probably are related in part to differences in dietary levels of S, Mo, Fe, Se, and Zn (16).

Cu toxicity in humans seems highly unlikely, except by accidental contamination of foodstuffs, as no cases of chronic disorders traceable to excessive Cu intakes have been reported. However, metabolic Cu intoxication in humans is a well-known pathological condition termed Wilson's disease. The primary defect is thought to be failure of the liver to remove albumin-bound Cu from the plasma for incorporation into ceruloplasmin because of a genetically controlled absence of the necessary liver enzyme system. The result is massive accumulation of liver Cu, liver cir-

rhosis, renal damage, reduced plasma ceruloplasmin, and elevated levels of Cu in brain and kidney. Administration of chelating agents to induce urinary excretion of Cu have been employed to minimize tissue damage. High dietary Zn is under study as a therapeutic measure in patients with Wilson's disease.

❏ MANGANESE (Mn)

Mn was recognized as a dietary essential for animals in 1931 (64). Although the widespread occurrence of Mn in foodstuffs makes a deficiency less likely than for many other mineral elements, sufficient examples exist of practical problems with Mn deficiency in animals and birds to justify detailed consideration. The metabolism, functions and deficiency, and toxicity signs of Mn have been reviewed in detail (14, 65).

Tissue Distribution

The total body supply of Mn is less than that of most other required minerals; for example, the total Mn content of adult humans is only 1% of the amount of Zn and 20% of Cu. It is widespread throughout the body and tends not to accumulate in liver and other tissues in high concentrations when ingested in large amounts, in contrast to most other trace elements. Bone, kidney, liver, pancreas, and pituitary gland have the highest concentration. Bone Mn content is more responsive to dietary intake than that of other tissues; it represents 25% of the total body content in one study with pullets and was less mobilizable from the skeleton than from liver, skin, feathers, and muscle. A large proportion of soft tissue Mn is present in labile intracellular forms, but in bone it is associated primarily with the inorganic fraction.

Functions

Mn is essential for formation of chondroitin sulfate, a component of mucopolysaccharides of bone organic matrix. Thus, it is essential for normal bone formation. Mn is necessary for prevention of ataxia and poor equilibrium in newborn animals and birds. Biochemical and histological evidence relating to the role of Mn in this realm is lacking except for the presence of a structural defect in the inner ear of affected animals. This abnormality appears to be related to defective cartilage mucopolysaccharide formation. Many glycosyl transferases, enzymes of importance in synthesis of polysaccharides and glycoproteins, require Mn for activity. The effects of Mn deficiency on bone and cartilage formation appear to be explained on this basis.

Mn is a component of the metalloenzyme, pyruvate carboxylase and activates phosphoenolpyruvate carboxykinase and, as such, plays a role in carbohydrate metabolism. Mn is necessary as a cofactor in the enzyme that catalyzes the conversion of mevalonic acid to squalene and stimulates synthesis of cholesterol and fatty acids in rat liver. Thus, it plays a vital role in lipid metabolism. Mn stimulates arginase activity in mammals and in vitro it activates a variety of other enzymes. The biological significance of these in vitro studies remains to be determined.

Metabolism

Absorption.   The mode and control of Mn absorption from the GI tract are poorly understood. The amount absorbed appears to be proportional to the amount ingested, and absorption usually is less than 10%. Excessive dietary Ca or P reduces Mn absorption. However, both urinary and fecal excretion of parenterally administered radioactive Mn is greater in rats previously fed a low Ca diet than those fed a high Ca diet. Although this mainly may reflect the greater bone resorption of rats fed low Ca, thereby resulting in less Mn retention by bone, the results illustrate that dietary Ca and P content affects not only Mn absorption but also Mn tissue losses. Divalent Mn is absorbed about as well as the oxide, carbonate, chloride and sulfate salts. Mn absorption is increased in Fe deficiency.

Transport and Storage.   Mn is absorbed from the GI tract as Mn^{++} oxidized to Mn^{+++}, transported rapidly to all tissues, and finally concentrated in mitochondria-rich tissues. Liver, pancreas, and brain mitochondria have been shown to accumulate radioactive Mn in many species. Mn is carried in blood as Mn^{+++}, loosely bound to a plasma β_1-globulin (other than transferrin), and is removed from blood quickly, first appearing in mitochondria and later in the nuclei of cells. The exact role of Mn in the metabolism and function of mitochondria is unknown, but Mn deficiency is associated with alterations in their structure and metabolism (60, 65). Mn content of milk and fetuses and of eggs reflects closely dietary intake, illustrating the dissimilarity between Mn and such minerals as Fe and Cu in transport across mammary and reproductive tissues.

Excretion.   The main route of Mn excretion is via the bile, with smaller amounts lost through pancreatic secretions and sloughed intestinal mucosal cells and still smaller amounts in urine and sweat. Much of the bile Mn is reabsorbed. Bile concentration parallels that of blood; this may explain the failure of body tissues to accumulate large concentrations of Mn. Thus, excretion rather than absorption is the primary means by which body Mn homeostasis normally is maintained.

Deficiency Signs

Many different skeletal abnormalities are associated with Mn deficiency in several animal species. These abnormalities undoubtedly all are related to the role of Mn in mucopolysaccharide synthesis in bone organic matrix. Lameness, shortening and bowing of the legs, and enlarged joints are common in Mn-deficient rodents, pigs, cattle, goats, and sheep, and perosis or slipped tendon is common in poultry (Fig. 12.12). Choline deficiency also produces perosis (see Ch. 15). This condition includes malformation of the tibiometatarsal joint, bending of the long bones of the leg, and slipping of the gastrocnemius tendon from its condyle. Parrot beak, shortened and thickened legs and wings—manifestations of the same defect in bone formation and often termed chondrodystrophy—are common signs of Mn deficiency in birds. Impairment in calcification of bones in Mn-deficient animals is not a factor in the bone malformations. Although plasma alkaline phosphatase sometimes is reduced in Mn-deficient animals, no change occurs in the composition of bone ash, except an occasionally observed decline in Mn concentration. Eggshell thickness and strength also are reduced in Mn deficiency. The ataxia and poor coordination and balance observed commonly in newborn mammals and newly hatched birds whose dams have been fed Mn-deficient diets is irreversible and is related to abnormal bone formation of the inner ear bones during prenatal life. In chicks, the characteristic head retraction sometimes is referred to as the "star-gazing" posture. A genetically related congenital ataxia of mice caused by defective development of inner ear bones has been shown to be preventable by Mn supplementation of the maternal diet at a specific time in gestation. This represents a unique example of an interaction between a nutrient and a mutant gene affecting bone development.

Rats fed Mn-deficient diets during growth and pregnancy produce pups whose liver activities of these two enzymes and plasma concentrations of glucose are less than in pups of control dams, suggesting that

Figure 12.12 *Manganese deficiency. Top. Litter from a sow fed 0.5 ppm of Mn. The pigs showed weakness and a poor sense of balance at birth. Center. A 132-day-old gilt fed 0.5 ppm Mn since she weighed 8 lb. Note increased fat deposition caused by low Mn diet. Courtesy of W. M. Beeson, Purdue University. Bottom. Perosis in the chick, which results in enlargement and malformation of the hock joint.*

glucose homeostasis may be compromised in neonates by Mn deficiency (66).

Delayed estrus, poor conception, decrease in litter size, and livability have been reported in farm and laboratory animals, and decreased egg production and hatchability occur in birds deprived of Mn. In males, Mn deficiency produces absence of libido and failure in spermatogenesis (14).

Newborn guinea pigs from Mn-deprived dams show marked hypoplasia of the pancreas and adult Mn-deficient guinea pigs show changes in pancreas histology and impaired glucose tolerance (67). Whether this effect of Mn on the pancreas and glucose tolerance is related to some specific effect on insulin production or to an indirect action through the presence of Mn in pyruvate carboxylase, which is involved in gluconeogenesis, is not known. The blood of diabetics is low in Mn and administration of Mn to these subjects has a hypoglycemic effect. Thus, Mn appears to play a role in glucose metabolism, but its practical importance in this role in animal nutrition is not known. Mn deficiency has been reported to be associated with reduced liver and bone lipids in rats, but the exact role of Mn in lipid metabolism remains unknown.

Although Mn deficiency is not considered probable in humans, Schroeder *et al.* (68) have suggested the possibility of a relationship between several human disorders and Mn nutrition. The relatively high levels of Mn in many foods commonly available to man in relation to metabolic requirements would suggest that such relationships are unlikely but worthy of examination.

Toxicity

High dietary levels of Mn are tolerated well by most species; the toxic effects of Mn appear to be related more to interference with utilization of other minerals than to a specific effect of Mn itself. Rats, poultry, and calves show no ill effects of diets containing 820 to 1,000 ppm Mn, but pigs show reduced growth at 500 ppm. The reduced growth rate associated with excess Mn is a reflection mainly of reduced appetite.

Ca and P utilization are affected adversely by excess Mn. Rickets has been produced in rats fed 1.73% Mn in the diet, and hypoplasia of tooth enamel has been observed in rats, cows and pigs fed excess Mn. Fe deficiency anemia is produced in cattle, pigs, rabbits, and sheep fed 1,000 to 5,000 ppm Mn. In the presence of adequate dietary intake of all nutrients, 1,000 ppm Mn appears to be the maximum tolerable level, while for poultry and swine, 2,000 and 400 ppm are the upper limits (16). Neurological disorders and behavioral changes have been observed in workers mining Mn ores.

❏ SELENIUM (Se)

Selenium was recognized as a toxic mineral many years before its essentiality for animals and birds was discovered. Schwarz and Foltz (69) first reported in 1957 that Se prevents liver necrosis in rats and in the same year it was shown also that it prevents exudative diathesis in chicks. The following year Muth *et al.* (70) cured muscular dystrophy in lambs with supplemental Se. All of these lesions previously had been known to be produced by vitamin E deficiency (see Ch. 14). Thus, a new era of nutrient interrelationships was developed. Knowledge of Se and vitamin E in nutrition and metabolism has been reviewed extensively (14, 16, 71).

Tissue Distribution

Se is present in all cells of the body, although the concentration generally is less than 1 ppm; thus, the total body supply is relatively low. Liver, kidney, and muscle generally contain the highest concentrations of Se, and the values for these and other tissues are affected by dietary intake (Tables 12.4, 12.5). Concentration of Se in liver and kidney of animals fed toxic levels (5–10 ppm) may be as high as 5–7 ppm.

Functions

Noguchi *et al.* (72) and Rotruck *et al.* (73) provided data elucidating the specific biochemical functions of Se. Scientists at Michigan State University (74) provided quantitative data on the response of domestic animals to supplemental Se.

Se is a component of the enzyme glutathione peroxidase (GSH-Px) and in this role is involved in catabolism of peroxides arising from tissue lipid oxidation. Thus it plays a central role in maintaining integrity of cellular membranes. GSH-Px is present in all tissues with activity highest in liver and red blood cells, intermediate in heart, kidney, lung, stomach, adrenal glands, pancreas, and adipose tissue and lowest in brain, skeletal muscle, eye lens, and testis (71). Se is a constituent of other enzymes in microorganisms, so eventually it may be shown to perform additional functions in animals. Se also is

TABLE 12.4 Selenium content of the longissimus muscle of pigs fed diets from different sources in the USA.[a]

SOURCE[b]	DIET SE, PPM	MUSCLE SE, PPM, DRY BASIS
Arkansas	0.152	0.817
Idaho	0.086	0.392
Illinois	0.036	0.223
Indiana	0.052	0.232
Iowa	0.235	0.977
Michigan	0.040	0.206
Nebraska	0.330	1.178
New York	0.036	0.163
North Dakota	0.412	1.430
South Dakota	0.493	1.893
Virginia	0.027	0.118
Wisconsin	0.178	0.501
Wyoming	0.158	1.098

[a]Ku *et al.* (74).
[b]Corn-soybean meal diets of similar composition.

required for normal pancreatic morphology and through this effect on pancreatic lipase production is responsible for normal absorption of lipids and tocopherols from the GI tract. Whether the effect of Se on the pancreas is really only a manifestation of its role as a component of glutathione peroxidase is still not entirely clear.

Metabolism

Absorption.   The main site of Se absorption is from the duodenum. It is not absorbed from the rumen or abomasum of sheep or the stomach of pigs. It is absorbed relatively efficiently either from natural Se-containing feedstuffs or as inorganic selenite (35–85%). Absorption of Se in ruminants probably is largely as selenomethionine and selenocystine as a result of the incorporation of inorganic dietary Se into amino acids by rumen microflora. Because Se-depleted animals retain more Se than adequately fed animals, it has been suggested that increased absorption occurs in response to tissue needs. However, excretion also is responsive to tissue needs. Pigs fed Se as a component of sweet clover grown on coal ash high in Se retain more tissue Se than pigs fed equal amounts of inorganic Se, suggesting that plant Se is more available (75).

TABLE 12.5 Selenium content of tissues of pigs fed Se at different levels from sodium selenite.[a]

TISSUE	DIETARY SE, PPM				
	0.05[b]	0.10	0.15	0.25	1.05
	. . . tissue se, ppm fresh basis . . .				
Longissimus muscle	0.05	0.08	0.09	0.11	0.13
Myocardium	0.11	0.21	0.21	0.23	0.33
Liver	0.14	0.51	0.57	0.59	0.80
Kidney	1.37	2.07	2.06	1.95	2.10

[a]Groce *et al.* (74).
[b]Corn-soybean meal basal diet.

Transport and Storage. After absorption, Se is transported in the plasma in association with a plasma protein and enters all tissues where it is stored mainly as selenomethionine and selenocystine. Se is incorporated into RBCs, leucocytes, myoglobin, nucleoproteins, myosin, and several enzymes, including cytochrome c and aldolase.

Excretion. Tissue Se is relatively labile as illustrated by its rapid loss from tissues of animals fed low-Se diets following consumption of high-Se diets. Loss occurs via the lungs, feces and urine. The proportion excreted by each route depends on the route of administration, tissue levels and animal species. In sheep, injected Se is excreted mainly in the urine in proportion to the amount administered; fecal loss is small and constant with dosage level; expired Se is similar to fecal loss at low levels of administration, but rises with dosage level and exceeds fecal loss by several fold at high dosage levels (76). Orally administered Se is excreted in feces in largest quantities at low intake levels. As intake rises, fecal loss remains relatively stable and expired Se increases steadily; urinary loss rises at moderate levels of supplementation, then declines.

Fecal losses represent mostly unabsorbed Se, but also that excreted via the bile, pancreatic duct and intestinal mucosal cells. Arsenic (As), which is known to reduce absorption of Se from the GI tract, also increases bile and urinary excretion of Se when As is injected.

The form in which Se is provided in the diet has an important effect on its absorption. Scott (77) summarized the utilization of plant vs. animal sources of Se and concluded that the generally superior utilization of plant Se results from the presence of Se in the inorganic form in plants; animal tissues contain Se mainly in the organic form as selenomethionine and selenocystine.

The sulfate ion has important effects on Se metabolism under some conditions. Urinary excretion of Na selenate is increased by parenterally or orally administered sulfate. The effect of sulfate is less marked when Se is provided as selenite than as selenate; sulfate probably has no effect on utilization of Se provided in the organic form. The similar chemical and physical characteristics of Se and S in relation to metabolism have been reviewed (78).

Placental transfer of Se is extensive in all species studied as evidenced by prevention of musuclar dystrophy in lambs and calves by Se administration to the pregnant dam and by radioactive tracer studies. Selenomethionine is transferred more readily to the fetus than inorganic Se.

Deficiency Signs

Several deficiency diseases of animals and birds that were earlier considered to be from vitamin E deficiency more recently have been shown to be preventable by Se, as well. These include nutritional muscular dystrophy (NMD) in lambs, poultry, pigs, and calves (see Fig. 12.13); exudative diathesis (ED) in poultry, and liver necrosis in rats and pigs. Encephalomalacia in chicks is cured or prevented by vitamin E or antioxidants, but not by Se.

Se-responsive NMD is common in calves and lambs in many parts of the world. Allaway *et al.* (79) have mapped geographic areas with soil Se deficiency and Se excess in the USA (see Fig. 12.16). Undoubtedly,

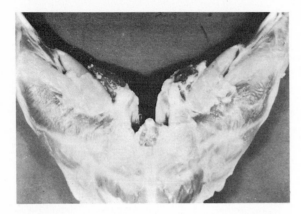

Figure 12.13 *Se deficiency in ruminants. Top. Severe nutritional muscular dystrophy (white muscle disease) in a lamb carcass. Most severely affected muscles are identified with arrows. Courtesy of J. E. Oldfield, Oregon State University. Middle. Stiffness in a calf causing it to stand in a urinating position with its back arched and its tail raised. The calf is standing on the tips of its hoofs. Bottom. A calf suffering an attack of shortness of breath has accelerated breathing, fluctuating flanks, and degeneration of the respiratory muscles. Courtesy of M. Hidiroglou, Animal Res. Institute, Ottawa, Canada.*

widely differing levels of soil Se are present in other parts of the world as well. Affected lambs may show a stiff gait and arched back giving rise to the name stiff lamb disease. Severe cases result in death. Injection or oral administration of vitamin E or Se to the pregnant or lactating dam or the newborn protects against NMD. Postmortem examination reveals whitish streaks in the striated muscle, which are caused by degeneration of the muscle fiber (Zenker's degeneration) and account for the common name, white muscle disease. If the heart muscle is affected, sudden death may occur. This is an increasingly common problem in growing pigs and often is referred to as mulberry heart disease. Animals with NMD show drastic rises in blood plasma concentrations of several enzymes that normally are intracellular but are released into the plasma when tissue damage occurs. Such enzymes include glutamic oxaloacetic transaminase (GOT) and lactic dehydrogenase isoenzymes (LDH). In pigs, the chief target organ, in addition to the heart muscle, is the liver. Massive liver necrosis and sudden death is a common sign of vitamin E-Se deficiency in growing pigs (see Fig. 14.7). Serum ornithine carbamyltransferase is elevated because of liver cell damage which releases the intracellular enzyme into the blood. Vitamin E supplementation of the diet of pigs fed marginal Se prevents this liver damage. The syndrome in pigs is called hepatosis dietetica and has become a practical field problem in Scandinavia, New Zealand, and the USA. This is due, presumably, to soil depletion of Se or changes in methods of fertilization or harvesting and processing of cereal grains which may affect their tocopherol or Se content or biological availability. Corn grown on low-Se soil fertilized with Se contains a higher level of Se than that grown on adjacent unfertilized plots, and the Se is available biologically for chicks.

Chicks fed diets deficient in Vitamin E and Se develop ED which is prevented by supplementation with either nutrient. ED is characterized by accumulation of subcutaneous fluids on the breast, resulting from escape of blood constituents to the extracellular spaces after capillary damage. Noguchi *et al.* (72) showed that glutathione peroxidase activity in plasma of Se-deficient chicks declined to less than 10% of normal within about 5 days. The activity of this enzyme correlates well with the protection by Se of chicks from ED. Vitamin E, although it protects against ED in the absence of Se, has no effect on glutathione peroxidase activity. Thus, the metabolic role of Se in protecting against ED is distinct from that of vitamin E. Plasma glutathione peroxidase acts as the first line of defense against peroxidation of lipids in the capillary membrane by destroying peroxides formed in the absence of vitamin E. Peroxidation of membrane lipids is prevented with adequate vitamin E, thus blocking the destruction of the capillary membranes. In its absence, Se functions to prevent peroxidation by its presence in glutathione peroxidase. Thus, the disruption of capillary membrane integrity, which results in ED, is prevented by either vitamin E or Se, but by slightly different mechanisms.

Se deficiency in chicks fed adequate vitamin E results in pancreatic degeneration and fibrosis, which impedes vitamin E absorption from the GI tract. Gries and Scott (80) have shown that the pancreas is the target organ for Se deficiency in chicks, as skeletal muscle, heart muscle, liver, and other tissues are unaffected if vitamin E is adequate.

Infertility in cattle, sheep, and birds has been reported to respond favorably to Se feeding or injection. Knowledge is incomplete as to whether such effects are related distinctly to Se or whether a sparing effect on the vitamin E requirement is involved, although experiments with rats over a successive generation have demonstrated reduced fertility in females and males even in the presence of adequate vitamin E. Thus, inconsistent results in farm animals may reflect differences in tissue stores of Se and vitamin E as well as species differences.

The addition of inorganic Se to the diets of swine, chickens, beef cattle, and sheep within the USA has been approved by the Food and Drug Administration as a means of controlling Se-deficiency diseases. The approved levels vary with animal species and stage of the life cycle.

Toxicity

Animals grazing on seleniferous soils or fed crops grown on these soils develop a fatal disease known as blind staggers or alkali disease. This syndrome was described in horses as early as 1856 and since has been studied in other species. Soils containing more than 0.5 ppm Se potentially are dangerous to livestock as the plants harvested from them may contain 4 ppm or more. Blind staggers is characterized by emaciation, loss of hair, soreness and sloughing of hooves, and eroding of the joints of long bones leading to lameness; heart atrophy, liver cirrhosis, anemia, excess salivation, grating of the teeth, blindness, paralysis, and death.

In poultry, egg production and hatchability are reduced and deformities are common, including lack of eyes and deformed wings and feet. Abnormal embryonic development also is common in rats, pigs, sheep, and cattle fed excess Se.

Diets containing 5 ppm of Se produce toxic signs in most species. High-protein diets tend to protect against Se toxicity, and inorganic sulfate has been reported to relieve the growth depression in rats fed 10 ppm Se. Arsenic (As) added to the feed or drinking water alleviates Se toxicity in dogs, pigs, cattle and chicks. Liver succinic dehydrogenase activity in rats is reduced by high Se and restored by As. This is the only enzyme known to be affected by excess Se. The mode of action by which toxicity symptoms are brought about is unknown.

Se toxicity in humans, even those living in seleniferous areas, is not considered likely because of food distribution patterns and the wide variety of foodstuffs consumed by most human populations.

❏ OTHER TRACE ELEMENTS

In addition to those already discussed in detail, other elements may be considered essential, based on the broad definition that their absence from the diet results in metabolic or functional abnormalities in one or more tissues of an animal species. These are chromium (Cr), fluorine (F), molybdenum (Mo), and silicon (Si), and possibly aluminum (Al), arsenic (As), boron (B), bromine (Br), lithium (Li), cadmium (Cd), nickel (Ni), lead (Ph), tin (Sn), and vanadium (V) (10, 11, 13).

A detailed description of the tissue distribution, functions, metabolism, and deficiency signs of these minerals in animals is beyond the scope of this chapter. Excellent detailed coverage has been provided by Underwood (14) and in the books edited by Comar and Bronner (81). The complex subject of interactions between and among mineral elements has been addressed by Mills (82). Only selected references are included in the present discussion to explain the reasoning on which each of the mineral elements has been interpreted as being essential. Much more information is available on toxic effects, especially of As, Cd, F, and Mo. Toxic aspects of these and other minerals are considered in Ch. 13.

Chromium (Cr)

Evidence that Cr might be required by animals was reported in 1954 when synthesis of cholesterol and fatty acids by rat liver was shown to be increased by Cr. In 1959, Schwarz and Mertz (83) demonstrated the importance of trivalent Cr in glucose utilization. This since has been shown to be related to the presence of Cr as a cofactor in insulin. Cr utilization not only depends on its valence (trivalent is utilized, hexavalent is not) but on its chemical form. Mertz (84) showed that radioactive Cr transfer to the rat fetus was accomplished only when Cr was incorporated into yeast and not when it was administered to the mother as inorganic salts. Mertz (85) and Schroeder (86) both concluded that trivalent Cr is required for normal carbohydrate and lipid metabolism. The requirement for Cr is increased in humans with an impaired glucose tolerance. Cr in nutrition has been reviewed (87), but no clear evidence has been found for a practical need for Cr supplementation of diets for animals fed typical natural ingredients.

Fluorine (F)

F can qualify as an essential nutrient for animals and humans mainly on the basis of its preventative effect against dental caries. Navia *et al.* (88) concluded that supplemental F in the drinking water should be provided during or shortly after tooth eruption for maximum cariostatic effects. No reports of a positive growth response to F addition to F-low diets appeared until 1972 when Schwartz and Milne (89) obtained improved growth in rats by applying strict control of dietary and environmental contamination. Although low levels in the diet or in drinking water (1 ppm) protect against dental caries (tooth decay), higher levels produce mottled tooth enamel and enlarged bones. Low dietary F has been reported to protect against osteoporosis in humans, but this point still is controversial as animal experiments have failed to support the observation. Growth and remodeling of bones is affected by the level of dietary F, so the conditions under which F is beneficial or harmful to bone and teeth may be related not only to level of F intake but to other unexplained factors. High dietary Ca depresses F uptake of bone; probably other dietary variables also are important.

The adverse effects of industrial F pollution on animals has been reviewed and documented (90). Excellent reviews of F in nutrition are available (14, 16, 17, 91, 92).

Molybdenum (Mo)

Evidence that Mo is essential for animals was reported in 1953 when it was shown to be a component of the metalloenzyme, xanthine oxidase (93). Later, chicks, turkey poults, and lambs were shown to perform more favorably when Mo was added to semipurified diets. The growth response in lambs was obtained using a basal diet containing 0.36 ppm Mo, which resulted in a 2.5-fold improvement in daily gain. Because most feedstuffs contain considerably more Mo, it is not surprising that Mo generally has not been recognized as an essential nutrient. Mo in animal nutrition has been reviewed (94). Its presence in feeds at toxic levels is of greater practical concern. Dietary levels of Cu, Zn, S, Ag, Cd, and S-containing amino acids have major effects on the susceptibility of animals to Mo toxicosis (20).

Silicon (Si)

Si has been recognized since 1973 as an essential nutrient for chicks. It is the most abundant element in the earth's crust, next to oxygen, is present in large amounts in plants and, as a result, is ingested in large quantities by animals. Absorption occurs as monosilicic acid, which represents only a small fraction of the total Si ingested. Carlisle (95) first reported a growth response in chicks fed Si by using purified diets prepared carefully to minimize Si contamination and by raising the animals in a rigidly controlled environment low in Si. Subsequently, Schwarz and Milne (96), using similarly controlled conditions, obtained a 25–34% increase in growth of rats by Si supplementation to a low-Si purified diet. Si appears to be involved in some way in the initiation of the mineralization process in bones. From a practical view point, adverse effects of high Si intake rather than Si deficiency appear to be of greater importance.

Urinary calculi appear more frequently in grazing cattle as Si content of the forage increases; prairie hay, which contains more Si than alfalfa hay, increases the incidence of calculi. Increasing water intake and urine volume by feeding a high NaCl-containing diet reduces or eliminates siliceous calculi (16). The essentiality and toxic roles of Si in animal and human nutrition have been reviewed (16, 97).

❏ ADDITIONAL POSSIBLY REQUIRED MINERALS

Many mineral elements are ubiquitous in nature and for many of those commonly present in animal and human tissues no metabolic role has been discovered. Some appear to be harmless, some toxic. Among them, Al, As, B, Br, Cd, Li, Ni, Pb, Sn and

V have been reported to be required by one or more animal species.

Sorenson et al. (4) found that the concentration of Al in tissues changes in a circadian rhythm and with other changes in biological activity. It accumulates in regenerating bone, stimulates enzyme systems involved with succinate metabolism, and has been reported essential for fertility in female rats (16). These observations provide indirect evidence for an essential role of Al in nutrition, but if a metabolic requirement does exist, it has not been quantified. The role of Al in nutrition has been reviewed thoroughly (98).

Supplementation of As to purified diets has been reported to increase growth of chicks, decrease neonatal mortality in rats and improve birth weight and decrease neonatal mortality in goats.

Schwarz and Spallholz (cited in 6) found that rats fed a highly purified diet containing less than 0.4 ppb Cd showed a growth depression when maintained in a metal-free environment. This is the first evidence of a metabolic requirement for Cd; the overwhelming research emphasis has been toxicology of Cd ingestion.

A dietary requirement for Ni first was reported in chicks; deficiency has also been produced in pigs, goats, rats (8), and sheep (9). Deficiency signs have been varied, but include decreased hematocrit, abnormalities in the liver, reproductive problems, high neonatal mortality and depressed growth, serum proteins, liver and serum lipids, and dietary N utilization. The metabolic bases for these diverse effects of Ni deficiency have not been established, but all reports taken together suggest the possibility of inadequate Ni when the diet contains less than 40 ppb Ni and when environmental contamination is controlled with filtered air and carefully prepared Ni-free diets are fed throughout a lifetime or through more than one generation (16).

A single report (12) of a growth response to dietary Sn in rats kept in plastic isolators to prevent environmental contamination is the basis on which Sn is considered as a possibly required element for animals. The wide uses of Sn in food containers and in industry has stimulated far more research on Sn toxicosis than on Sn requirements.

It has been reported that reproductive efficiency is impaired by a deficiency of V. Several other reports have shown beneficial effects of V on rats, chicks, and others have described tissue uptake and movement of V (16). V stimulates the rate of glucose transport into rat adipocytes, possibly by activating the insulin-sensitive transport system for glucose.

Shechter and Kerlich (10) reported that V ions mimic the effect of insulin on glucose oxidation in rat adipocytes and suggested that the effect is due mainly to the presence of vanadyl tetravalent ions produced within the cells and not, primarily, to inhibition of the Na pump. The demonstration of an effect of V on glucose metabolism in intact animals remains to be done, but such a possibility seems reasonable. As with many other trace elements, V toxicity has received detailed attention; its toxic action appears to be exerted through inhibition of an array of enzymes.

Barium (Ba) may be required for growth of some species; bromine (Br) may be required for growth of mice and chicks; cadmium (Cd) may be required for growth of rats and rubidium (Rb) and cesium (Cs) may replace part of the K requirement. None of these effects qualify any of these minerals, on the basis of present knowledge, as dietary essentials according to the criteria outlined by Cotzias (99).

Future research with the aid of more sensitive analytical methods and more carefully controlled nutritional and environmental variables may enable the reclassification of one or more of the ubiquitous and, in some instances, toxic minerals as essential nutrients.

Associated with the complexities of interactions between and among mineral elements and between mineral elements and other dietary constituents are the problems of bioavailability. Further advances in knowledge of essential elements and their identification will require careful methodology and interpretation of data obtained under conditions in which efficiency of entrance into and excretion from the body may be affected by bioavailability (100). The advancing technology of stable isotope use (101) in animals and humans may prove to be highly useful in addressing these questions.

Further confirmation is needed to establish these and other minerals as dietary essentials, but clearly, newer and more sensitive analytical methods and closer control of environmental contamination along with a greater understanding of mineral interrelationships, favor the possibility of discovering additional essential minerals for animals and humans. These prospects are explored in several publications (13, 14, 16, 18, 97, 102–104).

❏ SUMMARY

Modern analytical techniques permit detection of minute traces of minerals in animal tissues. The list of trace minerals known to be required by animals continues to grow. The following are known to be required by one or more animal species for normal life processes: cobalt (Co), iodine (I), iron (Fe), copper (Cu), zinc (Zn), manganese (Mn), selenium (Se), chromium (Cr), fluorine (F), molybdenum (Mo), and silicon (Si). Others possibly required, based on limited evidence are aluminum (Al), arsenic (As), boron (B), bromine (Br), cadmium (Cd), lithium (Li), nickel (Ni), lead (Pb), tin (Sn), and vanadium (V). Minerals known to be required as well as those for which no metabolic requirement has been established tend to accumulate in body tissues in direct proportion to dietary intake. Excessive concentrations, even of required minerals, can produce adverse effects.

Trace elements function as activators of enzyme systems or as constituents of organic compounds. Many complex interactions have been identified among and between trace minerals, between and among trace and macromineral elements, and between trace elements and vitamins. Regional distribution of some trace minerals in soils has been described. Such information is useful in identifying problem areas for trace mineral deficiencies and excesses in animals and humans. Trace minerals most likely to be deficient in animals fed commonly used feedstuffs are Fe, Mn, Co, (required as a constituent of vitamin B_{12}), I (supplied easily as iodized salt), Zn (requirement increased by high dietary Ca), Cu (only in regions where soil Mo is high), and Se (only in regions where soil Se is low). Feed manufacturers often add trace amounts of one or more of these minerals to macromineral supplements to insure an adequate intake of each.

❑ REFERENCES

1. Stika, K. M. and G. H. Morrison. 1981. *Fed. Proc.* **40**:2115.

2. Fox, M. R. S. and S. H. Tao. 1981. *Fed. Proc.* **40**:2130.

3. Carlisle, E. 1972. *Fed. Proc.* **31**:700.

4. Sorenson, J. R. J., I. R. Campbell, L. B. Tepper, and R. D. Lingg. 1974. *Environ. Health Perspective* **8**:3.

5. Nielsen, F. H., D. R. Myron, and E. O. Ulthus. 1977. In *Trace Element Metabolism in Man and Animals,* III, M. Kirchgessner (ed.). Technical Univ., Munich, W. Germany.

6. Friberg, L. F. 1985. *Cadmium and Health: A Toxicological and Epidemiological Appraisal. Vol. 1.* CRC Press, Boca Raton, FL.

7. Nielsen, F. H. and D. A. Ollerich. 1974. *Fed. Proc.* **33**:1767.

8. Nielsen, F. H. and H. H. Sandstead. 1974. *Amer. J. Clin. Nutr.* **27**:515.

9. Spears, J. W., E. E. Hatfield, R. M. Forbes, and J. E. Koenig. 1978. *J. Nutr.* **108**:313.

10. Shechter, Y. and S. J. D. Kerlich. 1980. *Nature* **284**:556.

11. Dubyak, G. R. and A. Kleinzeller. 1980. *J. Biol. Chem.* **255**:5306.

12. Schwarz, K., D. B. Milne, and E. Vinyard. 1970. *Biochem. Biophys. Res. Commun.* **40**:22.

13. Nielsen, F. H. 1984. *Ann. Rev. Nutr.* **4**:21.

14. Underwood, E. J. 1977. *Trace Elements in Human and Animal Nutrition,* 4th ed. Academic Press, N.Y.

15. Sandsted, H. 1982. Requirements and Function of Trace Elements. In *Ann. Rev. Nutr.,* Vol. 2. Annual Reviews, Inc., Palo Alto, CA.

16. National Research Council. 1980. *Mineral Tolerances of Domestic Animals.* Natl. Acad. Sci., Washington, D.C.

17. Mertz, W. 1986. *Trace Elements in Human and Animal Nutrition,* 5th ed. Vols. 1 and 2. Academic Press, Orlando, Fl.

18. Levander, O. A. and L. Cheng. 1980. Micronutrient Interactions: Vitamins, Minerals and Hazardous Elements. *Ann. N.Y. Acad. Sci.* **355**:1–372, Academic Press, N.Y.

19. Kubota, J. 1980. Ch. 12 in *Applied Soil Trace Elements,* B. E. Davies (ed.). John Wiley and Sons, N.Y.

20. Underwood, E. J. and J. F. Filmer. 1935. *Aust. Vet. J.* **11**:84.

21. Smith, S. E., B. A. Kock, and K. L. Turk. 1951. *J. Nutr.* **44**:455.

22. Askew, H. D. and J. Watson. 1943. *New Zeal. J. Sci. Tech.* **A25**:81.

23. Dinussen, W. E., E. W. Klosterman, E. L. Lasley, and M. L. Buchanan. 1953. *J. Animal Sci.* **12**:623.

24. Matovinovic, J. 1983. *Ann. Rev. Nutr.* **3**:341.

25. Gross, J. 1962. In *Mineral Metabolism,* Vol. II, Part B. Academic Press, N.Y.

26. Ammerman, C. B., et al. 1964. *J. Nutr.* **84**:107.

27. Perdomo, J. T., R. H. Harms, and L. R. Arrington. 1966. *Proc. Soc. Exp. Biol. Med.* **122**:758.

28. Suzuki, H., T. Higuchi, K. Sawa, S. Ohtaki, and Y. Horiuchi. 1965. *Acta Endocrinol* **50**:161.

29. Baker, H. J. and J. R. Lindesy. 1968. *JAVMA* **153**:1618.

30. Wolff, J. 1969. *Am. J. Med.* **47**:101.

31. Todd, W. R., C. A. Evehjem, and E. B. Hart. 1934. *Amer. J. Physiol.* **107**:146.

32. Tucker, H. F. and W. D. Salmon. 1955. *Proc. Soc. Exp. Biol. Med.* **88**:613.

33. Prasad, A. S. 1979. *Zinc in Human Nutrition.* CRC Press, Inc., Boca Raton, Fl.

34. Cousins, R. J. 1979. *Nutr. Rev.* **37**:97.

35. Cousins, R. J. 1979. *Amer. J. Clin. Nutr.* **32**:339.

36. DiSilvestro, R. A. and R. J. Cousins. 1983. *Ann. Rev. Nutr.* **3**:261.

37. Doyle, J. J. and J. E. Spaulding. 1978. *J. Animal Sci.* **47**:398.

38. Murphy, E. W., B. W. Willis, and B. K. Watt. 1975. *J. Amer. Dietet. Assoc.* **66**:345.

39. Chester, J. K. 1978. *World Rev. Nutr. Dietetics* **32**:135.

40. Cousins, R. J. 1982. In *Clinical, Biochemical and Nutritional Aspects of Trace Elements,* A. S. Prasad (ed.). Liss, N.Y.

41. Solomons, N. W. and R. J. Cousins. 1983. In *Absorption and Malabsorption of Mineral Nutrients,* I. H. Rosenberg and N. W. Solomons, (eds.). Liss, N.Y.

42. Pekas, J. C. 1968. *J. Animal Sci.* **27**:1559.

43. Apgar, J. 1985. *Ann. Rev. Nutr.* **5**:43.

44. Prasad, A. S., et al. 1963. *J. Lab. Clin. Med.* **62**:84.

45. Park, J. H., C. J. Grandjean, M. H. Hart, S. H. Erdman, P. Pour, and J. A. Vanderhoos. 1986. *Amer. J. A. Physiol.* **251**:E273.

46. Smith, S. E. and E. J. Larson. 1946. *J. Biol. Chem.* **163**:29.

47. Hsu, F. S., L. Krook, W. G. Pond, and J. R. Duncan. 1975. *J. Nutr.* **105**:112.

48. Hamilton, R. P., M. R. S. Fox, B. E. Fry, A. O. L. Jones, and R. M. Jacobs. 1979. *J. Food Sci.* **44**:738.

49. NRC. 1974. *Nutrients and Toxic Substances in Water for Livestock and Poultry.* NAJ-NRC, Washington, D.C.

50. Moore, C. V. and R. Dubach. 1962. In *Mineral Metabolism,* Vol. II, Part B. Academic Press, N.Y.

51. Moore, C. V. 1951. *Harvey Lect.* **55**:67.

52. Dallman, P. R. 1986. *Ann. Rev. Nutr.* **6**:13.

53. Tophan, R. W., H. Woodruff, and M. C. Walker. 1981. *Biochem.* **20**:319.

54. Furugouri, K. 1978. In *CRC Handbook Series in Nutrition and Food,* Section E, Nutritional Disorders. CRC Press, Boca Raton, Florida.

55. Hahn, P. F., et al. 1943. *J. Exp. Med.* **78**:169.

56. Hart, E. B., et al. 1928. *J. Biol. Chem.* **77**:797.

57. NRC. 1977. *Medical and Biological Effects of Environmental Pollutants Copper.* Natl. Acad. Sci., Washington, D.C.

58. O'Dell, B. L. 1976. In *Trace Elements in Human Health and Disease, Vol. I.* A. S. Prasad (ed.). Academic Press, N.Y.

59. Cartwright, G. E. and M. M. Wintrobe. 1964. *Amer. J. Clin. Nutr.* **14**:224; **15**:94.

60. Hurley, L. S. 1976. In *Trace Elements in Human Health and Disease,* Vol. II, pp. 301–314. Academic Press, N.Y.

61. Cooke, B. C. 1983. In *Recent Advances in Animal Nutrition,* W. Haresign (ed.). Butterworths, London, England.

62. Braude, R. 1967. *World Rev. Animal Prod.* **3**:69.

63. Gipp, W. F., et al. 1973. *J. Nutr.* **103**:713.

64. Waddell, J., H. Steenback, and E. B. Hart. 1931. *J. Nutr.* **4**:53.

65. Leach, R. M., Jr. 1976. In *Trace Elements in Human Health and Disease,* Vol. II, pp. 235–248. Academic Press, N.Y.

66. Baly, D. L., C. L. Keen, and L. J. Hurley. 1985. *J. Nutr.* **115**:872.

67. Schrader, R. E. and G. J. Everson. 1968. *J. Nutr.* **94**:269.

68. Schroeder, H. A., J. J. Balassa, and I. J. Tipton. 1966. *J. Chronic Dis.* **19**:545.

69. Schwarz, K. and C. M. Foltz. 1957. *J. Amer. Chem. Soc.* **79**:3293.

70. Muth, O. H., J. E. Oldfield, L. F. Remmert, and J. R. Schubert. 1958. *Sci.* **28**:1090.

71. Ganther, H. E., et al. 1976. In *Trace Elements in Human Health and Disease,* Vol. II, pp. 165–234. Academic Press, N.Y.

72. Noguchi, T., A. H. Cantor, and M. L. Scott. 1973. *J. Nutr.* **103**:1502.

73. Rotruck, J. T., et al. 1973. *Sci.* **179**:588.

74. Ku, P. K., W. T. Ely, A. W. Groce, and D. E. Ullrey. 1972. *J. Animal Sci.* **46**:559.

75. Mandizodsa, K. T., et al. 1979. *J. Animal Sci.* **49**:535.

76. Lopez, P. C., R. L. Preston, and W. H. Pfander. 1968. *J. Nutr.* **94**:219.

77. Scott, M. L. and A. H. Cantor. 1972. *Proc. Cornell Nutr. Conf.,* p. 66. Cornell University, Ithaca, N.Y.

78. Levander, O. A. 1976. In *Trace Elements in Human Health and Disease,* Vol. II, pp. 135–163. Academic Press, N.Y.

79. Allaway, W. H., D. P. Moore, J. E. Oldfield, and O. H. Muth. 1966. *J. Nutr.* **88**:401.

80. Gries, C. L. and M. L. Scott. 1972. *J. Nutr.* **102**:1287.

81. Comar, C. L. and F. Bronner. 1962–72. *Mineral Metabolism,* Vols. I, II, III. Academic Press, N.Y.

82. Mills, C. F. 1985. *Ann. Rev. Nutr.* **5**:173.

83. Schwarz, K. and W. Mertz. 1959. *Arch. Biochem. Biophys.* **85**:292.

84. Mertz, W. 1969. *Physiol. Rev.* **49**:163.

85. Mertz, W. 1967. *Fed. Proc.* **26**:186.

86. Schroeder, H. A. 1968. *Amer. J. Clin. Nutr.* **21**:230.

87. National Research Council. 1974. *Chromium.* NAS-NRC, Washington, D.C.

88. Navia, T. M., et al. 1976. In *Trace Elements in Human Health and Disease,* II, p. 249. Academic Press, N.Y.

89. Schwarz, K. and D. B. Milne. 1972. *Bioinorganic Chem.* **1**:331.

90. Krook, L. and G. A. Maylin. 1979. *Cornell Vet.* **69** (Suppl. 8).

91. NRC. 1974. *Effects of Fluoride in Animals.* NAS-NRC, Washington, D.C.

92. Spencer, H., et al. 1980. *Ann. NY Acad. Sci.* **355**:181–194. Academic Press, N.Y.

93. Rickert, D. A. and W. W. Westerfeld. 1953. *J. Biol. Chem.* **203**:915.

94. Underwood, E. J. 1976. In *The Biology of Molybdenum,* W. Chappel and K. Peterson (eds.). Marcel Dekker, Inc., N.Y.

95. Carlisle, E. M. 1972. *Science* **178**:619.

96. Schwarz, K. and D. B. Milne. 1972. *Nature* **239**:333.

97. Nielsen, F. H. 1976. In *Trace Elements in Human Health and Disease,* Vol. II, pp. 379–399. Academic Press, N.Y.

98. Life Sciences Research Office. 1975. *Evaluation of the Health Aspects of Aluminum Compounds and Food Ingredients.* Life Sciences Research Office. Federation of American Societies for Experimental Biology, Bethesda, MD. SCOG-43 Contract No. FOA223-75-2004.

99. Cotzias, G. C. 1967. Proc. First Annual Trace Substances in Environmental Health. Univ. Missouri, Columbia, MO.

100. Forbes, R. M. and J. W. Erdman, Jr. 1983. *Ann. Rev. Nutr.* **3**:213.

101. Matthews, D. E. and D. M. Bier. 1983. *Ann. Rev. Nutr.* **3**:309.

102. Schroeder, H. A. 1973. In *Essays in Toxicology,* Vol. 4, pp. 107–199. Academic Press, N.Y.

103. Schroeder, H. A. and M. Mitchener. 1975. *J. Nutr.* **105**:421.

104. Hamilton, E. I. 1982. *Fed. Proc.* **40**:2126.

13

Toxic
Minerals

ALL MINERALS, INDEED ALL nutrients, may be toxic to animals when ingested in excess amounts. The margin of safety between the minimum amount required in the diet and the amount that produces adverse effects varies among minerals and according to conditions. For example, NaCl may produce convulsions and death in pigs if fed at only 4 to 5 times the required concentration in the diet when access to water is restricted, but the tolerance is much greater with adequate water intake. On the other hand, although the amount of Zn required by pigs is about 25–50 ppm in the diet, 20 to 40 times this concentration is required to produce toxic signs.

Many minerals may be shown to be toxic under experimental conditions, but only a few are of practical importance because of their wide distribution in the environment or their pronounced toxic properties.

The rapid advances in multielement analysis of animal and plant tissues using techniques such as neutron activation, spark-source spectrometry, and inductively coupled plasma emission atomic absorption spectroscopy have allowed approaches to trace element toxicities and interactions never before possible.

Schroeder *et al.* (1–5) have discussed the concepts of mineral toxicity and suggested the possibility of toxicity to animals of a wide array of trace minerals, some of which are ubiquitous. Our discussion here is limited to some of the minerals that represent more pressing practical problems for animals and humans and about which considerable knowledge is available. These minerals include Pb, Cd, Hg, F, and Mo. Other minerals that may be hazardous to health under some conditions also are discussed. A review of mineral tolerances of domestic animals (6) provides detailed narrative and tabular information on the effects of ingestion of toxic and excessive levels of required minerals. This review and the book edited by Mertz (6a) should be consulted for specific information on all of the required and highly toxic minerals as well as on those widespread in the environment but of limited concern as toxicants. Maximum tolerable levels of required and toxic minerals in the diet of domestic animals are shown in Table 13.1 (6).

❏ LEAD (Pb)

Lead (Pb) poisoning in humans was recognized several hundred years ago and became a clinical problem in Western Europe in the seventeenth and eighteenth centuries where cooking utensils, other household articles and water pipes contained high concentrations of Pb (7). In more recent times, Pb poisoning in children became more common as a result of ingestion of high-Pb paint, which flaked and peeled from walls and fixtures, and of eating and drinking from utensils made of high-Pb clay (8, 9); chronic Pb poisoning in people of all ages is a threat whenever the water supply passes through tanks and pipes soldered with Pb (10). Pb toxicity presently is considered the most common cause of accidental death by poisoning in humans and animals world-wide (8, 10). Pb toxicity also may occur in areas where contamination results from agricultural spray residues or near smelting plants, mines and roadways, the latter as a result of tetraethyl lead from motor fuels (the use of low-Pb gasoline in late-model automobiles in the US is based on this hazard) (10).

Signs of Pb toxicity include pallor, lassitude, anorexia, and irritability in children and adults but the most definitive symptoms are anemia elevated blood Pb levels and urinary excretion of α-amino-levulinic acid in humans and animals (10). Pb toxicity affects several organs and tissues. Microcytic, hypochromic anemia is produced in Pb toxicity as a result of a decrease in survival time of red blood cells (excessive hemolysis) and a decrease in red cell formation from a block in heme synthesis. RBC from Pb-intoxicated animals show stippling and nucleation. In the kidney, pathological changes occur, resulting in amino aciduria, glycosuria, and hyperphosphaturia. Necrosis, hemorrhage, and ulceration of the stomach and small intestine occur in animals, and, in the nervous system, petechial hemorrhages and loss of myelin from nerve sheaths in the brain accompanied by cerebrocortical softening after prolonged exposure have been reported. Pb toxicity also affects the skeleton, causing osteoporosis in sheep (13) and reduced bone matrix formation and excess resorption of mineralized bone in children and rabbits (14). Enlarged joints of long bones are common in swine (15) (Fig. 13.1) and horses. In pigs (15), a low-Ca diet (0.7%, in the presence of 1,000 ppm of Pb, caused greater uptake of Pb by the tissues and more severe symptoms of toxicity than a high-Ca diet (1.2%). Pb toxicity causes petechial hemorrhages and necrosis in the liver of horses, dogs and pigs. The main clinical signs of toxicity and the main pathological effects have been listed by NRC (6) for various animal species.

Pb may be absorbed into the body via the GI tract, lungs, and skin (10). Absorption from the GI tract is low (20%), and the percentage absorbed does not seem to be affected by level of Pb in the diet. Retention of inhaled Pb in the body is 37–47% (16). Dietary factors influencing Pb toxicity have been enumerated and discussed (6, 10, 17–19).

Continuous oral administration of Pb produces its highest concentration in the skeleton (up to 90% of body burden), with smaller amounts in liver and kidney and still smaller concentrations in other tissues (7–15). Tissue uptake of Pb is affected by dietary Ca and P level; for example, high Ca-P depresses tissue Pb in pigs and rats (15, 16). Pb is transported

TABLE 13.1 Maximum tolerable levels of dietary minerals for domestic animals.[a]

| | SPECIES | | | | | |
ELEMENT	CATTLE	SHEEP	SWINE	POULTRY	HORSE	RABBIT
Aluminum,[b] ppm	1,000	1,000	200*	200	200*	200*
Antimony, ppm	—	—	—	—	—	70–150
Arsenic, ppm						
Inorganic	50	50	50	50	50*	50
Organic	100	100	100	100	100*	100*
Barium,[b] ppm	20*	20*	20*	20*	20*	20*
Bismuth, ppm	400*	400*	400*	400*	400*	2,000
Boron, ppm	150	150*	150*	150*	150*	150*
Bromine, ppm	200	200*	200	2,500	200*	200*
Cadium,[c] ppm	0.5	0.5	0.5	0.5	0.5*	0.5*
Calcium,[d] %	2	2	1	0.4 (Laying hen) 1.2 (Other)	2	2
Chromium, ppm						
Chloride	1,000*	1,000*	1,000*	1,000	1,000*	1,000*
Oxide	3,000*	3,000*	3,000*	3,000	3,000*	3,000*
Cobalt, ppm	10	10	10	10	10*	10*
Copper, ppm	100	25	250	300	800	200
Fluorine,[e] ppm	40 (Young) 40 (Mature dairy) 50 (Mature beef) 100 (Finishing)	60 (Breeding) 150 (Finishing)	150	150 (Turkey) 200 (Chicken)	40*	40*
Iodine, ppm	50[f]	50	400	300	5	—
Iron, ppm	1,000	500	3,000	1,000	500*	500*
Lead,[c] ppm	30	30	30	30	30	30*
Magnesium, %	0.5	0.5	0.3*	0.3*	0.3*	0.3*
Manganese, ppm	1,000	1,000	400	2,000	400*	400*
Mercury,[c] ppm	2	2	2	2	2*	2*
Molybdenum, ppm	10	10	20	100	5*	500
Nickel, ppm	50	50*	100*	300*	50*	50*
Phosphorus,[d] %	1	0.6	1.5	0.8 (Laying hen) 1.0 (Other)	1	1
Potassium, %	3	3	2*	2*	3*	3*
Selenium, ppm	2*	.2	2	2	2*	2*
Silicon,[b] %	0.2*	0.2	—	—	—	—
Silver, ppm	—	—	100*	100	—	—
Sodium chloride, %	4 (Lactating) 9 (Nonlactating)	9	8	2	3*	3*
Strontium, ppm	2,000	2,000*	3,000	30,000 (Laying hen) 3,000 (Other)	2,000*	2,000*
Sulfur, %	0.4*	0.4*	—	—	—	—
Tin, ppm	—	—	—	—	—	—
Titanium,[e] ppm	—	—	—	—	—	—
Tungsten, ppm	20*	20*	20*	20	20*	20*

TABLE 13.1 (*Continued*).

ELEMENT	SPECIES					
	CATTLE	SHEEP	SWINE	POULTRY	HORSE	RABBIT
Uranium, ppm	—	—	—	—	—	—
Vanadium, ppm	50	50	10*	10	10*	10*
Zinc, ppm	500	300	1,000	1,000	500*	500*

[a]The text (6) should be consulted prior to applying the maximum tolerable levels to practical situations. Continuous long-term feeding of minerals at the maximum tolerable levels may cause adverse effects. The listed levels were derived from toxicity data on the designated species. The levels identified by an * were derived by interspecific extrapolation. Dashes indicate that data were insufficient to set a maximum tolerable level (Table 1, reference 6).
[b]As soluble salts of high bioavailability. Higher levels of less-soluble forms found in natural substances can be tolerated.
[c]Levels based on human food residue considerations.
[d]Ratio of calcium to phosphorus is important.
[e]As sodium fluoride or fluorides of similar toxicity. Fluoride in certain phosphate sources may be less toxic. Morphological lesions in cattle teeth may be seen when dietary fluoride for the young exceeds 20 ppm, but a relationship between the lesions caused by fluoride levels below the maximum tolerable levels and animal performance has not been established.
[f]May result in undesirably high iodine levels in milk.
[g]No evidence of oral toxicity has been found.

in blood as an aggregate of Pb phosphate which is adsorbed to the surface of red blood cells. Major routes of Pb excretion are the GI tract and kidneys. That lost through the GI tract largely is via the bile. Urinary Pb output is proportional to blood Pb concentration. There is no direct evidence for kidney tubular secretion of Pb.

Increased dietary Ca, P, Fe, Mg, Zn, and vitamin E reduce Pb toxicity, while Hg, Cd, Mo, Se, F, and vitamin D aggravate it. Although there are conflicting reports on the effect of dietary protein on Pb toxicity, the weight of evidence suggests that signs of Pb toxicity are minimized in animals fed a marginal level of protein. Much still remains unknown concerning the importance of nutrient interrelationships in the response to high Pb intake in humans and animals.

❏ CADMIUM (Cd)

Cadmium (Cd) is toxic to a wide range of animal life and has specific adverse effects on the testes and kidney. Cd metabolism has been reviewed (6, 20, 21). Cd occurs geologically in Zn ores and is used widely in industry in the production of batteries, pigments and stabilizers and in electroplating (6). The atmosphere around some cities of the USA contains a significant amount of Cd (as high as 6.2 mg Cd/m^3), and water may be an important dietary source. Vegetables, fruits, and nuts are poor sources of Cd, but some seafoods and cereal grain by-products exceed 1 ppm Cd.

Total Cd in tissues of adults in the USA has been estimated at 30 mg, with 10 mg in kidney and 4 mg in liver. Kubota *et al.* (22) detected Cd in less than half of the human blood samples tested; the concentration of Cd in samples with detectable amounts was less than 1 mcg/dℓ in 83% of the cases. Cd concen-

Figure 13.1 *Lameness and flexed carpal joints in a pig fed 1,000 ppm of lead. Courtesy of L. Krook, Cornell, University.*

tration of testes, liver, spleen, kidneys, teeth, and hair of calves is increased by high levels of dietary Cd, but mammary transfer is low.

Specific adverse effects of Cd, when fed to experimental animals, include kidney damage and hypertension (23) and microcytic, hypochromic anemia (24, 25). The anemia and growth depression can be alleviated partially by concomitant oral or parenteral administration of additional Fe. Parisek (26) showed that Cd injection into the testes of male rats causes tissue necrosis and sterility; in pregnant females, it causes destruction of placenta and reproductive failure.

Cd toxicity is alleviated partially by high dietary Zn, Fe, and Ca; a complex interaction is apparent between levels of dietary Cu, Fe, and Zn in protecting against Cd toxicity. Low dietary Ca exacerbates the effects of Cd in reducing bone Ca content. Metallothionein in liver, kidneys and intestinal mucosa is involved with the complex interactions between Cd, Cu, and Zn (27, 28).

A series of unrelated compounds protect the testes against injected Cd. These include Zn, Se, cysteine, glutathione, and estrogen. The mode of protection is unknown, although it has been suggested (20, 28) that Se may protect by forming relatively unstable Se salts of Cd which are stored harmlessly in the body. In this regard, there is evidence that Cd in turn, may protect against Se toxicity (29). Diet supplementation with Zn, Cu, and Mn produces a reduced uptake of Cd by liver, kidney, and whole body in Japanese quail fed a diet containing Cd at a level similar to that ingested normally by humans and domestic animals.

More information is needed to ascertain the importance of environmental Cd contamination in human and animal health, but more complete knowledge of Cd metabolism and intoxication clearly should be a high priority goal for nutritionists and toxicologists.

❏ MERCURY (Hg)

The toxicity of mercury (Hg) has been recognized for many years; it is a hazardous environmental contaminant because of its uses in industry and agriculture (20, 30). Its occurrence in nature and its toxic properties have been reviewed in depth (6, 30–32).

Hg combines preferentially with –SH groups and in this way inhibits enzyme systems containing such groups. Hg accumulates in the lysosomes within cells and has been associated with their rupture; this has been suggested as the basis for the cell destruction by Hg, as destruction of lysosomes releases hydrolytic enzymes. Hg poisoning produces kidney necrosis and death. Concomitant administration of Se protects against the necrosis and improves survival (33). The reason for this protection by Se is not clear, although it may be related to formation of relatively insoluble compounds of low toxicity, such as $HgSeO_3$, which are stored in the body, or that Se catalyzes Hg to change to a less damaging form (6).

Organic Hg compounds such as methyl Hg and phenyl Hg are more toxic than inorganic Hg compounds such as $HgCl_2$. All of these compounds cause accumulation of Hg in liver and kidney, severe growth depression in rats (34) and decreased egg production and hatchability in chickens (35). Vitamin E protects against the toxic effects of methyl Hg in rats (36) and Japanese quail (37). Whether the protective effects of vitamin E and of Se against Hg toxicity have a common metabolic basis is unknown. The only known functions of vitamin E and Se are related to the prevention of cellular oxidative damage (38).

Hg content of hair, fingernails, and teeth gives a useful index of the degree of exposure of humans and animals. Kidneys consistently have a higher Hg concentration than all other tissues in humans (39). Urinary excretion is less than fecal excretion, although genetic differences have been observed among chickens. Some of the fecal Hg is a result of excretion through the bile.

Knowledge of the forms in which Hg is present in body tissues is meager. Living organisms can methylate Hg compounds and methyl Hg is retained in tissues longer than inorganic forms. The conversion of Hg compounds to methyl Hg by microorganisms has been suggested as a factor in the high concentration of Hg present in fish (40). The high concentration of Hg in fish apparently is not a result of recent environmental contamination because samples of fish stored for many years also have been shown to be high in Hg.

The specific antidote for acute Hg poisoning is dimercaprol which, in conjunction with proteins such as those in milk and eggs, binds Hg still in the GI tract (6). The practical dangers of Hg poisoning in humans and animals appear to be the result of a few specific industrial practices and processes, and the awareness of these problems should minimize such problems in the future.

❏ FLUORINE (F)

Aside from its role in preventing dental caries, fluorine (F) can be considered a toxic mineral for humans and animals. The tissue distribution, metabolism, and toxic effects of F have been described in detail (6, 20, 41, 42). Chronic fluorosis has been reported from several parts of the world mostly as a result of F-containing dusts from steel mills and other industries processing F-rich substances (such as reduction of aluminum ore), and secondarily in association with the use of high-F rock phosphate as mineral supplements for animals. Krook and Maylin (43) described chronic F poisoning in cattle raised adjacent to an industrial aluminum smelting plant in Canada. Stained teeth of fluorotic cattle are shown in Fig. 13.2. Toxic effects in humans exposed to F in air, water, or food are as follows (44): 1 ppm F in water reduces dental caries, but 2 ppm or more F induces mottled enamel, 8 ppm in water induces osteosclerosis in some subjects, and 110 ppm in food or water produces growth retardation and kidney changes; 20–80 mg/day or more ingested from water or air produces crippling fluorosis, and 2.5 g or more in an acute oral dose is fatal. Detailed discussion of the effects of F on teeth is inappropriate here, but may be found in several reviews (44, 45).

The effects of high F on bone are somewhat contradictory; reported effects of fluorosis in animals range from osteosclerosis to osteoporosis. Jowsey

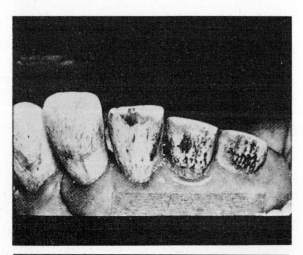

Figure 13.2 *Stained teeth of fluorotic cattle. Vegetative staining is typical of excessive fluorine intake at moderate levels. University of Tennessee photograph.*

et al. (46) reported increased bone formation, and Ramberg et al. (47) reported increased bone resorption in response to F. Forsyth et al. (48) fed levels of up to 450 ppm of F in the presence of 1.2% or 0.5% Ca (Ca:P ratio kept constant at 1.2:1) to pigs through two generations; they found that high F did not increase bone density but did cause mottled bone and interfered with collagen metabolism. The lower level of Ca-P was associated with greater F retention in bone, but there was no evidence of soft tissue lesions or of hyperostosis. Growth rate was depressed by high F, but high F in the presence of high dietary Ca-P did not reduce growth. Newborn pigs from sows, fed high F had decreased length, volume, and weight and increased F concentrations of humerus, demonstrating the effective placental transfer of F.

F is a potent enzyme inhibitor. Fatty acid oxidase activity in kidney is decreased in fluorosis, suggesting impaired lipid metabolism. Carbohydrate metabolism is disturbed also. In general, all animals can tolerate slightly higher intakes of F from rock phosphate or phosphatic limestones than from more water-soluble sources (6). High dietary Ca, Mg, or Al or a high concentration of Ca in the water, when F is administered in the water, inhibit the toxic effects of F (6, 49).

Almost complete absorption of soluble F from the GI tract occurs. F tends to follow the distribution of Cl in the body; it crosses cell membranes freely and thus leaves the blood quickly after absorption. Some F enters red blood cells so that about 25% of total blood F is within the red cells. The skeleton takes up F readily. Absorbed F that escapes retention in the skeleton is excreted mainly in the urine, but also to a smaller extent in sweat and by re-excretion into the GI tract. Urinary excretion in cattle and sheep normally represents 50–90% of the dietary intake, depending on the solubility and the proportion of F absorbed. Milk F concentrations are affected only slightly by dietary F (6), although pigs nursing sows fed high F do show increased bone F concentration (48). Although the beneficial effect of small amounts of F on teeth is recognized, ingestion of excessive F induces characteristic bone and teeth lesions and should be avoided in animals and humans.

❏ MOLYBDENUM (Mo)

Although molybdenum (Mo) is recognized as a required nutrient (see Ch. 12) it is of more concern as a toxic mineral. Mo toxicity first was recognized in England when it was reported (50) that cattle grazing certain pastures high in Mo developed severe diarrhea. The syndrome became known as peat scours or teart and later was found to be prevented by Cu supplementation of the diet. Subsequently, Dick (17) reported that high Mo and sulfate intake produced Cu deficiency in ruminants. Thus, the primary toxic effect of Mo intake is the precipitation of Cu deficiency.

Striking species differences exist in susceptibility to high Mo intakes. Cattle appear to be the most susceptible, sheep less so, and horses and pigs still less. Mo has been fed at 1,000 ppm in the diet of pigs for 3 mo. with no ill effects; levels of 50–100 ppm produce severe diarrhea in cattle. Poultry, guinea pigs, rabbits, and rats are intermediate between pigs and cattle in their tolerance to high Mo. Signs of toxicity, in addition to diarrhea in cattle and rats, include anemia, dermatosis, anorexia, deformed front legs in rabbits, and reduced lactation and testicular degeneration in several species (20).

Manifestations of Mo toxicity in sheep include decreased liver and plasma Cu, reduced crimp and pigmentation of the wool, anemia, and alopecia. Newborn lambs from affected ewes show enzootic ataxia (swayback), resulting from demyelination of nerves (6).

Liver alkaline phosphatase activity is decreased in kidney and intestine of Mo intoxicated rats, and liver sulfide oxidase activity is decreased. This interference with S metabolism has been suggested as being a factor in the mechanism of Mo toxicity. The observed relationship of dietary sulfate level to Mo tolerance fits this suggestion. Mo-Cu-sulfate interrelationships have been reviewed in detail by Underwood (20). The reduction in liver sulfide oxidase activity in Mo toxicity may lead to precipitation of insoluble cupric sulfide, rendering Cu physiologically unavailable.

Species differences in both absorption and excretion of Mo probably account for differences in tolerance to high dietary Mo. Some of this apparent species variability in susceptibility to excess Mo may be due to variations in concurrent dietary intakes of Cu, Zn, S, Al, Cd, and S-containing amino acids (6). Hexavalent forms of Mo present in forages are water soluble and well absorbed by cattle; Mo is absorbed more rapidly by pigs than by cattle; but is lost quickly in the urine of pigs. Mo content of milk of ruminants is increased by high-Mo forage; milk Mo of ewes grazing forage containing 1 ppm Mo was 10 mcg/ℓ

compared to 980 mcg/ℓ in milk of ewes grazing forage containing 3 ppm Mo (52). The Mo of milk apparently is bound entirely to xanthine oxidase, so that Mo concentration is proportional to enzyme activity.

The chemical form in which Mo exists in blood is unknown, although it is present both in red cells and in plasma and is a constituent of the enzyme, xanthine oxidase. The proportion in red cells varies from 70% at low Mo intake to much lower values as dietary Mo increases. The absorption of Mo from the GI tract is reduced greatly by the presence of high dietary sulfate; this in turn affects the concentration of Mo in blood and tissues (29).

The practical importance of Mo as a toxic mineral appears to relate mainly to cattle and sheep grazing pastures in areas of the world with high soil Mo contents. Such areas are widespread and of significant worldwide concern; molybdenosis has been reported in cattle grazing in such widely separated geographic locations as England, New Zealand, Ireland, and the western USA.

❏ OTHER MINERALS

Schroeder et al. (1–4, 53), NRC (6), and Browning (54) have characterized several trace minerals as to their innate toxic effects as judged by growth, life span and carcinogenic activity in mice. Table 13.2 summarizes the results obtained in this extensive series of experiments. Based on records of weight gain, longevity and incidence of malignant tumors in rats and mice, Schroeder has concluded that the following minerals appear to have innate toxicity: Cd, Pb, F, Se, Te, Ti, As, Ge, Sn, Nb, Sb, Ni, Sc, Cr^{+6}, Ga, Y, Rh, Pd, and In. Moreover, each of the required minerals is toxic when fed in excess of needs, if any (see Chs. 11 and 12). Schroeder and Mitchener (1) have suggested that suppression of growth rate induced in mice by some of the toxic elements is in the following order: $Ga > Y > Sc > In > Cr^{+6} > Pd > Rh$. The following have been shown to be tumerogenic: Se, Ni, Pd, and Rh.

In addition, the following elements have had additional toxic properties ascribed to them (6, 55, 56, 57). Aluminum (Al) interferes with P availability in non-ruminants although it has only minor effects in ruminants (57).

Excess Al has three potential toxic effects: decreased absorption of a number of elements and of lipids from and decreased motility of the GI tract; pulmonary damage if inhaled; systemic toxicity if ab-

TABLE 13.2 Toxic properties of various trace minerals having no known dietary requirements.[a]

TRACE ELEMENT	CONCENTRATION IN DRINKING WATER MG/LITER	TEST SPECIES	WEIGHT GAIN REDUCTION	LIFE SPAN REDUCTION	CARCINOGENIC
Cadmium (Cd)	5	mice	no	yes	no
Cadmium	5	rats	no	yes	no
Lead (Pb)	5	mice	no	yes	no
Lead	5	rats	no	yes	no
Lead	25	rats	no	no	no
Selenate (Se^{+6})	0.02	rats	no	no	yes
Selenite (Se^{+4})	0.02	rats	yes	yes	no
Selenite	0.02	mice	no	no	—
Tellurium (Te)	0.02	rats	no	no	no
Tellurium	0.02	mice	yes	yes	no
Titanium (Ti)	5	mice	no	yes	no
Arsenic (As)	5	mice	no	yes	no
Arsenic	5	rats	no	no	no
Germanium (Ge)	5	mice	no	yes	no
Germanium	5	rats	no	yes	no
Tin (Sn)	5	mice	no	no	no
Tin	5	rats	no	yes	no
Vanadium (V)	5	mice	no	no	no
Vanadium	5	rats	no	no	no
Zirconium (Zr)	5	mice	no	no	no
Zirconium	5	rats	no	no	no
Niobium (Nb)	5	mice	yes	yes	no
Niobium	5	rats	no	no	no
Antimony (Sb)	5	mice	yes	yes	no
Antimony	5	rats	no	yes	no
Fluorine (F)	10	mice	no	no	no
Nickel (Ni)	5	mice	no	no	no
Scandium (Sc)	5	mice	yes	no	no
Chromium (III) (Cr^{+6})	5	mice	no	no	no
Chromium (VI) (Cr^{+3})	5	mice	yes	no	no
Gallium (Ga)	5	mice	yes	yes	no
Yttrium (Y)	5	mice	yes	no	no
Rhodium (Rh)	5	mice	yes	no	yes
Palladium (Pd)	5	mice	yes	no	yes
Indium (In)	5	mice	yes	no	no

[a]From Schroeder *et al.* (1–4, 53). Se, V, F, Ni, and perhaps others may be required under some conditions.

sorbed, including brain damage, skeletal decalcification, and anemia. Evidence linking Al toxicity to Alzheimer's disease in humans is inconclusive and requires further research (58). Antimony (Sb) reduces mean life span of female rats with no evidence of carcinogenesis or tumorigenesis. Arsenic (As) attaches to sulfhydryl groups of protein and trivalent As specifically blocks lipoate-dependent enzymes (18) and results in vomiting, diarrhea, cellular necrosis, and death in a few days after a single toxic dose. Inorganic As ingested by ruminants and non-ruminants is methylated and excreted in the urine. Chronic As toxicity is unlikely and seldom reported, probably because As is bound loosely to tissue protein and excreted quickly by the kidney. Barium (Ba) is highly toxic when absorbed, but it never occurs free in nature, so the danger of ingesting soluble forms of Ba is small. Barium sulfate is used in taking x-ray photographs of the GI tract, but it is so nearly insoluble that it is non-toxic. Barium chloride, carbonate, and sulfide are toxic and their ingestion results in paralysis of the central nervous system, intense myocardial stimulation, skeletal muscle tumors, and death (6), Beryllium (Be), bismuth (Bi), boron (B), bromine (Br), rubidium (Rb), silicon (Si), silver (Ag), strontium (Sr), thallium (Tl), tungsten (W), uranium (U), and vanadium (V) have also been shown to be toxic when consumed in excess amounts (53, 56, 59). Rubium (Rb) and cesium (Cs) can replace K as a nutrient for growth of yeast and sea urchin eggs so, as in the case of other trace elements, the distinction of toxicity and essentiality is often difficult. Tungsten (W) depresses growth and decreases life span in chicks but not rats (5) and causes death by respiratory paralysis.

❑ RADIONUCLIDES IN NUTRITION

Considerable public and medical concern has been voiced about the effects of exposure to radioactive isotopes of minerals on human and animal health. The public response to the accidental escape of radioactive substances from nuclear power plants, at Three Mile Island in Pennsylvania in 1980 and at Cherynobyl in the USSR in 1986, typifies the high degree of anxiety and concern about the dangers of radioactivity in the environment. This general subject is outside the realm of our discussion, except for a consideration of the consequences of contamination of the food chain with dangerous radionuclides. For example, the presence of ^{131}I and ^{90}Sr

in food products, especially milk, has led to an appreciable body of literature on the physiological effects. No attempt is made here to enumerate these effects in detail.

Chronic effects of low levels of radiation of mammals include increased incidence of leukemia, cancer, and genetic mutations (60). Although the distribution of the rare earth minerals (61) in nature is widespread, their significance in animal and human nutrition is in doubt.

The protective ability of animal organisms against uptake of ^{90}Sr and other radionuclides, as well as potentially toxic rare earths, is important. Of course, the use of radioactive isotopes as tracers in studying metabolism of minerals is an established practice in nutrition research. The hazards must be recognized, however. The preferential utilization of Ca over ^{90}Sr has been determined in many species. Hardy *et al.* (62) compared the skeletal and soft-tissue burdens of Mg, Si, ^{90}Sr, Ba, and ^{226}Ra in pigs and sheep at various stages of growth in relation to Ca burden. Ca utilization by pigs was 47% and 17% by sheep, but utilization of all other minerals was considerably less.

A measure of the discrimination by the body against these minerals is the observed ratio (OR) which is an expression of the overall discrimination in the movement of two elements from a source into a biological system. Table 13.3 shows the OR of each of these nuclides as the nuclide to Ca ratio in the whole body divided by the nuclide to Ca ratio in the diet. The pig and sheep both clearly discriminate against stable Sr, ^{90}Sr, Ba, and ^{226}Ra, as evidenced by the low OR values. The pig discriminated against

TABLE 13.3 Ratio of nuclide to Ca in whole body and in diet of pigs and sheep (observed ratio, OR).[a]

NUCLIDE/CA	NUCLIDE/CA IN WHOLE BODY/ NUCLIDE:CA IN DIET (OR)	
	PIG	SHEEP
Sr/Ca	0.14	0.45
^{90}Sr/Ca	0.17	0.20
^{226}Ba/Ca	0.02	0.62
Ra/Ca	0.01	0.52

[a]Hardy *et al.* (62).

Br 7 times more effectively than against Sr, and against [226]Ra 14 times more than against Sr. In contrast, the sheep showed little difference in OR for Sr, Ba, and Ra. More [226]Ra and Ba occurred in soft tissue than in bone in the pig, but in the sheep only 3–4% was found in soft tissues. Thus, species differences occur apparently not only in relative utilization of rare earths but in tissue distribution. With our present knowledge we cannot generalize about the response to be expected to contamination of diets of humans and animals with potentially hazardous rare earths, either stable or radioactive isotopes.

❏ POTENTIAL POLLUTION OF THE ENVIRONMENT BY MINERALS

Based on amounts of minerals present in the earth's crust and their use patterns in industry, Bowen (60) divided minerals into four categories with respect to relative pollution potential: very high, high, moderate, and low. Minerals considered to have very high potential for pollution were Ag, Au, Cd, Cr, Cu, Mg, Pb, Sb, Sn, Ti, Zn. This classification is of only limited use in relation to human and animal nutrition and metabolism because of the ever-changing nature of technology which results in variable exposure to specific minerals. Advances in sophisticated methodology for studying trace elements in biological tissues will enhance the monitoring of these changes. The concept of patterns of movement of toxic minerals in the environment in response to changing technology must be recognized by nutritionists and biologists concerned with controlling pollution while providing an adequate feed and food supply.

❏ SUMMARY

All minerals may be toxic to animals and humans when ingested in excess amounts. Minerals discussed in this chapter include either those not known to be required for normal life processes of animals or some required in extremely small amounts. The list includes minerals whose presence in the environment creates practical problems of toxicity for animals and humans and about which considerable knowledge is available. Such minerals include lead (Pb), cadmium (Cd), mercury (Hg), fluoride (F), and molybdenum (Mo). In addition, the following minerals have had toxic properties ascribed to them: aluminum (Al), antimony (Sb), arsenic (As), barium

(Ba), beryllium (Be), bismuth (Bi), boron (B), bromine (Br), rubidium (Rb), selenium (Se), silicon (Si), silver (Ag), strontium (Sr), thallium (Tl), tungsten (W), uranium (U), and vanadium (V). Some of these toxic minerals have received attention as possible dietary essentials for humans and animals. In fact, the reader will recognize that several of the minerals listed in this chapter as toxic, also have been shown to be required nutrients—that is, F, Mo, Se, Si. Future research may result in the reclassification of an additional one or more of the toxic and/or ubiquitous minerals as essential nutrients.

❏ REFERENCES

1. Schroeder, H. A. and M. Mitchener. 1971. *J. Nutr.* **101**:1431.

2. Schroeder, H. A., J. J. Balassa, and W. H. Vinton, Jr. 1964. *J. Nutri.* **83**:239.

3. Schroeder, H. A., and J. J. Balassa. 1967. *J. Nutr.* **92**:245.

4. Schroeder, H. A., et al. 1968. *J. Nutr.* **95**:95.

5. Schroeder, H. A. and M. Mitchener. 1975. *J. Nutr.* **105**:421.

6. National Research Council. 1980. *Mineral Tolerance of Domestic Animals.* Natl. Acad. Sci., Washington, D.C.

6a. Mertz, W. 1986. *Trace Elements in Human and Animal Nutrition,* 5th ed. Academic Press. N.Y.

7. Aub, J. C., Faihall, A. S. Minot, and P. Reznikoff. 1962. *Lead Poisoning. Medicine Monography,* Vol. 7. William and Wilkins, Baltimore, MD.

8. Reddick, L. P. 1971. *Southern Med. J.* **64**:446.

9. Lin-Fu, J. S. 1970. U.S. Public Health Serv. Publ. No. **2108**:1.

10. Quarterman, J. 1986. In *Trace Elements in Human and Animal Nutrition,* 5th ed., W. Mertz (ed.). Academic Press, Orlando, FL, p. 281.

11. U.S. Dept. Health, Education and Welfare. 1973. DHEW Pub. No. (HSM) **73**:10005.

12. National Research Council. 1972. *Lead: Airborne Lead in Perspective.* Natl. Acad. Sci., Washington, D.C.

13. Clegg, F. G. and J. M. Rylands, 1966. *J. Comp. Path.* **76**:22.

14. Hass, G. M., D. V. L. Browan, R. Eisentein, and A. Hemmons. 1964. *Amer. J. Path.* **45**: 691.

15. Hsu, F. S., L. Krook, W. G. Pond, and J. R. Duncan. 1975. *J. Nutr.* **105**:112.

16. Levander, O. A. and L. Cheng (eds.). 1980. Micronutrients Interactions: Vitamins, Minerals and

Hazardous Elements. *Ann. N.Y. Acad. Sci.* **355**:1–372.

17. Forbes, R. M. and G. C. Sanderson. 1978. Ch. 16, in *The Biogeochemistry of Lead in the Environment.* Elseiever/North-Holland Biomedical Press, N.Y., N.Y.

18. Ammerman, C. B., S. M. Miller, K. R. Fish, and S. L. Hansard II. 1977. *J. Animal Sci.* **44**:485.

19. Smith, J. C. 1976. In *Trace Elements in Human Health and Disease,* Vol. II, Essential and Toxic Elements, p. 443. Academic Press, N.Y.

20. Underwood, E. J. 1977. *Trace Elements in Human and Animal Nutrition,* 4th ed. Academic Press, N.Y.

21. Kostial, K. 1986. In *Trace Elements in Human and Animal Nutrition,* 5th ed., *W. Mertz* (ed.). Academic Press, Orlando FL., p. 319.

22. Kubota J., V. A. Lazar, and F. L. Losee. 1968. *Arch. Environ. Health* **16**:788.

23. Schroeder, H. A., et al. 1966. *Arch. Environ. Health* **13**:788.

24. Pond, W. G., E. F. Walker, Jr., and D. Kirtland. 1973. *J. Animal Sci.* **36**:1122.

25. Cousins, R. J., A. K. Barber, and J. R. Trout. 1973. *J. Nutr.* **103**:964.

26. Parizek, J. 1960. *J. Reprod. Fert.* **1**:294; **7**:263; **9**:111.

27. Cousins, R. J. 1979. *Environ. Health Perspect.* **28**:131.

28. Whanger, P. D., J. W. Ridlington, and C. L. Holcomb. 1980. *Ann. N.Y. Acad. Sci.* **355**:333.

29. Flegal, K. and W. G. Pond. 1979. *J. Nutr.* **110**:1255.

30. Peakall, D. B. and R. J. Lovett. 1972. *Biosci.* **22**:20.

31. Montague, P. and K. Montague. 1971. *Mercury.* The Gruin Co., Inc. N.Y.

32. Clarkson, T. W. 1976. In *Trace Elements in Human Health and Disease,* Vol. II, Essential and Toxic Elements, pp. 453–475. Academic Press, N.Y.

33. Parizek, J. and J. Kalouskova. 1980. *Ann. N.Y. Acad. Sci.* **355**:347.

34. Johnson, S. L. and W. G. Pond. 1974. *Nutr. Reports Internatl.* **9**:135.

35. Emerick, R J., S. Palmer, C. W. Carlson, and R. A. Nelson. 1976. *Fed. Proc.* **355**:577(abstr.).

36. Welsh, S. O. 1979. *J. Nutr.* **109**:1673.

37. El-Begearmi, M. M., H. E. Ganther, and M. L. Sunde. 1977. *Poult. Sci.* **56**:1711.

38. Ganther, H. E. 1980. *Ann. N.Y. Acad. Sci.* **35**:212.

39. Joselow, M. M., L. J. Goldwater, and S. B. Weinberg. 1967. *Arch. Environ. Health.* **15**:64.

40. Jensen, S. and A. Jernelov. 1969. *Nature* **223**:753.

41. National Research Council. 1971. *Flourides. Biological Effects of Atmospheric Pollutants.* Natl. Acad. Sci., Washington, D.C.

42. National Research Council. 1974. *Effects of Fluorides in Animals.* Natl. Acad. Sci., Washington, D.C.

43. Krook, L. and G. A. Maylin. 1979. *Cornell Vet.* **69**(Suppl. 8).

44. Bhussry, B. R., et al. 1970. In *Fluorine and Human Health.* World Health Organization, Geneva, Switzerland.

45. Adler, P. 1970. In *Fluorine and Human Health.* World Health Organization, Geneva, Switzerland.

46. Jowsey, J. R., R. F. Schenk, and F. W. Reutter, 1968. *J. Clin. Endocrine. Metab.* **28**:869.

47. Ramberg, C. F., Jr., et al. 1970. *J. Nutr.* **100**:981.

48. Forsyth, D. M., W. G. Pond, and L. Krook. 1972. *J. Nutr.* **102**:1639.

49. Spencer, H., L. Dramer, and D. Osis. 1980. *Ann. N.Y. Acad. Sci.* **355**:181.

50. Ferguson, W. S., A. H. Lewis, and S. J. Watson. 1938. *Nature* **141**:553.

51. Dick, A.T. 1953. *Austral. Vet. J.* **29**:233; 1954, **30**:196.

52. Hogan, K. G. and A. J. Hutchinson. 1965. *New Zealand J. Agr. Res.* **8**:625.

53. Schroeder, H. A., et al. 1963. *J. Nutr.* **80**:39; 1965, **86**:51; **86**:31; 1967, **92**:334; 1968.

54. Browning, E. 1961. *Toxicity of Industrial Metals.* Butterworth and Co., Ltd., London.

55. Mertz, W. 1968. In *Trace Elements in Human and Animal Nutrition,* 5th ed., W. Mertz (ed.). Academic Press, Orlando, FL, p. 371.

56. Nielsen, F. H. 1986. In *Trace Elements in Human and Animal Nutrition,* 5th ed., W. Mertz (ed.). Academic Press, Orlando, FL. p. 415.

57. Valdivia, R., C. B. Ammerman, C. J. Wilcox, and P. R. Henry. 1978. *J. Animal Sci.* **47**:1351.

58. Alfrey, A. C. 1986. In *Trace Elements in Human and Animal Nutrition,* 5th ed., W. Mertz (ed.). Academic Press, Orlando, FL. p. 399.

59. Schroeder, H. A., M. Mitchener, J. J. Balassa, M. Kanisawa, and A. P. Nason. 1968. *J. Nutr.* **95**:95.

60. Bowen, H. J. M. 1966. *Trace Elements in Biochemistry.* Academic Press, N.Y.

61. Kyker, G. C. 1962. In *Mineral Metabolism,* Vol. II, Part B. Academic Press, N.Y.

62. Hardy, E. J., Rivera, I. Fisenore, W. Pond, and D. E. Hogue. 1970. In *Health and Safety Laboratory,* pp. 183–190. U.S. Atomic Energy Commission Symp., N.Y.

14

Fat-Soluble Vitamins

THE TERM VITAMIN WAS coined in 1912 by Funk (1) who suggested that food contained special organic constituents that prevented certain of the classical human diseases of that time—beriberi, pellagra, rickets, and scurvy. Since that time a long list of vitamins has been identified and characterized.

Vitamins are required in minute quantities for normal body function, yet each has its own specific function and the omission of a single vitamin from the diet of a species that requires it produces specific deficiency symptoms and results ultimately in death of the animal. Although many of the vitamins function as coenzymes (metabolic catalysts), others have no such role but perform other essential functions. The known vitamins can be divided on the basis of solubility properties into fat-soluble and water-soluble. The fat-soluble vitamins—A, D, E, and K—are considered in this chapter and the water-soluble vitamins are considered in Ch. 15.

❏ VITAMIN A

Structure

Vitamin A is required in the diet of all animals thus far studied. It can be provided as the vitamin or as its precursor, carotene. The nomenclature and formulas for vitamin A and many different carotenes are described in detail by Harris (2) and Goodwin (3).

The structures of vitamin A alcohol and β-carotene are shown (Fig. 14.1) (4). Vitamin A is composed of a β-ionone ring and an unsaturated side chain. β-carotene is composed of two vitamin A molecules joined as shown.

Vitamin A can occur as the alcohol (retinol), as shown, as the aldehyde (retinal), or as the acid (retinoic acid) in the free form or esterfied with a fatty acid (for example, as vitamin A palmitate). It can occur as the all *trans* form (as shown), all *cis* form or as a mixture of *cis* and *trans* forms. The *trans* form of retinol is considered to have 100% biological activity. Biological activities of two isomers of retinal, expressed as a percentage of potency of all *trans* retinol are all *trans*, 91, and 2-mono *cis* (neo), 93.

More than 500 carotenoid pigments exist in nature in addition to β-carotene (3), but plants contain no vitamin A. Carotenoids differ from each other in the configuration of the ring portion of the molecule. They include α- and γ-carotene, cryptoxanthin, zeaxanthin, and xanthophyll. The vitamin A precursors must be modified to release biologically available vitamin A. Zeaxanthin and xanthophyll possess no vitamin A activity, but others have some activity, the amount depending on the animal species. For the rat the relative biopotency of retinol is 100; β-carotene, 50; α-carotene, 25; γ-carotene, 14; and cryptoxanthin, 29.

Vitamin A activity originally was expressed as international units (IU), determined in a bioassay with β-carotene as a standard. Later, an additional standard was established based on retinyl acetate; thus, there were two standards, one for preformed vitamin A and one for provitamin A. One IU of preformed vitamin A was 0.344 μg of retinyl acetate (0.3 μg of retniol) and one IU of provitamin A was 0.6 μg of β-carotene. Bieri and McKenna (5) reviewed the history of expressing values for fat-soluble vitamins and described the currently accepted expression of dietary vitamin A, D, E, and K. Vitamin A is expressed in retinol equivalents (μg). One retinol equivalent = $0.167 \times$ β-carotene or $0.084 \times$ other provitamin A. Thus, the total vitamin A value of a food or mixed diet is:

$$\text{retinol equivalents (μg)}$$
$$= \text{μg retinol} + \frac{\text{μg β-carotene}}{6}$$
$$+ \frac{\text{μg other provitamin A}}{12}$$

The conjugated double bonds in vitamin A and carotene cause a characteristic yellow color. Exposure to ultraviolet light destroys the double bonds and the biological activity of vitamin A and its precursors. Some enzymes present in natural feedstuffs destroy carotenoids, but esterified vitamin A is more stable than retinol or retinal. The stability of vitamin A added to feeds can be increased by covering minute droplets of vitamin A with gelatin or wax or by adding an antioxidant such as ethoxyquin to the feed; the antioxidant is oxidized in preference to vitamin A. In current nutrition practice in the USA, most vitamin A is supplied by synthetic sources which can be produced very economically.

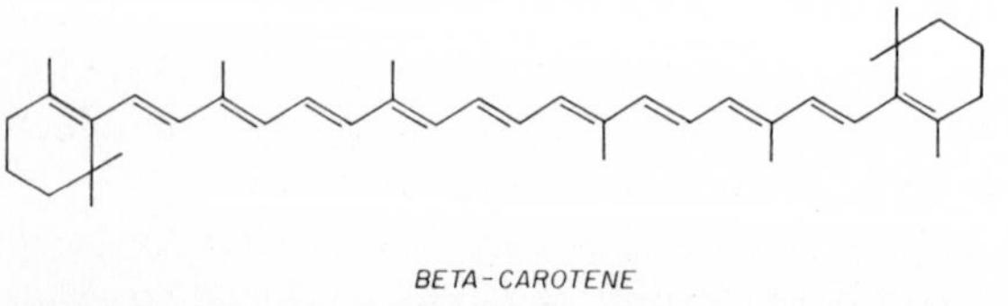

BETA-CAROTENE

Figure 14.1 *Upper. Structure of vitamin A, the term used as the generic descriptor of all β-ionone derivatives. The compound (R = —CH₂OH), also known as vitamin A, vitamin A alcohol, vitamin A₁, vitamin A₁ alcohol, axerophthol, or axerol, should be designated all-trans retinol. Lower. The structure of β-carotene (provitamin A) (4).*

Functions

At least three distinct functions of vitamin A have been identified (6). Vitamin A is required (as retinol) for normal night vision (formation of rhodopsin or visual purple in the eye); this is the only specific chemical reaction that has been identified. Vitamin A combines as a prosthetic group of rhodopsin which breaks down on exposure to light. This reaction is part of the physiological process of sight. Vitamin A is required for normal epithelial cells which line or cover body surfaces or cavities—respiratory, urogenital and digestive tracts, and skin; and it is required for normal bone growth and remodeling (normal osteoblastic activity). In addition, vitamin A may play a primary role in the synthesis of glycoproteins.

Deficiency Signs

The practical significance of hypovitaminosis A (vitamin A deficiency) is greater perhaps than for any other vitamin (7, 8, 9). Because one function of vitamin A is to allow formation of rhodopsin in the eye, night blindness is a symptom of vitamin A deficiency in all animals studied. The degree of failure in dark adaptation has been used as a measure of the quantative needs in humans and some animals.

The essentiality of vitamin A for normal epithelium creates a wide variety of deficiency symptoms in animals deprived of the vitamin (Fig. 14.2). Some of the common deficiency signs in various animals are: xerophthalmia in children and in growing animals (this condition is characterized by dryness and irritation of the cornea and conjunctiva of the eye and results in cloudiness and infection), keratinization of respiratory epithelium, resulting in greater severity of respiratory infections; reproduction difficulties, including abortions and birth of weak offspring, and associated thickening of vaginal epithelium; repro-

Figure 14.3 *Vitamin A-deficient chick showing xerophthalmia. Courtesy of Poultry Sci. Dept, Cornell U.*

ductive failure in males because of effects on spermatogenic epithelium; embryonic death in chicks and mammalian embryos; poor growth in surviving young, uric acid deposits in kidneys, heart, liver and spleen and keratinization of epithelium of respiratory tract of chicks and xerophthalmia in chicks (Fig. 14.3) and mammals. Xerophthalmia remains a major public health problem in developing countries (8). Oomen (9) classified the stages of xerophthalmia in human infants and presented photographs depicting the appearance of the eye in each case, ranging from night blindness to the more permanent scarring effects involving the cornea.

The importance of vitamin A in normal bone formation relates to a variety of deficiency signs which, although seemingly unrelated, have a common basis involving abnormal skeletal development. Gallina et al (10) provided evidence in calves that vitamin A deficiency produces increased osteoblastic activity. This agrees with earlier reports in other species. Nervous disorders such as unsteady gait, ataxia and convulsions occur as a result of partial occlusion of the spinal cord by the surrounding vertebral column in growing animals. Exophthalmia (Fig. 14.4) and elevated cerebrospinal fluid pressure exist in vitamin A deficiency, apparently as a result of excess pressure on the brain stem associated with a constricted spinal column and optic foramen. Blindness and skeletal abnormalities occur in deficient newborn pigs. A wide range of additional manifestations. (Table 14.1) (11) of vitamin A deficiency have been reported, but there is no definitive knowledge as to the exact mode

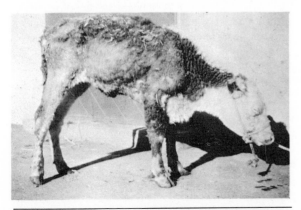

Figure 14.2 *Severe vitamin A deficiency in a calf. Animal shows excessive lacrimation, a lethargic appearance, and appears to have diarrhea and some respiratory involvement. Courtesy of Chas. Pfizer Co.*

Figure 14.4 *Heifer showing exophthalmia or bulging eye condition due to high cerebrospinal fluid pressure and partial closure of the optic foramen. Courtesy of L. A. Moore, USDA.*

of action on which the metabolic changes are based. Bone changes occurring in vitamin A deficiency are associated with changes in chondroitin sulfate, mucopolysaccharide synthesis, and increased urinary excretion of inorganic sulfate in rats. Vitamin A deficiency increases bone thickness, but results in less Ca deposition and more glycosaminoglycan (GAG). This increase in GAG is apparently due to an increase in the amount of sulfated GAG in bone resulting from a defect in degradation of GAG (12). Vitamin A metabolism has been linked with vitamin E (as an antioxidant in the stability of biological membranes); vitamin D (in bone metabolism); sterols (deficiency reduces cholesterol synthesis); squalene (deficiency increases squalene synthesis); and coenzyme Q or ubiquinone (deficiency increases ubiquinone synthesis in liver). Vitamin A deficiency in rats causes adrenal gland atrophy and reduced gluconeogenesis. Vitamin A is involved in some manner with biosynthesis of adrenal steroids and of glycogen. Vitamin A deficiency may be related to kidney stone formation in rats (13), based on the observed reduction in urinary Ca excretion, and is associated with altered Fe metabolism, including reduced plasma Fe and sometimes anemia (14). The effect does not appear to be caused by increased red blood cell destruction.

Metabolism

Vitamin A from synthetic sources or animal tissues in feedstuffs is present primarily as the palmitate ester which is hydrolyzed by pancreatic enzymes that are activated by bile salts. Free vitamin A is incorporated into the lipid micelles (see Ch. 9) and reaches the microvilli of the upper jejunum where it is transferred into the mucosal cell by active transport as retinol. Within the mucosal cell it is re-esterified to palmitate and other esters, incorporated into chylomicrons and transported to the lymph (15–17) for storage in the liver parenchymal cells as retinyl esters. Release of vitamin A from the liver is preceded by hydrolysis to free retinol by retinyl palmitate hydrolase. This enzyme is increased in activity by 100-fold during vitamin A deficiency, suggesting that it is important in maintaining serum vitamin A concentrations. Vitamin A is transported from the liver to peripheral tissues as free retinol bound to retinol-binding protein (RBP). RBP has been characterized in a wide variety of animals.

Carotenoids are split within the rat intestinal mucosal cell by a specific enzyme (18) to form retinal which is reduced to retinol. Some retinol is converted to retinal and retinoic acid and absorbed into the portal blood as a glucuronide. Tissues other than intestinal mucosal cells are capable of splitting carotenoids to vitamin A. Liver contains an enzyme with the same properties as the β-carotene-splitting enzyme of the intestine (19) and lung and kidney also may be involved. The details of absorption in other species are less well known. Species differences seem certain, as some animals deposit very little carotene in depot fat even though their diets are high in carotenoids, but others have appreciable amounts of carotene in their depot fat and milk. Rats, cats, dogs, sheep, goats, and guinea pigs apparently convert most or all carotene to vitamin A, but cattle (especially Guernseys and Jerseys), horses, some rabbits, chickens, and humans have blood and depot fats high in carotenoids if dietary carotenoids are high. In fact, chickens absorb only hydroxycarotenoids unchanged and deposit them in tissues. A wide variation in efficiency exists even between species considered to be efficient converters of carotenoids to vitamin A. For example, the pig is only one-third as efficient as the rat in converting β-carotene to vitamin A. Some recycling of vitamin A by enterohepatic circulation occurs, but this probably is not a major conservation mechanism.

The degree of absorption of vitamin A and its precursors varies, depending on the animal species and type of diet. Apparent absorbability of vitamin A in dairy cattle fed a variety of forages averaged 78% in one report (20). There is considerable degradation

TABLE 14.1   Vitamin A deficiency signs in animals.[a]

ABNORMALITY	ANIMALS STUDIED	ABNORMALITY	ANIMALS STUDIED
General		*Liver*	
Anorexia	Rat, fowl, farm animals	Metaplasia of bile duct	Rat
Growth failure and weight loss	Rat, fowl, farm animals	Degeneration of Kupffer cells	Rat
Xerosis of membranes	Rat, fowl		
Roughened hair or feathers	Rat, birds, farm animals	*Nervous system*	
Infections	Rat, birds, farm animals	Incoordination	Rat, bovine, pig
		Paresis	Rat, pig
Death	Rat, birds, farm animals	Nerve degeneration or twisting	Rat, dog, rabbit, bovine, bird, pig
Eyes		Constriction of optic foramina	Bovine, dog
Night blindness	Rat, farm animals	Bone formation	
Xerophthalmia	Rat, bovine	Defective modeling	Dog, bovine
Keratomalacia	Rat	Restriction of brain cavity	Dog
Opacity of cornea	Rat, bovine		
Loss of lens	Rat, bovine	*Reproduction*	
Papilloidema	Bovine	Degeneration of testes	Rat
Constriction of optic nerve	Bovine, dog	Abnormal estrus cycle	Rat, bovine
		Resorption of fetuses	Rat
Respiratory system		*Congenital abnormalities*	
Metaplasia of nasal passages	Fowl	Anophthalmia	Pig, rat
		Microophthalmia	Pig, rat
Pneumonia	Rat, bovine	Cleft palate	Pig, rat
Lung abscesses	Rat	Aortic arch deformation	Rat
GIT		Kidney deformities	Rat
Metaplasia of forestomach	Rat	Hydrocephalus	Rabbit, bovine
Enteritis	Rat, farm animals	*Miscellaneous*	
Urinary system		Increased cerebro-spinal fluid pressure	Bovine, pig
Thickened bladder wall	Rat	Cystic pituitary	Bovine
Cystitis	Rat		
Urolithiasis	Rat		
Nephrosis	Rat		

[a]Adapted from Roels (11).

in the rumen. In humans, vitamin A absorption and storage may be improved by adding fat to a low-fat diet.

The distribution of vitamin A, its esters and carotenoids in human blood serum during absorption from the GI tract is summarized in Table 14.2 (21). The liver hydrolyzes the retinyl ester and free retinol is carried by the blood complexed to RBP to tissues that require it for normal function. In vitamin A deprivation, liver stores are depleted even though the release of RBP by the liver is inhibited. Wright and Hall (22) reported that total liver vitamin A can be estimated, within limits, from plasma vitamin A concentration in several species of animals fed diets containing vitamin A levels ranging from deficient to toxic.

Many nutrients affect vitamin A concentrations in plasma and liver. Protein deficiency and Zn deficiency (8, 23) decrease vitamin A concentrations in plasma and liver; excess vitamin E interferes with the conversion of β-carotene to vitamin A (24). Liver concentrations, in general, are of more diagnostic value in assessing vitamin A status than are blood concentrations.

Liver biopsy techniques have been developed for use in cattle as a means of studying vitamin A requirements (Fig. 14.5). The turnover rate of vitamin A in liver of beef cattle has been estimated. Protein level of the diet does not affect vitamin A turnover rate significantly. Kohlmeier and Burroughs (25) suggested that cattle entering finishing lots with 20–40 µg/g of vitamin A in the liver have sufficient reserves for 90–120 days under normal feeding conditions and that no dietary vitamin A is required for good feedlot performance if plasma vitamin A is maintained above 25 µg/ml and liver vitamin A exceeds 2 µg/g. This claim is still controversial. Such factors as vitamin A

destruction in feedstuffs and initial stores of liver vitamin A will, of course, affect the level of dietary vitamin A needed to maintain these minimum tissue levels. The data apply here to cattle, but the same type of consideration must be applied to other species when determining appropriate levels of supplementation.

Protein ingestion affects vitamin A utilization. Protein deficiency causes reduced vitamin A concentrations of plasma and reduced liver storage. Signs of vitamin A deficiency may appear in protein-deficient animals even in the presence of adequate liver vitamin A storage. This has been suggested to result from reduced transport of vitamin A from liver because of reduced serum albumin, the carrier protein for vitamin A in blood. Impaired conversion of carotene to vitamin A in protein deficiency also may occur, but the dominant factor appears to be a defect in transport (11).

There is evidence that fat-soluble vitamins play a role in the release of hormones and in their cellular functions and conversely that growth hormone may exert a positive effect on tissue uptake and storage of vitamin A (26).

Thyroid function is affected by vitamin A intake. Vitamin A deficiency reduces thyroxin secretion and causes thyroid hyperplasia. Conversely, thyroxin stimulates conversion of carotenoids to vitamin A and increases storage of vitamin A, but also increases depletion of vitamin A reserves when a vitamin A-deficient diet is fed.

There is increasing evidence (3) that β-carotene and the carotenoid canthaxanthin inhibit the growth of skin tumors. The protective effect has been reported with β-carotene addition to the diet or, in one report, by topical application. The effect may be related to the fact that carotenoids quench free radical

TABLE 14.2 Distribution of retinol, vitamin A esters, and carotenoids in human blood serum during absorption.[a]

SERUM FRACTION	VITAMIN A		CAROTENOIDS, %
	RETINOL, %	ESTER, %	
Chylomicrons	5.3	7.5	0
Lipoprotein Sf 10-100	3.9	79.4	0
Lipoprotein Sf 3-9	20.2	8.6	78.3
Other proteins	70.6	4.4	21.7

[a]From Krinsky et al. (21).

Figure 14.5 *Liver biopsy. Top: Liver sample being aspirated with a syringe. Bottom: Sample of liver obtained. Courtesy of J. F. Bone, Oregon State U.*

formation. The use of carotenoids in treating photosensitization is also related to the oxygen quenching property. The anticancer effect of β-carotene is under study in a long-term human investigation (27).

Oral contraceptives in humans elevate blood vitamin A concentrations, possibly by an effect of the estrogen component of the formulation on increasing the levels of retinol binding protein (RBP). The rapidly advancing capabilities of hormone assays of blood and tissues offer exciting possibilities for identifying more completely the role of the endocrine system in affecting the metabolism of vitamins and other nutrients in humans and animals.

Vitamin A is transported readily by the mammary gland to the milk of swine and goats. Cattle transfer both vitamin A and carotene to the milk in response to dietary intake, the proportions depending partly on breed. Vitamin A concentration of human milk tends to be related to maternal intake of the vitamin.

Toxicity

Vitamin A is not excreted readily, so long-term ingestion of amounts larger than needed or acute dosage with a large excess may result in toxic symptoms. The toxic range is reached when daily intake reaches 50–500 fold the metabolic requirement. Death has been reported in humans after a single dose of 500,000–1,000,000 IU of vitamin A. Chronic toxicity manifests itself as anorexia, weight loss, skin thickening, scaly dermatits, swelling and crusting of the eyelids, patchy hair loss, hemorrhaging, decreased bone strength, spontaneous bone fractures, thinning of the bone cortex, and death. Excess mucous forms and normal keratinization is inhibited in hypervitaminosis A. The bone changes described in young pigs fed excess vitamin A have been attributed to destruction of epiphyseal cartilage and decreased matrix formation in the presence of normal remodeling. Excess vitamin A may cause disruption of lipoprotein membranes. Plasma and liver levels of vitamin E are reduced in animals fed excess vitamin A, but the effect seems to be related to reduced absorption of vitamin E rather than to interference with tissue metabolism (24).

The dietary levels causing toxic symptoms will vary in accordance with species, age, body store, degree of absorbability, and degree of conversion of carotene to vitamin A where the free vitamin is not fed. In pigs, toxic symptoms include rough hair coat, hyperirritability and sensitivity to touch, petechial hemorrhages over the legs and abdomen, cracked, bleeding skin above the hooves, blood in urine and feces, loss of control of legs, periodic tremors, and death.

Excess vitamin A during pregnancy results in malformed young in rats, mice, and pigs, but less so for guinea pigs and rabbits. During early gestation an excess induces embryonic death, but, if begun later in gestation, abnormalities may occur, the severity and type differing according to species. In pigs, a single excess dose of vitamin A injected on day 18 or 19 of pregnancy causes cleft palate, abnormal skulls and skeleton, and, sometimes, eyelessness in the newborn. Injection of the same dose before or after this stage of development has no such effect. Clearly, the effect is related to the relative rate of growth and differentiation of a particular organ at the time the excess vitamin A is given.

❑ VITAMIN D

Structure

Several sterols have biological vitamin D activity, but only two, vitamin D_2 (irradiated ergosterol or calciferol) and vitamin D_3 (irradiated 7-dehydrocholesterol) are of major importance. Most mammals can use either vitamin D_2 or D_3 efficiently, but birds utilize D_2 only one-seventh as efficiently as they do D_3. The structures of vitamins D_2 and D_3 and their sterol precursors are shown in Fig. 14.6 (28).

Ergosterol is the chief plant source and 7-dehydrocholesterol is found in animal tissues. Ultraviolet light converts each provitamin to its respective biologically active form. Exposure of harvested green forage to sunlight for several hours converts plant sterols to vitamin D_2. Similarly, exposure of animals to sunlight for a few minutes/day is sufficient to convert skin sterols to vitamin D_3, thus eliminating the need for a dietary source under most conditions.

Functions

Vitamin D was named by McCollum (29), who showed that it differed from vitamin A, which had been also named by McCollum (30). Vitamin A was named on the basis of the presence of a substance present in butter fat and cod liver oil which was required for growth of animals fed what was otherwise a chemically defined diet. McCollum realized that the antirachitic activity of cod liver oil was distinct from its antixerophthalmia activity and subsequently determined that vitamin A and D were two distinct fat-soluble compounds with different curative functions. Shortly thereafter, Steenbock and Black (31) discovered that ultraviolet light caused an alteration of some substances in animals and that ultraviolet irradiation of not only animals but of their feed prevented or cured rickets. This fascinating account of early classical research discoveries of vitamin D and its functions is detailed by DeLuca (28). Historical perspective, physiology of vitamin D action, discovery of the vitamin D endocrine system, current knowledge of vitamin D metabolism, and functions of its metabolities have been summarized (28, 32, 33).

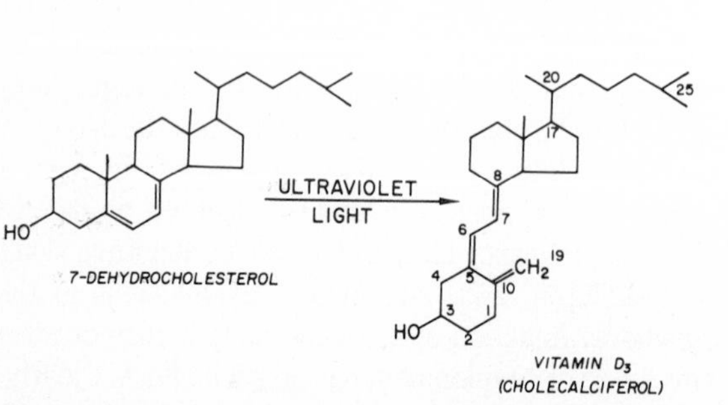

The general functions of vitamin D are to elevate plasma Ca and P to levels that will allow normal bone mineralization and that will prevent the tetany that results if plasma Ca falls appreciably below normal. Vitamin D, in conjunction with parathyroid hormone (PTH), prevents tetany by elevating plasma Ca concentration. Normal plasma Ca levels are achieved by adjusting intestinal transport of Ca from ingested sources and by release of Ca from bone. Stimulation of the active transport of Ca and P across the intestinal epithelium involves the active form of vitamin D. PTH stimulates Ca absorption indirectly by stimulating the production of an active form of vitamin D, 1,25 dihydroxy cholecalciferol (1,25-$(OH)_2D_3$) under conditions of hypocalcemia. There is evidence for an action of 1,25-$(OH)_2D_3$ in stimulating reabsorption of Ca from kidney tubules. Thus, intestinal absorption, bone resorption and renal tubule reabsorption of Ca and P represent the three reservoirs available for maintenance of plasma Ca and P within limits compatible with normal bone mineralization and neuromuscular tone.

One or more Ca-binding proteins are involved in Ca transport. Wasserman and colleagues (34) isolated a Ca-binding protein from intestinal mucosa of several species (birds, rats, dogs, cattle, pigs, monkey, guinea pigs) which requires vitamin D. However, there appears to be at least one other factor functioning in Ca transport. DeLuca (35) suggested that Ca-dependent ATPase, alkaline phosphatase, and actin likely may be factors induced by 1,25$(OH)_2D_3$ to function in Ca transport. Further work is needed to define the exact nature of the mode of action of

Figure 14.6 *The structures of vitamins D_2 and D_3 and their sterol precursors. Courtesy H. F. DeLuca, U. Wisconsin (28).*

$1,25(OH)_2D_3$ in stimulating Ca absorption from the GI tract (36).

Metabolism

Although the importance of vitamin D in normal Ca and P metabolism has been recognized for many decades, great strides have been made during the past few years in understanding the metabolic reactions of vitamin D and the importance of vitamin D metabolites in various tissues and organs of the body. Current knowledge of vitamin D metabolism has been detailed (28, 32, 33, 37, 38). The sequential alterations in vitamin D in the body are illustrated in Fig. 14.7 (33). Vitamin D absorbed from the intestines or made in the skin by ultraviolet radiation is carried to the liver where it is hydroxylated to produce 25-hydroxyvitamin D_3 (25-OH-D_3), the main circulating form of vitamin D. Significant hydroxylation also occurs in other tissues, including lung, intestine, and kidney (33). There does not appear to be a direct action of 25-OH-D_3 on any target tissue. Rather, further transformation is needed; metabolism to 1,25-$(OH)_2D_3$ and 24,25-$(OH)_2D_3$ occurs exclusively in the kidney. These final products are delivered by the blood to the target tissues of intestine, bone and elsewhere in the kidney where they carry out their functions. Thus, the metabolically active forms of vitamin D are considered to be hormones. Both steps in the conversion of vitamin D to 1,25-$(OH)_2D_3$ and 24,25-$(OH)_2D_3$ are under the control of mixed function of monoxygenase enzymes in the microsomes of the liver and in the mitochondria of the kidney. The formation of hydroxylated metabolites of vitamin D_3 from skin and diet has been summarized (33). In addition to these metabolites of vitamin D, more

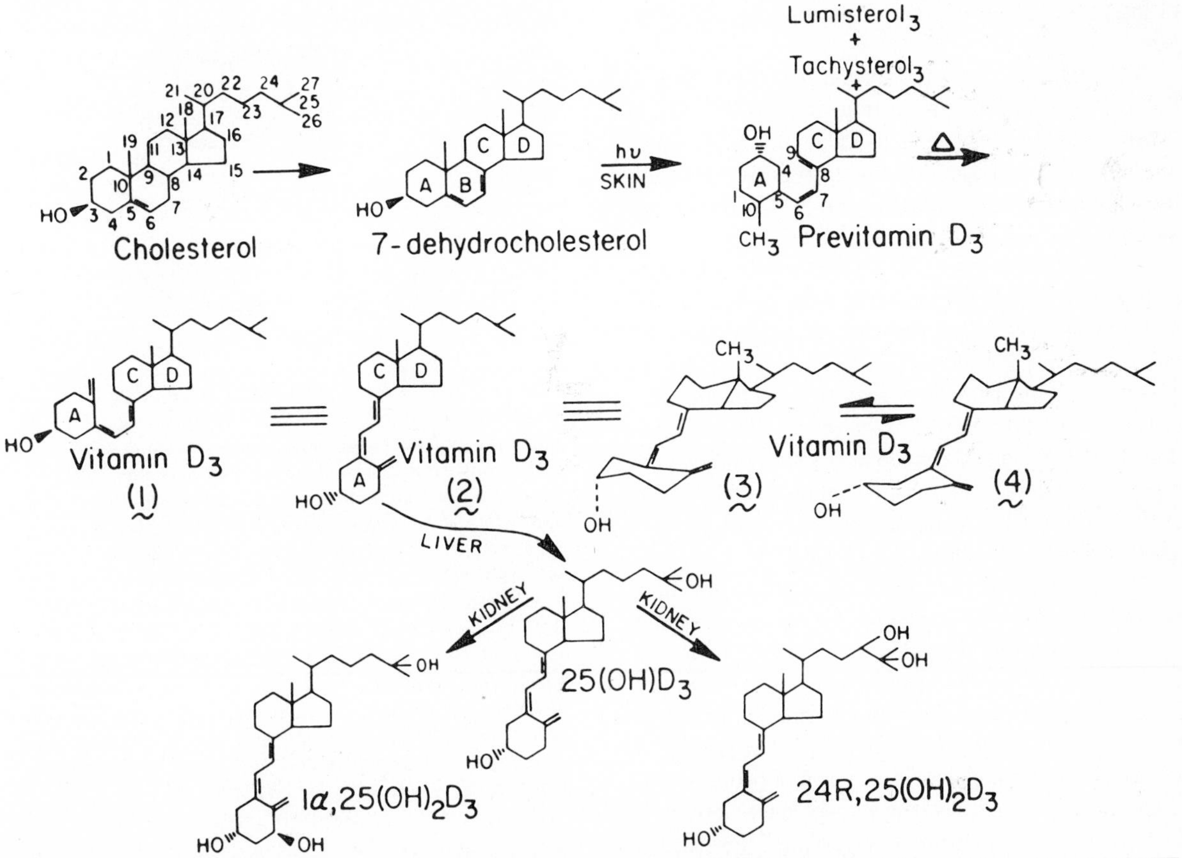

Figure 14.7 Key vitamin D sterols. (Top line) Vitamin D is produced from 7-dehydrocholesterol via previtamin D as a consequence of the uv-mediated opening of the B-ring. (Middle line) Summary of the evolution of the conformational representations of vitamin D. Structure 1 or 2 resulted from original chemical analysis; structures 3 and 4 represent results of recent studies (232, 233) indicating the conformational mobility of the A-ring. (Bottom line) Structure of the three principal metabolites; hv = ultraviolet light irradiation. By permission from Henry and Norman (33).

than twenty other compounds are produced under certain conditions (33); their physiological roles are unknown. They include $1,25,25\text{-}(OH)_3D_3$, $25\text{-}OH\text{-}D\text{-}26,23\text{-}lactone$, calcitroic acid, and cholecalcitroic acid.

High dietary Ca decreases the production of $1,25\text{-}(OH)_2D_3$ by the kidney, and low dietary Ca stimulates it. Regulation of $1,25\text{-}(OH)_2D_3$ synthesis is related also to serum Ca concentration, through the action of parathyroid hormone (PTH) which catalyzes the conversion of $25\text{-}OH\text{-}D_3$ to $1,25\text{-}(OH)_2D_3$. Thus, $1,25\text{-}(OH)_2D_3$ appears to be the ideal compound for treatment of diseases related to parathyroid insufficiency. Various analogs of this very expensively isolated and purified compound are receiving attention for use in clinical problems of Ca homeostasis in humans and animals.

Nephrectomized animals cannot make significant amounts of $1,25\text{-}(OH)_2D_3$ and, therefore, do not respond to physiological doses of vitamin D in terms of increased Ca absorption or serum Ca concentration.

Although it is generally agreed that the kidney is the principal site of production of $1,25(OH)_2D_3$, a number of other cell types, including bone, placenta, intestine, and yolk sac, have been reported to make the conversion of $25(OH)D_3$ to $1,25(OH)_2D_3$ or $24,25(OH)_2D_3$ (33).

Administration of $1,25\text{-}(OH)_2D_3$ to nephrectomized animals induces the same response as in normal animals, suggesting that this compound does not have to be metabolized further for metabolic activity. The specific biochemcial events that occur after localization of $1,25\text{-}(OH)_2D_3$ in the target tissue to produce the physiological response are under study currently. The overall mechanism of vitamin D movement in the body and functions of its metabolities are diagrammed schematically in Fig. 14.8.

The concept of vitamin D as a precursor to a steroid hormone, $1,25(OH)_2D_3$, has been extended to the increased knowledge of receptors for $1,25(OH)_2D_3$ in target organs, analogous to receptors for insulin, estrogen, and other hormones in target tissues (37). Bone cells apparently respond to $1,25(OH)_2D_3$ by modulating an array of proteins, including collagen and alkaline phosphatase, required for bone mineralization and remodeling. There is also new evidence that $1,25(OH)_2D_3$ may be involved in immunology by modulating production of antibody-producing B cells or helper T cells.

In addition to dietary vitamin D status as a regulator of $25(OH)D_3$ metabolism, dietary Ca and P, estrogen, parathyroid hormone, calcitonin, and pi-

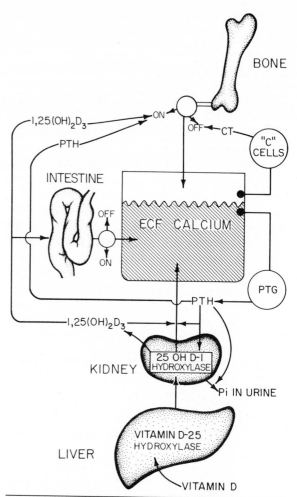

Figure 14.8   *The Ca homeostatic mechanism diagrammatically represented involving the vitamin D endocrine system. In response to hypocalcemia, the parathyroid glands secrete parathyroid hormone. The parathyroid hormone in turn binds to the kidney and bone. In the kidney it stimulates production of $1,25\text{-}(OH)_2D_3$. The $1,25\text{-}(OH)_2D_3$ then stimulates intestinal absorption of Ca and together with the parathyroid hormone stimulates the mobilization of Ca from bone and renal reabsorption of Ca. The resultant rise in plasma (ECF) Ca shuts off secretion of the parathyroid hormone. If Ca rises above the normal value of 10 mg per deciliter, calcitonin (CT) is secrete "C" cells of the thyroid. This hormone blocks the mobilization of Ca from bone, thereby suppressing plasma Ca concentration. Courtesy H. F. DeLuca, U. Wisconsin (51).*

tuitary hormones, including growth hormone, have been shown to play a role. Obviously, the complex regulation of vitamin D metabolism is still incompletely understood and complete knowledge of all of the interacting forces will require further study, the details of which are beyond the scope of this discussion.

Vitamin D is stored mainly in the liver, but also in kidney and lung and perhaps in other tissues. Placental and mammary transfer are limited, when compared with vitamin A, but sufficiently high levels are present in the newborn and milk of most species to prevent early rickets. Only limited data are available on quantitative transfer of vitamin D across placental and mammary tissue. DeLuca (38) has summarized evidence suggesting that Ca can be mobilized from bone and intestine of some animal species during pregnancy and lactation by a vitamin D-independent mechanism and that the young vitamin D deficient rat pup is not responsive to the administration of $1,25\text{-}(OH)_2D_3$. Therefore, it appears that factors other than vitamin D may be involved in Ca mobilization during pregnancy and lactation.

Although the vast majority of research has been directed at determining the effect of vitamin D on Ca and P metabolism, available evidence also indicates that vitamin D promotes absorption from the GI tract of Be, Co, Fe, Mg, Sr, Zn, and, perhaps, still other elements. It is not known whether the effect is caused by vitamin D-dependent protein carriers, or by other mechanisms.

Deficiency Signs

The main effect of a deficiency of vitamin D is abnormal skeletal development. Normal calcification cannot occur in the absence of adequate Ca and P. Therefore, either a deficiency of vitamin D, which results in impaired utilization of Ca, or a deficiency of Ca or of P, will produce similar abnormalities in the skeleton (the roles of Ca and P are discussed in Ch. 11).

The term applied to vitamin D deficiency in young, growing animals is rickets; the comparable condition in adults is osteomalacia. In each instance inadequate calcification of organic matrix occurs, which results in lameness, bowed and crooked legs (Fig. 14.9), spontaneous fractures of long bones and ribs, and beading of the ribs. In growing animals the bone ash is reduced (Ca:P tends to remain constant), and weight gain may be depressed. In adults, negative mineral balance occurs, and bone ash concentration declines.

Species differences exist in the response to deprivation of vitamin D by dietary means or protection from ultraviolet light (sunlight). Calves and pigs can grow normally on a level of vitamin D in the diet that quickly produces rickets in chicks. Pheasants and turkeys have a higher vitamin D requirement than chicks. The difference in species requirements may be related to growth rate, as animals and birds with very rapid growth tend to be more susceptible to rickets. Protein source affects the vitamin D requirement of pigs. Soybean protein, high in phytate, is associated with a higher vitamin D requirement than milk protein.

Serum Ca concentration tends to be reduced in vitamin D deficiency, although hormonal mechanisms (parathyroid hormone and calcitonin) are quite efficient in maintaining a relatively constant range. Although parathyroid hormone is under the influence of vitamin D, calcitonin is not. Spanos and MacIntyre (39) summarized the relationship between vitamin D and calcitonin in nutrition. Calcitonin produces hypocalcemia and hypophosphatemia by inhibiting bone resorption. During growth, lactation, and pregnancy, calcitonin and $1,25\text{-}(OH)_2D_3$ concentrations in plasma are high. It has been suggested that by opposing the resorptive action of $1,25\text{-}(OH)_2D_3$ on bone, calcitonin preserves the integrity of the skeleton and directs the action of $1,25\text{-}(OH)_2\text{-}D_3$ to the GI tract to meet the need for Ca. Serum alkaline phosphatase may be increased in vitamin D-deficiency rickets. This enzyme is present in bone and is associated with bone resorption. Holick et al. (40) suggested a mechanism of preferential translocation by a binding protein of vitamin D_3 formed in the skin of animals by photosynthesis whereby the synthesis, storage and slow, steady release of vitamin D_3 from skin to the circulation is accomplished. Thus, the skin serves as

Figure 14.9 *Lameness and sore joints in pig fed a vitamin D-deficient diet and kept indoors without access to sunlight.*

the site of synthesis, reservoir for storage of pro D_3 and the organ where the slow dermal conversion of pro D_3 to D_3 occurs.

Vitamin D deficiency can be prevented by only a few minutes of exposure to direct sunlight, although skin pigmentation affects the amounts of sunlight required to prevent rickets; white-skinned animals require less sunlight than dark-skinned ones. Loomis (41) has suggested that skin color in humans is an adaptation that provides for protection against rickets in inhabitants of northern regions as well as protection against excess vitamin D synthesis in skin of inhabitants of equatorial regions.

Toxicity

Excess vitamin D causes abnormal deposition of Ca in soft tissues. This Ca is resorbed from bone, resulting in brittle bones subject to deformation and fractures. Ca deposits are frequent in kidneys, aorta, and lungs. Such lesions can be produced in rats with dosages of 300,000 to 600,000 IU, in chicks with 4,000,000 IU/kg of diet and in pigs at 250,000 IU/animal/day for 30 days. Human infants show toxic signs with levels as low as 3,000–4,000 IU/day (only 10 times the requirement). Hypervitaminosis D can lead to death, usually from uremic poisoning resulting from severe calcification of kidney tubules. Excess vitamin D during pregnancy apparently does not cause severe abnormalities in the fetus, but is not harmless, as premature closing and shortening of the skull bone and abnormal teeth have been observed in newborn rabbits whose dams were given excess vitamin D.

During the past few years several plants indigenous to widely different geographic areas have been found to produce signs resembling those of vitamin D toxicity in animals. Wasserman and Nobel (42) have summarized the isolation and identification of the toxic substances in these calcinogenic plants and their physiologic effects on animals. The problem was first recognized more than 20 years ago in Argentina in cattle and eventually was found to be due to consumption of a plant, *Solanum malacoxylon*, which contains glycosides of $1,25$-$(OH)_2$-D_3. Subsequently, cattle and horses grazing a shrub in Florida, *Cestrum diurnum*, showed the same clinical signs and the plant was found to contain the same or similar metabolite of $1,25$-$(OH)_2$-D_3. Cattle and sheep in Germany and Austria are affected similarly by consuming a plant called *Trisetum flavescens* and cattle

in Jamaica, Hawaii, India, and New Guinea are similarly afflicted after consuming plants of unknown identity. The signs in all cases include weight loss, stiffness of forelimbs, arching of back, emaciation, hypercalcemia and hyperphosphatemia, and death. The ingestion of a source of $1,25$-$(OH)_2$-D_3 bypasses the normal regulatory step (the kidney), thereby stimulating excess synthesis of intestinal Ca-binding protein and causing excessive amounts of Ca and P to be retained. Haschek *et al.* (43) described the pathogenesis of vitamin D toxicity and concluded that the osteocytic death and osteonecrosis is a direct toxic action of vitamin D, since hypoparathyroidism and hypercalcitoninism, which occur secondarily to hypercalcemia, could not account for the appearance of bone cell death which occurred within one day of vitamin D overdose.

❏ VITAMIN E

Vitamin E first was recognized as a fat-soluble factor necessary for reproduction in rats (44). Alpha tocopherol, the most active biological form of vitamin E, was isolated by Evans *et al.* (45). Other forms of tocopherol have been designated with prefixes such as β and γ. The structure of α-tocopherol is shown in Fig. 14.10 (4).

Other compounds with chemical structures similar to tocopherols are found in animal tissues, but have limited biological activity. The chemistry and biochemistry of vitamin E have been detailed (46). Vitamin E is very unstable; its oxidation is increased by the presence of minerals and of polyunsaturated fatty acids (PUFA) and decreased by esterification to form tocopheryl acetate. The d-isomer is more active than the l-form. Most commercially available vitamin E is available as dl-α tocopheryl acetate.

Knowledge of vitamin E nutrition and metabolism has been summarized in several other reviews (17, 47–50).

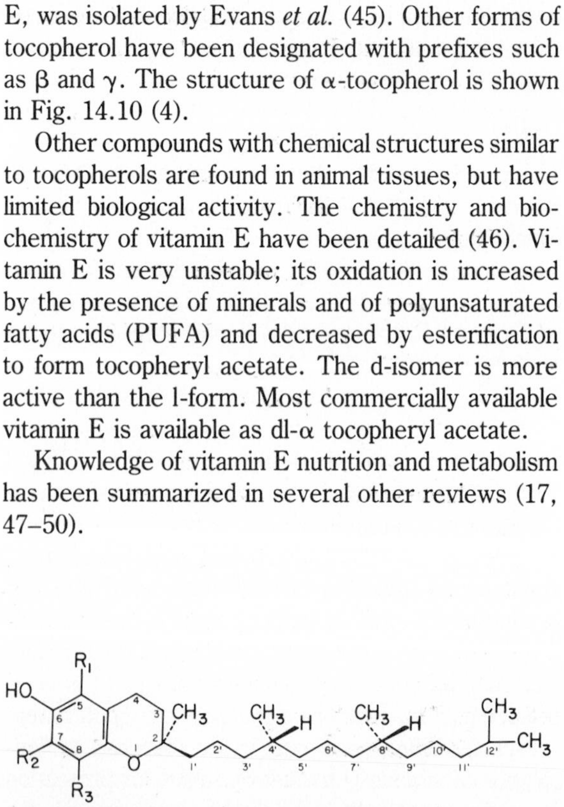

Figure 14.10 Structure of vitamin E (4).

Functions

In 1969 (17) the activity of α-tocopherol was classified under two main headings, effects attributable to the hydroxy group of the molecule (antioxidant effect) and effects brought about by metabolities of α-tocopherol. Current concepts of the biochemical functions of vitamin E include its role as a biological free radical scavenger (50, 51), in nucleic acid and protein metabolism (52), and in mitochondrial metabolism (53).

The antioxidant effect of vitamin E and its action as a free radical scavenger can explain most of the effects of vitamin E deficiency in animals. It is important in maintenance of the integrity of cellular membranes. The recognition that the mineral, Se, can protect against most vitamin E deficiency signs has led to an enormous body of literature aimed at elucidating the relationship between the two nutrients. These interrelationships are described in greater detail in Ch. 12.

There is growing evidence (52) that vitamin E influences the synthesis of specific proteins. However, the exact role of vitamin E in protein synthesis still is unknown. The activity of several enzymes is affected by vitamin E deficiency. In many cases, activity is increased, suggesting that the vitamin may serve as a repressor for the synthesis of certain enzymes. Some 30 enzymes have been reported to increase in activity during vitamin E deficiency, while a decrease in activity has been observed for at least 10. It has been suggested the vitamin E may function in regulation of gene transcription, but such a possibility requires further testing.

Vitamin E has been shown to affect several mitochondrial and microsomal functions, some of them associated with the ability to oxidize. Corwin (53) suggested that part of the vitamin E molecule can serve a reduction-oxidation function to protect S and Se proteins and, perhaps, to transfer single electrons at the mitochondrial membrane and at other cell organelles. By its membrane localization vitamin E helps to maintain compartmentalization and permeability of membranes (54). Vitamin E modulates synthesis of prostaglandin synthesis; in some tissues synthesis is increased and in some it is decreased by vitamin E deficiency. Low vitamin E decreases the production of prostaglandins by microsomes from muscle, testes, and spleen while it increases their production by blood platelets. The mechanism by which vitamin E shows these effects is unknown.

Massive vitamin E supplementation of wellbalanced diets increases antibody production (especially IgG) against a variety of antigens in several species of animals. It also increases protection of chickens against *E. coli* infection and mice against *D. pneumoniae* infection (55). The mode of action of these observed effects of vitamin E on the immune response in the laboratory and the practical importance of these effects under field conditions remain to be determined. Detailed biochemical studies of vitamin E metabolism presently underway in many laboratories can be expected eventually to clarify the uncertainties still remaining in the total role of vitamin E in nutrition.

Deficiency Signs

The manifestations of vitamin E deficiency are varied and some are species specific, but can be divided into three broad categories as follows: reproductive failure; derangement of cell permeability; and muscular lesions (myopathies).

Reproductive failure associated with vitamin E deficiency can be related to embryonic degeneration, as in the rat and bird, or to sterility from testicular atrophy as in the chicken, dog, guinea pig, hamster, and rat, or to ovarian failure in female rats.

Derangement of cell permeability may affect liver, brain, kidney, or blood capillaries. Liver necrosis occurs in vitamin E deficiency of rats and pigs (Fig. 14.11), but Se can prevent it, even in the absence of supplemental vitamin E. Red blood cell hemolysis occurs in vitamin E-deficient rats, chicks, and human infants; kidney degeneration in deficient mink,

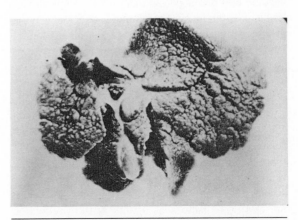

Figure 14.11 *Necrotic liver from pig fed a vitamin E-Se deficient diet.*

monkeys, and rats; and steatitis (inflammation of adipose tissue) in chicks, mink, and pigs. Kidney degeneration and steatitis were prevented by Se in the species studied.

Two common manifestations of vitamin E deficiency in chicks are encephalomalacia (abnormal Purkinje cells in cerebullum) and exudative diathesis (ED). Se prevents ED but not encephalomalacia. In encephalomalacia, incoordination and ataxia result from hemorrhages and edema in the cerebellum. Synthetic antioxidants, such as ethoxyquin and DPPD, prevent encephalomalacia. Polyunsaturated FA enhance the incidence of encephalomalacia in chickens fed diets marginal in vitamin E. In ED severe edema results from increased capillary permeability. A bluish-green subcutaneous exudate resulting from blood protein loss is evident on the breast of affected birds preceding death.

Nutritional muscular dystrophy (NMD, stiff-lamb disease, white muscle disease, muscular dystrophy) is common is growing lambs, calves, pigs, chicks, turkeys, and rabbits fed vitamin E-deficient diets. The lesions involve degeneration of skeletal muscle fiber (Zenker's degeneration) which are seen grossly as whitish streaks on the surface of muscles. Degeneration of heart muscle (Mulberry heart disease) and of liver (liver necrosis) are common in vitamin E-deficient pigs. Sudden death is a common occurrence in calves and in affected pigs, which show the heart and liver lesions on necropsy. In NMD, peroxidation of muscle tissues and activities of lysosomal enzymes are increased. Glutamic oxalacetic transaminase (SGOT) in blood serum is increased drastically in animals with NMD. This is an index of damage to muscle or heart tissue resulting in release of this enzyme into the blood, although it is not specific for NMD. A common sign of vitamin E deficiency in the turkey is myopathy of the gizzard as well as of heart and skeletal muscles. Se can prevent these lesions as well as those of liver, heart, and skeletal muscle in most types of NMD in mammals. NMD of birds apparently is only partly responsive to Se. The amino acid cysteine has a primary role in prevention of NMD in chicks as NMD is increased by factors that deplete body cysteine and decreased by factors that spare it. It has been suggested that cysteine and vitamin E act two different ways to prevent NMD in chicks. The complete story on vitamin E, cysteine, Se, and other factors as agents in the prevention of NMD in birds and animals is being unraveled gradually.

Metabolism

Absorption, Transport, and Storage. The absorption of vitamin E has been reviewed by Gallo-Torres (56, 57). The site of greatest absorption is in the jejunum in mammals. Tocopherols are absorbed mainly by micelle formation in the presence of bile salts. Both the d- and l-isomers are absorbed, but the d-isomer has a relative potency 1.2 times that of the racemic mixture. Esterified tocopherols are absorbed less efficiently than the unesterified vitamin; hydrolysis of esters is nearly complete in the GI tract lumen. Absorption of tocopherol is enhanced by solubilization in medium-chain triglycerides compared with long-chain triglycerides, and unsaturated fatty acids reduce tocopherol absorbability. Degree of absorption of ingested tocopherols has been estimated at 10 to 36% in humans and probably approaches this range of values in animals. Both bile and pancreatic secretions and needed for optimum tocopherol absorption. Tocopherols are absorbed into the lymphatics and are transported as a part of lipoproteins.

Plasma concentration of tocopherols is affected by rate of removal from plasma and retention in individual tissues; total plasma lipid and β-lipoprotein contents are positively correlated with plasma tocopherol level. Vitamin E also is transported in the red blood cell, localized in the cell membrane. Rapid exchange of tocopherol occurs between plasma and red blood cells. The dynamics of vitamin E transport between tissues has been detailed, (58). Storage occurs in liver, skeletal muscle, heart, lung, kidney, spleen, and pancreas in similar amounts and in pituitary, testes, and adrenals in even higher concentrations. Because tocopherols are fat soluble, concentrations are expressed best as units/g of fat rather than as units/g of tissue. The wide tissue distribution of tocopherol would be expected in view of its role in preventing peroxidation and in maintaining cell membrane integrity.

Interrelationships Between Vitamin E and Other Nutrients. Several authors (50, 59–61) have summarized the current knowledge of interrelationships of vitamin E with other nutrients. The following nutrients have been shown to affect the vitamin requirement of animals: Se, polyunsaturated fatty acids (PUFA), S-amino acids, Fe, vitamin A, vitamin C, choline, and Zn.

Se—Several vitamin E deficiency diseases, including muscular dystrophy, liver necrosis, myocardial lesions, and chick ED can be prevented by Se. The metabolic basis for the protective action of Se appears to be related to the prevention by Se of lipid peroxidation in vitamin E deficient animals. Se is a component of the enzyme, glulathione peroxidase, which catalyzes the destruction of peroxides, which are a product of lipid peroxidation in the absence of the antioxidant action of vitamin E (see Ch. 12 for details).

PUFA—Vitamin E requirement is increased as the concentration of PUFA in body tissues increases. This relationship is based on the antioxidant properties of vitamin E and the greater susceptibility of PUFA to peroxidation due to the higher proportion of double bonds in the unsaturated carbon chain of the FA. Attempts to define vitamin E requirements in terms of an optimum ratio to PUFA have not yielded a satisfactory value, presumably because of differences in tissue stores of vitamin E and PUFA and, perhaps, to lack of linearity in the optimum ratio with changes in concentration of vitamin E. Young dogs fed vitamin E-deficient diets with safflower oil (high in PUFA) have been reported to develop browning of the fat around the intestine, hemolysis of RBC, and depressed plasma tocopherol in direct relation to dietary fat level; however, other work has failed to demonstrate that high levels of vitamin E can prevent this pigment formation. Testes, heart, adipose tissue, adrenal, brain, skeletal muscle, and bone marrow accumulate large amounts of fluorescent pigment in vitamin E-deficient animals fed PUFA. There is strong evidence that vitamin E is a preventative. For example, Reddy *et al.* (62) found that rats fed 10% lard-1% cod liver oil diets without vitamin E for 4 mo. accumulate twice the fluorescent pigments in adipose tissue as those fed the same diet but supplemented with vitamin E. Furthermore, adipose tissue of rats fed cod liver oil, which is higher in PUFA than corn oil, had three times the fluorescence of adipose tissue from those fed corn oil. Fluorescent pigments in adipose tissue extracts may be the products of in vivo lipid peroxidation. A proposed pathway of formation of fluorescent (ceroid) pigment has been described (62). Dietary supplementation of vitamin E has been shown (63) to improve the oxidative stability of pork from pigs fed the fortified diet.

The apparent increase in consumption of fats high in PUFA in the USA increases the possibility that vitamin E may tend to be a limiting nutrient in human nutrition. Harman (64) suggested that peroxidation (free radical reactions) of adipose tissues play a significant role in aging. He hypothesized that human productive lifespan could be extended by dietary manipulation to reduce peroxidation in body tissues.

Lifespan of mice is shortened as much as 10% by increasing the amount and/or degree of unsaturation of dietary fat (64); several antioxidants reduce the incidence of congenital malformation (mostly skeletal deformities) in vitamin E-deficient rats.

S-amino acids—Cystine prevents liver necrosis in animals fed vitamin E deficient diets. The protective effect is due apparently to the reducing (antioxidant) properties of the sulfhydryl group of S-amino acids.

Fe—Neonatal animals and humans given supplemented Fe in the presence of a suboptimal intake of vitamin E or of a low plasma tocopherol level induced by a high PUFA diet may develop vitamin E deficiency anemia. Hemolytic anemia, characterized by low hemoglobin, high recticulocyte count, and changes in red blood cell morphology has been reported in premature infants with low plasma vitamin E. Newborn pigs marginally deficient in vitamin E may show signs of Fe toxicity and death when given a normal intramuscular dose of Fe for prevention of Fe-deficiency anemia. The adverse effects of Fe on vitamin E status may be due to increased peroxidation of PUFA in red blood cells.

Vitamin A—Vitamin E reduces depletion of liver vitamin A and appears to spare vitamin A by its antioxidant properties, although this suggested mechanism is not accepted universally. High levels of vitamin A increase the vitamin E requirement. Signs of vitamin A toxicity may be alleviated by increased vitamin E ingestion. The mechanisms involved in vitamin A–E interactions have been reviewed recently (49). The relationships may be of practical importance only outside the range of normal vitamin A intakes.

Vitamin C—Some inhibition of lipid peroxidation in tissues of vitamin E deficient animals has been shown by vitamin C administration. It reduces the incidence of ED in chickens. However, a sparing effect of vitamin C on vitamin E is not a consistent finding, and its apparent protective role may be one of sparing Se by improving its absorption from the GI tract which, in turn, protects tissues from lipid peroxidation. The nutritional roles of vitamins E and C and their possible interactions remain to be completely understood (50).

Choline—The liver lesions associated with choline deficiency have been reported to be prevented by supplemental vitamin E. It was suggested (59) that lipid peroxidation may be a lesion of choline deficiency, which would then be expected to respond favorably to vitamin E.

Vitamin B_{12}—Recent evidence suggests that vitamin E is required for the conversion of vitamin B_{12} to its coenzyme, S'-deoxyadenosyl-cobalamin, which is necessary for the metabolism of methylmalonate. This could explain the inverse relationship between serum tocopherol and vitamin B_{12} concentration reported in human patients (65).

Zn—Deficiency of either Zn or vitamin E is associated with testes degeneration and increased arachidonic acid in testes lipids (65). Recent data obtained in rats fed diets of differing Zn and vitamin E content showed that peroxidation precedes hemolysis in vitamin E-deficient red blood cells and that Zn stabilizes the red cell membrane against cellular changes following peroxidation. Other data from chicks fed a low Zn diet (66) support the hypothesis that Zn plays a role analogous to that of vitamin E in stabilizing cell membrane structure and thereby reducing peroxidative damage. Further research is needed to determine the biochemical interactions between these two nutrients and to quantify the effect of dietary level of one on the dietary requirements of the other.

Tengerdy (55) has suggested the possibility that vitamin E, through its stimulatory effect on the immune system, might have a beneficial effect on aging, which is known to be accompanied by a decreased functioning of the immune system. Such a relationship deserves further study as a possible mechanism in addition to that of reduced peroxidation of body tissues, to explain a potential benefit of vitamin E in longevity.

Placental and Mammary Transfer of Vitamin E

The placental transfer of vitamin E is inefficient (67); whereas FA cross the placenta more efficiently. Therefore, a reduction of vitamin E-PUFA ratio in fetal tissues may predispose the newborn to vitamin E deficiency, but no information is available on the question. Some placental transfer of vitamin E does occur, but malformations have been observed in young rats fed low-vitamin E even though vitamin E was found in liver, blood and carcasses of the young.

The tocopherol content of the milk of both ruminant and non-ruminant animals is affected by concentration in the diet. Thus, susceptibility of newly weaned animals to vitamin E deficiency is dependent on the

body stores they have accumulated in response to the diet of the dam during gestation and lactation.

Toxicity

Few reports have been made of vitamin E toxicity in animals or humans. Scattered descriptions of hemorrhagic syndromes, nervous disorders, edema, changes in endocrine glands, and antagonism of vitamin K have appeared in experimental animal research, but detailed pathology of hypervitaminosis E is not available. Human adults have tolerated oral doses of 1 g/day for months without undesired effects. Apparently the range of safe level of intake is wider than for other fat-soluble vitamins, but the wholesale consumption of vitamin E as well as of all nutrients should be avoided.

❏ VITAMIN K

Structure

A hemorrhagic syndrome was described in 1929 in chicks fed a diet low in sterols, and in 1935 Dam (68) showed that the missing factor was a fat-soluble vitamin which he named vitamin K. Vitamin K really is a group of compounds. The structure of the two most important natural sources of vitamin K, phylloquinone (vitamin K_1) and menaquinone (vitamin K_2) are shown in Fig. 14.12 (4). Vitamin K_1 is common is green vegetables and vitamin K_2 is a product of bacterial flora in the GI tract of animals and humans. A synthetic, menadione (vitamin K_3), is used widely commercially; its structure also is shown.

Menaquinone also can occur as menaquinone-6,7,8, or 9; that is, the side chain may contain more than 4 isoprene units shown. Apparently the liver converts these forms of vitamin K to vitamin K_2, suggesting that this is the metabolically active form.

Functions

Vitamin K is required for normal blood clotting. Specifically, it is required for synthesis of prothrombin in the liver. It is not a component of prothrombin, but acts on enzyme systems involved in prothrombin synthesis and in the synthesis of other factors involved in the total blood clotting mechanism. Olson (70) suggested that vitamin K acts by influencing messenger RNA formation needed for prothrombin synthesis. Such a role could help to explain the rapid synthesis of prothrombin that occurs in vitamin K-

PHYLLOQUINONE (K₁)

MENAQUINONE (K₂)

MENADIONE (K₃)

Figure 14.12 *Structure of vitamin K.*

deficient animals treated with vitamin K (2–6 h). Vitamin K is involved in at least four steps in clot formation: a plasma thromboplastin component (Factor IX), a tissue thromboplastin component (Factor VII), "Stuart" factor (Factor X), and prothrombin (Factor II). The exact mode of action in each reaction is unknown.

The clotting mechanism (Table 14.3) is stopped by oxalate and citrate, which precipitate Ca^{++}, and by heparin, which apparently blocks formation of the Stuart factor.

Current knowledge of vitamin K metabolism and the details of its function in blood coagulation has been summarized by Olson (69). He described the biosynthesis of prothrombin; the distribution, requirements, purification, and mechanism of action of vitamin K-dependent γ-glutamyl carboxylase; the absorption and metabolism of vitamin K, and the action of vitamin K antagonists. The unique role of the amino acid, γ-carboxyglutamic acid as a compound of prothrombin in vitamin K metabolism was described. New knowledge on the importance of the utilization and reutilization of vitamin K for the carboxylation of peptide-bound glutamate residues in the vitamin K-dependent proteins was emphasized. Eight of these proteins are involved in blood coagulation. Suffice it to say that, although the end result of vitamin K deficiency in animals and humans is a

failure in blood coagulation, the biochemical complexities are still under study in this fast-moving field of molecular biology.

Deficiency Signs

A deficiency of vitamin K results in prolonged blood clotting time, generalized hemorrhages, and death in severe cases. Often, subcutaneous hemorrhages appear over the body surface, giving a blotchy, bluish, mottled appearance to the skin. The clotting time of the blood is a good index of vitamin K status. A normal clotting time of a few seconds may be extended to several minutes in vitamin K-deficient animals.

The microflora of the intestinal tract normally produce adequate vitamin K to meet the metabolic needs of the host. The vitamin is obtained either by absorption from the lower GI tract after synthesis or by coprophagy (feces eating), which serves as an important means of supplying nutrients to many animal species. Barnes and Fiala (71) showed that prevention of coprophagy in rats produced vitamin K deficiency. Nutritionists have not, until recently, concerned themselves greatly with supplying supplemental vitamin K in the diet, because the GI tract microflora play such an important role in synthesizing vitamin K. However, newer technology has created problems with deficiency of vitamin K under practical condition. Chicks fed sulfaquinoxaline to control coccidiosis develop vitamin K deficiency. This sulfa drug is an antagonist of vitamin K. Pigs fed in wire floor cages, in which access to feces is reduced, develop

TABLE 14.3   Vitamin K involvement in blood clotting.

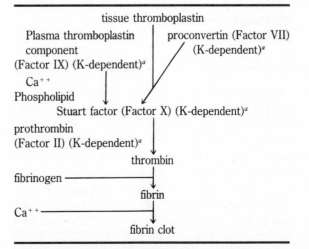

[a]Synthesis of each is inhibited by vitamin K antagonists.

increased prothrombin clotting times and growing-finishing pigs fed 60–65% cane sugar developed deficiency symptions. Field reports of a hemorrhagic syndrome preventable by supplemental vitamin K in growing-finishing swine suggest that vitamin K deficiency is an increasingly serious practical problem. Several factors may be contributing to this increase. Mycotoxins (from moldy grain) may antagonize vitamin K; increased confinement feeding of swine has been associated with less use of pasture and forages that are high in vitamin K; and the use of slotted floors lessens the opportunity for coprophagy. Clearly, much remains to be discovered concerning factors that affect vitamin K requirement and that produce deficiencies.

Metabolism

Absorption and Utilization. The naturally occurring and synthetic vitamin K's are absorbed most efficiently in the presence of dietary fat and bile salts, and menadione requires bile salts for absorption. The efficiency of absorption of vitamin K depends on the form in which the vitamin is combined as well as on the specific isomer involved. The mechanisms by

which vitamin K is transported in blood are not defined clearly, probably because of the variable solubility in water vs fats of the several compounds having vitamin K activity.

The biological activity of several compounds showing vitamin K potency is listed in Table 14-4. The activity of menadione and its derivatives depends on the relative stabilities of the preparations used and on whether or not sulfaquinoxaline is present in the test diet. Menadione and its derivatives are less effective than phylloquinone in counteracting the antagonistic effects of sulfaquinoxaline. Menadione is very reactive and may be toxic; for this reason, and because of its lower biological activity, it is used far less commonly in feeds than are its derivatives.

Vitamin K compounds are very unstable under alkaline conditions. Menadione dimethylpyrimidinol bisulfate is more stable as well as higher in biological activity than menadione.

Vitamin K Antagonists and Inhibitors

A well-known natural antagonist of vitamin K is dicoumarol, often present in weather-damaged sweet clover hay. The presence of dicoumarol in hay or silage causes massive internal hemorrhages and death in calves. Another important antagonist of vitamin K is Warfarin®, which is a competitive inhibitor of menaquinone (K_2). The inhibition of vitamin K function by Warfarin has resulted in the large scale marketing of Warfarin as a rat poison. The effect of Warfarin in increasing clotting time can be reversed by simultaneously increasing the amount of K_2 given to the animal.

The structures of dicoumarol and of Warfarin are shown below.

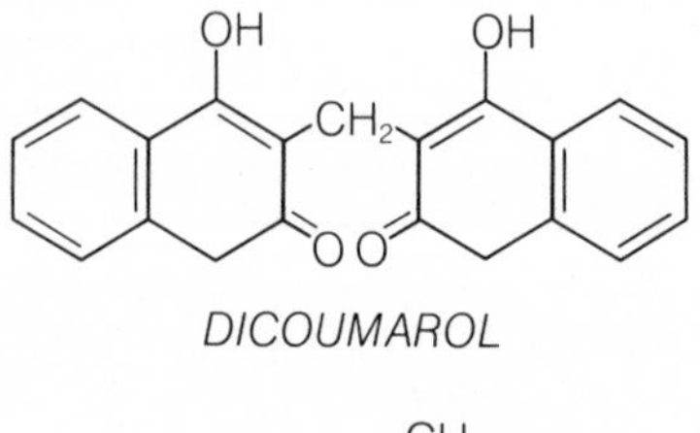

TABLE 14.4 Relative biological activity of several forms of vitamin K.[a]

	ACTIVITY RELATIVE TO THAT OF NATURAL VITAMIN K_1 (PHYLLOQUINONE-4)
Phylloquinone-1	5
Phylloquinone-2	10
Phylloquinone-3	30
Phylloquinone-4	100
Phylloquinone-5	80
Phyloquinone-6	50
Menaquinone-2	15
Menaquinone-3	40
Menaquinone-4	100
Menaquinone-5	120
Menaquinone-6	100
Menaquinone-7	70
Menadione	40–150[b]
Menadione sodium bisulfate	50–150[b]
Menadione dimethylpyrimidinol bisulfate	100–160[b]

[a]From P. Griminger. 1966. Vitamins and Hormones 24:605.
[b]Activity depends on relative stabilities of preparations used and on presence or absence of sulfaquinoxaline in the test diet.

DICOUMAROL

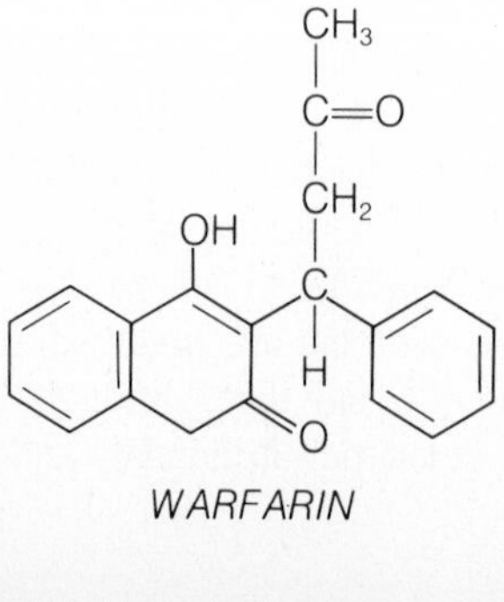

WARFARIN

Other vitamin K antagonists, including α-tocopheryl quinone, sulfaquinoxaline (previously discussed), and some napthoquinone derivatives as well as other substances, including butylated hydroxtoluene, salicylate, and high doses of vitamins A and E may be of importance in affecting the dietary requirement for vitamin K (69).

Toxicity

Phylloquinone and menaquinone derivatives are nontoxic even in high dosage levels, but menadione is toxic to the skin and respiratory tract of several animal species; its bisulfate derivatives are not. Menadione given in prolonged high doses produces anemia, porphyrinuria, and other abnormalities in animals and chest pains and shortness of breath in humans.

❑ SUMMARY

Vitamins are organic compounds required in minute quantities for normal body functions. The known vitamins can be divided on the basis of solubility properties into fat-soluble and water-soluble. The fat-soluble vitamins are A, D, E, and K. Storage in body tissues allows consumption of deficient diets over a longer period of time than for water-soluble vitamins before deficiency signs appear.

Vitamin A can be provided as the vitamin or its precursor, carotene. Many carotenoid pigments exist in nature, but β-carotene is biologically the most active. Vitamin A activity is expressed in retinal equivalents (μg). One retinal equivalent = $0.167 \times$ β-carotene or $0.084 \times$ other provitamin A. Vitamin A is required for normal night vision, normal epithelial cells and normal bone growth and remodeling, and it may play a primary role in the synthesis of glycoproteins. Vitamin A deficiency results in xerophthalmia (irritation of the cornea and conjunctiva of the eye), keratinization of respiratory epithelium, reproductive failure in males, embryonic death, and poor growth in surviving young.

Vitamin D_2 (irradiated ergosterol or calciferol) and vitamin D_3 (irradiated 7-dehydrocholesterol) are the two major sterols with vitamin D activity. Most animals use either vitamin D_2 or vitamin D_3 efficiently, but birds require vitamin D_3. Ultraviolet light converts each provitamin to its biologically active form. Vitamin D functions to elevate plasma Ca and P levels for normal bone mineralization and prevention of tetany produced by hypocalcemia. The active metabolite of vitamin D (1,25 dihydroxycholecalciferol) is produced by the kidney under conditions of hypocalcemia, and stimulates intestinal absorption, bone resorption, and possibly kidney tubular reabsorption of Ca and P to maintain plasma Ca within normal limits. Deficiency of vitamin D results in inadequate bone calcification (rickets in growing animals and osteomalacia in adults); thus dietary Ca deficiency and vitamin D deficiency produce the same signs. Vitamin D deficiency can be prevented by only a few minutes of daily exposure to direct sunlight.

Vitamin E was first recognized as a fat-soluble factor needed for reproduction in rats. Alpha tocopherol is the most biologically active form of vitamin E. Functions of vitamin E include its role as a biological free radical scavenger and as an antioxidant. There is evidence that vitamin E influences the synthesis of specific proteins and of prostaglandins. Vitamin E deficiency results in reproductive failure, derangement of cell permeability, and muscular lesions. Deficiency causes encephalomalacia and exudative diathesis in chicks, muscular dystrophy in several animals species, and liver necrosis and cardiac muscle degeneration in pigs and calves. Muscular dystrophy and liver necrosis caused by vitamin E deficiency can be prevented by dietary Se. Other nutrients shown to affect the vitamin E requirement include polyunsaturated fatty acids, S-amino acids, Fe, vitamin A, vitamin C, choline, and Zn.

Vitamin K is really a group of compounds; the two most common forms are phylloquinone (vitamin K_1) and menaquinone (vitamin K_2). Vitamin K_1 is common in green vegetables and vitamin K_2 is a product of bacterial flora in the gastro-intestinal tract of animals and humans. Vitamin K is required for normal blood clotting (for synthesis of prothrombin by the liver). Vitamin K deficiency results in prolonged blood clotting time and generalized hemorrhages. The microflora of the gastrointestinal tract normally produce adequate vitamin K to meet metabolic needs of the host animal, but newer technology such as feed additives that alter intestinal microflora and the use of wire floor cages to prevent access to feces, may create the need for greater attention to meeting the vitamin K needs of animals.

❑ REFERENCES

1. Funk, C. 1912. *J. State Med. London*, **20**:341.
2. Harris, R. S. 1967. In *The Vitamins*, Vol. I, 2nd ed. Academic Press, N.Y.
3. Goodwin, T. W. 1986. *Ann. Rev. Nutr.* **6**:273.

4. International Union of Nutritional Sciences Committee. 1979. *J. Nutr.* **110**:8.

5. Bieri, J. G. and M. C. McKenna. 1981. *Amer. J. Clin. Nutr.* **34**:289.

6. Moore, T. 1960. *Vitamins and Hormones*, **18**:499.

7. Follis, R. H. 1958. *Deficiency Disease*. C. C. Thomas Pub. Springfield, IL.

8. Tielsch, J. M. and A. Sommer. 1984. *Ann. Rev. Nutr.* **4**:183.

9. Oomen, H. A. P. C. 1976. Ch. 9 in *Present Knowledge in Nutrition*, 4th ed. The Nutrition Foundation, Inc. Washington, D.C.

10. Gallina, A. M., et al. 1972. *J. Nutr.* **100**:129.

11. Roels, O. A. 1967. In *The Vitamins*, Vol 1, 2nd ed. Academic Press, N.Y.

12. Navia, J. M. and S. S. Harris. 1980. *Ann. N.Y. Acad. Sci.* **355**:45.

13. Zile, M., H. F. DeLuca, and H. Ahrens. 1972. *J. Nutr.* **102**:1255.

14. Hodges, R. E., R. B. Rucker, and R. H. Gardner. 1980. *Ann. N.Y. Acad. Sci.* **355**:58.

15. Ullrey, D. E. 1972. *J. Animal Sci.* **35**:648.

16. Morii, H. and H. F. DeLuca. 1967. *Amer. J. Physiol.* **213**:358.

17. Boguth, W. 1969. *Vitamins and Hormones.* **27**:1.

18. Goodman, D. S., H. S. Huang, M. Kansi, and T. Shiratori. 1967. *J. Biol. Chem.* **242**:3543.

19. Olson, J. A. and O. Hayaishi. 1965. *Proc. Natl. Acad. Sci. U.S.* **54**:1364.

20. Wing, J. M. 1969. *J. Dairy Sci.* **52**:479.

21. Krinsky, N. I. et al. 1958. *Arch. Biochem. Biophys.* **73**:233.

22. Wright, K. E. and R. C. Hall, Jr. 1979. *J. Nutr.* **109**:1063.

23. Smith, J. C., Jr. 1980. *Ann. N.Y. Acad. Sci.* **355**:62.

24. Smith, J. C., Jr. 1980. *Ann. N.Y. Acad. Sci.* **355**:62.

25. Kohlmeier, R. H. and W. Burroughs. 1970. *Ann. N.Y. Acad. Sci.* **30**:1012.

26. Ahluwalia, G. S., L. Kaul, and B. S. Ahluwalia. 1980. *J. Nutr.* **110**:1185.

27. Mathews-Roth, M. M. 1985. *Pure Appl. Chem.* **57**:717.

28. DeLuca, H. F. 1979. *Nutr. Rev.* **37**(6):161.

29. McCollum, E. V., N. Simmonds, J. E. Becker, and P. G. Shipley. 1982. *J. Biol. Chem.* **53**:293.

30. McCollum, E. V. and M. Davis. 1913. *J. Biol. Chem.* **15**:167.

31. Steenbock, H. and A. Black. 1924. *J. Biol. Chem.* **61**:405.

32. Norman, A. W. 1980. *Vitamin D. Molecular Biology and Clinical Nutrition*. Marcel Dekker, Inc., N.Y.

33. Henry, H. L. and A. W. Norman. 1984. *Ann. Rev. Nutr.* **4**:493.

34. Wasserman, R. H. and J. J. Faher. 1977. In *Calcium Binding Proteins and Calcium Function*, pp. 292–302, R. H. Wasserman et al. (eds). Elsevier North-Holland, Inc., N.Y. N.Y.

35. DeLuca, H. F. 1978. *Ann. N.Y. Acad. Sci.* **307**:356.

36. Taylor, A. N. 1980. In *Vitamin D. Molecular Biology and Clinical Nutrition*, p. 321. Marcel Dekker, Inc., N.Y.

37. Haussler, M. R. 1986. *Ann Rev. Nutr.* **6**:527.

38. DeLuca, H. F. 1980. *Nutr. Rev.* **38**(5):169.

39. Spanos, E. and I. MacIntyre. 1980. In *Vitamin D. Molecular Biology and Clinical Nutrition*, p. 489. Marcel Dekker, Inc., N.Y.

40. Holick, M. F., H. K. Schnoes, and H. F. DeLuca. 1971. Identification of 1,25-digydroxycholecalciferol, a Form of Vitamin D_3 Metabolically Active in the Intestine. *Proc. Natl. Acad. Sci.* **68**:803.

41. Loomis, W. F. 1967. *Science* **157**:501.

42. Wasserman, R. H. and T. A. Nobel. 1980. In *Vitamin D. Molecular Biology and Clinical Nutrition*, p. 455. Marcel Dekker, Inc., N.Y.

43. Haschek, W. M., L. Krook, F. A. Kallfelz, and W. G. Pond. 1978. *Cornell Vet.* **68**(3):324.

44. Evans, H. M. and K. S. Bishop. 1922. *J. Metabolic Res.* 1:319, 335.

45. Evans, H. M., J. H. Emerson, and G. A. Emerson. 1936. *J. Biol. Chem.* **113**:319.

46. Machlin, L. J. 1980. *Vitamin E. A Comprehensive Treatise*, pp. 1–660. Marcel Dekker, Inc., N.Y.

47. Horwitt, M. K., C. C. Harvey, and E. M. Harmon. 1968. *Vitamins and Hormones* **26**:487.

48. Witting, L. A. 1970. In *Progress in Chemistry of Fats and Other Lipids* **9**:517.

49. Bieri, J. G. 1984. Ch. 16 in *Present Knowledge in Nutrition*, 5th ed., pp. 226–240. The Nutrition Foundation, Washington, D.C.

50. McCay, P. B. 1985. *Ann. Rev. Nutr.* **5**:323.

51. McCay, P. B. and M. M. King. 1980. Part 5E in *Vitamin E. A Comprehensive Treatise*, p. 289. Marcel Dekker, N.Y.

52. Catignani, G. L. 1980. Section 2 in *Vitamin E. A Comprehensive Treatise*, p. 318. Marcel Dekker, N.Y.

53. Corwin, L. M. 1980. Section 3 in *Vitamin E. A Comprehensive Treatise*, p. 332. Marcel Dekker, N.Y.

54. Molennaar, I., C. E. Hulstaert, and M. J. Hardonk. 1980. Part 5G in *Vitamin E. A Comprehensive Treatise*, p. 372. Marcel Dekker, N.Y.

55. Tengerdy, R. P. 1980. Chapter 8 in *Vitamin E. A Comprehensive Treatise*, p. 429. Marcel Dekker, N.Y.

56. Gallo-Torres, H. E. 1980. Part 5A in *Vitamin E. A Comprehensive Treatise*, p. 170. Marcel Dekker, N.Y.

57. Gallo-Torres, H. E. 1980. Part 5B in *Vitamin E. A Comprehensive Treatise*, p. 193. Marcel Dekker, N.Y.

58. Kayden, H. J. and L. Bjornson. 1972. *Ann. N.Y. Acad. Sci.* **203**:127.

59. Draper, H. H. 1980. Part 5D in *Vitamin E. A Comprehensive Treatise*, p. 272. Marcel Dekker, N.Y.

60. Machlin, L. J. and E. Gabriel. 1980. *Ann. N.Y. Acad. Sci.* **355**:98.

61. Arnrich, L. and V. A. Arthur. 1980. *Ann. N.Y. Acad. Sci.* **355**:109.

62. Reddy, K., B. Fletcher, and A. Tappel. 1973. *J. Nutr.* **103**:908.

63. Tsai, T. C., G. H. Wellington, and W. G. Pond. 1978. *J. Food Sci.* **43**:193.

64. Harman, P. 1969. *J. Amer. Geriatrics Soc.* **17**:721.

65. Machlin, L. J. and E. Gabriel. 1980. Interactions of Vitamin E with Vitamin C, Vitamin B_{12} and Zn. *Ann. N.Y. Acad. Sci.* **355**:98.

66. Bettger, W. J., et al. 1980. *J. Nutr.* **110**:50.

67. Nitowski, H. M., K. S. Hsu, and H. H. Fordon. 1962. *Vitamins and Hormones* **20**:559.

68. Dam, H. 1935. *Biochem. J.* **29**:1273.

69. Olson, R. E. 1984. *Ann. Rev. Nutr.* **4**:281.

70. Olson, R. E. 1964. *Science* **145**:926.

71. Barnes, R. H. and G. Fiala. 1958. *J. Nutr.* **68**:603.

15

Water-Soluble Vitamins

UNLIKE THE FAT-SOLUBLE VITAMINS, water-soluble vitamins (except B_{12}) are not stored in appreciable quantities in body tissues. They must be supplied in the diet on a day-to-day basis for those animals having a GI tract in which microbial synthesis is not a prominent feature. In ruminants under normal conditions the water-soluble vitamin requirement is met almost entirely from microbial synthesis in the rumen and lower GI tract; in herbivores such as the horse and rabbit, microbial synthesis occurs in the colon or cecum. Thus, the nutritionist need not be concerned about providing routinely a dietary source for these species. However, for pigs, poultry, and other simple-stomached animals, including humans, a dietary source is essential.

Most of the water-soluble vitamins are required in minute amounts. They are all organic compounds, but are unrelated to each other in structure. Most function as metabolic catalysts, usually as coenzymes. All produce profound aberration in metabolism if unavailable to the tissues in sufficient amounts. Because of their ready excretion by the kidney, acute toxicity of the water-soluble vitamins is unlikely.

Each water-soluble vitamin will be discussed as to structure, function and deficiency signs. The IUNS Committee on Nomenclature (1) provides rules for naming vitamins. These rules are needed to minimize confusion and misinterpretation in discussing vitamin nutrition and are followed here.

❏ THIAMIN (ANEURIN, B₁)

Structure

Thiamin consists of one molecule of pyrimidine joined with one of thiazole. Williams (2) established its structure, as shown:

THIAMIN

$$Me—N=C—NH_2 \quad S—CH_2—CH_2—OH$$

The compound 3-(4-amino-2-methylpyrimidin-5-ylmethyl)-5-(2-hydroxyethyl)-4-methylthiazolium, formerly known as vitamin B₂, vitamin F, aneurin (e) or thiamine, should be designated *thiamin*. Its use in phrases such as "thiamin activity" and "thiamin deficiency" represent preferred usage (1).

Functions

Thiamin is phosphorylated in the liver to form coenzymes, cocarboxylase or thiamin pyrophosphate (TPP) and lipothiamide (LTPP). TPP is involved in the decarboxylation of α-keto acids. Among the reactions in which TPP participates, the decarboxylation of pyruvic acid to acetaldehyde is important and can be illustrated as:

$$\text{Pyruvic acid} \xrightarrow{\text{TPP}} \text{acetaldehyde} + CO_2$$

LTPP is involved in oxidative decarboxylation of α-ketoglutarate and other metabolites of the citric acid cycle.

The pig is somewhat unique in that it stores appreciable thiamin in its tissues. This accounts for the fact that pork is an excellent source of dietary thiamin.

A thiamin-binding protein has been identified in chicken egg and liver and in pregnant rat blood plasma (3, 4). It has been suggested that its presence in plasma may play a role in the transfer of thiamin across the placenta. Estrogen induces its synthesis in liver and modulates the concentration in blood plasma.

Deficiency Signs

In thiamin deficiency, blood pyruvic acid and lactic acid concentrations increase; this has been used in the assessment of thiamin status. Because pyruvic acid is a key metabolite in energy utilization in the citric acid cycle (see Fig. 7.1), it is evident that thiamin deficiency seriously disturbs carbohydrate and lipid metabolism.

The immediate effect of a thiamin deficiency is a reduction in appetite (anorexia). In humans, the thiamin deficiency syndrome, beriberi, has been recognized for centuries. The syndrome includes numbness of extremities, weakness and stiffness in the thighs, edema of the feet and legs, unsteady gait, rigidity and paralytic symptoms, and pain along the spine. Brain glial cells have impaired ability to synthesize fatty acids and cholesterol in thiamin deficiency; this impairment has been suggested as the basis for degenerative changes seen in glial cells in deficient animals. In animals, the classical disease is polyneuritis in chicks (retraction of the head; Fig. 15.1) and rats (walking in circles). Bradycardia (slow heart rate) is a common manifestation in all species studied and myocardial damage results in dilation of the heart (Fig. 15.2) and heart failure in swine. Body temperature is reduced and the adrenal gland is enlarged. Whether or not the symptoms of thiamin deficiency, including the heart lesion, result from pyruvic or lactic acid accumulation or are due to other factors is not certain. It has been suggested recently that changes in liver aminotransferase activities in thiamin deficient animals may be due to accumulation of pyruvic acid or other metabolites. The most com-

Figure 15.1 *Polyneuritis in the chick showing the typical retraction of the head and rigidity of the legs as well as the marked effect on growth. Courtesy of Poultry Sci. Dept., Cornell U.*

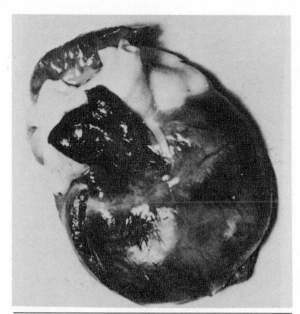

Figure 15.2 *Enlarged flabby heart from a thiamindeficient pig. Courtesy of D. E. Ullrey, Michigan State U.*

mon assessment of thiamin nutritional status is the measurement of erythrocyte transketolase activity.

Antagonists

There are several compounds that resemble thiamin in chemical structure but have no thiamin activity. Addition to the diet or injection of these antimetabolites* results in thiamine deficiency which can be overcome by increasing the thiamin intake. One such thiamin antagonist is pyrithiamin.

Many foods, especially certain fish and sea foods, contain significant amounts of a group of enzymes, thiaminases, which split the thiamin molecule and render it ineffective biologically. Chastek paralysis, a disease in silver foxes first reported in 1940, later was shown to be caused by thiaminases in raw fish being fed. These enzymes are heat labile, so that cooking of foods containing them destroys the antithiamin activity.

Thiamin is heat labile, especially in alkaline conditions. Toxicity has not been reported, presumably

*The concept of antimetabolites in nutrition has been reviewed by Woolley (1959; *Sci.* **129**:615). Antimetabolites are used in clinical medicine (for example, in control of certain types of cancer) and in nutritional research.

because of the rapid loss of excess thiamin in the urine.

☐ RIBOFLAVIN (LACTOFLAVIN, B_2)

Structure

Riboflavin is a yellow fluorescent pigment consisting of ribose and isoalloxazine. The compound 7,8-dimethyl-10-(1'-D-ribityl)isoalloxazine, formerly known as vitamin B_2, vitamin G, lactoflavin(e), or riboflavine, should be designated *riboflavin*. Its use in phrases such as "riboflavin activity" and "riboflavin deficiency" represent preferred usage (1).

RIBOFLAVIN

$$CH_2-(CHOH)_3-CH_2OH$$

Riboflavin was synthesized in 1935. It is heat stable but destroyed readily by light. Riboflavin, riboflavin 5-phosphate (also called flavin mononucleotide or FMN) and flavin adenine dinucleotide (FAD) are the only naturally occurring substances with riboflavin activity, although several synthetic derivatives show some activity (5).

Functions

Riboflavin functions in the coenzymes, FAD and FMN, which occur in a large number of enzyme systems. The interconversions of these biologically active forms can be illustrated as follows;

flavokinase
Riboflavin + ATP ⟶ FMN + ADP

FAD pyrophosphyorylase
FMN + ATP ⟶ FAD + pyrophosphate

FMN and FAD are present in most if not all animal cells and occur as coenzymes in the flavoprotein enzyme systems such as oxidases (aerobic dehydrogenases) and anaerobic dehydrogenases. Both FAD and FMN are related closely in several reactions with niacin coenzymes, coenzyme I (NAD), and coenzyme II (NADP).

Deficiency Signs

The primary general effect, as with most of the water-soluble vitamin deficiencies, is reduced growth rate in young animals. Various pathological lesions accompany a deficiency. In rats, conjunctivitis, corneal opacity, and vascularization of the cornea are common signs of deficiency; skin lesions and hair loss—related to a failure in regeneration of hair follicles—may occur. Corneal opacity (cataracts) associated with riboflavin deficiency in rats appears to occur only on high galactose diets. Humans with cataracts have a higher incidence of biochemical riboflavin deficiency and abnormal galactose tolerance (6). The exact biochemical basis for the formation of cataracts in animals fed riboflavin-deficient high galactose diets remains uncertain. Galactose metabolism does not seem to be affected by riboflavin deficiency. Mature female rats fed riboflavin-deficient diets have abnormal estrous cycles and give birth to a high proportion of pups with congenital malformations of the skeleton. In deficient dogs, fatty infiltration of the liver and corneal opacity have been reported. Changes in the cornea also have been reported as typical of riboflavin deficiency in pigs; in addition, hemorrhages of the adrenals, kidney damage, anorexia, vomiting, and birth of weak and stillborn piglets have been reported in deficient swine. Erythrocyte glutathione reductase (EGR), a flavin-dependent enzyme, is widely accepted as an indicator of riboflavin status (7). Riboflavin-deficient swine have a high EGR activity coefficient and produce stillborn and weak piglets (8). A specific sign of deficiency in poultry is curled-toe paralysis (Fig. 15.3), which results from degenerative changes in the myelin sheaths of the nerve fibers.

Fatty acid oxidation by liver mitochondria of riboflavin deficient rats is decreased rapidly, apparently as a result of a reduction in acyl-CoA dehydrogenase activity. Riboflavin has not been shown to be required for activity of other enzymes involved in fatty acid beta-oxidation. Riboflavin deficiency in baby pigs results in depressed liver glutathione peroxidase activity (9). The role of riboflavin in vitamin E-Se nutrition (Se is a constituent of glutathione peroxidase) in animals and humans needs further study.

In mature ruminants the microflora of the rumen synthesize sufficient riboflavin and other water-soluble vitamins (as well as vitamin K) to eliminate a dietary need under most conditions. Young preruminant animals (lambs and calves) have a dietary requirement early in life, however, and deficiency

Figure 15.3   *Curled-toe paralysis in a riboflavindeficient chick, a typical sign of a severe deficiency. Courtesy of Chas. Pfizer Co.*

signs can be induced with synthetic milk diets. Diets low in riboflavin produce lesions in the corners of the mouth and on the lips, anorexia, loss of hair, and diarrhea in calves and lambs. The type of diet fed to immature ruminants appears to be a controlling factor in the development of rumen microbial populations that synthesize riboflavin.

Riboflavin deficiency has also been reported in monkeys, mice, cats, horses, and other species; the symptoms resemble in one or more ways those described for other animals. Riboflavin deficiency has been reported to cause moderate suppression of antibody production in rats and pigs (10).

In humans, riboflavin deficiency causes lesions of the lips and mouth (angular stomatitis), insomnia, irritability, scrotal dermatitis, conjunctivitis, and burning of the eyes. There is evidence for a need for riboflavin-dependent oxidoreductase systems in the activation of vitamin B_{12} and for a reduction in pyridoxine enzyme systems in riboflavin deficiency. These are just two among several interactions that are known to exist among pairs of B-vitamins.

Metabolism

Riboflavin is absorbed rapidly by phosphorylation in the intestinal mucosal cell, and is used directly by cells throughout the body. The maintenance requirement is dependent mainly on excretion rather than decomposition. A half life of 16 days has been reported for the rat under normal conditions; turnover is accelerated with high riboflavin diets (11).

Dietary composition and environmental temperature may affect the dietary requirement. High-fat diets or low-protein diets tend to increase the requirement, and the requirement of growing pigs has been reported to be increased by high environmental temperature.

Toxicity

Riboflavin toxicity is extremely unlikely because of its rapid loss in urine. Rats given 560 mg/kg of body weight in an intraperitoneal injection show some mortality from kidney damage, but such a massive dose certainly is not physiological. High-protein diets may be toxic in riboflavin deficiency. This may be related to the reduction in D-amino acid oxidase activity of liver observed in riboflavin deficiency.

Analogs and Antagonists

Some analogs show riboflavin activity. At least four derivatives of isoalloxazine have about half the biological activity of riboflavin for rats. A long list of other isoalloxazine derivatives have no activity. Several analogs of riboflavin have been shown to be inhibitors of riboflavin. These include isoriboflavin (5,6-dimethyl-9-D-1'-ribitylisoalloxazine), dinitrophenazine, galactoflavin, and D-araboflavin. Many riboflavin antagonists inhibit growth of tumors and/or pathogenic bacteria and in this role, of course, can be extremely valuable medically.

❑ NIACIN (NICOTINIC ACID)

The human disease, pellagra, was traced to a deficiency of a factor in yeast. Since then the importance of niacin as the specific nutrient involved has been clarified further in animals as well as in humans (12–14).

Structure

Niacin (nicotinic acid) and its amide derivative have the following structures, shown below.

The term *niacin* should be used as the generic descriptor for pyridine 3-carboxylic acid and derivatives exhibiting qualitatively the biological activity of nicotinamide. Thus, phrases such as "niacin activity" and "niacin deficiency" represent preferred usage (1).

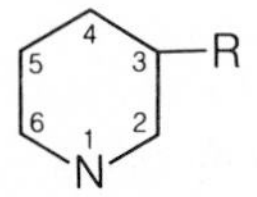

The compound pyridine 3-carboxylic with (R = —COOH), also known as niacin or vitamin PP, should be designated *nicotinic acid*.

The compound with (R = —CONH$_2$), also known as niacinamide or nicotinic acid amide, should be designated *nicotinamide*.

Niacin and niacinamide are equivalent to each other in biological activity for animals and humans. Both are very stable in heat, light, and alkali, and, therefore, are stable in feeds.

Niacin is the accepted generic description for pyridine 3-carboxylic acid and derivatives showing the qualitative nutritional activity of nicotinic acid. Nicotinamide is the amide of nicotinic acid. All forms of niacin are expressed as nicotinamide equivalents in terms of milligram or microgram equivalents of nicotinamide (1).

Functions

Niacin functions as a constituent of two important coenzymes that act as codehydrogenases. These enzymes are NAD (nicotinamide adenine dinucleotide) and NADP (nicotinamide adenine dinucleotide phosphate). These niacin-containing enzymes are important links in the transfer of hydrogen from substrates to molecular oxygen, resulting in water formation. As such, they are vital in several chemical reactions that occur in animal tissues.

NAD and NADP probably combine with a variety of protein carriers (apoenzymes) with specificity for a particular reaction. Thus, a large number of substrates can be dehydrogenated. All animal cells contain NAD and NADP; the ratio of the two varies among tissues. NAD is convertible to NADP and vice versa. Similarly, many of the reactions above that involve NAD and NADP are reversible. The enzymes (NAD and NADP) are reduced to the di-hydro forms which are, in turn, dehydrogenated by flavin (riboflavin-containing) enzymes.

Deficiency Signs

The general sign of niacin deficiency is reduced growth and appetite. Specific deficiency signs in animals include diarrhea, vomiting, dermatitis, unthriftiness, and an ulcerated intestine (necrotic enteritis) in swine; poor feathering, a scaly dermatitis and, sometimes, "spectacled eye" (Fig. 15.4) in chicks; and a peculiar darkening of the tongue (black tongue) and mouth lesions in dogs. In humans, a bright red tongue, mouth lesions, anorexia, and nausea are the common syndrome of pellagra.

Niacin present in most cereal grains is not available biologically for the pig and other simple-stomached animals (15–17). Apparently there are several bound forms of niacin containing peptides and complex carbohydrates. One of the bound forms in wheat is termed niacytin, which contains peptides, hexoses, and pentoses. This helps to account for the high incidence of pellagra among human populations subsisting on diets composed mainly of cereal grains.

Adult ruminants are not fed supplemental niacin under normal conditions because of the synthesis by rumen microflora. Niacin deficiency has been produced in calves, and some evidence suggests that milk production of high producing dairy cows and daily weight gain and feed utilization of feedlot cattle may be improved, at least during the first few weeks of the finishing period, by 50 to 500 ppm of supplemental niacin. These preliminary reports must be verified and the responses quantified; the environ-

mental and feeding conditions under which a beneficial response to niacin and other B-vitamin supplementation can be expected need to be identified. Robinson (18) has summarized the evidence supporting the view that intestinal synthesis of niacin in humans may provide some of the metabolic requirement for the vitamin under some conditions.

Niacin-Tryptophan Interrelationships

If animals are deprived of dietary niacin, the metabolic requirement for the vitamin can be met by conversion of tryptophan, an amino acid, to niacin (see Ch. 7). If tryptophan is provided in the diet in slight excess of the amount needed for tissue protein synthesis, the excess can be used to satisfy the niacin requirement. The synthesis of 1 mg of nicotinamide in this way requires about 60 mg of tryptophan for the pig and humans. The efficiency of conversion probably varies with species and with dietary and metabolic states. For example, Harmon *et al.* (19) showed that the dietary niacin requirement of growing pigs was higher when the diet contained corn protein instead of milk protein, presumably because of the lower tryptophan availability from corn in addition to the known lack of availability of niacin from corn. N_1-methylnicotinamide and N_1-methyl-6-pyridine-nicotinamide are the main excretory products of niacin in the pig, dog, rat, and humans, but in the chick it is dinicotinyl-ornithine. Ruminants appear to excrete the vitamin largely unchanged. Levels of niacin metabolites in urine often are used in studies of niacin requirements and metabolism.

Analogs and Antagonists

Several compounds related structurally to niacin possess some vitamin activity. These include several fatty acid esters of niacin and 3-hydroxyxanthranilic acid, an intermediate in the conversion of tryptophan to niacin. The structures of 13 known metabolites of niacin were illustrated in a review (13).

Mice fed 3-acetyl-pyridine show signs of niacin deficiency, although it appears to have some vitamin activity for normal dogs. Considerable variation exists among species in utilization of or antagonism by various analogs of niacin.

Effects of Massive Doses of Niacin

Large doses of niacin sometimes are prescribed for schizophrenia and in efforts to induce cerebrovas-

Figure 15.4 *"Spectacled eye" in a niacin-deficient chick illustrating the loss of feathers around the eye. Courtesy of M. L. Sunde, Univ. of Wisconsin.*

cular dilation in patients with senile ataxia. Similar doses (3 to 9 g daily) of nicotinic acid reduce serum cholesterol in patients with hypercholesterolemia. While such high intakes of niacin are effective in decreasing mobilization of fatty acids from adipose tissue and increasing utilization of muscle glycogen stores, similar effects have been reported on cardiac muscle metabolism. Long-term results of niacin doses of 3 g per day given for therapy of coronary heart disease in men with previous heart attacks failed to show a clear benefit on mortality. Furthermore, long-term high dose niacin therapy may be associated with liver damage, multiple enzyme changes, gastrointestinal disturbance, and elevated serum uric acid and glucose (12). Therefore, the wisdom of dietary supplementation of niacin at this level for animals appears in doubt, although this kind of information is limited.

❏ PANTOTHENIC ACID (PANTOYL-β-ALANINE)

A growth factor for yeast was first identified as pantothenic acid. Later (20, 21), it was prepared from liver, and since has been shown to be required by a large number of animal species.

Structure

The structure of pantothenic acid, the peptide of a butyric acid derivative and β-alanine, is shown:

PANTOTHENIC ACID

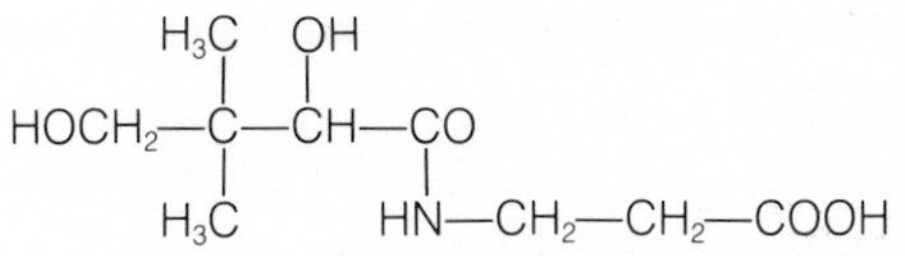

The compound, N-(2,4-dihydroxy-3,3-dimethyl-1-oxobutyl)-β-alanine, formerly known as pantoyl-β-alanine, should be designated *pantothenic acid*. It use in phrases such as "pantothenic acid activity" and "pantothenic acid deficiency" represent preferred usage (1).

Usually it is present as the Ca or Na salt of the d-isomer (active form) of pantothenic acid. The Ca salt is the most common form in which the vitamin is added to diets because it is less hygroscopic than the Na salt.

Functions

Pantothenic acid functions as a component of coenzyme A (CoA)—the coenzyme required for acetylation of numerous compounds in energy metabolism. The role of CoA in metabolism of fatty acids was discussed in Ch. 9. CoA is required in the formation of two-C fragments from fats, amino acids, and carbohydrates for entry into the citric acid cycle and for synthesis of steroids.

The synthesis and metabolism of CoA has been reviewed (22). The pathway of CoA synthesis involves pantothenate → 4'-phosphopantothenic acid → 4' phosphopantothenyl cysteine → 4'-phosphopantetheine → diphospho CoA → CoA. The degradation of CoA is not well known.

Absorption of amino acids from the GI tract somehow involves vitamin B_6, but the mechanisms are not clear; no specific enzyme systems requiring pyridoxal phosphate are known.

A deficiency of pantothenic acid precludes the synthesis of CoA because the CoA molecule contains pantothenic acid at 10% of its weight. The structure of CoA is shown:

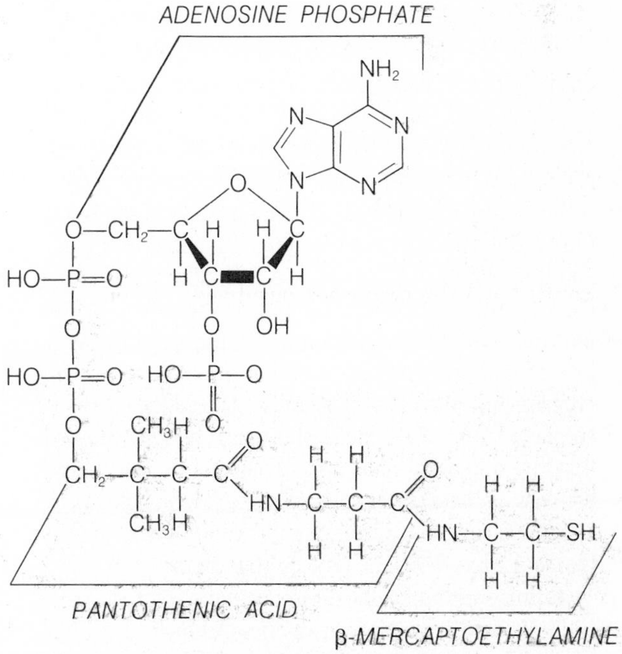

COENZYME A

The transformations of lipids and carbohydrates that involve S-acylated CoA include: hydrolysis of the thiol ester bond; racemization; dehydrogenation;

reduction; hydration; carboxylation; condensation reactions; and transferases.

The concentration of CoA in liver is increased by fasting and the proportion that is acylated is increased. This increase in the proportion of acylated CoA is brought about by the increase in tissue free fatty acids resulting from fasting. Endocrine changes such as the decrease in ratio of insulin to glucagon which occurs in diabetes also increases acylated CoA in liver through the effect on mobilization of free fatty acids from tissue lipid stores. The data illustrate that nutritional and endocrine changes have a striking effect on CoA metabolism which in turn provides a mechanism by which the liver can adjust quickly to changing needs for tissue fatty acid synthesis and oxidation.

Deficiency Signs

In addition to causing reduced growth rate as a generalized effect in all animals studied, pantothenic acid deficiency results in dermatitis in chicks, graying of the hair (achromotrichia) in rats and foxes, hemorrhaging and degeneration of the adrenal cortex of rats and mice, fetal death and resorption in rats, nervous derangement, skin lesions, lymphoid cell necrosis in the thymus, degeneration of duodenal mucosal cells and vacuolation of pancreatic acinar cells in chicks (23). In guinea pigs, diarrhea, rough hair coat, anorexia, and enlarged and hemorrhagic adrenals have been reported. A striking feature of pantothenic acid deficiency is fatty infiltration of the liver. Other signs in dogs are vomiting, gastritis, enteritis, and hemorrhage of the thymus and kidney. A prominent feature of deficiency in pigs is the effect on the nervous system. In addition to the impaired growth, loss of hair and enteritis noted in other species, the deficient pig develops a peculiar gait called "goosestepping" (Fig. 15.5). Follis and Wintrobe (24) showed that the abnormal gait was a result of degenerative damage to various nerves. Slow growth, anorexia, and impaired sow productivity result when pantothenic acid is deficient (25) in sow diets.

Ruminants normally do not require dietary pantothenic acid because of rumen synthesis, but deficiency has been produced in calves by feeding a synthetic milk diet low in the vitamin. Signs of deficiency are rough hair coat, dermatitis, anorexia, loss of hair around the eyes (spectacle eye), and demyelinization of the sciatic nerve and spinal cord.

Pantothenic acid appears to be related closely to

Figure 15.5 *"Goose-stepping" in a pig fed a pantothenic acid-deficient diet. Courtesy of W. M. Beeson, Purdue University.*

antibody production. Reduced formation of antibodies to several types of antigens in rats (26) and pigs (10, 25) and to tetanus toxoid in humans (27) has been observed in pantothenic acid deficiency.

Although clearcut deficiency of pantothenic acid has not been described in humans, deficiency signs have been induced by feeding a pantothenic acid antagonist (omega-methyl-pantothenic acid). Signs include fatigue, apathy, gastrointestinal disturbances, cardiovascular instability (tachycardia and variable blood pressure), and increased susceptibility to infections. Caution must be used in interpreting results of experiments in which vitamin antagonists are used to induce deficiency of the vitamin to confirm that biochemical or morphological lesions are due to the vitamin deficiency and not to the effects of the antagonist itself.

❑ VITAMIN B$_6$

Birch and Gyorgy (28) first established the properties of a component of a crude concentrate that was found to cure dermatitis in rats fed diets supplemented with thiamin and riboflavin. This compound was named pyridoxine. The International Committee on Nomenclature (1) now recommends that the term Vitamin B$_6$ be used for all 3-hydroxy-2-methyl pyridine derivatives showing qualitatively the biological activity of pyridoxine. The structures of the major compounds with vitamin B_6 activity (pyridoxine, pyridoxal, and pyridoxamine) are shown:

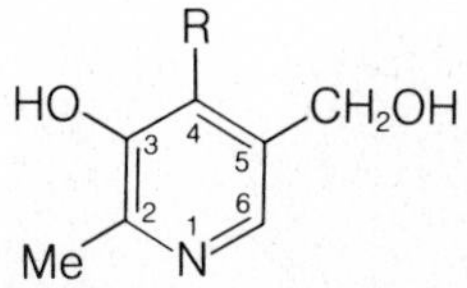

Phrases such as "vitamin B_6 activity" and "vitamin B_6 deficiency" represent preferred usage (1).

The compound with (R = Ch_2OH), 3-hydroxy-4,5-bis(hydroxy-methyl)-2-methyl-pyridine, formerly known as vitamin B_6, adermin, or pyridoxol, should be designated *pyridoxine*. The term "pyridoxine" is not synonymous with the generic term "vitamin B_6."

The compound with formula (R = HCO), also known as pyridoxaldehyde, should be designated *pyridoxal*.

The compound with (R = CH_2NH_2), 3-hydroxy-4-methylamino-5-hydroxymethyl-2-methylpyridine, should be designated *pyridoxamine*.

The chemistry of each of these forms of vitamin B_6 and the biosynthesis and metabolic interconversions of them have been described (29–31). A specific enzyme is involved in each conversion and niacin and riboflavin both are associated with one or more reactions as components of coenzymes (NADP and FMN, respectively). Vitamin B_6 is stable to heat, light and alkali solutions and maintains its activity well in mixed diets.

Functions

Vitamin B_6 functions as a coenzyme of a vast array of enzyme systems associated with protein and nitrogen metabolism. Metabolic roles of vitamin B_6 and human requirements for it have been reviewed (31). Methods used in vitamin B_6 analysis and in assessment of vitamin B_6 status of humans and animals have been summarized (7, 32).

As early as 1945 the B_6 requirement was recognized to increase with high dietary protein. This is explained by the fact that pyridoxal phosphate is the coenzyme of transaminases, which must be increased in activity to metabolize increased quantities of dietary protein. Sauberlich (30) tabulated a list of more than 50 pyridoxal-5[1]-phosphate-dependent enzymes and the reactions catalyzed and has listed the major types of enzymatic reactions involving pyridoxal phosphate-dependent enzymes as follows:

transamination; decarboxylation, racemization (not in animal tissues); amine oxidation; aldol reaction; cleavage; dehydration (deamination); and desulfhydration.

Aspartic transaminase (glutamic oxaloacetic transaminase) is the most abundant transaminase in mammalian tissues. Amino acid decarboxylases are widespread in micro-organisms, but the following are important in animal tissues: glutamic acid decarboxylase, cysteine-sulfonic acid decarboxylase, and aromatic L-amino acid decarboxylases. Tryptophan metabolism is dependent to a great extent on pyridoxal phosphate dependent enzymes, and a vitamin B_6 deficiency results in urinary excretion of abnormal metabolites of tryptophan: xanthurenic acid, kynurenine, and 3-hydroxykynurenine. Tyrosine and phenylalanine metabolism also involve a number of pyridoxal phosphate-dependent enzymes and deaminases (dehydrases) requiring pyridoxal phosphate are important in catabolism, especially of serine, threonine, and homoserine. Many phosphorylases in animal tissues contain pyridoxal phosphate, and total phosphorylase activity in skeletal muscle in rats is decreased in vitamin B_6 deficiency.

Vitamin B_6 is absorbed chiefly as pyridoxal after hydrolysis of pyridoxal phosphate by alkaline phosphatase in the lumen of the GI tract (33). Pyridoxal crosses the intestinal wall and accumulates in tissue more rapidly than pyridoxine and pyridoxamine. Vitamin B_6 circulates in the plasma as pyridoxal phosphate complexed to albumin; albumin-bound pyridoxal phosphate is not transported into cells.

The bioavailability (absorption from the GI tract) of vitamin B_6 varies widely among feed sources and may be as low as 50% in dry-heated cereals. It has been postulated that the reduced bioavailability of vitamin B_6 may be the result of the formation of complexes with proteins, amino acids or reducing sugars and of degradation products during food processing. Yen *et al.* (34) have suggested that a chick growth assay is more sensitive than plasma enzyme assay as an indicator of biologically available B_6 in heated corn and soybean meal.

Vitamin B_6 is involved somehow in red blood cell formation, probably because pyridoxal phosphate is required for porphyrin synthesis. B_6 is also important in the endocrine system; deficiency affects activities of growth hormone, insulin, and gonadotrophic, adrenal, thyroid, and sex hormones, but the mechanisms are not understood fully. The defective cellular transport of amino acids in vitamin B_6 deficient animals is believed to be due to the reduced pituitary growth hormone levels associated with the vitamin B_6 depletion (35). Growth hormone secretion is stimulated by dopamine which is produced from dopa decarboxylase of which pyridoxal phosphate is a coenzyme.

Deficiency Signs

The most common sign of B_6 deficiency involves the nervous system. Convuslions have been observed in all species studied. Demyelinization of the peripheral nerves, swelling and fragmentation of the myelin sheath, and later other degenerative changes occur. The convulsive seizures observed in B_6-deficient animals have resulted in many studies of brain metabolites and enzymes. The administration of γ-aminobutyric acid temporarily controls the seizures in B_6-deficient animals.

Vitamin B_6 deficiency results in reduced antibody response to various antigens in rats, guinea pigs (36), and pigs (10, 37, 63, 64), and reduces immunocompetence in progeny of depleted female rats (64). The mechanisms of immunosuppression induced by B_6 deficiency are unknown.

In some animal species, vitamin B_6 deficiency results in skin lesions on the feet, around the face and ears (acrodynia), atrophy of the hair follicles and abscesses and ulcers around the sebaceous glands from secondary infection in rats, mice, and monkeys (38). Skin lesions have not been reported in B_6-deficient swine, calves, or poultry.

Vitamin B_6 is required for normal reproduction in the rat and for normal egg laying and hatchability in hens. It is synthesized by rumen bacteria and evidence has been shown for some intestinal synthesis in simple-stomached animals. Although deficiency of B_6 is unlikely in farm animals because of its wide distribution in feedstuffs, the pig fed a B_6-deficient experimental diet exhibits the classical symptoms of deficiency, including convulsive seizures, poor growth, a brown exudate around the eyes, and low urinary excretion of the vitamin. The deficient chick shows depressed growth and abnormal feathering (Fig. 15.6). The B_6 requirement of humans is increased during pregnancy and in women receiving oral contraceptives. Oral lesions similar to those of riboflavin deficiency were alleviated by vitamin B_6 therapy and low plasma pyridoxal phosphate levels were increased by vitamin B_6 (39). It has been proposed that pyridoxal phosphate may function in steroid hormone action by serving as a ligand for binding the

Figure 15.6 B_6 *deficiency in chicks. Growth of the deficient chick on the right is greatly depressed and feathering is abnormal. Courtesy of G. E. Combs.*

transporting steroid-receptor complexes between the cytoplasm and nucleus where the hormones influence gene expression (40, 41). A need for increased vitamin B_6 intake during pregnancy of domestic animals has not been established.

Vitamin B_6 deficiency produces a wide variety of changes related to lipid metabolism including reduced carcass fatness, fatty liver, and elevated plasma lipids and cholesterol. The metabolic mechanism by which these effects occur in B_6 deficiency is unclear.

Oxalic acid is excreted in large quantities in the urine of B_6-deficient animals and humans; it is derived from metabolism of glycerine, serine, alanine, and other compounds that, under normal conditions, are metabolized to compounds other than oxalic acid.

Pyridine-2-carboxylic acid (picolinic acid) content of the rat pancreas is increased by increasing dietary vitamin B_6 content. Picolinic acid, a metabolite of tryptophan, appears to be an important Zn-binding ligand in the intestinal tract and pancreas, although this function is controversial.

Toxicity and Analogs

Vitamin B_6 toxicity is very unlikely; rabbits, rats and dogs tolerate doses up to 1 g/kg body weight (42). High doses given orally or parenterally produce convulsions, impaired coordination, paralysis, and death. All three forms of the vitamin are absorbed readily from the GI tract and are distributed widely in tissues. Most of an administered dose appears in the urine with negligible amounts found in feces or sweat. The major excretory product of B_6 in animals is 4-pyridoxic acid, which is derived directly from pyridoxal (31).

Structural analogs, including 4-deoxypyridoxine and 2-methyl-pyridoxine, function as B_6 antagonists in animals, and agents such as hydrazones, hydroxylamines, and semicarbazides form inactive complexes with pyridoxal or pyridoxal phosphate and produce vitamin B_6 deficiency signs (43), including convulsions in humans and animals. Gregory (44) showed that epsilon-pyridoxyl lysine, a complex formed between vitamin B_6 aldehydes and lysine during food storage, produces vitamin B_6 deficiency signs when fed at low levels to rats. Further work is needed to determine the practical significance of the formation of complexes of B_6 with other feed constituents in processed feeds and foods.

❑ VITAMIN B_{12} (CYANOCOBALAMIN)

Vitamin B_{12} is the most recently discovered vitamin. It was first known as the animal protein factor (APF) because animals fed diets not containing animal protein were prone to the hematological and neurological signs that were later shown to be prevented or cured by vitamin B_{12}. It has been shown to be present in animal tissues and excreta, although probably it is not formed by animal or plant tissues. The only known primary source of vitamin B_{12} is from microorganisms; it is synthesized by a wide range of bacteria but not in appreciable amounts by yeast and fungi. The chemistry and properties of B_{12} (63) and the early history of the association of vitamin B_{12} with Co and with folacin have been reviewed (45, 46).

Structure

The compound, α-(5,6-dimethylbenzimidazolyl) cobamide cyanide, is designated vitamin B_{12} or cyanocobalamin. Several derivatives, including hydroxycobalamin and nitritocobalamin, also have B_{12} activity (1). The structure for cyanocobalamin is shown. The term *vitamin B_{12}* should be used as the generic descriptor for all corrinoids exhibiting qualitatively the biological activity of cyanocobalamin. Thus, phrases such as "vitamin B_{12} activity" and "vitamin B_{12} deficiency" represent preferred usage (1).

The compound, Co α-[α-(5,6-dimethylbenzimidazoloyl)]-Co β-cyanocobamide, formerly known as vitamin B_{12}, vitamin B_{12} or cyanocobalamine should be designated *cyanocobalamin*.

The compound, Co α-[α-(5,0-dimethylbenzimidazoloyl)]-Co β-hydroxocabalamide, formerly known

as vitamin B_{12b}, or vitamin B-12b, should be designated *hydroxocobalamin*.

The compound, Co α-[α-(5,6-dimethylbenzimidazoloyl)]-Co β-aquacobamide, the conjugated acid of hydroxocobalamin, formerly known as vitamin B_{12a}, or vitamin B-12a, should be designated *aquacobalamin*.

The compound, Co α-[α-(5,6-dimethylbenzimidazoloyl)]-Co β-nitritocobamide, formerly known as vitamin B_{12c}, or vitamin B-12c, should be designated *nitritocobalamin*.

Vitamin B_{12} is a dark red crystalline compound, unstable at temperatures above 115° for 15 min, unstable to sunlight and stable within the pH range of 4–7 at normal temepratures. It contains Co and P in a 1:1 molar ratio.

The vitamin was isolated first in 1948 (47, 48). Since then a variety of isolation sources have been used with high yields coming from fermentation liquors of streptomycin, aureomycin or by special fermentations carried out with selected microorganisms.

Functions

Vitamin B_{12} functions as a coenzyme in several important enzyme systems. These include isomerases (mutases), dehydrases, and enzymes involved in methionine biosynthesis. The oxidation of propionate in animal tissues involves a series of reactions requiring B_{12} as well as pantothenic acid as components of coenzymes. Vitamin B_{12} is a component of a coenzyme for the enzyme, methylmalonyl-CoA isomerase, which catalyzes the conversion of methylma-lonyl-CoA to succinyl-CoA, which in turn is converted to succinate for entrance into the TCA cycle.

Vitamin B_{12} is linked closely with another water-soluble vitamin, folacin, in the synthesis of methionine in both bacterial and animal cells. Vitamin B_{12} deficiency leads to secondary folacin deficiency and methionine alleviates it.

The effect of vitamin B_{12} deficiency on folate metabolism is explained by the reduced reaction of a folic acid derivative (CH_3-H_4Pte-Glu) with homocysteine by the vitamin B_{12}-dependent enzyme, methyltransferase, and by its effect on liver folate levels. Methionine also increases liver folacin uptake and concentration. The interrelationships between folacin, vitamin B_{12}, and methionine in metabolism have been described (46, 49). Niacin (as NAD) is involved in the series of reactions as well.

Either vitamin B_{12} or folacin deficiency interfers with intestinal absorption of nutrients. Changes in the epithelial cells of the intestine, along with shortened villi are observed. In the vitamin B_{12} deficiency of pernicious anemia, increased bacterial populations occur in the upper small intestine due to achlorhydria.

A more complete understanding of the role of vitamin B_{12} in animal metabolism and its relationship to folacin awaits further study, but the general statement can be made that it is a component of coenzymes required for methyl-group synthesis and metabolism and that it is required for nucleoprotein synthesis in tandem with folic acid. Methionine appears to be the key factor regulating cellular uptake of folate; in the presence of low methionine, folate becomes trapped as 5-methyl-tetrahydrofolate, as in vitamin B_{12} deficiency.

Several amino acid interconversions involve enzyme systems associated with vitamin B_{12} and folacin. Folate coenzymes serve as acceptors or donors of one-carbon units in an array of reactions involved in amino acid and nucleotide metabolism, which are diagrammed in the review by Shane and Stokstad (46). Methionine synthetase is one of the three mammalian enzymes known to require vitamin B_{12} as a cofactor, along with methylmalonyl-CoA mutase and leucine 2,3-aminomutase.

Absorption, Transport, Storage, and Excretion of Vitamin B_{12}

Vitamin B_{12} absorption requires the presence of an enzyme secreted by the mucosal cells of the stomach and upper small intestine (cardiac region of the stom-ach in humans; pyloric region of stomach and upper duodenum of pigs and probably other animals) (50). This enzyme has been designated the intrinsic factor (IF), and in its absence B_{12} deficiency occurs. IF from one species may inhibit absorption of B_{12} in another species. For example, IF from pig stomach renders orally administered B_{12} less available to chicks and rats.

The B_{12}-IF complex passes down the GI tract to the ileum where it is complexed further with Ca and Mg ions and is adsorbed to the surface of the mucosa. It then is disassociated from the Ca or Mg by an apparently specific releasing enzyme contained in the intestinal secretions, and the B_{12} is absorbed. The exact mechanism by which it passes through the mucosal cell membrane is not known, but it has been suggested that it passes through the cell membrane by pinocytosis before the complex is broken by the releasing enzyme. After reaching the blood, B_{12} is bound to an α-globulin designated as transcobalamin I, or if injected, to a β-globulin designated transcobalamin II, from which it is subsequently shifted to transcobalamin I. The exact role of each form in the transport and storage of B_{12} is not known.

The amount of B_{12} not needed for immediate use is stored in liver and other tissues. in humans, 30–60% is stored in liver, 30% in muscle, skin, and bone and smaller amounts in other tissues (50). When the protein-binding-capacity of the blood serum for B_{12} is surpassed, excretion of the free vitamin occurs through the kidney and bile. More B_{12} is excreted daily in the bile in humans than is contained in the blood. The daily fecal excretion is less than the daily bile excretion, showing that reabsorption of a high proportion of B_{12} from the GI tract occurs.

Deficiency Signs

Although B_{12} is distributed widely in animal tissues and products, a deficiency is likely when simple stomached animals are maintained for long periods of time on diets entirely of plant origin. Sufficient microbial synthesis of vitamin B_{12} occurs in the small intestine of vegetarians to protect partly against a vitamin B_{12} deficiency (51). Hygenic practices in food handling also may have an effect on vitamin B_{12} status of humans. In ruminants, whose rumen microflora are capable of synthesizing the vitamin for use by the host, a B_{12} deficiency can be induced by feeding a Co-deficient diet. Because Co is a constituent of the B_{12} molecule, the vitamin cannot be synthesized when Co is not available. The relationships between B_{12}

and Co in ruminants have been detailed in reviews by Underwood (52) and Church *et al.* (53) and are discussed in Ch. 13.

Growth failure is a general symptom of deficiency in all animal species studied. In B_{12}-deficient chicks, poor feathering, kidney damage, impaired thyroid function, lower level of sulfhydryl groups in the thyroid, perosis, depressed plasma proteins, and elevated blood non-protein N and glucose occur (50). Eggs from B_{12}-deprived hens fail to hatch; embryos die at about day 17 and show multiple hemorrhages, fatty livers, enlarged hearts and thyroids, and lack of myelination of the sciatic nerves and spinal cord. Humans with pernicious anemia associated with vitamin B_{12} deficiency signs may have an abnormal electroencephalogram.

Baby pigs deprived of B_{12} show rough hair coats, incoordinated hind leg movements, normocytic anemia and enlarged liver and thyroids. Sows fed B_{12}-deficient diets during gestation have a high incidence of abortion, small litters, abnormal fetuses, and inability to rear the young. In deficient rats, retarded heart and kidney development, fatty liver, reduced blood sulfhydryl compounds, a decrease in activities of liver cytochrome oxidase and dehydrogenases, and an increase in liver CoA activity occur (42). The increased pantothenic acid content of liver in B_{12} deficiency is a general observation among the animal species studied. Vitamin B_{12} deficiency in humans is manifested by a megaloblastic anemia (pernicious anemia), but is observed mainly when absorption is impaired by the absence of IF.

Breast-fed human infants nursing vegetarian mothers may show signs of vitamin B_{12} deficiency, including anemia, skin pigmentation, apathy, retardation, involuntary movements, and methylmalonic aciduria (54). Mothers of these infants have mild anemia, megaloblastic bone marrow, and low plasma and milk vitamin B_{12} concentrations.

Co-deficient cattle and sheep develop deficiency signs reversible by B_{12}. Signs include reduced appetite, emaciation, anemia, fatty liver, birth of weak young, and reduced milk production. Ketosis, a relatively common disease of lactating dairy cattle, may be related to a metabolic deficiency of B_{12}, which interferes with the metabolism of propionate. Only a small proportion of B_{12} synthesized in the rumen is absorbed and, of the total vitamin B_{12} analogs produced in the rumen, only a small fraction have biological activity. Vitamin B_{12} analogs also may be produced in significant amounts by small intestinal bacteria and result in vitamin B_{12} insufficiency for the host.

Blood plasma contains several vitamin B_{12} binding proteins (human plasma contains three, trancobalamin I, II, and III) whose role is not entirely clear. One suggested role is that of providing a selective mechanism for removal of analogs of vitamin B_{12} from the body by excretion in the bile, another is that of leaching out vitamin B_{12} from intra and extra cellular bacteria, thereby imparting antibacterial action. Much remains unknown about the importance of vitamin B_{12} carrier proteins in nutrition.

The literature reports no evidence that vitamin B_{12} given in large doses causes acute or chronic toxicity.

❏ FOLACIN

Structure

The compound, monopteroylglutamic acid (folic acid) has the structure shown:

The term folacin should be used as the generic description for folic acid and related compounds with biological activity of folic acid (1). Folic acid derivatives with the glutamic acid residue combined through a peptide bond with one or more additional residues are designated folic acid derivatives with biological activity (1): tetrahydrofolic acid; 5-formyltetrahydrofolic acid; 10-formyltetrahydrofolic acid; or 5-methyltetrahydrofolic acid.

Functions

The relationship of folacin to B_{12} metabolism was emphasized in the previous section. Folic acid and its derivatives take part in a variety of metabolic reactions involving incorporation of single-C units into large molecules. The metabolically active form of folacin is tetrahydrofolic acid, which is a constituent of a coenzyme associated with metabolism of single-

C fragments. A dietary source of folacin is converted by the body tissues to tetrahydrofolic acid, which is known to be required for the biosynthesis of purines, pyrimidines, glycine, serine, and creatine. Folacin also may be concerned with synthesis of the enzymes, choline oxidase, and xanthine oxidase, and is involved in choline and methionine metabolism. Other suggested roles of folacin in metabolism which are less well documented include: ascorbic acid biosynthesis in rats; porphyrin portions of metal porphyrin enzyme synthesis; and regulation of metal ions in the body.

Absorption, Storage, and Excretion

Considerable intestinal synthesis of folic acid and its derivatives occurs, and humans and animals may absorb significant quantities. Folacin is absorbed freely from the GI tract and carried to all tissues of the body. Absorption is an active process. The liver contains high concentrations of folacin and apparently is the main site of conversion of folic acid into 5-formyltetrahydrofolic acid, along with the bone marrow. Vitamin B_{12} enhances the conversion.

Folic acid excretion occurs in urine, feces and sweat. Sweat constitutes a major route of loss of folic acid in humans, but in animals whose sweat glands are less well developed (pig, cow, sheep), most of the excretion occurs in feces and urine. Methyltetrahydrofolate (MTHF), the main form of folacin in plasma, is transported to non-hepatic tissues where it is demethylated and then returned to the liver as non-methyl folate. Some of the non-methyl folate is excreted in the bile and thus is subject to reabsorption. Thus, the maintenance of normal plasma folate levels depends on enterohepatic circulation. Of course, much of the fecal excretion is of microbial origin in the GI tract.

Deficiency Signs

The most prominent sign of folacin deficiency in humans and animals, aside from reduced growth rate, is a macrocytic, hyperchromic anemia, leucopenia, and thrombocytopenia. The anemia produced by folacin deficiency is indistinguishable from that of vitamin B_{12} deficiency (46). Resistance of animals to infections is affected by folacin; for example, monkeys show increased resistance to experimental poliomyelitis when suffering from chronic deficiency, and deficient rats show impairment of antibody response to murine typhus.

Folacin deficiency causes abnormal fetuses in pregnant rats. The central nervous system and the skeleton appear to be the most affected. Immature ruminants have been shown to require folacin in the diet, although a deficiency is unlikely because of the high content of most feedstuffs.

Folic acid antagonists such as aminopterin and amethopterin have been shown to inhibit cell division in normal and abnormal tissues, presumably because of their effect on purine and pyrimidine synthesis.

Because folacin is distributed widely in nature, it is unlikely to be deficient in common diets for birds and animals. However, antagonists create the possibility for deficiency when they are present in the diet by accident or as antimicrobials.

❏ BIOTIN

Biotin was first recognized as a growth factor for yeast. Later, rats fed raw egg white developed skin lesions and loss of hair, which were found to be cured by a protective factor in liver, now known to be biotin. Biotin was isolated first from egg yolks (29), and later from liver. The chemistry, isolation and biosynthesis of biotin have been reviewed (29, 56).

Structure

The structure of biotin, formerly known as vitamin H or coenzyme R, is shown:

$$BIOTIN$$

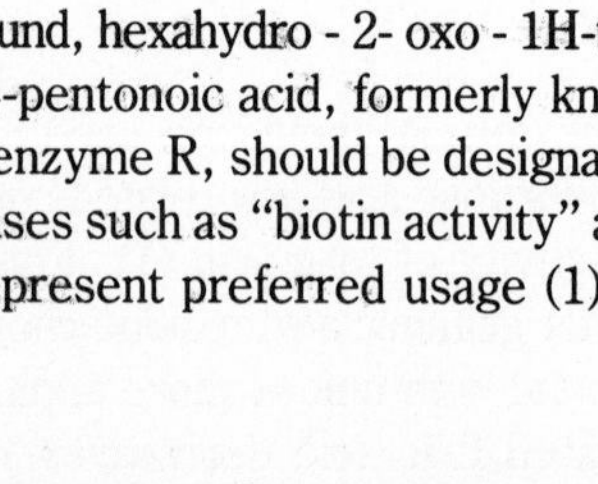

The compound, hexahydro - 2- oxo - 1H-thieno[3,4-d] imidazole-4-pentonoic acid, formerly known as vitamin H or coenzyme R, should be designated *biotin*. Its use in phrases such as "biotin activity" and "biotin deficiency" represent preferred usage (1).

Functions

Biotin is a component of several enzyme systems and, as such, participates in the following reactions: conversion of propionyl CoA to methylmalonyl-CoA;

degradation of leucine; fat metabolism; and trans-carboxylation reactions. Its metabolic role has been reviewed (55).

Biotin has been suggested to be involved in aspartic acid synthesis, in deamination of amino acids, and somehow involved in the activities of malic enzyme and ornithine transcarboxylase. The effects of biotin deficiency on protein, carbohydrate, and lipid metabolism probably can be explained on the basis of its involvement in the reactions listed above rather than on some general basis.

Deficiency Signs

A deficiency of biotin is unlikely under normal dietary conditions because the quantitative requirement of most animal species is low relative to the biotin content of common feedstuffs and because microbial synthesis in the GI tract provides a source of biotin for ruminants and for simple-stomached animals that practice coprophagy.

Deficiency in rats is characterized by a progressive scaly dermatitis and alopecia (56). Biotin is needed for normal reproduction in female and male rats. Deficiency in females results in birth of young with abnormalities of the heart and circulatory system, and in deficient males development of the genital system is retarded. Dermatitis and perosis are the chief signs of biotin deficiency in chicks and turkey poults. Biotin deficiency is aggravated when pantothenic acid also is deficient in the diet of rats and chicks. Biotin deficiency has been produced experimentally in young pigs resulting in alopecia, seborrheic skin lesions, hind leg spasticity, and cracked hooves. Experimental biotin deficiency signs among healthy humans eating normal diets are unconvincing. However, biotin deficiency signs have been described in human patients given total parenteral nutrition of a mixture not containing biotin (57). Signs included skin rash, hair loss, pallor, lethargy, and irritability. Within two weeks following the beginning of daily ingestion of 10 mg of biotin, rash was gone, hair growth had started, and irritability was relieved. Inherited deficiencies of each of the three mitochondrial biotin-containing carboxylases have been reported in humans (55).

Deficiency signs have been produced in chicks, rats, pigs, fish, hamsters, mink, guinea pigs, and other species fed raw egg white. A protein-like constituent of egg white, avidin, forms a stable complex with biotin in the GI tract and renders the biotin unavailable for absorption. Avidin is destroyed by moist heat and the avidin-biotin complex also is destroyed by steaming for 30–60 min, so that biotin deficiency is not likely in animals fed cooked egg protein.

Biotin deficiency symptoms have been reported recently in swine under field conditions. Cunha (58) suggested that the increased use of slotted floors may be a factor, because coprophagy may be reduced. If so, we have an example of the effects of changing technology on the need for continued reappraisal of the nutrient requirements of animals under practical conditions of production.

There is no evidence for significant toxicity signs from oral or parenteral administration of massive doses of biotin in animals.

❏ CHOLINE

Choline was first isolated from hog bile in 1849 and its structure was reported in 1867. The chemistry and metabolism of choline have been reviewed (59). Choline is distributed widely in animal tissues as free choline, acetylcholine, and as a component of phospholipids including lecithin and sphingomyelin. The structure of free choline is shown:

$$HO—CH_2CH_2—\overset{+}{N}\underset{CH_3}{\overset{CH_3}{<}}—CH_3$$

The compound with formula $(CH_3)_3\ N\ +\ CH_2CH_2OH$ should be designated *choline*. Its use in phrases such as "choline activity" and "choline deficiency" represents acceptable usage (1).

Choline added to feeds usually is supplied as choline chloride or choline dihydrogen citrate. Choline chloride or choline dihydrogen citrate. Choline chloride is extremely hygroscopic and therefore is often added to the diet as a 70% aqueous solution.

Functions

Choline has the following broad functions: it is a structural component of tissues (in lecithin, sphingomyelin); it is involved with transmission of nerve impulses as a component of acetylcholine; it supplies biologically labile methyl groups; it has lipotropic effects (prevents accumulation of liver fat); it facilitates the formation and secretion of chylomicrons in the intestine. Unlike most other water-soluble vitamins, there is no good evidence that choline or its derivatives are required as co-factors in enzymatic reactions although lysophosphatidyl-choline has been found to be required for activation of glycosyltransferases in membranes.

The importance of choline as a component of phospholipids is clear from the discussion in Ch. 9 on Lipids. Because phospholipids are essential components of cell membranes and lipoproteins, it is not surprising that choline deficiency causes abnormalities in cell structure and function. Therefore, the effect of choline in modifying phospholipid level and composition seems to be the best available explanation for much of its broad impact on cell physiology and biochemistry.

Its role as a component of acetylcholine is vital, as acetylcholine is the compound responsible for transmitting nerve impulses. Brain acetylcholine levels are directly related to blood levels. It has been suggested that dietary choline may affect brain acetylcholine concentration not only by increasing acetylcholine synthesis, but also by affecting the acetylcholine receptor membranes which are rich in choline and ethanolamine phosphatides. The main physiological effects of acetylcholine are peripheral vasodilation, contraction of skeletal muscle, and slowing of the heart rate. Acetylcholine is hydrolyzed to choline and acetic acid by cholinesterases. The acetylation of choline to acetylcholine is driven by an enzyme system requiring CoA.

Choline serves as a donor of methyl groups in transmethylation reactions. Labile methyl groups may come from choline or from its oxidation products, betaine aldehyde, betaine, and dimethylglycine.

Labile methyl groups, although for a time considered essential in the diet, are synthesized in body tissues from other one-C fragments. Folic acid is involved in the metabolism of these one-C fragments from which methyl groups are derived, and vitamin B_{12} is required in the transfer of methyl groups from one metabolite to another once they are formed.

Deficiency Signs

The manifestations of choline deficiency probably are related to interference with all of its distinct functions. As choline is a component of phospholipids, a deficiency is associated with fatty liver. Other signs of choline deficiency are hemorrhagic kidneys and other tissues of rats and other species and perosis in chicks. The accumulation of lipids in the liver (fatty liver syndrome) in choline deficiency is common to all species studied. Liver fat accumulation is associated with a depressed level of serum lipids, and a change in membrane and in conformational structure of lipoproteins needed for lipid transport from liver to other tissues. Such an action of choline would explain the reduced serum lipid levels observed in choline deficiency.

Dietary methionine can replace choline completely for prevention of fatty liver in rats and pigs. The choline requirement consists of two parts—one that is indispensible and one for which methionine can be substituted. In young animals this can occur only if methionine is provided in excess of that needed for tissue protein synthesis; that available above the amount needed for tissue growth can supply labile methyl groups for choline synthesis from ethanolamine.

The choline requirement is reduced when the diet limits growth by a deficiency of another nutrient. Fat increases the requirement and caloric restriction reduces it. In fact, the fatty liver and hemorrhagic kidneys produced in rats fed a choline-deficient diet are prevented by restricting the fat and carbohydrate of the diet to reduce growth.

In perosis of choline-deficient chicks, the symptoms are the same as seen in Mn and biotin deficiencies. In swine, choline deficiency causes an abnormal gait in growing pigs and reproductive failure in adult females in addition to the fatty liver and hemorrhages noted for other species.

No direct evidence exists for choline deficiency in humans, but a considerable effort has been devoted to studying the possible relationship between fatty infiltration of the liver in alcoholics and choline nutrition; pharmacological doses of choline have been given successfully to patients with brain disorders associated with deficiencies of cholinergic tone. The relationship between alcoholic liver cirrhosis and nutrition is a complex one in which choline appears to be only one of a number of factors.

Reports of choline toxicity have not been found in the literature.

❑ ASCORBIC ACID (VITAMIN C)

A factor in citrus fruits capable of preventing scurvy in humans was recognized many years ago. The isolation of L-ascorbic acid and its characterization as a water-soluble vitamin have been reviewed (60).

Structure

The structure of L-ascorbic acid is shown:

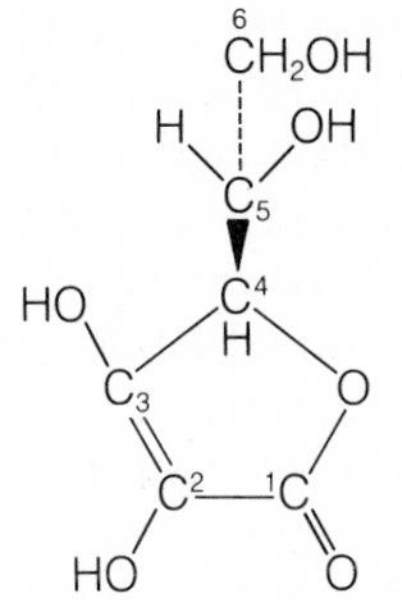

The term *vitamin C* should be used as the generic descriptor for all compounds exhibiting qualitatively the biological activity of ascorbic acid. Thus, phrases such as "vitamin C activity" and "vitamin C deficiency" represent preferred usage (1).

The compound, 2,4-didihydro-L-threo-hexano-1,4-lactone, formerly known as vitamin C, cevitamic acid or hexuronic acid, should be designated L-*ascorbic acid* or *ascorbic acid*. The trivial name *ascorbic acid* represents preferred usage (1).

The compound, L-threo-hexano-1,4-lactone, should be designated L-*dehydroascorbic acid* or *dehydroascorbic acid*. The trivial name *dehydroascorbic acid* represents preferred usage (1). Both the reduced and oxidized forms of L-ascorbic acid are physiologically active.

Functions

L-ascorbic acid is formed from D-glucose by the following reactions: D-glucose → D-glucuronic acid → L-gulonic acid → L-gulono-gamma-lactone → L-ascorbic acid. Animals that cannot synthesize vitamin C lack the enzyme, L-gulonolactone oxidase, which is responsible for the conversion of L-gulono-gamma-lactone to L-ascorbic acid.

Ascorbic acid is involved in several important metabolic converions, which may be summarized as follows: it is involved directly with a number of enzymes catalyzing oxidation and reduction (electron transport) reactions. Ascorbic acid, itself easily oxidized and reversibly reduced, serves as a reducing agent. It is required to maintain normal tyrosine oxidation and for normal collagen metabolism. Specifically, it is required for the formation of hydroxyproline from proline (61) and hydroxylysine from lysine (62). The hydroxylation reaction occurs only when the amino acids are in peptide linkage in collagen. Ascorbate

does not participate in the hydroxylation reaction, but is required to keep enzyme-bound Fe^{++} in the reduced form.

It is required as a co-substrate in certain mixed-function oxidations, as in the conversion of dopamine to norepinephrine (62). L-ascorbic acid can be replaced by D-ascorbic acid, isoascorbic acid, or glucoascorbic acid in this reaction. It is required along with ATP for the incorporation of plasma Fe into ferritin. ATP, ascorbate, and Fe appear to form an activated complex which allows release of ferric Fe from a tight complex with plasma transferrin for incorporation into tissue ferritin.

Because ascorbic acid is not stored in appreciable quantities in body tissues, it must be supplied almost on a day-to-day basis for those species unable to synthesize it. Most mammalian and avian species are able to synthesize it from glucose in adequate amounts, but a growing list of species is known to develop a deficiency when dietary ascorbate is withheld. Humans, other primates and the guinea pig are the classical examples of animals unable to synthesize vitamin C. Other species now known to require a dietary source are the Indian fruit bat, red-vented bulbul, the flying fox, and some non-mammals, such as rainbow trout, Coho salmon, two species of locust, and the silkworm. Although the pig synthesizes ascorbic acid, some evidence (63, 64) suggests that a growth response may be obtained by supplemental vitamin C in growing-pig diets under some conditions.

Deficiency Symptoms

The first sign of vitamin C deficiency is a depletion of tissue concentrations of the vitamin. Early signs, known as scurvy in humans, include edema, weight loss, emaciation, and diarrhea. Specific structural defects occur in bone, teeth, cartilage, connective tissues, and muscles. These defects can be explained largely by a failure in collagen formation in these tissues, including defective matrix formation in bones. Hemorrhages are seen commonly in muscles and in the gums as a result of increased capillary fragility. Hemorrhage, fatty infiltration, and necrosis may occur in the liver, and the spleen and kidney are damaged by hemorrhage. The adrenal gland is enlarged, congested, and infiltrated with fat. Adrenal hormone secretions are affected markedly. Biochemical changes in vitamin C deficiency include increased formation of mucopolysaccharides in connective tissue, increased hyaluronic acid in repair tissue of animals with scurvy, and decreased incorporation of sulfate into mucopolysaccharides. Vitamin C deficiency is associated with decreased serum protein concentration and anemia, prolonged blood clotting time, and delayed wound healing.

The role of ascorbic acid in Ca and P metabolism apparently is related to its association with bone matrix formation. Ca and P cannot be deposited normally in bone when matrix formation is impaired by vitamin C deficiency. Ascorbic acid enhances Fe absorption and has less predictable though generally beneficial effects on utilization of S, F, and I.

Deficiency signs in humans resemble those reported in animals. Because of the generally recognized reduction in plasma ascorbic acid concentration and reduced urinary excretion of ascorbic acid in the presence of infectious disease, some have suggested that higher than recommended levels should be ingested in times of illness or stress. Pauling (65) has suggested that levels several times the NRC recommended levels are effective in prevention of the common cold. This claim has not been supported by the research of others and must be rejected. Although the toxicity level of ascorbic acid apparently is many-fold greater than the requirement, evidence suggests that chronic ingestion of 5–50 times those levels recommended may increase susceptibility to scurvy when vitamin C is withdrawn (66). Moreover, there is evidence of impaired phagocyte bactericidal activity associated with the administration of large doses of vitamin C. Claims of benefits in humans consuming megavitamin doses of vitamin C (several times the recommended level of 45 mg/day) have been made; it appears that the evidence does not justify the practice. The vitamin C content of plasma of farm animals able to synthesize the vitamin averages 0.3 to 0.4 mg/dℓ; this level is similar to that of plasma of humans consuming 45 mg of vitamin C daily. Adverse effects of high levels in the diet of animals not considered to have a dietary ascorbic acid requirement may reduce utilization of Cu and, perhaps, other trace elements to a marked degree. Therefore, indiscriminate ingestion of large doses of ascorbic acid in animals and humans should be avoided, even though tissue storage is limited and tolerance is high.

❏ MYO-INOSITOL

Inositol is a common and abundant constituent of plant materials. Phytic acid, a major source of P in many cereal grains and other seeds, is the hexa-

phosphoric acid ester of inositol, but phytase enzymes needed to hydrolyze phytic acid to release free inositol are absent or limiting in normal digestive secretions. Nevertheless, inositol is present in abundant amounts in available form. Intestinal synthesis by microflora of the GI tract also provides considerable inositol.

The compound cyclohexitol, also known as inositol or mesoinositol, should be designated *myoinositol*. Its use in phrases such as "myo-inositol activity" and "myo-inositol deficiency" represents acceptable usage (1).

Myo-inositol (inositol) is essential for the growth of cells in tissue cultures and has been reported to be required for the growth of gerbils, rats, and other animals under certain conditions (67). Tissue synthesis of inositol has been demonstrated in mammals. The structure of inositol is shown. Early work on dietary inositol was directed toward its role as a lipotropic factor for animals. Recently, the emphasis has been on the influence of dietary inositol on the levels of free inositol and its phospholipid derivitives in mammalian cells and the metabolic basis for the accumulation of fat in the liver of deficient animals. In mammalian cells, inositol exists mainly in its free form, and is bound to phospholipid as phosphatidylinositol (PI). Its concentration in animal tissues is increased by dietary inositol. Impaired release of plasma lipoprotein, increased fatty acid mobilization from adipose tissue, and enhanced liver fatty acid synthesis are all suggested as factors in dietary inositol deficiency. Cellular phosphoinositides tend to be high in arachidonic acid, which suggests special importance for inositol in biological membranes. Available data (67) lead to the conclusion that inositol has important functions in lipid metabolism not heretofore appreciated in animal nutrition.

The chemistry, biogenesis, and occurrence of deficiency effects in animals, and pharmacology and toxicology of inositol have been received (67–70).

MYO-INOSITOL

❏ PABA

Para-aminobenzoic acid (PABA) was first discovered as an essential growth factor for microorganisms.

Although isolated reports have been made of a beneficial effect on animals by addition of PABA to the diet, no clear-cut evidence for a dietary requirement exists. Thus, PABA shares with inositol the status of being a questionable candidate for classification as a vitamin. It is synthesized abundantly in the intestine and the fact that it is a growth factor for some microorganisms suggests that a shortage in the diet of some animals may affect performance indirectly by limiting the synthesis of other vitamins.

The structure of PABA is shown.

p-AMINOBENZOIC ACID

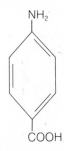

The compound should be designated *p-aminobenzoic acid*. Its use in phrases such as "*p*-aminobenzoic acid activity" and "*p*-aminobenzoic acid deficiency" represents acceptable usage (1).

Interactions of Vitamins with Other Nutrients

Although more than 30 years have passed since the discovery of the newest member of the water-soluble vitamin group (B_{12}), sporadic reports persist in the literature of unidentified factors that improve performance of animals and birds fed diets adequate in all known nutrients. Possibly one or more undiscovered organic compounds in nature are dietary essentials for animals and, therefore, will be classified as vitamins. The nature of such compounds, their distribution in nature, and the amounts and conditions in which they are required are yet to be determined.

Nutritional interrelationships of vitamins with trace elements were discussed in Chs. 12 and 13 and with other vitamins in Ch. 14 and in previous sections of this chapter. Detailed accounts of these interactions are available for in-depth knowledge. Suffice it to say that the field of nutrition has reached heightened complexity and an increased awareness of the importance of delicate interrelationships between and among specific nutrients must be a high priority goal in animal and human nutrition as the future unfolds. Progress in identifying and quantifying these inter-

actions can be expected to be enhanced by the availability of newer laboratory methods and greater analytical capabilities (7).

❑ SUMMARY

Water-soluble vitamins are all organic compounds, but are unrelated to each other in structure. Unlike the fat soluble vitamins, they are not (except B_{12}) stored in appreciable quantities in body tissues and, therefore, must be supplied in the diet daily for those animals whose gastrointestinal tract does not provide appreciable microbial synthesis. Water-soluble vitamins include the following compounds: thiamin (B_1), riboflavin (B_2), niacin (nicotinic acid), pantothenic acid, vitamin B_6 (pyridoxine, pyridoxal and pyridoxamine), vitamin B_{12} (cyanocobalamin), folacin (folic acid or monopteroylglutamic acid), biotin, choline, vitamin C (ascorbic acid), myoinositol, and p-aminobenzoic acid.

Most of the water-soluble vitamins function as metabolic catalysts, usually as coenzymes. Profound aberrations in metabolism occur if they are unavailable to the tissues in sufficient amounts. For example, thiamin deficiency produces neurological disturbances, including beriberi in humans (numbness of extremities, unsteady gait, edema of feet and legs), polyneuritis in chicks (retraction of the head), and bradycardia (slow heart rate) in all species studied.

Rapid kidney excretion of water-soluble vitamins ingested in excess of requirements makes day-to-day administration necessary and toxicity signs unlikely. Some water-soluble vitamins such as biotin may be synthesized by microflora in the gastrointestinal tract of non-ruminant animals in amounts sufficient to meet requirements; ruminant animals generally do not need supplemental dietary water-soluble vitamins owing to synthesis by rumen microflora.

Vitamin C is synthesized in the tissues of most animals, but some species, including humans, monkeys, and guinea pigs, require a dietary source.

Nutritional interrelationships among water-soluble vitamins and between vitamins and macro and trace minerals are numerous. More complete knowledge of these interrelationships must be a high priority goal for the future.

❑ REFERENCES

1. International Union of Nutritional Sciences. Committee on Nomenclature. 1980. *J. Nutr.* **110**:8.
2. Williams, R. R. and J. K. Cline. 1936. *J. Amer. Chem. Soc.* **58**:1504.

3. Adiga, P. R. and K. Muniyappa. 1978. *J. Steroid Biochem.* **9**:829.

4. Muniyappa, K., U. S. Murthy, and P. R. Adija. 1978. *J. Steroid Biochem.* **9**:888.

5. Horwitt, M. K. 1972. In *The Vitamins*, 2nd ed. Academic Press, N.Y.

6. Bhat, K. S. and C. Gopalan. 1974. *Nutrition Metabol.* **17**:1–8.

7. Sauberlich, H. E. 1984. *Ann. Rev. Nutr.* **4**:377.

8. Frank, G. R., J. M. Bahi, and R. A. Eastu. 1984. *J. Animal Sci.* **59**:1567.

9. Brady, P. S., et al. 1979. *J Nutr.* **109**:1615.

10. Harmon, B. G., et al. 1963. *J Nutr.* **79**:269.

11. Yang, Chung-Shu and D. B. McCormick. 1967. *J. Nutr.* **93**:445.

12. Roe, D. A. 1973. *A Plague of Corn: The Social History of Pellagra.* Cornell Univ. Press, Ithaca, N.Y.

13. Darby, W. J., K. W. McNutt, and E. N. Todhunter. 1975. *Nutr. Rev.* **33**:289.

14. Kodicek, E., R. Braude, S. K. Kon, and K. G. Mitchell. 1956. *Brit. J. Nutr.* **10**:51.

15. Chadhuri, D. K. and E. Kodicek. 1960. *Brit. J. Nutr.* **41**:35.

16. Luce, W. G., E. R. Peo, and D. B. Hudman. 1966. *J. Nutr.* **88**:39; 1967. *J. Animal Sci.* **26**:76.

17. Yen, J. T., A. S. Jensen, and D. H. Baker. 1977. *J. Animal Sci.* **45**:269.

18. Robinson, F. A. 1966. *The Vitamin Co-Factors of Enzyme Systems.* Pergamon Press Ltd., London.

19. Harmon, B. G., D. E. Becker, A. H. Jensen, and D. H. Baker. 1969. *J. Animal Sci.* **28**:848.

20. Elvehjem, C. A. and C. J. Koehn. 1934. *Nature* **134**:1007.

21. Lepkovsky, S. and T. H. Jukes. 1936. *J. Biol. Chem.* **114**:109.

22. Wright, L. D. 1976. Ch. 22 in *Present Knowledge of Nutrition*, 4th ed., p. 226. The Nutrition Foundation, Washington, D.C.

23. Gries, C. L. and M. C. Scott. 1972. *J. Nutr.* **102**:1269.

24. Follis, R. H., Jr. and M. M. Wintrobe. 1945. *J. Expt. Med.* **81**:539.

25. Miller, E. R. and E. T. Kornegay. 1983. *J. Animal Sci.* **57**(suppl. 2):315.

26. Pruzansky, T. and A. E. Axelrod. 1955. *Proc. Expt. Biol. Med.* **89**:323.

27. Hodges, R. E., W. B. Bean, M. A. Ohlson, and R. E. Bleiler. 1962. *Amer. J. Clin. Nutr.* **11**:85.

28. Birch, T. W. and P. Gyorgy. 1936. *Biochem. J.* **30**:304.

29. Harris, S. A. 1968. In *The Vitamins*, Vol. II. Academic Press, N.Y.

30. Sauberlich, H. E. 1968. In *The Vitamins*, Vol. II. Academic Press, N.Y.

31. Ink, J. L. 1984. *Ann. Rev. Nutr.* **3**:289.

32. Lehlem, J. E. and R. D. Reynolds. 1981. *Methods in Vitamin B-6 Nutrition*, pp. 1–401. Plenum Press, N.Y.

33. Mehansho, H., M. W. Hamm, and L. M. Henderson. 1979. *J. Nutr.* **109**:1542.

34. Yen, J. T., A. H. Jensen, and D. H. Baker. 1976. *J. Animal Sci.* **42**:866.

35. Heindel, J. J. and T. R. Riggs. 1978. *Amer. J. Physiol.* **235**:E316.

36. Axelrod, A. E., S. Hopper, and D. A. Long. 1965. *J. Nutr.* **74**:58.

37. Tobson, L. C. and M. R. Schwarz. 1980. Ch. 10 in *Vitamin B-6 Metabolism and Role in Growth*, p. 205, G. P. Tryfiates (ed.). Food and Nutrition Press, Inc., Westport, CT.

38. Weber, R., H. Wieser, and O. Wiss. 1968. In *The Vitamins*, Vol. II. Academic Press, N.Y.

39. Cleary, R. E., L. Lumeng, and T. K. Li. 1975. *Amer. J. Obstet. Gynecol.* **121**:25.

40. Cake, M. H., D. M. DiSorbo, and G. Litwack. 1978. *J. Biol. Chem.* **253**:4886.

41. Cidlowski, J. A. and J. W. Thanassi. 1979. *Biochem.* **18**:2378.

42. Coates, M. E. 1968. In *The Vitamins*. Academic Press, N.Y.

43. Gregory, J. F., III and J. R. Kirk. 1981. *Nutr. Rev.* **39**:1.

44. Gregory, J. F., III. 1980. *J. Nutr.* **110**:995.

45. Underwood, E. J. 1975. *Nutr. Rev.* **33**:65.

46. Shabe, B. and E. L. R. Stokstad. 1985. *Ann. Rev. Nutr.* **5**:115.

47. Rickes, E. L., et al. 1948. *Science* **107**:396.

48. Smith, E. L. and L. E. J. Parker. 1948. *Biochem. J.* **43**:viii.

49. Stokstad, E. L. R. 1976. Ch. 20 in *Present Knowledge in Nutrition*, 4th ed., p. 204. The Nutrition Foundation Inc., N.Y.

50. Reisner, E. H. 1968. In *The Vitamins*. Academic Press, N.Y.

51. Albert, M. J., V. I. Mathan, and S. J. Baker. 1980. *Nature* **283**:781.

52. Underwood, E. J. 1977. *Trace Elements in Human and Animal Nutrition*. Academic Press, N.Y.

53. Church, D.C. (ed.). 1979. *Digestive Physiology and Nutrition of Ruminants*, Vol. 2—Nutrition. 2nd ed. O & B Books, Inc. Corvallis, OR.

54. Higginbottom, M. C., L. Sweetman, and W. L. Nyhan. 1978. *New Eng. J. Med.* **299**:317.

55. Sweetman, L. and W. L. Nyhan. 1986. *Ann. Rev. Nutr.* **6**:317.

56. Gyorgy, P. and B. W. Langer. 1968. In *The Vitamins*, Vol. II, 2nd ed. Academic Press, N.Y.

57. Mock, D. M., et al. 1981. *New Eng. J. Med.* **304**:820.

58. Cunha, T. J. 1971. *Feedstuffs* **43**(9):20.

59. Kuksis, A. and S. Mookerjea. 1978. *Nutr. Rev.* **36**:201.

60. Englard, S. and S. Seifter. 1986. *Ann. Rev. Nutr.* **6**:365.

61. Mapson, L. W. 1967. In *The Vitamins*, Vol. I. Academic Press, N.Y.

62. Barnes, M. J. and E. Kodicek. 1972. *Vitamins and Hormones* **30**:1.

63. Cromwell, G. L., V. W. Hays, and J. R. Overfield. 1970. *J. Animal Sci.* **31**:63.

64. Yen, J. T. and W. G. Pond. 1981. *J. Animal Sci.* **53**:1292.

65. Pauling, L. 1971. *Vitamin C and the Common Cold.* W. H. Freeman and Co., San Francisco.

66. Sorensen, D. I., M. M. Devine, and J. M. Rivers. 1974. *J. Nutr.* **104**:1041.

67. Holub, B. J. 1986. *Ann. Rev. Nutr.* **6**:563.

68. Alam, S. Q. 1971. In *The Vitamins*, Vol. III. 2nd ed. Academic Press, N.Y.

69. Cunha, T. J. 1971. In *The Vitamins*, Vol. III, 2nd ed. Academic Press, N.Y.

70. Milhorat, A. T. 1971. In *The Vitamins*, Vol. III, 2nd ed. Academic Press, N.Y.

71. Levander, O. A. and L. Cheng. 1980. Micronutrient Interactions: Vitamins, Minerals and Hazardous Elements. *Ann. N.Y. Acad. Sci.* **355**:1–372.

16

Non-Nutritive Feed Additives and Growth Stimulators

FEED ADDITIVES ARE DEFINED as feed ingredients of a non-nutritive nature that stimulate growth or other types of performance (such as egg production), improve the efficiency of feed utilization, or may be beneficial to the health or metabolism of the animal. Many of the compounds listed as feed additives would be classified as drugs (a substance used as a medicine). Of the commonly used feed additives, many are antimicrobial agents—compounds that include antibiotics, antibacterial agents, and antifungal agents. Hormone-like substances may also be included. Growth stimulators may be feed additives, but may also include such things as some hormones or hormone-like chemicals that may be administered subcutaneously or intramuscularly rather than orally.

Feed additives are used extensively in the USA, although perhaps less so than in the 1950s and 1960s. There is a trend toward reduced utilization because of pressure from various groups that believe usage of antibiotics, in particular in animal feeds, may be detrimental to humans, although current evidence does not indicate such a problem (1).

❑ FEED LABELING AND MEDICATED FEED

Current estimates are that 80–85% of manufactured feeds are medicated and that about 80% of the eggs and meat consumed in the USA come from animals fed medicated feed at one time or other during their lifetimes. In the USA all commercially produced feeds must be registered at the state level and be labeled; unfortunately labeling requirements are not standard throughout the country. In any case, if the feed contains any additive not on the GRAS (generally recognized as safe) list, the feed is under the control of the Food and Drug Administration. The FDA requires very extensive documentation on safety, efficacy, and tissue residues before it approves use of a new drug. When approved and put into use, any feed containing such a drug must contain appropriate labels (2) that contain the word medicated directly following and below the product name. The purpose of the medication must be stated, the names and amounts of the active ingredients must be listed, a warning statement (when required by the FDA) for a withdrawal period before slaughter for human food, conditions against misuse, and appropriate directions must be given for use of the feed. Custom-mixed feeds are subject to the same requirements.

Problems do arise with the use of medicated feeds from time to time. In addition to outright mistakes that may be made in the manufacturing process (of which several highly publicized cases have occurred), one of the big problems is inadvertent contamination in the feed mill when a non-medicated feed is mixed and processed in equipment following a batch of medicated feed. It is difficult to remove all traces of previous feed from the various pieces of equipment used in feed mills. Another common problem is the use of medicated feeds in combinations not approved for feeding to animals other than those on the approved list. These situations may develop as a result of requests by local veterinarians and/or nutritionists for a "special mix" of medicated feeds for their clients. If any of the parties knowingly produces and feeds an illegal mix, they are liable for legal action by the FDA.

❑ TYPES OF FEED ADDITIVES

Many different types of feed additives have been fed to domestic animals at one time or another, but many of them have not withstood the test of time and careful experimentation as well as of practical usage. Additives have come and gone as a result of such factors as cost, tissue residues, toxicity, or, what is more common, no beneficial response by the animal. The non-nutritive additives used as production improvers in the USA at the present time are the antibacterial agents—antibiotics, arsenicals, and nitrofurans—and hormones or hormone-like compounds intended to stimulate gain and improve feed efficiency in young, rapidly growing animals. With the primary exceptions of buffers, monensin, and lasalocid, mature animals do not respond with improved performance.

Additives listed in Table 16.1 are only those for which the manufacturer claims improved growth or feed efficiency—with the exception of Tylosin, which is fed to beef cattle to control abscessed livers in the feedlot. There are many other additives of a more specific nature that may find usage in special situations, such as control of internal and external parasites, insect pests, and those used for a wide variety of infectious diseases. The various additives classed as drugs and controlled by the FDA are listed in an industry publication, *The Feed Additive Compendium* (2). The current issue (1987) lists 55 different compounds as currently being approved. Information is taken from the *Federal Register* (3), a publication of Congress, which provides periodic updates on feed additives as well as many other things. There are 18 compounds listed in Table 16.1. Since the previous edition of this book, one antibiotic (lasalocid) has been added to this list, three antibiotics have been deleted (bacitracin, erythromycin, and oleandomycin), and one hormone-like product (thyroprotein) has been deleted.

In nearly all cases feed additives approved as production improvers are used at very low levels. For example, if we look in *The Feed Additive Compendium* for chlortetracycline use with swine, we find that its use is permitted at a level of 10–50 g/ton to promote growth and improve feed efficiency. At a level of 50–100 g/ton, it may be used for prevention of bacterial swine enteritis, to maintain weight gain in the presence of atrophic rhinitis, for reduction of the incidence of cervical abscesses, and to prevent bacterial swine enteritis during times of stress. At a level of 100–200 g/ton it is used for treatment of bacterial swine enteritis; at a level of 200 g/ton as an aid in reducing spread of leptospirosis (when fed as the sole medication); at a level of 400 g/ton as an aid in reducing shedding of leptospirae; as an aid in reducing the abortion rate of swine and the mortality rate of newborn pigs when leptospirosis is present.

Most drugs are approved for more than one use level, but the higher levels are in most cases for the control of some type of disease or parasite. In addition, these approved drugs can be used for many other purposes than to improve production, such as prevention or treatment of coccidiosis in poultry, swine, sheep, and cattle. Other uses include the treatment of chronic respiratory disease in poultry, infectious sinusitis and non-specific infectious enteritis (blue comb) in poultry, control of swine dysentery, reduction in number of liver condemnations due to abscesses in cattle, diarrhea in a number of species, stomach and/or intestinal worms in a number of species, blackhead in turkeys, breast blisters in broilers, fowl cholera, fowl typhoid, paratyphoid and pullorum in chickens, bloat in cattle, fly control in cattle, and so on.

It should be noted that quite a few of these drugs may be used in combination with other controlled products. The various listings are too detailed to give here, but the reader should be aware that it is illegal to use any combination of controlled drugs that has not been approved by the FDA.

Note (Table 16.1) that very few additives have been approved for horses, rabbits, sheep, and ducks. The primary reason for this is the cost in relation to potential sales volume. The approval procedure must be done with each species. Thus, if projected sales do not indicate sufficient volume to justify the cost, no approval will be requested. This is especially true for drugs that are approved for use with cattle, but might be effective for sheep and goats. Quite often some of the research will be done with sheep and later with cattle, but very seldom is the drug put up for approval for sheep. Fortunately, rulings by the FDA on minor species may help to rectify this problem.

❑ ANTIMICROBIAL DRUGS

Antibiotics are compounds produced by one microorganism that inhibit the growth of another organism; they are the most widely used of the antimicrobial drugs. A list of those in common use in the USA as feed additives for domestic species is shown in Table 16.1. Chlortetracycline, oxytetracycline, penicillin, and bacitracin zinc have enjoyed wider usage than

most of the other antibiotics, although there are many others and new antibiotics are continually being isolated and studied. Usage of penicillin is greatly restricted now, and the approved usage of various sulfa drugs (not antibiotics) also is very limited. Arsenicals and nitrofurans are used primarily for poultry and swine. When used as growth promotants, these various additives are added to feed at low levels. Therapeutic levels (for treating disease) normally are considerably higher.

Antibiotics are still in use, where allowed by law, because they usually give a response in terms of growth, improved feed efficiency, and, generally, improved health. The response in growth and improved feed efficiency is apt to be variable among animal species, and from time to time and place to place. For example, there is little or no response in new animal facilities, in very clean surroundings, or in germ-free animals raised under aseptic conditions. The response that may be expected in young pigs is shown in Table 16.2 and that for growing and fattening cattle in Table 16.3. Improvements have been shown of 15–16% in daily weight gain and 6.5–6.9% in feed efficiency in weanling pigs fed antibiotics in studies completed between 1950 and 1977 (5) and between 1978 and 1985 (6). Corresponding improvements in growing-finishing pigs during both time intervals were 3.6–4% for gain and 2.1–2.4% for feed efficiency.

Evidence indicates that most growing antibiotic-fed animals eat more than control animals receiving the same diet without antibiotics. Thus, this may largely account for the improved growth and efficiency. When animals are given the same amount of food with and without antibiotics, those fed antibiotics have usually not gained any faster. Evidence does indicate that antibiotics may have a sparing effect on dietary needs for some amino acids and B-complex vitamins in young chicks, pigs or rats, the beneficial response being greater when diets contain submarginal or minimal levels of those nutrients.

It has been suggested that this nutrient-sparing effect may be a result of (a) stimulation of microorganisms of the GI tract which favor nutrient synthesis, (b) suppression of organisms which compete for critical nutrients, or (c) improved nutrient absorption from the GI tract as a result of thinner, healthier intestinal walls seen in antibiotic-fed animals. Another possibility is that growth may be enhanced as a result of stimulation of various enzyme

TABLE 16.1   Some feed additives commonly used for improving animal performance in the USA.

NAME[a]	APPROVED FOR USE WITH	APPROVED DOSE LEVEL[b]	
		G/TON OF FEED	OTHER MEASURE OF DOSE
Arsanilic acid or	poultry	90	0.01%
Na arsanilate	swine	45–90	0.005–0.01%
Bacitracin methylene	poultry	4–50	
disalicylate*	laying chickens	10–25	
	swine	10–30	
Bacitracin zinc*	poultry	4–50	
	swine	20–40	
	cattle		
			35–70 mg/head/day
Bambermycins*	broilers, growing turkeys	1–2	
	swine	2–4	
Carbadox	swine	10–25	
Chlortetracycline*	poultry	10–50	
(Aureomycin)	calves		25–70 mg/head/day or 0.1 mg/ lb BW/day
	feedlot cattle		70 mg/head/day
	dairy cows		70 mg/head/day
	lambs	20–50	
	horses		85 mg/head/day
	swine	10–50	
Dichlorvos	swine	334–500	
Furazolidone	poultry	7.5–10	
	baby pigs	100–200	
	sows	150	
Ipronidazole	turkeys		0.00625% of diet
Lasalocid*	cattle	10–30	or 100–360 mg/head/day
	cattle on pasture		60–200 mg/head/day
Lincomycin*	broilers	2–4	
Melengestrol acetate	beef heifers		0.25–0.50 mg/head/day
Monensin*	cattle	5–30	or 50–360 mg/head/day
	cattle on pasture		24–400 g/ton of supplement
Oxytetracycline*	growing chicks		
(Terramycin)	and turkeys	5–7.5	
	laying chickens	10–100	
	laying turkeys	10–100	
	swine, 10–30 lb	25–50	
	30–200lb	7.5–10	
	calf starters and		
	milk replacers		0.5–5.0 mg/lb body weight/day
	calves	25–75	
	feedlot cattle		75 mg/hd/day
	beef cattle		75 mg/hd/day
	dairy cattle	75	
	sheep	10–20	
	rabbits	10	

TABLE 16.1 (*Continued*).

NAME[a]	APPROVED FOR USE WITH	APPROVED DOSE LEVEL[b]	
		G/TON OF FEED	OTHER MEASURE OF DOSE
Penicillin*	chickens, turkeys	2.4–50	
	swine	10–50	
Roxarsone	chickens		0.0025–0.005% of diet
	turkeys	22.7–45.4	
	swine		0.0025–0.00375% of diet
Tylosin*	growing chicks	4–50	
	laying chickens	20–50	
	swine		
	starter feeds	20–100	
	grower feeds	20–40	
	finisher feeds	10–20	
	beef cattle	8–10	
Virginiamycin*	broilers	5–15	
	swine	5–10	

[a]Many of these drugs are approved for use with other drugs or at higher levels for disease control.
[b]For up-to-date approvals, see Anon. (2).
*Antibiotics

systems. It also has been suggested that antibiotics improve performance by their antiurease action which results in reduced ammonia production in the GI tract. Ammonia is toxic to cells and may increase cell turnover in the GI tract epithelium. A third effect proposed is that of disease control, particularly control of organisms causing subclinical or non-specific diseases; this seems a likely factor because healthy animals respond very little to antibiotics. Note the response of runt pigs shown in Table 16.2.

In addition to some expected improvement in gain and feed efficiency, the feeding of antimicrobial drugs usually will reduce the incidence of diarrhea expected in young animals, especially in young mammals deprived of colostrum. Animals fed the drugs are also less prone to go off feed, and enterotoxemia and death loss are less apt to occur in lambs fed high-grain rations. In beef cattle the incidence of abscessed livers is usually greatly reduced in antibiotic-fed cattle on high-grain rations.

TABLE 16.2 Effects of antibiotics on growth and feed efficiency in pigs of different weights[a]

INITIAL WT, KG	NO. OF EXPERIMENTS	GROWTH RESPONSE, %	FEED UTILIZATION RESPONSE, %
<11.4	13	19.6	4.1
11.4–13.6	37	15.6	0.9
13.7–15.9	41	15.0	2.6
16.0–18.2	34	14.3	7.8
18.3–22.7	44	10.5	4.2
>22.7	46	8.7	4.1
Runt pigs	12	82 (30–154)	11 (4–23)

[a]From Wallace (4); a variety of antibiotics were used in these experiments.

TABLE 16.3   Effect of low-level feeding of antibiotics to beef cattle.[a]

ITEM	GROWING-WINTERING		FINISHING	
	CONTROL	ANTIBIOTIC[b]	CONTROL	ANTIBIOTIC[b]
Daily gain, kg	0.56	0.61	1.16	1.24
Feed/unit gain	12.70	12.02	9.85	9.37
Number of animals	5352		2354	
Av. initial wt, kg	228		310	
Av. days on trial	112		117	
Gain response, %	8.9		6.7	
Feed conversion response, %	5.4		4.9	

[a]From Wallace (4).

[b]Continuous low level at about 70/mg/head/day. Antibiotics involved were chlortetracycline, oxytetracycline, and bacitracin.

Ionophore Antibiotics

Only two antibiotics have been approved for use with beef cattle in recent years. These are monensin and lasalocid, two of several antibiotics produced by various strains of *Streptomyces* bacteria. They are referred to as polyether ionophore antibiotics because these compounds interfere with passage of ions through various membranes. A great deal of literature has been generated on these products (7). Initially, they were approved for use with poultry as cocciodiostats; later, it was learned that they were effective production improvers for cattle as well as cocciodiostats for cattle and sheep.

These two compounds have a number of general effects. Although the effects of monensin and lasalocid are not identical, in general they both cause a shift in rumen volatile fatty acids to relatively more propionic acid accompanied by less loss of energy as methane, resulting in more efficient gain of growing animals or, what is unusual, increased weight gain of mature animals. The exact reason for the improved efficiency remains speculative, but it appears to be related to reduction in rumen degradation of protein and an increase in post-ruminal digestion of starch. Energy losses in feces and urine are reduced in most instances. Monensin, but apparently not lasalocid, has been shown to be effective as an inhibitor of rumen bloat, possibly because it acts to control protozoal growth. Monensin has also been shown to result in a reduced retention of Na and an increased retention of K in lambs (8), and one paper suggests

that it will prevent the development of ruminal parakeratosis, a problem that sometimes appears in animals fed high-grain or pelleted diets.

Examples of some experimental data on these two antibiotics are given in Table 16.4. Note that monensin results in a reduction in feed consumption, little effect on gain in feedlot cattle and an improvement in feed efficiency (feed:gain). There also appears to be a slight additive effect when fed to animals given implants of growth promotants, such as (in this case) Ralgro and Synovex. On pasture, monensin generally results in increased liveweight gain. When research has been done with cattle on forage rations fed in confinement, feed intake may stay the same or be reduced and liveweight gain may usually be increased slightly.

Data shown for lasalocid indicate essentially the same response with feedlot cattle as for monensin. In most instances, it appears likely that either product could be substituted for the other.

General Comments on Antibiotics

Some comment on continued use of antibacterial drugs in animal feeds is required at this point. Individuals and organizations that object to the continuous use of low levels in animal feeds do so on the basis that resistant pathogenic strains of microorganisms might develop which could be harmful to humans. In the USA, antibiotics have been widely used for about 30 years as feed additives. While it is true that microbial resistance to antibiotics was shown from the first (indeed some microorganisms may come to require an antibiotic), no convincing, documented instance has been shown where more virulent pathogens have been isolated as a result of feeding low levels of antibiotics to animals (1). As a matter of fact, the evidence shows that resistant strains are nearly always less virulent (11, 12). Those who object to antibiotic feeding ignore the considerable amount of favorable evidence for antibiotics and the experience and advice of respected scientists (1). Although it is true that antibiotics and other drugs are sometimes used in lieu of good management practices, the beneficial response to antibiotics in livestock enterprises attests to the assertion that the cost in productivity in animal agriculture in the USA would be considerable if routine use of antibiotics were not allowed. The ratio of benefit:risk, a common measure used to evaluate drugs, is greatly in favor of continued use of antibiotics.

❏ HORMONES

Many different hormones have been fed or injected into animals at one time or another with the intent of increasing growth or milk production or to modify the normal fattening processes. This list includes growth hormone, natural or synthetic adrenal cortical hormones, natural and synthetic estrogens, androgens, progestogens, androgen-estrogen combinations, thyroid and antithyroid compounds.

At one time, diethylstilbestrol (DES) was widely used as either an oral feed additive or as a subcutaneous implant for cattle or as an implant for sheep, but its use is allowed no longer in the USA because of potential residue problems. With swine, hormones have not shown any consistent benefit. For practical usage with calves and feedlot cattle, compounds of interest would include hexestrol, synthetic estrogen used outside the USA; melengestrol acetate, a synthetic progestogen used orally for heifers; zeranol

TABLE 16.4 Effect of monensin and lasalocid on performance of cattle.

	MEASURE OF PERFORMANCE		
TREATMENT	FEED CONSUMED, KG/DAY	DAILY GAIN, KG/DAY	FEED TO GAIN RATIO
Feedlot cattle[a]			
Controls	8.27	1.09	8.09
Monensin	7.73	1.10	7.43
Controls	8.89	1.14	8.01
Monensin	8.65	1.18	7.43
Implant	9.61	1.28	7.63
Monensin + implant	8.97	1.32	6.85
Pasture cattle[a]			
Controls		0.61	
Monensin		0.69	
Feedlot cattle[b]			
Control	8.68	0.99	8.75
Lasalocid, 30 g/ton	8.27	1.02	8.09
Lasalocid, 45 g/ton	8.09	1.04	7.79
Monensin, 30 g/ton	8.09	1.03	7.93

[a]Data excerpted from a review (9) that is a compilation of many different experiments done in many different places.
[b]Data from Berger *et al.* (10) from cattle (48/treatment) fed a 60% high-moisture corn, 30% corn silage diet (dry basis).

(Ralgro®), said to be an anabolic agent, which is implanted; Synovex, a combination of estrogen and progesterone, used as an implant; Rapid Gain®, a combination of testosterone and estrogen, used as an implant; and Steer-oid®, a combination of progesterone and estradiol used as an implant. Most of these products also appear to work well for feedlot lambs, although much lower dosages are required.

In ruminants the various natural or synthetic hormones appear to produce a response which results from increased N retention accompanied by an increased intake of feed. The result is, usually, an increased growth rate, an improvement in feed efficiency and, frequently, a reduced deposition of body fat which may, at times, result in a lower carcass grade for animals fed to the same weight as nontreated animals.

Currently, there is a considerable amount of research interest in the use of intramuscular injections of growth hormone for lactating cows. Proper dosage will stimulate increased feed consumption and milk production. It is not an approved drug for use at the time this was written (Winter, 1987).

Thyroid-active hormones have been used from time to time, particularly with cattle. It has been demonstrated amply that thyroprotein or iodinated casein, which produces the same physiological response, may be used over short periods of time to stimulate milk production, particularly when cows are past their peak of production. Continued use during the remainder of a normal lactation is not apt to result in any improvement in milk production, and withdrawal will result in a prompt decrease in milk production. Thus, there is little current interest in use of such products and they are no longer approved for use with lactating dairy cows. No beneficial response is likely in growing and fattening animals. Antithyroid compounds also have been used on the assumption that a decrease in thyroid activity might be beneficial in the fattening process. Some studies have shown favorable response, particularly with respect to improved feed efficiency, but others have not and there is no current interest (or approved use) in such feeding products.

❑ OTHER FEED ADDITIVES

β-Adrenergic Agonists

Recently there has been active interest in the possibility of using orally effective synthetic β-adrener-

gic agonists (β-agonists) as a means of repartitioning nutrients to favor lean meat and reduce fat deposition. These compounds are catecholamine derivitives that have some pharmacological properties similar to those of epinephrine. The basis for the physiological effect appears to be the action of β-agonists on β-adrenergic receptors located on cell membranes to effect stimulation of cyclic adenosine monophosphate (AMP) production within the cell (13). The mechanism by which this response alters lipid metabolism in adipose tissue and decreases protein turnover in skeletal muscle is still unclear, but data reported from work with lambs, steers, chicks, and swine all show improvements in carcass leanness of animals fed the agents (14). Two such agents are clenbuterol and cimaterol, both similar in structure to epinephrine. The total impact of this family of compounds on the livestock industry as a means of improving efficiency of lean meat production will depend on economic and biological factors not yet completely ascertained and on the regulatory obstacles to their clearance for use in food animal production.

Zeolites

Zeolites are crystalline, hydrated aluminosilicates of alkali and alkaline earth cations that possess infinite three-dimensional structures. They are able to gain and lose water reversibly and to exchange some of their constituent cations without a major change in structure (15). There are some 50 species of natural zeolites present in sedimentary deposits of volcanic origin around the world (16). Clinoptilolite is probably most abundant in nature and has received attention in animal nutrition because of its cation-binding properties (17). Research from Japan, USSR, Czechoslovakia, USA, and other countries provides evidence for improved body weight gain and efficiency of feed utilization of ruminant and non-ruminant animals fed diets supplemented with 1–5% clinoptilolite. The physiologic basis for the observed responses are unknown, but probably are related to the ammonia and other cation-binding capacities of clinoptilolite. Clinoptilolite protects rats, pigs, and sheep against acute ammonia toxicity and against the toxic effects of Cd and Pb. The positive growth response is not obtained consistently; the variable response may be associated with differences in purity, particle size, or physico-chemical variation in the raw ore. The ultimate usefulness of these natural mineral ores as feed additives for livestock production will be determined by the success of researchers and livestock producers in identifying the conditions under which positive responses to supplementation are obtained.

Miscellaneous Additives

A variety of feed additives is used from time to time for specific purposes which may or may not be related to stimulation of growth or other forms of production. For example, activated carbon has shown some promise for reducing absorption of certain pesticides that may be contaminants in the diet. A variety of anthelmintics are used routinely as medicinals for control of stomach and intestinal worms. Antioxidants have some value in reducing oxidation of nutrients such as vitamin E and unsaturated fats with the result that dietary requirements of vitamin A and E may be reduced. Sodium bentonite, a clay, is used as a pellet binder and shows some promise of improving N utilization in ruminants. A variety of surface-active compounds are used for prevention and treatment of bloat in ruminants. Various buffers such as $NaHCO_3$ aid in the prevention of indigestion following sudden ration changes in ruminants and may help to relieve the low-fat milk problem in dairy cows. Other buffers are useful in prevention and treatment of urinary calculi. Various feed flavors are used in different animal rations, although published research data are not overly encouraging, but suggest that the effect is mainly on preference when a choice of rations is given rather than on total feed consumption. Enzymes have been tried extensively for chicks, pigs, and ruminants, but results generally have not been encouraging. Organic iodides have value for prevention of foot rot in cattle. Drugs that inhibit methane production may have some potential for ruminants if non-toxic ones can be developed. Live yeast cultures and dried rumen cultures sometimes are promoted, but with little factual evidence of their worth.

❏ SUMMARY

Feed additives have very important functions in modern day diets. The various antibiotics or antimicrobials allow more rapid growth and/or more efficient performance because of control of subclinical disease. Hormones or hormone-like compounds may be quite effective in stimulating more rapid gain or other changes in productivity. A host of other additives are used commonly for very specific purposes ranging from pellet binders to control of specific parasites.

❏ REFERENCES

1. Various authors. 1986. Public Health Implications of the Use of Antibiotics in Animal Agriculture. *J. Animal Sci.* **62** (Suppl. 3):1–106.
2. Anonymous. 1987. *Feed Additive Compendium.* Miller Pub. Co., Minnetonka, MN, and The Animal Health Institute, Alexandria, VA.
3. Federal Register. Superintendent of Documents. Government Printing Office, Washington, D.C.
4. Wallace, H. D. 1970. *J. Animal Sci.* **31**:1118.
5. Hays, V. W. 1979. In *Drugs in Livestock Feed*, Vol. I, pp. 29–36. Tech. Rep. Office of Technology Assessment, Congress of the United States, Washington, D. C.
6. Zimmerman, D. R. 1986. *J. Animal Sci.* **62** (Suppl. 3):6.
7. Various authors. 1984. Symposium on Monensin in Cattle. *J. Animal Sci.* **58**:1461–1539.
8. Kirk, D. J., L. W. Greene, G. T. Schelling, and F. M. Byers. 1985. *J. Animal Sci.* **60**:1479.
9. Goodrich, R. D., et al. 1984. *J. Animal Sci.* **58**:1484.
10. Berger, L. L., S. C. Ricke, and G. C. Fahey, Jr. 1981. *J. Animal Sci.* **53**:1440.
11. Hirsch, D. C. and N. Wiger. 1978. *J. Animal Sci.* **31**:1102.
12. Kiser, J. S. 1976. *J. Animal Sci.* **42**:1058.
13. Fain, J. N. and J. A. Garcia-Sainz. 1983. *J. Lipid Res.* **24**:945.
14. Dalyrmple, R. H., P. K. Baker, and C. A. Riche. 1984. Proc. Georgia Nutr. Conf., Univ. of Georgia, Athens, GA. p. 111.
15. Sheppard, R. A. 1984. In *Zeo Agriculture—Use of Natural Zeolites in Agriculture and Aquaculture*, p. 31. W. G. Pond and F. A. Mumpton (eds.). Westview Press, Boulder, CO.

17

Factors Affecting Nutrient Intake, Requirements, Utilization, and Nutritional Status

THERE ARE MANY DIFFERENT factors which affect nutrient requirements of animals and/or the extent of nutrient utilization. Some of these have been mentioned in earlier chapters and others will be discussed in this chapter. The intent here is to point out some of these factors; no effort will be made to provide a detailed discussion on the various topics.

❏ GENETIC FACTORS

Genetics probably plays a more important role in nutrient utilization than many readers realize. As a matter of fact, more than 270 "inborn errors of metabolism" are recognized in humans, many of which are controlled genetically, but only about 30 of them can be treated by dietary modifications (1). Only a few situations in animals are known in which genetic differences result in higher or lower nutrient requirements for specific situations. These include a strain of cattle that have a high Zn requirement, mice known to have high requirements for some B-vitamins, and sheep that require larger amounts of Fe. Such conditions are controlled by qualitative genes.

Marked improvement has occurred in recent decades in several domestic animal species in growth rates and efficiency of nutrient utilization. Such changes are the result of increasing gene frequency (caused by selection) of groups of genes that produce a quantitative response, although the overall heritability of such improvement is not exceedingly high. Such genetic improvement may not, necessarily, be a result of a change in nutrient utilization so much as in overall improvement in animal health, resistance to stress and disease, or in greater adaptation to a particular type of environment. Nevertheless, the net result is an improvement in animal productivity. An example with swine is shown in Table 17.1. Note the considerable improvement in rate and efficiency of gain

TABLE 17.1 Effect of genetic improvement on swine growth and efficiency. Data are from a test station at Ames, IA.

ITEM	YEAR 1956	1976	CHANGE, %
Data on boars			
Daily gain, lb	1.89	2.13	12.7
Feed efficiency[a]	0.338	0.394	16.6
Backfat, in.	1.46	0.79	−45.9
Carcass data on barrows[b]			
Backfat, in.	1.64	1.24	−24.3
Loineye area, in.²	3.22	5.20	61.5
Ham + loin, % of carcass	32.3	34.2	5.9

[a]Expressed as lb gain/lb feed consumed.
[b]Barrow slaughter weight was increased from 200 to 220 lb between these dates; this would tend to increase backfat thickness and loineye area.

accompanied by a reduction in backfat in boars, and the reduction in backfat and increased size of the loineye area and increased proportion of ham + loin in barrows. Similar and probably more marked changes have occurred in poultry which have been made possible by greater selection pressures in species which produce many offspring per year. Such changes can be produced in cattle and sheep, but genetic progress is much slower because of the lesser opportunity for selection pressure.

❏ NUTRITIONAL INDIVIDUALITY

An important concept the reader should appreciate is that not all similar animals respond in an identical manner to a given diet (or other environmental conditions). Examples have been shown in previous chapters of differences in responses of animals in digestibility, growth rates, taste responses, and so on. Although such individual responses have been known to occur for many, many years, good explanations for the differences are only rarely forthcoming. Such variations have been documented in laboratory animals and humans by Williams (2–4). These examples show clearly that a wide range in requirements for a variety of different nutrients may be expected at times, even in related animals from closely inbred strains of laboratory rats. Obviously, this variability in nutrient utilization presents great problems in the field of human nutrition, requiring the development and dissemination of needed information on this subject and more training in nutrition of people in the medical field. With domestic animals, except for some pets, the common practice would be to cull animals that do not perform adequately, whether the cause be an excessive requirement for nutrients or for other reasons. The incidence of occurrence of domestic animals with very high (or low) nutrient requirements is documented inadequately at this time, but it is a subject that is certainly worthy of further study.

❏ VEGETARIAN DIETS

A growing number of North Americans consume diets devoid of or very low in animal products in response to ethnic, religious, and social beliefs. It should be pointed out that there are several types of so-called vegetarian diets. A strict vegetarian is one who eats foods of plant origin exclusively. A lactovegetarian

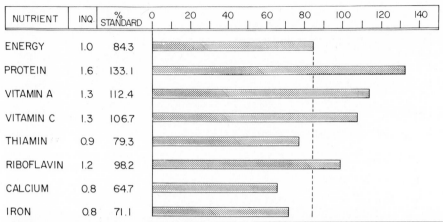

Figure 17.1 *Aggregate of food consumed in the United States as determined by the 1965–66
household consumption survey using the USDA basic four education system. The remaining 15%
of kilocalories were contributed by sugar, fats, oils, carbonated beverages, and alcohol. The
results were analyzed using nutrient density with U.S. RDA's and 2,100 Kcal as standards.
From Hanson and Wyse (10).*

consumes milk and milk products in addition to plant products, an ovovegetarian consumes eggs in addition to plant products, and a lactoovovegetarian consumes both milk products and eggs in addition to plant products.

The nutritional wisdom of these drastic changes from the dietary norm in the USA can be argued both pro and con. Major segments of the human population of the world survive and reproduce while consuming foods almost exclusively of plant origin. However, the nutritional deficiencies that may result are receiving increased attention. For example, vegetarian

children less than two years of age have retarded height and weight which, although it may be reversed later, may be associated with anemia, rickets, and failure to thrive (5). Furthermore, vitamin B_{12} deficiency has been reported in breast-fed infants of strict vegetarians (6), and formation of cataracts in humans and animals have been implicated with suboptimal intakes of nutrients likely to be low in plant foodstuffs (7).

On the other hand, chronic degenerative diseases including cancer of the colon and cardiovascular disease may be less likely in vegetarians. The higher

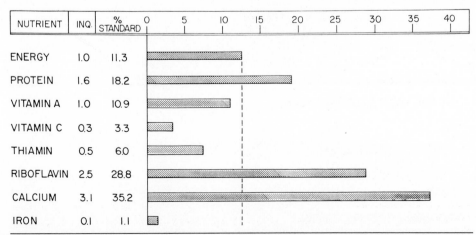

Figure 17.2 *The average contribution to the daily nutritional needs of milk and milk products
as consumed. From Hanson and Wyse (10).*

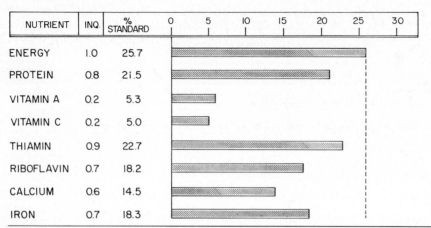

Figure 17.3   *The average of contribution to the daily nutritional needs of bread and cereal products as consumed. From Hanson and Wyse (10).*

incidence of colon cancer in populations who consume diets high in animal products than in those consuming higher cereal diets may be related to the higher fiber content of cereal diets or to their lower fat and/or protein content. The daily fecal excretion of bile acids and neutral sterols is lower in vegetarians, suggesting a metabolic basis for the difference (8). Plasma lipids are lower in vegetarians than in persons consuming a typical USA diet (9); elevated plasma lipids have been implicated in development of atherosclerosis and heart attacks in humans.

In the typical USA human diet of 2,100 Kcal, about 11% of the energy is derived from milk and milk products, 26% from breads and cereals, 36% from beef, pork, poultry, fish, and nuts and 12% from fruits and vegetables. The remaining 15% is from sugar, fats, oils, carbonated beverages, and alcohol (10). The percentages of the daily human requirement for energy, protein, Ca, Fe, and selected vitamins for this type of a diet are shown in Fig. 17.1. Protein, vitamin A, and vitamin C intakes are 133, 112, and 107% of the recommended intakes for persons consuming the typical diet, while thiamin, Ca, Fe, and riboflavin intakes are below recommended levels.

Figures 17.2–17.5 depict the percentage of recommended daily allowances (RDA) of each of the above nutrients contributed by milk and milk products, bread and cereal products, meat and meat substitutes, and fruits and vegetables, respectively, as

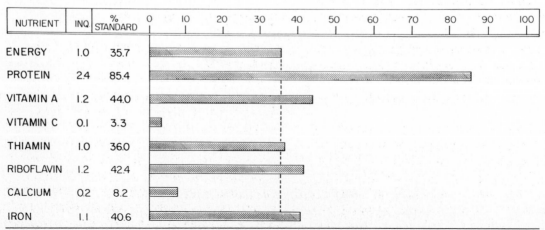

Figure 17.4   *The average contribution to the daily nutritional needs of meat and meat substitutes as consumed. From Hanson and Wyse (10).*

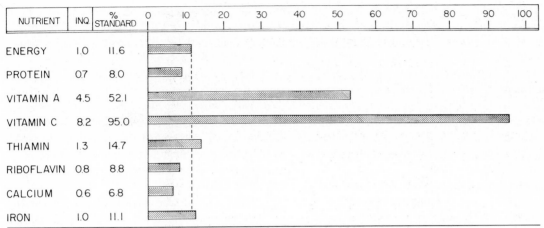

Figure 17.5 *The average contribution to the daily nutritional needs of fruits and vegetables as
consumed. From Hanson and Wyse (10).*

consumed. Milk products and meat together supply
more than 100% of the protein requirement, 70% of
the riboflavin requirement, 54% of the vitamin A
needs, and 42% of thiamin requirements. Milk products alone supply 35% of the Ca required and meat
alone provides 85, 44, 36, 42, and 41% of the protein,
vitamin A, thiamin, riboflavin, and Fe requirements,
respectively. In contrast, bread, cereal products,
fruits, and vegetables combined provide less than
30% of the protein requirement and 37, 27, 21, and
29% of the thiamin, riboflavin, Ca, and Fe requirements, respectively. These food groups do, however, supply more than 60% of the vitamin A requirement and 100% of the vitamin C.

Strict vegetarian diets fail to meet daily requirements for several critical nutrients unless there is
careful selection of foodstuffs and fortification with
Ca, Fe, and several B-vitamins. Although trace minerals are not considered in the data presented, plants
provide marginal amounts of several elements including I, Zn, and, in some locations, Se. Animal
products are not only generally higher in trace minerals, but provide them in more biologically available
forms.

The livestock and poultry industries depend heavily on plant feedstuffs to meet animal requirements
for growth, reproduction, and lactation. For example, a typical diet for growing pigs in the USA consists
of corn (or corn and cereal by-products), soybean
meal, and mineral and vitamin supplements. It has
been demonstrated amply that successful lifecycle
production can be achieved with all-plant diets. However, it is generally easier to meet the needs for

limiting amino acids in rapidly growing animals by
including animal products in the diet. In many instances it is a common practice to use synthetic
sources of lysine or methionine in formulas for broilers or young pigs. Vitamin B_{12} must be obtained
either from microbial sources (yeast, bacteria) or
animal tissues because it is not found in plant tissues.

The ability of a vegetarian diet to sustain life and
productive functions cannot be questioned. The prac-
ticality of providing optimum nutrition without using
animal products depends on careful foodstuff selection coupled with daily supplements of concentrated
sources of Ca, Fe, I, and selected vitamins and other
trace elements, often at a high economic cost.

❏ ORGANIC TOXINS IN FOODS

Many, many different poisonous plants are recognized, and relatively large numbers of animals are
affected by poisons each year. Poisoning in humans
is less apt to occur, but a sizeable number of cases
occur every year, also. Animals, in general, have the
ability to detect and reject many plants that may have
adverse effects on them. In many instances poisoning
occurs when food availability is reduced. However,
animals cannot always detect potentially toxic plants.
Two prime examples of potent toxins that animals
do not appear to detect are nitrates (often found in
toxic or lethal amounts in grass species fertilized
heavily with N or in drouth stunted plants) or prussic
acid (toxicity frequently occurs when sorghum spe-

cies have been stunted by drouth or the plants have been frosted).

In the case of human food, contamination of raw foods by toxic molds is a major cause of toxicity as it is with animals. The molds may be difficult to detect and toxins frequently are not inactivated by normal cooking methods. Many different problems resulting from ingestion of contaminated foods have been documented (11). In addition to this, growth of toxic bacteria in canned foods or fresh foods cause many cases of illness and some fatalities every year.

Many readers probably do not realize that a high percentage of food plants contain organic toxins of one type or another (11, 12). It is rather common knowledge that legume seeds contain inhibitors of one type or another, that *Brassica* species contain goitrogens, and that both may cause problems. However, many other common food plants may contain potent toxins. For example, carrots contain carotatoxin, myristicin, and estrogens; onions a mixture of toxic allyl di- and trisulfides; olives, tannins, and benzo(a)pyrene; potatoes, especially if exposed to sunlight, solanine. If a careful analysis is done with techniques which are quite sensitive, toxins can be identified in almost any food or feed. Fortunately, the toxins are in such low concentrations or the plants make up such a small proportion of the diet that no harm results from ingestion.

Many things are toxic. Several animal species are subject to water intoxication (which may be fatal) if enough water is consumed by a partially depleted animal. Except for some chemicals that may gradually accumulate in tissues, eventually reaching a concentration which is harmful, most toxic reactions are dose related; that is, increasing size of dose (amount ingested) is more apt to result in a toxic reaction or a more severe reaction. Fortunately, with a few exceptions, human food is quite safe.

❏ NUTRITION AND DISEASE

There is relatively little information relating the nutritional state of domestic animals to either prevention or treatment of infectious diseases. The general opinion seems to be that well-fed animals are more susceptible to viral infections than poorly fed animals, evidence having been cited on cattle to the effect that the incidence of hoof-and-mouth disease is greatest in well-fed cattle while the disease occurs in a mild form during periods of starvation (13). On the other hand, well-fed animals are said to be more

resistant to bacterial and parasitic infections. Note that for the most part the data on this topic are of an epidemiological nature rather than from research studies designed to bear on this problem.

In a number of research studies, protein deficiencies have resulted in an impaired immune response to bacteria, viruses and fungi (14). Likewise, vitamin deficiencies, particularly vitamin A, have been linked with increased susceptibility to infectious diseases. In dogs, experimental obesity has been reported to result in reduced resistance to both bacterial and viral infections (15).

Perhaps the relationship between nutrition and chronic disease is illustrated best by Fig. 17.6. In a disease like hemophilia, the genetic determinant accounts for 100% of the illness and no nutritional control is possible. With phenylketonuria, the affected person has a genetic deletion of the enzyme phenylalanine hydroxylase. Because it is involved in the synthesis of tyrosine, it is possible for dietary intervention to readjust phenylalanine-tyrosine ratios and effect some control of the disease. On the other end of the curve, scurvy is 100% controllable by nutrition, but diseases such as pellagra and rickets, although primarily nutritional, do have some genetic component.

❏ EVALUATING THE NUTRITIONAL STATUS OF AN ANIMAL

Now that the reader has had an opportunity to go through the preceding chapters dealing with the metabolism and deficiency symptoms of the various required nutrients, it is probably desirable to recap and condense some of the information relating to evaluation of the nutritional status of animals. By way of a review, Table 17.2 lists in brief form the primary deficiencies encountered for most of the required nutrients.

Nutritional deficiencies result in chronic problems, with few exceptions, and they may take days, weeks, or months to develop as contrasted to acute problems with some diseases or metabolic disturbances that may develop in hours or days. What is the best method to evaluate nutritional status? There is no simple answer to that question because the answer will depend upon the problem encountered, the species of animal involved, the level, stage, and type of production, complications with other deficiencies or excesses, stresses, and other unknown factors. Some

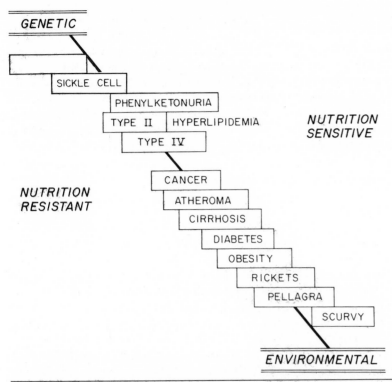

Figure 17.6 *The reciprocal genetic and environmental determinants of 13 diseases as shown on a linear scale. The extent to which nutritional intervention can modify the disease is indicated by the degree of displacement of each bar to the right of the line. Reproduced by permission of R. E. Olson (16).*

of the methods that are useful are discussed briefly in succeeding sections.

Animal Productivity

Human health workers normally base evaluation of growth on standard charts for weight and height at a given age by sex with some consideration for body type. With domestic animals, height at the withers, birth weights, weaning weights, or weights at other times are useful measures. Gain also may be expressed as weight per day of age or rate of gain during some particular period of rapid growth.

Nutrient deficiencies of any type will, sooner or later, result in some reduction in weight gain, although the specific cause may vary considerably from nutrient to nutrient. Young, rapidly growing animals will normally show deficiency symptoms in a much shorter period of time than older animals, partly because the tissue reserves are usually low and partly because the need for nutrients during rapid growth is quite high as compared to a mature animal. In fact,

as indicated in Table 17.2 and the various chapters on the nutrients, mature animals may be quite resistant to developing clinical symptoms of deficiencies of a number of the nutrients.

As with growth, other measures of productivity such as work (exercise), milk production, egg production, and so on, will often be affected by deficiencies. The deficiency may not be severe enough to produce any specific clinical signs, although a thorough biochemical evaluation might provide information needed to establish a biochemical lesion.

Reproducing animals often are affected by deficiencies that may result in such symptoms as thin-shelled eggs, low hatchability, embryonic death, and so forth in poultry or in delayed estrus, many unbred animals, resorption, abortions, birth of stillborn young, low birth weights, weak, unthrifty young, and so on, in mammalian species. Nutrient demands during reproduction and/or lactation are higher than for periods of near maintenance. Depending upon the nutrient involved, the dam (mother) will direct nutrients toward the fetus and sacrifice her body tissues in the

TABLE 17.2 Major nutritional deficiency symptoms.

NUTRIENT	CLINICAL SYMPTOMS[a]
Protein	Kwashiorkor or with low energy, marasmus, black hair turns red and is brittle (H); poor productivity, low fertility, birth of underweight young with poor livability, poor milk production, low blood albumin and/or blood urea, unkempt appearance.
Lysine	White barring of primary wing feathers (T).
Methionine	Fatty Liver (YS).
Other amino acids	No specific symptoms have been observed in farm animals.
Essential fatty acids	Poor growth (YC, YS, YCh), skin lesions (YC, YS).
Carbohydrates	No specific symptoms unless associated with low energy intake.
Energy	Low productivity, loss of body weight, stillborn young, poor or nil milk production, poor fertility. Usually associated with deficiencies of other nutrients such as protein and minerals such as P.
Water-soluble vitamins	
Thiamin	Beriberi, edema, heart failure (H); polynuritis (YCh); opistothonus, anorexia, high blood pyruvic acid; blindness (C).
Riboflavin	Facial dermatitis, insomnia, irritability (H); lesions of the eye, anorexia, vomiting, birth of weak or stillborn young (S); curled-toe paralysis (YCh); diarrhea, loss of hair (YC, YSh).
Niacin	Pellegra (H); diarrhea, vomiting, dermatitis around the eye (YCh), poor growth.
Pyridoxine	Convulsions, anorexia, poor growth, brown exudate around eyes (YS); abnormal feathering (YCh).
Pantothenic acid	Poor growth, graying of hair in some species; dermatitis, embryonic death (YCh); loss of hair, enteritis, goose-stepping, incoordination in walking (YS).
Biotin	Dermatitis, perosis (YCh, YT).
Choline	Perosis, fatty liver (YCh, YT); abnormal gait, reproductive failure in females, hemorrhagic kidneys, fatty liver (S).
Folacin	Anemia, gastrointestinal disturbances, impaired coordination (H); anemia in other species.
Cobalamin	Anemia, poor feathering, perosis (YCh); low hatchability, fatty livers, enlarged hearts (Ch, T); rough hair coats, incoordinated hind leg movements, anemia, abortion, other reproductive problems (S).
Vitamin C	No problems in domestic animals; scurvy (H).
Fat-soluble vitamins	
Vitamin A	Xeropthalmia, night blindness, permanent blindness (all species); diarrhea, convulsions, high cerebrospinal fluid pressures (Y); incoordination, reproductive failure in males, abortion or birth of weak or dead young (C).
Vitamin D	Rickets in young, osteomalacia in adults, lameness and sore joints, crooked legs, spontaneous fractures of long bones (Y); negative mineral balance, low bone ash (A).
Vitamin E	Nutritional muscular dystrophy (Y), fetal reabsorption, sterility, testicular atrophy (C, CH, T), liver necrosis (YS), fragile red blood cells (YS, YSh); encephalomalacia, exudative diathesis (YCh).
Vitamin K	Slow blood clotting; subcutaneous hemorrhages.
Macrominerals	
Calcium	Rickets, osteoporosis, poor growth; muscle cramps, convulsions (H).
Phosphorus	Rickets (Y), osteoporosis (A), anorexia, pica, low fertility.
Magnesium	Anorexia, poor productivity, tetany; weak crooked legs (S).
Potassium	Muscular weakness, paralysis (H); abnormal electrocardiograms, unsteady gait, weakness, pica.
Sodium	Anorexia, muscle cramps, mental apathy (H); dehydrated appearance, craving for salt, weight loss.
Chlorine	Depressed growth.
Sulfur	Reduced gain or loss of weight (C, Sh), loss of wool (Sh).

TABLE 17.2 (*Continued*).

NUTRIENT	CLINICAL SYMPTOMS[a]
Trace minerals	
Chromium	Impaired ability to metabolize glucose.
Cobalt	Primarily ruminants; symptoms similar to cobalamin; emaciation, anemia, fatty degeneration of the liver.
Copper	Anemia; when coupled with high Mo and/or sulfate, swayback or enzootic neonatal ataxia, loss of pigment in hair or wool (C, Sh); bone abnormalities, cardiovascular lesions, reduced egg production, reproductive failure.
Flourine	Excessive tooth decay (H).
Iron	Anemia and associated poor productivity; very common in young pigs.
Manganese	Lameness and shortening and bowing of the legs, enlarged joints (Y); perosis (YCh, T); reduced egg shell thickness (ACh, T); weakness, poor sense of balance; crooked calf disease (C); poor fertility (C).
Molybdenum	Reduced growth rates (not common).
Nickel	Prenatal mortality, unthriftiness, decreased growth rate (YCh, T, YS), poor N retention (YSh).
Selenium	Nutritional muscular dystrophy (Y), exudative diathesis (YCh, T); liver necrosis (YS); heart failure (YC); retained placenta (AC).
Zinc	Poor growth, anorexia, parakeratotic lesions on head, neck, belly and legs (C, Sh, S); perosis, abnormal feathering (YCh, T); poor testicular development, slow wound healing (H, other species).

[a]Y, young; A, adults; H, humans; C, cattle, Ch, chickens; S, swine; Sh, sheep; T, turkeys.

process. However, at some point before the deficiency becomes life threatening to the dam, usually she will interrupt a pregnancy by resorption or abortion or by production of small, unthrifty, young. Even if the fetus survives to birth, milk production, especially vital colostrum, may not be adequate to provide the necessary immunity or the milk supply may be insufficient to produce a normal rate of growth or the dam may cease lactation altogether not long after parturition if the deficiency is severe enough.

Nutritional History

If information is available on the type and amount of diet consumed by an animal, often such data can be used to establish a possible cause or to rule out other possibilities. Such information may be possible to obtain on animals fed in confinement, but it is often not available on free ranging animals. Nevertheless, some attempt should be made to provide background data any time that it can be obtained. Feed samples also should be obtained for possible future analyses. Information should be obtained on the eating habits such as amount consumed, frequency of eating, consumption of concentrates or roughages, and evidence of pica or other abnormal eating habits such as wood chewing.

Physical Examinations

Animals that do not feel well will not groom their hair or feathers as often (if at all) as do normal animals, the result being that the hair looks dry (no mucus from the saliva or, for feathers, oil from the oil gland in birds) and uncared for. Neither do they participate in mutual grooming as well animals might. Also, animals that get up after lying down, normally will stretch to relieve muscle strains whereas sick animals usually do not do this. Observation of ruminant animals will indicate if normal rumination is taking place during non-eating periods. If the animal moves about, evidence may be seen for some change in normal coordination of movement; a number of deficiencies result in lameness or some neurological interference with muscular movements. Nutrient deficiencies that cause dermatitis can be detected by visual examination of the skin, feathers, hair, or wool. Manifestations such as goose-stepping in swine from pantothenic acid deficiency, retracted head from thiamin deficiency, encephalomalacia in chicks from vitamin E deficiency, of polioencephalomalacia in ruminants from a metabolic deficiency of thiamin, are examples of deficiencies that can be detected readily by gross physical examinations. Other problems such as vitamin A deficiency may be detected by evidence of exophthalmia, excessive lacrimation or examination of the interior of the eye with an opthalmascope. Goiter is a clear cut indication of thyroid malfunction, although not necessarily of a simple iodine deficiency.

Tissue Analyses

Blood.   Data on blood may be useful in some instances, but not in all deficiencies (see Ch. 4). Low blood glucose and high plasma free fatty acids are correlated (although not highly) to inadequate energy consumption in cattle. Plasma albumen is correlated negatively to protein intake as is plasma urea. Blood mineral levels are not correlated highly to current consumption unless the body is grossly deficient because of the homeostatic mechanisms which attempt to maintain normal physiological levels of Ca, P, Mg, Na, and K. The same comments generally apply to the various trace minerals. Ceruloplasmin (Cu-containing enzyme) is useful for Cu, and circulating thyroid hormones may be used for iodine.

Hair.   Hair, of course, is an easy tissue to obtain from an animal. A fair number of studies have been done on animals, particularly cattle, indicating that hair is a reflection of past consumption of a number of the trace minerals, but it does not appear to be precise enough for common usage.

Bone.   Bone analyses—either individual minerals or total bone ash—can serve as a good means of evaluating the Ca-P status of an animal or a group of animals. Of course, bone samples are not so easily taken from a living animal as are blood or hair. X-ray films also can be used to evaluate density of bone, but the availability of the equipment and costs associated make it an expensive method, but one that might be used on highly valued animals.

Organ Tissues.   Liver and kidney tissues are storage sites for most of the trace minerals and a number of the vitamins. For experimental animals, data from these organs can be very useful in determining the body storage for such nutrients. Liver biopsy techniques are available for animals (and humans). Tissue samples (if large enough) can be subjected to histological or chemical evaluations.

Urine.   Although urine analyses are used extensively in human medicine and health work, they are not used routinely with domestic animals. The presence of ketones in urine in large amounts may be indicative of primary or secondary ketosis, especially in lactating cows or does. The presence of any appreciable quantity of Mg is indicative of an adequate level of consumption. In cases involving urinary calculi, urine samples may be informative. In the event that multichannel analyzers ever become available commonly in the animal field, probably more use will be made of urine samples. In the human field, analyses often are conducted on vitamins or their metabolites to evaluate the status for niacin, riboflavin, and thiamin. Urea, albumin, and creatine and/or creatinine are used to assess the protein status, iodine is useful for thyroid status, and glucose is normally included as an indicator of diabetes (17).

❏ SUMMARY

Many different factors may alter nutrient needs or utilization in animals fed a given diet. Genetic factors certainly are important as are unexplained differences in similar individuals. Disease and stress may alter nutrient metabolism, but our knowledge of this topic in domestic animals is quite deficient. Nutritional status of animals can be evaluated in many different ways. Clinical examinations, tissue analyses, digestive tract function, and others may be useful for specific nutrients, but different nutrients may require different procedures because of variations in tissue storage, metabolism, or excretion.

❏ REFERENCES

1. Wong, P. W. and D. Y. Hsia. 1973. In *Modern Nutrition in Health and Disease,* 5th ed. Lea & Febiger, Philadelphia, PA.

2. Williams, R. J. 1956. *Biochemical Individuality: The Basis for the Genetotrophic Concept.* John Wiley, NY.

3. Williams, R. J. 1971. *Nutrition Against Disease.* Pitman Pub. Corp., NY.

4. Williams, R. J. 1979. Nutritional Individuality. *J. Nutr. Acad.* **11**(11):8.

5. Anonymous. 1979. *Nutr. Rev.* **37**(4):108.

6. Anonymous. 1979. *Nutr. Rev.* **37**(5):142.

7. Bounce, G. E. 1979. *Nutr. Rev.* **37**(11):337.

8. Anonymous. 1975. *Nutr. Rev.* **33**(5):136.

9. Anonymous. 1975. *Nutr. Rev.* **33**(9):285.

10. Hanson, R. G. and B. W. Wyse. 1978. In *Plant and Animal Products in the U.S. Food System,* pp. 136–148. Nat. Acad. Sci., Washington, DC.

11. Mickelsen, O., M. G. Yang and R. S. Goodhart. 1973. In *Modern Nutrition in Health and Disease,* 5th ed. Lea & Febiger, Philadelphia, PA.

12. Hall, R. L. 1977. *Nutr. Today* **12**(6):6.

13. Church, D. C. (ed.). 1972. *Digestive Physiology and Nutrition of Ruminants,* Vol. 3. O & B Books, Inc., Corvallis, OR.

14. Wannemacher, R. W., Jr. 1980. *Feedstuffs* **52**(23):16.

15. Newberne, P. M., V. R. Young, and J. F. Gravlee. 1969. *Brit. J. Exp. Pathol.* **50:**172.

16. Olson, R. E. 1978. *Nutr. Today* **13**(4):18.

17. Barnes, L. A., et al. 1981. *Nutrition and Medical Practice.* AVI Pub. Co., Inc., Westport, CN.

PART 3

APPLIED ANIMAL NUTRITION

18

Feeding Standards and the Productive Functions

❏ INTRODUCTION

Feeding standards are statements or quantitative descriptions of the amounts of one or more nutrients needed by animals. Use of such standards dates back to the early 1800s. There has been a gradual development over the years to the point where nutrient requirements for farm animals may be specified with a high degree of accuracy, particularly for growing chicks and pigs; although there are still many situations where nutrient needs cannot be specified with great accuracy for animals, nutrient needs of most animals are far better understood than for man. This is due to the simple fact that people do not lend themselves to the type of experimentation needed to collect good quantitative data.

In the USA the most widely used standards are those published by the various committees of the National Research Council (NRC). These standards (see Appendix tables on nutrient requirements) are continually revised and reissued at intervals of a few years. In England the standards in use are developed by the Agricultural Research Council (ARC). Other countries have similar bodies which update information and make recommendations on animal nutrient requirements.

❑ TERMINOLOGY USED IN FEEDING STANDARDS

Feeding standards usually are expressed in quantities of nutrients required/day or as a percentage of a diet; the former being used for animals given exact quantities of a diet and the latter more commonly when rations are fed ad libitum. With respect to the various nutrients, most are expressed in weight units, as percentages or ppm. Some vitamins—A, D, E—are usually given in international units, although carotene may be given in mg and vitamin E in ppm. Protein requirements are most frequently given in terms of digestible protein (DP) or crude protein although amino acids could be substituted for protein in non-ruminant species when adequate information is at hand. Energy is expressed in a variety of different forms (see Ch. 10). The NRC uses ME for poultry, DE for swine and horses, DE, ME and TDN for sheep, ME, TDN and NE_m and NE_g for beef cattle and, for dairy cattle, values are given for DE, ME, TDN, NE_m and NE_g for growing animals with additional values as NE_l for lactating cows (see Appendix tables). The ARC uses ME almost exclusively and other European countries use ME in newly developed standards. Regardless of the units used, feeding standards are based on some estimate of animal needs and have been derived from data obtained from a great many experimental studies conducted under a wide variety of conditions with a diverse list of feedstuffs.

Some comments are in order regarding the use of NE_m and NE_g for beef cattle and growing dairy cattle and NE_l for lactating cows by the NRC publications. If one looks at the tables on feed composition in the respective publications, it is apparent that values are given in this energy terminology for almost all of the feedstuffs listed except for mineral supplements. The reader should be aware that most of these NE values have been calculated from older data that were given originally as TDN (in the USA) as there is a wealth of older data expressed in this form; some values also have been derived from DE and ME. Only a limited number of feedstuffs have been evaluated directly in terms of ME, NE_m, NE_g, or NE_l. However applicable these values may be for these respective classes of cattle, recalculating from existing data does not necessarily improve the original data.

As pointed out in Ch. 10, energy (for adult animals) is required in relation to body weight$^{0.75}$ rather than in direct proportion to body weight. All current feeding standards recognize this approach, although not all emphasize it in their descriptions. For the other nutrients, Crampton (1) suggested some time ago that energy should be used as the base value and that other nutrients should be specified in relation to the amount of available energy consumed. Crampton suggested that all animals have a requirement for maintenance of 19 g of digestible protein/100 Kcal of DE. Although this approach probably is applicable, it has not been used widely in calculating protein requirements except for poultry where calorie:protein ratios have been shown to have practical significance. Because most animals tend to eat to meet energy needs, if we go from a moderate energy concentration to a high energy concentration in the diet, feed consumption will decline; thus, more protein is needed per unit of diet, but the calorie:protein ratio may not change. However, with herbivores, DP is influenced markedly by dry matter intake. Thus, if DM intake is increased, DP declines as a result of abrasion in the lower GI tract, but DE intake may remain essentially unchanged. As a result, relationships between caloric intake and protein requirements are more obscure when a wide range of ration types is considered.

The NRC poultry committee did at one time express protein needs in relation to energy, but this approach is no longer used; in the other NRC publications, recommendations on protein needs are calculated on the basis of need/unit of $BW^{0.75}$, with additional amounts included for milk production.

In the case of mineral requirements, P need is sometimes computed in relation to protein intake (NRC beef). Ca need is based on P requirements and body size with additional amounts for lactation or egg production of laying birds. Other mineral requirements generally are specified on the basis of metabolic size. Some vitamins, particularly thiamin and niacin, are known to be required in relation to energy needs, while riboflavin and B_6 needs are more directly related to protein intake.

Computation of nutrient needs in relation to energy seems to be a very sound approach for non-ruminant species. Certainly, if protein is required in direct relation to energy, then it should be feasible to relate the needs of most other nutrients to energy consumption. It is to be hoped that in the future more of the NRC committees will recognize the value of relating nutrient needs to energy concentration of the diet as our nutritional information becomes more precise.

METHODS OF ESTIMATING NUTRIENT NEEDS

Nutrient requirements of animals are evaluated and computed on the basis of many different types of information. With respect to energy, animals needs may be based on calorimetric studies modified as necessary with data from feeding experiments under practical environmental conditions. Although calorimetric data provide useful information on fasting or basal metabolism or energy expenditure of closely confined animals, such data do not appear to give good estimates of the energy expenditure of grazing animals because field studies indicate a considerably higher energy requirement than do calorimetric studies; the increase, in many cases, is caused by increased activity associated with grazing. In addition, the effect of environmental changes in temperature, solar radiation, wind, humidity, and other stressing factors are difficult to quantify, so we are faced with the need to conduct feeding experiments under natural environmental and management conditions.

One limitation of feeding trials is that estimating energy gain or loss by the animal is difficult (see Ch. 10). We can easily calculate the energy value of milk or eggs produced and, in a long experiment, slight changes in body energy may not cause much of an error in estimating the energy needs of the animal, but such errors may be relatively large in short-term studies. This problem can be overcome partially by using data obtained from slaughter experiments (see Ch. 10).

With protein and the major minerals, one method used at times to calculate requirements is designated as the factorial method. This method is based on back calculations of utilization using amounts excreted in urine and feces and, for lactating animals, amounts secreted in milk. The computations used in calculating protein requirements are too complex to justify a complete explanation here; the reader is referred to ARC (2) for more details, but a simple example will be given for Ca. In this method the net requirement of Ca for maintenance and growth is calculated as the sum of the endogenous losses (fecal + urinary) and the quantity retained in the body. To determine the dietary requirement, the net requirement is divided by an average value of availability (expressed as a decimal). For example, a heifer of 318 kg (700 lb) gaining 0.45 kg/day (1 lb) might have endogenous losses of 5 g of Ca/day and retain 3 g/day; its net requirement would be 8 g Ca/day. For an animal of this weight, average availability of Ca

would be about 40%, thus the animal's dietary requirement for Ca would be $8 \div 0.4 = 20$ g/day.

The factorial approach suffers from the fact that endogenous losses are difficult to estimate because endogenous losses are those originating from body tissues and must be estimated by feeding an animal a diet free of soluble Ca (or whatever nutrient is of interest) or by use of radioisotope procedures. In addition, availability of dietary nutrients is not a fixed biological quantity and may vary with age, source of the nutrient and other dietary or environmental factors. Factorial estimates of requirements generally are lower than those derived from feeding trials or balance studies.

With respect to vitamins, balance studies are of little value because excretory metabolites of some vitamins are difficult to measure or have not been identified; thus, data must be obtained from feeding trials or some measure of animal productivity. Data on blood levels, tissue storage, freedom from deficiency signs and symptoms, and ability of the animal to produce at maximal levels are used to specify vitamin requirements.

INACCURACIES IN FEEDING STANDARDS

For the nutritionist, feeding standards provide a useful base from which to formulate diets or estimate feed requirements of animals. However, they should not be considered as the final answer on nutrient needs, but should be used as a guide. Current NRC recommendations are specified in terms believed (by the committees) to be minimum requirements for a population of animals of a given species, age, weight, and productive status. Some of the earlier versions were called allowances and, as such, included a safety factor on top of what was believed to be required.

It is well known that animal requirements vary considerably, even within a relatively uniform herd. The expected distribution of nutrient requirements for animals in a broad population is represented by the typical bell-shaped curve (Fig. 18.1). Of course, where any producer is concerned, he is not likely to be dealing with a population of animals with such a symmetrical distribution, and the curve is likely to be skewed in one direction or the other (Fig. 18.2). Even if the population were symmetrical, it is not practical to attempt to provide a nutrient intake that would be sufficient for 100% of the population, even for humans. The end result will be overfeeding a few

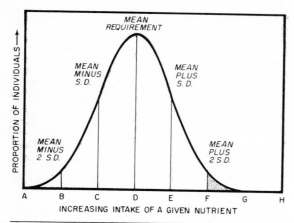

Figure 18.1 *Distribution of the nutrient requirements of a hypothetical population. The statistical unit of variation is known as the standard deviation (S.D.). An intake of F, obtained by adding two S.D. to the mean value, would cover the requirements for nearly all (97.5%) of the individuals in this* **theoretical** *population. The colored region shows the small proportion of healthy individuals (2.5%) not covered by the allowance.*

animals that have low requirements and underfeeding some that have high requirements. With most domestic animals, we would probably cull out those that do poorly for some reason or other, possibly because some of them have extraordinarily high requirements for a specific nutrient. If we can identify individual animals (such as dairy cows) that have high requirements and are high producers, then it may

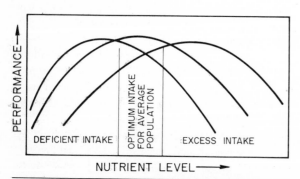

Figure 18.2 *A theoretical example of how nutritional requirements may be shifted for individuals or groups of animals by any of a number of causative factors. The usual objective for animal production would be to supply nutrients within the optimum zone, but it may not be easy to achieve this objective in all cases because the optimum zone will vary with different populations and environmental conditions.*

be feasible to provide supplementary nutrients without grossly overfeeding the whole herd.

As suggested in Fig. 18.2, excess nutrients may result in depressed animal production and, in a few cases, outright toxicity or death. In any event from the point of view of cost, it is not desirable to feed more than is required.

It is quite obvious from the literature that management and feeding methods may alter an animal's needs or efficiency of feed utilization apart from known breed differences in nutrient metabolism and requirements. In addition, most current recommendations provide no basis for increasing intake in severe weather or reduction in mild climates. Nor is any allowance made for the effect of other stresses such as disease, parasitism, surgery, and so on. Frequently, beneficial effects of additives or feed preparatory methods are not considered (if known). Thus, we may have many variables that may alter nutrient needs and nutrient utilization, and these variables are often difficult to include quantitatively in feeding standards, even when feed quality is well known.

☐ NUTRITIONAL NEEDS AND THE PRODUCTIVE FUNCTIONS

The remainder of this chapter will be devoted to some general discussion relating the effect of various productive functions to nutrient requirements, followed by sections on individual species and classes of animals.

Maintenance

Maintenance may be defined as the condition in which an animal is neither gaining or losing body energy (or other nutrients). With productive animals, there are only a few times when maintenance is desired; it is approximated closely or attained in adult male breeding animals other than during the breeding season and, perhaps, for a few days or weeks in adult females following the cessation of lactation and before pregnancy increases requirements substantially. However, as a reference point for evaluating nutritional needs, maintenance is a standard benchmark. Other things being equal, nutrient needs are minimal during maintenance. In field conditions during dry periods of the year, we may find that range animals may need to expend considerable energy just to obtain enough plant material for consumption as opposed to the amount of energy expended when forage growth is more lush, but this does not alter the fact that nutrient needs are less during maintenance than when an animal is performing some productive function.

Growth and Fattening

Growth, as measured by increase in body weight, is at its most rapid rate early in life. When expressed as a percentage increase in body weight, the growth rate declines gradually until puberty, followed by an even slower rate until maturity. As animals grow, different tissues and organs develop at differential rates and it is quite obvious that the conformation of most newborn animals is different from that of adults; this differential development has, no doubt, some effect on changing nutrient requirements. Growth rate decreases because the biological stimulus to grow is lessened, because young animals cannot continue to eat as much/unit of metabolic size and, as measured by increase in body weight, because relatively more of the tissue of older animals is fat, which has a much higher caloric value than muscle tissue (see Ch. 10).

Nutrient requirements/unit of body weight or metabolic size are greatest for very young animals; these needs taper off gradually as the growth rate declines and as the animal approaches maturity. In young mammals, nutrient needs are so great that, because the capacity of the GI tract is relatively limited in space and function, they must have milk (or a milk replacer) and additional highly digestible food to approach maximal growth rates. As the young mammal grows, quality of the diet generally decreases as more and more of its food is from non-milk sources with the result that digestibility is lower and the dry matter of food is used less efficiently.

Dry matter consumption for all young animals is usually far greater/unit of body weight during their early life than in later periods. This high level of feed consumption provides a large margin above maintenance needs, thus allowing a high proportion to be used for growth and development of the young animal. Due to differences in capability of the GI tract for food utilization and because the rate, duration, and character of body growth vary with age and animal species, nutrient requirements may be quite different for different animal species. Nevertheless, it is characteristic for all species that nutrient requirements (in terms of nutrient concentration/unit of diet) are higher for the very young and then decline gradually as the animal matures. Naturally, total food

and nutrient consumption are less for young animals because of their smaller size.

Nutrient deficiencies show up quite rapidly in young animals, particularly when the young are dependent in the early stages of life on tissue reserves obtained while in utero. With few exceptions, tissue reserves in newborn animals are low. Milk or other food may be an inadequate nutrient source so that deficiencies may occur frequently until the food supply changes or the young animal develops a capability to eat the existing food supply. The young pig is an example. Fe reserves are low and rapid growth soon depletes body reserves; because milk is a poor source of Fe, young pigs often become anemic unless supplemented with Fe.

Young mammals are dependent on an intake of colostrum early in life. In the first few hours after birth, the intestinal tract is permeable to large molecules such as proteins. Colostrum has a large supply of globulins and other proteins that provide nutrition as well as a temporary supply of antibodies which increase resistance to many diseases greatly. In addition, colostrum is a rich source of most of the vitamins and trace minerals, and the young animal's tissues can be supplied rapidly with needed nutrients which may not have been provided adequately in utero.

From a production point of view, nutrient requirements/unit of gain are least and gross efficiency is greatest when animals grow at maximal rates, even though more fat may be deposited by fast gainers. However, net efficiency (nutrient needs above maintenance) may not be altered greatly. In a number of instances it may not be desirable or economical to attempt to achieve maximal gain. For example, if we want to market a milk-fed veal calf at an early age, maximum gain and fattening are desired. On the other hand if the calf is being grown out for a herd replacement, then less than maximal gain will be just as satisfactory and considerably cheaper.

The biological stimulus to grow cannot be suppressed greatly in young animals without resultant permanent stunting. It is possible to maintain young animals for a period during which they do not increase body energy reserves, yet they will—if other nutrients are adequate—continue to increase in stature. Following a period of subnormal growth caused by energy restriction, most young animals will gain weight at faster than normal rates when given adequate rations. This response is termed compensatory growth. This phenomenon has practical application when young calves are wintered at low to moderate levels (submaximal). When new grass is available in the spring or if they are put in the feedlot, weight gain occurs at a very rapid rate initially. Efficiency for the total period and especially for a given amount of gain is greater, however, if the animal is fed at near maximal rates, but this practice (deferred feeding) may allow the use of much cheaper feedstuffs or deferred marketing and, as a result, be a profitable management procedure.

Work

Experimental studies with humans and animals indicate that work results in an increased energy demand in proportion to the work done and the efficiency with which it is accomplished (3). Carbohydrates are said to be more efficient sources of energy for work than fats (4). With respect to protein, balance studies show little, if any, increase in N excretion in horses or humans as a result of muscular exercise (3, 4). Although this evidence has been obtained in a number of studies, data on men indicate reduced quality and quantity of work when protein intake is on the low side, but still above maintenance levels. It is a common belief that hard workers need more protein, and it is a typical practice in competitive athletics to feed performers high levels of meat and other high-protein foods. Perhaps some of the effect on performance is psychological.

If sweating occurs, work may be expected to increase the need of N and Cl, particularly. P intake should be increased during work because it is a vital nutrient in many energy-yielding reactions. Likewise, the B-vitamins involved in energy metabolism,

particularly thiamin, niacin, and riboflavin, probably should be increased as work output increases, although data on this subject are not clear.

Reproduction

Although nutrient needs of animals for reproduction generally are considerably less critical than during rapid growth, certainly they are more critical than for an adequate level of maintenance. If nutrient deficiencies occur prior to breeding, they may render animals sterile, or result in low fertility, silent estrus, or failure to establish or maintain pregnancy.

It has been demonstrated many times that underfeeding (energy, protein) during growth will result in delayed sexual maturity, and that both underfeeding and overfeeding (energy) usually will result in reduced fertility as compared to that of animals fed on a moderate intake. Of the two, overfeeding is usually more detrimental to fertility.

Energy needs for most species during pregnancy are more critical during the last third of the term. This fact is illustrated by data on cattle shown in Table 18.1; daily energy deposits increase quite rapidly between day 200 and 280. Although the data in Table 18.1 show that only a relatively small amount of the cows' energy requirements are needed for reproduction, other information indicates a somewhat greater need. Pregnant animals have a greater appetite and will spend more time grazing and searching for food than non-pregnant animals. Furthermore, the basal metabolic rate of pregnant animals is higher; the increase over maintenance is called the heat increment of gestation. By the end of preg-

TABLE 18.1 Deposition of various nutrients in the fetus, uterine tissues, and mammary gland of the cow at different stages of pregnancy.[a]

| DAYS AFTER CONCEPTION | UTERINE AND FETAL DEPOSITS (PER DAY) | | | | MAMMARY GLAND, g PROTEIN/DAY |
	ENERGY, Kcal	PROTEIN, g	Ca, g	P, g	
100	40	5			
150	100	14	0.1		
200	235	34	0.7	0.6	7
250	560	83	3.2	2.7	22
280	940	144	8.0	7.4	44
Approximate net daily maintenance requirement of 1000 lb cow	700	300	8	12	

[a]From data of Moustgaard (5).

nancy, the basal rate is about 1.5-fold that of similar non-pregnant cows.

Protein deposition in the products of conception follows the same trend as energy, but protein is relatively more critical for development of the fetus in the late stages than early in pregnancy as is true for Ca, P, and other minerals and vitamins.

Inadequate nutrition of the mother during pregnancy may have variable results, depending on the species of animal, the degree of malnutrition, the nutrient involved and the state of pregnancy. Nutrient deficiencies are more serious usually in late pregnancy although there may be exceptions to this. With a moderate deficiency, fetal tissues tend to have a priority over the mother's tissues; thus, body reserves of the mother may be withdrawn to nourish the fetus. A very severe deficiency, however, usually will result in partial depletion of the mother's tissues and such detrimental effects as resorption of the fetus, abortion, malformed young, or birth of dead, weak, or undersized young with, sometimes, long-term effects on the mother. When the mother's tissues are depleted of critical nutrients, then tissue storage in the young animal almost always is low, nutrients secreted in colostrum also are low, milk production may be nil, and survival of the young animal is much less certain than when nutrition of the mother is at an adequate level.

Lactation

Heavy lactation probably results in more nutritional stress in mature animals than any other production situation, with the possible exception of heavy, sustained muscular exercise. During a year, high-producing cows or goats typically produce milk with a dry matter content equivalent to 4–5 fold that in the animal's body, and some animals reach production levels as high as 7X body dry matter. High-producing cows give so much milk that normally it is impossible for them to consume enough feed to prevent weight loss during peak periods of lactation.

Milk of most domestic species contains 80–88% water; thus, water is a critical nutrient needed to sustain lactation. All nutrient needs are increased during lactation because milk components are either supplied directly via the blood or synthesized in the mammary gland and, thus, are derived from the animal's tissues or more directly from food consumed; all recognized nutrients are secreted to some extent in milk. The major components of milk are fat, protein, and lactose with substantial amounts of ash,

primarily Ca and P. Milk yield varies widely between and within species. In cows, peak yields occur usually between 60 and 90 days after parturition and then gradually taper off; thus the peak demand for nutrients follows the typical milk flow characteristic for the species concerned. Milk composition and quantity in ruminants, particularly the fat content and, to a lesser extent, the protein and lactose, may be altered by the type of diet. In monogastric species diet may affect fat, mineral, and vitamin composition of milk.

Limiting water or energy intake of the lactating cow (and probably of any other species) results in a marked drop in milk production, whereas protein restriction has a less noticeable effect, particularly during a short period of time. Although deficiencies of minerals do not affect milk composition markedly, they will result in rapid depletion of the lactating animal's reserves. The needs of elements such as Cu, Fe, and Se will be increased during lactation, even though they are found in very low concentrations in milk. The effects of marked nutrient deficiencies during lactation often will carry over into pregnancy and the next lactation.

❏ NUTRITION AND THE PRODUCTIVE FUNCTIONS—RUMINANTS

Space is set aside in this section for some discussion of nutrition as affected by different productive functions for specific classes of domestic animals. Comments will not be made on each class within each species but, rather, only on those classes of animals in which nutritional problems are more critical in normal livestock production. Omissions of this nature are not meant to imply that nutrition may not be critical in all stages of the life cycle, but it is obvious that some stages of the life cycle are more critical than others, and these differences justify the selectivity used in the following discussions.

Young Ruminants

Young ruminant animals existing on milk or liquid milk substitutes frequently are referred to as preruminants because rumen function is not a dominant factor in food utilization. Rather, most of the liquid ingesta passes into the lower part of the stomach (abomasum) and on into the small intestine rather than into the rumen. This being the case, the nutrient requirements of these young animals are similar—both qualitatively and quantitatively—to non-ruminant species. As opposed to an older animal with a functioning rumen, preruminants require a dietary source of essential amino acids and fatty acids and of vitamin K and the various B-complex vitamins. These are dietary nutrients not normally needed by ruminants because the microbial population of the stomach and gut synthesizes adequate amounts of these organic nutrients. The point at which a preruminant animal develops a functioning rumen is dependent upon species and age, but is also affected markedly by the supply of milk and availability of palatable feedstuffs or forage. Young calves can be weaned successfully to dry feed at three weeks of age and young lambs by four weeks, providing the dry feed is palatable and has a satisfactory nutrient content. More commonly, young animals begin to consume solid feed gradually, milk makes up less and less of their daily diet, and the rumen develops gradually in size and function.

Most of the nutritional data on preruminants has been developed with dairy calves taken from the cow at an early age. In order to feed these calves, milk replacers have been developed that allow satisfactory performance at a cost usually less than use of grade A fluid milk. Milk replacers are available also for lambs and may be used to feed orphan lambs or extra lambs when a ewe has produced twins or triplets.

Milk replacers usually are based on use of relatively large amounts of dried skim milk supplemented with ingredients such as lard, starch, glucose, soy flour, dried whey, or buttermilk, and with sources of the vitamins and minerals and feed additives such as antibiotics. Quality of protein is a critical factor as low quality proteins are utilized poorly and may cause digestive disturbances. It is necessary also to avoid too much carbohydrate in the form of starch or sucrose because the young animal does not have the gastrointestinal enzymes to digest much starch and has no sucrase for digestion of sucrose. High levels of whey result in diarrhea, either due to the excess lactose or high ash content. Fats (except highly saturated sources) from a variety of sources can be used, as can protein from sources such as soy flour, fish meal, yeasts, and so on, although milk sources are preferred if cost is not prohibitive and especially if maximum growth is desired.

Except where veal calves with light-colored meat are being raised, all young animals on milk replacers should have supplementary dry feed avialable by at least 10 days of age. Mixtures can be made up preferably of rolled grains and other appropriate supplementary feeds such as alfalfa hay, molasses, and soybean meal when cost allows. Young animals do not use urea efficiently as a source of N. Good to excellent quality forage should also be available at an early age.

Feedlot Cattle

The cattle feedlot industry has become a highly specialized segment of agriculture, particularly in areas where there are large numbers of feeder cattle accompanied by surplus grain production. Many feedlots are in existence with capacities on the order of 30–40 thousand head and one or two with capacities of 100,000 head or more; with an annual turnover of about $2\frac{1}{2}$ times capacity, these feedlots account for the majority of fat cattle marketed at the present time in the USA.

Cattle coming into these feedlots range in size from 90 to 450 kg (200 to 1,000 lb) or more and in age from a few months to well over a year; thus, nutritional requirements and management problems vary tremendously. Because the cattle may come from many different farms and ranches, one of the biggest problems is the stresses imposed during marketing and transportation to the feedlot, exposure to new diseases and parasites, and adaptation of these cattle to their new environment. These various stresses can result in severe sickness and in high death losses if management is not at a high level.

In addition, ruminant animals need time to adapt to unfamiliar feedstuffs. The time required primarily is because rumen microorganisms, which predigest the feed, develop into populations that reflect the composition of the feed. This takes time and means that animals should not be changed suddenly from one diet to quite a different one, particularly when going from a roughage diet to one high in readily available carbohydrates, which cause the most problems.

From strictly a nutritional point of view, except for the problem of adaptation, problems in the feedlot are more often of a management than of a strictly nutritional nature because many of these large feedlots use nutrition consultants. Nutritional problems that crop up are related to the practice of pushing cattle too fast onto high-grain rations. This may result in indigestion and founder. Mineral nutrition may be ignored, which, in the case of Ca and P imbalance, may result in urinary calculi. In addition, it is not uncommon to use by-product or waste feedstuffs for which no good quantitative nutritional data are available.

As a result of the large numbers of animals involved, a high degree of mechanical handling of feed is required. With usual price relationships in the USA, it is cheaper to feed rations high in grains and other concentrates than to feed roughages with low energy availability. This type of diet is prone to cause digestive disturbances and disease and requires care in formulating diets and in the feeding management of these cattle.

The need for efficient feed conversion to minimize feed costs has resulted in the widespread use of grains processed in various ways. Although processed grains usually are more digestible and produce more efficient gains, they also are more likely to result in digestive disturbances if used improperly in finishing diets.

Wintering Beef Cows

Beef cows often are wintered on high proportions of straw, stover, grass hay, winter range, or other low-quality roughages. Dry beef cows can be wintered on such feedstuffs because their nutrient requirements are modest compared to lactating dairy cows or growing animals. Nutrients that usually are of concern include protein, energy, minerals and, at times, vitamin A. Although protein requirements are low, the protein content and digestibility in low-quality roughages also are low, so some supplementary feed often is needed, particularly in late gestation and lactation. Energy may or may not be of concern depending on quality of the roughage. Most low-quality roughages are deficient in P and often in Ca and Mg and some of the trace minerals such as I. Vitamin A may be of concern, particularly where cows have been on dry forage for several months, resulting in depletion of reserves in the liver.

During lactation, nutrient needs increase appreciably. If cows are underfed to a great extent, milk production will be reduced markedly, and more problems may be expected with rebreeding. Better quality hays, silages, or other roughage should be fed during lactation to avoid these problems. Young calves can often be creep fed profitably while cows are in winter quarters, particularly if feed supply for the cow is inadequate in quantity or quality.

Care is required in providing supplemental N for cows on poor quality roughage. Urea, a common supplementary form of N for cattle, must be fed along with some readily available carbohydrate (starch or sugars) in order to achieve satisfactory utilization and to prevent urea toxicity.

Dairy Cows

The nutrition of lactating dairy cows is much more critical than that of beef cows because dairy cows produce at a much higher level and, partly, because they have less time to recover between lactations.

Dairy cows often are prone to milk fever and ketosis, particularly cows in their third and subsequent lactations. Milk fever is a result of abnormal Ca metabolism early in lactation. It can be controlled moderately well by careful management of the Ca:P ratio, taking care not to have excess Ca and to have adequate levels of P. Treatment prior to parturition with massive doses of vitamin D or its active metabolite, 1,25-dihydroxycholecalciferol, is helpful. Ketosis appears to be a result of faulty energy metabolism often accompanied by low energy intake; it often occurs during peak milk flow. Its incidence often can be reduced by increasing energy intake during the latter stages of gestation, and, thus, having the cow adapted to a rapid increase in feed following parturition. Feeding of good-quality roughage and adequate total energy are factors that appear to reduce the incidence of ketosis.

Energy intake in lactating cows can be increased by increasing grain in the diet, but eventually this results in reduced roughage consumption. Reduced roughage intake, especially accompanied by feeding of heat-treated grains, usually causes a reduced milk-fat percentage. When milk is sold on the basis of its fat content, this is, obviously, undesirable. Consequently, the usual practice is to feed cows between 40 and 60% of their diet as roughage. Use of ground and pelleted roughage also must be restricted because milk fat percentage is apt to decline if they make up a high proportion of the diet.

Where the common practice is to feed high-quality legume hay or excellent grass or legume silage, protein intake usually is not a problem in dairy cows. However, where other roughages such as corn silage are fed, protein intake frequently can be borderline to low. This is apt to lead to reduced milk production if continued for several weeks. Trace minerals as well as some of the major minerals must be of more concern in dairy cows than in many other livestock classes.

Feedlot Lambs

Many fat lambs go to market directly off the ewe. Others that are late, small, or poor doers may be fattened on grass, wheat pasture in the Midwest, or in large commercial feedlots. Feedlot lambs have many of the same problems that cattle do; namely, they may be stressed considerably in the process of getting on feed in a new environment. Adaptation time when they are fed new diets is just as essential to lambs as for cattle. Fortunately, lambs will gain well and finish satisfactorily on considerably less grain than cattle, particularly if high-roughage pelleted rations are feasible to use.

Lambs given sudden access to high-grain diets, especially if large amounts of wheat are used, are subject to acute indigestion and often to enterotoxemia caused by bacterial toxins; use of low levels of antibiotics is helpful in these situations. Lambs also are subject to urinary calculi if fed excess P in relation to Ca.

Energy consumption is not a problem in lambs provided rations are palatable and in a satisfactory physical form. Lambs often are underfed on protein; they often respond to levels above those suggested by NRC and, in addition, are apt to have leaner carcasses when fed more protein, a desirable characteristic in terms of the human diet. Other than the factors mentioned, nutrition of feedlot lambs usually is not critical since the time factor is relatively short. If a lamb comes into the feedlot deficient in some nutrient, then some action may be required to alleviate the problem.

Ewes

Nutrition problems of ewes, for the most part, are less likely than for most other ruminants. This is due partly to the fact that the usual management practice (at least in the USA) is to feed a much better quality forage to ewes than beef cows commonly receive. This comment may not apply to sheep production in dryland areas.

Nutrition prior to and during the breeding season may have a substantial influence on the number of lambs born. If ewes are maintained in moderate flesh, but on an increasing plane of nutrition at breeding (called flushing), they usually will have more lambs than if managed in other ways. Overfeeding for too

long a period will, however, reduce embryo survival and the number of lambs born.

A second critical period for ewes is in late gestation. Ewes carrying multiple fetuses have a markedly reduced stomach capacity so that food consumption decreases at a time when a greater nutrient supply is vital. This can result in pregnancy disease, a form of ketosis accompanied by acidosis. Pregnancy disease largely can be prevented by increasing the energy intake of such ewes by means of a gradually increasing concentrate intake during the last six weeks of gestation.

Although lactating ewes occasionally do have milk fever, it is quite rare as compared to the incidence in lactating cows. Nutritional requirements increase substantially while the ewe is lactating, particularly so when more than one lamb is being nursed. Obviously, the ewe needs an increased intake of protein, energy, and major minerals found in milk.

❏ SWINE

Estimates of quantitative nutrient requirements for each phase of the life cycle have been tabulated by NRC (6). As with other species the nutrient requirements suggested must be considered only as guidelines as differences in genetic potential and environmental or climatic conditions may be expected to affect the requirement for each nutrient.

Gestation

The nutrient requirements for the sow during gestation are influenced by two separate productive functions—the need for maintaining the pregnant sow and the provision of an adequate nutrient supply for the developing fetuses. In general, nutrient requirements in early gestation are modest as compared to late gestation and, particularly, lactation.

It is possible, at least with some nutrients, to obtain normal reproduction through one reproductive cycle on a diet that is clearly inadequate for the dam. For example, results with sows fed protein-free diets during gestation show that the dam can draw on her own reserves to meet the needs of the fetuses for growth and survival. However, such a diet cannot be considered adequate because it does not satisfy the long-term requirements of both dam and fetuses.

Pregnant sows will consume far more feed voluntarily than required and will become obese if intake is not restricted to ca. 1.8–2.3 kg of a high-concentrate diet/day (6,600 Kcal of DE). The amount of restriction needed is dependent upon the size and condition of the animal, of course.

Lactation

The nutrient output in sow milk during a five-week lactation is much greater than the nutrient deposition in fetuses and placental membranes during a 114-day gestation period. Therefore, as with ruminants, nutrient requirements of the sow for lactation are far more demanding than for gestation. While the sow can draw on her own body reserves for milk production, complete or partial lactation failure results if nutrient restriction is severe or prolonged. In general, a deficiency of a particular nutrient is manifested more by a reduction in total milk production than by a decreased concentration of that nutrient in the milk.

The most striking effect of level of intake on total milk production is with energy. If the lactating sow is not allowed to eat at or near ad libitum, milk production declines. In the well-fed sow, milk production increases as litter size increases, up to the point at which her genetic capacity for milk production is reached. Mature sows raising large litters often will consume 6.8–9.0 kg (15–20 lb) or more/day of a high-concentrate diet (3,600 Kcal of ME/kg) at the peak of lactation (4–5 weeks postpartum). Daily yield of milk, which has a dry matter content of ca. 20% (compared to 13% for bovines), may range from 5.5–9.0 kg (12–20 lb) or more during the 4th or 5th week of lactation.

The energetic efficiency of lactation is higher when milk is produced by current energy intake than by dependence on body fat reserves. Therefore, in practical feeding the highest efficiency of energy utilization is achieved by controlled feeding during gestation to minimize mobilization of depot fats for milk production.

Inadequate protein (essential amino acids) intake also will result in reduced milk production, although the effect is less marked than for energy. Deficiencies of other required nutrients also may affect milk production, although to a lesser degree than for protein and energy.

Preweaning

The nutrient requirements of the suckling pig, except for Fe, normally are met by sow milk during the first 2–3 weeks. After this time rapid growth of the pig, combined with the decline in milk yield after week five, necessitates the provision of supplemental creep feed if maximum growth is to be attained. The protein content of the creep feed, as a percentage of diet, does not have to be as high as that of sow milk. The carbohydrate source must be palatable and low in fiber to encourage consumption. For this reason, cane sugar, dried molasses, or glucose are often added at a level of 5–10 + % of the diet. Non-nutritive sweeteners, such as saccharin or monosodium glutamate, are also used, but at a much lower concentration. Although the energy concentration of the creep diet is not especially critical, the addition of 5–10% fat to the diet improves palatability and encourages early consumption.

The introduction of a dry, well-balanced diet early enough so that the suckling pig consumes enough for maximum weight gain is a major consideration during the preweaning period. Although consumption during this period is negligible as compared to later periods, a small amount may greatly increase growth of young pigs.

Removal of the pig from the sow earlier than four weeks of age can be considered early weaning. The younger the pig at weaning, the more critical are the dietary requirements. Pigs weaned at birth and deprived of colostrum must be fed a highly fortified diet, kept in a warm, sanitary environment and be given parenteral (other than orally) antibody protection (porcine γ-globulin) for a reasonable chance of survival. Cow's milk can serve as a substitute for sow milk, although its lower caloric density does not allow maximum weight gain. Liquid sow milk substitutes of higher caloric density can be used. Composition of one such diet is (g/l of finished milk): casein, 44.3; glucose, 44.1; lard, 33.0; soy lecithin, 2.0; minerals and vitamins. Baby pigs utilize casein 5–10% more efficiently than soybean protein, presumably due to limitations in digestive enzyme capacity in early life. Liquid diets must be fed at frequent intervals (minimum of 4X daily) to provide adequate intake for reasonable growth and to avoid digestive problems. If an adequate dry diet is available, young pigs can be weaned to dry diets at a few days of age.

Growing Period [Early Postweaning]

This stage of the life cycle of the pig is set arbitrarily as the period from weaning (usually 5–6 weeks) to ca. 45 kg live weight (12–16 weeks of age). During this period nutrient requirements are less critical than at earlier stages, but more critical than during the finishing period. The changes in nutrient requirements as the pig matures are related to changes in growth rate and body composition. Fat concentration of the body increases rapidly at the expense of water and, although the percentage of protein remains rather stable, the calorie:protein ratio in the body increases steadily to market weight. Full-feeding of growing pigs on a high-energy diet (1,500 Kcal DE/lb or 3,300 Kcal/kg) results in maximum rate of gain and efficiency of feed utilization. Limited feeding will produce a leaner carcass, but the slower growth rate reduces energetic efficiency because of the higher proportion of daily energy intake needed for maintenance. Feeding a protein-deficient diet during the growing period results in a fatter carcass; feeding protein in excess of the requirement, however, may not result in a leaner carcass. Females and intact males have a higher carcass lean content than barrows and also require a higher percentage of protein in the diet.

In addition to nutritional factors, the physical form of the diet is important. Pelleting certain types of diets, especially those containing barley and other fibrous grains, may improve growth and efficiency of feed utilization. In addition, fineness of grind and dustiness of the feed contribute to variations in performance of growing pigs.

Finishing Period [45–90 kg]

The same principles and problems in meeting nutrient requirements during the growing period apply during the finishing period. However, the quantitative requirements for nutrients other than energy are less (as a percentage of the diet) during the finishing period. The total daily feed requirement is considerably greater during the finishing period not only because of larger body size but also because of the higher feed requirement/unit of body weight gain; this is a reflection of increased fat disposition which requires considerably more energy/unit of gain.

Limiting feeding of finishing swine to 70–80% of ad libitum intake reduces carcass fatness, but also reduces rate and efficiency of gain due to the greater proportion of daily intake needed for maintenance. The system of feeding used for finishing will, therefore, be dictated by the economic relationship between carcass value of lean vs. fat pigs and the price of feed and labor.

The finishing pig, as well as the growing pig, tends to select proportions of grain and protein supplement appropriate to metabolic needs when the two feed sources are offered separately. It is more common, however, to feed complete diets as pellets, meal, or in liquid or paste form.

While by far the greatest tonnage of feed in a swine enterprise is devoted to finishing pigs, this stage of the life cycle is the least critical in terms of meeting specific nutrient requirements of growing finishing-pigs.

❏ POULTRY

It should be recognized that chickens and turkeys eat to satisfy their energy needs provided the ration allows them to do so. There are, of course, exceptions to this rule, particularly where heavy breed layers are concerned, when birds have a tendency to overeat. Where this is a problem, it is the general practice to subject the birds to some degree of feed restriction during both the growing and production periods.

The major ingredients that are integral parts of poultry rations at the present time in the USA are corn, as the primary energy source, and soybean meal as the major protein supplement. These major ingredients, usually available in plentiful supply, allow rapid growth or high egg production with very efficient feed conversion. However, corn-soy rations are deficient in some nutrients* for chickens; these nutrients are normally supplied by alfalfa meal, other feedstuffs or concentrated supplements.

A number of satisfactory substitutes may be available. For example, milo and wheat certainly may be used when priced economically. Similarly, cottonseed meal, fish meal, or meat and bone meal may be used as protein sources.

Note that the nutrient requirements of chickens and turkeys are understood more completely and quantitated with greater precision than is the case for other species. Because this is so and because a higher percentage of poultry feed is prepared commercially, nutrient problems may (should) be less likely than for other species.

Broilers

Because of the very rapid growth of chicks, nutrient needs are more critical than for older birds. In newly hatched chicks body reserves of nutrients such as

---

*Amino acids: methionine; macrominerals: Ca, P, Na, Cl; trace minerals: I, Mn, Se, Zn; vitamins: all fat- and water-soluble vitamins except choline.

the various vitamins and minerals may be low. Thus, in order to obtain maximum growth rates and to avoid nutrient deficiencies, more attention must be paid to quality of protein and adequacy of the essential amino acids, especially methionine and lysine, and provision must be made for adequate supplementation of the necessary minerals and vitamins.

Probably in no other area does the concept that birds eat to satisfy their energy needs apply more than in the feeding of broiler chicks. Because of the increased demands made for efficiency of production, both energy and protein contents of the diet are most important. Accordingly, diets containing variable protein and energy levels, called multiple stage rations, are used at different ages during the 8-week broiler growing period. Generally, it is recognized that protein requirement decreases with age and the indiscriminant use of these feeds without regard to protein level results in poor feed utilization and increased cost. Further, virtually all broiler feeds are now fed in pelleted or crumblized form and switching to mash feeds should be avoided. Supplemental fats from vegetables or animal sources are used widely as concentrated energy sources when the cost makes it feasible to include them in broiler rations. However, when the energy content of the ration is increased, feed consumption usually will be reduced; thus, high-energy diets require a greater concentration of all other nutrients, providing digestibility and absorption are not altered.

The importance of the diet as a carrier of non-nutritional factors cannot be underestimated. For example, the diet is the usual vehicle for administration of medicants such as antibiotics or coccidiostats. It is also the means for obtaining the yellow pigmented skin demanded by most consumers. Skin pigmentation is related to the xanthophyll content of the feed. Both yellow corn and alfalfa meal are good sources of this substance, and any dietary change that lowers xanthophyll intake must be corrected.

Laying Hens

In feeding layers, both energy and protein are important, but probably to a lesser degree than noted for broilers. In addition, protein quality is less important than for broilers. Under normal conditions mash-type feeds may replace pelleted feeds used with broilers. However, once pellets are used they should be continued as hens prefer the physical texture of pelleted feeds.

In general, rations now in use are considered complete diets from the standpoint of providing all nutrients required for egg production. Dietary protein intake is related to the daily protein requirement for egg production. Accordingly, because of the usual decrease in laying with age, diets often are formulated to meet these variable production rates. Higher protein levels are required during the earlier production periods when higher rates of lay are prevalent. Therefore, lower protein diets should not be used during early periods of production. This type of feeding program is termed phase feeding.

Ca frequently is a critical nutrient in layer diets. The presence of Ca in adequate amounts insures good eggshell quality. Protein and P contents also may fall into this category. Any factor decreasing food intake can affect shell quality adversely. The presence of certain feedstuffs in diets also may influence egg quality. For example, the use of cottonseed meal can have a deleterious effect on internal egg quality as evidenced by the presence of olive-green yolks and pink albumen; therefore, its use should be curtailed.

Turkeys

Most systems employed with chickens are also used with turkeys. Protein requirements are considerably greater than for chickens and the use of multiple stage diets is much more prevalent. As feed costs increase relative to product price, interest in feeding for compensatory growth has occurred. By feeding poults low-protein diets during their early growth period, more efficient gains are possible during later growth stages with the end result that overall gains are obtained with less protein consumption.

Pelleted diets often are used for feeding breeder turkeys. In general, systems and practices are similar to those used with chickens. Breeder diets need to be fortified, especially with the required vitamins (A, D, E, riboflavin, pantothenic acid, biotin, and folic acid) and several trace minerals (Mn, Se, Zn) in order to insure the production of viable poults.

❏ HORSES

Horses in the USA are raised for pleasure or work rather than as meat or milk producing animals. Consequently, management goals are somewhat different from most livestock species in that horsepeople are more concerned with raising animals that can perform various athletic endeavors with competitive efficiency. The horse production areas of primary importance are reproduction, lactation, growth and work.

Reproduction [Conception-Gestation]

Reproductive efficiency in horses averages approximately 60–65% nationally, a level which is considerably lower than that of other livestock species. This poor performance can be attributed to a variety of causes such as updating the breeding season due to establishment of mandatory January 1 birthdates by many breed registries and to poor breeding farm management.

In regard to management improvement, researchers have established that reproductive efficiency of mares and stallions can be improved by increasing their plane of nutrition beginning about 60–80 days prior to breeding. The flushing of breeding animals that have been maintained in a slightly thrifty wintering condition stimulates the mare's reproductive system. Many times the additional nutrients are all that is required for the mare's cycling pattern to become more regular and for normal ovulation to occur. Quite possibly, many wintering diets provide only for normal body maintenance (neglecting the reproductive processes in favor of essential body functions), causing reproductive activity to remain somewhat dormant. Diet mismanagement (over or under feeding) prior to any flushing period may reduce the beneficial effects of such a feeding program. In addition, it is known that over 60% of the foal fetus is produced during the last 80–90 days of gestation; therefore, it is wise to increase a pregnant mare's plane of nutrition to meet this increased demand. These feeding practices will help to insure improved reproductive performance and production of foals by dams having adequate body reserves to meet the stresses of heavy lactation.

Lactation

As with most species the lactation period (3–5 mo.) places the heaviest demands on a broodmare and results in a marked increase in nutritional requirements. Milk production by a 500 kg mare may range from 14 kg/day early in the lactation period to peak production of 17 kg/day at 2–3 mo. Mare's milk generally is lower in fat, protein, and ash and higher in sugar than cow's milk. On a dry matter basis, mare's milk averages about 61.50%, 22.00%, 13.12%, and 3.80% sugar, protein, fat, and ash, respectively.

In view of the fact that the mare is producing large quantities of milk for an extended time period, it is essential to increase her plane of nutrition. In the case of a 545 kg (1,200 lb) mare, her daily feed intake should be increased from about 7.9 kg (maintenance to 11.8 kg, and should provide an additional 14 Mcal of DE, 0.55 kg digestible protein, 30.8 g Ca and 26.9 g P in order to prevent the mare from drawing on her body stores to an excessive extent during lactation.

Growth

Nutritional demands of immature horses for optimal growth follow general patterns similar to other livestock species. Of primary importance in feeding young foals is the fact that they have a limited digestive tract capacity. Hence, consideration must be given to feeding concentrated diets of high quality to insure intake of adequate quantities of required nutrients. Average birth weights of foals of light horse breeding run from 36–45 kg (80–100 lb); average daily gains may be 1 kg/day for very young foals maturing at 545 kg body weight and may range down to 0.7 kg/day for weanlings and to 0.35 kg/day and 0.18 kg/day for yearlings and two-year olds, respectively.

Mare's milk contains about 19–22% protein on a dry basis, and foals require a relatively high protein concentration in their diet (19–22% preweaned, 16% weanling, 13–14% yearling and 12% for two-year old). Studies of dietary amino acid requirements have indicated lysine as the most limiting in many foal diets. It appears that a minimum of 0.75% dietary lysine will support optimal growth in young horses.

Similar to protein requirements, foals require higher dietary concentrations of digestible energy during the early growing period with a diminished concentration required as they become older. This is due partially to the increasing capacity of the digestive tract and the establishment of an active bacterial population in the lower gut of older foals.

Minerals of primary importance in foal nutrition are Ca and P because of their involvement in the growing bones. Research has shown that foals require about 0.8% and 0.6% dietary Ca and P, respectively, with these values gradually declining with age. Ca and P fed in a 1.25–2:1 ratio will provide for optimum bone mineralization; extremely wide ratios (excessive amounts of P) are associated with abnormal bone development in foals. Additional mineral needs usually will be met by normal dietary feedstuffs or by inclusion of 0.25% trace-mineralized salt in the diet.

Vitamin D is frequently added to foal diets because of its importance for absorption of dietary Ca. Other fat-soluble vitamins (A and E) also generally are added to foal rations. The mature horse is able to acquire much of its B-vitamin needs through microbial synthesis in the gut, but intestinal synthesis in the immature foal is not adequate to meet dietary needs. Therefore, it is essential that young horses receive dietary B-vitamin supplementation as well as vitamins A, D, and E. In most situations vitamin premixes or commercial vitamin supplements added to the diet will alleviate problems of vitamin deficiency.

Foals usually are not weaned until 4–5 mo. of age; however, many managers have discovered that providing nursing foals with a high quality creep feed allows for less milk demand from the dam and greater opportunity for foals to grow to their genetic potential. In addition, creep-fed foals are less likely to be affected by the post-weaning slump observed in foals during the period of adapting from primarily a milk diet to a solid food diet. Recent research has shown that foals may be weaned from the mare at one month of age, providing they have access to adequate amounts of properly formulated milk replacer. Early-weaned or orphaned foals grow more slowly than their non-weaned comrades during the first year; however, they will usually compensate during their second year. Generally, early-weaned and normally weaned foals cannot be differentiated by two years of age if strict management practices are followed.

Work

In domestic livestock in the USA, athletic performance or work is one productive function that is rather unique to horses although this is not true in many undeveloped countries. Work by modern horses would include such things as carrying a rider for varying distances at various speeds over a variety of terrains. This would include such activities as racing, jumping, trail riding, cutting, rodeo events, or ranch work.

Unfortunately, most equine nutritionists are forced to classify nutrient requirements for work into three categories: light, moderate, and strenuous. These categories are relics of the past when work by draft horses was defined in terms of weight pulled for a given duration at a given speed (usually at a walk). Today, it is more difficult to establish a precise definition for work because most horses work for short time periods with their degree of exertion ranging from mild activity to near exhaustion. The preceding problems have lent themselves to the development of "horse feeding"as an art with scientific application being made only in very recent years.

Many voids exist in discussing the nutrients re-

quired by horses for work. The current energy, vitamin, and mineral requirements for work are in need of further investigation. It is assumed that protein requirements increase with work, however, not to the same degree as other nutrients. In most cases the additional feed supplied to meet increased energy demands will contain adequate protein. Contrary to many beliefs, mature performance horses do not require high protein diets to function at optimum capacities.

Most B-vitamins are associated with energy metabolism; consequently, their requirement increases with increased energy consumption and utilization during work. The O_2-carrying capacity of the blood is of importance in conditioning a performance horse. Vitamin E and Se have been associated with red blood cell fragility and muscle tissue capillary integrity. Because Fe also is associated with red blood cell production, it should receive due consideration in evaluating diets of performance horses.

There are a limited number of ways to evaluate the ability of a ration to provide adequate nutrients for strenuous athletic activity. Maintenance of body weight is an obvious positive sign and, since O_2-carrying capacity is vital, the packed cell volume and red blood cell count are reasonably good indicators of the adequacy of a ration.

In general terms diets for working horses should provide for increased DE, vitamin, and mineral concentrations with increased total daily protein, but not necessarily increased dietary protein concentration above that of maintenance (12%).

Many times coming two-year olds are placed in preparatory training for the race track, show ring or other activities during the later part of their yearling year. It is wise to insure that young horses in this situation are not only fed to meet their requirements for maintenance and growth but also fed to meet the additional nutrient needs for performing their required athletic functions. If these additional needs are not met, body development may be delayed or inhibited.

❏ SUMMARY

Feeding standards are the outgrowth of vast amounts of experimentation with animals. They are intended to specify quantitative nutritive requirements of different animal classes and species at a given age, rate of growth, and/or a specific productive function. In general, current standards are very satisfactory guidelines, but they must be revised continually as health or management are improved or genetic changes are made which allow more rapid growth or higher levels of production which, in turn, may alter nutrient needs.

❏ REFERENCES

1. Crampton, E. W. 1965. *J. Nutr.* **82**:353.
2. ARC. 1980. *The Nutrient Requirements of Ruminant Livestock*. Commonwealth Agr. Bureaux, London, England.
3. Brody, S. 1945. *Bioenergetics and Growth*. Hafner Pub. Co., NY.
4. Mitchell, H. H. 1962. *Comparative Nutrition of Man and Domestic Animals*. Academic Press, NY.
5. Moustgaard, J. 1959. In *Reproduction in Domestic Animals*. Academic Press, NY.
6. NRC. 1979. *Nutrient Requirements of Swine*. Nat. Acad. Sci., Washington, DC.

19

Factors Affecting
Feed Consumption

❏ INTRODUCTION

There is a considerable amount of interest in the various factors affecting feed consumption by animals. This is understandable in view of the economic factors related to feed intake and cost of production. A great mass of evidence shows clearly that the gross efficiency of production can be increased greatly in growing, fattening, or lactating animals if their consumption can be maintained at a high level without any major health problems. An example of this is shown in Table 19.1. Although these data are not applicable universally, they illustrate clearly the principle in question: that the maintenance requirement of animals gaining at a slow rate represents a much greater percentage of the total feed required than for animals gaining at more rapid rates. In this instance maintenance accounted for 75%, 59%, and 48% of total energy for cattle gaining 0.45, 0.91, and 1.36 kg/day, respectively.

Other costs are incurred at low levels of productivity, such as additional labor and additional time that money is tied up and less efficient use of facilities and equipment. High-level production is not without its costs, however, as animals are more prone to metabolic diseases and disorders that do not occur with a high frequency in animals producing at more moderate rates; for example, milk fever, ketosis, and acute indigestion in cattle. In addition, higher quality feed ingredients and more costly diets usually are required to attain high levels of productivity; however, the net cost is apt to be less for high rates of production in any situation where intensive animal production is practiced. Thus, the need to attain high levels of productivity provides the impetus for studying and learning about factors that influence feed intake.

There are a number of situations in which it is desirable to limit feed intake. For example, it is often convenient to self-feed different classes and species of animals, but often the desired or needed feed consumption is considerably less than ad libitum intake. The need of wintering beef cows for supplemental protein is a good example, or the need to restrict feed consumption by pregnant sows. The same situation could apply to diets designed for any species where the animal is primarily in a maintenance situation, that is, adult animals under no productive stress. Consequently, more information is needed on factors that tend to inhibit as well as stimulate food consumption.

❏ PALATABILITY AND APPETITE

Palatability is a term frequently misused. A quick and simple definition would be the overall acceptance and relish with which an animal consumes any given feedstuff or diet; obviously, this is not a very quantitative measure. Palatability is, essentially, the result of a summation of many different factors sensed by the animal in the process of locating and consuming food and it depends upon appearance, odor, taste, texture, temperature, and, in some cases, auditory properties of the food. These various factors are, in turn, affected by the physical and chemical nature of the food; the effect on individual animals may be modified by physiological or psychological differences. In research on palatability, it usually is measured by giving animals a choice of two or more feeds so that they can express a preference. **Appetite,** on the other hand, generally refers to internal factors (physiological or psychological) that stimulate or inhibit hunger in the animal. The effects of different variables on appetite or palatability are discussed in succeeding sections.

Taste

In taste research the basic tastes are described as sweet, sour, salty, and bitter along with what is called the common chemical sense, which means that animals may detect certain chemicals that do not fall in one of these four classes. Most of the taste research has been done with pure chemicals in water solutions or when added to feedstuffs. However, in the usual environment the animal is only occasionally exposed to a pure chemical and most tastes are a result of complex mixtures of organic and inorganic compounds which frequently defy description. In addition, odor frequently has a pronounced effect on taste perception.

Much research on taste in humans and animals such as the rat has been conducted, but relatively few papers are available on the domestic farm species;* thus, only a limited amount of information is available on them. Research with domestic animals shows clearly that their responses are not typical of human responses, leading to the assumption that sensations perceived by humans for a given chemical may be quite different than for many animals, although there is no way to prove this theory conclusively.

Animals are able to taste chemicals that dissolve partially because of taste buds located primarily on the tongue, but also on the palate, pharynx, and other parts of the oral cavity. Lower animals may have external taste buds on antennae, feet, and other appendages. On the tongue, different areas are sensitive to different tastes. In humans the tongue is particularly sensitive to sweet and salty flavors at the tip and front edges. On the sides, it is more sensitive to sour, and at the back, bitter. The number of taste buds varies greatly among species. It is said that averages are: chicken, 24; dog, 1,700; humans,

*See bibliography covering years from 1556–1966 in Kare and Maller (2).

TABLE 19.1 Energy required to produce 340 kg (750 lb) of gain on 500 steers at three rates of gain.[a]

| DAILY GAIN, kg (lb) | DAYS ON FEED | AV. WT, kg (lb) | NET ENERGY REQUIRED | | CORN EQUIVALENT, kg × 10³ |
			FOR MAINTENANCE, Mcal	FOR GAIN, Mcal	
0.45 (1.0)	700	340 (750)	2,156,000	708,500	1,707.7
0.91 (2.0)	350	340 (750)	1,078,000	740,250	1,176.6
1.36 (3.0)	234	340 (750)	720,720	782,730	1,018.8

[a]From McCullough (1).

9,000; pig and goat, 15,000; and cattle, 25,000. The number of taste buds does not necessarily reflect taste sensitivity as the chicken will reject certain flavored solutions that apparently are imperceptible to cattle.

With the four basic tastants in water solutions, sheep show a positive preference only for a few sugars in water solutions; cattle have a strong preference for sweets and a moderate preference for sour flavors; deer show a strong preference for sweets and moderate to weak preference for sour and bitter flavors; and goats tend to show a preference for all four taste classes. The concentration of the solution has a marked effect on preference or rejection. Other information indicates that sheep and cattle prefer grasses with high organic acid content, and Arnold (3) has shown that a variety of organic compounds common to some plants resulted in a reduced intake by sheep. Other data with cattle indicate that some complex volatile biochemicals may have a marked effect on taste preferences of similar forages (4). Salt-deficient sheep, however, have a marked preference for various Na salts, and it has been shown that ruminant animals will choose to graze on grasses that have been fertilized with P and N in preference to those not so fertilized. Pigs have a pronounced liking for sweets, and chickens show a positive response to a wide variety of plant or animal tissue components, but have little or no liking for some sugars, although they will consume xylose, which may cause toxic reactions.

Human taste has been shown to be affected by a variety of factors such as age, sex, physiological condition (pregnancy, for example), and disease. Information of this type is almost non-existent in domestic animals, although some is available on rats and dogs. It has been demonstrated that buck deer have a stronger preference for sour compounds than does,

and bucks show a preference for bitter compounds such as quinine, although does do not. Very likely, domestic species may show the same type of response.

It is well known that there are great differences in the ability of different humans to detect low concentrations of different tastants and, when detected, in the response—that likes and dislikes for foods and fluids vary widely. The same principle undoubtedly applies to animals. An example of the variability to be expected in similar sheep given different test solutions is presented in Table 19.2. Note the tremendous range in acceptibility of these different solutions, a situation that is typical of animal response to such tests.

A variety of different flavoring agents, which usually have moderate to strong odors also, are sold for use in commercial feeds. Many times they are added to animal feeds on the assumption that if it smells good to humans it ought to taste and smell good to animals. It is very probable that a substantial amount of money is wasted as a result, although a limited amount of published information indicates that some commercial favoring agents have resulted in increased feed consumption in some situations. Flavors (and odors) are likely to be of less consequence when animals do not have a choice of feedstuffs than when a variety of feedstuffs are available at one time. There is some indication that flavor association may be useful in increasing feed consumption. This has been shown by feeding a sow a flavoring agent which is secreted in milk. Providing the same flavor in dry feed for the young pig may increase consumption of the dry feed.

Odors

Odors are produced by volatile compounds and, as the reader will know, there is a tremendous variety

TABLE 19.2   An example of variation in response of sheep to different chemical solutions when given a choice between the chemical solution and tap water.[a]

CHEMICAL IN TEST SOLUTION	CONSUMPTION OF TEST SOLUTION, % OF TOTAL					
	SHEEP NO.					
	1	2	3	4	5	AV.
Sucrose, 15%	95	24	30	82	8	48
Lactose, 1.3%	73	54	42	46	68	56
Maltose, 2%	8	61	33	44	21	33
Glucose, 5%	69	88	27	71	90	69
Saccharin, 0.037%[b]	36	34	7	28	57	32
Sodium chloride, 2.5%[b]	8	23	14	22	29	19
Quinine HCl, 0.0063%[b]	51	80	23	27	43	45
Urea, 0.16%[b]	20	46	60	64	48	48

[a]From Goatcher (5).
[b]Those identified with * are a second set of sheep.

that may be produced by food and feed. At the present time there is little agreement as to a single broad classification of odors such as we find in taste.

It is conceded that most animals have a keener sense of smell than humans do, but quantitative information at this time is not adequate to predict the response of an animal. Some of the best research with domestic species (sheep) has been reported by Arnold (3, 6). When various senses—smell, taste, or touch—were impaired by surgery, Arnold found that loss of the sense of smell did not increase consumption of any of five plant species and intake of two was decreased. Sheep were less apt to consume flowering heads, a fact also noted by others. When various odoriferous compounds were added to feed, Arnold found that the response depended on whether the animals had a choice or not, and the response (increased or decreased total consumption) was not predictable. Of six different compounds, only butyric acid increased consumption with and without a choice of feeds. A wide variety of odoriferous compounds may be objectionable to sheep at first, with the sheep reacting strongly, but eventually they overcame their objections and ate the feed even when other uncontaminated feed was available. This information would indicate that odor may serve as an attractant, but may not have a great deal of influence on total or eventual consumption.

Sight

It is recognized that many, although not all, animal species have better vision than man. However, the importance of sight as it affects food consumption in animals is not understood fully. Pangborn (7) points out that experimental evidence on humans indicates clearly that sight has a pronounced effect on taste, because individuals tend to associate different colors, shapes, and other visual cues with known flavors and odors. Sight in animals appears to be used more for orientation and location of food. Research with cattle and sheep shows no effect of coloring feeds red, green, or blue—indicating that they may be color blind.

Texture-Physical Factors

It is well known that the texture and particle size of feedstuffs may influence acceptability. Pelleted feeds are a good example, as most domestic and some wild ruminant species will readily take to pelleted feeds even though they may be completely unfamiliar with them. Particle size and texture also may have some effect as evidenced by the fact that many animals will take more readily to rolled or cracked grains than to whole grains. Feed preparatory methods that reduce dustiness usually result in an increased feed intake, as almost all animals discriminate against dust if given a chance to do so; this is probably one reason why succulent feeds are consumed readily compared to dry feed.

❏ APPETITE AND REGULATION OF FEED INTAKE

Appetite has been defined as the desire of an animal to eat and **satiety** as the lack of desire to eat. **Hunger** may be defined as the physiological state that results from the deprivation of food of a general or specific type and is abolished by the ingestion of these foods. Appetite is frequently quantitated by measuring the intake of food in a limited time span. An example of equipment used in appetite research is shown in Fig. 19.1.

All current theories agree that food intake is affected by factors operating to control intake over a long-term period and that other short-term controls operate to control the daily feed consumption. Discussion follows on some of the major areas of importance.

Long-Term Control

That animals have some means of controlling appetite over the long-term cannot be questioned. This is clearly demonstrated by the fact that, when adequate food of an acceptable nature is available, wild animals do not starve or overeat to a harmful extent, although humans and some domestic animals are exceptions. This seems to be particularly true for wild species that (with the exception of some arctic or hibernating species) seldom accumulate the amount of body fat seen in tame species. Some of the inputs believed to be involved in long-term appetite control include the physiological state of the animal such as lactation or estrus, the nitrogen status of the animal, environmental factors such as temperature and humidity, photoperiod and/or season, and production level and total energy demand. Very little is known about how these factors function except that the effects of season (low intakes in winter, high intakes in summer) may reflect photoperiod and, hence, be mediated at least in part by the pineal gland (8).

Short-Term Control

It has been demonstrated clearly that hunger and satiety centers are located in the hypothalamus (mid-brain). Studies with experimental animals have shown that lesions in the appropriate location (lateral hypothalamus) will cause temporary loss of appetite and lack of thirst, so this area appears to be responsible for initiation of feeding. By the same token, appropriate lesions in the ventromedial hypothalamus may cause an animal to overeat, indicating that this area inhibits appetite. Electrodes placed in these areas can be used to pinpoint electrical stimuli to cause the same effects so that the animal will eat during stimulation and quit eating as soon as the electrical stimulus is stopped.

Daily food intake is normally consumed in a number of discrete meals. The short-term controls that initiate and end each meal are accomplished, as presently known, either by neural receptors and afferent neurons that relay impulses from the gut, liver, and

Figure 19.1 *Apparatus designed to measure feed consumption of sheep in timed intervals to study periodic intake of feed. Courtesy of P. J. Wangsness, Pennsylvania State University.*

perhaps other organs into centers in the midbrain or by blood-born factors whose mechanisms are not presently fully understood.

Chemostatic Regulation of Appetite

In most non-ruminant species there is evidence that blood glucose concentration is related negatively to feed intake over the short-term, and that hunger contractions of the stomach are more pronounced when blood glucose is low. Administration of glucose solution into the stomach a few minutes prior to a meal may result in a marked delay in solid food intake of pigs and horses, but administration of glucose intravenously will have little effect when given about the same time as the meal starts. Either may affect subsequent meals (10, 11), so the current feeling is that the effect of glucose on appetite is more of an emergency type of control (11). In ruminant species such relationships do not hold because blood glucose concentration has little, if any relationship to feed intake. Data on ruminants indicate that blood insulin levels increase after feeding and that the level of insulin is influenced by the energy level of the diet

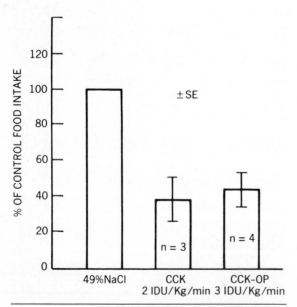

Figure 19.2 *Effect on food intake of CCK (natural cholecystokinin of porcine origin) and CCK-8 (synthetic cholecystokinin) infused into the jugular vein continuously of pigs over a 10-min. test meal time. Food consumption was depressed to about 40% of the controls. From Anika et al. (12). Courtesy of T. K. Houpt, Cornell University. From Anika et al. (12).*

and/or amount of food consumed (9). Some evidence shows that blood propionate levels are related negatively to feed intake as are rumen volatile fatty acids, where high concentrations in the dorsal sac may inhibit feeding.

There is ample evidence to illustrate that high osmotic pressure in the duodenum will inhibit appetite for a time. This effect can be produced by concentrated solutions of sugar or salt, so it is not an energy-related response (10).

Growth hormone will increase milk production and feed intake, but its normal role in hunger and satiety is unclear at present. The same comment applies to most other hormones. Some of the gastrointestinal peptide hormones (gastrin, cholecystokinin, and secretin) will depress intake in a dose-related manner when administered intravenously in various veins in the intestinal area (Fig. 19.2). In pigs, cholecystokinin levels in the blood are at least double after eating as before eating (12). Evidence is also available for cholecystokinin activity, which is produced and released within the brain, acting as a signal of satiety, but the normal mechanism triggering its release and satiety has not been established. Pentagastrin, a synthetic peptide with the activity of gastrin, appears to act on the brain to depress intake by sheep. Other opioid peptides administered in the central nervous system will stimulate feeding in sheep, but further information is required to understand how they fit into the overall scheme of appetite stimulation and control (11). No doubt other unidentified chemical factors have some effect on appetite in animals, but further time is required to develop more information.

Caloric Density and Physical Limitations of the GI Tract on Appetite

Most adult animals are capable of maintaining a relatively stable body weight over long periods of time. Likewise, young animals of a given species tend to grow at uniform rates. Both adults and growing young do this in spite of marked variation in physical activity and energy expenditure, indicating that the animal is able to adjust energy intake to energy expenditure by some unknown means of appetite control. If no other problems interfere—such as nutrient deficiencies, disease, and so on—animals eat to meet their caloric needs. If the diet is diluted by water, then a much greater volume will be consumed. By the same token, if the diet is diluted with undigestible ingre-

TABLE 19.3   Effect of energy level on performance of finishing broilers from 4.5 to 8 weeks of age.[a]

RATION ENERGY, ME, Mcal/kg	CONSUMPTION OF FEED, kg	ENERGY, Mcal	FEED CONVERSION	DAILY GAIN, g
2.81	2.30	6.46	2.80	34.2
2.98	2.31	6.87	2.65	36.3
3.10	2.31	7.17	2.45	39.3
3.14	2.22	6.98	2.39	38.8
3.18	2.20	7.02	2.35	39.1
3.31	2.18	7.20	2.32	39.1
3.79	2.09	7.90	2.14	40.6

[a]From Combs and Nicholson (14).

dients, then the animal will eat more up to a point at which its GI tract can no longer accommodate the bulk in the diet. This principle is illustrated in Table 19.3 with chickens and graphically in Fig. 19.3. In Table 19.3 note that feed consumption declines gradually as energy content of the diet is increased over a rather narrow range, although total energy intake increased in this example. Feed conversion also was improved as energy concentration in the diet increased. These principles are recognized in the nutrition of non-ruminant species, and diets are adjusted to provide more or less optimum caloric density for a given production function. For example, if one wishes to control energy intake of pigs, it can be done by diluting the ration with alfalfa hay.

The effect of feeding growing-fattening pigs increasing amounts of alfalfa hay in pelleted diets is shown in Table 19.4. In contrast to most instances where pelleted diets have been fed, especially high roughage for ruminants, feed consumption did not increase (and even decreased). In this instance the alfalfa may have had an inhibitory effect on appetite. DE consumption decreased accompanied by less efficient feed use. However, backfat thickness was reduced with added alfalfa.

In ruminant species, where a large proportion of the diet is composed of roughages—pasture, hay, silages—the relationship is less clearly understood by most producers, probably because so many different factors affect the optimum caloric density for a given class and species of animals. Factors such as physical density of the feed, particle size, amount of indigestible residue, solubility of the dry matter of the feed, rapidity of rumen fermentation, and level

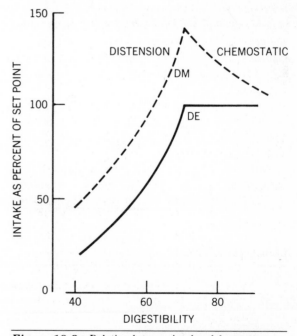

Figure 19.3 *Relation between intake of dry matter (DM) or digestible energy (DE). Data fitting this model are obtained when a concentrate diet is diluted with a bulky filler or coarse forage. Similar results have been obtained for cattle, sheep and rats. The constancy of energy intake in high density diets is determined by the set point of metabolism; below the inflection point gut fill, or the time spent eating and/or ruminating becomes limiting so that the animal is not able to eat up to the level of its appetite. From Van Soest (13).*

TABLE 19.4   Effect of percentage of roughage in the diet on feed consumption of pigs.[a]

ITEM	DIETARY ALFALFA, %			
	0	20	40	60
Daily feed consumed, kg	3.0	3.0	3.2	2.7
Daily gain, kg	0.86	0.73	0.63	0.41
Feed efficiency	3.6	4.1	5.0	6.7
Daily DE intake, Mcal	8.91	7.80	7.40	5.50
Av. backfat, cm	3.9	3.5	3.2	2.9

[a]From Powley et al. (15).

and frequency of feeding influence rate of passage through the GI tract. This, in turn, influences the amount of space in the stomach and gut for the next meal. For example, it has been demonstrated many times that consumption of low-quality roughages such as straw and poor hay can be increased markedly by addition of protein supplements and, sometimes, with P or molasses. Such forage usually is deficient in both N and P for adequate rumen digestion and small amounts of readily available carbohydrate tend to stimulate cellulose digestion in the rumen. Other nutrients required by rumen microorganisms would be expected to have the same effect (Mg and S, for example). By way of another example, pelleting of low-quality roughages will almost always increase consumption greatly due to more rapid digestion and passage out of the rumen.

With the very low quality roughages (straws, stovers, etc.), only moderate amounts of supplemental feed will result in depressed roughage consumption. This phenomenon is illustrated in Table 19.5. In this instance note that 1.2 kg of a barley-alfalfa supplement depressed ad libitum consumption of barley straw, and that increasing levels continued to depress straw consumption, although total organic matter increased gradually.

As a result of these factors, pinpointing a precise value at which increasing caloric density of a ration would result in a reduced intake of dry matter or energy would be most difficult. Age is a factor also, as young lambs or calves are less able to handle high-roughage diets than older animals. With respect to dairy cows, Conrad *et al.* (17) concluded that 67% digestible dry matter was the lowest ration digestibility at which lactating cows producing moderate amounts of milk could regulate energy intake (no longer physically limiting), whereas other work has shown that energy intake of dairy heifers was maintained when the ration (pelleted) was above 56% digestible dry matter (18).

TABLE 19.5   Effect of supplemental feeds on consumption by cattle of barley straw.[a]

ITEM	SUPPLEMENTAL FEED/DAY, KG[b]					
	1	1.5	3.0	4.5	6.0	7.5
Organic matter intake, kg/day						
Straw[c]	4.18	3.66	3.24	3.37	2.91	2.04
Supplement	—	1.20	2.40	3.60	4.80	6.00
Total	4.18	4.86	5.64	6.97	7.71	8.06
Straw OM intake, g/kg BW	12.0	10.6	9.4	9.7	8.4	5.9
Total OM intake, g/kg BW	12.0	14.0	16.3	20.1	22.2	23.3
Crude protein, % of whole diet	4.1	7.0	8.7	9.7	10.7	12.3

[a]From Horton and Holmes (16).
[b]Supplement was a 1:2 mixture of barley and dried alfalfa.
[c]Straw was fed ad libitum.

Two sets of data illustrating the effect of caloric density on energy intake are shown in Table 19.6. The data on steers illustrate clearly the curvilinear effect on energy intake as the caloric density goes from low to high. At the low end, physical limitations of the GI tract are, most likely, limiting intake to less than would be consumed otherwise. At the two highest energy concentrations, feed and energy intake were reduced considerably, probably because of abnormal rumen fermentation or appetite inhibition by some chemical factor produced in or present in the GI tract. In the example with lambs, dry matter was almost the same with each of these rations which were composed of varying amounts of barley, oats and oat hulls. However, estimated ME intake and carcass gain were highest with the most concentrated ration (79.5% DE). Note also that dry matter found in the forestomach and gut after slaughter increased progressively as the caloric density of the rations decreased. These data illustrate the physical limitation effect of a roughage (oat hulls) that is of low digestibility. With respect to these lambs the high energy ration had not, apparently, reached the point of diminishing returns as it did with the steers.

The bulk density (weight/unit of volume) of a diet may have a marked effect on feed consumption. This is illustrated in Fig. 19.4. In this particular instance the diets were formulated to be isocaloric but with different densities. Note that volume of feed consumed increased as the density decreased and that energy consumption (TDN) also decreased as density decreased. Feed processing such as pelleting, cubing, chopping or grinding results in increased density of most feeds.

The point (in terms of caloric density) at which an animal will have satisfied its energy demand may be expected to be quite variable with different classes and species of animals because energy needs will vary with productive functions. Thus, a lactating cow will have a greater demand than a pregnant, nonlactating cow, which, in turn, will have a higher requirement than an animal that is neither pregnant nor lactating. Rapid growth will stimulate a greater need for energy as will various environmental factors and stressing situations.

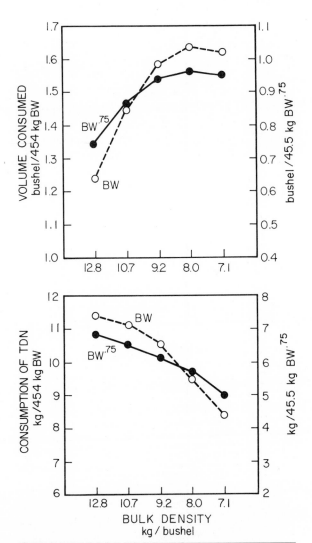

Figure 19.4 *Graphs illustrating the effect of changing bulk density on volume (upper) and energy consumption (lower) by cattle. The diets were presumed to be isocaloric. From Kellems and Church (21).*

❏ INHIBITION OF APPETITE

As the reader has probably concluded, control of appetite is a complex mechanism with inputs from a variety of different sources. In addition to the various theorized mechanisms, appetite is affected generally by factors that interfere with the normal functions of the GI tract or by many different diseases that affect non-GI tract tissues and organs.

Nutritionally, it has been known for many, many years that a high-protein meal (in humans, at least) tends to dull the appetite. This is believed to be related to the prolonged and relatively high heat increment resulting from the metabolism of amino acids. Fat also is inhibitory, presumably because a high-fat meal does not pass out of the stomach rapidly and fat entering the duodenum triggers hormonal

TABLE 19.6   Effect of caloric density on feed and energy intake of ruminant species.

ITEM	EXPERIMENTAL DATA										
Steers[a]											
Roughage in ration, %	100	90	80	70	60	50	40	30	20	10	0
DE, Kcal/g	2.50	2.62	2.81	2.92	3.02	3.08	3.21	3.25	3.36	3.46	3.60
Dry matter intake, g/kg BW$^{0.75}$	94	91	98	97	91	97	98	87	85	71	46
DE intake, Kcal/kg BW$^{0.75}$	235	242	276	282	276	299	316	282	288	245	166
Lambs[b]											
DE, %	65.2		71.6		74.9		76.6		79.5		
Calculated ME, Mcal/kg	2.36		2.59		2.71		2.73		2.82		
Dry matter intake, kg/day	1.06		1.03		1.00		1.00		1.02		
ME intake, Mcal/day	2.50		2.66		2.71		2.73		2.88		
Carcass gain, g/day	105		118		121		125		143		
Dry matter in forestomach, g	1287		1302		818		816		503		
Dry matter in hind gut, g	265		236		226		220		188		

[a]Data from Parrott *et al.* (19).
[b]Data from Andrews *et al.* (20).

mechanisms that may cause restriction of the pylorus, resulting in a slow emptying of the stomach.

In human nutrition and dietetics there is a great interest in appetite inhibitors (called anorectics) that are often used in weight reduction programs. Many different compounds have been used at one time or another, but most of those currently in use are amines similar to or derived from amphetamine; these compounds are stimulatory to the central nervous system, but, at the same time, result in some inhibition of appetite. Undesirable side effects occur frequently and, in addition, many people develop tolerance to the effect on appetite after a period of a few weeks. Generally, these chemical inhibitors have not been proven to be very successful and there are many conditions where their use is contra-indicated.

Feed intake for animals is more commonly limited by caloric dilution—dilution of rations with feedstuffs of low digestibility—or by restricting intake by reducing the daily allowance. Feed intake can be restricted partially in other ways. For example, feed provided in a physical form not preferred—such as a dusty meal—nearly always will reduce feed intake. Unpalatable ingredients can be used, for example, diammonium phosphate or quinine. With ruminant species, salt (NaCl) has been used successfully to restrict intake, but this would be hazardous with birds and pigs because they are relatively susceptible to salt toxicity. Research in the early 1950s demonstrated that salt, when mixed with protein supplements such as cottonseed meal, can be fed for several months to cattle or sheep without detrimental results if water is not restricted. Salt may be needed in a concentration of 20–30% of the mixture to restrict protein supplement consumption to about one kg/day for cattle. The exact amount depends on availability of other feedstuffs and the age of the animal. Fat has been used to restrict intake of concentrates and, nutritionally, is probably preferable to dilution with salt as the excess salt, even though it may not be harmful, is wasted from a nutritional point of view and may increase urinary loss of other electrolytes.

❏ FACTORS AFFECTING FEED INTAKE

Some knowledge of expected feed intake is required in any situation where ad libitum intake is allowed—that is, for high-producing or fast-gaining animals. If we assume that suggested nutrient allowances are reasonably accurate, then we must know how much feed is likely to be consumed in order to arrive at the desired concentration of nutrients in any ration provided to an animal. To put it another way, if we assume that a cow requires 1.5 kg of protein/day, we must know how much feed is consumed in order to arrive at a desired percentage of protein in the diet if we do not want to over- or under-feed the cow. As the reader may have concluded, several factors may affect the amount of feed consumed by an animal. These are discussed briefly in subsequent sections.

Body Weight

As indicated in Ch. 10, energy requirements of adult animals are related, more or less, to body weight raised to the 0.75 power. Thus, an increase in body size from, let us say, 1,000 lb to 1,100 lb, does not increase energy requirements by 10%, but by a lesser amount, 7.4%.* However, body weight, by itself, is not always highly related to feed intake, particularly when we are dealing with fattening animals. For example, beef animals just starting on feed are apt to have relatively little body fat (10% +) and may be expected to consume on the order of 2.5–2.75% of body weight/day. When they are approaching market condition with, perhaps, 25–30% of body tissues being fat, feed consumption is apt to be more nearly 2.2% of body weight/day. This is a reflection of the fact that energy need (and feed consumption) is related more nearly to lean body mass than to total body weight; also, more fat has been deposited in the abdominal cavity, thus reducing the amount of space that may be occupied by the GI tract and the feed that it contains.

Individuality of Animals

Anyone who has had experience with individually fed animals realizes that they do not all eat alike and may readily show pronounced likes and dislikes when they have the opportunity to express themselves. It is well known also that hormonal differences may result in hyperexcitable or phlegmatic animals, with resultant effects on activity and feed consumption. Such differences make it difficult to predict how much some of these animals may consume. In modern day ag-

---

*$1,000^{0.75} = 177.8$; $1,100^{0.75} = 191.0$; the difference, $13.2 = 7.4\%$ increase over 177.8.

riculture, catering to such individual animal variation may not be feasible, even though we should be aware that it exists.

Type and Level of Production

All young animals have what we might call a 'biological urge' to grow and growth cannot be impeded greatly without an adverse effect on eventual size and/or productivity. Almost invariably, those animals having the most rapid growth rates have the best appetites. Ample evidence shows also that pregnancy and lactation result in a stimulation of appetite. With respect to lactating animals, appetite is not correlated completely with production. Some cows, for example, have the ability to lactate at very high levels, yet do not have the appetite to go along with it, with the result that they may lose a considerable amount of body weight during peak lactation. On the other hand, some animals will not deplete body reserves greatly in order to produce milk. Considerable variation among animals is found in this respect.

Miscellaneous Factors

Hot ambient temperatures, especially along with high humidity, have an inhibitory effect on appetite. On the other hand, cold temperatures usually stimulate appetite. Diet characteristics can modify these influences somewhat, although not greatly.

Health of the animal is certainly a factor of great consequence. Most infectious diseases result in a reduced feed intake, more or less related to the severity of the infection. Likewise, intestinal para-sites such as ascarids, usually result in reduced feed consumption, often for prolonged periods of time. Metabolic problems such as ketosis, bloat, and diarrhea result in restricted feed consumption.

Stresses (in addition to disease or parasites) usually will reduce consumption. Such stresses as crowding (lack of adequate space), noise and disturbances, and excessive handling tend to keep animals excited and reduce feed consumption.

Proper design for feed bunks, mangers and water supplies can encourage increased intake. Cleanliness of feed and water containers may have a pronounced effect, also, as most animals object to dirt, sour feed, molds, and manure in or near their feed or water. Inadequate water supplies, particularly if the water is contaminated or foul-tasting or has a high dissolved solids content (see Ch. 6), will reduce feed consumption.

❏ EXPECTED FEED INTAKE

Expected Feed Intake of Cattle

The total feed consumption of cattle, as with other ruminants, is highly dependent upon the quality of the roughage being consumed. As an approximate guide, the information in Table 19.7 can be used, bearing in mind that many different factors may modify the values given. For example, it is clear that young, rapidly growing animals will consume more/unit of size than adult animals, particularly if fed high quality roughages. Also, adult animals with high

TABLE 19.7 Expected roughage consumption by cattle.

FEEDSTUFF	USUAL RANGE IN ENERGY		DRY MATTER INTAKE, % BODY WT/DAY
	TDN, %	DE, MCAL/KG	
Lush, young legume, grass pasture; barn-dried grass	70+	3.10+	2.75–3.5
Well-eared corn silage; high quality sorghum silage	70	3.10	2.0–2.5[a]
Moderate quality, actively growing pasture	60–65	2.65–2.87	2.5–3.2
Grass and grass-legume silage of good quality	55–60	2.43–2.65	2.0–2.5[a]
Good quality legume hays	50–55	2.20–2.43	2.5–3.0
Grass hay from mature plants; regrowth pasture	45–50	1.98–2.20	1.5–2.0
Poor quality grass hays; dormant pasture	40–45	1.76–1.98	1.0–1.5
Cereal and grass straws	35–40	1.54–1.76	1.0 or less

[a]Cattle will only rarely eat as much dry matter from silage as when the same crop is preserved in other forms.

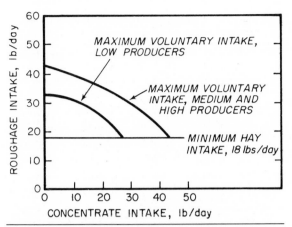

Figure 19.5 *Estimated maximum voluntary intake of roughages [90% dry matter] by 1200 lb cows at varying concentrate intakes. From Dean et al. (22). By permission of Lea & Febiger.*

physiological needs, such as lactating cows, may consume forage at the upper limits or even exceed the values shown in the table, but those with low requirements will not consume nearly as much. Feed preparation, such as pelleting, may increase consumption greatly as will proper supplementation of low quality roughages. Silages are only rarely consumed at levels approaching that of high quality hay, even though the digestibility of the silage may be quite good; the high water content may be partially responsible as well as the high acid content.

Conrad *et al.* (17) maintain that consumption by dairy cows of rations of low digestibility is in direct proportion to body weight rather than in proportion to metabolic size (BW$^{0.75}$). Equations developed by Conrad can be used to predict maximum feed intake and minimum allowable digestibility in the rations. These equations are:

Maximum feed intake (values in lb)

$$= 10.7 \, (BW/1000) + 0.058 \, BW^{0.75}$$
$$+ 0.33 \text{ milk production} + 0.53$$

Minimum allowable digestibility (values in lb)

$$= \frac{(0.058 \, BW^{0.75} + 0.33 \text{ milk production} + 0.53)}{\text{maximum feed intake}}$$

where BW = body weight. These formulas have worked out well in practice.

Figure 19.5 illustrates the range in forage con-

sumption that may be expected by dairy cows given various levels of concentrates. As indicated in this figure, small amounts of concentrates may not depress forage consumption; they may even increase consumption of low quality roughages; however, as a general rule, increased concentrate consumption will result in a gradual reduction in roughage intake and in total dry matter consumption, although energy intake will nearly always increase as concentrates are added. For dairy cows, most nutritionists recommend 35–55% concentrate in the total ration for optimum utilization of roughage and near-maximum energy intake. For finishing beef cattle, the amount of concentrate fed in the USA in current practice is apt to be about 60–90%, depending on the quality of the roughage and on feed preparation methods used on both roughage and concentrates.

With respect to total feed consumption, young animals would be expected to consume relatively more than older animals. Young Holstein calves may be expected to consume 3.2–3.4% of body weight at 2 mo. of age of a complete feed and to consume about 3% at 6 months of age. After this their feed intake will decline gradually. NRC (24) recommen-

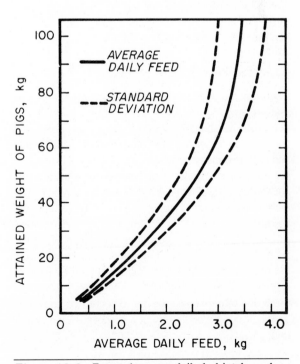

Figure 19.6 *Expected average daily feed intake and range for full-fed pigs when fed according to NRC standards. From NRC (24).*

dations for finishing beef steers are somewhat lower. Suggested maximum dry matter intake ranges from 2.96% for lightweight calves to 2.2% for calves weighing 450 kg. For yearling steers, values given range from 3.2% of body weight for animals weighing 135 kg decreasing to 2.36% for those weighing 454 kg. Of course, the caloric and bulk densities will have a marked effect on maximum consumption. Mature cattle will not normally be fed diets with such high caloric density as fattening cattle. NRC suggestions for lactating cows giving 10 kg of milk/day are only 2% of body weight/day of dry matter, much lower than a dairy cow would be expected to consume.

Expected Feed Intake of Sheep

Experiments carried out under calorimetric conditions indicate that sheep will consume roughages at about the same level/unit of metabolic size ($BW^{0.75}$) as cattle. However, because their actual size is considerably smaller, the amount, when expressed as percentage of body weight, will be greater. NRC values (see Appendix tables) indicate consumption of total ration by finishing lambs to be about 4.3% of body weight at 30 kg (66 lb) ranging down to 3.5% at 55 kg (121 lb). This level of consumption may be exceeded when lambs are fed high-roughage, pelleted rations. NRC values for other sheep classes are given in the appropriate tables.

Expected Feed Intake of Swine

Feed consumption of growing pigs from weaning to market weight (18–100 kg; 40–220 lb) may be expected to be about 2.0–3.2 kg/day (4.5–7 lb). Consumption level will be affected markedly by physical and caloric density as well as other factors discussed previously. A graphic presentation of typical feed consumption is shown in Fig. 19.6. Note that average daily consumption is about 5% of body weight, although it is higher for young pigs and decreases gradually as the pigs get older and fatter. Mature animals, except for lactating sows, usually are limit fed to about 1.8–2.3 kg (4–5 lb) daily as they usually will become too fat unless a low-energy ration is used. Lactating sows may be expected to consume 3–4% of body weight/day of a moderate energy ration.

Expected Consumption of Chickens

Expected feed consumption of mixed sexes of broiler chicks on typical rations and with favorable conditions

TABLE 19.8   Expected feed consumption of broiler chicks, mixed sexes.[a]

AGE IN WEEKS	AV. BODY WEIGHT,		FEED/BROILER/WEEK	
	LB	G	LB	G
1	0.26	118	0.29	132
2	0.57	259	0.43	195
3	1.02	463	0.72	327
4	1.53	695	0.94	427
5	2.06	935	1.07	486
6	2.67	1212	1.26	572
7	3.33	1512	1.45	658
8	3.98	1807	1.62	735

[a]Anonymous (25).

is illustrated in Table 19.8. As with other species, growth rate declines as does feed consumption/unit of body weight as animals age. With respect to laying hens, feed consumption is affected markedly by size of the hen and by her level of egg production. With 2.3 kg (5 lb) birds producing at a level of 60–70%, daily feed consumption will be about (24–25 lb) 10.9–11.3 kg/100 birds.

❑ SUMMARY

Many different factors affect feed consumption by animals. Changes in taste, odors, physical texture, and so on, will normally alter consumption. In general, animals tend to regulate their diet by the need for energy, although selectivity of dietary components has a marked effect on consumption of protein, minerals and vitamins. Animals that require more feed—such as in lactation, heavy work, rapid growth—have greater appetites, but the specific mechanisms that control appetite have yet to be elucidated. Expected feed intake is important when diets are designed for a specific purpose. If consumption is less than anticipated, then nutrient concentration must be higher in order to meet nutritional needs.

❑ REFERENCES

1. McCullough, M. E. 1973. *Feedstuffs* **45**(7):34.
2. Kare, M. R. and O. Maller (eds.). 1967. *The Chemical Senses and Nutrition*. The Johns Hopkins Press, Baltimore, MD.

3. Arnold, G. W. 1970. In *Physiology of Digestion and Metabolism in the Ruminant.* Oriel Press, Newcastle-Upon-Tyne, England.

4. Aderibigbe, A. O., D. C. Church, R. B. Frakes, and R. G. Petersen. 1982. *J. Animal Sci.* **54:**164.

5. Goatcher, W. D. 1969. M. S. Thesis, Oregon State Univ., Corvallis, OR.

6. Arnold, G. W. 1966. *Austral. J. Agr. Res.* **17:**531.

7. Pangborn, R. M. 1967. In *The Chemical Senses and Nutrition.* The Johns Hopkins Press, Baltimore, MD.

8. Suttie, J. M., R. N. B. Kay, and E. D. Goodall. 1984. *Livestock Prod. Sci.* **11:**529.

9. Lofgren, P. A. and R. G. Warner. 1972. *J. Animal Sci.* **35:**1239.

10. Houpt, T. R. 1984. *J. Animal Sci.* **59:**1345.

11. Grovum, W. L. 1987. In *The Ruminant Animal,* p. 202, D. C. Church (ed.). Prentice-Hall, Inc., Englewood Cliffs, N.J.; Della-Ferra, Mary Anne and C. A. Baile. 1984. *J. Animal Sci.* **59:**1362.

12. Anika, S. M., T. R. Houpt, and K. A. Houpt. 1981. *Amer. J. Physiol.* **240:**R310.

13. Van Soest, P. J. 1982. *The Nutritional Ecology of the Ruminant.* O & B Books, Inc., Corvallis, OR.

14. Combs, G. F. and J. L. Nicholson. 1964. *Feedstuffs* **36**(34):17.

15. Powley, J. E., et al. 1981. *J. Animal Sci.* **53:**308.

16. Horton, G. M. J. and W. Holmes. 1976. *Animal Prod.* **22:**419.

17. Conrad, H. R., A. D. Pratt, and J. W. Hibbs. 1964. *J. Dairy Sci.* **47:**54.

18. Montgomery, M. J. and B. R. Baumgardt. 1965. *J. Dairy Sci.* **48:**569.

19. Parrott, C., H. Loughhead, W. H. Hale, and C. B. Theurer. 1968. Arizona Cattle Feeders Day Report, Univ. of Arizona, Tucson.

20. Andrews, R. P., M. Kay, and E. R. Ørskov. 1969. *Animal Prod.* **11:**173.

21. Kellems, R. O. and D. C. Church. 1981. Proc. West. Sec. Amer. Soc. *Animal Sci.* **32:**26.

22. Dean, G. W., D. L. Bath, and S. Olayide. 1969. *J. Dairy Sci.* **52:**1008.

23. NRC. 1984. *Nutrient Requirements of Beef Cattle.* Nat. Acad. Sci., Washington, D.C.

24. NRC. 1973. *Nutrient Requirements of Swine.* Nat. Acad. Sci., Washington, D.C.

25. Anonymous. 1972. Poultry Management and Business Analysis Manual. Maine Ext. Serv. Bul. 566.

20

Feedstuffs for Animals

IN THE STUDY OF animal nutrition and feeding, we need to be concerned with feedstuffs (or feeds) because they are the raw material that is essential for animal production. With domestic animals used for production of food or fiber, we are concerned with the efficient conversion of feedstuffs to useful products for man's use or enjoyment. Consequently, some understanding of the chemical and nutritional composition of important classes of feedstuffs will provide a better understanding of applied animal nutrition.

A tremendous variety of feedstuffs is used for animal feeding throughout the world, the variety of a given location depending on the local products that are grown or harvested and the class and species of animals involved. Well over 2,000 different products have been characterized to some extent for animal feeds, not counting varietal differences in various forages and grains.

The desirability of a given feedstuff is dependent upon a number of different factors. Cost is an important item and, generally, products fed to animals are either those that are not edible for humans or those that are produced in excess of human needs in a given location or country. With our imperfect systems of distribution, a grain that may be surplus in the USA might well be in high demand for human use in some other area of the world. Thus, it is only in relatively recent times that livestock have been fed large quantities of edible food grains.

323

Other factors affecting value of a feedstuff will include acceptability by the animal, ability of a given animal species or class to utilize a given product, the nutritional content, and the handling and milling properties of the product.

The number of feedstuffs is so great that it is not feasible to cover many individual feeds in any detail in this book. Rather, we will deal with major differences of feedstuffs in the various classes (next section) with occasional emphasis on individual items. Readers desiring more detailed information can refer to NRC (1), to IFI (2), or to older publications such as Morrison (3). Other publications providing tabular data on feed and forage composition include an FAO publication on tropical feeds (4), one from the University of Florida on Latin American feeds (5) and one (6) on by-products and unusual feedstuffs.

❏ CLASSIFICATION OF FEEDSTUFFS

A **feedstuff** may be defined as any component of a diet that serves some useful function. Most feedstuffs provide a source of one or more nutrients, but ingredients may be included to provide bulk, reduce oxidation of readily oxidized nutrients, to emulsify fats, provide flavor, color or other factors related to acceptability, rather than serving strictly as a source of nutrients. Generally, medicinal compounds usually are excluded. One classification scheme is given below:

ROUGHAGES

Permanent pasture and range plants
Temporary pasture plants
Soilage or green chop
Cannery and food crop residues

DRY FORAGES AND ROUGHAGES

Hay
  Legume
  Non-legume (primarily grasses)
  Cereal crop hays
Straw and chaff
Fodder, stover
Other products with >18% crude fiber
  Corn cobs
  Shells
  Sugar-cane bagasse
  Cottonseed hulls
  Cotton gin trash
  Animal wastes

SILAGES

Corn
Sorghum
Grass
Grass-legume
Legume
Miscellaneous

CONCENTRATES (ENERGY SOURCES)

Cereal grains
Milling by-products (primarily from cereal grains)
Molasses of various types
Seed and mill screenings
Beet and citrus pulps
Animal and vegetable fats
Whey
Miscellaneous
  Brewery by-products
  Waste from food processing plants
  Cull fruits, vegetables, and nuts
  Garbage
  Roots and tubers
  Bakery waste

PROTEIN CONCENTRATES

Oilseed meals
  Cottonseed, soybean, linseed, etc.
Animal meat or meat and bone meals
Marine meals
Avian by-product meals
Seeds (whole) from plants
Milling by-products
Distillers and brewers dried grains
Dehydrated legumes

Single-cell sources (bacteria, yeast, algae)
Non-protein nitrogen (urea, etc.)
Dried manures
MINERAL SUPPLEMENTS
VITAMIN SUPPLEMENTS
NON-NUTRITIVE ADDITIVES

Antibiotics
Antioxidants
Buffers
Colors and flavors
Emulsifying agents
Enzymes
Hormones
Medicines
Miscellaneous

The relative value (in very general terms) of some groups of feedstuffs is given in Table 20.1. This is intended to give the reader a quick understanding of the nutrient concentration found in these sources. Note that there would be many exceptions with such a simple classification, particularly with regard to the mineral elements. Nevertheless, it is a simple matter to go down one of the columns, such as energy, and note quickly that there are appreciable differences in different feed sources. More details on composition are presented in later sections.

❏ ROUGHAGES

Roughages are the primary foods for all herbivorous animals existing under natural conditions; such food provides the major portion of their diet for most if not all of the year. Harvested and stored roughages (hays, silages and other forms) are utilized by humans to increase animal productivity under conditions that would not allow it otherwise in nature. Thus, for farm animals roughages are of primary interest for ruminants and horses. Although other species such as swine can survive on roughage, productivity with no other source of feed would be too low to be economical in our current economy.

Nature of Roughages

To most livestock feeders, a **roughage** is a bulky feed that has a low weight/unit of volume. This is probably the best means of classifying a feedstuff as a roughage, but any means of classifying roughages has its limitation because, due to the nature of the products we are dealing with, there is a great variability in physical and chemical composition. Most feedstuffs classed as roughages have a high crude fiber (CF) content and a low digestibility of nutrients such as crude protein and energy. If we attempt, as does NRC (1), to classify all feedstuffs as roughages that have >18% CF and/or with low digestibility, immediately we find exceptions. Corn silage is a good example; nearly always it has >18% CF, but the TDN content of well-eared corn silage is about 70% on a dry basis. Lush young grass is another example. Although its weight/unit volume may be relatively low and fiber content relatively high, it digestibility is quite high. Soybean hulls are another exception for ruminants.

Most roughages have a high content of cell-wall material (see Ch. 3). The cell-wall fraction may have a highly variable composition, but contains appreciable amounts of lignin, cellulose, hemicellulose, pectin, polyuronides, silica, and other components. In contrast, roughages generally are low in readily available carbohydrates as compared to cereal grains.

The amount of lignin is a critical factor with respect to digestibility. Lignin is an amorphous material associated closely with the fibrous carbohydrates of the cell wall of plant tissue. It limits fiber digestibility, probably because of the physical barrier between digestive enzymes and the carbohydrate in question. Removal of lignin with chemical methods increases digestibility greatly by rumen microorganisms and, probably, by cecal organisms. Lignin content of plant tissue increases gradually with maturity of the plant and a high negative correlation exists between lignin content and digestibility, particularly for grasses, although somewhat less for legumes. There is evidence that the silica content of plant tissue is related negatively to fiber digestibility.

The protein, mineral, and vitamin contents of roughages are highly variable. Legumes may have 20% or more crude protein content, although a third or more may be in the form of non-protein N. Other roughages, such as straw, may have only 3–4% crude protein. Most others fall between these two extremes.

Mineral content may be exceedingly variable; most roughages are relatively good sources of Ca and Mg, particularly legumes. P content is apt to be moderate to low, and K content high; the trace minerals vary greatly depending on plant species, soil and fertilization practices.

TABLE 20.1   Nutrient contributions of major feedstuff groups.[a]

| | RELATIVE VALUE | | | | | | |
| | | | MINERALS | | VITAMINS | | |
FEEDSTUFF	PROTEIN	ENERGY	MACRO	TRACE	FAT-SOL.	B-COMPLEX	BULK
High-quality roughage	+ +	+ +	+ +	+ +	+ + +	+	+ + +
Low-quality roughage	+	+	+	+	−	−	+ + + +
Cereal grains	+ +	+ + +	+	+	+	+	+
Grain millfeeds	+ +	+ +	+ +	+ +	+	+ +	+ +
Feeding fats	−	+ + + +	−	−	−	−	−
Molasses	+	+ + +	+ +	+ +	−	+	−
Fermentation products	+ + +	+ +	+	+ +	−	+ + + +	±
Oil seed proteins	+ + +	+ + +	+ +	+ +	+	+ +	+ +
Animal proteins	+ + + +	+ + +	+ + +	+ + +	+ +	+ + +	+

[a]Relative values are indicated by number of + . Feeding values (nutrient content and availability) of any product depends on many different factors which are discussed in the text.

In overall nutritional terms, roughages may range from very good nutrient sources (lush young grass, legumes, high-quality silage) to very poor feeds (straws, hulls, some browse). The nutritional value of the very poor often can be improved considerably by proper supplementation or by some feed preparatory methods. However, the feeder must use some judgement in selecting the appropriate roughage for a given class and species of animal.

Factors Affecting Roughage Composition

A number of factors may affect roughage composition and nutritive value. Maturity at harvest (or grazing) has one of the most pronounced effects. One relatively detailed example of stage of maturity on composition and digestibility of orchard grass (*Dactylis glomerata*) is shown in Table 20.2. Many other examples are available in the literature. In Table 20.2 note the rapid decline in crude protein; in Fig. 20.1 the same type of decline in digestibility is shown for alfalfa and four grass species. A gradual decline occurs also in ash and soluble carbohydrates and an increase in lignin, cellulose, and CF, all during a six-week period. Digestibility declines, also, as these changes in plant composition occur. The changes that occur will depend on the plant species and on the environment in which the plant is grown. For example, if the growing season progresses rather rapidly from cool spring weather to hot summer weather, changes in plant composition will be more

rapid than when the weather remains cool during plant maturation, especially in a cool season grass. In plants such as alfalfa (*Medicago sativa*), which has quite different growing habits than grass, rapid changes take place as the plant matures and blooms. Crude protein contents given by NRC publications indicate the following values (% on dry basis) for second cuttings: immature, 21.5; prebloom, 19.4; early bloom, 18.4; mid-bloom, 17.1; full bloom, 15.9; and mature, 13.6. Corresponding changes in TDN range from 63 to 55%. Part of these differences are due to the fact that the plant loses leaves as it matures, and leaves have a higher nutrient value than the remainder of the plant. As plants mature, there is a decline in concentration of Ca, K, and P and for most of the trace minerals.

For many years soil fertility and fertilization practices have been known to have a pronounced effect on quality of forage and crops produced. In addition, some alterations in plant composition may occur as a result of these factors, although the differences are much less dramatic than those changes associated with increased maturity, and results given in the literature show many discrepancies in responses to fertilizer. In pastures with mixed plant species, one obvious change that may occur as a result of fertilization is an alteration in the vegetative composition because some plants respond more to fertilizer than others. If a grass-legume mixture is fertilized with high levels of N, for instance, this practice is apt to kill out the legume or to stimulate the grass much more than the legume. Fertilization of grasses with N tends to increase total, non-protein, and nitrate N of the plants. However, nitrate levels usually drop off rapidly after fertilization. K content and, perhaps, some other minerals may increase in response to N; however, the marked increase in plant growth that may be obtained by high levels of N may be expected to result in some dilution of most mineral elements, particularly during the first few days or weeks of rapid growth after fertilization.

Digestible protein is apt to be increased and, in some instances, palatability and dry matter intake may increase in response to fertilization with N, although not all data agree on some of these points. Fertilization studies have shown, in general, that plant concentration of most of the mineral elements may be increased by fertilization with the element in question. P use may increase palatability when used alone or in combination with N. Thus, results to date indicate that soil fertility and/or fertilization practices may alter nutrient concentration and consumption of forage plants.

Harvesting and storage methods may have a marked effect on nutritive value of roughages, particularly when forage cut for hay is unduly bleached by the sun or damaged by dew and/or rain. Sun bleaching results in a rapid loss of carotenes, although this is of less consequence than it used to be because of the low cost and common usage of synthetic vitamin A. Leaching by rain will result in losses in soluble carbohydrates and N, and added handling required would normally result in additional loss of leaves. Any harvesting method used for legumes that reduces leaf loss will help to maintain nutritive value. With respect to storage, hays may lose a considerable amount of original nutritive value if stored too wet with resultant heating and mold formation. Otherwise, there is relatively little nutritive loss if the hay is stored in dry conditions over a period of several years. The same comment applies to silages;

TABLE 20.2   Effect of stage of maturity on composition and digestibility of orchard grass.[a]

	STAGE OF MATURITY			
ITEM	6–7″ HIGH CUT 5/19 PASTURE	8–10″ HIGH CUT 5/31 LATE PASTURE	10–12″ HIGH CUT 6/14 EARLY HAY	12–14″ HIGH CUT 6/27 MATURE HAY
Composition, %				
Crude protein	24.8	15.8	13.0	12.4
Ash	9.3	6.8	7.1	7.2
Ether extract	4.0	3.5	3.9	4.2
Organic acids	6.3	6.0	5.4	5.0
Total carbohydrates[b]	49.9	63.0	64.4	63.1
Sugars	2.1	9.5	5.4	2.4
Starch	1.2	9.5	0.8	0.9
Alpha cellulose	19.5	19.8	19.1	27.7
Beta and gamma cellulose	3.4	5.4	3.8	2.5
Pentosans	15.1	15.8	16.8	18.1
Nitrogen-free-extract	35.0	45.7	44.2	41.2
Lignin	5.7	5.0	6.2	8.1
Crude fiber	26.9	28.2	31.8	35.0
Digestibility, %				
Dry matter	73	74	69	66
Crude protein	67	63	59	59
Crude fiber	81	77	71	68

[a] From Ely *et al.* (7).
[b] Total carbohydrates = (crude fiber + NFE) − (lignin + organic acids)

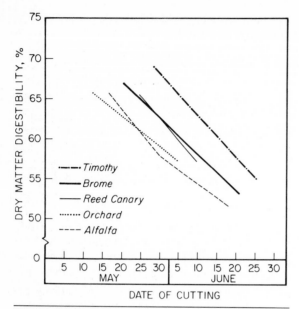

Figure 20.1 *Effect of maturity on dry matter digestibility of first cutting forages.*

well-preserved silages will keep for a number of years without much effect on nutritive value.

Latitude, along with accompanying effects of temperature and light intensity, may have an appreciable effect on plant composition and nutritive value. Not a great deal of information is available on this subject, but data do indicate that nutritive value of forage cut on a given date is apt to be higher as we go away from the equator toward the poles (northern or southern).

❏ PASTURE AND GRAZED FORAGES

A wide variety of vegetation is utilized by herbivorous animals. With respect to agricultural production, herbage usually is divided into native and cultivated species, the latter being utilized to improve productivity, to extend the period of high-quality grazing, or to improve the versatility of crop production.

Herbage may also be divided into the following classes:

Grasses—members of the family Gramineae (6,000 + species)
   Cool season grasses—grasses that make their best growth in the spring and fall
   Warm season grasses—grasses that grow slowly in

the early spring and grow most actively in early summer, setting seed in summer or fall
Legumes—members of the family Leguminosae (14,000 + species)
Forbs—primarily broadleaf, non-woody, plants
Browse—woody plants consumed in some degree by ruminants, particularly selective eaters such as deer and antelope

Grasses

Grasses are by far the most important plant family that humans are concerned with agriculturally, because the grass family not only includes all of the wild and cultivated species used for grazing but also the cultivated cereal grains and sorghum species. However, in this section we will be concerned only with grass as a forage, and will not consider it from an agronomic point of view. The discussion also will be very general because of the tremendous numbers of grasses of importance.

As a food for grazing animals, grass has many advantages. Most grass species are quite palatable when immature and only a few are high toxic for any appreciable part of the grazing season. Grasses of one type of another have the ability to grow in most environments in which herbivores can survive, arctic regions being one notable exception. Futhermore, nutrients supplied in grasses roughly provide amounts that more or less parallel animal needs during a yearly life cycle of reproduction and production, except during mid-winter in cold climates.

Some more or less typical values for chemical composition are illustrated in Table 20.2. Early in the growing season, grasses—especially cool season species—have a very high water content and an excess of protein for ruminant animals. The result is that animals may have diarrhea and, because of the low dry matter content, may have difficulty in obtaining a maximum intake of energy. Grass proteins usually are high in the amino acid, arginine, and also contain appreciable amounts of glutamic acid and lysine. If N application is liberal, and particularly if S is deficient, there is apt to be a high level of NPN in the form of amino acids and amides and a relative deficiency of the S-containing amino acids. High nitrate also may result from fertilization. Toxic symptoms may occur at levels of about 0.07% nitrate N (dry matter basis) and amounts on the order of 0.22% may be fatal to ruminants; however, if ruminants are adapted and fed on high-nitrate grasses continuously, toxicity is less likely because rumen microorganisms are capable of reducing nitrate to ammonia which is well utilized.

In comparison with legumes such as alfalfa (which is known as lucerne in countries outside of North America), the protein content of grasses is nearly always lower, particularly in mature plants. Digestible energy is high (i.e., 70 + %) in young grass, but declines rapidly with maturity. Mature plants, especially those that are weather leached, will be low in digestible energy and protein, as well as in other solubles such as carbohydrates and some of the minerals and in carotene; thus, this type of plant material may not meet the animal's needs, even when productive requirements are quite low.

Mineral content of grasses may vary considerably depending on the species and soil fertility, particularly. Of those elements of concern to ruminants, grasses usually are adequate in Ca, Mg, and K, but are apt to be borderline or deficient in P. Trace minerals also vary considerably; evidence from Canada indicates that 80% or more of forage species measured contained less than levels generally considered adequate for ruminants. Ranges and typical values to be expected are shown in Table 20.3. It should be pointed out that mineral concentration is not a good measure of availability to the animal. Very little good information is available on mineral availability from different feedstuffs.

The desirability of different grasses depends on the local environment and their growing habits and on animal needs. Considerable differences may exist in the composition of grasses that fall into the cool- or warm-season classes. Generally, cool-season grasses mature at slower rates and their quality deteriorates less rapidly than do warm-season grasses. Lush, young grass usually is quite palatable, but palatability declines for most species as the plants mature, and most animals object to the seed heads of many grass species. Quality differences between species of grasses become more evident with maturity. Furthermore, regrowth of grass in the fall usually is not as nutritious as spring grass, partly due to the lower concentration of soluble carbohydrates.

Cultivated grasses held in high esteem include perennial ryegrass (*Lolium perenne*), Italian ryegrass (*Lolium multiforum*), orchard grass (*Dactylis glomerata*), blue grass (*Poa* spp), and smooth brome grass (*Bromus inermus*). Others considered less desirable include Bermuda grass (*Cynodon dactylon*), foxtail (*Alopecurus pratensis*), bent (*Agrostis* spp), and tall fescue (*Festuca arundinacea*). In addition to varying in growth habits, these species may vary in nutrient composition, palatability and digestibility. Tropical and subtropical species that have found appreciable use in various countries include Buffelgrass (*Cen-*

TABLE 20.3 Range and typical mineral concentrations for pasture grasses and alfalfa plants.

MINERAL ELEMENT	GRASSES			ALFALFA		
	LOW	TYPICAL	HIGH	LOW	TYPICAL	HIGH
Major elements, % of dry matter						
Ca	<0.3	0.4–0.8	>1.0	<0.60	1.2–2.3	>2.5
Mg	<0.1	0.12–0.26	>0.3	<0.1	0.3–0.4	>0.6
K	<1.0	1.2–2.8	>3.0	<0.4	1.5–2.2	>3.0
P	<0.2	0.2–0.3	>0.4	<0.15	0.2–0.3	>0.7
S	<0.1	0.15–0.25	>0.3	<0.2	0.3–0.4	>0.7
Trace elements, ppm of dry matter						
Fe	<45	50–100	>200	<30	50–200	>300
Co	<0.08	0.08–0.25	>0.30	<0.08	0.08–0.25	>0.3
Cu	<3	4–8	>10	<4	6–12	>15
Mn	<30	40–200	>250	<20	25–45	>100
Mo	<0.4	0.5–3.0	>5	<0.2	0.5–3.0	>5
Se	<0.04	0.08–0.1	>5	<0.04	0.08–0.1	>5
Zn	<15	20–80	>100	<10	12–35	>50

chrus ciliarus L.,), Rhodegrass (*Chloris gayana*), Kikuyugrass (*Pennisetum clandestinum*), Pangola digitgrass (*Digitaria decumbens*), Panicgrass (*Panicum maximum*; several strains are grown), Paragrass (*Brachiaria multica*), Napiergrass (*Pennisetum purpureum*), and Molassesgrass (*Melinis minutiflora*). Kikuyugrass is from Hawaii, the others are from Africa. In the right environment these grasses may be very productive in a tropical or subtropical climate.

In many regions in North America, some of the cereals are used for pasture, particularly winter wheat, with lesser use of barley, oats, and rye. These plants can be pastured during the winter and early spring with little or no effect on grain yield, provided soil conditions permit. The forage of these plants is quite high in readily available carbohydrates (50 + %) and crude protein is high. Extensive use of such pasture is made in the southwestern states of the USA, particularly for growing calves and lambs.

Several sorghum species are used for pasture or harvested forage. Sudan grass (*Sorghum vulgare sudanense*) is one of the more common ones used in the USA, but others, such as Johnson grass (*Sorghum halepense*), find some use. Sudan-sorghum hybrids have been developed. These species are utilized by some producers because they can be sown during early summer in temperate areas and will produce late summer and fall pastures. They are prone to have high levels of glycosides which can be converted to hydrocyanic acid (a highly toxic product), particularly following drought or frost damage, so care must be used if these conditions occur while pasture is in use.

Legumes

Many different legumes are utilized by grazing animals, although the cultivated legumes comprise a much smaller group than do cultivated grasses. In overall usage, alfalfa (*Medicago sativa*) is by far the most common legume used for pasture, hay-crop silage, and hay in North America. Alfalfa finds much favor because of its high yield, its persistence as a perennial crop, and because of its high palatability and excellent nutrient content.

Other legumes that find extensive usage for pasture or hay include clovers such as ladino or red (*Trifolium pratense*), white (*T. repens*) and subterranean (*T. subterraneum*), as well as common lespedeza (*Lespedeza striata*), lupines (*Lupinus* spp) and vetches (*Vicia* spp).

Legumes have higher protein contents than grasses, particularly in more mature plants. Fiber in the stems tends to be particularly high and soluble carbohydrates relatively low. The leaves are rich sources of nutrients, but stems are of much less value, especially in mature plants. Changes in plant composition with maturity are largely a result of increased lignification and increased fiber in the stems because of a reduced leaf:stem ratio. Compared to grasses, legumes have characteristically high concentrations of Ca, Mg, and S (Table 20.3) and, frequently, Cu. They tend to be lower in Mn and Zn than grasses. On the whole, legumes are palatable, although most are bitter and may require some adaptation before they are consumed readily by cattle.

Some legumes, particularly alfalfa and white, ladino and red clover, are prone to cause bloat in grazing ruminants, especially cattle. Bloat is caused primarily by foam-producing compounds from the plant, of which cytoplasmic proteins and, perhaps, pectins are the most important. Foam in the rumen (see ref. 8) causes entrapment of normal rumen gases which cannot be eliminated, resulting in a gradual increase in rumen pressures and, if not relieved, eventual suffocation of the animal. Research evidence indicates that alfalfa plants can be selected to have a lower content of the proteins that are involved in bloat production.

Native Pastures and Range

Pastures and rangeland comprised of uncultivated native forage plants cover vast areas of land in regions of the world where the environment, soil or topography rule out intensive agricultural methods. These areas usually contain a wide range of grasses, sedges, forbs and browse. The nutrient properties of these various plants vary widely and, in addition, there are apt to be distinct seasonal patterns of use by different grazing animals. The subject is too complex to discuss here; for more information, the reader is referred to Heath *et al.* (9) or Morley (10).

Miscellaneous Forage Plants

In some areas and for some specific seasonal usage, plants such as the cabbage family (*Brassica* spp) are used extensively. Kale, cabbage, and rape are included in this group. Rape, for example, is planted sometimes for use as fall pasture by sheep. The tops of root crops such as beets and turnips also are used as forage. As a part of the total resource, however, these crops account for a very small percentage of the total.

HARVESTED DRY ROUGHAGES

In temperate areas roughages stored in the dried form are the most common type used for feeding during the time of year when grazing is not available or for feeding of confined animals. Roughages harvested in the form of long hay or bales require a relatively high labor input and present difficulties in handling. Fortunately, machinery currently available allows rather complete mechanization in operations where it is financially feasible (see Figs. 20.2 to 20.5). Continual improvement is being made in such equipment.

HAYS

Hay—from grasses or legumes—is grown and harvested almost exclusively for animal usage. Haymaking has been practiced for many centuries, and much information has been accumulated on the nutritive value of hays as affected by many different factors too numerous to discuss in detail here. Although haymaking is the most common method of conserving green crops, its relative importance has declined somewhat in recent years because of in-

Figure 20.3 Equipment designed for convenience in feeding loose hay. Courtesy of the Hesston Corporation.

creased use of green chop (feeding of freshly cut plants) and forage crops in silage.

The usual intent in haymaking is to harvest the crop at a more or less optimum stage of maturity in order to capture a maximal yield of nutrients/unit of land without damage to the next crop. To make good hay the water content of the plant material must be reduced to a point low enough to allow storage without marked nutritional changes. Moisture content of green herbage may range from 65 to 85% or more, depending on maturity and the plant species. For hay to keep satisfactorily in storage, the water content must be reduced to about 15% or less.

Losses in Haymaking

It is impossible to cut, dry, and move hay into storage without losses occurring in the process. However, it may be possible to harvest more units of nutrients/unit of land than could be obtained by grazing because of trampling and feed refusal resulting from contamination by dung and urine and to selective grazing of some species of plants. Both the quality and quantity of field-cured hay that can be harvested depends on such factors as maturity when cut, method of handling, moisture content, and weather conditions during harvest. For example, rain on freshly cut hay will cause little damage; however, when hay is partially dried, rain is very damaging. Early cut hay in many areas is often of low quality because of rain and resultant spoilage, leaching and leaf loss. One report indicates dry matter losses ranging from about 6% for artificially dehydrated hay

Figure 20.2 Equipment designed for ease and convenience of handling loose hay. Courtesy of the Hesston Corporation.

Figure 20.4 *A square hay baler, a type which has been long used for baling hay which may be sold by the producer. Courtesy of J. I. Case Implement Co.*

up to about 33% for rain-damaged field-cured hay. Another report indicated the following losses: plant respiration losses (before plant is dry), 3.5% in 24 h; leaching by rain, 5–14%; and leaf shattering in legume hays, 3–35%. thus, very substantial amounts of dry matter may be lost in haymaking under adverse conditions; an average loss of 15–20% is not abnormal for legume hays.

Changes During Drying

Ample evidence shows that rapid drying, provided it is not accompanied by excessively hot temperatures, results in the least changes in chemical components of forage. Machines such as crimpers (or conditioners) have been developed to crush the stems of plants like alfalfa and speed up the drying process. If drying is slow in the field, stack or bale, appreciable changes may occur as a result of activity by plant enzymes and microorganisms or because of oxidation. After the plant is cut, the cells continue to function for a time with the result that soluble carbohydrates may be oxidized. Oxidative reactions may continue for some time, depending on the temperature and how the hay is stored. The most obvious change is a loss of pigmentation as plants lose carotenes by oxidation. Proteins may be modified as some hydrolysis occurs, resulting in relatively greater amounts of NPN, primarily amino acids. Slow drying almost always is accompanied by excessive

Figure 20.5 *Large round bales formed by this machine reduce the number of bales that must be handled, but they must be handled with mechanical equipment. Courtesy of the Hesston Corporation.*

TABLE 20.4 Composition and digestibility of green ryegrass and material from the same field which was dried artificially or made into wilted or unwilted silage.[a]

ITEM	FRESH GRASS	DRIED GRASS	WILTED SILAGE	UNWILTED SILAGE
Composition of dry matter				
Organic matter, %	90.8	92.0	92.2	91.7
Total water-soluble carbohydrate, %	9.2	8.4	trace	trace
Cellulose, %	24.2	24.3	25.0	26.8
Hemicellulose, %	14.0	13.3	12.9	13.1
Total N, %	2.85	2.99	3.09	3.08
Gross energy, Kcal/g	4.59	4.55	4.46	4.89
Digestibility, %				
Energy	67.4	68.1	67.5	72.0
Cellulose	75.2	75.5	76.5	80.6
Hemicellulose	59.4	57.7	59.9	63.2
N	75.2	71.0	76.5	76.4

[a]From Beever *et al.* (11). In this experiment the fresh grass was quick-frozen so that it could be fed at the same time as the other forms.

mold growth which reduces the palatability and nutritive value of hay, and in some cases, the molds may be toxic.

Hay stored in the stack or bale while too wet to dry rapidly may undergo enough fermentation to result in marked temperature increases (largely because of growth of thermophilic molds), which may cause browning and, sometimes, spontaneous combustion. Newly baled alfalfa hay should have no more than 25 to 30% moisture to avoid these problems. Excess heating or molding results in a marked reduction in digestibility of protein and energy.

If drying is not complicated by weather factors, relatively little change in the composition takes place between green plant and hay, nor is there any pronounced effect on nutrient utilization (see Table 20.4). Animals generally ingest dry matter from fresh herbage at a slower rate than for hay, and some slight differences may occur in rumen fermentation, digestibility and site of digestion in ruminants, but the differences appear to be inconsequential.

Thus, we see that drying need not have any great effect on forage utilization. However, in practice, we must expect some loss of leaves in legumes and reduced soluble carbohydrates. Hay, if made from moderately mature plants, will have lower protein and digestible energy than young herbage, but is apt to be better than very mature herbage. Nutritive properties of hays are, then, similar to those or forages, but with slightly to greatly reduced values depending on freedom from weather damage and method of harvesting.

❏ ARTIFICIALLY DRIED FORAGE

Rapid drying is required for good haymaking. At one time in the USA and northern Europe, particularly in areas where weather was a problem, considerable interest was shown in barn drying. This is accomplished by circulating air through the hay after storage. Although a very good product can be produced, interest has declined with greater usage of silage and recent developments in bale-handling machinery.

Dehydration of herbage with appropriate machinery is a viable industry both in the USA and some areas of northern Europe. In the USA, alfalfa is the primary crop that is dehydrated, but in Europe, grasses or grass-clover mixtures are used more commonly. In making dehydrated alfalfa the herbage is cut at a prebloom stage, dried quickly at hot temperatures, ground, and sometimes pelleted. Because carotene and xanthophyll pigments are important for poultry feeds, the product often is stored using inert gases such as N_2 to reduce oxidation. Herbage so processed is high in crude protein and quite digestible, moderately low in fiber and has a high carotene content. The relatively low fiber content makes such feedstuffs more suitable for species such as poultry and swine and, in the USA, a high proportion of dehydrated alfalfa goes into commercial diets for these species. For poultry the carotenes and xanthophylls serve to increase pigmentation of the skin of broilers or the yolk of eggs. Protein and other nutrients are also important. For swine, particularly sows, nutrients of interest are the vitamins, Ca, and trace minerals. These feeds serve very well for horses or ruminants, but generally are more expensive/unit of nutrients provided as compared to other roughage sources.

STRAWS AND CHAFF

An appreciable amount of straw and chaff is available for animal feed in most farming areas, although much less than in the days when stationary threshing machines were used for harvesting cereal grains. Straw consists mainly of the stems and variable amounts of leaves of plants that remain after the removal of the seeds. Chaff consists of the small particles removed from the seed head along with limited amounts of small or broken grains.

The primary supply of straw and chaff comes from the small cereal grains—wheat, barley, rye, rice, oats—but, in some areas, substantial amounts may be available from the grass or legume seed industry and from various miscellaneous crops. As a whole, straws are very low in digestible protein, very high in fiber and, usually, lignin, and are poor feed, although some are of less value than others. For example, values given from NRC (1) for winter wheat straw (dry basis) are: crude protein, 3.2%; crude fiber, 40.4%; and digestible energy (cattle), 1.92 Mcal/kg or 47% TDN (these energy values are too high in the writer's opinion). Of the various cereal straws, that from oats is regarded as the best, partly because the grain is often harvested before it is fully ripe. As a feedstuff, straws are best used as a diluent in high-concentrate rations or as the basal feed for wintering cattle when properly supplemented with deficient nutrients—protein, vitamin A, minerals. Even though straws are low in metabolizable energy, the energy derived from that which is digested and from the heat increment (see Ch. 10) provides energy that can be used for animals, such as pregnant cows, which have a low productive requirement.

MISCELLANEOUS

In the USA nearly all of the grain from corn and sorghum now is field-harvested and often the cobs or threshed seed heads are left in the field, along with a substantial amount of grain at times. This material provides a useful resource which should be utilized, even though it is of low quality. The nutritive problems here are the same as with straws, and some supplementary feeding is required to supply needed minerals, carotene and protein. Protein may be less critical than with straws.

Other roughage sources are available in some areas. In cotton growing areas, cottonseed hulls and cotton gin trash are available in substantial amounts and these are consumed readily by ruminants. In addition, roughage sources such as pineapple greenchop, pineapple juice presscake, pineapple stump meal, rice mill feed, sugarcane bagasse, and sugarcane strippings may be available where the base crops are grown (6).

HARVESTED HIGH-MOISTURE ROUGHAGES

Green Chop (Soilage)

Green chop (or soilage) is herbage that has been cut and chopped in the field and then fed to livestock in confinement. Plants used in this manner include the forage grasses, legumes, sudan grass and other sorghum family species, the corn plant, and, at times, residues of food crops used for human consumption.

Although this is one of the simplest means of mechanically harvesting herbage (Fig. 20.6), it requires constant attention to animal needs as opposed to other methods of harvesting herbage. A major advantage of use of green chop is that more usable nutrients can be salvaged/unit of land than with other methods such as pasturing, haymaking, or ensiling. Thus, it is sometimes feasible to harvest in this manner rather than using such crops in other ways, provided land productivity is high (this reduces harvesting costs). When herbage growth outruns daily need, the excess can be made into hay or silage before it becomes too mature for efficient usage. Weather, of course, is less of a factor than in haymaking.

Data, in general, indicate that beef cattle fed soilage will gain as well as when pastured using intensive systems such as short-term rotations or strip grazing

Figure 20.6 *One type of forage harvested utilized in making silage or for green chop. Courtesy of Deer & Co.*

Figure 20.7 *A view of the face of a bunker (pit, trench) silo, a type used in many areas for storage of large amounts of silage. This type facilitates equipment usage in both filling and unloading. Courtesy of Bill Fleming, Beef Magazine.*

and that dairy cows do equally well when fed soilage as when fed alfalfa preserved in other ways. Practical experience has indicated that optimal usage is obtained when green chop is fed along with hay or silage rather than by itself, partly because total dry matter consumption tends to be greater.

Silage

Silage has been used for feeding animals, primarily ruminants, for many years (Fig. 20.7). It is the material produced by controlled fermentation of high-moisture herbage. When such material is stored under anaerobic conditions and, if the supply of fermentable carbohydrates is adequate, sufficient lactic acid is produced to stabilize the mass so that fermentation stops. If undisturbed, silage will keep for an indefinite period. Alternate methods, primarily used in Europe, require the addition of strong acids that lower the pH, thus preventing fermentation, or the use of formaldehyde with or without organic acids such as propionic. Such combinations inhibit most fermentation that would otherwise occur.

Good silage is a very palatable product which is utilized well (see Table 20.4), and excellent results may be obtained with high-producing animals such as lactating cows. In addition to any advantages in harvesting or in nutritive properties, the fermentation that occurs usually will reduce greatly the nitrate

content, if nitrate is present, and other toxic materials, such as hydrocyanic acid, will be reduced in amount. However, the reader should remember that fermentation requires energy, thus there are losses caused by ensiling so that the overall nutrient content of material in the silo after ensiling is less than that of the material that went into the silo. This may or may not be reflected in normal analytical data.

Most silage in the USA is made from the whole corn plant (*Zea mays*) or from any of a number of sorghum varieties in areas where rainfall is insufficient for growing corn. Grass, grass-legume, or legume silages are used extensively because technology is adequate to produce very good silage from these crops. For that matter, palatable and nutritious silage can be produced from a wide variety of herbage, including weeds and low-moisture herbage. Some of the nutritional characteristics of principal silage crops will be discussed in later sections.

Chemical Changes During Fermentation

Chemical changes during silage fermentation are rather complex and a complete discussion is beyond the scope of this book. For further information, the reader is referred to other sources (9,12).

The chemical changes are the result of plant enzyme activity and action of microbes present on the herbage or which find their way into it from other routes. The plant enzymes continue to be active for the first few days after cutting while oxygen is available, resulting in some metabolism of soluble carbohydrates to CO_2 and water and the production of heat. Optimum temperatures during fermentation are said to be between 80° and 100°F. Excessive heat is objectionable, but is not likely if the silage is well packed to exclude most of the air.

Plant proteins are broken down partially by cellular enzymes, resulting in an increase in NPN compounds such as amino acids. Anaerobic microorganisms multiply rapidly, using sugars and starches as primary energy sources and producing mainly lactic acid with lesser amounts of acetic acid and small amounts of others such as formic, propionic, and butyric; little butyric acid is present in well-preserved silage. Continued action occurs on N-containing compounds with further solubilization and production of ammonia and other NPN compounds (Table 20.5). The level of lactic acid rises in well-preserved corn or sorghum silage, eventually reaching levels of 7–8%, and the pH drops to about 4.0, depending on buffering capacity and dry matter content of the crop in question. Grass silages will usually have a higher pH (~4.5). If the silage is too wet or the supply of soluble carbohydrates too low, the pH will not go this low, allowing the development of clostridia bacterial species, relatively large

amounts of butyric acid, and further fermentation of NPN compounds, resulting in production of amines such as tryptamine, histamine, and others. These amines have undesirable odors and tastes (i.e., rotten) and they may be toxic. On the other hand, if the mass is too dry or poorly packed, excess heating may occur, and molds may develop, producing unpalatable and, sometimes, toxic silage.

For most crops, dry matter contents of about 35% and a soluble carbohydrate content of 6–8% (dry basis) are near optimal for silage making. Consequently, if grass or legume silage is to be made, usually it is wilted some before ensiling. If direct-cut herbage is used, usually it will be too wet for good silage, allowing clostridia bacteria to multiply. When herbage such as grass or legumes is direct-cut and ensiled, preservatives, or sterilants may be added. Additional dry matter from sources such as ground corn cobs, straw, hay, and so on, may be used to soak up some of the moisture and soluble carbohydrates may be added in the form of grain or molasses; these provide useful insurance when making grass-legume silage. Silage sterilants such as formic acid, sulfur dioxide, or sodium metabisulfite may be ad-

TABLE 20.5　Composition and nutritive value of third cutting alfalfa harvested as hay, low-moisture and high-moisture silage.[a]

ITEM	HAY	WILTED FORAGE[b]	LOW-MOISTURE SILAGE	GREEN CHOP[b]	HIGH-MOISTURE SILAGE
Dry matter, %	92.6	58.1	59.0	28.8	28.1
Others on DM basis					
Crude protein, %	20.6	18.1	20.4	19.8	21.6
Cellulose, %	34.0	33.3	37.4	30.3	37.9
Soluble carbohydrates, %	7.8	5.2	2.5	3.8	3.7
Total N, %	3.3	2.9	3.3	3.2	3.4
Soluble N, % of total N	31.8	37.2	51.1	32.6	67.0
NPN, % of total N	26.0	28.4	44.6	22.6	62.0
Volatile fatty acids, %					
acetic			0.4		4.2
propionic			0.05		0.14
butyric			0.002		0.11
pH			4.7		4.7
Dry matter intake,					
g/day/kg body wt	25.3		21.8		25.8
Digestibility, %					
Dry matter	64.5		59.0		59.5
Nitrogen	77.5		63.0		72.8
Cellulose	58.8		60.4		64.3

[a]Taken from Sutton and Vetter (13).
[b]Wilted herbage used to make low-moisture silage and the green chop was used for the high-moisture silage.

vantageous where moisture content is high, but are of doubtful value in silage made from wilted grasses or legumes or from corn or sorghum plants.

Losses from Ensiling

Losses occur during ensiling because of fermentative activity and resultant heat produced. Obviously, these may be quite variable. Gaseous losses are said to range from 5–30% of original dry matter. Most of the losses originate from soluble and highly digestible nutrients with the result that silage (Table 20.5) is almost certain to contain a higher percentage of fibrous and insoluble ingredients.

Very substantial amounts of seepage may occur in high-moisture silage, particularly where the dry matter content is less than 30%. Above this level such losses are moderate to low. Seepage moisture contains many soluble nutrients, and such losses must be avoided if silage feeding is to be highly efficient. Further losses occur from molding. Molding nearly always takes place around the perimeter and on top of the silage. Data on alfalfa silage indicate spoilage losses on the order of 4–12% of original dry matter ensiled. Such material is not only unpalatable but may also be toxic. Obviously, overall losses may be quite variable, but, when field losses are included, total losses may be expected to be about 20–25% of herbage dry matter present in the field.

❑ NUTRITIVE PROPERTIES OF SILAGES

One of the nutritive problems associated with feeding silages is that consumption of dry matter in the form of silage nearly always is lower than when the same crop is fed as hay, and this seems to apply whether the crop in question is legume, grass, or other herbage. Intake of silage usually is greater as the dry-matter content increases. Data covering 70 different silages (14) indicate that ad libitum intake was correlated positively with the dry matter, N, and with lactic acid as a percentage of total acids. Intake was negatively correlated with acetic acid content and ammonia as a percentage of total N. Intake was related positively to digestibility for legumes, but negatively for grasses other than ryegrass. This information would indicate that maximum intake should be achieved with silage containing just enough moisture to allow for preservation with minimum pro-

duction of ammonia and acetic acid, which tend to increase at higher moisture contents (see Table 20.5).

Differences in digestibility and in animal performance between direct cut or wilted silage and hay have been inconsistent. Some investigations indicate that digestibility of energy is improved enough by ensiling to compensate for the reduced intake. Unfortunately, errors in analyzing silage have been included in many experimental reports; if silage is typically dried in an oven, substantial amounts of volatile materials are lost, thus giving a low value for nutrient content of silage as fed and an underestimate of organic matter intake and digestibility.

Grass-Legume Silages

Grass or legume silages are, normally, high in crude protein (20 + %) and carotene, but only moderate in digestible energy. This combination is too high in protein for most ruminants and more nearly optimum results may be expected by supplementing grass sil-

Figure 20.8 An illustration of gas-tight silos which have become widely used in recent years. These silos are useful also for storage of high-moisture grain. Courtesy of the A. O. Smith Co.

Figure 20.9 *A plastic bag used for silage making. Such equipment costs much less initially than other types, but it is a temporary solution if silage will be used continually. This type of silo does have the advantage that it can be located in different areas.*

than does high-moisture silage. It is used to a great extent in the USA for dairy cows. This type of silage is made best in air-tight silos now in common use in many areas (Fig. 20.8) or with reusable plastic bags (Fig. 20.9).

Corn and Sorghum Silage

Corn silage is the most popular silage in the USA in areas where the corn plant grows well. It is becoming more popular in other areas of the world because, except for sugar cane, maximum yields of digestible nutrients/unit of land can be harvested from this crop. In addition, the corn plant can be handled mechanically at a convenient time of the year. A host of research reports have appeared on this subject.

Well-made corn silage is a very palatable product with a moderate to high content of digestible energy, but it usually is low to moderate in digestible protein, particularly for the amount of energy contained. Although corn silage contains much grain (up to 50% in well-eared crops), maximum growth rates or milk yields cannot be obtained without energy and protein supplementation.

The effect of stage of maturity on nutritive value of corn silage is shown in Table 20.6. Note that the crude fiber declines and NFE increases as the corn becomes more mature; this is a reflection of the increased grain content. Digestibility of energy was quite constant due to the offsetting effect of increasing energy from grain vs. the lower digestibility of the more mature stalk. No information was given in this paper on total yield, but the data show clearly

age with some form of energy (grains) or by diluting the protein by feeding some other form of low-protein roughage.

Digestibility (Table 20.5), retention of N, and efficiency of utilization of N for growth or lactation generally are lower with silage than with dry crops of comparable composition. This may be related to the presence of many different forms of non-protein N found in silage.

Low-moisture silage, often called haylage, is a very palatable feed, probably because it tends to have relatively less acetic acid and less N in the form of ammonia and other NPN compounds (Table 20.5)

TABLE 20.6   Effect of maturity on nutritive value of corn silage as fed.[a]

	STAGE OF MATURITY			
ITEM	SOFT DOUGH	MED.-HARD DOUGH	EARLY DENT	GLAZED AND FROSTED
Dry matter, % as fed	24	27	32	39
Crude protein, % of DM	8.0	7.7	7.8	8.0
Crude fiber, % of DM	24.0	20.9	17.8	16.6
NFE, % of DM	58.4	62.9	65.9	68.3
Dry matter intake, % body wt/day	1.66	2.02	1.90	1.71
Gross energy digestibility, %	67.7	68.1	65.7	65.0
Protein digestibility, %	53.7	53.9	53.8	54.6
Energy balance, Kcal/day	962	3285	2870	2341

[a]Data from Colovos *et al.* (15). Silage fed ad libitum along with a small amount of molasses-urea supplement.

that intake and digestibility were greater for the medium-to-hard dough stage.

Research in recent years has shown that some additives may improve corn silage. Treatment at ensiling time with limestone (0.5–1%) or other Ca salts tends to buffer the acids produced during fermentation and results in a very substantial increase in lactic acid production and, usually, an improvement in intake and animal performance. Likewise, addition of urea (0.5–1%) or anhydrous ammonia to corn silage will increase the crude protein content and has worked out well for dairy cows, particularly. The value of the added N will depend, somewhat, on fertilization practices used on the crop as heavy fertilization with N will increase the N content of the plant.

These same general comments apply to sorghum silage. As a rule sorghum silage has a somewhat lower nutritive value than corn silage. This is a result of lower digestibility and lower sugar content of the stalk, and the passage through the GI tract of the small seeds if not broken up during ensiling. When the seeds have been partially broken, then sorghum silage is comparable to corn silage if the grain content is comparable.

Miscellaneous Silages

A wide variety of other herbaceous material has been used to make silage. Waste from canneries processing food crops such as sweet corn, green beans, green peas, and various root or vegetable residues have been used successfully. Residues of this type are difficult to use on a fresh basis because of a variable daily supply or because they are available for only short periods of time. Ensiling is advantageous in that it tends to result in a more uniform feed and a known supply provides for more efficient planning. Some low-quality roughages such as grass straws can be ensiled and, when additives such as molasses, urea, and NaOH are added, a reasonably palatable and digestible product can be produced.

Silage Use in Tropical Climates

According to the literature very little use is made of silage in most tropical countries. However, there is adequate evidence that silage of satisfactory quality can be made from grasses such as Elephant grass (*Pennisetum purpureum*) and several of the Panic grasses and forage cereals. Wilkinson (16) points out that tropical grasses generally contain lower levels of water-soluble carbohydrates than do temperate

species. He suggests that at least 3% (fresh weight) of soluble carbohydrates should be present to ensure adequate production of lactic acid and to avoid the undesirable secondary fermentations resulting in high butyric acid production. Because of the low soluble carbohydrate content, grasses need to be wilted, but over-wilting prior to ensiling can occur easily under tropical conditions. In one study with forage maize (corn), it was shown that losses associated with silage production were (those measured): mechanical losses in the field, 6%; respiration and fermentation during storage, 7%; surface waste, 7%; during removal from storage, 5%. Wilkinson pointed out that silos to be used in the tropics should be designed so that they are long and narrow to minimize the face area exposed between feeding times and thus reduce deterioration of the silage.

❏ HIGH-ENERGY FEEDSTUFFS

Feedstuffs included in this class are those that are fed or added to a ration primarily for the purpose of increasing energy intake or to increase energy density of the ration. Included are the various cereal grains and some of their milling by-products and liquid feeds—primarily molasses and mixtures in which molasses predominates—and fats and oils.

High energy feedstuffs generally have low to moderate levels of protein. However, several of the high-protein meals could be included on the basis of available energy. Furthermore, on the basis of energy/unit of dry matter we could include some of the roots and tubers; because of their high water content usually they are considered separately. The same comments apply to fluid milk.

Energy from high-energy feedstuffs is supplied primarily either by readily available carbohydrates—sugars and/or starches—or by fat. Depending upon the type of diet and the class of animal involved, feedstuffs in this class may make up a substantial percentage of an animal's total diet. As such, other nutrients provided by these feeds—amino acids, minerals, vitamins—must be considered also, but quantitatively these nutrients are of less concern than the available energy.

❏ CEREAL GRAINS

Cereal grains are produced by members of the grass family (Gramineae) grown primarily for their seeds. A tremendous tonnage is produced in the USA primarily for feed as shown in Table 20.7. Of course, some of these grains go into human food. For example, corn may be consumed as popped corn, corn flakes, corn flour, corn starch, corn syrup, or corn oil, but the amount used in this manner is much less than goes into animal feed. Wheat and rice are grown primarily for human consumption, although substan-

tial amounts of wheat may go into animal feed in the USA when price and supply allow it. Barley and oats, although good feeds, are becoming relatively less important because they do not yield as well as some of the other feed grain plants. Other grains such as millet and rye find only limited use as feeds. A wheat-rye cross, triticale, is produced in only small quan-

TABLE 20.7   Feedgrains, protein sources, and by-product feedstuffs fed to animals in the USA.[a]

FEEDSTUFF		AMOUNT CONSUMED, ESTIMATE FOR 1985
		---Million metric tons---
Feed supply		305.6
Feed grains		145.6
Corn (maize)	117.6	
Grain sorghums	14.0	
Oats and Barley	13.6	
Wheat and Rye		12.1
Oilseed meals		22.4
Grain protein feeds		3.0
Other by-product feeds		16.5
Total fed		202.4
Manufactured Feeds		---1,000 metric tons---
Animal protein		
Tankage and meat meal		1,480
Fish meal and solubles		237
Commercial dried milk products		106
Non-commercial milk products		83
Oilseed meals		
Soybean		18,002
Cottonseed		1,646
Linseed		115
Peanut		102
Sunflower		435
Grain proteins		
Brewers dried grains		404
Distillers dried grains		748
Gluten feed and meal		1,576
Other feeds		
Alfalfa meal		850
Dried beet pulp, w/wo molasses		1,360
Rice millfeed		558
Wheat millfeed		4,588
Molasses, inedible		2,500
Fats and oils		591
Miscellaneous by-product feeds		1,308

[a]Data from USDA and Anonymous (17).

tities for animal feed. Of the total grains (not counting byproducts) fed in 1985, corn accounted for 74.7%, and this was in a year when much more wheat was fed than the usual practice.

Average values for some nutrients in cereal grains are given in Table 20.8. Note here that relatively small differences occur between grains and identifying them on the basis of their chemical composition would be difficult at times. Although grains usually are said to be less variable in composition than roughages, many factors influence nutrient composition and, thus, feeding value for a given grain. For example, factors such as soil fertility and fertilization, variety, weather and rainfall, and insects and disease may all affect plant growth and seed production so that average book values may not be meaningful. With wheat, for example, if a hot, dry period occurs while the grain is ripening, shriveled, small seeds may result; although they may have a relatively high protein content, the starch content is apt to be much lower than usual, the weight per bushel will be low, and the feeding value appreciably lower.

Although crude protein content of feed grains is relatively low, ranging from 8–12% for most grains, we may find some lower than this and, particularly with wheat, some may be much higher, sometimes as high as 22% crude protein. Sorghum grains are also quite variable.

Of the nitrogenous compounds, 85–90% is in the form of proteins; most cereal grains are moderately low to deficient for monogastic species in lysine and often in tryptophan (corn) and threonine (sorghum and rice) and in methionine for poultry, whose requirement is higher than that for pigs.

The fat content may vary greatly, ranging from less than 1% to more than 6% with oats usually having the most and wheat the least. Most of the fat is found in the seed embryo. Seed oils are high in linoleic and oleic acids, both unsaturated fatty acids that tend to become rancid quickly, particularly after the grain is processed.

The carbohydrates in grains, with the exception of the hulls, are primarily starch with small amounts of sugars. The starch, which makes up most of the endosperm, is highly digestible, providing hull permeability allows access of digestive juices. Starch from the different grains has specific physical characteristics that can be identified by microscopic examination, and the size of starch granules varies from grain to grain. Minor differences are noted in chemical characteristics, some of which have not been understood well with respect to animal utilization.

Hulls of seeds have a substantial effect on feeding value. Most hulls (or seed coats) must be broken to some extent before feeding for efficient utilization, particularly for ruminant animals. Barley and oats sometimes are known as rough grains because of the very fibrous hulls that are relatively resistant to digestion. Rice hulls are almost totally indigestible. For more details on the cereal grains, see Church (18).

Corn (*Zea mays*)

In areas where it grows well, corn will produce more digestible nutrients/unit of land than any other grain crop (Fig. 20.10). Yields of corn on small acreages have approached 400 bushels/acre (11 + tons). In addition, corn is a very digestible and palatable feed, being relished by all domestic animals. Essentially 100% of corn grain is harvested mechanically (Fig. 20.11).

The chemical composition of corn has been studied in detail. Zein, a protein in the endosperm, makes up about half the total protein in the kernel of most varieties. This protein is low in many of the essential amino acids but particularly so for lysine and tryptophan; the total protein of corn is deficient in these amino acids for non-ruminant species and requires supplementation for adequate performance. The low tryptophan (which is a precursor for niacin) plus the low niacin content will lead, eventually, to a niacin deficiency and pellagra in monogastric animals depending on corn as a major dietary constituent (see Ch. 15). N fertilization has been shown to increase

Figure 20.10 *A field of corn (maize), a crop used to feed millions of animals when harvested in different ways. Photo courtesy of R. W. Henderson.*

TABLE 20.8 Average composition of the major cereal grains, dry basis.[a]

ITEM	CORN, DENT	OPAQUE-2 CORN	WHEAT HARD WINTER	WHEAT SOFT WHITE	RICE, WITH HULLS	RYE	BARLEY	OATS	SORGHUM (MILO)
Crude protein, %	10.4	12.6	14.2	11.7	8.0	13.4	13.3	12.8	12.4
Ether extract, %	4.6	5.4	1.7	1.8	1.7	1.8	2.0	4.7	3.2
Crude fiber, %	2.5	3.2	2.3	2.1	8.8	2.6	6.3	12.2	2.7
Ash, %	1.4	1.8	2.0	1.8	5.4	2.1	2.7	3.7	2.1
NFE, %	81.3	76.9	79.8	82.6	75.6	80.1	75.7	66.6	79.6
Total sugars, %	1.9		2.9	4.1		4.5	2.5	1.5	1.5
Starch, %	72.2		63.4	67.2		63.8	64.6	41.2	70.8
Essential amino acids, % of DM									
Arginine	0.45	0.86	0.76	0.64	0.63	0.6	0.6	0.8	0.4
Histidine	0.18	0.44	0.39	0.30	0.10	0.3	0.3	0.2	0.3
Isoleucine	0.45	0.40	0.67	0.44	0.35	0.6	0.6	0.6	0.6
Leucine	0.99	1.06	1.20	0.86	0.60	0.8	0.9	1.0	1.6
Lysine	0.18	0.53	0.43	0.37	0.31	0.5	0.6	0.4	0.3
Phenylalanine	0.45	0.56	0.92	0.57	0.35	0.7	0.7	0.7	0.5
Threonine	0.36	0.41	0.48	0.37	0.25	0.4	0.4	0.4	0.3
Tryptophan	0.09	0.16	0.20		0.12	0.1	0.2	0.2	0.1
Valine	0.36	0.62	0.79	0.56	0.50	0.7	0.7	0.7	0.6
Methionine	0.09	0.17	0.21	0.19	0.20	0.2	0.2	0.2	0.1
Cystine	0.09	0.22	0.29	0.34	0.11	0.2	0.2	0.2	0.2
Minerals, % of DM									
Calcium	0.02		0.06	0.09	0.06	0.07	0.06	0.07	0.04
Phosphorus	0.33		0.45	0.34	0.45	0.38	0.35	0.30	0.30
Potassium	0.33		0.57	0.44	0.25	0.52	0.63	0.42	0.39
Magnesium	0.12		0.11	0.11	0.11	0.13	0.14	0.19	0.22

[a]Analytical data taken from NRC publications.

TABLE 20.9 Relative values (dry basis) of different cereal grains as given by NRC publications.

GRAIN	DIGESTIBLE PROTEIN, CATTLE	ENERGY				
		TDN		ME CHICKENS	NE_m CATTLE	NE_g CATTLE
		CATTLE	SWINE			
Corn, #2 dent	100	100	100	100	100	100
Barley	131	91	88	77	93	95
Milo	95	88	96	103	81	83
Oats	132	84	79	74	76	77
Wheat, hard red winter	152	97	99	90	95	96

protein content and decrease protein quality, due primarily to an increase in the zein fraction.

The energy value of corn is used as a standard of comparison for other grains (Table 20.9). Thus, if the relative energy value of corn is taken at 100, the value of other cereal grains is usually lower. This is partially accounted for because of the low fiber content of the corn kernel and the high digestibility of its starch. Wheat compares favorably with corn, but diets composed of a high percentage of wheat often promote lower feed intake, particularly by ruminants.

Figure 20.11 *A modern corn picker which shells the corn as it is picked in the field. Courtesy of the Deutz-Allis Corp.*

White and yellow corn have similar compositions except that yellow corn has a much higher content of carotene and xanthophylls, vitamin A precursors. Both white and yellow corn are fair sources of vitamin E, but low in the B-vitamins and devoid of vitamin D. Corn is very deficient in Ca. Although the P content is relatively high, much of it is in the form of phytic acid P, which has a low availability to most monogastric animals. Trace elements are relatively low to deficient.

Several genetic mutants of corn have been isolated and are being developed. One of these known as opaque-2 is of particular interest because it has a high level of lysine and increased levels of most other essential amino acids (see Table 20.8). This change results from a reduction in zein and an increase in glutelin, a protein found both in the endosperm and germ. The result is an improvement in the quality of the corn protein. Performance of monogastric species may be improved considerably by the use of this mutant. It is questionable if opaque-2 is of added value for ruminants. Yields of opaque-2 are not equivalent to common corn nor are prices proportionately higher, so interest of corn producers has not resulted in a marked increase in production of this mutant.

A second mutant of interest is known as floury-2. Although it also has higher levels of lysine and some of the other essential amino acids, comparative experiments do not indicate it to be as good as the opaque-2 strain. Other experimental mutants include those designated as high-fat, high-amylose, and brown midrib.

Grain Sorghum (*Sorghum vulgare*)

Sorghum is a hardy plant that is able to withstand heat and drought better than most grain crops. In addition, it is resistant to pests such as root worm and the corn borer, and is adaptable to a wide variety of soil types. Consequently, sorghum is grown in many areas where corn does not do well. Sorghum yields less than corn, where corn thrives. The seed from all varieties is small and relatively hard, and usually requires some processing for good animal utilization.

A wide range of sorghum varieties (all *Sorghum vulgare*) are used for seed production. These include milo, various kafirs, sorgo, sumac, millet, hegari, darso, feterita and cane. Milo is a favorite in drier areas because it is a short plant adaptable to harvesting with grain combines. Development of hybrid varieties that have higher yields has increased production greatly in recent years.

Chemically, grain sorghums are similar to corn. Protein content averages about 11%, but is apt to be quite variable; lysine and threonine are the most limiting amino acids. Content of other nutrients is similar to that of corn. Feeding trials indicate that sorghum grains are worth somewhat less than corn (Table 20.9), although some data indicate a higher value. Some bird-resistant varieties, whose seed coats are high in tannin, are not well liked by most animals.

Wheat (*Triticum* spp)

Wheat is not often grown intentionally for animal feed in North America, and almost all commonly grown varieties were developed with flour milling qualities in mind rather than feeding values. All harvesting is done mechanically in North America (Fig. 20.12, see page 356). On a world-wide basis about 20% of the wheat produced is used as feed. The hard winter wheats are high in protein, averaging 13–15%, but the soft white wheats have less protein (Table 20.8). The amino acid distribution is better than that of most cereal grains, and wheat is a very palatable and digestible feed, having a relative value equal to or better than corn for most animals. Feeding wheat to ruminants requires some caution because wheat is more apt than other grains to cause acute indigestion in animals unadapted to it. Some processing (grinding, rolling) is required to optimal utilization. When available for feed, it can be substituted equally for corn on the basis of digestible energy.

Barley (*Hordeum vulgare* or *H. distichon*)

Barley is grown widely in Europe and in the cooler climates of North America and Asia. Although a small amount goes into human food and a substantial amount is used in the brewing industry in the form of malt, most of it is used for animal feeding.

Barley contains more total protein and higher levels of lysine, tryptophan, methionine, and cystine than corn, but its feeding value is appreciably less in most cases, due to the relatively high fiber content of the hull and the lower digestible energy. Barley is a very palatable feed for ruminants, particularly when rolled before feeding, and few digestive problems result from its use. Hull-less varieties are roughly comparable to corn and, thus, more suitable for swine and poultry feeding; however, not much hull-less barley is produced. A new high-lysine barley containing 25% more lysine than common barley shows promise as an energy source for monogastric species; this would allow a saving in supplemental protein.

Oats (*Avena sativa*)

Oats represent only about 4.5% of the total world production of cereal grains, most of the production being concentrated in northern Europe and America. The protein content of oats is relatively high and the amino acid distribution is more favorable than for corn, but oats are not used widely for feeding of swine or poultry because of the hull which makes up about one-third of the seed. The hull is quite fibrous and poorly digested. Even when ground, the result is a very bulky feed. Including a high percentage in the diet does not allow for optimal feed intake for growing poultry or swine, although oats have some value in protecting young pigs from stomach ulcers. For ruminants and horses, oats is a favored feed for breeding stock, one well liked by animals. However, for feedlot cattle oats do not supply sufficient energy for maximal gains. Oat groats (whole seed minus the hull) have a feeding value comparable to corn, but the price usually is not favorable for animal use.

Triticale

A relatively new cereal grain, triticale, shows promise as a swine feed. Triticale is a hybrid cereal derived from a cross between wheat (*Triticum duriem*) and rye (*Secale cereale*). Its feeding value as an energy source is comparable to that of corn and other cereal grains for swine. Triticale can replace all of the grain sorghum and part of the soybean meal in diets for growing pigs. Total protein content tends to be higher than that of corn and grain sorghum and similar to that of wheat.

Comparative Value of Grains

Some information already has been given on this topic (Table 20.9), but some additional information is in order. Animal research on the feed grains has gone on for many years, and research papers still appear at fairly frequent intervals. For example, data from three relatively recent reports are given in Table 20.10. These data are shown to illustrate the problem of comparative evaluation. In the first two experiments, pigs were fed the test grains in addition to a basal diet believed to have an excess of required nutrients other than energy. In the third, pigs were fed grain plus a mineral-vitamin supplement. The latter experiment would be a better estimate of the energy *and* amino acid contribution, while the former would be only a measure of energy contribution.

Another comparison is shown in Table 20.11, in which dairy cows were fed complete diets with 60% of the dry matter from rolled barley, wheat, or oats. Despite the fact that cows fed wheat ate more feed and those fed oats had the lowest digestibility of organic matter (done with indidators; possibly in error?), those fed the oats produced more milk or fat-corrected milk during the test period.

In the writer's opinion, comparative trials always should include a "standard," such as corn. In addition,

TABLE 20.10 Comparative value of cereal grains for pigs.

	GRAINS						
MEASUREMENT	CORN	OATS	WHEAT	BARLEY	TRITICALE	MILO	REF.
Daily gain,[a] g	293	253					19
Feed conversion	1.17	1.36					
Dig. energy, Kcal/g	3.43	2.84					
Daily gain,[a] g			251	230			20
Feed conversion			1.25	1.27			
Dig. energy, Kcal/g			3.82	3.76			
Dig. energy,[b] Kcal/g	3.80		3.71	3.38	3.60		21
Dig. energy, Kcal/g	4.06	3.21	3.96	3.46		3.82	NRC

[a]Grains were fed at an average of 1.5% of body weight in addition to a basal diet fed at 3% of body weight/day. All nutrients except energy were considered to be fed in excess of requirements.
[b]Grains were fed only with a mineral and vitamin supplement.

TABLE 20.11   Response of lactating dairy cows to feeding complete diets with 60% rolled barley, wheat, or oats.[a]

ITEM	BARLEY	WHEAT	OATS
Dry matter intake, kg/day	16.89	18.10	17.69
Organic matter digestibility, %	68.9	73.5	61.0
Daily FCM production, kg	24.6	24.9	27.6

[a]After Moran (22).

if we are dealing with complete diets, the non-test portion of the diet should be adjusted to compensate for deficiencies of the grains. This should provide more reliable data for comparative purposes.

❏ MILLING BY-PRODUCTS OF CEREAL GRAINS

The milling of cereal grains for production of flour, starch, or other products results in production of a number of by-products that are used primarily by the commercial feed trade. Details of milling procedures, seed composition and more complete descriptions of by-products may be found in other references (23).

Milling by-products from wheat account for about 25% of the kernel. They are classified and named on the basis of decreasing fiber as bran, middlings (or mill run), shorts, red dog, and feed flour. These are relatively bulky and laxative feeds, particularly bran, but are quite palatable to animals. The bran and middlings are from the outer layers of the seed and contain more protein than the grain. Protein quality is improved somewhat, although these products are apt to be deficient in lysine and methionine as well as some other essential amino acids. These outer layers of the seed are relatively good sources of most of the water-soluble vitamins, except for niacin, which is entirely unavailable. These feedstuffs are low in Ca and high in P and Mg. The bulk of the production of wheat by-products is used in swine and poultry rations; although when bran is available, it is a favored feed in rations for dairy cows, all breeding classes of ruminants and for horses.

Corn milling by-products are somewhat different than wheat by-products because corn is often milled for purposes other than flour production. When milled for corn meal, hominy feed is produced, a product that consists of corn bran (hulls), corn germ and part of the endosperm. It is similar to corn meal

but higher in protein and fiber. Some wet-milling processes are used for various purposes resulting in by-products such as corn gluten meal, corn gluten feed, germ meal, corn solubles, and bran. The gluten meal is a high-protein product. Of these by-products, hominy feed is most valuable as an energy feed and it is used in a wide variety of diets. It is quite digestible but of variable energy value depending on its fat content.

Milling by-products of barley, sorghum, rye, and oats are similar, more or less, to those of wheat or corn and of comparable nutritional value. With rice, the bran may be of good quality, but is apt to be quite variable because of inclusion of hulls. The bran tends to become rancid rapidly because of its relatively high content of unsaturated fats.

❏ LIQUID ENERGY SOURCES

Molasses

Molasses is a major by-product of sugar production, the bulk of it coming from sugar cane. About 25–50 kg of molasses results from production of 100 kg of refined sugar. Molasses also is produced from sugar beets and other products as shown in Table 20.12; hemicellulose extract (wood molasses, Masonex) is a somewhat similar product.

Molasses is essentially an energy source and the main constituents are sugars. Cane molasses contains 25–40% sucrose and 12–25% reducing sugars with total sugar content of 50–60% or more. Crude protein content normally is quite low (3 ± %) and variable, and the ash content ranges from 8–10%, largely made up of K, Ca, Cl, and sulfate salts. Molasses is a good source of the trace elements, but has only a moderate to low vitamin content. In commercial use molasses is adjusted to about 25% water content, but may be dried for mixing into dry diets.

TABLE 20.12 Analytical and TDN values of different sources of molasses.[a]

| | SOURCE OF MOLASSES | | | | | |
ITEM	CANE[b]	BEET	CITRUS	CORN	SORGHUM	REFINERS
Standard Brix, deg.	79.5	79.5	71.0	78.0	78.0	79.5
Total solids, %	75	76	65	73	73	73
Crude protein, %	3.0	6.0	7.0	0.5	0.3	3.0
Ash, %	8.1	9.0	6.0	8.0	4.0	8.2
Total sugars, %	48–54	48–52	41–43	50	50	48–50
TDN, %	72	61	54	63	63	72

[a]From Anonymous (24).
[b]Also known as blackstrap molasses.

One of the problems in molasses feeding is that such products (except for corn molasses) are quite variable in composition. Age, type, and quality of the cane, soil fertility, and system of collection and processing have a bearing on composition of molasses. As an example, the Ca content of 11 samples of cane molasses ranged from 0.3 to 1.68% (25).

Molasses is utilized widely as a feedstuff, particularly for ruminants. In the USA alone about 2.5 million tons are used annually and large amounts are used in Europe and in other areas where it is produced. The sweet taste makes it appealing to most species. In addition, molasses is of value in reducing dust, as a pellet binder, as a vehicle for feeding medicants or other additives, and as a liquid protein supplement when fortified with a N source. The cost often is attractive as compared to grains. Most molasses products are limited in use, however, because of milling problems (sticky consistency of molasses) or because levels exceeding 15–25% of the diet are apt to result in digestive disturbances, diarrhea, and inefficient animal performance. The diarrhea largely is a result of the high level of various mineral salts in most molasses products. The problem is not due to sugar content, because pigs or ruminants can utilize comparable amounts of sugar supplied in other forms. High-test molasses, which has a lower ash content, can be fed at very high levels to either pigs or cattle without any particular problem, but not much high-test molasses is available for animal feeding.

Other Liquid Feeds

Whey, a by-product of cheese or casein production, is used similarly to dried skim milk. It may be bought as is (no processing), condensed, or dried. The high lactose and mineral content may be laxative, so the amount that can be used is limited. Whey is relatively low in protein (13–17% dry basis), although the protein is of high biological value. It is an excellent source of B-vitamins. Delactosed whey is available in some areas.

Various other liquids may be used in feeds or liquid protein supplements. However, with the exception of propylene glycol, nearly all would be classed as protein sources because they contain >20% CP on a dry basis.

❏ OTHER HIGH-CARBOHYDRATE FEEDSTUFFS

Root Crops

Root crops used in feeding animals, particularly in northern Europe, include turnips, mangolds, swedes, fodder beets, carrots, and parsnips. These crops may be dug and left lying in the field to be consumed as desired when used as animal feed. The bulky nature of these feeds limits their use for swine and poultry, so most are fed to cattle and sheep.

Root crops are characterized by their high water (75–90 + %), moderately low fiber (5–11% dry basis), and crude protein (4–12%) contents. These crops tend to be low in Ca and P and high in K. The carbohydrates range from 50–75% of dry matter and are mainly sucrose which is highly digestible by ruminants and non-ruminants. Animals (sheep, cattle) not adapted to beets or mangolds (both *Beta vulgaris*) tend to be subject to digestive upsets, probably because of the high sucrose content.

A tropical root crop (*Manihot esculenta*) called cassava, yucca, manioc, tapioca, or mandioca is of great potential importance as a livestock feed. It is ninth in world production of all crops and fifth among tropical crops, and has been shown in experimental plots to be capable of yielding 75–80 tons/hectare/year which is many times greater than can be produced by rice, corn, or other grains adapted to the tropics (25). Although it is strictly a tropical plant, significant amounts of cassava are used at the present in the USA and Europe for livestock feeding. Cassava root contains approximately 65% water, 1–2% protein, 1.5% crude fiber, 0.3% fat, 1.4% ash, and 3% NFE. Thus, its dry matter largely is readily available carbohydrates. Dried cassava is equal in energy value to other root crops and tubers and can be used to replace all of the grain portion of the diet for growing-finishing pigs if the amount of supplemental protein is increased to compensate for the low protein content of cassava. It can be used as the main energy source in diets of gestating and lactating swine. The stalk and leaf portion of the plant is utilized well by ruminants, but is too high in fiber for non-ruminants.

Freshly harvested cassava roots and leaves may be high in prussic acid (hydrocyanic acid). Oven-drying at 70–80°C, boiling in water, or sun-drying are effective in reducing the HCN content of freshly harvested cassava. As improved harvesting and processing methods for cassava are developed, large-scale commercial production of cassava can be expected to make a significant contribution to the world energy feed supply for animals.

Tubers

Surplus or cull white potatoes (*Solanum tuberosum*) are used for feeding cattle or sheep in areas where commercial potato production occurs. Pigs and chickens do poorly on raw potatoes, but cooking improves digestibility of the starch so that it is comparable to corn starch. Potatoes are high in digestible energy (dry basis), which is derived almost entirely from starch. Water content is about 78–80%; crude protein content is low, and the quality of the protein is poor. The Ca content is usually low. Potatoes and particularly potato sprouts contain a toxic compound, solanin, which may cause problems if potatoes are fed raw or ensiled. In cattle finishing rations, cull potatoes frequently are fed at a level to provide up to half of the dry matter intake.

Various by-products of potato processing are available in some areas as high percentages of white potatoes are processed to some extent before entering the retail trade in the USA. Potato meal is the dried raw meal of potato residue left from the processing plants. Potato flakes are residues remaining after cooking, mashing, and drying; potato slices are the residue after raw slices are dried with heat; and potato pulp is the by-product remaining after extraction of starch with cold water. The raw meals have about the same relative nutrition values as raw cull potatoes. A product called dried potato by-product meal is produced in some areas; it contains the residue of food production such as off-color french fries, whole potatoes, peelings, potato chips, and potato pulp. These are mixed, limestone is added, and the mixture dried with heat. Potato slurry is a high-moisture product remaining after processing for human food; it contains a high amount of peel. Generally, the value of these potato products is comparable roughly to that of raw or cooked cull potatoes, depending on how the by-product is dried. However, residues of the potato chip processing may have much higher levels of fat, so the energy value may be increased accordingly. For swine, cooked potato products are restricted usually to 30% or less of the ration.

Dried Bakery Product

This is a product produced from reclaimed (unused) bakery products; candy, nuts, and so on. While relatively little is available, it is an excellent feed as most of the energy is derived from starch, sucrose and fat. It is utilized well by pigs and is a preferred ingredient in starter rations. A wide variety of unconsumed bakery products make very satisfactory feeds for swine or ruminants. Where available, it is often used in dairy feed mixes.

Dried Beet and Citrus Pulp

Dried beet pulp is the residue remaining after extraction of sugar from sugar beets. Molasses may be added before drying and the product may be sold in shredded or pelleted form. The physical nature and high palatability make it a favored feed for cattle or sheep and it has a feeding value comparable to cereal grains. Unfortunately, the supply continues to decrease because fewer and fewer sugar beets are being produced.

Citrus pulp is a somewhat similar product (but with a lower energy value) remaining after the juice is extracted from citrus fruits; it includes peel, pulp, and seeds. Citrus pulps are used primarily as feedstuffs for cattle or sheep.

❑ FATS AND OILS

Surplus animal fats and, occasionally, vegetable oils frequently are used in commercial feed formulas, depending on relative prices. A variety of different products are available and these have been described as to composition and source by the American Association of Feed Control Officials. For the most part, feeding fats are animal fats derived by rendering of beef, swine, sheep, or poultry tissues. Vegetable oils generally command better prices for use in producing margarine, soap, paint, and other industrial products so that usually they are priced out of use in animal feeding.

Although most animals need a source of the essential fatty acids (see Ch. 9), these are supplied in sufficient amounts in natural feedstuffs and supplementation is not required except when low-fat energy sources are used. Fats are added to rations for several reasons. As a source of energy, fats are highly digestible, and digestible fat supplies about 2.25X that of digestible starch or sugar; thus, they have a high caloric value and can be used to increase energy density of a ration. Fats often tend to improve rations by reducing dustiness and increasing palatability. There is some evidence that fats will reduce bloat in ruminants. In addition, the lubrication value on milling machinery is often of interest. Fats are subject to oxidation (see Ch. 9) with development of rancidity which reduces palatability and may cause some digestive and nutritional problems. Feeding fats usually have antioxidants added, especially if the fats are not to be mixed into the diet and fed immediately.

Adding fat at low to moderate levels sometimes can increase total energy intake through improved palatability, although animals usually consume enough energy to meet their demand when it is physically possible. In swine and poultry diets, 5–10% fat is often added to creep diets for pigs or to broiler rations. Amounts above 10–12% usually will cause a sharp reduction in feed consumption, so concentration of other nutrients may need to be increased in order to obtain the desired consumption.

For ruminants, high levels of fats are used in milk replacers; depending on the purpose of the replacer, it may contain 10–30% added fat. Ruminants on dry feed, however, are less tolerant of high fat levels than are non-ruminants. Concentrations of more than 7–8% are apt to cause digestive disturbances, diarrhea, and greatly reduced feed intake. In practice, 2–4% fat may be added in finishing rations for cattle,

and some fat occasionally is added to rations for lactating dairy cows.

❑ PROTEIN CONCENTRATES

Protein is one of the critical nutrients, particularly for young, rapidly growing animals and high-producing adults, although it may be secondary to energy or other nutrients at times. In addition, protein supplements usually are more expensive than energy feeds, so optimal use is a must in any practical feeding system. Most energy sources, except for fat, starch, or refined sugar, supply some protein, but usually not enough to meet total needs except for adult animals. Furthermore, for monogastric animals the quality of protein from a given source rarely is adequate to sustain maximal production with minimal amounts of protein.

Protein supplements (>20% crude protein) are available from a wide variety of animal and plant sources, and non-protein N sources such as urea and ammonium phosphates are available from synthetic chemical manufacturing processes. It is beyond the scope of this book to detail all of the available sources; refer to Pond and Maner (25) for more detailed discussion and data on amino acid composition of some of the less well-known protein sources. Table 20.13 contains data on composition of a few common protein supplements.

Protein Supplements of Animal Origin

Protein supplements derived from animal tissues are obtained primarily from inedible tissues from meat packing or rendering plants, from surplus milk or milk by-products or from marine sources. Those of animal origin include meat meal, meat and bone meal, blood meal and feather meal; milk products include dried skim and whole milk and dried buttermilk; fish products include whole fish meal made from a variety of species, meals made from residues of fish or other seafood and fish protein concentrate.

Meat Meal, Meat and Bone Meal, Blood Meal

These animal by-products are used almost exclusively for swine, poultry and pet diets in the USA, although they may be used for ruminants in some areas. Palatability is moderate to good. However, the quality of meat or meat and bone meal varies considerably depending upon dilution with bone and tendonous tissues and on methods and temperatures

TABLE 20.13 Composition of several important protein supplements.

ITEM	ALFALFA, DEHY.	DRIED SKIM MILK	MEAT MEAL	FISH MEAL, HERRING	FEATHER MEAL	COTTONSEED MEAL, SOL. EXT.	SOYBEAN MEAL, SOL. EXT.	BREWERS GRAINS, DEHY.
Dry matter, %	93.1	94.3	88.5	93.0	91.0	91.0	89.1	92.0
Other components, %[a]								
Crude protein	22.1	36.0	55.0	77.4	93.9	45.5	52.4	28.1
Fat	3.9	1.1	8.0	13.6	2.6	1.0	1.3	6.7
Fiber	21.7	0.3	2.5	0.6	0.0	14.2	5.9	16.3
Ash	11.1	8.5	21.0	11.5	3.5	7.0	6.6	3.9
Ca	1.63	1.35	8.0	2.2	0.4	0.2	0.3	0.29
P	0.29	1.09	4.0	1.7	0.5	1.1	0.7	0.54
Essential amino acids								
Arginine	0.97	1.23	3.0	4.5	6.9	4.6	3.8	1.4
Cystine		0.48	0.4	0.9	4.1	0.7	0.8	
Histidine	0.43	0.96	0.9	1.6	0.6	1.1	1.4	0.5
Isoleucine	0.86	2.45	1.7	3.5	4.8	1.3	2.8	1.6
Leucine	1.61	3.51	3.2	5.7	8.7	2.4	4.3	2.5
Lysine	0.97	2.73	2.6	6.2	2.0	1.7	3.4	1.0
Methionine	0.32	0.96	0.8	2.3	0.6	0.5	0.7	0.4
Phenylalanine	1.18	1.60	1.8	3.1	4.8	2.2	2.8	1.4
Threonine	0.97	1.49	1.8	3.2	5.1	1.3	2.2	1.0
Tryptophan	0.54	0.45	0.5	0.9	0.7	0.5	0.7	0.4
Valine	0.11	2.34	2.2	4.1	7.8	1.9	2.8	1.7

[a]Composition on dry basis. Data from NRC publications.

used in processing. Biological value of the proteins is lower, generally, than for fish or soybean meal. Growth studies with pigs indicate that these products are best used as a part rather than the total source of supplemental protein. Blood meal is a high-protein source (80–85% CP, dry basis), but it is quite deficient in isoleucine and is best used as a partial supplementary protein source, also.

Poultry By-Products

A number of by-product meals are produced, but the most important one is feather meal. This meal is quite high in protein (85%) and, when diets are formulated to adjust for its amino acid deficiencies, it is a satisfactory protein for non-ruminants as well as ruminants. Hair meals could also be produced in this manner. Both feathers and hair require more extensive cooking (to make their proteins digestible) than other by-product animal meals.

Milk Products

Dried skim or whole milk, although excellent protein sources, usually are quite expensive as compared to other feedstuffs. These products are used primarily in milk replacers or in starter rations for young pigs or ruminants. The quality of dried milk can be impaired by overheating during the drying process (drum drying), therefore spray-dried milk is preferred. Poor quality milk, when used in milk replacers, is apt to lead to diarrhea and digestive disturbances.

Marine Protein Sources

Fish meals are primarily of two types—those from fish caught for making meal and those made from fish residues processed for human food or other industrial purposes. Herring or related species provide much of the raw material for fish meals. These fish have a high body oil content, much of which is removed in preparation of the finished fish meal.

Good quality fish meals are excellent sources of proteins and amino acids, ranking close to milk proteins. The protein content is high (see Table 20.13), and it is highly digestible. Fish meals are especially high in essential amino acids, including lysine, which are deficient in the cereal grains. In addition, fish meal normally is a good source of the B-vitamins and most of the mineral elements. As a result, fish meal is a highly favored ingredient for swine and poultry feeds, although the cost of such meal is considerably higher in most areas than for other protein sources except milk. Some fish meal is used for ruminants in Europe, but very little is used for this purpose in North America. Some use of fat-extracted meals appears feasible in milk replacers.

The quality of fish may be variable due to factors such as partial decomposition before processing or overheating during processing. Excess oil may lead to rancidity and inadequate drying may allow molding. Even with good quality meal, high levels, when fed to swine, may result in fishy flavored pork if extraction of fat from the meal is incomplete.

❑ PLANT PROTEIN CONCENTRATES

The most important commercial sources of plant protein concentrates are derived from soybeans and cottonseed with lesser amounts from peanuts, flax (linseed), sunflower, sesame, safflower, rapeseed, various legume seeds, and other miscellaneous sources of lesser importance. Meals made from the seeds mentioned (except for some beans, peas) are called oilseed meals because these seeds are all high in oils that have a number of important commercial uses.

Three primary processes are used for removing the oil from these seed crops. These are known as expeller (screw press), prepress-solvent and solvent extraction. In the expeller process the seed, after cracking and drying, is cooked for 15–20 minutes, then extruded through dies by means of a variable pitch screw. This results in rather high temperatures which may cause reduced biological value of the proteins. The solvent-extracted meals are extracted with hexane or other solvents, usually at low temperatures. In the prepress-solvent process the seed oils are removed partially with a modified expeller process and then extracted with solvents; this usually is done with seeds containing more than 35% oil as they are not suitable commercially for direct solvent extraction.

As a group the oilseed meals are high in crude protein, most being over 40% (Table 20.13), and they are standardized before marketing by dilution with hulls or other material. A high percentage of the N is present as true protein (95 ± %) which is highly digestible and of moderate to good biological value, although usually of lower value than good an-

imal protein sources. Most meals are low in cystine and methionine and have a variable and usually low lysine content; soybean meal being an exception in lysine content. The energy content varies greatly, depending on processing methods; solvent extraction leaves less fat and, thus, reduces the energy value. Ca content is low usually, but most are high in P content although half or more is present as phytin P, a form poorly utilized by monogastrics. These meals contain low to moderate levels of the B-vitamins and are low in carotene and vitamin E.

Soybean Meal

Whole soybeans (*Glycine max*) contain 15–21% oil which is removed by solvent extraction or by a combination of mechanical procedures and solvent extraction. In processing the meal is toasted, a procedure that improves the biological value of its protein; the protein content is standardized at 44% or 50% by dilution with soybean hulls. Soybean meal is produced in large amounts in the USA and elsewhere and is a highly favored feed ingredient as it is quite palatable, highly digestible, of high energy value and results in excellent performance when used for different animal species. Methionine and lysine are the most limiting amino acids for swine and poultry and the B-vitamin content is low. In overall value soybean meal is the best plant protein source available in any quantity.

As with most other oil seeds, soybeans have a number of toxic, stimulatory and inhibitory substances. For example, a goitrogenic material is found in the meal and its long-term use may result in goiter in some animal species. It also may contain antigens that are especially toxic to young preruminants. Of major concern in non-ruminant species is a trypsin-inhibitor material that inhibits digestibility of protein. Fortunately, this inhibitor and other factors (saponins and a hemagglutinin) are inactivated by proper heat treatment during processing. Soybeans also contain genistein, a plant estrogen which may account, in some cases, for part of their growth-promoting properties.

Currently, there is interest in feeding whole soybeans after appropriate heat processing (100°C for 3 minutes) to inactivate the trypsin inhibitors. This whole bean product is known in the feed trade as full fat soybean meal; it contains about 38% CP, 18% fat, and 5% CF. Heating-extruding equipment has been developed for on the farm processing and its use appears feasible in relatively small operations. Such meal has found some favor in dairy cow diets and, in moderate amounts, in diets for swine and poultry. Heat-treated soybeans can be used to replace all of the soybean meal in corn-soy diets from growing-finishing pigs.

Cottonseed Meal

Due to the growth habits of cotton (*Gossypium* spp), cottonseed meal (CSM) is available in many areas where soybeans do not grow, particularly in some areas in South America, northern Africa, and Asia. CSM protein is of good, although variable, quality. Most meals are standardized (in the USA) at 41% crude protein. The protein is low in cystine, methionine and lysine, and the meal is low in Ca and carotene, although palatable for ruminants. CSM is less well liked by swine and poultry; nevertheless, it finds widespread use in animal feeds, although its use is more limited by various problems than that of soybean meal.

The cotton seed (and CSM) contains a yellow pigment, gossypol, which is relatively toxic for non-ruminant species, particularly young pigs and chicks. In addition, feeding CSM results in poor egg quality because gossypol tends to produce green egg yolks. Sterculic acid, which is found in CSM, can cause egg whites to turn pink.

Gossypol is found bound to free amino groups in the seed protein or in a free form which can be extracted with solvents. The free gossypol is the toxic form. Gossypol toxicity can be prevented in most instances by addition of ferrous sulfate and other iron salts. Choice of an appropriate processing method such as prepress-solvent extraction or more complicated extraction methods can remove most of the free gossypol. Further improvement can be made by plant breeding. Gossypol is produced in glands that can be reduced in size or removed by genetic changes in the plant. Meals from glandless seeds have resulted in good performance in poultry, although not for young pigs when given most of their supplementary protein from CSM (26). Biologically tested meals that are screened by feeding to hens are available in some areas, but at a higher price than normal meals.

Other Oilseed Meals

Linseed meal is made from flax seed (*Linum usitatissimum*), which is produced for the drying oils it contains. Linseed meal accounts for only a small part of the total plant proteins produced in the USA. The crude protein content is relatively low (35%) and is deficient in lysine. Although favored in ruminant diets, linseed meal is used sparingly for most species.

A substantial amount of peanuts (*Arachis hypogaea*) is grown worldwide (second to soybeans among seed legumes), mostly for human consumption. Peanut meals are quite deficient in lysine and the protein is low in digestibility. Peanuts contain a trypsin inhibitor, as do many beans, and they may be contaminated with molds such as *Aspergillus flavus*, which produces potent toxins (aflatoxins) that are detrimental, particularly to young animals.

Safflower (*Carthamus tinctorius*) is a plant grown in limited amounts for its oil. The meal is high in fiber and low in protein unless the hulls are removed. The protein is deficient in S-containing amino acids and lysine. This meal finds most use in ruminant rations because of the fiber content and inferior amino acid content.

Sunflowers (*Helianthus annuus*) are produced for oil and seeds, primarily in northern Europe and Russia as they will grow in relatively cool climates, although production is increasing in North America. The meals, although high in protein, are high in fiber and have not produced performance in swine or dairy cows comparable to that obtained with other protein sources.

Rapeseed meal (from *Brassica napus* or *B. campestris*) is of interest because it grows in more northern climates than most oilseed plants. Most rapeseed meals are about 40% crude protein with an amino acid pattern similar to that of other oilseed meals. Use of rapeseed meal from older varieties of rape is limited, at least in monogastric species, by the content of goitrogenic substances common to members of the mustard family. These meals also tend to be unpalatable. However, newer varieties and improved processing methods have resulted in meals of much better quality and improved palatability.

Other Plant Protein Sources

Coconut or copra meal, the residue after extraction and drying the meat of the coconut, is available in many areas of the world. The crude protein content is low (20–26%) and of variable digestibility. It can be used to partially supply protein needs of most species.

Field beans and peas of a number of species are sometimes available for animal feeding, although they may be grown primarily for human food. These seeds generally contain about 22–26% protein and the pro-

TABLE 20.14.   Chemical composition of some grain legumes.

ITEM	MOISTURE, %	COMPOSITION, % OF DM				
		PROTEIN	ETHER EXTRACT	FIBER	ASH	NFE
Chickpeas (forage)	11.8	19.6	4.0	9.5	3.2	63.7
Cowpeas	11.0	26.4	2.0	4.8	3.9	62.9
Dry beans	11.0	26.8	1.5	4.7	3.8	63.2
Field beans	11.0	26.3	2.2	8.8	3.8	58.9
Field peas	10.1	28.8	1.7	6.7	2.8	60.0
Pigeon peas	11.0	23.5	1.9	9.0	3.9	61.7

teins tend to be deficient in S-containing amino acids as well as tryptophan. Some seeds contain toxic factors, such as trypsin inhibitors, as well as other toxins. Because of the toxins and poor protein quality, use in feed for monogastric species is limited unless they are processed to inactivate some of the inhibitors. Some of these grain legumes hold promise as complete energy-protein feeds for swine in tropical areas of the world. Their favorable chemical composition is illustrated by data in Table 20.14. Considerable research effort currently is being expended to identify high-yielding varieties and to develop economical methods of destroying inhibitors and toxins. Recent work suggests that autoclaving or extruding are satisfactory methods for some bean species.

Distillery and Brewery By-Products

By-products of the distilling and brewing industries find some use as animal feed. The main products are wet or dried distillers and brewers grains. The protein content is higher than that of the original grain and energy values are similar to barley grain. Distillers dried solubles is an excellent source of B-vitamins and trace elements. Dried brewers grains has relatively high crude protein content (26%), but is low in starch and digestible energy. Dried distillers grain by-products are used more for ruminants and horses, but the solubles are used in all animal feeds when available.

New and Miscellaneous Protein Sources

As the world protein shortage becomes more acute, efforts continue to identify and develop additional sources for use in livestock feeding. Potential sources include animal wastes, seaweed, and single cell protein products such as algae, bacteria, and yeasts.

Animal and poultry wastes (feces and urine) have potential value as animal feed. To date, it appears that ruminants are best able to utilize them and until technological advances provide the knowledge needed to convert these waste products to feed useful to other species, cattle and sheep probably will be the main avenue of utilization. Current research efforts are aimed at possible utilization of microbial populations grown on animal wastes as a means of improving the nutritive value of these wastes for other animal species.

Algae is an attractive possibility as a protein source, except for the high moisture content. Preliminary results with cultivated fresh water algae indicate a potential for about 10 times as much protein/unit of land area as soybeans. Algae contains about 50% protein, 6–7% fiber, 4–6% fat, and 6% ash. A major problem, of course, is how to harvest and dry a product of this type. A particularly promising blue-green algal feedstuff is *Arthrospira platensis,* which contains more than 60% protein of high biological value.

Seaweed is plentiful in many areas of the world, but most research work indicates that it is not a good source of either energy or protein and should be used mainly as a mineral supplement which should not exceed 10% of the diet. It contains about 2% Ca, 0.4–0.5% P and is a good source of Fe and is extremely high in I.

There is interest also in preparing leaf protein concentrates from crops such as alfalfa because of its high yield of protein per unit of land. This is still in the development stage. It might be noted that various trypsin inhibitors have been found in a variety of leaf extracts (27).

It seems quite likely that single cell protein sources (yeasts, bacteria) may become much more important in the future as animal feeds. Yeasts and/

or bacteria can be grown on many different kinds of wastes. This offers particular advantages if the wastes are quite dilute and if means of concentrating and harvesting the microorganisms can be developed. Some yeast is used at this time in animal feeds, but the prices are relatively high. Bacterial proteins also are on the market, being produced from soluble wastes from breweries or wood pulping (paper) operations. Feeding values have not been well characterized for most animal species at this time, but preliminary data indicate that such products can be used satisfactorily for ruminant animals and, possibly, for non-ruminants as well.

❏ NONPROTEIN-NITROGEN [NPN]

NPN includes any compounds that contain N but are not present in the polypeptide form of precipitable protein. Organic NPN compounds would include ammonia, amides, amines, amino acids, and some peptides. Inorganic NPN compounds would include a variety of salts such as ammonium chloride and ammonium sulfate. Although some feedstuffs, particularly some forages, contain substantial amounts of NPN, from a practical point of view, NPN in formula feeds usually refers to urea or, to a lesser extent, such compounds as the ammonium phosphates, mainly because other NPN compounds often are too costly to use for feeding of animals at the present time, and those such as ammonium sulfate are not suitable sources of N.

NPN, especially urea, is primarily of interest for feeding of animals with a functioning rumen. The reason for this is that urea is hydrolyzed rapidly to ammonia which is then incorporated into amino acids and microbial proteins by rumen bacteria which are utilized later by the host. Thus, the animal, itself, does not utilize urea directly.

A variety of factors must be considered in utilizing urea in feeds, but complete discussion of the subject is too complex for this chapter (see ref. 7). Urea, if consumed too rapidly, may be toxic or lethal. Furthermore, urea must be fed with some readily available carbohydrate for good utilization and to prevent toxicity, and some adaptation time is required for the animal. Where livestock management is good and feed is formulated and mixed properly, urea can provide a substantial amount of the supplemental N required, even to the point where it supplies all of the N in purified diets. In practical rations current recommendations are that not more than one-third of the total N be supplied by urea. Most states require

labeling of feed tags with maximal amounts of urea as a protective measure for the buyer.

In non-ruminants the only microorganisms that can convert urea to protein are found in the lower intestinal tract at a point where absorption of amino acids, peptides, and proteins is believed to be rather low or non-existent. Research with pigs, poultry, horses and other species indicates that some ^{15}N from urea can be recovered in amino acids and proteins from body tissues, probably as a result of its incorporation into tissue amino acids by various known pathways of amination and transmaination. However, little if any net benefit is to be expected from feeding urea to non-ruminants. The most likely situation in which it might be useful would be when the supply of essential amino acids was adequate and the non-essentials in short supply; then supplementing with urea might be of some slight benefit.

❏ MINERAL SUPPLEMENTS

Although minerals make up only a relatively small amount of the diet of animals, they are vital to the animal and, in most situations, some diet supplementation is required to meet needs. Of course, all of the required mineral elements are needed in an animal's diet, but needed supplementary minerals will vary according to the animal species, age, production, diet, and mineral content of soils and crops in the area where grown. Generally, those minerals of concern include common salt (NaCl), Ca, P, Mg, and, sometimes, S of the macrominerals and, of the trace elements, Cu, Fe, I, Mn, and Zn and, in some places, Co and Se. Most energy and N sources—fat and urea being two marked exceptions—provide minerals in addition to the basic organic nutrients, but the flexibility needed in formulating diets usually requires more concentrated sources of one or more mineral elements. Some of these sources are discussed briefly.

Mineral Sources

Common salt (NaCl) is required for good animal production except in areas where the soil and/or water are quite saline. It is a common practice to add 0.25 to 0.5% salt to most commercial feed formulas, although this probably is more than actually is required for most species. Salt often is fed ad libitum, particularly to ruminants and horses, because their requirement probably is higher than for swine or poultry, and different feeding methods lend them-

TABLE 20.15   Composition of a typical trace-mineralized salt and its contribution to the diet when included at a level of 0.5%.

MINERAL[a]	AMOUNT IN SALT MIXTURE, %	AMOUNT PROVIDED IN COMPLETE DIET WHEN 0.5% INCLUDED, ppm
NaCl	Not less than 97.000 or more than 99.000	5000
Cobalt	Not less than 0.015	0.70
Copper	0.023	1.15
Iodine	0.07	3.50
Iron	0.117	5.4
Manganese	0.225	11.25
Sulfur	0.040	2.0
Zinc	0.008	0.40[b]

[a]Ingredients are: Salt, cobalt carbonate, copper oxide, calcium iodate, iron carbonate, manganese oxide, sodium sulfate, zinc oxide; yellow prussate of soda (sodium ferrocyanide) added as an anticaking agent. If selenium is added, FDA regulations specify 20 ppm for beef and dairy cattle and 30 ppm for sheep.
[b]This amount supplies only about 1% of the needs of swine.

selves to this practice. Excess salt may be a problem for all species, but particularly for swine and poultry because they are much more susceptible to toxicity than other domestic species, especially if water consumption is restricted.

In many cases salt is used as a carrier for some of the trace elements (see Table 20.15). Additional sources of the trace elements can be added to feedstuffs as inorganic salts in areas where they are known to be needed, or feedstuffs high in a needed mineral can be used in the feed formula.

Ca and P are required in large amounts by the animal body and many feedstuffs are deficient in one or both of these elements. Some of the common supplements are shown in Table 20.16. Most sources of Ca are well utilized by different animal species. Although net digestibility may be low, particularly in older animals, there is little difference between Ca sources. This statement does not apply to P, however, because sources differ greatly in availability. In plants about half of the P is bound to phytic acid and P in the product, phytin, is utilized poorly by monogastric species. The usual recommendation is to consider only half of plant P available to monogastric species although ruminants utilize it very well. Marked differences exist also in the biological availability of inorganic sources. Phosphoric acid and the mono-, di-, and tri-calcium phosphates are utilized efficiently. Sources such as Curacao Island and colloidal (soft) phosphates are utilized less well by most animals. Some sources are high in fluoride and must be defluorinated to prevent toxicity when the supplement is fed for an extended period of time.

Of course, some differences exist in utilization of some of the inorganic salts and oxides of different elements. For example, Mg in magnesite is used very poorly; Fe from ferric oxide is almost com-

TABLE 20.16   Some common supplements for Ca, P, and Mg.

MINERAL SOURCE	Ca, %	P, %	Mg, %
Bone meal, steamed	24–29	12–14	0.3
Bone black, spent	27	12	
Dicalcium phosphate	23–26	18–21	
Tricalcium phosphate	38–39	19–20	
Defluorinated rock phosphate[a]	31–34	13–17	
Raw rock phosphate[b]	24–29	13–15	
Sodium phosphate		22–23	
Soft phosphate	18	9	
Curacao phosphate	35	15	
Diammonium phosphate		20	
Oyster shell	38		
Limestone[c]	38		
Calcite, high grade	34		
Gypsum	22		
Magnesium oxide			60–61

[a]Usually less than 0.2%F.
[b]2–4% F.
[c]Dolomite limestone contains up to 10% or more Mg.

pletely unavailable, and I from some organic compounds such as diiodosalicylic acid, although it is absorbed, is also almost all excreted. Se from plant sources is more available biologically than that from inorganic sources. Legume forage and animal and fish proteins are excellent sources of the trace elements.

There is some interest in utilization of chelated trace minerals. Chelates are compounds in which the mineral atom is bound to an organic complex (hemoglobin, for example). Feeding of chelated minerals has been proposed on the basis that chelates will prevent the formation of insoluble complexes in the GI tract and reduce the amount of the particular mineral that will be required in the diet. Limited evidence indicates that this works sometimes (with Zn in poultry diets) but not in all, and the cost/unit of mineral is appreciably higher. Further data are required to know how well chelated trace minerals will work out for all species.

Figure 20.12   *Grain combines being used to harvest wheat in the Pacific Northwest. Photo by R. W. Henderson.*

❑ VITAMIN SOURCES

Nearly all feedstuffs contain some vitamins, but vitamin concentration varies tremendously because it is affected by harvesting, processing, and storage conditions as well as plant species and plant part (seed, leaf, stalk). As a rule, vitamins are destroyed quickly by heat, sunlight, oxidizing conditions, or storage conditions that allow mold growth. Thus, if any question arises of adequacy of a diet, it is better to err on the positive side than to have a diet that is deficient.

As a general rule, vitamins likely to be limiting in natural diets are: vitamins A, D, E, riboflavin, pantothenic acid, niacin, choline, and B_{12}, depending on the species and class of animal with which we are concerned. For adult ruminants only A, D, and E are of concern; A is the most likely to be deficient. Vitamin K and biotin can be a problem for both swine and poultry under some conditions, in addition to those vitamins listed previously.

Fat-Soluble Vitamins

The best sources of carotene and vitamin A are green plants and organ tissues such as liver meal. Commercially, most vitamin A now is produced synthetically at such low prices that the cost of adding it to rations is negligible and there is no economic reason not to add it where any likelihood of a need exists. High quality forages are good sources of vitamin D;

very high activity is obtained from fish liver oils or meals and irradiated yeast or animal sterols are common sources. Vitamin E is found in highest concentrations in the germ or germ oils of plants and in moderate concentrations in green plants or hay. Vitamin K is available in synthetic form (see Ch. 14) and, where gut synthesis is not adequate, it can be added at reasonable costs.

Water-Soluble Vitamins

Animal and fish products, green forages, fermentation products, oil seed meals, and some seed parts are good sources of the water-soluble vitamins. The bran layers of cereal grains are fair to moderate sources, and roots and tubers are poor to fair sources. Commercially, some of the crystalline vitamins or mixtures used for humans are prepared from liver and yeast or other fermentation products and some are produced synthetically. Thus, these various sources can be used to meet vitamin needs in animal rations. Vitamin B_{12} is produced only by microorganisms; it is stored in animal tissues and is found in fermentation products and in animal manures. Animal and fish products are good sources.

❑ SUMMARY

A vast variety of plant, animal, microbial, mineral, and synthetic feed ingredients are available in our modern world to use in animal diets. Although many of these items are used only in small amounts or for specific situations, improved knowledge of animal nutrition has allowed more complete utilization of many products that were unmarketable at one time. Unfortunately, even with all of the sophisticated analytical equipment available, a limiting feature in utilization of feedstuffs is the dependence on book analytical values of non-standardized feed ingredients. Feeds actually used may be quite different than expected—partly because of natural variation when harvested or manufactured and partly because some organic components, particularly vitamins and fatty acids, may deteriorate with time in storage. Another important factor is that in many instances digestibility values are calculated values which may not always be accurate. Last, but not least, animal utilization, particularly with ruminants, is highly dependent upon the level of feeding because digestibility and body metabolism will change as the quantity of a nutrient changes in the diet.

❏ REFERENCES

1. NRC. 1982. *United States-Canadian Tables of Feed Composition,* 3rd revision. Nat. Acad. Sci., Washington, D.C.

2. IFI. 1984. *IFI Tables of Feed Composition.* P. V. Fonnesbeck, H. Lloyd, R. Obray, and S. Romesburg (eds.). International Feedstuffs Institute, Utah State Univ., Logan, UT.

3. Morrison, F. F. 1956. *Feeds and Feeding,* 22nd ed. The Morrison Pub. Co., Clairmont, Alberta, Canada.

4. Gohl, B. 1975. *Tropical Feeds.* FAO, Rome, Italy.

5. McDowell, L. R., *et al.* 1974. *Latin American Tables of Feed Composition.* Dept. of Animal Science, Univ. of Florida, Gainesville, FL.

6. Bath, D. L., *et al.* 1980. *By-product and Unusual Feedstuffs in Livestock Rations.* West Regional Ext. Publ. 39.

7. Ely, R. E., E. A. Kane, W. C. Jacobson, and L. A. Moore. 1953. *J. Dairy Sci.* **36**:334.

8. Church, D. C. (ed.). 1988. *The Ruminant Animal.* Prentice-Hall, Inc., Englewood Cliffs, N.J.

9. Heath, M. E., D. S. Metcalf, and R. F. Barnes (eds.). 1973. *Forages,* 3rd ed. Iowa State Univ. Press, Ames, IA.

10. Morley, F. H. W. (ed.). 1981. *Grazing Animals.* Elsevier Scientific Pub. Co., Amsterdam and New York.

11. Beever, D. E., D. J. Thomson, E. Pfeffer, and D. G. Armstrong. 1971. *Brit. J. Nutr.* **26**:123.

12. Watson, S. J. and M. J. Nash. 1960. *The Conservation of Grass and Forage Crops.* Oliver and Boyd, Edinburgh, Scotland.

13. Sutton, A. L. and R. L. Vetter. 1971. *J. Animal Sci.* **32**:1256.

14. Wilkins, R. J., K. J. Hutchinson, R. F. Wilson, and C. E. Harris. 1971. *J. Agr. Sci.* **77**:531.

15. Colovos, N. F., *et al.* 1970. *J. Animal Sci.* **30**:819.

16. Wilkinson, J. M. 1983. *World Animal Rev.* **45** (Jan.–March):37.

17. USDA. 1985. *Agricultural Statistics.* U.S. Government Printing Office, Washington, D.C.; Anonymous, 1986. *Feedstuffs 1986 Reference Issue (July).* Miller Pub. Co., Minnetonka, MN.

18. Church, D. C. (ed.). 1984. *Livestock Feeds and Feeding,* 2nd ed. Prentice-Hall, Inc., Englewood Cliffs, N.J.

19. DeGoey, L. W. and R. C. Ewan. 1975. *J. Animal Sci.* **40**:1052.

20. Wu, J. F. and R. C. Ewan. 1979. *J. Animal Sci.* **49**:1470.

21. Cornejo, S. J. Potocnjak, J. H. G. Holmes, and D. W. Robinson. 1973. *J. Animal Sci.* **40**:1052.

22. Moran, J. B. 1986. *Animal Prod.* **43**:27.

23. Anonymous. 1980. *Millfeed Manual.* Millers's National Fed., Chicago, IL.

24. Anonymous. 1978. *Liquid Ingredients Handbook.* Nat. Feed Ingredients Assoc., Des Moines, IA.

25. Pond, W. G. and J. H. Maner. 1984. *Swine Production and Nutrition.* AVI Pub. Co., Westport, CT.

26. LaRue, D. C., D. A. Knabe, and T. D. Tanskley, Jr. 1985. *J. Animal Sci.* **60**:495.

27. Humpfries, C. 1980. *J. Sci. Food Agr.* **31**:1225.

21

Feed Preparation
and Processing

FEED REPRESENTS THE MAJOR cost in
animal production. Even with sheep, which
typically consume more forage than other domestic
species, feed may represent 55 + % of total
production costs; with poultry, a value of 75–80%
might be more appropriate. Thus, it is imperative
to supply an adequate diet—in terms of nutrient
content—and to prepare the diet in a manner that
will encourage consumption without waste and
allow high efficiency of feed utilization.

Feed processing may be accomplished by physical,
chemical, thermal, bacterial, or other alterations of
a feed ingredient before it is fed. Feeds may be
processed to alter the physical form or particle
size, to preserve, to isolate specific parts, to
improve palatability or digestibility, to alter nutrient
composition or to detoxify.

Generally, feed preparatory methods become more
important as level of feeding increases and when
maximum production is desired. This is so because
heavily fed animals become more selective and
because, in ruminants, digestibility tends to
decrease as level of feeding increases. The latter
occurs primarily because feed does not remain in
the GI tract long enough for maximal effect of the
various digestive processes. Feed preparation may
become more important for larger animal
production units with greater mechanization. This

applies particularly to roughage because long or baled hay is less convenient to handle than chopped, pelleted, or cubed hay.

Feed preparatory methods that are used for swine and poultry are relatively simple as compared to the variety that is available for ruminant feeds. Thus, the bulk of the discussion in this chapter will deal with ruminants with brief sections on non-ruminant species. Also, the discussion will deal primarily with roughages and grains and not with methods that are used for processing of oil seed meals, grain by-products, and similar feedstuffs.

❏ GRAIN PROCESSING METHODS

Grain processing methods can be divided conveniently into dry and wet processes or into cold and hot processing. Heat is an essential part of some methods, but it is not utilized at all in others. Likewise, added moisture is essential in some methods but may even be detrimental in others. Examples of milo processed in different ways are shown (Fig. 21.1) and various methods are listed and discussed later.

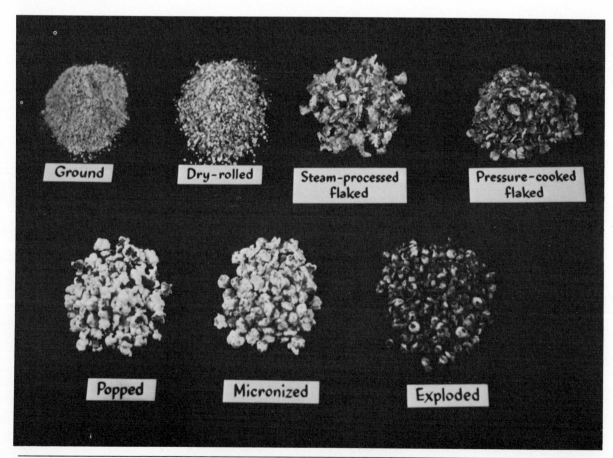

Figure 21.1   *Examples of sorghum grain processed by several different methods. Courtesy of W. H. Hale, University of Arizona.*

❏ COLD PROCESSING METHODS

Methods (or machinery) used for cold processing include rollermills, hammermills, soaking, reconstitution, ensiling at high moisture content, and preservation with added chemicals. Comments follow on the different methods.

Rollermill Grinding

Rollermills act on grain by compressing it between two corrugated rolls that can be screwed together to produce smaller and smaller particles. With grains like corn, wheat, or milo, the product can range in size from cracked grain to a rather fine powder. With the coarse grains—barley and oats—the product may range in size from a flattened seed to a relatively fine-ground product, but the hulls will not be ground as well as with other types of grinding mills. Rollermills produce a less dusty feed than a hammermill. If not ground too finely, the physical texture is very acceptable to most species. Rollermills are not used with roughage.

Hammermills

A hammermill processes feed with the aid of rotating metal bars (hammers) that blow the ground product through a metal screen. The size of the product is controlled by changing the screen size. These mills will grind anything from a coarse roughage to any type of grain, and the product size will vary from particles similar to cracked grain to a fine powder. There may be quite a bit of dust lost in the process and the finished product is usually more dusty than with a rollermill.

Soaked Grain

Grain soaked for 12–24 h in water has long been used by livestock feeders. The soaking, sometimes with heat, softens the grain which swells during the process, making a palatable product that should be rolled before using in finishing rations. Research results do not show any marked improvement as compared to other methods. Space requirements, problems in handling and potential souring have discouraged large scale use.

Reconstitution

Reconstitution is similar to soaking and involves adding water to mature dry grain to raise the moisture content to 25–30% and storage of the wet grain in an oxygen-limiting silo for 14–21 days prior to feeding. This procedure has worked well with sorghum in particular, resulting in improved gain and feed conversion (Table 21.1) by cattle fed high-concentrate rations when whole grain was used.

TABLE 21.1   Examples of effect of grain processing on steer performance.

ITEM[a]	AV. DAILY GAIN, kg	DAILY FEED INTAKE, kg	FEED TO GAIN RATIO, kg
Mili, dry rolled	1.28	10.31	8.02
vs. steam-flaked	1.41	10.60	7.64
Sorghum grain, dry rolled	1.00	8.26	8.21
vs. reconstituted	1.20	8.40	7.02
Barley, dry rolled	1.31	9.44	7.22
vs. steam-flaked	1.41	10.31	7.32
Corn, dry rolled	1.38	9.17	6.70
vs. pressure cooked	1.52	9.53	6.33
Whole corn, reconstituted	1.18	9.31	7.85
vs. steam-flaked	1.20	9.22	7.66
Whole corn	1.25	7.01	5.62
vs. whole steamed	1.31	7.57	5.79
vs. steam-flaked	1.33	6.71	5.06

[a]All except the last comparison excerpted from Church (1); the last comparison is from Ramirez (2); in this last example, the feed intake is expressed on a dry matter basis. Comparisons among treatments only should be made as listed because the other treatments may have been done in a different location at a different time.

High-Moisture Grain

This term refers to grain harvested at a high moisture content (20–35%) and stored in a silo to preserve the grain because it would spoil unless it is ensiled or treated with chemicals. It may be ground before ensiling or ground or rolled before feeding. This is a particularly useful procedure when weather conditions do not allow normal drying in the field and it obviates the need to dry the grain artificially. Storage costs may be relatively high, but high-moisture grain produces good feedlot results, comparable to some of the processing methods discussed. Feed conversion, particularly, is improved. Wet grains are not as flexible to sell once ensiled.

Acid Preservation of High-Moisture Grains

With higher fuel costs increased interest has developed in eliminating artificial drying of newly harvested cereal grains. Data with barley or corn for pigs and research with corn or sorghum for beef cattle show promise for the use of acids to preserve high-moisture grains. Thorough mixing of 1–1.5% propionic acid, mixtures of acetic-propionic acids or formic-propionic acids into high-moisture (20–30%) whole corn or other cereal grains retards molding and spoilage without affecting animal performance appreciably, compared with that obtained with dried grains.

❑ HOT PROCESSING METHODS

Methods that have been used in recent years for heat processing grains and other products (such as oilseed meals, pet food, and so on) include steam rolling, steam flaking, popping, micronizing, roasting, pelleting, and extruding. Pressure cooking and exploding are methods that have been tried at the feedlot level. However, cost of the equipment and maintenance problems have discouraged continued use. Information available to the author indicates that micronizing and roasting are not being used (Winter, 1987) at the present time, and that popping is on its way out. Comments on methods in use follow.

Steam-Rolled and Steam-Flaked Grains

Steam-rolled grains have been used for many years, partly to kill weed seeds. The steaming is accomplished by passing steam up through a tower above the rollermill. Grains are subjected to steam for only a short time (3–5 min.) prior to rolling. Most results indicate little if any improvement in animal performance as compared to dry rolling, but use of steam does allow production of larger particles and fewer fines.

Steam-flaked grains are prepared in a similar manner but with relatively rigid quality controls. Grain is subjected to high-moisture steam for a sufficient time to raise the water content to 18–20%, and the grain is then rolled to produce a rather flat flake. Feedlot data with cattle indicate that best response is produced with thin flakes that apparently allow more efficient rupture of starch granules and produce a more desirable physical texture. Corn, barley, and sorghum usually give a good response in terms of increased gain; although feed efficiency is improved with corn and sorghum, barley shows little improvement.

Pelleting

Pelleting is accomplished by grinding the feed and then forcing it through a thick die. Feedstuffs usually are, but not always, steamed to some extent prior to pelleting. Pellets can be made in different diameters, lengths, and hardnesses and have been commercially available for many years. All domestic animals generally like the physical nature of pellets, particularly as compared to meals, and a high percentage of poultry and swine feeds are pelleted. However, results with ruminants on high-grain diets have not been particularly favorable because of decreased feed intake even though feed efficiency is usually improved over other methods. Pelleting the ration fines (finely ground portions of a ration) frequently is desirable because the fines often will be refused otherwise. Supplemental feeds such as protein concentrates are pelleted in many instances so they can then be fed on the ground or in windy areas with little loss. One example of a pellet mill is shown (Fig. 21.2).

Popping and Micronizing

Most readers are familiar with popped corn which is produced by action of dry heat, causing a sudden expansion that ruptures the endosperm of the grain. This process increases gut and rumen starch utilization, but results in a low-density feed. Consequently, it usually is rolled before feeding to reduce bulk. Micronizing is essentially the same as popping, except that heat is provided in the form of infrared energy.

Figure 21.2   *One example of a pellet mill. Pellet mills can be used to pellet a wide variety of feeds-stuffs, although roughage and cereal grains must usually be ground prior to pelleting. Courtesy of Sprout-Waldron Corporation.*

Extruding

Extruded grains are prepared by passing the grain through a machine with a spiral screw that forces the grain through a tapered head. In the process the grain is ground and heated, producing a ribbon-like product. Results with cattle on high-grain rations are similar to those with other processing methods. With animal feeds, extruding is generally restricted to pet foods.

❏ FEED PROCESSING FOR NON-RUMINANTS

Swine and Poultry

Grinding and pelleting are the most common means of preparing feed for these two classes of animals. Generally, results show that grinding to a medium to moderately fine texture results in better performance than when grains are finely ground. Feed particles of different ingredients should be of a similar size so that animals do not sort out the course particles and leave the fines. Digestibility of grains by swine generally is improved by grinding, and finely ground (0.16 cm screen size) grain promotes improved efficiency as compared with coarse grinding (1.27 cm screen or larger) in a hammermill. How-

ever, finely ground feed is associated with an increased incidence of stomach ulcers in pigs.

Pelleting usually results in improved gain, partly because animals tend to eat more in a given period. Efficiency often is improved, sometimes because of less feed wastage with pellets. A common practice, particularly for poultry, is to pellet meal diets and then roll them, producing a product called crumbles. The texture of crumbles is well liked, particularly if pellets are quite hard. It should be noted that birds fed pellets tend to exhibit more cannibalism than those given feed in mash form.

Research data with swine indicate that pelleting generally improves gain and feed efficiency (5–10%) of the feed grains that are low in fiber—corn, wheat, sorghum—but it has less effect on barley and oats. Although oats are improved considerably by medium-to-fine grinding, pelleting may improve efficiency with little or no effect on daily gain. Pelleting is of less interest for older hogs which do not need to produce at maximal rates.

Other feed preparatory methods have been used with varying degrees of success for both pigs and poultry. With barley, soaking and treatment with different enzymes may result in some improvement, but little use is being made currently of these methods, partly because little barley is fed to poultry, and the improvement for swine probably does not justify the expense. Steam flaking and reconstitution may improve digestibility for pigs, but have little effect on gain.

Other Animals

Feed processing done on horse feed is more a matter of convenience for the feeder or to avoid dust, mold, and so on, because horses are not normally fed at levels equivalent to that for a fast-growing chick or a high-producing cow and efficiency is not as important a factor. Horse feeders are prone to use rolled or coarsely cracked grains with liberal amounts of molasses to avoid problems with dust. Some pelleted or cubed hays are fed, but only as a small percentage of the total roughage fed to horses. Cubed hay has, occasionally, resulted in problems with choking.

Rabbits, a species of only moderate commercial importance in the USA, usually are fed pelleted, mixed feeds and/or long roughages. Commercial growers use pelleted feeds because of convenience and to reduce waste. A substantial amount of pet food is either pelleted or processed through extruders that alter the physical form as well as cook the food.

❑ GRAIN PROCESSING FOR RUMINANTS

Grain processing is done primarily to improve digestibility and efficiency of utilization because grain is in a physical form that can be handled mechanically with few problems. Improvement in animal utilization usually can be obtained by various means that break up the hull or waxy seed coat and improve digestibility of starch in the endosperm. Some methods may provide a more favorable particle size and/or density that facilitates more optimal passage through the rumen and that may, also, improve palatability. For a method to be effective, it must (a) reduce wastage or (b) increase consumption and rate of gain or (c) be utilized more efficiently. As indicated, grain (or roughage) is expected to give greater returns/unit of cost when feed intake of grain is high. Animals on a maintenance diet normally would not be fed much grain and any improvement in efficiency normally would not return the added cost.

In diets typically in use at this time in the USA, grain and other concentrates in finishing rations for cattle may account for 60–95% of the total intake. The need and benefits of grain processing can be shown clearly in most instances when higher levels of grain are fed ad libitum. Selected examples of research trials with different grains are shown in Table 21.1. Some research evidence indicates that whole corn grain may be an exception to this general rule when corn makes up a high percentage of the diet. It appears that the size and density of the corn grain is a factor; furthermore, cattle apparently masticate whole corn well enough so that much of it will be partly broken before swallowing. Steaming or steam-flaking may improve utilization of corn slightly, but probably not enough to warrent the added expense. Usually, as the percentage of roughage in the diet increases, the physical nature of the concentrate becomes less important, although processing still may influence digestibility and efficiency.

Economics of Feed Processing

The relatively higher energy costs experienced in recent years have increased interest in minimizing feed processing costs or in obtaining the maximum return per unit of cost for processing. At the present time, the methods listed in Table 21.2 are those most commonly used for processing feed. Pelleting is used mainly for feed supplements or protein supplements which may be fed to a variety of animals.

TABLE 21.2 Fossil fuel energy use for some feed processing methods.[a]

PROCESS	Mcal/ton
Drying corn	240
Propionic acid	200
Grinding corn	40
Pelleting corn	80
Steam flaking corn	120
Dehydrating and pelleting alfalfa	1,800
Drying wet beet pulp	1,750

[a]Data from Ward (3).

Current fuel costs are higher in proportion to grain costs than when most of the methods were developed. An estimate of the fuel needs (Mcal) needed for several procedures is given in Table 21.2. Note that the greatest use of fuel is required to dry very wet materials such as green forage (alfalfa) or wet beet pulp, whereas a procedure such as grinding requires relatively little energy.

The actual costs of processing feed are not easy to compute and are apt to vary considerably from installation to installation. One writer (4) recently calculated that overt costs for dryrolling, hammermilling, and steam flaking to be $1.79, $2.34, and $5.19/ton, respectively. Overt costs were made up of normal, fixed, and variable costs. It was pointed out that hidden costs were very difficult to calculate (not included). They were such items as shrink (dust, moisture losses, feed spoilage, spills), fires and explosions or other property losses, equipment and or system downtime, and product quality-customer satisfaction items.

The data in Table 21.3 suggest that grain processing (more than dry rolling) normally does not result in any marked increase in daily gain of cattle and that the primary benefit is some improvement in feed efficiency. Of course, good processing can stimulate feed consumption just as poor processing may depress feed consumption, and many reports show appreciable differences in gain (1). Wastage may be reduced by good processing.

The relative value of different grain processing methods for feedlot cattle have been calculated by Schake and Bull (5) and are shown in Table 21.4, based on daily gains and efficiencies shown in Table 21.3 which were compiled from a number of experimental trials done in Texas. Note that flaking, re-

TABLE 21.3 Daily gain and feed conversion used to establish costs in Table 21.4.[a]

METHOD	CORN			SORGHUM		
	GAIN, lb	FC,[b] lb	FC, %[c]	GAIN, lb	FC,[b] lb	FC, %[c]
Dry ground or rolled	2.62	5.79	—	2.50	6.09	—
Steam flaked	2.68	5.36	7.46	2.65	5.60	8.11
Reconstituted	2.61	5.33	7.97	2.54	5.34	12.32
Early harvested						
Ground, ensiled	2.57	5.14	11.14	2.64	5.52	9.35
Acid treated	2.68	5.56	3.97	2.45	5.60	8.11

[a]Data from Schake and Bull (5).
[b]FC = feed conversion.
[c]% improvement in FC of grain dry matter compared to dry processing.

constitution, or early-harvesting all resulted in some improvement in feed efficiency when compared to dry ground or rolled grain. However, because of higher costs for equipment, power, storage (early-harvesting requires that all the grain be purchased at one time), and so on, the most efficient methods did not necessarily result in the greatest net value/ton of grain. Note that larger feedlots had some advantage in costs for flaking and reconstitution, but not with early-harvested grain whether ensiled or acid-treated.

Feed Processing for Dairy Cows

Feed processing may result in somewhat different responses in dairy cows than for growing or finishing cattle or lambs. Generally, feeding lactating cows high-grain rations, particularly heat-treated grains, or all of their roughage in ground or pelleted form results in reduced rumen acetate proportions (in relationship to propionic acid) and lower milkfat percentages. Total milkfat production may not be decreased because feedstuffs which are capable of causing low milkfat may also stimulate increased total milk production. When milk is sold on the basis of its fat percentage (an archaic method, unfortunately), then use of heat-treated grains or pelleted roughages may need to be restricted. Most commonly, lactating cows are fed concentrates in which the grains have been coarsely ground or steam-rolled. However, pelleted feeds are fed in milking parlors in many operations because cows will eat more pellets in a short period of time while being milked. Pelleting also avoids some of the dust otherwise encountered in such sit-

uations. Some dairy farmers utilize ground and ensiled high-moisture grains, particularly corn.

Grain Processing for Sheep

Very few benefits can be shown for processed grains fed to sheep (1). Ration sorting can be reduced and pelleting may reduce wastage or sorting. Otherwise, sheep—finishing lambs or ewes—chew grains (with the possible exception of sorghums) well enough that processing is not necessary. In addition, it is not a common practice to feed as much grain (as a % of the diet) as to cattle, so any possible benefits would be reduced because of this standard practice. In some feedlots it is a common practice (but less common than in the recent past) to pellet finishing rations. This allows greater use of roughages and such diets can be self fed.

☐ ROUGHAGE PROCESSING FOR RUMINANTS

Baled Roughage

Baling is still one of the most common methods of handling roughage, particularly where it is apt to be sold or transported some distance. Baling has a considerable advantage over loose hay stacked in the field or roughage in other less dense forms. Although baled hay now can be handled mechanically, it still requires considerably more hand labor than many other feedstuffs. Furthermore, considerable waste may occur in feeding, depending on how it is fed (feed bunks, on the ground) and on the level of feeding. Heavily fed animals such as dairy cows may be quite selective so that stems will not be consumed. Thus, nearly always a high loss occurs in feeding baled hays. Consumption is not adequate for high levels of performance (Table 21.5) when baled hay provides the only feed for ruminants.

Chopped and Ground Roughage

Chopping or grinding puts roughage in a physical form in which it can be handled easily by some mechanical equipment, tends to provide a more uniform product for consumption, and usually reduces feed refusals and waste. However, additional expense may be incurred by grinding and loss of dust may be appreciable from grinding in hammermills. This dust loss sometimes is reduced in commercial mills by spraying fat on bales before they are ground. Ground hays are, as a rule, quite dusty and may not be consumed readily. Adding molasses, fat or water usually will improve intake. Chopping produces a physical texture of a more desirable nature than grinding, but chopped hay does not lend itself as well to incorporation into mixed feeds as does ground hay.

Grinding as well as pelleting or cubing results in a feed with less of a coarse physical texture. This may or may not be an advantage; it is less likely to be with herbivorous species.

Pelleting

Pelleted roughages are readily consumed by ruminants, provided they are not too dense to eat readily, nor too soft, which results in too many fines. Roughages such as long hay must be ground before pelleting—a slow, costly process compared to similar treatment of grains. Thus, cost of processing is a bigger item than for most other feed processing methods. Pelleting usually gives the greatest relative increase in performance for low-quality roughages. This appears to result from an increase in density with more rapid passage through the GI tract and not to any great improvement in digestibility. Pel-

TABLE 21.4   1980 costs for processing grain in feedlots in Texas.[a]

ITEM[b]	CORN		SORGHUM	
	FEEDLOT SIZE		FEEDLOT SIZE	
	5,000	20,000	5,000	20,000
Dry rolling				
Cost/ton, $	2.57	1.74	2.53	1.71
Steam flaking				
Cost/ton, $	9.79	6.37	9.37	6.31
Net value/ton, $	0.24	2.83	0.12	2.70
Reconstituted				
Cost/ton, $	6.11	3.79	5.91	3.68
Net value/ton, $	4.43	5.92	7.71	9.12
Early-harvested, ground and ensiled				
Cost/ton, $	12.55	11.45	11.86	10.82
Net value/ton, $	0.60	0.87	−1.36	−1.11
Early-harvested, and acid treated				
Cost/ton, $	15.69	14.01	14.89	13.24
Net value/ton, $	−9.35	−8.50	−5.42	−4.59

[a]From Schake and Bull (5).
[b]Cost estimates include initial investments for equipment, variable costs and interest on fixed and variable costs. Net value per ton is a reflection of these costs and of improvements in gain and/or feed conversion, which would allow more cattle to be fed on a given amount of grain.

TABLE 21.5   Effect of roughage processing on animal performance of cattle.[a]

ITEM	AV. DAILY GAIN, kg (lb)		DAILY DRY MATTER INTAKE, kg (lb)		FEED/UNIT OF GAIN
Coastal Bermuda grass					
long	0.33	(0.73)	4.67	(10.30)[b]	17.0
vs. ground	0.50	(1.11)	6.07	(13.38)[b]	13.9
vs. pelleted	0.66	(1.45)	6.53	(14.4)[b]	11.3
Alfalfa hay					
baled	0.29	(0.63)	4.31	(9.5)	15.1
chopped	0.28	(0.62)	4.22	(9.3)	15.1
pelleted	0.78	(1.73)	6.49	(14.3)	8.3
Alfalfa hay					
baled	0.67	(1.48)	6.14	(13.5)	9.1
cubes	0.86	(1.90)	6.65	(14.7)	7.8
haylage	0.77	(1.70)	6.79	(15.0)	8.9

[a]Data excerpted from ref. 1.
[b]Feed intake as fed.

leted roughages are metabolized somewhat differently; as a result of more rapid passage out of the rumen, less cellulose is digested and relatively less acetic acid is produced with relatively greater digestion in the intestines. Utilization of metabolizable energy usually is more efficient. Pelleted high-quality roughages will produce performance (gain in weight) in young cattle (see Table 21.5) or lambs almost comparable to high-grain feeding. An example is shown in Fig. 21.3 of the change in density achieved with grinding and pelleting.

Cubed Roughages

Cubing is a relatively new process in which dry hay is forced through dies that produce a square product (ca. 3 cm in size) of varying lengths. Grinding before cubing is not required, but usually water is sprayed on the dry hay as it is cubed. Field cubers have been developed (Fig. 21.4), and stationary cubers are used to process hay from stacks or bales. Alfalfa hay produces the best cubes. Research data (1) indicate that cubes will produce satisfactory performance in cattle, provided they are not too hard. Although cubes have some advantages, particularly that they can be handled with mechanized feeding equipment, they have never been as popular as expected. A partial answer may be that it is difficult to detect low quality hay (visually) after it has been cubed.

Chemical Treatments

Poor quality forage and other materials (wood, sugar cane bagasse, pineapple waste, and so on) high in cellulose represent a substantial resource for animal feed. Such materials are not very digestible, so there has been a considerable amount of research on this subject with the intent of improving animal utilization.

Figure 21.3   An example of the densification of alfalfa hay which can be achieved by baling, grinding and pelleting (left to right). Each sample contains 2.27 kg of hay.

Figure 21.4 *One type of portable hay cuber. These machines produce a product (cubes) which facilitate handling, transportation and feeding of roughages. Courtesy of Deer & Co.*

TABLE 21.6 Effect of ammoniation of wheat straw on intake and digestibility by sheep.[a]

| | | TREATED STRAW | | |
| | | | HMAWS[b] | |
ITEM	UNTREATED STRAW	STACK AMMONIATION	DIRECT FED	AIRED
Straw DM intake, % of body weight	1.16	1.56	1.69	2.00
Straw DM digestibility, % Fed adlibitum	39.4	47.6	53.1	58.4
Straw cellulose dig., %	57.7	63.8	63.3	68.1
Straw hemicellulose dig., %	47.6	55.4	75.6	79.0

[a]From Streeter and Horn (6).
[b]HMAWS = high-moisture ammoniated wheat straw. All straws were fed with a supplement containing soybean meal, ground corn, molasses, minerals, and salt.

TABLE 21.7   Effect of treating wheat straw with alkaline hydrogen peroxide on intake and digestibility by sheep.[a]

ITEM	UNTREATED STRAW		TREATED STRAW	
	LOW WS	HIGH WS	LOW WS	HIGH WS
Intake, g/day				
Dry matter	2,271	1,297	2,234	2,526
Crude protein	302	180	303	390
Digestibility, % of intake				
Dry matter	68.4	58.0	82.7	70.7
Crude protein	74.4	75.0	78.6	71.7
Cellulose	53.8	37.5	78.0	84.0

[a]Data after Kerley *et al.* (7). Wheat straw made up ca. 33% of the diet in the Low WS and ca. 52% in the High WS diets. The remainder of the diet was composed of ground corn, soybean meal, urea, molasses, minerals, and vitamins.

Methods have ranged from soaking straws in alkali solutions for up to a month to treatments involving heat, pressure, and chemicals.

The state of the art at this time is that digestibility of a roughage such as cereal straw can be increased a moderate amount (i.e., dry matter digestibility from about 40 to 50±%) by spraying with NaOH solutions or ensiling with NaOH, molasses, water, and so on, but costs in North America are not such that it is a feasible method at this time. In areas where roughage is in shorter supply, it may be a feasible method; as a matter of fact, several processing plants have been built in northern Europe.

Another method that shows potential is treatment with anhydrous ammonia. This process will add N to the straw that can be used to some extent by rumen microorganisms. One example, believed to be representative of the published literature, is shown in Table 21.6. In this instance sheep were fed a diet made up primarily of straw plus a supplement. Untreated straw was fed as a negative control and straw was treated by direct ammoniation in the bale (which was covered), or high-moisture straw was treated in a similar manner and either fed directly out of the sacks used for storage or allowed to air out before being fed. As with most other experiments with ammoniated poor quality roughage, treatment generally increases consumption of the roughage, digestibility of dry or organic matter is improved as is the digestibility of cellulose and hemicellulose. Animal live-

weight gain is usually improved to a moderate degree.

Another possible treatment is the use of alkaline hydrogen peroxide (AHP). AHP will cause some solubilization of lignin in highly lignified forages such as straw. One example of research is shown in Table 21.7. In this case treatment of straw with AHP increased dry matter intake markedly for the high-straw diet. In addition, treatment increased the digestibility of dry matter and cellulose markedly.

❑ SUMMARY

Various feed processing methods have been developed that will reduce waste, discourage selectivity of ingredient consumption, and usually increase feed consumption and efficiency of feed utilization. Feed processing is of particular importance for animals consuming feed at high levels and for animals expected to perform at high levels of production. However, higher relative fuel costs have resulted in more selectivity of processing methods because efficiency of fuel use is not always comparable for the different procedures. With roughages, some degree of processing is required when they are incorporated into complete diets, allowing mechanization of the mixing and feed distribution systems. Feed wastage can be reduced considerably by processing baled or long hays, but the costs also will be increased substantially. Newer methods of chemically treating low-quality roughages may be feasible economically. Use of anhydrous ammonia on low-quality roughages (which are also low in crude protein) will generally result in increased consumption of the roughage, some improvement in digestibility of dry matter, and some utilization of the ammonia as a N source for rumen microorganisms. Although not yet fully evaluated, treatment of low-quality roughages with alkaline hydrogen peroxide (which solubilizes some of the lignin) appears to result in a marked increase in digestibility of the fibrous carbohydrates in roughages that are, otherwise, not well utilized without extensive chemical treatments.

❏ REFERENCES

1. Church, D. C. (ed.). 1984. *Livestock Feeds and Feeding,* 2nd ed. Prentice-Hall, Inc., Englewood Cliffs, N.J.
2. Ramirez, R. G., et al. 1985. *J. Animal Sci.* **61**:1.
3. Ward, G. W. 1981. Unpublished data. Colorada State University, Ft. Collins, CO.
4. McEllhiney, R. R. 1986. *Feed Management* **37**(11):30.
5. Schake, L. M. and K. L. Bull. 1980. Texas Agr. Expt. Sta. Tech. Rpt. 81–1.
6. Streeter, C. L. and G. W. Horn. 1984. *J. Animal Sci.* **59**:559.
7. Kerley, M. S., *et al.* 1986. *J. Animal Sci.* **63**:868.

22

Diet
Formulation

HUGO VARELA-ALVAREZ

DIET FORMULATION IS AN important aspect
of animal production. The success of any animal
production enterprise depends greatly on proper
feeding and nutrition based on economic rations.
The animal production practitioner should have a
good knowledge of different aspects of nutrition,
feeding, feedstuffs interactions and limitations, as
well as the economics of production and feeding.
Diet formulation, properly carried out, is the result
of this knowledge. Some of the mathematical
techniques required in diet formulation are quite
simple, although for complex diets they can
become complicated. However, with the advent of
personal computers and ready access to
appropriate software, even the techniques needed
for complex rations can be used by almost anyone
with the proper nutritional knowledge. Some of the
simple techniques, as well as the basics for
complex diet formulation, are presented.

❏ INFORMATION NEEDED

Several types of information are required for an organized approach to diet formulation before any mathematical manipulation can be done. These are discussed briefly.

Nutrient Requirements of the Animal

The first step is to arrive at some estimate of the nutrient requirements of the animal for which the ration is intended. Nutrient requirements for animals are expressed in terms of energy, protein (and amino acids), mineral elements, vitamins, and fiber. Specification of nutrient requirements can be found in different sources. In the USA, the National Research Council (NRC) recommendations are the most commonly used guides for nutrient requirements (1–3). Tables from these publications are given in the Appendix.

The reader should understand that these recommendations should be modified when the formulator has knowledge indicating a change should be made. For example, high-producing dairy cows may need more liberal nutrient allowances or, we may need adjustment to compensate for weight loss or, in a cold climate, energy needs may be higher than NRC recommendations.

Feedstuffs and Feedstuffs Analysis

The next step is to list all the available feedstuffs (as in Table 22.1) to be considered in the diet for the particular animal in question. The nutrient analysis of feedstuffs is essential. How satisfactory the diet will be depends on the reliability of the feedstuff analysis. Updated analytical data on feedstuffs are preferred where available; if not, average composition data can be used from the NRC tables (Appendix) or composition data from any other reliable source. Diets are only as good as the analytical information used to formulate them. In the case of feedstuffs utilized for monogastrics, it may be appropriate to include "available" nutrients as opposed to "total" nutrients (as in the case of P and amino acids).

Some feedstuffs are usable due to digestibility or palatability for each species and class of animals. Therefore, both the feedstuff analysis and the maximum percentage allowances of a particular feedstuff for a diet should be considered in formulation. For example, in some cases we could use urea for adult ruminants instead of a protein feed, but for monogastric species or for milk replacer formulas, based on our present knowledge, we would not consider

urea at all. In areas where one of the trace minerals in native forages is quite low, we would consider a supplement of the deficient minerals, whereas normally it might be ignored in routine diet formulations.

Furthermore, we must consider whether the feedstuff should be processed and, if so, in what manner and at what cost? Is it a palatable feedstuff or will the mixture be palatable? Does the ingredient present a problem in handling, mixing, or storing?

Obviously, it takes a fund of knowledge and experience to answer these questions. The ability to answer these questions correctly is essential for a practicing nutritionist. For our purposes, the beginner need not address such questions as posed in the previous paragraph as time and experience will help provide the answers that cannot be covered in this chapter.

❏ MECHANICS OF DIET FORMULATION

When the number of nutrients specified is small, diet formulation can be adequately carried out through simple calculations. The calculations involved in this type of formulation are simple and few. However, as the number of nutrient specifications and/or the number of feedstuffs available increases, the mathematics are quite involved. The various techniques for diet formulation that are currently in use are illustrated in the following sections.

Pearson's Square

Use of Pearson's square is a simple procedure that allows us to mix two feedstuffs with different nutrient concentrations and come up with a mix of the desired total concentration. For the Pearson's square to work, the desired diet nutrient concentration must be between the nutrient concentrations of the two feedstuffs. Suppose we have a protein source such as cottonseed meal (CSM) with 40.9% crude protein (CP) and corn with 8.8% CP, and we need a mixture of the two that will have 18% CP. As shown in the illustration, we compare the CP percentage of each feed on the left with the desired percentage in the middle of the square. The lesser value is subtracted from the greater value, and the answer, in parts of a mixture rather than in percentage, is recorded diagonally, but read horizontally.

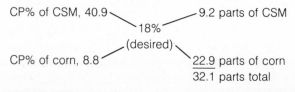

TABLE 22.1   Feedstuff composition on as fed basis. (Data from NRC publications.)

FEED REFERENCE NUMBER	DM, %	$ /ton[a]	CP, %	DE, Mcal/ kg	Ca, %	P, %	LYS, %	METH, %
Vit-Min premix	100	900	—	—	—	—	—	—
Alfalfa meal 1-00-023	92	137	17.5	2270	1.44	0.22	0.73	0.20
Fish meal 5-02-000	93	310	72.3	2500	2.29	1.70	5.70	2.10
Wheat 4-05-268	87	120	14.1	3220	0.05	0.37	0.31	0.20
Corn 4-02-935	89	77	8.8	3325	0.02	0.28	0.24	0.20
Wheat middlings 4-05-205	88	83	16.0	2940	0.12	0.90	0.69	0.20
Soybean meal 5-04-604	89	209	44.0	3090	0.29	0.65	2.93	0.70
Tallow 4-00-409	99	220	—	7900	—	—	—	—
Dical. phosphate 6-01-080	100	292	—	—	23.70	18.84	—	—
Limestone 6-02-632	100	72	—	—	36.07	0.02	—	—
L-Lysine	100	4080	76.9	—	—	—	76.9	—
Meth hydroxy an.	100	3420	74.4	—	—	—	—	74.4
Salt	100	66	—	—	—	—	—	—

[a] 1 ton = 1000 kg

Answer:

9.2 parts of CSM and 22.9 parts of corn, or

% of CSM in mix = (9.2/32.1) × 100 = 28.66

% of grain in mix = (22.9/32.1) × 100 = 71.34

Check for CP:

28.66% CSM × 40.9% CP = 11.72%

71.34% corn ×   8.8% CP =   6.28%

                         18.00%

                         total CP

                         in the mix

The same procedure can be used for energy, minerals, and so on. Furthermore, calories, ppm, or other units of measurement can be used in place of percentages.

Sometimes we might want to have the exact amounts of two major nutrients, such as CP and energy. We can accomplish this by going through three Pearson's squares. Suppose we want a final mix with 12% CP and 74% TDN. We have corn with 8.8% CP and 81% TDN, CSM with 40.9% CP and 68.6% TDN, and oat hay with 8.1% CP and 53.8% TDN. For this we must have a minimum of three feedstuffs. First, we go through two squares and get a mix exact for each nutrient—in this example we

will do CP first. We must have one mix with 12% CP and greater than 74% TDN, and one mix with 12% CP and less than 74% TDN. We proceed as shown.

Mix 1.   12% CP, > 74% TDN.

CP% of CSM, 40.9   3.2 = 9.97% × 0.686

                        (TDN% in CSM)

              12%   Compute

          (desired)   TDN

                              = 6.84

CP% of Corn, 8.8   28.9 = 90.03% × 0.81

                      32.1 parts

                      (TDN% in corn) = 72.93

                                      79.77

Mix 2.   12% CP, < 74% TDN.

CP% of CSM, 40.9   3.9 = 11.89% × 0.686

                              = 8.16

              12%

CP% of oat hay, 8.1   28.9 = 88.11% × 0.538

                     32.8 parts   = 47.40

                                       55.56

Then solve for TDN.

Mix 3.   12% CP and 74% TDN.

TDN% in Mix 1, 79.77 ⟍ ⟋ 18.44 = 76.17%
74%
(desired)
TDN% in Mix 2, 55.56 ⟋ ⟍ 5.77 = 23.83%
24.21 parts

Calculate ingredient composition:

CSM% in Mix 1, 9.97 ×
          (76.17% of Mix 1 in Mix 3) =   7.594
CSM% in Mix 2, 11.89 ×
          (23.83% of Mix 2 in Mix 3) =   2.833
CSM in Mix 1 and Mix 2.   10.427

Corn% in Mix 1, 90.03 ×
          (76.17% of Mix 1 in Mix 3) = 68.57
Oat% in Mix 2, 88.11 ×
          (23.83% of Mix 2 in Mix 3) = 21.00

Check CP   = (10.427 × 0.409 + 68.57 × 0.088
          + 21 × 0.081)
          = 4.27 + 6.03 + 1.70 = 12.00

Check TDN = (10.427 × 0.686 + 68.57 + 0.81
          + 21 × 0.538)
          = 7.16 + 55.54 + 11.30 = 74.00

As the reader can see, this procedure works very well to produce a mix with *exact specifications* for two nutrients. If we want to add more nutrients, it will require more than three squares. Diets that have exact requirements for more than two nutrients are tedious to formulate by hand.

Simultaneous Equations

Some individuals prefer to solve simple diet formulation using simultaneous equations. The amounts of the ingredients will be the unknowns. For the same problem as with the single Pearson's square, the approach would be:

$$X = \% \text{ of CSM in mix}$$
$$Y = \% \text{ of corn in mix}$$
$$X + Y = 100$$
          (equation for total amount of each feedstuff)
$$0.409X + 0.088Y = 18 \quad \text{(equation for CP)}$$

To solve this problem it is necessary to multiply the members of the first equation ($X + Y = 100$) by a unit that will allow one of the unknowns (X or Y) in the second equation to factor out. Thus, if we multiply it by 0.088 we have:

Amount equation times 0.088:
$$0.088X + 0.088Y = 8.8$$
CP equation $0.409X + 0.088Y = 18.0$
Subtract from it $0.088X + 0.088Y = 8.8$
The answer is $0.321X = 9.2$

Then $X = 9.2/0.321 = 28.66$ and substituting the value of X in the amount equation, we obtain
$$28.66 + Y = 100$$
$$Y = 100 - 28.66 = 71.34$$

The answer, obviously, is the same as with the Pearson's square method. The reader should keep in mind that for this system to work, the number of equations should be equal to or larger than the number of unknowns.

Mathematical Programming

Mathematical programming is widely used in the USA, both on a private basis and by public institutions. The first large-scale, public service to provide feed programming and forage testing in the USA was started at The Pennsylvania State University in January, 1959.

With the Pearson's Square and the simultaneous equations methods, the mix obtained is of a predetermined CP percentage or a predetermined energy level. The amounts of the ingredients considered for the mix are therefore fixed. In reality, the percentage of protein required or the amount of energy in a diet is considered a minimum, and therefore the final mix should have "at least" the required amount of the nutrient. Sometimes the specified nutrient is required within a range, that is, at least some minimum quantity, but less than a maximum quantity. These two methods, the Pearson's Square and the simultaneous equations, cannot handle inequalities or ranges, and both methods are independent of price. When price is considered, optimization is done by trial and error.

In cases of multiple nutrient requirements, multiple feed sources, price consideration, and requirements being greater than and/or less than some level, diet formulation should be done by mathematical programming. This technique, when properly used, helps to achieve both a nutritionally balanced diet and economic optimization, because it allows for simultaneous consideration of economical and nutritional parameters (4, 5).

Nutritionists should have a good knowledge of diet specifications, should be familiar with formulation and interpretation of results, and should think of the solution process, that is, the mathematical manipulation as a "black box." Nutritionists (or students in this case) need not be concerned with the mechanics of the mathematical solution of the linear programming matrix. Diet formulation by mathematical programming should be treated as an interactive process, in which the nutritionist should verify, interpret, and reformulate, if necessary, all diet formulas.

With the availability of microcomputers, mathematical programming can be performed quite easily if the programming is done properly. We use the term "programming" as the planning of "economic" activities for the sake of optimization, subject to some constraints. There exist a large number of computer programs for the solution of mathematical programming problems, so a detailed explanation of the mathematics involved is not given here. Further information may be found in other sources (6–8).

Least-Cost Formulation

A great percentage of production cost is due to feed, thus diet formulation using least-cost techniques has been used extensively during the past 20 years. For any of the mathematical programming techniques to work, formulation of the problem should be done properly. Once the formulation of the problem is stated, then we can use any linear programming package to solve the diet formulation. Once we have a solution, it is one of the functions of the nutritionist to verify if the solution conforms with nutritional knowledge.

Example. To illustrate the problem statement for a least-cost formulation, the following steps of this technique are presented. Let us formulate a diet for growing pigs (20–35 kg).

STEP 1: DETERMINE THE ANIMAL'S DIETARY REQUIREMENTS from the NRC tables (given in Appendix). They are 16% CP; 3380 Kcal DE/kg; 0.60% Ca; 0.50% P; 0.70% lysine; 0.45% methionine. There are other nutrient specifications, but for this example only these requirements will be utilized.

STEP 2: DETERMINE ANY OTHER RATION RESTRICTIONS. It is a common practice with both swine and poultry rations to add a vitamin-trace mineral package (premix) as a needed supplement. We will add the premix at a rate of 5 kg/ton or 0.5%. We will also specify the addition of 5% dehydrated alfalfa (16.3% CP), 10% wheat (hard red spring), and 1.5% fish meal (herring). For the remainder of the diet, we will choose from corn, wheat middlings, soybean meal, tallow, dicalcium phosphate, limestone, L-lysine, methionine hydroxy analog, and salt. Our required ingredients, price per ton, and their nutrient compositions are presented in Table 22.1. Note that in the case of amino acid supplements the amount of protein content is equal to the amount of the amino acid (or sum of amino acids) supplied.

STEP 3: STATE THE PROBLEM IN EQUATION FORM, as follows: Let X_1, X_2, X_3, X_4, X_5, X_6, X_7, X_8, X_9, X_{10}, X_{11}, X_{12}, and X_{13} be the non-negative quantities of the vitamin-mineral premix, alfalfa meal, fish meal, wheat, corn, wheat middlings, soybean meal, tallow, dicalcium phosphate, limestone, L-lysine, methionine hydroxy analog, and salt, respectively. They will be mixed to yield 100 units of a minimum cost diet that will satisfy all the specified nutritional requirements. It also will consider the constraints on the first four ingredients.

Using the crude protein content of the different feedstuffs under consideration, we can say that there are $0X_1$ units of protein in X_1 units of vitamin-mineral premix, $0.175X_2$ units in X_2 units of alfalfa meal, $0.723X_3$ units in X_3 units of fish meal, $0.141X_4$ units in X_4 units of wheat, $0.088X_5$ units in X_5 units of corn, $0.16X_6$ units in X_6 units of wheat middlings, $0.44X_7$ units in X_7 units of soybean meal, $0X_8$ units in X_8 units of tallow, $0X_9$ units in X_9 units of dicalcium phosphate, $0X_{10}$ units in X_{10} units of limestone, $0.769X_{11}$ in X_{11} units of L-lysine, $0.744X_{12}$ units in X_{12} units of methionine hydroxy analog, and $0X_{13}$ units in X_{13} units of salt. Expressing it in an equation form we will have:

$$0X_1 + 0.175X_2 + 0.723X_3 + 0.141X_4$$
$$+ 0.088X_5 + 0.16X_6 + 0.44X_7 + 0X_8 + 0X_9$$
$$+ 0X_{10} + 0.769X_{11} + 0.744X_{12} + 0X_{13} > 16$$

This equation states that the sum of the contribution of protein by each ingredient should be greater than or equal to 16, which is the minimum requirement of CP in this diet. This also implies that

$$X_1 + X_2 + X_3 + X_4 + X_5 + X_6 + X_7 + X_8$$
$$+ X_9 + X_{10} + X_{11} + X_{12} + X_{13} = 100$$

That is, that the sum of all ingredients should be equal to 100 units, thus having a diet with a minimum of 16% CP. The equation that includes the sum of all ingredients would be called the "Amount" equation.

The difference between mathematical programming and simultaneous equations is that in mathematical programming we work with equalities and inequalities at the same time, while in simultaneous equations all are equalities. By handling inequalities, mathematical programming allows us to handle ranges for ingredients or nutritional specifications.

The rest of the equations (constraints) for the nutritional requirements are:

Energy:
$$0X_1 + 2270X_2 + 2500X_3 + 3220X_4$$
$$+ 3325X_5 + 2940X_6 + 3090X_7$$
$$+ 7900X_8 + 0X_9 + 0X_{10} + 0X_{11}$$
$$+ 0X_{12} + 0X_{13} > 338000$$

The figure 338000 comes from the fact that the specified requirement for energy is 3380 Kcal DE/kg; because we are formulating a 100 kg diet, then the total content of energy will be at least $3380 \times 100 = 338,000$ Kcal DE.

Ca:
$$0X_1 + 0.0144X_2 + 0.0229X_3 + 0.0005X_4$$
$$+ 0.0002X_5 + 0.0012X_6 + 0.0029X_7$$
$$+ 0X_8 + 0.237X_9 + 0.3507X_{10} + 0X_{11}$$
$$+ 0X_{12} + 0X_{13} > 0.6$$

P:
$$0X_1 + 0.0022X_2 + 0.017X_3 + 0.0037X_4$$
$$+ 0.0028X_5 + 0.009X_6 + 0.0065X_7 + 0X_8$$
$$+ 0.1884X_9 + 0.002X_{10} + 0X_{11} + 0X_{12}$$
$$+ 0X_{13} > 0.5$$

Lysine:
$$0X_1 + 0.0073X_2 + 0.057X_3$$
$$+ 0.0031X_4 + 0.0024X_5 + 0.0069X_6$$
$$+ 0.0293X_7 + 0X_8 + 0X_9 + 0X_{10}$$
$$+ 0.769X_{11} + 0X_{12} + 0X_{13} > 0.7$$

Methionine:
$$0X_1 + 0.002X_2 + 0.021X_3$$
$$+ 0.002X_4 + 0.002X_5 + 0.002X_6$$
$$+ 0.007X_7 + 0X_8 + 0X_9 + 0X_{10}$$
$$+ 0X_{11} + 0.744X_{12} + 0X_{13} > 0.45$$

STEP 4: SET THE RESTRICTIONS FOR INDIVIDUAL FEEDSTUFFS.

Vitamin-mineral premix	$X_1 = 0.5$
Alfalfa meal	$X_2 = 5$
Fish meal	$X_3 = 1.5$
Wheat	$X_4 = 10$

STEP 5: SET UP THE OBJECTIVE FUNCTION. Construct the equation dealing with the price of the diet. Price in dollars/ton or any other unit does not affect the results. As long as the prices for each ingredient are in the same units ($/kg, $/ton, $/cwt), the cost of the resulting diet formula will be correct. We add all the prices and state the minimum cost diet as the objective function in the following way:

$$900X_1 + 137X_2 + 310X_3 + 120X_4 + 77X_5$$
$$+ 83X_6 + 209X_7 + 220X_8 + 292X_9 + 72X_{10}$$
$$+ 4080X_{11} + 3420X_{12} + 66X_{13}$$
$$= \text{minimum price}$$

STEP 6: UTILIZING ANY APPROPRIATE LINEAR PROGRAMMING SOFTWARE RUN THE DIET FORMULATED. The final set up will be:

Minimize Price:
$$900X_1 + 137X_2 + 310X_3$$
$$+ 120X_4 + 77X_5 + 83X_6$$
$$+ 209X_7 + 220X_8 + 292X_9$$
$$+ 72X_{10} + 4080X_{11} + 3420X_{12}$$
$$+ 66X_{13}$$

such that:

$$X_1 + X_2 + X_3 + X_4 + X_5 + X_6 + X_7 + X_8$$
$$+ X_9 + X_{10} + X_{11} + X_{12} + X_{13}$$
$$= 100 \quad \text{(Amount)}$$

$$0X_1 + 0.175X_2 + 0.723X_3 + 0.141X_4$$
$$+ 0.088X_5 + 0.16X_6 + 0.44X_7 + 0X_8 + 0X_9$$
$$+ 0X_{10} + 0.769X_{11} + 0.744X_{12} + 0X_{13}$$
$$> 16 \quad \text{(Protein)}$$

$$0X_1 + 2270X_2 + 2500X_3 + 3220X_4 + 3325X_5$$
$$+ 2940X_6 + 3090X_7 + 7900X_8 + 0X_9 + 0X_{10}$$
$$+ 0X_{11} + 0X_{12} + 0X_{13} > 338000 \quad \text{(Energy)}$$

$$0X_1 + 0.0144X_2 + 0.0229X_3 + 0.0005X_4$$
$$+ 0.0002X_5 + 0.0012X_6 + 0.0029X_7 + 0X_8$$
$$+ 0.237X_9 + 0.3607X_{10} + 0X_{11} + 0X_{12} + 0X_{13}$$
$$> 0.6 \quad \text{(Ca)}$$

$$0X_1 + 0.0022X_2 + 0.017X_3 + 0.0037X_4$$
$$+ 0.0028X_5 + 0.009X_6 + 0.0065X_7 + 0X_8$$
$$+ 0.1884X_9 + 0.002X_{10} + 0X_{11} + 0X_{12} + 0X_{13}$$
$$> 0.5 \quad \text{(P)}$$

TABLE 22.2 Diet composition and analysis (as Fed).

		RUN 1	RUN 2
X_1	Vitamin-mineral premix	0.5000	0.5000
X_2	Alfalfa meal	5.0000	5.0000
X_3	Fish meal (herring)	1.5000	1.5000
X_4	Wheat (hard red spring)	10.0000	10.0000
X_5	Corn	—	41.8823
X_6	Wheat middlings	67.9875	20.0000
X_7	Soybean meal (44%)	3.4641	12.6562
X_8	Tallow	10.1408	6.7764
X_9	Dicalcium phosphate	—	0.2482
X_{10}	Limestone	1.1007	1.0001
X_{11}	L-Lysine	—	—
X_{12}	Methionine Hydroxy Analog	0.3068	0.2368
X_{13}	Salt	—	0.2000
	Amount, kg	100.0000	100.0000
	Price/ton	125.2653	127.8827
	DE, Kcal/kg	3380.0000	3380.0000
	Protein, %	16.0000	16.0000
	Ca, %	0.6000	0.6000
	P, %	0.7081	0.5000
	Lysine, %	0.7236	0.7623
	Methionine, %	0.4500	0.4500

$$0X_1 + 0.0073X_2 + 0.057X_3 + 0.0031X_4$$
$$+ 0.0024X_5 + 0.0069X_6 + 0.0293X_7 + 0X_8$$
$$+ 0X_9 + 0X_{10} + 0.769X_{11} + 0X_{12} + 0X_{13}$$
$$> 0.7 \quad \text{(Lysine)}$$
$$0X_1 + 0.002X_2 + 0.021X_3 + 0.002X_4$$
$$+ 0.002X_5 + 0.002X_6 + 0.007X_7 + 0X_8 + 0X_9$$
$$+ 0X_{10} + 0X_{11} + 0.744X_{12} + 0X_{13}$$
$$> 0.45 \quad \text{(Methionine)}$$

$X_1 = 0.5$ (vitamin-mineral premix)

$X_2 = 5$ (alfalfa meal)

$X_3 = 1.5$ (fish meal)

$X_4 = 10$ (wheat)

STEP 7: FROM THE RESULTS OF THIS RUN (Run 1 in Table 22.2), VERIFY IF THE DIET IS APPROPRIATE. We can see that in this case we have too much wheat middlings and no salt. The reader should note that this was done on purpose to illustrate the need for verification. We should specify an upper limit of 20% wheat middlings, and include salt within a range of 0.2 and 0.5% in our diet. Therefore, we have to include the following additional equations (constraints) to our initial formulation:

$X_6 < 20$ upper limit for wheat middlings

$X_{13} > 0.2$ lower limit for salt

$X_{13} < 0.5$ upper limit for salt

Then, we run the program again.

After verifying the new diet (Run 2, Table 22.2), we may decide that this ration is acceptable. Notice that because of the new constraints, this new diet has a higher price than the first one ($127.8827 vs. $125.2653), but it will be *the lowest cost diet given those constraints.* Also, in the second run we obtained a lower tallow and limestone content as well as an increase in soybean meal. With the *proper mathematical formulation and interactive interpretation of the results,* we can arrive at a satisfactory formulated diet that is lowest cost for a particular set of requirements and constraints.

TABLE 22.3   Opportunity prices for run 1 diet.

FEEDSTUFFS NOT INCLUDED IN DIET		PRICE, $/ton	FEEDSTUFF WOULD BE USED IF PRICE IS BELOW, $/ton
X_5	Corn	77	73.207
X_9	Dicalcium phosphate	292	12.440
X_{11}	L-lysine	4080	165.292

Most linear programming software packages will give us, in addition to the properly balanced diet, a table with feedstuffs opportunity prices or "shadow prices," that is, a list of those feedstuffs not included in the diet and the price at which each would be included within the constraints specified. This information will help us in determining which are the "bargain" prices if we want to buy other feedstuffs. The opportunity prices (shadow prices) for the diet of Run 1 in Table 22.2 are presented in Table 22.3.

Maximum Profit Formulation

With this procedure, both the nutritional requirements and the animal performance are considered. Basically, the formulation contains all known feeding and nutrition inputs and animal production outputs. In this method we utilize feedstuffs based on cost and composition, animal performance (kg of milk, or daily gain) as a function of nutrients, and total animal product output. The animal product output is treated as an income, and price of feed as an expense. The objective is to maximize profit. This type of formulation requires knowledge of the maximum daily dry matter intake (DMI) of the animal, production response to nutrient intake, and daily nutrient requirements for maintenance.

Example.   To illustrate this technique, a diet will be formulated to achieve maximum profit, formulating a diet to support an optimum level of milk production in a cow with a good dairy potential. The cow has a weight of 600 kg, and is in her first lactation.

In this case, minimum daily requirements for maintenance and growth for the lactating cow are obtained from the NRC tables. These requirements are: net energy for lactation (NE_l), 12.36 Mcal/day; crude protein, 0.881 kg/day; Ca, 0.0264 kg/day; P, 0.0204/day. We will also specify salt within a range of 0.05 to 0.1 kg/day.

The optimum level of milk production and max-

imization of returns are interdependent; we want to maximize the amount of money that is left after we subtract feed price from milk sales, so the solution will include the amounts of each feedstuffs that should enter into the formula and also the optimal amount of milk to be produced. Requirements for production are dependent on amount of milk produced and milk butterfat. In this case we will be working with fat corrected milk (FCM) at 3.5% butterfat.

In dairy cows, milk production response to NE_l intake is quadratic (9, 5), as described in Fig. 22.1. The procedure for incorporating that selected curvilinear milk production response into our mathematical programming setup is to linearize portions of that curve, and then specify them as inequalities. These linearized values are presented in Table 22.4.

For the formulation of this diet, the objective function will be to maximize the difference between the income from milk and the expense of feed. Because the diet is being formulated on a dry matter basis

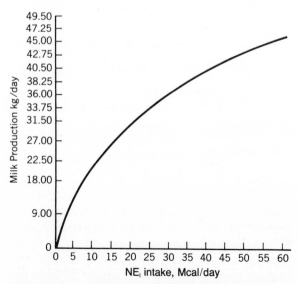

Figure 22.1   *Milk production response to NEl intake.*

TABLE 22.4 Linear representation of milk production response to net energy for lactation (NE_l).

PORTION	MILK PRODUCTION PORTION, kg	AMOUNT OF MILK, kg	NE LACTATION /kg MILK, Mcal
P_1	0.00– 9.00	9.00	0.33
P_2	9.00–18.00	9.00	0.51
P_3	18.00–22.50	4.50	0.77
P_4	22.50–27.00	4.50	1.10
P_5	27.00–31.50	4.50	1.21
P_6	31.50–33.75	2.25	1.34
P_7	33.75–36.00	2.25	1.70
P_8	36.00–38.25	2.25	2.38
P_9	38.25–48.25	10.00	3.22

we have to convert the prices of the feedstuffs from as fed to a dry matter basis. The price per kg of X_1 will be \$90/ton divided by dry matter percent of X_1 then divided by 1000 (1000 kg/ton)—that is, $(90/0.89)/1000 = 0.1011$. Using the prices (dry matter basis) presented in Table 22.5, and using \$0.25 per kg of milk as the selling price, the objective function will look like this:

$$\text{Maximize profit:} \quad 0.25\text{MILK} - 0.1056X_1$$
$$- 0.0865X_2 - 0.292X_3$$
$$- 0.072X_4 - 0.2348X_5$$
$$- 0.1419X_6 - 0.1348X_7$$
$$- 0.1254X_8 - 0.066X_9$$

In this equation, "MILK" is the optimum amount of milk to be produced per cow per day.

The amount of energy supplied by the feed minus the energy required for production must be greater than or equal to the energy required for maintenance and growth. The equation for energy (NE_l) will be as follows:

$$1.89X_1 + 2.42X_2 + 2.07X_5 + 2.66X_6 + 1.21X_7$$
$$+ 1.70X_8 - 0.33P_1 - 0.51P_2 - 0.77P_3$$
$$- 1.1P_4 - 1.21P_5 - 1.34P_6 - 1.7P_7 - 2.38P_8$$
$$- 3.22P_9 > 12.36$$

The next point to consider will be to estimate total milk production. Total milk production will be the variable "MILK." Therefore, if from total milk

production we subtract the milk from each portion of production, the results must be equal to zero:

$$\text{MILK} - P_1 - P_2 - P_3 - P_4 - P_5 - P_6 - P_7$$
$$- P_8 - P_9 = 0$$

This equation ensures that the amount of "MILK" is restricted by the milk produced under each portion of production, otherwise the amount could go very high because the object is to maximize profit.

To set the limits on each portion of production, as presented in Table 22.4, the following equation must be set:

$$P_1 < 9.00 \quad \text{1st portion}$$
$$P_2 < 9.00 \quad \text{2nd portion}$$
$$P_3 < 4.50 \quad \text{3rd portion}$$
$$P_4 < 4.50 \quad \text{4th portion}$$
$$P_5 < 4.50 \quad \text{5th portion}$$
$$P_6 < 2.25 \quad \text{6th portion}$$
$$P_7 < 2.25 \quad \text{7th portion}$$
$$P_8 < 2.25 \quad \text{8th portion}$$
$$P_9 < 10.00 \quad \text{9th portion}$$

If we assume that the production requirements for protein, Ca and P are linear, that is, directly proportional to the amount of milk, then these equations can be written in such a way that the amount of protein (or Ca or P) supplied by the feedstuffs minus the amount of protein required for production (protein per kg of milk times "MILK") is greater

TABLE 22.5 Feed composition on a dry matter basis. (Data from NRC Publications)

| | | AS FED | | | DRY MATTER BASIS | | | | | |
FEEDSTUFF	REFERENCE NUMBER	DM, %	$/ ton[a]	$/kg	NE_l, Mcal /kg	ME_m, Mcal /kg	NE_g, Mcal /kg	CP, %	Ca, %	P, %
X_1 Barley	4-07-939	89.0	94	0.1056	1.89	2.12	1.45	10.7	0.05	0.36
X_2 Corn	4-02-931	89.0	77	0.0865	2.42	2.24	1.55	10.0	0.02	0.35
X_3 Dical. Phos.	6-01-080	100.0	292	0.2920	—	—	—	—	23.70	18.84
X_4 Limestone	6-02-632	100.0	72	0.0720	—	—	—	—	36.07	0.02
X_5 Soybean meal	5-04-604	89.0	209	0.2348	2.07	2.09	1.43	51.5	0.36	0.75
X_6 Cottonseed	5-01-608	93.0	132	0.1419	2.66	2.41	1.69	24.9	0.15	0.73
X_7 Alfalfa hay	1-00-063	89.0	120	0.1348	1.21	1.24	0.68	16.0	1.35	0.22
X_8 Corn silage	3-08-154	27.9	35	0.1254	1.70	1.56	0.99	8.0	0.27	0.20
X_9 Salt		100.0	66	0.0660	—	—	—	—	—	—

[a]1 ton = 1000 kg

than or equal to the requirement of protein for cow maintenance and growth. According to the NRC tables, a cow needs 0.074, 0.0026, and 0.0019 kg of CP, Ca, and P per kg of milk (3.5%FCM), respectively.

Maximum dry matter intake equations can be set directly, that is, the sum of all feedstuffs being less than certain maximum dry matter intake, or we can set the equation dependent on production, similar to the way we have set the energy equation. Here we will set it in the former way:

$$X_1 + X_2 + X_3 + X_4 + X_5 + X_6 + X_7 + X_8 + X_9 < \text{MDMI}$$

In this equation MDMI is the maximum dry matter intake. The figure used here is 3.7% of the body weight of the animal, that is, $600 \times 0.037 = 22.2$ kg dry matter.

The rest of the equations are set in the same way as in the least-cost formulation problem. The final maximum-profit formulation will be:

Maximize profit:
$$0.25\text{MILK} - 0.1056X_1$$
$$- 0.0865X_2 - 0.292X_3$$
$$- 0.072X_4 - 0.2348X_5$$
$$- 0.1419X_6 - 0.1348X_7$$
$$- 0.1254X_8 - 0.066X_9$$

such that
$$X_1 + X_2 + X_3 + X_4 + X_5 + X_6 + X_7 + X_8$$
$$+ X_9 < 22.2 \quad \text{(dry matter intake)}$$

$$1.89X_1 + 2.42X_2 + 2.07X_5 + 2.66X_6 + 1.21X_7$$
$$+ 1.70X_8 - 0.33P_1 - 0.51P_2 - 0.77P_3$$
$$- 1.1P_4 - 1.21P_5 - 1.34P_6 - 1.7P_7 - 2.38P_8$$
$$- 3.22P_9 > 12.36 \quad \text{(energy)}$$

$$0.107X_1 + 0.1X_2 + 0X_3 + 0X_4 + 0.515X_5$$
$$+ 0.249X_6 + 0.16X_7 + 0.08X_8 + 0X_9$$
$$- 0.074\text{MILK} > 0.881 \quad \text{(protein)}$$

$$0.0005X_1 + 0.0002X_2 + 0.237X_3 + 0.3607X_4$$
$$+ 0.0036X_5 + 0.0015X_6 + 0.0135X_7$$
$$+ 0.0027X_8 + 0X_9 - 0.0026\text{MILK}$$
$$> 0.0264 \quad \text{(Ca)}$$

$$0.0036X_1 + 0.0031X_2 + 0.1884X_3 + 0.002X_4$$
$$+ 0.0075X_5 + 0.0073X_6 + 0.0022X_7 + 0.002X_8$$
$$+ 0X_9 - 0.0019\text{MILK} > 0.0204 \quad (P)$$

$$\text{MILK} - P_1 - P_2 - P_3 - P_4 - P_5 - P_6 - P_7$$
$$- P_8 - P_9 = 0$$

$$P_1 < 9.00 \quad \text{(1st portion)}$$
$$P_2 < 9.00 \quad \text{(2nd portion)}$$
$$P_3 < 4.50 \quad \text{(3rd portion)}$$
$$P_4 < 4.50 \quad \text{(4th portion)}$$
$$P_5 < 4.50 \quad \text{(5th portion)}$$
$$P_6 < 2.25 \quad \text{(6th portion)}$$
$$P_7 < 2.25 \quad \text{(7th portion)}$$
$$P_8 < 2.25 \quad \text{(8th portion)}$$
$$P_9 < 10.00 \quad \text{(9th portion)}$$

$$X_9 > 0.05 \quad \text{(lower limit of salt)}$$
$$X_9 < 0.10 \quad \text{(upper limit of salt)}$$

As with the least-cost formulation, maximum-profit formulation has to be run with a linear programming software package and the result should be interpreted and modified accordingly. After running this formulation for the first time the diet does not contain any forage (Run 1, Table 22.6). We will explain how to correct this in the next section.

The reader should note that when diets are formulated on a dry matter basis, the formulation also should include the prices on a dry matter basis. Failure to use prices on a dry matter basis will give erroneous results that do not satisfy the maximum-profit property. When the result is obtained it should be converted to an as fed basis.

Under a maximum-profit formulation we obtain a ration together with the optimum level of production for maximum profit. The reader should note that the *mathematical statement of the diet and the revision of the results* are **important components** for an appropriate diet formulation.

Proportions in Mathematical Programming Formulation

In diet formulations the nutritionist wants to fulfill not only the quantity of a given nutritional requirement of an animal, but also to specify the proportion in which some feedstuff must be in the diet, or the proportion that two nutrients should be present in the diet. Examples of these are the proportion of forage to concentrate, or the proportion of Ca to P in dairy rations.

TABLE 22.6   Diet composition and analysis.

		RUN 1		RUN 2	
	FEEDSTUFF	DRY MATTER	AS FED	DRY MATTER	AS FED
X_1	Barley, kg	0.000	0.000	0.000	0.000
X_2	Corn, kg	10.085	11.331	6.772	7.610
X_3	Dicalcium phosphate, kg	0.000	0.000	0.030	0.030
X_4	Limestone, kg	0.316	0.316	0.217	0.217
X_5	Soybean meal, kg	0.000	0.000	2.921	3.282
X_6	Cottonseed, kg	11.749	12.634	3.330	3.581
X_7	Alfalfa hay, kg	0.000	0.000	0.000	0.000
X_8	Corn silage, kg	0.000	0.000	8.880	31.828
X_9	Salt, kg	0.050	0.050	0.050	0.050
	Profit, \$/cow/day	7.748		6.709	
	Optimum milk, kg/day	41.257		38.379	
	Feed, kg/cow/day	22.200	24.331	22.200	46.600
	Energy, NE_l, Mcal	55.658		46.389	
	CP, kg	3.934		3.721	
	Ca, kg	0.134		0.126	
	P, kg	0.121		0.093	
	Cottonseed in concentrate, %	52.925		25.000	
	Forage : concentrate	0:100		40:60	

Example.   Reformulate the previous diet in such a way that the forage to concentrate ratio is between 40:60 and 50:50; also, include an upper limit for whole cottonseed such that it cannot exceed 25% of the concentrate.

To specify that the diet requires a forage to concentrate ratio between 40:60 and 50:50, ***we need to formulate:*** first, we write an expression that specifies the ***forage,*** that is, $X_7 + X_8$; then, we represent the ***total diet*** by the expression

$$X_1 + X_2 + X_3 + X_4 + X_5 + X_6 + X_7 + X_8 + X_9$$

the ratio between the first and second equation gives us the proportion of forage in the diet. The lower ratio can be represented as:

$$\frac{X_7 + X_8}{X_1 + X_2 + X_3 + X_4 + X_5 + X_6 + X_7 + X_8 + X_9} > 0.4$$

Multiplying both sides by $(X_1 + X_2 + X_3 + X_4 + X_5 + X_6 + X_7 + X_8 + X_9)$, we get:

$$X_7 + X_8 > 0.4(X_1 + X_2 + X_3 + X_4 + X_5 + X_6 + X_7 + X_8 + X_9)$$

Performing the multiplication on the right-hand side and then subtracting from the left side, we obtain:

$$-0.4X_1 - 0.4X_2 - 0.4X_3 - 0.4X_4 - 0.4X_5$$
$$- 0.4X_6 + 0.6X_7 + 0.6X_8 - 0.4X_9$$
$$> 0 \quad \text{(forage} > 40\%)$$

This linear equation then can be used in mathematical programming to specify the lower limit. With the following equation for the upper limit, the diet will have the range of 40–50% forage in the final form:

$$-0.5X_1 - 0.5X_2 - 0.5X_3 - 0.5X_4 - 0.5X_5$$
$$- 0.5X_6 + 0.5X_7 + 0.5X_8 - 0.5X_9$$
$$< 0 \quad \text{(forage} < 50\%)$$

With these manipulations we can set specified percentages of any nutrient in a diet whose total amount is determined by the formulation—that is, it is a part of the optimal solution. This formulation is used to set ratios of an individual or a group of feedstuffs with respect to the total or part of the diet, to set ratios of individual nutrients with respect to the diet or any other nutrient. These manipulations are necessary because ratios (proportions) and percentages are not additive and, therefore, not linear. Linearity is essential for solving linear programming problems.

To specify that the whole cottonseed (X_6) must be less than 25% of the concentrate, we take the ratio of X_6 and the total concentrate ($X_1 + X_2 + X_3 + X_4 + X_5 + X_6 + X_9$) and make it less than 0.25:

$$\frac{X_6}{X_1 + X_2 + X_3 + X_4 + X_5 + X_6 + X_9} < 0.25$$

Multiplying both sides of this expression by the total concentrate ($X_1 + X_2 + X_3 + X_4 + X_5 + X_6 + X_9$) and then subtracting the right-hand side from X_6, we obtain:

$$-0.25X_1 - 0.25X_2 - 0.25X_3 - 0.25X_4 - 0.25X_5 + 0.75X_6 - 0.25X_9 < 0$$

After adding this equation and the two forages to concentrate equations to our original maximum-profit formulation, we obtain a new result (Run 2, Table 22.6). The diet in Run 2 complies with the constraints that the forage to concentrate ratio should be between 40:60 and 50:50, and that whole cottonseed should be less than 25% of the concentrate.

This procedure can be used with the simultaneous equations methods. Two things should be taken into consideration when using the simultaneous equations procedure: (a) the equations should have the "=" sign; (b) ranges are not possible, and therefore, the ratio should be set at some fixed point.

Formulating with NEm and NEg Values

Lofgreen and Garrett (11) proposed a system for expressing net energy requirements (NE) and feed values for beef cattle. This system separates the NE requirements for maintenance (NE_m) from those for gain (NE_g) and gives different energy values for feedstuffs used for these two functions. NE_g is applied only if the total energy intake is above that required for maintenance. NE_m and NE_g are not independent of each other. To handle this dependency with linear equations some mathematical manipulations are necessary. Let us illustrate how to formulate the energy requirement for beef cattle with the NE_m-NE_g system, using the following example.

Example. Using the feedstuffs in Table 22.5, formulate a minimum cost diet for a growing steer with the following daily requirement: a minimum 9.4 kg dry matter intake, 6.89 Mcal NE_m, 5.33 Mcal NE_g, 0.87 kg CP, 0.021 to 0.042 kg of Ca, 0.02 kg of P, and a minimum of 45% forage. We would also specify that salt must be included within a range of 0.03 and 0.06 kg.

The equation to specify crude protein is:

$$0.107X_1 + 0.1X_2 + 0.515X_5 + 0.249X_6 + 0.16X_7 + 0.08X_8 > 0.87$$

Dividing both sides by 0.87 we obtain:

$$\frac{0.107}{0.87}X_1 + \frac{0.10}{0.87}X_2 + \frac{0.515}{0.87}X_5 + \frac{0.249}{0.87}X_6$$
$$+ \frac{0.16}{0.87}X_7 + \frac{0.08}{0.87}X_8 > \frac{0.87}{0.87}$$

Let us examine the coefficient of each feedstuff: 0.107/0.87 for X_1 is the inverse of the amount of X_1 necessary to supply the 0.87 kg of protein required—that is, 0.87/0.107 = 8.1308 kg of X_1 are necessary to supply **all** the required protein; 0.44/0.87 is the inverse of the amount of X_2 necessary to supply the 0.87 kg of protein required—that is, 0.87/0.10 = 8.7 kg of X_2 are necessary to supply **all** the required protein; and so on with X_5, X_6, X_7, and X_8.

Based on this, we can construct an equation to specify NE requirement in which X_1, X_2, X_3, X_4, X_5, X_6, X_7, X_8, and X_9 have coefficients equal to the inverse of the total amount of each feedstuff required to supply **both** NE_m and NE_g.

The amount of X_1 necessary to supply all the NE requirement for maintenance is the amount of NE_m required divided by the amount of NE_m/kg in X_1 (6.89/2.12 = 3.25 kg); the amount of X_1 necessary to supply all the NE requirement for gain is the amount of NE_g required divided by the amount of NE_g/kg in X_1 (5.33/1.45 = 3.6759 kg). Therefore, the total amount of X_1 required to supply all the requirement of NE_m and NE_g will be: 3.25 + 3.6759 = 6.9259 kg. The inverse of this number will be 1/6.9259 = 0.144586. If a feedstuff does not have a NE_m and NE_g value, such as dicalcium phosphate, the inverse value is taken as zero ("0"). Table 22.7 presents the amounts of each ingredient necessary to supply NE_m and NE_g, and the inverse value that will be used as the coefficient for the equation to especify the NE (NE_m and NE_g) requirement.

TABLE 22.7 Amounts required to supply NE_m and NE_g and inverse of total $NE_m + NE_g$.

| FEEDSTUFF | AMOUNT REQUIRED TO SUPPLY **all** | | | INVERSE |
	NE_m	NE_g	$NE_m + NE_g$	$NE_m + NE_g$
X_1	3.2500	3.6759	6.9259	0.144586
X_2	3.0759	3.4387	6.5146	0.153501
X_3	—	—	—	0.000000
X_4	—	—	—	0.000000
X_5	3.2967	3.7173	7.0240	0.142371
X_6	2.8589	3.1538	6.0127	0.166313
X_7	5.5564	7.8382	13.3946	0.074656
X_8	4.4167	5.3838	9.8005	0.102036
X_9	—	—	—	0.000000

The equation to specify the requirement of **both** NE_m and NE_g will be:

$$0.144586X_1 + 0.153501X_2 + 0.142371X_5$$
$$+ 0.166313X_6 + 0.074656X_7 + 0.102036X_8 > 1$$

This procedure is tedious if done by hand, but a fast and accurate one if done by a computer. Formulating a diet under the Lofgreen-Garrett system with this approach is a simple and accurate method.

For our example the equation to especify dry matter intake will be:

$$X_1 + X_2 + X_3 + X_4 + X_5 + X_6 + X_7 + X_8$$
$$+ X_9 > 9.4$$

To specify the minimum 45% forage, we will divide the total forage ($X_7 + X_8$) by the total intake ($X_1 + X_2 + X_3 + X_4 + X_5 + X_6 + X_7 + X_8 + X_9$) and make it greater than or equal to 0.40:

$$(X_7 + X_8)/(X_1 + X_2 + X_3 + X_4 + X_5 + X_6 + X_7 + X_8 + X_9) > 0.45$$

Multiplying both sides of this expression by total dry matter intake and subtracting the right-hand side from ($X_7 + X_8$), we get:

$$-0.45X_1 - 0.45X_2 - 0.45X_3 - 0.45X_4$$
$$- 0.45X_5 - 0.45X_6 + 0.55X_7 + 0.55X_8$$
$$- 0.45X_9 > 0$$

The final formulation to produce a diet that is minimum cost for our example will be:

Minimize price $= 0.1056X_1 + 0.0865X_2 + 0.292X_3 + 0.072X_4 + 0.2348X_5 + 0.1419X_6 + 0.1348X_7 + 0.1254X_8 + 0.066X_9$

such that:

$$X_1 + X_2 + X_3 + X_4 + X_5 + X_6 + X_7 + X_8 + X_9$$
$$> 9.4 \quad \text{(dry matter intake)}$$

$$0.107X_1 + 0.1X_2 + 0.515X_5 + 0.249X_6 + 0.16X_7$$
$$+ 0.08X_8 > 0.87 \quad \text{(protein)}$$

$$0.144586X_1 + 0.153501X_2 + 0.142371X_5$$
$$+ 0.166313X_6 + 0.074656X_7 + 0.102036X_8$$
$$> 1 \quad \text{(NE)}$$

$$-0.45X_1 - 0.45X_2 - 0.45X_3 - 0.45X_4 -$$
$$- 0.45X_5 - 0.45X_6 + 0.55X_7 + 0.55X_8 - 0.45X_9$$
$$> 0 \quad \text{(minimum 40% forage)}$$

$$0.0005X_1 + 0.0002X_2 + 0.237X_3 + 0.3607X_4$$
$$+ 0.0036X_5 + 0.0015X_6 + 0.0135X_7 + 0.0027X_8$$
$$> 0.021 \quad \text{(lower limit of Ca)}$$

$$0.0005X_1 + 0.0002X_2 + 0.237X_3 + 0.3607X_4$$
$$+ 0.0036X_5 + 0.0015X_6 + 0.0135X_7 + 0.0027X_8$$
$$< 0.042 \quad \text{(upper limit of Ca)}$$

$$0.0036X_1 + 0.0031X_2 + 0.1884X_3 + 0.002X_4$$
$$+ 0.0075X_5 + 0.0073X_6 + 0.0022X_7 + 0.002X_8$$
$$> 0.02 \quad \text{(P)}$$

$X_9 > 0.03$ (lower limit of salt)

$X_9 < 0.06$ (upper limit of salt)

The results of this formulation after running it with a linear programming program are presented in Table 22.8.

Formulating Premixes and Supplements

Premixes are used in animal nutrition in small amounts to supply vitamins, trace minerals, or minerals in general, protein, amino acids, antibiotics, and drugs and medicine. As with diet formulation, premixes can be formulated using any of the techniques described previously. Proper analysis is required in order to obtain the desired final premix results, and prices are necessary when premixes are to be least-cost. In cases of limited raw materials the Pearson's Square or simultaneous equations can be used. The use of mathematical programming in premix formulation allows for the selection of the "best" (economically) raw materials within specified ranges.

❏ SUMMARY

Because feed represents a large percentage of the cost of production, diet formulation becomes a very important aspect of animal production. Diet formulation allows the nutritionist to develop a diet that can be eaten and utilized by the animal to provide an economically feasible level of production. For diets that contain few feedstuffs, and in which the nutritional parameters, such as energy, protein, and so on, are fixed, the techniques required are quite simple. In these cases the use of the Pearson's Square or simultaneous equations can be utilized. When diets become more complex and the optimum level of production is to be determined, mathematical programming is the technique of choice. With the advent of personal computers and the ready availability of mathematical programming software, the nutritionist does not need an in-depth knowledge of the mathematical methods required in mathematical programming. The techniques discussed here are easy and simple to use in diet formulation by both beginners and advanced animal nutritionists. One key point to remember is that *diet formulation by any technique requires interaction and revision;* that is, once formulated, the result should be revised and if not satisfactory it should be reformulated and recomputed, until the diet has all the desired technical nutritional specifications.

TABLE 22.8 Diet composition and analysis.

	FEEDSTUFF	DRY MATTER	AS FED
X_1	Barley, kg	0.000	0.000
X_2	Corn, kg	5.038	5.661
X_3	Dicalcium phosphate, kg	0.000	0.000
X_4	Limestone, kg	0.072	0.072
X_5	Soybean meal, kg	0.000	0.000
X_6	Cottonseed, kg	0.000	0.000
X_7	Alfalfa hay, kg	0.347	0.390
X_8	Corn silage, kg	3.883	13.918
X_9	Salt, kg	0.060	0.060
	Minimum price $	0.979	
	Feed, kg/day	9.400	20.100
	Energy, total NE_m, Mcal	17.774	
	total NE_g, Mcal	11.890	
	available NE_g, Mcal	7.280	
	CP, kg	0.870	
	Ca, kg	0.042	
	P, kg	0.024	
	Forage, %	45.000	

❑ REFERENCES

1. National Research Council. 1978. *Nutrient Requirements of Domestic Animals,* No. 3, Nutrient Requirements of Dairy Cattle, 5th rev. ed. Natl. Acad. Sci., Washington, DC.

2. National Research Council. 1979. *Nutrient Requirements of Domestic Animals,* No. 2, Nutrient Requirements of Swine, 8th rev. ed. Natl. Acad. Sci., Washington, DC.

3. National Research Council. 1984. *Nutrient Requirements of Domestic Animals,* Nutrient Requirements of Beef Cattle, 6th rev. ed. Natl. Acad. Sci., Washington, DC.

4. Church, D. C., W. G. Brown and A. T. Ralston. 1963. Evaluation of cattle fattening rations formulated with linear programming techniques. *J. Animal Sci.* **22**:898.

5. Dean, G. W., H. O. Carter, H. R. Wagstaff, S. O. Olayide, M. Ronning and D. L. Bath. 1972. *Production Functions and Linear Programming Models for Dairy Cattle Feeding.* Giannini Foundation Mon-

ograph No. 31, Dec. 1972. Ca. Agr. Exp. Sta. Univ. Ca. Agric. Publ. Berkeley, CA.

6. Cooper, L. and D. Steinberg. 1974. *Methods and Applications of Linear Programming.* W. B. Saunders Co., Philadelphia, PA.

7. Hadley, G. 1962. *Linear Programming.* Addison-Wesley Publ. Co., Reading, MA.

8. Varela-Alvarez, H. 1978. Description of an Introductory Course in Operations Research for Animal Science Students. M.A. Paper, Dept. of Statistics. The Pennsylvania State University, University Park, PA.

9. Blaxter, K. L. 1962. *The Energy Metabolism of Ruminants.* C. C. Thomas, Springfield, Ill.

10. Brokken, R. F. 1971. Programming models for use of the Lofgreen-Garrett net energy system in formulating rations for beef cattle. *J. Animal Sci.* **32**:685.

11. Lofgreen, G. P. and W. N. Garrett. 1968. A system for expressing net energy requirements and feed values for growing and finishing beef cattle. *J. Animal Sci.* **27**:793.

APPENDIX
Tables of Feed Composition and Animal Nutrient Requirements

The information provided here regarding the nutrient content of feedstuffs and animal requirements comes from National Research Council publications. Since the last edition of *Basic Animal Nutrition and Feeding,* there have been revisions of several of the species publications. Unfortunately, there are complications. The NRC Beef Committee has complicated matters by recalculating the energy values for most of the feedstuffs used for beef cattle. Most of the values are lower than for previous publications. In addition, they have increased recommended levels of dry matter intake and energy intake, and there are some differences in the tables for growing-fattening cattle compared to previous editions. Energy values given for cattle were taken from the NRC Beef publication with the exception that net energy for lactation values were taken from the last issue of the Dairy publication. If the Dairy publication (newest revision) is available before this book goes to press, it will be included.

Energy values were added for sheep because those listed in the latest Sheep publication (1985) are almost all appreciably lower than the values shown for beef cattle.

APPENDIX TABLE 1 Composition of feedstuffs commonly fed to cattle, sheep, and horses. Data from NRC Publications.

| | | | COMPOSITION, DRY BASIS, % | | | | | | ENERGY UTILIZATION, DRY BASIS, MCAL/KG | | | | | | | | | | | | |
| | | | | | | | | | CATTLE | | | | | | SHEEP | | | | | HORSES | |
FEED NAME AND DESCRIPTION	INTL. FEED NUMBER	TYPICAL DRY, %	CP	CF	NDF	ADF	Ca	P	DE	ME	NEm	NEg	NEl	TDN, %	DE	ME	NEm	NEg	TDN, %	DE	TDN, %
Alfalfa, fresh, late veg.	2-00-181	21	20.0	23	38	29	2.19	0.33	2.78	2.28	1.41	0.83	—	63	2.56	2.10	1.24	0.68	58	2.51	57
Alfalfa, fresh	2-00-196	24	20.0	26	—	—	1.96	0.30	2.69	2.27	1.31	0.61	1.37	61						2.42	55
Alfalfa, hay, S-C, early bloom	1-00-059	90	18.0	23	42	31	1.41	0.22	2.43	1.99	1.14	0.58	1.30	60	2.47	2.03	1.18	0.61	56		
Alfalfa, hay, S-C, mature	1-00-071	91	13.0	38	58	44	1.13	0.18	2.21	1.81	0.97	0.42	1.15	50	2.38	1.95	1.11	0.55	54		
Alfalfa, silage, wilted midbloom	3-00-217	38	15.5	30	47	35	—	—	2.56	2.10	1.24	0.68	1.25	58	2.56	2.10	1.24	0.68	58		
Alfalfa, silage, 30–50% dry matter	3-08-150	43	9.8	19	—	—	1.39	0.27	—	—	—	—	—	—							
Bakery waste, dried	4-00-466	92	10.7	1	—	2	0.14	0.26	3.92	3.22	2.21	1.52	2.06	89							
Barley grain	4-00-549	88	13.5	6	19	7	0.05	0.38	3.70	3.04	2.06	1.40	1.91	84	3.79	3.11	2.12	1.45	86	3.61	82
Barley grain, pacific coast	4-07-939	89	10.8	7	21	9	0.06	0.39	3.79	3.11	2.12	1.45	1.89	86	3.88	3.18	2.18	1.50	88	3.48	79
Barley straw	1-00-498	91	4.3	42	80	49	0.30	0.07	1.76	1.45	0.60	0.08	1.08	40	2.12	1.74	0.90	0.35	48	1.63	37
Bean, Navy, seeds	5-00-623	89	25.3	5	—	—	0.18	0.59	3.70	3.04	2.06	1.40	1.91	84	3.84	3.15	2.15	1.48	87		
Beet, Sugar, pulp, dehy.	4-00-669	91	9.7	20	54	33	0.69	0.10	3.26	2.68	1.76	1.14	1.79	74	2.96	2.43	1.60	1.04	67	2.86	65
Bermudagrass, fresh	2-00-712	34	12.0	26	—	—	0.53	0.21	2.65	2.17	1.31	0.74	—	60						2.20	50
Bermudagrass hay, SC	1-00-703	90	6.0	31	78	38	0.43	0.20	2.16	1.77	0.93	0.39	1.05	49	1.97	1.62	0.85	0.35	45		
Bluegrass, Kentucky fresh, early veg.	2-00-777	31	17.4	25	55	29	0.50	0.44	3.17	2.60	1.70	1.08	1.64	72	2.87	2.35	1.47	0.88	65	2.46	56
Bluestem, fresh, early veg.	2-00-821	27	12.8	25	—	—	0.63	0.20	3.00	2.46	1.57	0.97	—	68							
Brewers grains, dehy.	5-02-141	92	29.4	14	46	24	0.33	0.55	2.91	2.39	1.51	0.91	1.50	66	3.09	2.53	1.63	1.03	70	2.99	68
Brome, fresh, early veg.	2-00-892	34	18.0	24	56	31	0.50	0.30	3.26	2.68	1.76	1.14	1.54	74	3.53	2.89	1.94	1.30	80	3.00	68

Brome hay, late bloom, S-C	1-00-888	89	10.0	37	68	43	0.30	0.35	2.43	1.99	1.14	0.58	1.20	55						2.38	54
Citrus pulp, dehy.	4-01-237	91	6.7	13	23	22	1.84	0.12	3.62	2.97	2.00	1.35	1.76	82	3.70	3.04	2.06	1.40	84	2.99	68
Clover, Crimson, hay, S-C	1-01-328	87	18.4	30	—	—	1.40	0.22	2.51	2.06	1.21	0.64	1.35	57	2.43	1.99	1.14	0.58	55	2.16	49
Clover, Ladino, fresh, early veg.	2-01-380	19	27.2	14	—	—	1.93	0.35	3.00	2.46	1.57	0.97	1.59	68							
Clover, Ladino, hay, S-C	1-01-378	90	22.0	21	36	32	1.35	0.31	2.65	2.17	1.31	0.74	1.37	60	2.91	2.39	1.51	0.91	66	2.24	51
Clover, Red, fresh, early bloom	2-01-428	20	19.4	23			2.26	0.38	3.04	2.50	1.60	1.00	1.54	69	3.00	2.46	1.57	0.47	68	2.51	57
Clover, Red, hay, S-C	1-01-415	89	16.0	29	56	36	1.53	0.25	2.43	1.99	1.14	0.58	1.32	55	2.65	2.17	1.31	0.74	60	2.16	49
Corn, Dent, fodder	1-28-231	81	8.9	25	55	33	0.50	0.25	2.87	2.35	1.47	0.88	1.47	65	2.78	2.28	1.41	0.83	63	—	—
Corn, Cobs, ground	1-28-234	90	3.2	36	89	35	0.57	0.10	2.21	1.81	0.97	0.42	1.03	50	2.25	1.84	1.07	0.45	51	1.36	31
Corn distillers grains, dehy.	5-28-235	94	23.0	12	43	—	0.11	0.43	3.79	3.11	2.12	1.45	1.94	86	3.84	3.15	2.12	1.48	87	3.08	70
Corn ears, ground	4-28-238	87	9.0	9	—	—	0.07	0.27	3.66	3.00	2.03	1.37	1.84	83	3.66	3.00	2.03	1.37	83	3.26	74
Corn gluten, meal	5-28-241	91	46.8	5	37	9	0.16	0.50	3.79	3.11	2.12	1.45	—	86	3.88	3.18	2.18	1.50	88	—	—
Corn gluten feed	5-28-243	90	25.6	10	—	—	0.36	0.82	3.66	3.00	2.03	1.37	1.89	83	3.66	3.00	2.03	1.37	83	—	—
Corn grain, #2	4-02-931	88	10.1	2	—	—	0.02	0.35	3.97	3.25	2.24	1.55	2.03	90	3.84	3.15	2.15	1.48	87	3.87	88
Corn grain, flaked	4-28-244	86	11.2	1	—	—	—	—	4.19	3.44	2.38	1.67	—	95						—	—
Corn grain, high moisture	4-20-770	72	10.7	3	—	5	0.02	0.32	4.10	3.36	2.33	1.62	—	93						—	—
Corn silage, well-eared	3-28-250	33	8.1	24	51	28	0.23	0.22	3.09	2.53	1.63	1.03	1.59	70	3.09	2.53	1.63	1.03	70	—	—
Cotton, seed hulls	1-01-599	91	4.1	48	90	64	0.15	0.09	1.85	1.52	0.68	0.15	0.81	42	2.16	1.77	0.93	0.39	49	1.45	33
Cotton seeds	5-01-614	92	23.9	21	39	29	0.16	0.75	4.23	3.47	2.41	1.69	2.28	96						—	—
Cotton seed, meal, mech. extd., 41% protein	5-01-617	93	44.3	13	28	20	0.21	1.16	3.44	2.82	1.88	1.24	1.76	78	3.31	2.71	1.79	1.16	75	—	—
Cottonseed, meal, solv. extd., 41% protein	5-01-621	91	45.2	13	—	17	0.18	1.21	3.35	2.75	1.82	1.19	1.72	76	3.13	2.57	1.67	1.06	71	—	—
Fat, animal-poultry	4-00-409	99	—	—	—	—	—	—	7.80	6.40	4.75	3.51	5.25	177							
Fescue, Kentucky 31, fresh, early veg.	2-01-900	28	22.1	21	—	—	0.53	0.39					—		3.22	2.64	1.73	1.11	73	—	—
Fescue hay, S-C, early bloom	1-09-186	91	20.2	25	—	—	0.35	0.24					—		2.73	2.24	1.38	0.80	62	—	—
Fescue hay, S-C, early bloom	1-01-871	92	9.5	37	72	39	0.30	0.26	2.12	1.74	0.90	0.35	—	48							

APPENDIX TABLE 1 (Continued).

Feed Name and Description	Intl. Feed Number	Typical Dry, %	Composition, Dry Basis, % CP	CF	NDF	ADF	Ca	P	Cattle (Mcal/kg) DE	ME	NEm	NEg	NEl	TDN, %	Sheep (Mcal/kg) DE	ME	NEm	NEg	TDN, %	Horses DE	TDN, %
Flax, seed, solvent extd. (linseed meal)	5-02-048	90	38.3	10	25	19	0.43	0.89	3.44	2.82	1.88	1.24	1.74	78	3.48	2.86	1.91	1.27	79	3.04	69
Grass-legume silage	3-02-303	29	11.3	32	—	—	0.25	0.08	2.60	2.13	1.28	0.71	—	59	2.73	2.24	1.38	0.80	62	—	—
Lespedeza, common fresh, late veg.	2-26-028	32	16.4	32	—	—	—	—													
Milk, cattle, fresh	5-01-168	12	26.7	—	—	—	0.95	0.76	5.60	5.43	3.80	3.80	—	150							
Milk, sheep, fresh	5-08-510	19	24.7	—	—	—	1.05	0.79							6.00	5.82	4.07	1.61	—		
Millet, Foxtail, fresh	2-03-101	28	9.5	32	—	—	0.32	0.19	2.78	2.28	1.41	0.83	1.45	63							
Molasses, beet	4-00-668	78	8.5	—	—	—	0.17	0.03	3.48	2.86	1.91	1.27	1.72	79	3.40	2.78	1.85	1.22	77	3.17	72
Molasses, citrus	4-01-241	68	8.2	—	—	—	1.72	0.13	3.31	2.71	1.79	1.16	1.76	75	3.48	2.86	1.91	1.27	79		
Molasses, sugarcane	4-04-696	75	5.8	—	—	—	1.00	0.11	3.17	2.60	1.70	1.08	1.64	72	3.40	2.78	1.85	1.22	77	3.26	74
Oats, grain	4-03-309	89	13.3	12	32	16	0.07	0.38	3.40	2.78	1.85	1.22	1.74	77	3.44	2.82	1.88	1.24	78	3.34	76
Oats, grain, pacific coast	4-07-999	91	10.0	12	—	—	0.11	0.34	3.44	2.82	1.88	1.24	1.76	78						3.34	77
Oat hay, S-C	1-03-280	91	9.3	30	66	42	0.24	0.22	2.43	1.99	1.14	0.58	1.37	55	2.34	1.92	1.14	0.58	53		
Oat silage, dough stage	3-03-296	35	10.0	33	—	—	0.47	0.33	2.51	2.06	1.21	0.64	1.32	57						2.07	47
Oat straw	1-03-283	92	4.4	40	70	54	0.24	0.06	1.98	1.63	0.79	0.25	1.05	45	2.07	1.70	0.79	0.25	47	1.76	40
Orchard grass, fresh, early, veg.	2-03-439	23	18.4	25	55	31	0.58	0.54	3.17	2.60	1.70	1.08	1.52	72	2.95	2.42	1.54	0.94	67		
Orchard grass, hay, late bloom	1-03-428	91	8.4	37	72	45	0.26	0.30	2.38	1.95	1.11	0.55	1.10	54						2.42	55
Pea seeds	5-03-600	89	25.3	7	—	—	0.15	0.44	3.84	3.15	2.15	1.48	1.91	87							
Potato, tubers, fresh	4-03-787	23	9.5	2	—	—	0.04	0.24	3.57	2.93	1.97	1.32	1.81	81							
Potato, tubers, silage	4-03-768	25	7.6	4	—	—	0.04	0.23	3.62	2.97	2.00	1.35	1.81	82							
Poultry feathers, hydrolyzed	5-03-795	93	91.3	1	—	—	0.28	0.72	3.09	2.53	1.63	1.03	—	70							
Poultry manure, dehy.	5-14-015	90	28.2	13	38	15	9.31	2.52	2.29	1.88	1.04	0.49	—	52							

Feed	Int'l Ref. No.																				
Prairie plants, midwest, hay, S-C	1-03-191	92	5.8	34	—	—	0.43	0.15	2.25	1.84	1.00	0.45	—	51	—	—	—	—	—	2.02	46
Rape, fresh, early bloom	2-03-866	11	23.5	16	—	—	—	—	3.31	2.71	1.79	1.16	—	75	3.31	2.71	1.79	1.16	75	—	—
Rape, seed, meal, solvent extd.	5-03-871	91	40.6	13	—	—	0.67	1.04	3.04	2.50	1.60	1.00	1.57	69	3.26	2.68	1.76	1.14	74	—	—
Redtop, fresh	2-03-897	29	11.6	27	64	—	0.46	0.29	2.78	2.28	1.41	0.83	—	63	—	—	—	—	—	—	—
Redtop, hay, S-C, midbloom	1-03-886	94	11.7	31	33	18	0.63	0.35	2.51	2.06	1.21	0.64	1.35	57	2.47	2.03	1.18	0.61	56	—	—
Rice, bran	4-03-928	91	14.1	13	13	—	0.08	1.70	3.09	2.53	1.63	1.03	1.50	70	3.26	2.68	1.76	1.14	74	—	—
Rice, ground	4-03-938	89	8.9	10	71	55	0.07	0.32	3.48	2.86	1.91	1.27	—	79	—	—	—	—	—	—	—
Rice, straw	1-03-925	91	4.3	35	—	—	0.21	0.08	1.81	1.48	0.64	0.11	—	41	—	—	—	—	—	—	—
Rye, fresh	2-04-018	24	15.9	28	—	—	0.39	0.33	3.04	2.50	1.60	1.00	1.84	69	3.75	3.07	2.09	1.43	85	3.52	80
Rye, grain	4-04-047	88	13.8	3	—	—	0.07	0.37	3.70	3.04	2.06	1.40	—	84	1.98	1.63	0.79	0.25	45	—	—
Rye, straw	1-04-007	90	3.0	43	—	—	0.24	0.09	1.37	1.12	0.26	—	—	31	—	—	—	—	—	—	—
Ryegrass, Italian, fresh	2-04-073	25	14.5	24	—	—	0.65	0.41	2.65	2.17	1.31	0.74	—	60	—	—	—	—	—	—	—
Ryegrass, Italian, hay, S-C, early bloom	1-04-066	88	11.4	29	—	—	0.62	0.34	2.38	1.95	1.11	0.55	—	54	2.51	2.06	1.21	0.64	57	—	—
Ryegrass, Perennial, fresh	2-04-086	27	10.4	23	—	—	0.55	0.27	3.00	2.46	1.57	0.97	—	68	—	—	—	—	—	—	—
Ryegrass, Perennial, hay, S-C	1-04-077	86	8.6	30	41	30	0.65	0.32	2.65	2.17	1.31	0.74	—	60	—	—	—	—	—	—	—
Safflower seeds, meal, solvent extd.	5-04-110	92	25.4	32	58	41	0.37	0.81	2.51	2.06	1.21	0.64	1.23	57	2.47	2.03	1.18	0.61	56	—	—
Safflower seeds wo hulls, meal, solvent extd.	5-07-959	92	46.9	15	—	—	0.38	1.40	3.22	2.64	1.73	1.11	1.74	73	—	—	—	—	—	—	—
Sage, Black, browse, fresh	2-05-564	65	8.5	—	—	—	0.81	0.17	2.16	1.77	0.93	0.39	—	49	2.16	1.77	0.93	0.39	49	—	—
Saltgrass, hay, S-C	1-04-168	89	8.9	32	—	—	—	—	2.25	1.84	1.00	0.45	—	51	2.25	1.84	1.00	0.45	51	—	—
Sedge, hay, S-C	1-04-193	89	9.4	32	—	—	—	—	2.29	1.88	1.04	0.49	—	52	—	—	—	—	—	—	—
Sorghum, fodder	1-07-960	89	7.5	27	—	—	0.52	0.13	2.56	2.10	1.24	0.68	1.30	58	2.56	2.10	1.24	0.68	58	—	—
Sorghum, grain 8–10% protein	4-20-893	87	10.1	3	—	—	0.04	0.34	3.70	3.04	2.06	1.40	—	84	—	—	—	—	—	3.52	80
Sorghum, grain, flaked	4-16-295	85	10.1	3	—	—	0.04	0.34	4.06	3.33	2.30	1.60	—	92	—	—	—	—	—	—	—

APPENDIX TABLE 1 (Continued).

FEED NAME AND DESCRIPTION	INTL. FEED NUMBER	TYPICAL DRY, %	COMPOSITION, DRY BASIS, %						ENERGY UTILIZATION, DRY BASIS, MCAL/KG												
									CATTLE						SHEEP					HORSES	
			CP	CF	NDF	ADF	Ca	P	DE	ME	NEm	NEg	NEl	TDN, %	DE	ME	NEm	NEg	TDN, %	DE	TDN, %
Sorghum, grain, reconstituted	4-16-296	70	10.1	3	—	—	0.04	0.34	4.10	3.36	2.33	1.62	—	93						—	—
Sorghum, Milo, heads	4-04-446	90	10.0	9	—	—	0.13	0.25							3.70	3.04	2.06	1.40	84	—	—
Sorghum, silage	3-04-323	30	7.5	28	—	38	0.35	0.21	2.65	2.17	1.31	0.74	1.23	60	2.51	2.06	1.21	0.64	57	—	—
Sorghum, Sudangrass, fresh, early veg.	2-04-484	18	16.8	23	55	29	0.43	0.41	3.09	2.53	1.63	1.03	1.59	70	2.78	2.28	1.41	0.83	63	—	—
Sorghum, Sudangrass, hay, S-C	1-04-480	91	8.0	36	68	42	0.55	0.30	2.47	2.03	1.18	0.61	1.32	56	2.43	1.99	1.14	0.58	55	—	—
Sorghum, Sudangrass, Silage	3-04-499	28	10.8	33	—	—	0.46	0.21	2.43	1.99	1.14	0.58	1.32	55	2.34	1.92	1.07	0.52	53	—	—
Soybean, hay, S-C	1-04-538	94	17.8	30	—	—	1.26	0.27												—	—
Soybean, hulls	1-04-560	91	12.1	40	67	50	0.49	0.21	2.34	1.92	1.07	0.52	1.25	53	2.51	2.06	1.21	0.64	57	2.11	48
Soybean, seeds	5-04-610	92	42.8	6	—	—	0.27	0.65	2.82	2.31	1.44	0.86	1.79	64	2.38	1.95	1.11	0.55	54	2.64	60
Soybean, meal, solvent extd., 44% protein	5-20-637	89	49.9	7	—	—	0.33	0.71	4.01	3.29	2.27	1.57	2.18	91	4.14	3.40	2.35	1.65	94	4.05	92
Soybean, straw	1-04-567	88	5.2	44	70	54	1.59	0.06	3.70	3.04	2.06	1.40	1.86	84	3.88	3.18	2.18	1.50	88	3.60	82
Sunflower, seeds, meal, solvent extd.	5-09-340	90	25.9	35	40	33	0.23	1.03	1.85	1.52	0.68	0.15	0.96	42	1.90	1.56	0.72	0.18	43	—	—
Sunflower, seeds wo hulls, solvent extd.	5-04-739	93	49.8	12	—	—	0.44	0.98	1.94	1.59	0.75	0.22	1.47	44	1.98	1.63	0.75	0.25	45	3.12	71
Timothy, fresh, late veg.	2-04-903	26	18.0	32	—	—	0.39	0.32	2.87	2.35	1.47	0.88	1.47	65	3.35	2.75	1.82	1.19	76	—	—
Timothy, hay, S-C, late veg.	1-04-881	89	17.0	27	55	29	0.66	0.34	3.17	2.60	1.70	1.08	1.54	72	2.69	2.21	1.34	0.77	61	—	—
Timothy, hay, S-C, midbloom	1-04-883	89	9.1	31	67	36	0.48	0.22	2.73	2.24	1.38	0.80	1.54	62	2.87	2.35	1.47	0.88	65	—	—
									2.51	2.06	1.21	0.64	1.30	57	2.65	2.17	1.31	0.74	60	1.98	45

Feed	Ref. No.																			
Trefoil, Birdsfoot, fresh	2-20-786	24	21.0	25	—	—	1.91	0.22	2.91	2.39	1.51	0.91	1.72	66	2.78	2.28	1.41	0.83	63	—	—
Triticale, grain	4-20-362	90	17.6	4	—	—	0.06	0.33	3.70	3.04	2.06	1.40	—	84	3.79	3.11	2.12	1.45	86	—	—
Turnip, roots, fresh	4-05-067	9	11.8	12	44	34	0.59	0.26	3.75	3.07	2.09	1.43	1.94	85	3.11	—	—	—	—	—	—
Urea, 281% protein equivalent	5-05-070	99	287.0	—	—	—	—	—	—	—	—	—	—	—	—	—	—	—	—	—	—
Vetch, fresh, late veg.	2-05-108	22	20.8	28	48	33	—	—	2.51	2.06	1.21	0.64	1.40	57	2.60	2.13	1.28	0.71	59	—	—
Vetch, hay, S-C	1-05-106	89	20.8	31	51	15	1.18	0.32	3.09	2.53	1.63	1.03	1.59	70	2.43	1.99	1.14	0.58	55	2.94	67
Wheat, bran	4-05-190	89	17.1	11	—	—	0.13	1.38	—	—	—	—	—	—	3.13	2.57	1.67	1.06	71	—	—
Wheat, flour by-product (middlings)	4-05-205	89	18.4	8	—	—	0.13	0.99	3.04	2.50	1.60	1.00	1.84	69	3.62	2.97	2.00	1.35	82	—	—
Wheat, fresh, early veg.	2-05-176	22	28.6	17	52	30	0.42	0.40	3.22	2.64	1.73	1.11	1.67	73	3.31	2.71	1.79	1.16	75	—	—
Wheat, grain, hard red spring	4-05-258	88	17.2	3	—	—	0.04	0.43	3.92	3.22	2.21	1.52	—	89	3.97	3.25	2.24	1.55	90	3.83	87
Wheat, grain, hard red winter	4-05-268	88	14.4	3	—	—	0.05	0.43	3.88	3.18	2.18	1.50	2.03	88	3.88	3.18	2.18	1.50	88	3.83	87
Wheat, grain, soft red winter	4-05-294	88	13.0	2	—	—	0.05	0.43	3.92	3.22	2.21	1.52	—	89	3.88	3.18	2.18	1.50	88	—	—
Wheat, grain, soft white winter	4-05-337	89	11.3	3	14	—	0.07	0.36	3.92	3.22	2.21	1.52	2.03	89	3.92	3.22	2.21	1.52	89	3.83	87
Wheat, grain, soft white winter, pacific coast	4-08-555	89	11.2	3	—	—	0.10	0.34	3.88	3.18	2.18	1.50	—	88	3.92	3.22	2.21	1.52	89	—	—
Wheat, mill run	4-05-206	90	17.2	9	—	—	0.11	0.13	3.48	2.86	1.91	1.27	1.69	79	—	—	—	—	—	—	—
Wheat, silage, full bloom	3-05-185	25	8.1	31	—	—	—	—	2.60	2.13	1.28	0.71	—	59	—	—	—	—	—	—	—
Wheat, straw	1-05-175	89	3.6	42	70	54	0.18	0.05	1.81	1.48	0.64	0.11	1.01	41	1.81	1.48	0.64	0.11	41	1.50	34
Wheatgrass, Crested fresh, early veg.	2-05-420	28	21.5	22	—	—	0.46	0.34	3.31	2.71	1.79	1.16	—	75	3.31	2.71	1.79	1.16	75	—	—
fresh, post ripe	2-05-428	80	3.1	40	—	—	0.27	0.07	2.16	1.77	0.93	0.39	—	49	2.38	1.95	1.11	0.55	54	—	—
hay, S-C	1-05-418	93	12.4	33	—	36	0.33	0.21	2.34	1.92	1.07	0.52	—	53	2.34	1.92	1.07	0.52	53	—	—
Whey, cattle, dehy.	4-01-182	93	14.2	—	—	—	0.92	0.82	3.57	2.93	1.97	1.32	1.79	81	—	—	—	—	—	—	—
Whey, cattle, fresh	4-08-134	7	13.0	—	—	—	0.73	0.65	4.14	3.40	2.35	1.65	—	94	—	—	—	—	—	—	—
Yeast, Brewers, dehy.	7-05-527	93	46.9	3	—	—	0.13	1.49	3.48	2.86	1.91	1.27	1.79	79	—	—	—	—	—	3.30	75

APPENDIX TABLE 2   Composition and energy utilization of feedstuffs commonly fed to poultry and swine. Data from NRC publications.

FEED NAME AND DESCRIPTION	INTL. FEED NO.	COMPOSITION, AS FED					ENERGY UTILIZATION, AS FED Kcal/kg		
							POULTRY	SWINE	
		DM	CP	CF	Ca	P	ME	DE	ME
Alfalfa meal, dehy., 17% protein	1-00-023	92	17.5	24	1.44	0.22	1370	2580	2270
Bakery waste, dehy.	4-00-466	92	9.8	1	0.13	0.24	3862	—	—
Barley, grain	4-00-549	89	11.6	5	0.03	0.36	2640	3086	2870
Barley, grain, pacific coast	4-07-939	89	9.0	6	0.05	0.32	2620	3130	2940
Blood meal, spray or ring dried	5-00-381	93	88.9	1	0.06	0.09	3420	2690	1927
Brewers grains, dehy.	5-02-141	92	25.3	15	0.29	0.52	2080	1940	1710
Corn, dent, grain	4-02-935	89	8.8	2	0.02	0.28	3350	3525	3325
Corn and cob meal	4-02-849	85	7.8	10	0.04	0.21	—	3086	2500
Corn, distillers grain w/solubles, dehy.	5-28-236	93	27.4	9	0.17	0.72	2480	3568	3390
Corn, gluten feed	5-28-243	90	22.0	8	0.40	0.80	1750	3307	2400
Corn, gluten meal, 60% protein	5-28-242	90	62.0	1	0.23	0.50	3720	—	—
Corn, hominy feed	4-03-011	90	10.4	6	0.05	0.52	2896	3615	3365
Cotton, seeds, meal, solvent extd., 41% protein	5-07-872	90	41.4	14	0.15	0.97	2400	2630	2500
Fish, meal, anchovy	5-01-985	92	64.2	1	3.73	2.43	2580	3086	2450
Fish, meal, herring	5-02-000	93	72.3	1	2.29	1.70	3190	3086	2500
Fish, meal, menhaden	5-02-009	92	60.5	1	5.11	2.88	2820	2734	2230
Fish, solubles, condensed	5-01-969	51	31.5	—	0.30	0.76	1460	1686	1626
Meat meal	5-00-385	92	54.4	9	8.27	4.10	2000	2835	2408
Meat and bone meal	5-00-388	93	50.4	3	10.30	5.10	1960	2866	2434
Millet, pearl, grain	4-03-118	91	13.1	4	0.05	0.32	2554	—	—
Molasses, beet	4-00-668	79	6.1	—	0.13	0.06	—	2460	2320
Molasses, cane	4-04-696	74	2.9	—	0.82	0.08	—	2469	2343
Oats, grain	4-03-309	89	11.4	11	0.06	0.27	2550	2866	2668

APPENDIX TABLE 2 *(Continued)*.

FEED NAME AND DESCRIPTION	INTL. FEED NO.	COMPOSITION, AS FED					ENERGY UTILIZATION, AS FED Kcal/kg		
							POULTRY	SWINE	
		DM	CP	CF	Ca	P	ME	DE	ME
Oats, grain, pacific coast	4-07-999	91	9.0	11	0.08	0.30	2610	—	—
Peas, seed	5-03-600	90	23.8	5	0.11	0.42	2570	3527	3200
Poultry, feathers, meal, hydrolyzed	5-03-795	93	86.4	1	0.33	0.55	2360	2778	2270
Rape seed meal, solvent extd., low erucic acid	5-06-145	93	38.0	11	0.68	1.17	2000	—	—
Rice, bran	4-03-928	91	12.9	11	0.07	1.50	2100	3080	2200
Rice, grain	4-03-932	89	8.7	10	0.08	—	2990	2513	2360
Rye, grain	4-04-047	88	12.1	2	0.06	0.32	2626	3307	2712
Safflower, seeds, meal w/o hulls, solvent extd.	5-07-959	92	43.0	13	0.35	1.29	1921	—	—
Sorghum, grain, 8–10% protein	4-20-893	87	8.8	2	0.04	0.30	3288		
Sorghum, grain, Milo	4-04-444	89	8.9	2	0.03	0.28	—	3439	3229
Soybean, seeds, heat processed	5-04-597	90	37.0	5	0.25	0.58	3300	4056	3540
Soybean meal, dehulled, solvent extd.	5-04-612	90	48.5	4	0.27	0.62	2440	3860	3485
Soybean meal, solvent extd.	5-04-604	89	44.0	7	0.29	0.65	2320	3350	3090
Sunflower meal, w/o hulls, solvent extd.	5-04-739	93	45.4	12	0.37	1.00	2320	2998	2605
Triticale, grain	4-20-362	90	15.8	4	0.05	0.30	3163	—	—
Wheat, bran	4-05-190	89	15.7	11	0.14	1.15	1300	2513	2320
Wheat, middlings	4-05-205	88	16.0	8	0.12	0.90	1800	3050	2940
Wheat, shorts	4-05-201	88	16.5	7	0.09	0.81	2162	3175	2910
Wheat grain, hard red winter	4-05-268	87	14.1	2	0.05	0.37	2800	3483	3220
Wheat grain, soft white winter	4-05-337	89	10.2	2	0.05	0.31	3120	3659	3416
Whey, dehy.	4-01-182	93	12.0	—	0.97	0.76	1900	3439	3190
Yeast, Brewers, dehy.	7-05-527	93	44.4	3	0.12	1.40	1990	3135	2707

APPENDIX TABLE 3 Amino acid composition of selected feedstuffs.

	CRUDE PROTEIN, %	AMINO ACIDS, AS FED BASIS, %												
		ARGI-NINE	CYS-TINE	GLY-CINE	HISTI-DINE	ISO-LEUCINE	LEUCINE	LYSINE	METHIO-NINE	PHENYL-ALANINE	THREO-NINE	TRYP-TOPHAN	TYRO-SINE	VALINE
Forage—Roughage														
Alfalfa, dehy, 15% CP	15.2	0.60	0.17	0.70	0.30	0.68	1.10	0.60	0.20	0.80	0.60	0.40	0.40	0.70
Alfalfa, dehy, 20% CP	20.6	0.90	—	1.00	0.40	0.80	1.50	0.90	0.30	1.10	0.90	0.50	0.70	1.19
Alfalfa leaf meal, s-c	21.3	0.90	0.34	0.90	0.33	0.90	1.25	0.95	0.30	0.80	0.70	0.25	0.60	0.90
Grass, dehy	14.8	0.99	0.19	0.72	0.46	1.38	1.98	1.06	0.31	1.30	0.89	0.31	0.46	1.57
Energy Feeds														
Barley grain	11.6	0.53	0.18	0.36	0.27	0.53	0.80	0.53	0.18	0.62	0.36	0.18	0.36	0.62
Corn hominy feed	10.7	0.50	0.18	0.50	0.20	0.40	0.80	0.40	0.18	0.30	0.40	0.10	0.50	0.50
Corn germ meal	18.0	1.20	0.32	—	—	—	1.70	0.90	0.35	0.80	0.90	0.30	1.50	1.30
Corn grain	8.8	0.50	0.09	0.43	0.20	0.40	1.10	0.20	0.17	0.50	0.40	0.10	—	0.40
Millet grain	12.0	0.35	0.08	—	0.23	1.23	0.49	0.25	0.30	0.59	0.44	0.17	—	0.62
Oats grain	11.8	0.71	0.18	—	0.18	0.53	0.89	0.36	0.18	0.62	0.36	0.18	0.53	0.62
Potato meal	8.2	0.43	—	—	0.11	0.48	0.30	0.47	0.07	0.29	0.21	0.15	—	0.39
Rice grain w hulls	7.3	0.53	0.10	0.80	0.09	0.27	0.53	0.27	0.17	0.27	0.18	0.10	0.60	0.51
Rye grain	11.9	0.53	0.18	—	0.27	0.53	0.71	0.45	0.18	0.62	0.36	0.09	0.27	0.62
Sorghum grain, Milo	11.0	0.36	0.18	0.40	0.27	0.53	1.42	0.27	0.09	0.45	0.27	0.09	0.36	0.53
Wheat grain	12.7	0.71	0.18	0.89	0.27	0.53	0.89	0.45	0.18	0.62	0.36	0.18	0.45	0.53
Wheat shorts	18.4	0.95	0.20	0.40	0.32	0.70	1.20	0.70	0.18	0.70	0.50	0.20	0.40	0.77
Whey, dried	13.8	0.40	0.30	0.30	0.20	0.90	1.40	1.10	0.20	0.40	0.80	0.20	0.30	0.70

Plant Protein Sources

Brewers dried grains	25.9	1.30	—	—	0.50	1.50	2.30	0.90	0.40	1.30	0.90	0.40	1.20	1.60
Corn dist. solv., dehy.	26.9	1.00	0.60	1.10	0.70	1.50	2.10	0.90	0.60	1.50	1.00	0.20	0.70	1.50
Corn gluten meal	42.9	1.40	0.60	1.50	1.00	2.30	7.60	0.80	1.00	2.90	1.40	0.20	1.00	2.20
Cottonseed meal, solv.	50.0	4.75	1.00	2.35	1.25	1.85	2.80	2.10	0.80	2.75	1.70	0.70	0.80	2.05
Peanut meal, solv.	47.4	4.69	—	—	1.00	2.00	3.10	1.30	0.60	2.30	1.40	0.50	—	2.20
Rapeseed meal, solv.	39.4	2.16	—	1.88	1.05	1.43	2.63	2.09	0.76	1.49	1.65	0.48	0.83	1.90
Soybean meal, solv.	45.8	3.20	0.67	2.10	1.10	2.50	3.40	2.90	0.60	2.20	1.70	0.60	1.40	2.40
Sunflower meal, solv.	46.8	3.50	0.70	2.70	1.10	2.10	2.60	1.70	1.50	2.20	1.50	0.50	—	2.30
Yeast, Brewers dried	44.6	2.20	0.50	1.70	1.10	2.10	3.20	3.00	0.70	1.80	2.10	0.50	1.50	2.30

Animal and Fish Protein Sources

Blood meal	79.9	3.50	1.40	3.40	4.20	1.00	10.30	6.90	0.90	6.10	3.70	1.10	1.80	6.50
Buttermilk, dried	32.0	1.10	0.40	0.60	0.90	2.70	3.40	2.40	0.70	1.50	1.60	0.50	1.00	2.80
Casein, dried	81.8	3.40	0.30	1.50	2.50	5.70	8.60	7.00	2.70	4.60	3.80	1.00	4.70	6.80
Fish meal, anchovy	66.0	4.46	1.00	5.10	1.84	3.40	7.01	5.40	2.19	2.48	3.04	0.80	1.77	3.54
Fish meal, herring	70.6	4.00	1.60	5.00	1.30	3.20	5.10	7.30	2.00	2.60	2.60	0.90	2.10	3.20
Fish meal, menhaden	61.3	4.00	0.94	4.40	1.60	4.10	5.00	5.30	1.80	2.70	2.90	0.60	1.60	3.60
Liver meal	66.5	4.10	0.90	5.60	1.50	3.40	5.40	4.80	1.30	2.90	2.60	0.60	1.70	4.20
Meat meal	53.4	3.70	0.60	2.20	1.10	1.90	3.50	3.80	0.80	1.90	1.80	0.30	0.90	2.60
Meat and bone meal	50.6	4.00	0.60	6.60	0.90	1.70	3.10	3.50	0.70	1.80	1.80	0.20	0.80	2.40
Meat meal tankage	59.8	3.60	—	—	1.90	1.90	5.10	4.00	0.80	2.70	2.40	0.70	—	4.20
Milk, dried skim	33.5	1.20	0.50	0.20	0.90	2.30	3.30	2.80	0.80	1.50	1.40	0.40	1.30	2.20

APPENDIX TABLE 4 Vitamin content (ppm) of selected feedstuffs, fresh basis.

	CAROTENE	VITAMIN E	CHOLINE	NIACIN	PANTOTHENIC ACID	RIBOFLAVIN	THIAMIN	VITAMIN B$_6$	VITAMIN B$_{12}$
Plant Sources									
Alfalfa, dehy., 15% CP	102	98	1550	42	21	11	3.0	6.5	—
Alfalfa leaf meal, s-c	62	—	1600	55	33	15	—	11	—
Barley grain	—	11	1030	57	6.5	2.0	5.1	2.9	—
Brewers dried grains	—	—	1587	43	8.6	1.5	0.7	0.7	—
Corn dist. sol., dehy.	1	55	4818	115	21	17	6.8	10	—
Corn grain	4	22	537	23	5	1.1	4.0	7.2	—
Cottonseed meal, solv., 41% CP	—	15	2860	40	14	5.0	6.5	6.4	—
Oats grain	—	36	1073	16	13	1.6	6.2	1.2	—
Peanut meal, solv.	—	3	2000	170	53	11	7.3	10	—
Rice grain w hulls	—	14	800	30	3.3	1.1	2.8	—	—
Rye grain	—	15	—	1.2	6.9	1.6	3.9	—	—
Sorghum grain, Milo	—	12	678	43	11	1.2	3.9	4.1	—
Soybean meal, solv., 45% CP	—	3	2743	27	14	3.3	6.6	8.0	—
Wheat grain	—	34	830	57	12	1.2	4.9	—	—
Wheat middlings	—	58	1100	53	14	1.5	19	11	—
Yeast, brewers dried	—	—	3885	447	110	35	92	43	—
Animal Sources									
Buttermilk, dried	—	6	1808	9	30	31	3.5	2.4	0.02
Fish meal, herring	—	27	4004	89	11	9.0	—	3.7	219
Fish meal, menhaden	—	9	3080	56	9	4.8	0.7	—	0.1
Meat meal	—	1	1955	57	4.8	5.3	0.2	3.0	51
Meat and bone meal	—	1	2189	48	3.7	4.4	1.1	2.5	45
Liver meal	—	—	—	204	45	46	0.2	—	501
Milk, cow's, dried skim	—	9	1426	11	34	20	3.5	3.9	42
Whey, dried	—	—	20	11	48	30	3.7	2.5	0.03

APPENDIX TABLE 5 Mineral composition of salts and mineral supplements used in livestock rations, as fed basis, feed grade purity.[a]

NAME	BASIC CHEMICAL FORMULA	ELEMENTAL COMPOSITION, % FEED GRADE PRODUCTS										ACID-BASE REACTION
		Ca	Cl	F	K	Mg	Mn	N	Na	P	S	
Ammonium chloride	NH_4Cl		66.28					26.10				Acid pH 4.5–5.5
Ammonium phosphate												
monobasic	$(NH_4)H_2PO_4$			0.0025[b]				12.18		26.93		Acid pH 4.5
dibasic	$(NH_4)_2HPO_4$			0.0025[b]				21.21		23.48		Basic pH 8.0
Animal bone charcoal		27.1				0.5		1.4		12.7		
Animal bone meal, steamed		29.0				0.6	trace	1.9	0.5	13.6		
Calcium												
Calcium carbonate	$CaCO_3$	40.04										Basic
Limestone	$CaCO_3$	35.8				2.0	trace			trace		Basic
Limestone, dolomitic	$CaCO_3$	22.3			0.4	10.0	trace					Basic
Oyster shell	$CaCO_3$	38.0			0.1	0.3	trace		0.21	0.07		Basic
Calcium phosphates												
Monocalcium phosphate	$CaH_4(PO_4)_2$	15.9		0.0025[b]						24.6		Acid pH 3.9
Dicalcium phosphate	$CaHPO_4$	23.35		0.02						18.21		Acid pH 5.5
Tricalcium phosphate	$Ca_3(PO_4)_2$, CaO	38.76		0.18[b]						19.97		sl. Acid pH 6.9
Defluorinated rock phosphates		32.0		0.18[b]					4.0	18.0		
Gypsum	$CaSO_4$	29.44									23.55	Acid
Magnesium carbonate	$MgCO_3$	0.02				25.2						sl. Basic
Magnesium oxide	MgO					60.3			0.5			sl. Basic
Manganese sulfate	$MnSO_4 \cdot H_2O$, MnO						28.7				14.7	
Potassium chloride	KCl		47.6		52.4							Neutral pH 7.00
Sodium chloride	NaCl		60.66						39.34			Neutral
Sodium phosphate												
Monobasic	$NaH_2PO_4 \cdot H_2O$			0.0025[b]					16.6	22.40		Acid pH 4.4
Dibasic	Na_2HPO_4			0.0025[b]					32.39	21.80		Basic pH 9.0
Tripoly	$Na_5P_3O_{10}$			0.0025[b]					24.94	30.85		Basic pH 9.9

[a]Elemental content varies according to source; use guaranteed analysis where available.
[b]Maximum.

APPENDIX TABLE 6   Nutrient requirements of growing-finishing swine fed ad libitum: percent or amount per kilogram of diet.[a] (From 1979 NRC Publication on Swine)

	1–5[a]	5–10	10–20	20–35	35–60	60–100
LIVEWEIGHT, kg:						
EXPECTED DAILY GAIN, g:	200	300	500	600	700	800
EXPECTED EFFICIENCY, g gain/kg feed:	800	600	500	400	350	270
EXPECTED EFFICIENCY, FEED/GAIN:	1.25	1.67	2.00	2.50	2.86	3.75
Digestible Energy,[b] Kcal	3,700	3,500	3,370	3,380	3,390	3,395
Metabolizable Energy,[b] Kcal	3,600	3,400	3,160	3,175	3,190	3,195
Crude Protein,[c] %	27	20	18	16	14	13
Indispensable Amino Acids						
Lysine, %	1.28	0.95	0.79	0.70	0.61	0.57
Arginine, %	0.33	0.25	0.23	0.20	0.18	0.16
Histidine, %	0.31	0.23	0.20	0.18	0.16	0.15
Isoleucine, %	0.85	0.63	0.56	0.50	0.44	0.41
Leucine, %	1.01	0.75	0.68	0.60	0.52	0.48
Methionine + cystine,[d] %	0.76	0.56	0.51	0.45	0.40	0.30
Phenylalanine + tyrosine,[e] %	1.18	0.88	0.79	0.70	0.61	0.57
Threonine, %	0.76	0.56	0.51	0.45	0.39	0.37
Tryptophan,[f] %	0.20	0.15	0.13	0.12	0.11	0.10
Valine, %	0.85	0.63	0.56	0.50	0.44	0.41
Mineral Elements						
Calcium, %	0.90	0.80	0.65	0.60	0.55	0.50
Phosphorus,[g] %	0.70	0.60	0.55	0.50	0.45	0.40
Sodium, %	0.10	0.10	0.10	0.10	0.10	0.10
Chlorine, %	0.13	0.13	0.13	0.13	0.13	0.13
Potassium, %	0.30	0.26	0.26	0.23	0.20	0.17
Magnesium, %	0.04	0.04	0.04	0.04	0.04	0.04
Iron, mg	150	140	80	60	50	40
Zinc, mg	100	100	80	60	50	50
Manganese, mg	4.0	4.0	3.0	2.0	2.0	2.0
Copper, mg	6.0	6.0	5.0	4.0	3.0	3.0
Iodine, mg	0.14	0.14	0.14	0.14	0.14	0.14
Selenium, mg	0.15	0.15	0.15	0.15	0.15	0.10

APPENDIX TABLE 6   (*Continued*).

	1–5[a]	5–10	10–20	20–35	35–60	60–100
LIVEWEIGHT, kg:						
EXPECTED DAILY GAIN, g:	200	300	500	600	700	800
EXPECTED EFFICIENCY, g gain/kg feed:	800	600	500	400	350	270
EXPECTED EFFICIENCY, FEED/GAIN:	1.25	1.67	2.00	2.50	2.86	3.75

Vitamins

Vitamin A, IU	2,200	2,200	1,750	1,300	1,300	1,300
or β-carotene, mg	8.8	8.8	7.0	5.2	5.2	5.2
Vitamin D, IU	220	220	200	200	150	125
Vitamin E, IU	11	11	11	11	11	11
Vitamin K (menadione), mg	2.0	2.0	2.0	2.0	2.0	2.0
Riboflavin, mg	3.0	3.0	3.0	2.6	2.2	2.2
Niacin,[h] mg	22	22	18	14	12	10
Pantothenic acid, mg	13	13	11	11	11	11
Vitamin B_{12}, μg	22	22	15	11	11	11
Choline,[i] mg	1,100	1,100	900	700	550	400
Thiamin, mg	1.3	1.3	1.1	1.1	1.1	1.1
Vitamin B_6, mg	1.5	1.5	1.5	1.1	1.1	1.1
Biotin,[j] mg	0.10	0.10	0.10	0.10	0.10	0.10
Folacin,[j] mg	0.60	0.60	0.60	0.60	0.60	0.60

[a]Requirements reflect the estimated levels of each nutrient needed for optimal performance when a fortified grain-soybean meal diet is fed, except that a substantial level of milk products should be included in the diet of the 1–5 kg pig. Concentrations are based upon amounts per unit of air-dry diet (i.e., 90% dry matter).

[b]These are not absolute requirements but are suggested energy levels derived from diets containing corn and soybean meal (44% crude protein). When lower energy grains are fed, these energy levels will not be met; consequently, feed efficiency would be lowered.

[c]Approximate protein levels required to meet the need for indispensable amino acids when a fortified grain-soybean meal diet is fed to pigs weighing more than 5 kg.

[d]Methionine can fulfill the total requirement; cystine can meet at least 50% of the total requirement.

[e]Phenylalanine can fulfill the total requirement; tyrosine can meet at least 50% of the total requirement.

[f]It is assumed that usable tryptophan content of corn does not exceed 0.05%.

[g]At least 30% of the phosphorus requirement should be provided by inorganic and/or animal product sources.

[h]It is assumed that most of the niacin present in cereal grains and their by-products is in bound form and thus unavailable to swine. The niacin contributed by these sources is not included in the requirement listed. In excess of its requirement for protein synthesis, tryptophan can be converted to niacin (50 mg tryptophan yields 1 mg niacin).

[i]In excess of its requirement for protein synthesis, methionine can spare dietary choline (4.3 mg methionine is equal in methylating capacity to 1 mg choline).

[j]These levels are suggested. No requirements have been established.

APPENDIX TABLE 7 Daily nutrient requirements of growing-finishing swine fed ad libitum.[a] (From 1979 NRC Publication on Swine)

LIVEWEIGHT, kg: AIR-DRY FEED INTAKE, g:	1–5[a] 250	5–10 500	10–20 1,000	20–35 1,500	35–60 2,000	60–100 3,000
Digestible Energy,[b] Kcal	925	1,750	3,370	5,055	6,740	10,110
Metabolizable Energy,[b] Kcal	900	1,700	3,160	4,740	6,320	9,480
Crude Protein,[c] g	67.5	100	180	240	280	390
Indispensable Amino Acids						
Lysine, g	3.2	4.8	7.9	10.5	12.2	17.1
Arginine, g	0.8	1.3	2.3	3.0	3.6	4.8
Histidine, g	0.8	1.2	2.0	2.7	3.2	4.5
Isoleucine, g	2.1	3.2	5.6	7.5	8.8	12.3
Leucine, g	2.5	3.8	6.8	9.0	10.4	14.4
Methionine + cystine,[d] g	1.9	2.8	5.1	6.8	8.0	9.0
Phenylalanine + tyrosine,[e] g	3.0	4.4	7.9	10.5	12.2	17.1
Threonine, g	1.9	2.8	5.1	6.8	7.8	11.1
Tryptophan,[f] g	0.5	0.8	1.3	1.8	2.2	3.0
Valine, g	2.1	3.2	5.6	7.5	8.8	12.3
Mineral Elements						
Calcium, g	2.3	4.0	6.5	9.0	11.0	15.0
Phosphorus,[g] g	1.8	3.0	5.5	7.5	9.0	12.0
Sodium, g	0.25	0.5	1.0	1.5	2.0	3.0
Chlorine, g	0.33	0.7	1.3	2.0	2.6	3.9
Potassium, g	0.75	1.3	2.6	3.5	4.0	5.1
Magnesium, g	0.10	0.2	0.4	0.6	0.8	1.2
Iron, mg	38	70	80	90	100	120
Zinc, mg	25	50	80	90	100	150
Manganese, mg	1.0	2	3	3	4	6
Copper, mg	1.5	3	5	6	6	9
Iodine, mg	0.04	0.07	0.14	0.21	0.28	0.42
Selenium, mg	0.04	0.08	0.15	0.22	0.30	0.30

APPENDIX TABLE 7   *(Continued)*.

LIVEWEIGHT, kg: AIR-DRY FEED INTAKE, g:	1–5[a] 250	5–10 500	10–20 1,000	20–35 1,500	35–60 2,000	60–100 3,000
Vitamins						
Vitamin A, IU	550	1,100	1,750	1,950	2,600	3,900
or β-carotene, mg	2.2	4.4	7.0	7.8	10.4	15.6
Vitamin D, IU	55	110	200	300	300	375
Vitamin E, IU	2.8	5.5	11	17	22	33
Vitamin K (menadione), mg	0.50	1.1	2.2	3.3	4.4	6
Riboflavin, mg	0.75	1.5	3.0	3.9	4.4	7
Niacin,[h] mg	5.5	11	18	21	24	30
Pantothenic acid, mg	3.3	6.5	11	17	22	33
Vitamin B_{12}, μg	5.5	11	15	17	22	33
Choline,[i] mg	275	550	900	1,050	1,100	1,200
Thiamin, mg	0.33	0.65	1.1	1.7	2.2	3.3
Vitamin B_6, mg	0.38	0.75	1.5	1.7	2.2	3.3
Biotin,[j] mg	0.03	0.05	0.10	0.15	0.20	0.30
Folacin,[j] mg	0.15	0.30	0.60	0.90	1.2	1.8

[a]Requirements reflect the estimated levels of each nutrient needed for optimal performance when a fortified grain-soybean meal diet is fed, except that a substantial level of milk products should be included in the diet of the 1–5 kg pig. Concentrations are based upon amounts per unit of air-dry diet (i.e., 90% dry matter).

[b]These are not absolute requirements but are suggested energy levels derived from diets containing corn and soybean meal (44% crude protein). When lower energy grains are fed, these energy levels will not be met; consequently, feed efficiency would be lowered.

[c]Approximate protein levels required to meet the need for indispensable amino acids when a fortified grain-soybean meal diet is fed to pigs weighing more than 5 kg.

[d]Methionine can fulfill the total requirement; cystine can meet at least 50% of the total requirement.

[e]Phenylalanine can fulfill the total requirement; tyrosine can meet at least 50% of the total requirement.

[f]It is assumed that usable tryptophan content of corn does not exceed 0.05%.

[g]At least 30% of the phosphorus requirement should be provided by inorganic and/or animal product sources.

[h]It is assumed that most of the niacin present in cereal grains and their by-products is in bound form and thus unavailable to swine. The niacin contributed by these sources is not included in the requirement listed. In excess of its requirement for protein synthesis, tryptophan can be converted to niacin (50 mg tryptophan yields 1 mg niacin).

[i]In excess of its requirement for protein synthesis, methionine can spare dietary choline (4.3 mg methionine is equal in methylating capacity to 1 mg choline).

[j]These levels are suggested. No requirements have been established.

APPENDIX TABLE 8   Nutrient requirements of breeding swine: percent or amount per kilogram of diet.[a] (From 1979 NRC Publication on Swine)

	BRED GILTS AND SOWS; YOUNG AND ADULT BOARS[b]	LACTATING GILTS AND SOWS
Digestible Energy, Kcal	3,400	3,395
Metabolizable Energy, Kcal	3,200	3,195
Crude Protein,[c]%	12	13
Indispensable Amino Acids		
Arginine, %	0	0.40
Histidine, %	0.15	0.25
Isoleucine, %	0.37	0.39
Leucine, %	0.42	0.70
Lysine, %	0.43	0.58
Methionine + cystine,[d] %	0.23	0.36
Phenylalanine + tyrosine,[e] %	0.52	0.85
Threonine, %	0.34	0.43
Tryptophan,[f] %	0.09	0.12
Valine, %	0.46	0.55
Mineral Elements		
Calcium, %	0.75	0.75
Phosphorus,[g] %	0.60	0.50
Sodium, %	0.15	0.20
Chlorine, %	0.25	0.30
Potassium, %	0.20	0.20
Magnesium, %	0.04	0.04
Iron, mg	80	80
Zinc, mg	50	50
Manganese, mg	10	10
Copper, mg	5	5
Iodine, mg	0.14	0.14
Selenium, mg	0.15	0.15

APPENDIX TABLE 8 (*Continued*).

	BRED GILTS AND SOWS; YOUNG AND ADULT BOARS[b]	LACTATING GILTS AND SOWS
Vitamins		
Vitamin A, IU	4,000	2,000
or β-carotene, mg	16	8
Vitamin D, IU	200	200
Vitamin E, IU	10	10
Vitamin K (menadione), mg	2	2
Riboflavin, mg	3	3
Niacin,[h] mg	10	10
Pantothenic acid, mg	12	12
Vitamin B_{12}, μg	15	15
Choline, mg	1,250	1,250
Thiamin, mg	1	1
Vitamin B_6, mg	1	1
Biotin,[i] mg	0.1	0.1
Folacin,[i] mg	0.6	0.6

[a]Requirements reflect the estimated levels of each nutrient needed for optimal performance when a fortified grain-soybean meal diet is fed. Concentrations are based upon amounts per unit of air-dry diet (i.e., 90% dry matter).

[b]Requirements for boars of breeding age have not been established. It is suggested that the requirements will not differ significantly from that of bred gilts and sows.

[c]Approximate protein levels required to meet the need for indispensable amino acids when a fortified grain-soybean meal diet is fed. The true digestibilities of the amino acids were assumed to be 90%.

[d]Methionine can fulfill the total requirement; cystine can meet at least 50% of the total requirement.

[e]Phenylalanine can fulfill the total requirement; tyrosine can meet at least 50% of the total requirement.

[f]It is assumed that usable tryptophan content of corn does not exceed 0.05%.

[g]At least 30% of the phosphorus requirement should be provided by inorganic and/or animal product sources.

[h]It is assumed that most of the niacin present in cereal grains and their by-products is in bound form and thus unavailable to swine. The niacin contributed by these sources is not included in the requirement listed. In excess of its requirement for protein synthesis, tryptophan can be converted to niacin (50 mg tryptophan yields 1 mg niacin).

[i]These levels are suggested. No requirements have been established.

APPENDIX TABLE 9   Daily nutrient requirements of breeding swine.[a] (From 1979 NRC Publication on Swine)

	BRED GILTS AND SOWS; YOUNG AND ADULT BOARS	LACTATING GILTS AND SOWS		
AIR-DRY FEED INTAKE, g:	1,800[b]	4,000	4,750	5,500
Digestible Energy, Kcal	6,120[c]	13,580	16,130	18,670
Metabolizable Energy, Kcal	5,760[c]	12,780	15,180	17,570
Crude Protein, g	216	520	618	715
Indispensable Amino Acids				
Arginine, g	0	16.0	19.0	22.0
Histidine, g	2.7	10.0	11.9	13.8
Isoleucine, g	6.7	15.6	18.5	21.4
Leucine, g	7.6	28.0	33.2	38.5
Lysine, g	7.7	23.2	27.6	31.9
Methionine + cystine,[d]	4.1	14.4	17.1	19.8
Phenylalanine + tyrosine,[e] g	9.4	34.0	40.4	46.8
Threonine, g	6.1	17.2	20.4	23.6
Tryptophan,[f] g	1.6	4.8	5.7	6.6
Valine, g	8.3	22.0	26.1	30.2
Mineral Elements				
Calcium, g	13.5	30.0	35.6	41.2
Phosphorus,[g] g	10.8	20.0	23.8	27.5
Sodium, g	2.7	8.0	9.5	11.0
Chlorine, g	4.5	12.0	14.2	16.5
Potassium, g	3.6	8.0	9.5	11.0
Magnesium, g	0.7	1.6	1.9	2.2
Iron, mg	144	320	380	440
Zinc, mg	90	200	238	275
Manganese, mg	18	40	48	55
Copper, mg	9	20	24	28
Iodine, mg	0.25	0.56	0.66	0.77
Selenium, mg	0.27	0.40	0.48	0.55
Vitamins				
Vitamin A, IU	7,200	8,000	9,500	11,000
or β-carotene, mg	28.8	32.0	38.0	44.0
Vitamin D, IU	360	800	950	1,100
Vitamin E, IU	18.0	40.0	47.5	55.0
Vitamin K, mg	3.6	8.0	9.5	11.0
Riboflavin, mg	5.4	12.0	14.2	16.5
Niacin,[h] mg	18.0	40.0	47.5	55.0
Pantothenic acid, mg	21.6	48.0	57.0	66.0
Vitamin B_{12}, μg	27.0	60.0	71.2	82.5
Choline, mg	2,250	5,000	5,940	6,875
Thiamin, mg	1.8	4.0	4.8	5.5
Vitamin B_6, mg	1.8	4.0	4.8	5.5
Biotin,[i] mg	0.18	0.4	0.48	0.55
Folacin,[i] mg	1.08	2.4	2.8	3.3

*Footnotes are the same as for Appendix Table 8.

APPENDIX TABLE 10 Nutrient requirements of horses (daily nutrients per horse), ponies, 200 kg mature weight. (From 1978 NRC Publication on Horses)

	WEIGHT		DAILY GAIN		DIGESTIBLE ENERGY, Mcal	TDN		CRUDE PROTEIN		DIGESTIBLE PROTEIN		CALCIUM, g	PHOSPHORUS, g	VIT. A ACTIVITY, 1,000 IU	DAILY FEED[a]	
	kg	lb	kg	lb		kg	lb	kg	lb	kg	lb				kg	lb
Mature ponies, maintenance	200	440	0.0		8.24	1.87	4.12	0.32	0.70	0.14	0.31	9	6	5.0	3.75	8.2
Mares, last 90 days gestation			0.27	0.594	9.23	2.10	4.62	0.39	0.86	0.20	0.44	14	9	10.0	3.70	8.1
Lactating mare, first 3 months (8 kg milk per day)			0.0		14.58	3.31	7.29	0.71	1.56	0.54	1.19	24	16	13.0	5.20	11.5
Lactating mare, 3 months to weaning (6 kg milk per day)			0.0		12.99	2.95	6.50	0.60	1.32	0.34	0.75	20	13	11.0	5.00	11.0
Nursing foal (3 months of age)	60	132	0.70	1.54	7.35	1.67	3.68	0.41	0.90	0.38	0.84	18	11	2.4	2.25	5.0
Requirements above milk					3.74	0.85	1.87	0.17	0.37	0.20	0.44	10	7	0.0	1.20	2.7
Weaning (6 months of age)	95	209	0.50	1.10	8.80	2.0	4.40	0.47	1.03	0.31	0.68	19	14	3.8	2.85	6.3
Yearling (12 months of age)	140	308	0.20	0.44	8.15	1.85	4.07	0.35	0.77	0.20	0.44	12	9	5.5	2.90	6.4
Long yearling (18 months of age)	170	374	0.10	0.22	8.10	1.84	4.05	0.32	0.70	0.17	0.37	11	7	6.0	3.10	6.8
Two year old (24 months of age)	185	407	0.05	0.11	8.10	1.84	4.05	0.30	0.66	0.15	0.33	10	7	5.5	3.10	6.8

[a]Dry matter basis.

APPENDIX TABLE 11 Nutrient requirements of horses (daily nutrients per horse), 400 kg mature weight. (From 1978 NRC Publication on Horses)

	WEIGHT		DAILY GAIN		DIGESTIBLE ENERGY, Mcal	TDN		CRUDE PROTEIN		DIGESTIBLE PROTEIN		CALCIUM, g	PHOSPHORUS, g	VIT. A ACTIVITY, 1,000 IU	DAILY FEED[a]	
	kg	lb	kg	lb	Mcal	kg	lb	kg	lb	kg	lb	g	g	IU	kg	lb
Mature horses, maintenance	400	880	0.0		13.86	3.15	6.93	0.54	1.19	0.24	0.53	18	11	10.0	6.30	13.9
Mares, last 90 days gestation			0.53	1.17	15.52	3.53	7.76	0.64	1.41	0.34	0.75	27	19	20.0	6.20	13.7
Lactating mare, first 3 months (12 kg milk per day)			0.0		23.36	5.31	11.68	1.12	2.46	0.68	1.50	40	27	22.0	8.35	18.4
Lactating mare, 3 months to weaning (8 kg milk per day)			0.0		20.20	4.59	10.10	0.91	2.00	0.51	1.12	33	22	18.0	7.75	17.1
Nursing foal (3 months of age)	125	275	1.00	2.2	11.51	2.62	5.76	0.65	1.43	0.50	1.10	27	17	5.0	3.55	7.8
Requirements above milk					6.10	1.39	3.05	0.40	0.88	0.30	0.66	15	12	0.0	1.95	4.3
Weanling (6 months of age)	185	407	0.65	1.43	13.03	2.96	6.51	0.66	1.45	0.43	0.95	27	20	7.4	4.20	9.2
Yearling (12 months of age)	265	583	0.40	0.88	13.80	3.14	6.91	0.60	1.32	0.35	0.77	24	17	10.0	4.95	10.9
Long yearling (18 months of age)	330	726	0.25	0.55	14.36	3.26	7.17	0.59	1.30	0.32	0.70	22	15	11.5	5.50	12.2
Two year old (24 months of age)	365	803	0.10	0.22	13.89	3.16	6.95	0.52	1.14	0.27	0.59	20	13	11.0	5.35	11.8

[a]Dry matter basis.

APPENDIX TABLE 12   Nutrient requirements of horses (daily nutrients per horse), 500 kg mature weight. (From 1978 NRC Publication on Horses)

	WEIGHT		DAILY GAIN		DIGESTIBLE ENERGY, Mcal	TDN		CRUDE PROTEIN		DIGESTIBLE PROTEIN		CALCIUM, g	PHOSPHORUS, g	VIT. A ACTIVITY, 1,000 IU	DAILY FEED[a]	
	kg	lb	kg	lb		kg	lb	kg	lb	kg	lb				kg	lb
Mature horses, maintenance	500	1,100	0.0		16.39	3.73	8.20	0.63	1.39	0.29	0.64	23	14	12.5	7.45	16.4
Mares, last 90 days gestation			0.55	1.21	18.36	4.17	9.18	0.75	1.65	0.39	0.86	34	23	25.0	7.35	16.2
Lactating mare, first 3 months (15 kg milk per day)			0.0		28.27	6.43	14.14	1.36	2.99	0.84	1.85	50	34	27.5	10.10	22.2
Lactating mare, 3 months to weaning (10 kg milk per day)			0.0		24.31	5.53	12.16	1.10	2.42	0.62	1.36	41	27	22.5	9.35	20.6
Nursing foal (3 months of age)	155	341	1.20	2.64	13.66	3.10	6.83	0.75	1.65	0.54	1.19	33	20	6.2	4.20	9.2
Requirements above milk					6.89	1.57	3.45	0.41	0.90	0.31	0.68	18	13	0.0	2.25	4.9
Weanling (6 months of age)	230	506	0.80	1.76	15.60	3.55	7.80	0.79	1.74	0.52	1.14	34	25	9.2	5.00	11.0
Yearling (12 months of age)	325	715	0.55	1.21	16.81	3.82	8.41	0.76	1.67	0.45	0.99	31	22	12.0	6.00	13.2
Long yearling (18 months of age)	400	880	0.35	0.77	17.00	3.90	8.58	0.71	1.56	0.39	0.86	28	19	14.0	6.50	14.3
Two year old (24 months of age)	450	990	0.15	0.33	16.45	3.74	8.23	0.63	1.39	0.33	0.72	25	17	13.0	6.60	14.5

[a]Dry matter basis.

APPENDIX TABLE 13 Nutrient requirements of horses (daily nutrients per horse), 600 kg mature weight. (From 1978 NRC Publication on Horses)

	WEIGHT		DAILY GAIN		DIGESTIBLE ENERGY, Mcal	TDN		CRUDE PROTEIN		DIGESTIBLE PROTEIN		CALCIUM, g	PHOSPHORUS, g	VIT. A ACTIVITY, 1,000 IU	DAILY FEED[a]	
	kg	lb	kg	lb		kg	lb	kg	lb	kg	lb				kg	lb
Mature horses, maintenance	600	1,320	0.0		18.79	4.27	9.40	0.73	1.61	0.33	0.73	27	17	15.0	8.50	18.8
Mares, last 90 days gestation			0.67	1.47	21.04	4.78	10.52	0.87	1.91	0.46	1.01	40	27	30.0	8.40	18.5
Lactating mare, first 3 months (18 kg milk per day)			0.0		33.05	7.51	16.53	1.60	3.52	0.99	2.18	60	40	33.0	11.80	26.0
Lactating mare, 3 months to weaning (12 kg milk per day)			0.0		28.29	6.43	14.15	1.29	2.84	0.73	1.61	49	30	27.0	10.90	23.9
Nursing foal (3 months of age)	170	374	1.40	3.08	15.05	3.42	7.53	0.84	1.85	0.78	1.72	36	23	6.8	4.65	10.2
Requirements above milk					6.93	1.58	3.47	0.51	1.12	0.38	0.84	18	15	0.0	2.25	4.9
Weanling (6 months of age)	265	583	0.85	1.87	16.92	3.85	8.47	0.86	1.89	0.57	1.25	37	27	10.6	5.45	12.0
Yearling (12 months of age)	385	847	0.60	1.32	18.85	4.28	9.42	0.90	1.98	0.50	1.10	35	25	14.0	6.75	14.8
Long yearling (18 months of age)	475	1,045	0.35	0.77	19.06	4.33	9.53	0.75	1.65	0.43	0.95	32	22	13.5	7.35	16.2
Two year old (24 months of age)	540	1,188	0.20	0.44	19.26	4.38	9.64	0.74	1.63	0.39	0.86	31	20	13.0	7.40	16.3

[a] Dry matter basis.

APPENDIX TABLE 14 Nutrient concentrations in diets for horses and ponies expressed on 100% dry matter basis.[a] (From 1978 NRC Publication on Horses)

| | DIGESTIBLE ENERGY | | EXAMPLE DIET PROPORTIONS | | | | CRUDE PROTEIN, % | CAL-CIUM, % | PHOS-PHORUS, % | VITAMIN A ACTIVITY | |
| | | | HAY CONTAINING 2.2 Mcal/kg | | HAY CONTAINING 2.0 Mcal/kg | | | | | | |
	Mcal/kg	Mcal/lb	CONCEN-TRATE[b]	ROUGH-AGE	CONCEN-TRATE[b]	ROUGH-AGE				IU/kg	IU/lb
Mature horses and ponies at maintenance	2.2	1.0	0	100	10	90	8.5	0.30	0.20	1,600	725
Mares, last 90 days of gestation	2.5	1.1	25	75	35	65	11.0	0.50	0.35	3,400	1,550
Lactating mare, first 3 months	2.8	1.3	45	55	55	45	14.0	0.50	0.35	2,800	1,275
Lactating mare, 3 months to weaning	2.6	1.2	30	70	40	60	12.0	0.45	0.30	2,450	1,150
Creep feed	3.5	1.6	100	0	100	0	18.0	0.85	0.60		
Foal (3 months of age)	3.25	1.5	75	25	80	20	18.0	0.85	0.60	2,000	900
Weanling (6 months of age)	3.1	1.4	65	35	70	30	16.0	0.70	0.50	2,000	900
Yearling (12 months of age)	2.8	1.3	45	55	55	45	13.5	0.55	0.40	2,000	900
Long yearling (18 months of age)	2.6	1.2	30	70	40	60	11.0	0.45	0.35	2,000	900
Two year old (light training)	2.6	1.3	30	70	40	60	10.0	0.45	0.35	2,000	900
Mature working horses (light work)[c]	2.5	1.1	25	75	35	65	8.5	0.30	0.20	1,600	725
(moderate work)[d]	2.9	1.3	50	50	60	40	8.5	0.30	0.20	1,600	725
(intense work)[e]	3.1	1.4	65	35	70	30	8.5	0.30	0.20	1,600	725

[a]Values are rounded to account for differences among Appendix Tables 10.13 and for greater practical application.
[b]Concentrate containing 3.6 Mcal/kg.
[c]Examples are horses used in western pleasure, bridle path hack, equitation, and so on.
[d]Examples are ranch work, roping, cutting, barrel racing, jumping, and so on.
[e]Examples are race training, polo, and so on.

APPENDIX TABLE 15   Dietary minerals and vitamins for horses. (From 1978 NRC
Publication on Horses)

| | ADEQUATE LEVELS | | TOXIC LEVELS[a] |
	MAINTENANCE OF MATURE HORSES	GROWTH	
Calcium	—[b]	—[b]	
Phosphorus	—[b]	—[b]	
Sodium, %	0.35	0.35	
Potassium, %	0.4	0.5	
Magnesium, %	0.09	0.1	
Sulfur, %	0.15	0.15	
Iron, mg/kg	40	50	
Zinc, mg/kg	40	40	9,000
Manganese, mg/kg	40	40	*
Copper, mg/kg	9	9	*
Iodine, mg/kg	0.1	0.1	4.8
Cobalt, mg/kg	0.1	0.1	
Selenium, mg/kg	0.1	0.1	5.0
Fluorine, mg/kg	—	—	50+
Lead, mg/kg	—	—	80
Vitamin A	—[b]	—[b]	*
Vitamin D, IU/kg	275	275	150,000
Vitamin E, mg/kg	15	15	
Thiamin, mg/kg	3	3	
Riboflavin, mg/kg	2.2	2.2	
Pantothenic acid, mg/kg	15	15	

[a]Nutrients known to be toxic to other species but without adequate information on the horses are indicated
by *.
[b]See Appendix Tables 10.13.

APPENDIX TABLE 16 Daily nutrient requirements of sheep. (From 1985 NRC Publication on sheep)

| BODY WEIGHT | | WEIGHT CHANGE/DAY | | DRY MATTER PER ANIMAL[a] | | | ENERGY[b] TDN | | DE | ME | CRUDE PROTEIN | | Ca, | P, | VITAMIN A ACTIVITY, | VITAMIN E ACTIVITY, |
kg	lb	g	lb	kg	lb	% BODY WEIGHT	kg	lb	Mcal	Mcal	g	lb	g	g	IU	IU
Ewes[c]																
Maintenance																
50	110	10	0.02	1.0	2.2	2.0	0.55	1.2	2.4	2.0	95	0.21	2.0	1.8	2,350	15
60	132	10	0.02	1.1	2.4	1.8	0.61	1.3	2.7	2.2	104	0.23	2.3	2.1	2,820	16
70	154	10	0.02	1.2	2.6	1.7	0.66	1.5	2.9	2.4	113	0.25	2.5	2.4	3,290	18
80	176	10	0.02	1.3	2.9	1.6	0.72	1.6	3.2	2.6	122	0.27	2.7	2.8	3,760	20
90	198	10	0.02	1.4	3.1	1.5	0.78	1.7	3.4	2.8	131	0.29	2.9	3.1	4,230	21
Flushing—2 Weeks prebreeding and first 3 weeks of breeding																
50	110	100	0.22	1.6	3.5	3.2	0.94	2.1	4.1	3.4	150	0.33	5.3	2.6	2,350	24
60	132	100	0.22	1.7	3.7	2.8	1.00	2.2	4.4	3.6	157	0.34	5.5	2.9	2,820	26
70	154	100	0.22	1.8	4.0	2.6	1.06	2.3	4.7	3.8	164	0.36	5.7	3.2	3,290	27
80	176	100	0.22	1.9	4.2	2.4	1.12	2.5	4.9	4.0	171	0.38	5.9	3.6	3,760	28
90	198	100	0.22	2.0	4.4	2.2	1.18	2.6	5.1	4.2	177	0.39	6.1	3.9	4,230	30
Nonlactating—First 15 weeks gestation																
50	110	30	0.07	1.2	2.6	2.4	0.67	1.5	3.0	2.4	112	0.25	2.9	2.1	2,350	18
60	132	30	0.07	1.3	2.9	2.2	0.72	1.6	3.2	2.6	121	0.27	3.2	2.5	2,820	20
70	154	30	0.07	1.4	3.1	2.0	0.77	1.7	3.4	2.8	130	0.29	3.5	2.9	3,290	21
80	176	30	0.07	1.5	3.3	1.9	0.82	1.8	3.6	3.0	139	0.31	3.8	3.3	3,760	22
90	198	30	0.07	1.6	3.5	1.8	0.87	1.9	3.8	3.2	148	0.33	4.1	3.6	4,230	24
Last 4 weeks gestation (130–150% lambing rate expected) or last 4–6 weeks lactation suckling singles[d]																
50	110	180 (45)	0.40 (0.10)	1.6	3.5	3.2	0.94	2.1	4.1	3.4	175	0.38	5.9	4.8	4,250	24
60	132	180 (45)	0.40 (0.10)	1.7	3.7	2.8	1.00	2.2	4.4	3.6	184	0.40	6.0	5.2	5,100	26
70	154	180 (45)	0.40 (0.10)	1.8	40	2.6	1.06	2.3	4.7	3.8	193	0.42	6.2	5.6	5,950	27
80	176	180 (45)	0.40 (0.10)	1.9	4.2	2.4	1.12	2.4	4.9	4.0	202	0.44	6.3	6.1	6,800	28
90	198	180 (45)	0.40 (0.10)	2.0	4.4	2.2	1.18	2.5	5.1	4.2	212	0.47	6.4	6.5	7,650	30
Last 4 weeks gestation (180–225% lambing rate expected)																
50	110	225	0.50	1.7	3.7	3.4	1.10	2.4	4.8	4.0	196	0.43	6.2	3.4	4,250	26
60	132	225	0.50	1.8	4.0	3.0	1.17	2.6	5.1	4.2	205	0.45	6.9	4.0	5,100	27
70	154	225	0.50	1.9	4.2	2.7	1.24	2.8	5.4	4.4	214	0.47	7.6	4.5	5,950	28
80	176	225	0.50	2.0	4.4	2.5	1.30	2.9	5.7	4.7	223	0.49	8.3	5.1	6,800	30
90	198	225	0.50	2.1	4.6	2.3	1.37	3.0	6.0	5.0	232	0.51	8.9	5.7	7,650	32

NUTRIENTS PER ANIMAL

APPENDIX TABLE 16 (*Continued*).

BODY WEIGHT		WEIGHT CHANGE/DAY		DRY MATTER PER ANIMAL[a]			ENERGY[b]				NUTRIENTS PER ANIMAL						
							TDN		DE,	ME,	CRUDE PROTEIN		Ca,	P,	VITAMIN A ACTIVITY,	VITAMIN E ACTIVITY,
kg	lb	g	lb	kg	lb	% BODY WEIGHT	kg	lb	Mcal	Mcal	g	lb	g	g	IU	IU
First 6–8 weeks lactation suckling singles or last 4–6 weeks lactation suckling twins[a]																
50	110	−25 (90)	−0.06 (0.20)	2.1	4.6	4.2	1.36	3.0	6.0	4.9	304	0.67	8.9	6.1	4,250	32
60	132	−25 (90)	−0.06 (0.20)	2.3	5.1	3.8	1.50	3.3	6.6	5.4	319	0.70	9.1	6.6	5,100	34
70	154	−25 (90)	−0.06 (0.20)	2.5	5.5	3.6	1.63	3.6	7.2	5.9	334	0.73	9.3	7.0	5,950	38
80	176	−25 (90)	−0.06 (0.20)	2.6	5.7	3.2	1.69	3.7	7.4	6.1	344	0.76	9.5	7.4	6,800	39
90	198	−25 (90)	−0.06 (0.20)	2.7	5.9	3.0	1.75	3.8	7.6	6.3	353	0.78	9.6	7.8	7,650	40
First 6–8 weeks lactation suckling twins																
50	110	−60	−0.13	2.4	5.3	4.8	1.56	3.4	6.9	5.6	389	0.86	10.5	7.3	5,000	36
60	132	−60	−0.13	2.6	5.7	4.3	1.69	3.7	7.4	6.1	405	0.89	10.7	7.7	6,000	39
70	154	−60	−0.13	2.8	6.2	4.0	1.82	4.0	8.0	6.6	420	0.92	11.0	8.1	7,000	42
80	176	−60	−0.13	3.0	6.6	3.8	1.95	4.3	8.6	7.0	435	0.96	11.2	8.6	8,000	45
90	198	−60	−0.13	3.2	7.0	3.6	2.08	4.6	9.2	7.5	450	0.99	11.4	9.0	9,000	48
Ewe lambs																
Nonlactating—First 15 weeks gestation																
40	88	160	0.35	1.4	3.1	3.5	0.83	1.8	3.6	3.0	156	0.34	5.5	3.0	1,880	21
50	110	135	0.30	1.5	3.3	3.0	0.88	1.9	3.9	3.2	159	0.35	5.2	3.1	2,350	22
60	132	135	0.30	1.6	3.5	2.7	0.94	2.0	4.1	3.4	161	0.35	5.5	3.4	2,820	24
70	154	125	0.28	1.7	3.7	2.4	1.00	2.2	4.4	3.6	164	0.36	5.5	3.7	3,290	26
Last 4 weeks gestation (100–120% lambing rate expected)																
40	88	180	0.40	1.5	3.3	3.8	0.94	2.1	4.1	3.4	187	0.41	6.4	3.1	3,400	22
50	110	160	0.35	1.6	3.5	3.2	1.00	2.2	4.4	3.6	189	0.42	6.3	3.4	4,250	24
60	132	160	0.35	1.7	3.7	2.8	1.07	2.4	4.7	3.9	192	0.42	6.6	3.8	5,100	26
70	154	150	0.33	1.8	4.0	2.6	1.14	2.5	5.0	4.1	194	0.43	6.8	4.2	5,950	27
Last 4 weeks gestation (130–175% lambing rate expected)																
40	88	225	0.50	1.5	3.3	3.8	0.99	2.2	4.4	3.6	202	0.44	7.4	3.5	3,400	22
50	110	225	0.50	1.6	3.5	3.2	1.06	2.3	4.7	3.8	204	0.45	7.8	3.9	4,250	24
60	132	225	0.50	1.7	3.7	2.8	1.12	2.5	4.9	4.0	207	0.46	8.1	4.3	5,100	26
70	154	215	0.47	1.8	4.0	2.6	1.14	2.5	5.0	4.1	210	0.46	8.2	4.7	5,950	27
First 6–8 weeks lactation suckling singles (wean by 8 weeks)																
40	88	−50	−0.11	1.7	3.7	4.2	1.12	2.5	4.9	4.0	257	0.56	6.0	4.3	3,400	26
50	110	−50	−0.11	2.1	4.6	4.2	1.39	3.1	6.1	5.0	282	0.62	6.5	4.7	4,250	32
60	132	−50	−0.11	2.3	5.1	3.8	1.52	3.4	6.7	5.5	295	0.65	6.8	5.1	5,100	34
70	154	−50	−0.11	2.5	5.5	3.6	1.65	3.6	7.3	6.0	301	0.68	7.1	5.6	5,450	38

Body Wt (kg)	(lb)													
First 6–8 weeks lactation suckling twins (wean by 8 weeks)														
40	88	−100	2.1	4.6	5.2	1.45	3.2	6.4	5.2	306	0.67	8.4	5.6	4,000	32
50	110	−100	2.3	5.1	4.6	1.59	3.5	7.0	5.7	321	0.71	8.7	6.0	5,000	34
60	132	−100	2.5	5.5	4.2	1.72	3.8	7.6	6.2	336	0.74	9.0	6.4	6,000	38
70	154	−100	2.7	6.0	3.9	1.85	4.1	8.1	6.6	351	0.77	9.3	6.9	7,000	40
Replacement Ewe Lambs[e]														
30	66	227	1.2	2.6	4.0	0.78	1.7	3.4	2.8	185	0.41	6.4	2.6	1,410	18
40	88	182	1.4	3.1	3.5	0.91	2.0	4.0	3.3	176	0.39	5.9	2.6	1,880	21
50	110	120	1.5	3.3	3.0	0.88	1.9	3.9	3.2	136	0.30	4.8	2.4	2,350	22
60	132	100	1.5	3.3	2.5	0.88	1.9	3.9	3.2	134	0.30	4.5	2.5	2,820	22
70	154	100	1.5	3.3	2.1	0.88	1.9	3.9	3.2	132	0.29	4.6	2.8	3,290	22
Replacement Ram Lambs[e]														
40	88	330	1.8	4.0	4.5	1.1	2.5	5.0	4.1	243	0.54	7.8	3.7	1,880	24
60	132	320	2.4	5.3	4.0	1.5	3.4	6.7	5.5	263	0.58	8.4	4.2	2,820	26
80	176	290	2.8	6.2	3.5	1.8	3.9	7.8	6.4	268	0.59	8.5	4.6	3,760	28
100	220	250	3.0	6.6	3.0	1.9	4.2	8.4	6.9	264	0.58	8.2	4.8	4,700	30
Lambs Finishing—4 to 7 Months Old[f]														
30	66	295	1.3	2.9	4.3	0.94	2.1	4.1	3.4	191	0.42	6.6	3.2	1,410	20
40	88	275	1.6	3.5	4.0	1.22	2.7	5.4	4.4	185	0.41	6.6	3.3	1,880	24
50	110	205	1.6	3.5	3.2	1.23	2.7	5.4	4.4	160	0.35	5.6	3.0	2,350	24
Early Weaned Lambs—Moderate Growth Potential[f]														
10	22	200	0.5	1.1	5.0	0.40	0.9	1.8	1.4	127	0.38	4.0	1.9	470	10
20	44	250	1.0	2.2	5.0	0.80	1.8	3.5	2.9	167	0.37	5.4	2.5	940	20
30	66	300	1.3	2.9	4.3	1.00	2.2	4.4	3.6	191	0.42	6.7	3.2	1,410	20
40	88	345	1.5	3.3	3.8	1.16	2.6	5.1	4.2	202	0.44	7.7	3.9	1,880	22
50	110	300	1.5	3.3	3.0	1.16	2.6	5.1	4.2	181	0.40	7.0	3.8	2,350	22
Early Weaned Lambs—Rapid Growth Potential[f]														
10	22	250	0.6	1.3	6.0	0.48	1.1	2.1	1.7	157	0.35	4.9	2.2	470	12
20	44	300	1.2	2.6	6.0	0.92	2.0	4.0	3.3	205	0.45	6.5	2.9	940	24
30	66	325	1.4	3.1	4.7	1.10	2.4	4.8	4.0	216	0.48	7.2	3.4	1,410	21
40	88	400	1.5	3.3	3.8	1.14	2.5	5.0	4.1	234	0.51	8.6	4.3	1,880	22
50	110	425	1.7	3.7	3.4	1.29	2.8	5.7	4.7	240	0.53	9.4	4.8	2,350	25
60	132	350	1.7	3.7	2.8	1.29	2.8	5.7	4.7	240	0.53	8.2	4.5	2,820	25

[a]To convert dry matter to an as-fed basis, divide dry matter values by the percentage of dry matter in the particular feed.

[b]One kilogram TDN (total digestible nutrients) = 4.4 Mcal DE (digestible energy); ME (metabolizable energy) = 82% of DE.

[c]Values are applicable for ewes in moderate condition. Fat ewes should be fed according to the next lower weight category and thin ewes at the next higher weight category. Once desired or moderate weight condition is attained, use that weight category through all production stages.

[d]Values in parentheses are for ewes suckling lambs the last 4–6 weeks of lactation.

[e]Lambs intended for breeding; thus, maximum weight gains and finish are of secondary importance.

[f]Maximum weight gains expected.

APPENDIX TABLE 17 Nutrient concentration in diets for sheep; expressed on 100% Dry Matter Basis.[a] (From 1985 NRC Publication on Sheep)

BODY WEIGHT		WEIGHT CHANGE/DAY		ENERGY[b]			EXAMPLE DIET PROPORTIONS		CRUDE PROTEIN, %	CAL-CIUM, %	PHOS-PHORUS, %	VITAMIN A ACTIVITY, IU/kg	VITAMIN E ACTIVITY, IU/kg
kg	lb	g	lb	TDN[c], %	DE, Mcal/kg	ME, Mcal/kg	CONCENTRATE, %	FORAGE, %					
Ewes[d]													
Maintenance													
70	154	10	0.02	55	2.4	2.0	0	100	9.4	0.20	0.20	2,742	15
Flushing—2 weeks prebreeding and first 3 weeks of breeding													
70	154	100	0.22	59	2.6	2.1	15	85	9.1	0.32	0.18	1,828	15
Nonlactating—First 15 weeks gestation													
70	154	30	0.07	55	2.4	2.0	0	100	9.3	0.25	0.20	2,350	15
Last 4 weeks gestation (130–150% lambing rate expected) or last 4–6 weeks lactation suckling singles[e]													
70	154	180 (0.45)	0.40 (0.10)	59	2.6	2.1	15	85	10.7	0.35	0.23	3,306	15
Last 4 weeks gestation (180–225% lambing rate expected)													
70	154	225	0.50	65	2.9	2.3	35	65	11.3	0.40	0.24	3,132	15
First 6–8 weeks lactation suckling singles or last 4–6 weeks lactation suckling twins[e]													
70	154	−25(90)	−0.06 (0.20)	65	2.9	2.4	35	65	13.4	0.32	0.26	2,380	15
First 6–8 weeks lactation suckling twins													
70	154	−60	−0.13	65	2.9	2.4	35	65	15.0	0.39	0.29	2,500	15
Ewe Lambs													
Nonlactating—First 15 weeks gestation													
55	121	135	0.30	59	2.6	2.1	15	85	10.6	0.35	0.22	1,668	15
Last 4 weeks gestation (100–120% lambing rate expected)													
55	121	160	0.35	63	2.8	2.3	30	70	11.8	0.39	0.22	2,833	15
Last 4 weeks gestation (130–175% lambing rate expected)													
55	121	225	0.50	66	2.9	2.4	40	60	12.8	0.48	0.25	2,833	15

First 6–8 weeks lactation suckling singles (wean by 8 weeks)

55	121	−50	0.22	2.9	66	2.4	40	60	13.1	0.30	0.22	2,125	15

First 6–8 weeks lactation suckling twins (wean by 8 weeks)

55	121	−100	−0.22	3.0	69	2.5	50	50	13.7	0.37	0.26	2,292	15

Replacement Ewe Lambs[f]

30	66	227	0.50	2.9	65	2.4	35	65	12.8	0.53	0.22	1,175	15
40	88	182	0.40	2.9	65	2.4	35	65	10.2	0.42	0.18	1,343	15
50–70	110–154	115	0.25	2.6	59	2.1	15	85	9.1	0.31	0.17	1,567	15

Replacement Ram Lambs[f]

40	88	330	0.73	2.8	63	2.3	30	70	13.5	0.43	0.21	1,175	15
60	132	320	0.70	2.8	63	2.3	30	70	11.0	0.35	0.18	1,659	15
80–100	176–220	270	0.60	2.8	63	2.3	30	70	9.6	0.30	0.16	1,979	15

Lambs Finishing—4 to 7 Months Old[g]

30	66	295	0.65	3.2	72	2.5	60	40	14.7	0.51	0.24	1,085	15
40	88	275	0.60	3.3	76	2.7	75	25	11.6	0.42	0.21	1,175	15
50	110	205	0.45	3.4	77	2.8	80	20	10.0	0.35	0.19	1,469	15

Early Weaned Lambs—Moderate and Rapid Growth Potential[g]

10	22	250	0.55	3.5	80	2.9	90	10	26.2	0.82	0.38	940	20
20	44	300	0.66	3.4	78	2.8	85	15	16.9	0.54	0.24	940	20
30	66	325	0.72	3.3	78	2.7	85	15	15.1	0.51	0.24	1,085	15
40–60	88–132	400	0.88	3.3	78	2.7	85	15	14.5	0.55	0.28	1,253	15

[a]Values in Appendix Table 17 are calculated from daily requirements in Appendix Table 16 divided by DM intake. The exception, vitamin E daily requirements/head, are calculated from vitamin E/kg diet × DM intake.

[b]One kilogram TDN = 4.4 Mcal DE (digestible energy); ME (metabolizable energy) = 82% of DE.

[c]TDN calculated on following basis: hay DM, 55% TDN and on as-fed basis 50% TDN; grain DM, 83% TDN and on as-fed basis 75% TDN. Once desired or moderate weight condition is attained, use that weight category through all production stages.

[d]Values in parentheses are for ewes suckling lambs the last 4–6 weeks of lactation.

[f]Lambs intended for breeding thus, maximum weight gains and finish are of secondary importance.

[g]Maximum weight gains expected.

APPENDIX TABLE 18   Crude protein requirements for lambs of small, medium, and large mature weight genotypes[a] (g/d). (From 1985 NRC Publication on Sheep)

BODY WEIGHT, kg[b]	10	20	25	30	35	40	45	50
Daily Gain, g[b]								
Small Mature Weight Lambs								
100	84	112	122	127	131	136	135	134
150	103	121	137	140	144	147	145	143
200	123	145	152	154	156	158	154	151
250	142	162	167	168	168	169	164	159
300	162	178	182	181	180	180	174	168
Medium Mature Weight Lambs								
100	85	114	125	130	135	140	139	139
150	106	132	141	145	149	153	151	149
200	127	150	158	160	163	166	163	160
250	147	167	174	175	177	179	175	171
300	168	185	191	191	191	191	186	181
350	188	203	207	206	205	204	198	192
400	209	221	224	221	219	217	210	202
Large Mature Weight Lambs								
100	94	128	134	139	145	144	150	156
150	115	147	152	156	160	159	164	169
200	136	166	170	173	176	174	178	182
250	157	186	188	190	192	189	192	195
300	179	205	206	207	208	204	206	208
350	200	224	224	224	224	219	220	221
400	221	243	242	241	240	234	234	234
450	242	262	260	256	256	249	248	248

[a]Approximate mature ram weights of 95 kg, 115 kg, and 135 kg, respectively.
[b]Weights and gains include fill.

APPENDIX TABLE 19   Macromineral requirements of sheep, percentage of diet dry matter.[a] (From 1985 NRC Publication on Sheep)

NUTRIENT	REQUIREMENT
Sodium	0.09–0.18
Chlorine	—
Calcium	0.20–0.82
Phosphorus	0.16–0.38
Magnesium	0.12–0.18
Potassium	0.50–0.80
Sulfur	0.14–0.26

[a]Values are estimates based on experimental data.

APPENDIX TABLE 20   Micromineral requirements of sheep and maximum tolerable levels (ppm, mg/kg of diet matter).[a] (From 1985 NRC Publication on Sheep)

NUTRIENT	REQUIREMENT	MAXIMUM TOLERABLE LEVEL[b]
Iodine	0.10–0.80[c]	50
Iorn	30–50	500
Copper	7–11[d]	25[e]
Molybdenum	0.5	10[e]
Cobalt	0.1–0.2	10
Manganese	20–40	1,000
Zinc	20–33	750
Selenium	0.1–0.2	2
Fluorine	—	60–150

[a]Values are estimates based on experimental data.
[b]NRC (1980).
[c]High level for pregnancy and lactation in diets not containing goitrogens; should be increased if diets contain goitrogens.
[d]Requirements when dietary Mo concentrations are <1 mg/kg DM.
[e]Lower levels may be toxic under some circumstances.

APPENDIX TABLE 21 Net energy requirements of growing and finishing beef cattle (Mcal/day).[a]
(From 1984 NRC Publication on Beef)

BODY WEIGHT, kg:	150	200	250	300	350	400	450	500	550	600
NE$_m$ REQUIRED:	3.30	4.10	4.84	5.55	6.24	6.89	7.52	8.14	8.75	9.33
Daily gain, kg	NE$_g$ Required									
Medium-Frame Steer Calves										
0.2	0.41	0.50	0.60	0.69	0.77	0.85	0.93	1.01	1.08	
0.4	0.87	1.08	1.28	1.47	1.65	1.82	1.99	2.16	2.32	
0.6	1.36	1.69	2.00	2.29	2.57	2.84	3.11	3.36	3.61	
0.8	1.87	2.32	2.74	3.14	3.53	3.90	4.26	4.61	4.95	
1.0	2.39	2.96	3.50	4.02	4.51	4.98	5.44	5.89	6.23	
1.2	2.91	3.62	4.28	4.90	5.50	6.69	6.65	7.19	7.73	
Large-Frame Steers, Compensating Medium-Frame Yearling Steers and Medium-Frame Bulls										
0.2	0.36	0.45	0.53	0.61	0.68	0.75	0.82	0.89	0.96	1.02
0.4	0.77	0.96	1.13	1.30	1.46	1.61	1.76	1.91	2.05	2.19
0.6	1.21	1.50	1.77	2.03	2.28	2.52	2.75	2.98	3.20	3.41
0.8	1.65	2.06	2.43	2.78	3.12	3.45	3.77	4.08	4.38	4.68
1.0	2.11	2.62	3.10	3.55	3.99	4.41	4.81	5.21	5.60	5.98
1.2	2.58	3.20	3.78	4.34	4.87	5.38	5.88	6.37	6.84	7.30
1.4	3.06	3.79	4.48	5.14	5.77	6.38	6.97	7.54	8.10	8.64
1.6	3.53	4.39	5.19	5.95	6.68	7.38	8.07	8.73	9.38	10.01
Large-Frame Bull Calves and Compensating Large-Frame Yearling Steers										
0.2	0.32	0.40	0.47	0.54	0.60	0.67	0.73	0.79	0.85	0.91
0.4	0.69	0.85	1.01	1.15	1.29	1.43	1.56	1.69	1.82	1.94
0.6	1.07	1.33	1.57	1.80	2.02	2.23	2.44	2.64	2.83	3.02
0.8	1.47	1.82	2.15	2.47	2.77	3.06	3.34	3.62	3.88	4.15
1.0	1.87	2.32	2.75	3.15	3.54	3.91	4.27	4.62	4.96	5.30
1.2	2.29	2.84	3.36	3.85	4.32	4.77	5.21	5.64	6.06	6.47
1.4	2.71	3.36	3.97	4.56	5.11	5.65	6.18	6.68	7.18	7.66
1.6	3.14	3.89	4.60	5.28	5.92	6.55	7.15	7.74	8.31	8.87
1.8	3.56	4.43	5.23	6.00	6.74	7.45	8.13	8.80	9.46	10.10
Medium-Frame Heifer Calves										
0.2	0.49	0.60	0.71	0.82	0.92	1.01	1.11	1.20	1.29	
0.4	1.05	1.31	1.55	1.77	1.99	2.20	2.40	2.60	2.79	
0.6	1.66	2.06	2.44	2.79	3.13	3.46	3.78	4.10	4.40	
0.8	2.29	2.84	3.36	3.85	4.32	4.78	5.22	5.65	6.07	
1.0	2.94	3.65	4.31	4.94	5.55	6.14	6.70	7.25	7.79	
Large-Frame Heifer Calves and Compensating Medium-Frame Yearling Heifers										
0.2	0.43	0.53	0.63	0.72	0.81	0.90	0.98	1.06	1.14	1.21
0.4	0.93	1.16	1.37	1.57	1.76	1.95	2.13	2.31	2.47	2.64
0.6	1.47	1.83	2.16	2.47	2.78	3.07	3.35	3.63	3.90	4.16
0.8	2.03	2.62	2.98	3.41	3.83	4.24	4.63	5.01	5.38	5.74
1.0	2.61	3.23	3.82	4.38	4.92	5.44	5.94	6.43	6.91	7.37
1.2	3.19	3.97	4.69	5.37	5.03	6.67	7.28	7.88	8.47	9.03

[a]Shrunk liveweight basis.

APPENDIX TABLE 22   Protein requirements of growing and finishing cattle (g/day).[a]
(From 1984 NRC Publication on Beef)

BODY WEIGHT, kg:	150	200	250	300	350	400	450	500	550	600
Medium-Frame Steer Calves										
Daily gain, kg										
0.2	343	399	450	499	545	590	633	675	715	
0.4	428	482	532	580	625	668	710	751	790	
0.6	503	554	601	646	688	728	767	805	842	
0.8	575	621	664	704	743	780	815	849	883	
1.0	642	682	720	755	789	821	852	882	911	
1.2	702	735	766	794	822	848	873	897	921	
Large-Frame Steer Calves and Compensating Medium-Frame Yearling Steers										
0.2	361	421	476	529	579	627	673	719	762	805
0.4	441	499	552	603	651	697	742	785	827	867
0.6	522	576	628	676	722	766	809	850	890	930
0.8	598	650	698	743	786	828	867	906	944	980
1.0	671	718	762	804	843	881	918	953	988	1021
1.2	740	782	822	859	895	929	961	993	1023	1053
1.4	806	842	877	908	938	967	995	1022	1048	1073
1.6	863	892	919	943	967	989	1011	1031	1052	1071
Medium-Frame Bulls										
0.2	345	401	454	503	550	595	638	680	721	761
0.4	530	485	536	584	629	673	716	757	797	835
0.6	509	561	609	655	698	740	780	819	856	893
0.8	583	632	677	719	759	798	835	871	906	940
1.0	655	698	739	777	813	849	881	914	945	976
1.2	722	760	795	828	860	890	919	947	974	1001
1.4	782	813	841	868	893	917	941	963	985	1006

APPENDIX TABLE 22   *(Continued).*

BODY WEIGHT, kg:	150	200	250	300	350	400	450	500	550	600
Large-Frame Bull Calves and Compensating Large-Frame Yearling Steers										
0.2	355	414	468	519	568	615	661	705	747	789
0.4	438	494	547	597	644	689	733	776	817	857
0.6	519	574	624	672	718	761	803	844	884	923
0.8	597	649	697	741	795	826	866	905	942	979
1.0	673	721	765	807	847	885	922	958	994	1027
1.2	745	789	830	868	904	939	973	1005	1037	1067
1.4	815	854	890	924	956	986	1016	1045	1072	1099
1.6	880	912	943	971	998	1024	1048	1072	1095	1117
1.8	922	942	962	980	997	1013	1028	1043	1057	1071
Medium-Frame Heifer Calves										
0.2	323	374	421	465	508	549	588	626	662	
0.4	409	459	505	549	591	630	669	706	742	
0.6	477	522	563	602	638	674	708	741	773	
0.8	537	574	608	640	670	700	728	755	781	
1.0	562	583	603	621	638	654	670	685	700	
Large-Frame Heifer Calves and Compensating Medium-Frame Yearling Heifers										
0.2	342	397	449	497	543	588	631	672	712	751
0.4	426	480	530	577	622	665	707	747	787	825
0.6	500	549	596	639	681	721	759	796	832	867
0.8	568	613	654	693	730	765	799	833	865	896
1.0	630	668	703	735	767	797	826	854	881	907
1.2	680	708	734	758	781	803	824	844	864	883

[a]Shrunk liveweight basis.

APPENDIX TABLE 23   Calcium and phosphorus requirements of growing and finishing cattle (g/day).[a] (From 1984 NRC Publication on Beef)

BODY WEIGHT, kg	MINERAL	150	200	250	300	350	400	450	500	550	600
Medium-Frame Steer Calves											
Daily gain, kg											
0.2	Ca	11	12	13	14	15	16	17	19	20	
	P	7	9	10	12	13	15	16	18	19	
0.4	Ca	16	17	17	18	19	19	20	21	22	
	P	9	10	12	13	14	16	17	18	20	
0.6	Ca	21	21	21	22	22	22	22	23	23	
	P	11	12	13	14	15	17	18	19	20	
0.8	Ca	27	26	25	25	25	25	24	24	24	
	P	12	13	14	15	16	17	19	20	21	
1.0	Ca	32	31	29	29	28	27	26	26	25	
	P	14	15	16	16	17	18	19	20	21	
1.2	Ca	37	35	33	32	31	29	28	27	26	
	P	16	16	17	17	18	19	20	21	21	
1.4	Ca	42	39	37	35	33	32	30	29	27	
	P	17	18	18	19	19	20	20	21	22	
Large-Frame Steer Calves, Compensating Medium-Frame Yearling Steers, and Medium-Frame Bulls											
0.2	Ca	11	12	13	14	16	17	18	19	20	22
	P	7	9	10	12	13	15	16	18	20	21
0.4	Ca	17	17	18	19	19	20	21	22	23	24
	P	9	10	12	13	15	16	17	19	20	22
0.6	Ca	22	22	23	23	23	24	24	24	25	25
	P	11	12	13	15	16	17	18	20	21	22
0.8	Ca	28	27	27	27	27	27	27	27	27	27
	P	13	14	15	16	17	18	19	20	22	23
1.0	Ca	33	32	31	31	30	30	29	29	29	28
	P	14	15	16	17	18	19	20	21	22	23
1.2	Ca	38	37	36	35	34	33	32	31	30	30
	P	16	17	18	18	19	20	21	22	23	24
1.4	Ca	44	42	40	38	37	36	34	33	32	31
	P	18	18	19	20	20	21	22	22	23	24
1.6	Ca	49	47	44	42	40	38	37	35	34	32
	P	20	20	20	21	21	22	22	23	24	24
Large-Frame Bull Calves and Compensating Large-Frame Yearling Steers											
0.2	Ca	11	12	13	15	16	17	18	20	21	22
	P	7	9	10	12	13	15	17	18	20	21
0.4	Ca	17	18	19	19	20	21	22	23	24	25
	P	9	11	12	13	15	16	18	19	21	22

APPENDIX TABLE 23   (*Continued*).

BODY WEIGHT, kg	MINERAL	150	200	250	300	350	400	450	500	550	600
0.6	Ca	23	23	23	24	24	25	25	26	27	27
	P	11	12	14	15	16	18	19	20	22	23
0.8	Ca	28	28	28	28	28	29	29	29	29	30
	P	13	14	15	16	18	19	20	21	22	24
1.0	Ca	34	34	33	33	32	32	32	32	32	32
	P	15	16	17	18	19	20	21	22	23	24
1.2	Ca	40	39	38	37	36	36	35	35	34	34
	P	17	17	18	19	20	21	22	23	24	25
1.4	Ca	45	44	42	41	40	39	38	37	36	36
	P	18	19	20	20	21	22	23	24	25	26
1.6	Ca	51	49	47	45	44	42	41	40	39	38
	P	20	21	21	22	23	23	24	25	25	26
1.8	Ca	56	54	51	49	47	45	44	42	41	39
	P	22	22	22	23	23	24	25	25	26	26
Medium-Frame Heifer Calves											
0.2	Ca	10	11	12	13	14	16	17	18	19	
	P	7	9	10	11	13	14	16	17	19	
0.4	Ca	15	16	16	16	17	17	18	19	19	
	P	9	10	11	12	14	15	16	18	19	
0.6	Ca	20	20	19	19	19	19	19	19	19	
	P	10	11	12	13	14	16	17	18	19	
0.8	Ca	25	23	23	22	21	20	20	19	19	
	P	12	12	13	14	15	16	17	18	19	
1.0	Ca	29	27	26	24	23	22	20	19	19	
	P	13	14	14	15	16	16	17	18	19	
Large-Frame Heifer Calves and Compensating Medium-Frame Yearling Heifers											
0.2	Ca	11	12	13	14	15	16	17	18	20	21
	P	7	9	10	12	13	15	16	18	19	21
0.4	Ca	16	16	17	17	18	19	19	20	21	22
	P	9	10	11	13	14	15	17	18	20	21
0.6	Ca	21	21	21	21	21	21	21	21	22	22
	P	10	12	13	14	15	16	17	19	20	21
0.8	Ca	26	25	24	24	23	23	23	22	22	22
	P	12	13	14	15	16	17	18	19	20	21
1.0	Ca	31	29	28	27	26	25	24	23	23	22
	P	14	14	15	16	17	18	18	19	20	21
1.2	Ca	35	33	31	30	28	27	25	24	23	22
	P	15	16	16	17	17	18	19	20	20	21

*a*Shrunk liveweight basis.

APPENDIX TABLE 24   Mineral requirements and maximum tolerable levels for beef cattle. (From 1984 NRC Publication on Beef)

MINERAL	REQUIREMENT		MAXIMUM TOLERABLE LEVEL
	SUGGESTED VALUE	RANGE[a]	
Calcium, %	—	See Appendix Tables 23 and 27	2
Cobalt, ppm	0.10	0.07 to 0.11	5
Copper, ppm	8	4 to 10	115
Iodine, ppm	0.5	0.20 to 2.0	50
Iron, ppm	50	50 to 100	1000
Magnesium, %	0.10	0.05 to 0.25	0.40
Manganese, ppm	40	20 to 50	1000
Molybdenum, ppm	—	—	6
Phosphorus, %	—	See Appendix Tables 23 and 27	1
Potassium, %	0.65	0.5 to 0.7	3
Selenium, ppm	0.20	0.05 to 0.30	2
Sodium, %	0.08	0.06 to 0.10	10[b]
Chlorine, %	—	—	—
Sulfur, %	0.10	0.08 to 0.15	0.40
Zinc, ppm	30	20 to 40	500

[a]The listing of a range in which requirements are likely to be met recognizes that requirements for most minerals are affected by a variety of dietary and animal (body weight, sex, rate of gain) factors. Thus, it may be better to evaluate rations based on a range of mineral requirements and for content of interfering substances than to meet a specific dietary value.
[b]10% sodium chloride.

APPENDIX TABLE 25   Maximum tolerable levels of certain toxic elements for beef cattle. (From 1984 NRC Publication on Beef)

ELEMENT	MAXIMUM TOLERABLE LEVEL, ppm
Aluminum	1,000
Arsenic	50 (100 for organic forms)
Bromine	200
Cadmium	00.5
Fluorine	20 to 100
Lead	30
Mercury	2
Strontium	2,000

APPENDIX TABLE 26   Approximate total daily water intake of beef cattle. (From 1984 NRC Publication on Beef)

WEIGHT		TEMPERATURE IN °F (°C)[a]											
		40 (4.4)		50 (10.0)		60 (14.4)		70 (21.1)		80 (26.6)		90 (32.2)	
kg	lb	liter	gal	liter	gal	liter	gal	liter	gal	liter	gal	liter	gal
Growing Heifers, Steers, and Bulls													
182	400	15.1	4.0	16.3	4.3	18.9	5.0	22.0	5.8	25.4	6.7	36.0	9.5
273	600	20.1	5.3	22.0	5.8	25.0	6.6	29.5	7.8	33.7	8.9	48.1	12.7
364	800	23.8	6.3	25.7	6.8	29.9	7.9	34.8	9.2	40.1	10.6	56.8	15.0
Finishing Cattle													
273	600	22.7	6.0	24.6	6.5	28.0	7.4	32.9	8.7	37.9	10.0	54.1	14.3
364	800	27.6	7.3	29.9	7.9	34.4	9.1	40.5	10.7	46.6	12.3	65.9	17.4
454	1000	32.9	8.7	35.6	9.4	40.9	10.8	47.7	12.6	54.9	14.5	78.0	20.6
Wintering Pregnant Cows[b]													
409	900	25.4	6.7	27.3	7.2	31.4	8.3	36.7	9.7	—	—	—	—
500	1100	22.7	6.0	24.6	6.5	28.0	7.4	32.9	8.7	—	—	—	—
Lactating Cows													
409+	900+	43.1	11.4	47.7	12.6	54.9	14.5	64.0	16.9	67.8	17.9	61.3	16.2
Mature Bulls													
636	1400	30.3	8.0	32.6	8.6	37.5	9.9	44.3	11.7	50.7	13.4	71.9	19.0
727+	1600+	32.9	8.7	35.6	9.4	40.9	10.8	47.7	12.6	54.9	14.5	78.0	20.6

[a]Water intake of a given class of cattle in a specific management regime is a function of dry matter intake and ambient temperature. Water intake is quite constant up to 40°F (4.4°C).

[b]Dry matter intake has a major influence on water intake. Heavier cows are assumed to be higher in body condition and to require less dry matter and, thus, less water intake.

APPENDIX TABLE 27 Nutrient requirements of breeding cattle (metric). (From 1984 NRC Publication on Beef)

WEIGHT[a], kg	DAILY GAIN[b], kg	DAILY DM[c], kg	ENERGY DAILY ME, Mcal	ENERGY DAILY TDN, kg	ENERGY DAILY NEm, Mcal	ENERGY DAILY NEg, Mcal	ENERGY IN DIET DM ME, Mcal/kg	ENERGY IN DIET DM TDN, %	ENERGY IN DIET DM NEm, Mcal/kg	ENERGY IN DIET DM NEg, Mcal/kg	TOTAL PROTEIN DAILY, g	TOTAL PROTEIN IN DIET DM, %	CALCIUM DAILY, g	CALCIUM IN DIET DM, %	PHOSPHORUS DAILY, g	PHOSPHORUS IN DIET DM, %	VITAMIN A[d] DAILY, 1000's IU
Pregnant Yearling Heifers—Last Third of Pregnancy																	
325	0.4	7.1	14.2	3.9	8.04	NA[e]	2.00	55.2	1.15	NA[e]	591	8.4	19	0.27	14	0.20	20
325	0.6	7.3	15.7	4.3	8.04	0.77	2.15	59.3	1.29	0.72	649	8.9	23	0.32	15	0.21	20
325	0.8	7.3	17.2	4.8	8.04	1.67	2.35	64.9	1.47	0.88	697	9.5	27	0.37	16	0.22	20
350	0.4	7.5	14.8	4.1	8.38	NA	1.99	55.0	1.14	NA	616	8.3	20	0.27	15	0.21	21
350	0.6	7.7	16.5	4.6	8.38	0.81	2.14	59.1	1.28	0.71	674	8.8	24	0.32	16	0.21	22
350	0.8	7.8	18.1	5.0	8.38	1.76	2.34	64.6	1.46	0.88	720	9.3	27	0.35	17	0.22	22
375	0.4	7.8	15.5	4.3	8.71	NA	1.98	54.7	1.13	NA	641	8.2	21	0.27	15	0.19	22
375	0.6	8.1	17.2	4.8	8.71	0.86	2.13	58.8	1.27	0.70	697	8.6	25	0.31	17	0.21	23
375	0.8	8.2	19.0	5.2	8.71	1.86	2.32	64.1	1.45	0.86	743	9.1	27	0.33	18	0.22	23
400	0.4	8.2	16.1	4.5	9.04	NA	1.97	54.4	1.12	NA	664	8.1	22	0.27	16	0.20	23
400	0.6	8.5	18.0	5.0	9.04	0.90	2.12	58.6	1.26	0.69	721	8.5	25	0.30	18	0.21	24
400	0.8	8.6	19.8	5.5	9.04	1.95	2.31	63.8	1.44	0.85	764	8.9	28	0.33	18	0.20	24
425	0.4	8.6	16.8	4.6	9.36	NA	1.96	54.1	1.11	NA	687	8.0	23	0.27	17	0.20	24
425	0.6	8.9	18.7	5.2	9.36	0.94	2.11	58.3	1.25	0.69	743	8.4	26	0.30	18	0.20	25
425	0.8	9.0	20.7	5.7	9.36	2.04	2.30	63.5	1.43	0.84	786	8.8	28	0.31	19	0.21	25
450	0.4	8.9	17.3	4.8	9.67	NA	1.95	53.9	1.10	NA	710	8.0	23	0.26	18	0.20	25
450	0.6	9.2	19.4	5.4	9.67	0.98	2.10	58.0	1.25	0.68	765	8.3	26	0.29	19	0.21	26
450	0.8	9.4	21.5	5.9	9.67	2.13	2.29	63.3	1.42	0.84	807	8.6	28	0.30	20	0.21	26
Dry Pregnant Mature Cows—Middle Third of Pregnancy																	
350	0.0	6.8	11.9	3.3	6.23	NA	1.76	48.6	0.92	NA	478	7.1	12	0.16	12	0.18	19
400	0.0	7.5	13.1	3.6	6.89	NA	1.76	48.6	0.92	NA	525	7.0	13	0.17	13	0.17	21
450	0.0	8.2	14.3	4.0	7.52	NA	1.76	48.6	0.92	NA	570	7.0	15	0.17	15	0.18	23
500	0.0	8.8	15.5	4.3	8.14	NA	1.76	48.6	0.92	NA	614	7.0	17	0.19	17	0.19	25
550	0.0	9.5	16.7	4.6	8.75	NA	1.76	48.6	0.92	NA	657	6.9	18	0.19	18	0.19	27
600	0.0	10.1	17.8	4.9	9.33	NA	1.76	48.6	0.92	NA	698	6.9	20	0.20	20	0.20	28
650	0.0	10.7	18.9	5.2	9.91	NA	1.76	48.6	0.92	NA	739	6.9	22	0.21	22	0.21	30

Dry Pregnant Mature Cows—Last Third of Pregnancy

350	0.4	7.4	14.7	4.1	8.38	NA	1.98	54.7	1.13	NA	609	8.2	20	0.27	15	0.20	21
400	0.4	8.2	16.0	4.4	9.04	NA	1.96	54.1	1.11	NA	657	8.0	22	0.27	16	0.20	23
450	0.4	8.9	17.2	4.8	9.67	NA	1.94	53.6	1.10	NA	703	7.9	23	0.26	18	0.21	24
500	0.4	9.5	18.3	5.1	10.29	NA	1.92	53.1	1.08	NA	746	7.8	25	0.26	20	0.21	27
550	0.4	10.2	19.5	5.4	10.90	NA	1.91	52.8	1.07	NA	790	7.8	26	0.25	21	0.21	29
600	0.4	10.8	20.6	5.7	11.48	NA	1.90	52.5	1.06	NA	832	7.7	28	0.26	23	0.21	30
650	0.4	11.5	21.7	6.0	12.06	NA	1.89	52.2	1.05	NA	872	7.6	30	0.26	25	0.22	32

Two-Year-Old Heifers Nursing Calves—First 3–4 Months Postpartum—5.0 kg Milk/Day

300	0.2	6.9	16.6	4.6	9.30[f]	0.72	2.41	66.6	1.53	0.93	814[g]	11.8	26	0.38	17	0.25	27
325	0.2	7.3	17.4	4.8	6.64[f]	0.77	2.37	65.5	1.49	0.90	841[g]	11.5	27	0.37	18	0.25	28
350	0.2	7.8	18.1	5.0	9.98[f]	0.81	2.34	64.6	1.46	0.88	866[g]	11.2	27	0.35	19	0.24	30
375	0.2	8.2	18.9	5.2	10.31[f]	0.86	2.31	63.8	1.44	0.85	892[g]	10.9	28	0.34	19	0.23	32
400	0.2	8.6	19.7	5.4	10.64[f]	0.90	2.29	63.3	1.42	0.84	916[g]	10.7	28	0.33	20	0.23	34
425	0.2	9.0	20.4	5.6	10.96[f]	0.94	2.27	62.7	1.40	0.82	939[g]	10.5	29	0.32	21	0.23	35
450	0.2	9.4	21.1	5.8	11.27[f]	0.98	2.25	62.2	1.38	0.80	963[g]	10.3	29	0.31	22	0.23	37

Cows Nursing Calves—Average Milking Ability—First 3–4 Months Postpartum—5.0 kg Milk/Day

350	0.0	7.7	16.6	4.6	9.98[f]	NA	2.15	59.4	1.29	NA	814[g]	10.6	23	0.30	18	0.23	30
400	0.0	8.5	17.9	4.9	10.64[f]	NA	2.11	58.3	1.25	NA	864[g]	10.2	25	0.29	19	0.22	33
450	0.0	9.2	19.1	5.3	11.27[f]	NA	2.08	57.5	1.23	NA	911[g]	9.9	26	0.28	21	0.23	36
500	0.0	9.9	20.3	5.6	11.89[f]	NA	2.05	56.6	1.20	NA	957[g]	9.7	28	0.28	22	0.22	39
550	0.0	10.6	21.5	5.9	12.50[f]	NA	2.03	56.1	1.18	NA	1001[g]	9.5	29	0.27	24	0.23	41
600	0.0	11.2	22.6	6.2	13.08[f]	NA	2.01	55.5	1.16	NA	1044[g]	9.3	31	0.28	26	0.23	44
650	0.0	11.9	23.9	6.6	13.66[f]	NA	2.00	55.3	1.15	NA	1086[g]	9.1	33	0.28	27	0.23	46

Cows Nursing Calves—Superior Milking Ability—First 3–4 Months Postpartum—10.0 kg Milk/Day

350	0.0	6.2	18.5	5.1	13.73[f]	NA	3.00	82.9	2.03	NA	1009[g]	16.4	36	0.58	24	0.39	24
400	0.0	7.6	21.4	5.9	14.39[f]	NA	2.80	77.4	1.86	NA	1099[g]	14.4	37	0.49	25	0.33	30
450	0.0	9.1	23.2	6.4	15.02[f]	NA	2.56	70.7	1.66	NA	1186[g]	13.1	39	0.43	26	0.29	35
500	0.0	10.0	24.6	6.8	15.64[f]	NA	2.45	67.7	1.56	NA	1246[g]	12.4	40	0.40	28	0.28	39
550	0.0	10.9	25.8	7.1	16.25[f]	NA	2.38	65.8	1.50	NA	1299[g]	12.0	42	0.39	30	0.27	42
600	0.0	11.6	27.0	7.5	16.83[f]	NA	2.32	64.1	1.45	NA	1348[g]	11.6	43	0.37	31	0.27	45
650	0.0	12.4	28.2	7.8	17.41[f]	NA	2.28	63.0	1.41	NA	1394[g]	11.3	45	0.36	33	0.26	48

APPENDIX TABLE 27   (Continued).

Bulls, Maintenance and Regaining Body Condition

WEIGHT[a], kg	DAILY GAIN[b], kg	DAILY DM[c], kg	ENERGY DAILY ME, Mcal	ENERGY DAILY TDN, kg	ENERGY DAILY NE$_m$, Mcal	ENERGY DAILY NE$_g$, Mcal	ENERGY IN DIET DM ME, Mcal/kg	ENERGY IN DIET DM TDN, %	ENERGY IN DIET DM NE$_m$, Mcal/kg	ENERGY IN DIET DM NE$_g$, Mcal/kg	TOTAL PROTEIN DAILY, g	TOTAL PROTEIN IN DIET DM, %	CALCIUM DAILY, g	CALCIUM IN DIET DM, %	PHOSPHORUS DAILY, g	PHOSPHORUS IN DIET DM, %	VITAMIN A[d] DAILY, 1000's IU
<650	For growth and development use requirements for bulls in Tables 1, 2, and 3.																
650	0.4	12.3	24.3	6.7	9.91	2.06	1.98	54.8	1.13	0.57	904	7.4	25	0.20	23	0.19	48
650	0.6	12.6	26.7	7.4	9.91	3.21	2.11	58.4	1.25	0.69	957	7.6	27	0.21	24	0.19	49
650	0.8	12.8	28.7	7.9	9.91	4.40	2.24	62.0	1.37	0.79	998	7.8	29	0.23	25	0.20	50
700	0.4	13.0	25.7	7.1	10.48	2.18	1.98	54.8	1.13	0.57	942	7.3	26	0.20	25	0.20	51
700	0.6	13.4	28.2	7.8	10.48	3.40	2.11	58.4	1.25	0.69	994	7.4	29	0.22	26	0.20	52
700	0.8	13.5	30.3	8.4	10.48	4.66	2.24	62.0	1.37	0.79	1032	7.6	30	0.22	26	0.19	53
800	0.0	12.9	22.6	6.3	11.58	NA	1.75	48.4	0.91	NA	882	6.8	27	0.21	27	0.21	50
800	0.2	13.7	25.5	7.1	11.58	1.12	1.86	51.5	1.02	0.47	956	7.0	27	0.20	27	0.20	53
900	0.0	14.1	24.7	6.8	12.65	NA	1.75	48.4	0.91	NA	958	6.8	30	0.21	30	0.21	55
900	0.2	15.0	27.9	7.7	12.65	1.23	1.86	51.5	1.02	0.47	1031	6.9	31	0.21	31	0.21	58
1000	0.0	15.3	26.8	7.4	13.69	NA	1.75	48.4	0.91	NA	1032	6.8	33	0.22	33	0.22	60

[a]Average weight for a feeding period.

[b]Approximately 0.4 ± 0.1 kg of weight gain/day over the last third of pregnancy is accounted for by the products of conception. Daily 2.15 Mcal of NE$_m$ and 55 g of protein are provided for this requirement for a calf with a birth weight of 36 kg.

[c]Dry matter consumption should vary depending on the energy concentration of the diet and environmental conditions. These intakes are based on the energy concentration shown in the table and assuming a thermoneutral environment without snow or mud conditions. If the energy concentrations of the diet to be fed exceed the tabular value, limit feeding may be required.

[d]Vitamin A requirements per kilogram of diet are 2800 IU for pregnant heifers and cows and 3900 IU for lactating cows and breeding bulls.

[e]Not applicable.

[f]Includes .75 Mcal NE$_m$/kg of milk produced.

[g]Includes 33.5 g protein/kg of milk produced.

APPENDIX TABLE 28 Daily nutrient requirements of dairy cattle. (From 1978 NRC Publication on Dairy Cattle)

BODY WEIGHT, kg	BREED SIZE, AGE, wk	DAILY GAIN, g	FEED DM, kg	NE$_m$, Mcal	NE$_g$, Mcal	ME, Mcal	DE, Mcal	TDN, kg	TOTAL CRUDE PROTEIN, g	Ca, g	P, g	A, 1,000 IU	D, IU
Growing Dairy Heifer and Bull Calves Fed Only Milk													
25	S-1[a,b]	300	0.45	0.83	0.53	2.14	2.38	0.54	111	6	4	1.1	165
30	S-3	350	0.52	0.95	0.63	2.49	2.77	0.63	128	7	4	1.3	200
42	L-1	400	0.63	1.25	0.70	2.98	3.31	0.75	148	8	5	1.8	280
50	L-3	500	0.76	1.40	0.90	3.61	4.01	0.91	180	9	6	2.1	330
Growing Dairy Heifer and Bull Calves Fed Mixed diets													
50	S-10	300	1.31	1.45	0.57	3.91	4.45	1.01	150	9	6	2.1	330
50		400	1.40	1.45	0.76	4.36	4.94	1.12	176	9	6	2.1	330
50	L-3	500	1.45	1.45	0.96	4.82	5.42	1.23	198	10	6	2.1	330
50		600	1.45	1.45	1.16	5.01	5.69	1.29	221	11	7	2.1	330
50		700	1.45	1.45	1.35	5.36	5.95	1.35	243	12	7	2.1	330
75		300	2.10	1.96	0.58	5.17	6.05	1.37	232	11	7	3.2	495
75		400	2.10	1.96	0.77	5.56	6.53	1.46	254	12	7	3.2	495
75	S-19	500	2.10	1.96	0.98	5.96	6.94	1.55	275	13	7	3.2	495
75		600	2.10	1.96	1.17	6.36	7.31	1.64	296	14	8	3.2	495
75	L-10	700	2.10	1.96	1.37	6.71	7.67	1.72	318	15	8	3.2	495
75		800	2.10	1.96	1.56	7.08	7.94	1.80	341	16	8	3.2	495
Growing Dairy Heifers													
100		300	2.80	2.43	0.60	6.27	7.45	1.69	317	17	7	4.2	660
100		400	2.80	2.43	0.84	6.78	7.96	1.81	336	15	8	4.2	660
100	S-26	500	2.80	2.43	1.05	7.17	8.35	1.89	360	16	8	4.2	660
100		600	2.80	2.43	1.26	7.64	8.81	2.00	380	17	9	4.2	660
100	L-16	700	2.80	2.43	1.47	8.09	9.26	2.10	402	18	9	4.2	660
100		800	2.80	2.43	1.68	8.47	9.63	2.18	426	19	10	4.2	660
150		300	4.00	3.30	0.72	8.44	10.14	2.30	433	16	10	6.4	990
150		400	4.00	3.30	0.96	8.90	10.59	2.40	455	17	11	6.4	990
150	S-40	500	4.00	3.30	1.20	9.42	11.11	2.52	474	17	11	6.4	990
150		600	4.00	3.30	1.44	9.97	11.65	2.64	491	18	11	6.4	990
150	L-26	700	4.00	3.30	1.68	10.49	12.17	2.76	510	19	12	6.4	990
150		800	4.00	3.30	1.92	11.03	12.70	2.88	528	20	12	6.4	990
200		300	5.00	4.10	0.84	10.44	12.57	2.85	533	18	12	8.5	1320
200		400	5.20	4.10	1.12	11.20	13.41	3.04	571	19	13	8.5	1320
200	S-54	500	5.20	4.10	1.40	11.86	14.06	3.19	586	20	13	8.5	1320
200		600	5.20	4.10	1.68	12.39	14.59	3.31	604	21	14	8.5	1320

APPENDIX TABLE 28 (*Continued*).

BODY WEIGHT, kg	BREED SIZE, AGE wk	DAILY GAIN, g	FEED DM, kg	NEm, Mcal	NEg, Mcal	ME, Mcal	DE, Mcal	TDN, kg	TOTAL CRUDE PROTEIN, g	Ca, g	P, g	A, 1,000 IU	D, IU
200	L-36	700	5.20	4.10	1.96	13.01	15.20	3.45	620	21	14	8.5	1320
200		800	5.20	4.10	2.24	13.52	15.70	3.56	640	22	15	8.5	1320
250		300	5.89	4.84	0.93	12.05	14.55	3.30	610	20	15	10.6	1650
250		400	6.30	4.84	1.24	13.15	15.83	3.59	665	21	15	10.6	1650
250	S-69	500	6.30	4.84	1.55	13.81	16.49	3.74	678	22	16	10.6	1650
250		600	6.30	4.84	1.86	14.57	17.24	3.91	689	22	16	10.6	1650
250	L-47	700	6.30	4.84	2.17	15.20	17.86	4.05	704	23	17	10.6	1650
250		800	6.30	4.84	2.48	15.82	18.47	4.19	719	23	17	10.6	1650
300		300	6.67	5.55	1.02	13.64	16.47	3.74	671	20	15	12.7	1980
300		400	7.00	5.55	1.36	14.80	17.77	4.03	713	22	17	12.7	1980
300	S-83	500	7.20	5.55	1.70	15.69	18.74	4.25	746	23	17	12.7	1980
300		600	7.20	5.55	2.04	16.49	19.53	4.43	755	23	17	12.7	1980
300	L-57	700	7.20	5.55	2.38	17.07	20.11	4.56	771	24	18	12.7	1980
300		800	7.20	5.55	2.72	17.83	20.86	4.73	782	24	18	12.7	1980
350		300	7.23	6.24	1.08	15.27	18.34	4.16	701	22	16	14.8	2310
350	S-97	400	7.42	6.24	1.44	15.99	19.14	4.34	738	23	17	14.8	2310
350		500	8.00	6.24	1.80	17.42	20.81	4.72	804	25	18	14.8	2310
350		600	8.00	6.24	2.16	18.21	21.60	4.90	812	25	19	14.8	2310
350	L-67	700	8.00	6.24	2.52	18.88	22.26	5.05	826	25	19	14.8	2310
350		800	8.00	6.24	2.88	19.56	22.93	5.20	841	26	19	14.8	2310
400	S-115	200	7.26	6.89	0.76	14.85	17.94	4.07	692	21	16	17.0	2640
400		400	8.50	6.89	1.52	17.76	21.38	4.85	833	24	19	17.0	2640
400		600	8.60	6.89	2.28	19.61	23.24	5.27	856	25	20	17.0	2640
400	L-77	700	8.60	6.89	2.66	20.40	24.03	5.45	864	25	20	17.0	2640
400		800	8.60	6.89	3.04	21.11	24.73	5.65	876	26	21	17.0	2640
450		200	7.87	7.52	0.80	16.09	19.44	4.41	749	23	18	19.1	2970
450		400	9.00	7.52	1.60	19.02	22.84	5.18	867	26	20	19.1	2970
450		600	9.10	7.52	2.40	21.03	24.87	5.64	883	27	21	19.1	2970
450	L-87	700	9.10	7.52	2.80	21.82	25.66	5.82	892	27	21	19.1	2970
450		800	9.10	7.52	3.20	22.67	26.50	6.01	898	28	21	19.1	2970
500		200	8.46	8.14	0.84	17.30	20.90	4.74	788	24	19	21.2	3300
500		400	9.50	8.14	1.68	20.26	24.29	5.51	900	27	21	21.2	3300
500	L-98	600	9.50	8.14	2.52	22.26	26.28	5.96	903	27	21	21.2	3300
500		800	9.50	8.14	3.36	24.00	28.00	6.35	916	28	21	21.2	3300
550		200	9.05	8.75	0.88	18.50	22.34	5.07	835	25	19	23.3	3930

550	L-109	400	9.80	8.75	1.76	21.33	25.48	5.78	913	27	20	23.3	3930
550		600	9.80	8.75	2.64	23.28	27.51	6.24	914	27	20	23.3	3630
550		800	9.80	8.75	3.52	25.08	29.19	6.62	928	28	21	23.3	3630
600	L-127	200	9.58	9.33	0.90	19.60	23.68	5.37	879	25	18	25.4	3960
600		300	9.72	9.33	1.35	20.78	24.87	5.64	895	25	18	25.4	3960
600		400	10.00	9.33	1.80	22.22	26.45	6.00	918	26	19	25.4	3960
600		500	10.00	9.33	2.25	23.34	27.56	6.25	916	26	19	25.4	3960

Growing Dairy Bulls

100	S-26	500	2.80	2.43	1.05	7.17	8.35	1.89	361	16	8	4.2	660
100		600	2.80	2.43	1.26	7.64	8.81	2.00	381	17	9	4.2	660
100		700	2.80	2.43	1.47	8.09	9.26	2.10	403	18	9	4.2	660
100	L-15	800	2.80	2.43	1.68	8.47	9.63	2.18	427	19	10	4.2	660
100		900	2.80	2.43	1.89	8.84	10.00	2.27	450	20	10	4.2	660
150		500	4.00	3.30	1.15	9.42	11.11	2.52	476	18	11	6.4	990
150		600	4.00	3.30	1.38	9.91	11.59	2.63	497	19	11	6.4	990
150	S-38	700	4.00	3.30	1.61	10.30	11.98	2.72	520	20	12	6.4	990
150		800	4.00	3.30	1.84	10.84	12.52	2.84	539	21	12	6.4	990
150		900	4.00	3.30	2.07	11.47	13.14	2.98	555	21	13	6.4	990
150		1000	4.00	3.30	2.30	11.73	13.40	3.04	583	22	13	6.4	990
200	L-24	500	5.20	4.10	1.25	11.46	13.66	3.10	602	20	13	8.5	1320
200		600	5.20	4.10	1.50	12.01	14.21	3.22	622	21	14	8.5	1320
200		700	5.20	4.10	1.75	12.59	14.78	3.35	640	21	14	8.5	1320
200	S-48	800	5.20	4.10	2.00	13.07	15.26	3.46	660	22	15	8.5	1320
200		900	5.20	4.10	2.25	13.52	15.70	3.56	688	23	16	8.5	1320
200		1000	5.20	4.10	2.50	14.05	16.23	3.68	702	23	16	8.5	1320
250	L-31	500	6.30	4.84	1.35	13.44	16.11	3.65	684	22	16	10.6	1650
250		600	6.30	4.84	1.62	14.00	16.67	3.78	702	23	16	10.6	1650
250		700	6.30	4.84	1.89	14.62	17.28	3.92	718	23	17	10.6	1650
250	S-58	800	6.30	4.84	2.16	15.20	17.86	4.05	736	24	17	10.6	1650
250		900	6.30	4.84	2.43	15.78	18.43	4.18	753	25	17	10.6	1650
250		1000	6.30	4.84	2.70	16.13	18.78	4.26	778	25	18	10.6	1650
300	L-38	500	7.33	5.69	1.48	15.45	18.56	4.21	777	24	18	12.7	1980
300		600	7.40	5.69	1.77	16.13	19.27	4.37	800	25	19	12.7	1980
300		700	7.40	5.69	2.07	16.89	20.02	4.54	811	26	19	12.7	1980
300	S-68	800	7.40	5.69	2.36	17.51	20.63	4.68	827	26	19	12.7	1980
300		900	7.40	5.69	2.66	18.09	21.21	4.81	845	27	19	12.7	1980
300		1000	7.40	5.69	2.95	18.67	21.78	4.94	862	27	20	12.7	1980
350	L-45	500	8.10	6.54	1.60	17.27	20.71	4.70	828	25	19	14.8	2310
350		600	8.30	6.54	1.92	18.13	21.65	4.91	863	26	20	14.8	2310

APPENDIX TABLE 28 (*Continued*).

BODY WEIGHT, kg	BREED SIZE, AGE, wk	DAILY GAIN, g	FEED DM, kg	NE_m, Mcal	NE_g, Mcal	ME, Mcal	DE, Mcal	TDN, kg	TOTAL CRUDE PROTEIN, g	Ca, g	P, g	A, 1,000 IU	D, IU
350	S-79	700	8.30	6.54	2.24	18.93	22.44	5.09	873	27	20	14.8	2310
350		800	8.30	6.54	2.56	19.60	23.10	5.24	887	27	20	14.8	2310
350		900	8.30	6.54	2.88	20.22	23.72	5.38	903	28	20	14.8	2310
350	L-52	1000	8.30	6.54	3.20	20.89	24.38	5.53	917	28	21	14.8	2310
400		500	9.00	7.41	1.75	19.24	23.06	5.23	891	27	21	17.0	2640
400		600	9.00	7.41	2.10	20.00	23.81	5.40	902	27	21	17.0	2640
400	S-89	700	9.00	7.41	2.45	20.84	24.64	5.59	910	28	22	17.0	2640
400		800	9.00	7.41	2.80	21.60	25.40	5.76	921	28	22	17.0	2640
400		900	9.00	7.41	3.15	22.36	26.15	5.93	932	28	22	17.0	2640
400	L-60	1000	9.00	7.41	3.50	22.93	26.72	6.06	947	29	23	17.0	2640
450		200	8.41	8.27	0.76	17.20	20.77	4.71	762	23	19	19.1	2970
450		400	9.33	8.27	1.52	19.90	23.86	5.41	868	27	21	19.1	2970
450	S-90	600	9.50	8.27	2.28	21.83	25.84	5.86	898	28	22	19.1	2970
450		800	9.50	8.27	3.04	23.52	27.52	6.24	914	28	22	19.1	2970
450	L-67	1000	9.50	8.27	3.80	25.08	29.07	6.59	934	29	23	19.1	2970
500		100	8.26	8.95	0.40	16.90	20.41	4.63	740	22	18	21.2	3300
500		300	9.30	8.95	1.20	19.83	23.77	5.39	855	25	21	21.2	3300
500	S-111	500	10.00	8.95	2.00	22.22	26.45	6.00	941	28	23	21.2	3300
500		700	10.00	8.95	2.80	23.60	27.82	6.31	967	29	23	21.2	3300
500	L-74	900	10.00	8.95	3.60	25.56	29.76	6.75	973	29	23	21.2	3300
550		100	8.86	9.62	0.42	18.11	21.87	4.96	789	24	18	23.3	3630
550		300	10.20	9.62	1.25	21.29	25.62	5.81	935	28	22	23.3	3630
550	S-125	500	10.50	9.62	2.08	23.56	28.00	6.35	967	29	22	23.3	3630
550	L-82	700	10.50	9.62	2.91	25.51	29.94	6.79	976	29	22	23.3	3630
550		900	10.50	9.62	3.74	27.16	31.57	7.16	994	30	23	23.3	3630
600	S-149	100	9.42	10.27	0.43	19.27	23.28	5.28	833	25	19	25.4	3960
600		300	10.52	10.27	1.29	22.44	26.90	6.10	947	28	22	25.4	3960
600		500	10.80	10.27	2.15	24.72	29.28	6.64	980	29	23	25.4	3960
600	L-92	700	10.80	10.27	3.01	26.58	31.13	7.06	988	29	23	25.4	3960
650		100	9.96	10.90	0.44	20.37	24.60	5.58	875	26	20	27.6	4290
650		300	10.69	10.90	1.32	23.29	27.82	6.31	947	28	22	27.6	4290

650	L-102	500	11.10	10.90	2.20	25.75	30.44	6.90	992	29	23	27.6	4290
650		700	11.10	10.90	3.08	27.78	32.45	7.36	995	29	23	27.6	4290
700		100	10.51	11.53	0.45	21.50	25.97	5.89	918	27	21	29.7	4620
700		300	11.40	11.53	1.35	24.61	29.45	6.68	1005	29	23	29.7	4620
700	L-117	500	11.40	11.53	2.25	26.94	31.75	7.20	998	30	23	29.7	4620
700		700	11.40	11.53	3.15	28.99	33.78	7.66	1001	30	23	29.7	4620
750		100	11.02	12.14	0.45	22.53	27.21	6.17	960	28	22	31.8	4950
750	L-131	300	11.70	12.14	1.35	25.48	30.44	6.90	1024	30	23	31.8	4950
750		500	11.70	12.14	2.25	27.86	32.80	7.44	1014	30	23	31.8	4950
800		100	11.52	12.74	0.45	23.55	28.44	6.45	999	29	23	33.9	5280
800		300	12.00	12.74	1.35	26.35	31.44	7.13	1040	30	23	33.9	5280
800		500	12.00	12.74	2.25	28.62	33.68	7.64	1035	30	23	33.9	5280

Growing Veal Calves Fed Only Milk

35	—	500	0.67	0.98	0.90	3.17	3.52	0.80	173	7	4	1.5	231
45	L-1.0	800	1.06	1.36	1.52	5.04	5.60	1.27	259	8	5	1.9	297
55	L-2.8	900	1.20	1.55	1.73	5.74	6.38	1.45	292	11	7	2.3	363
65	L-4.4	1000	1.36	1.76	1.95	6.48	7.20	1.63	324	13	8	2.8	429
75	L-5.8	1050	1.48	1.96	2.10	7.05	7.83	1.78	334	15	9	3.2	495
100	L-9.2	1100	1.69	2.43	2.31	8.05	8.94	2.03	357	17	10	4.2	660
125	L-12.4	1200	1.95	2.88	2.64	9.30	10.33	2.34	392	19	11	5.3	825
150	L-15.4	1300	2.22	3.30	2.99	10.58	11.75	2.66	428	20	12	6.4	990

Maintenance of Mature Breeding Bulls

500	—	—	7.80	9.36	—	15.95	19.27	4.37	673	20	15	21	—
600	—	—	8.95	10.74	—	18.29	22.09	5.01	766	23	17	25	—
700	—	—	10.04	12.05	—	20.52	24.78	5.62	852	26	19	30	—
800	—	—	11.10	13.32	—	22.52	27.20	6.17	942	29	21	34	—
900	—	—	12.13	14.55	—	24.79	29.94	6.79	1017	31	23	38	—
1000	—	—	13.12	15.75	—	26.83	32.41	7.35	1093	34	25	42	—
1100	—	—	14.10	16.91	—	28.84	34.83	7.90	1169	36	27	47	—
1200	—	—	15.05	18.05	—	30.77	37.17	8.42	1244	39	29	51	—
1300	—	—	15.98	19.17	—	32.67	39.46	8.95	1316	41	31	55	—
1400	—	—	16.88	20.27	—	34.49	41.66	9.45	1386	43	33	59	—

aBreed size: S for small breeds (e.g., Jersey); L is for large breeds (e.g., Holstein).
bAge in weeks indicates probable age of S or L animals when they reach the weight indicated.

APPENDIX TABLE 29   Daily nutrient requirements of lactating and pregnant cows. (From 1978 NRC Publication on Dairy Cattle)

| BODY WEIGHT, kg | FEED ENERGY | | | | TOTAL CRUDE PROTEIN, g | CALCIUM, g | PHOSPHORUS, g | VITAMIN A, 1,000 IU |
	NE$_\ell$, Mcal	ME, Mcal	DE, Mcal	TDN, kg				
Maintenance of Mature Lactating Cows[a]								
350	6.47	10.76	12.54	2.85	341	14	11	27
400	7.16	11.90	13.86	3.15	373	15	13	30
450	7.82	12.99	15.14	3.44	403	17	14	34
500	8.46	14.06	16.39	3.72	432	18	15	38
550	9.09	15.11	17.60	4.00	461	20	16	42
600	9.70	16.12	18.79	4.27	489	21	17	46
650	10.30	17.12	19.95	4.53	515	22	18	50
700	10.89	18.10	21.09	4.79	542	24	19	53
750	11.47	19.06	22.21	5.07	567	25	20	57
800	12.03	20.01	23.32	5.29	592	27	21	61
Maintenance Plus Last 2 Months of Gestation of Mature Dry Cows								
350	8.42	14.00	16.26	3.71	642	23	16	27
400	9.30	15.47	17.98	4.10	702	26	18	30
450	10.16	16.90	19.64	4.47	763	29	20	34
500	11.00	18.29	21.25	4.84	821	31	22	38
550	11.81	19.65	22.83	5.20	877	34	24	42
600	12.61	20.97	24.37	5.55	931	37	26	46
650	13.39	22.27	25.87	5.90	984	39	28	50
700	14.15	23.54	27.35	6.23	1035	42	30	53
750	14.90	24.79	28.81	6.56	1086	45	32	57
800	15.64	26.02	30.24	6.89	1136	47	34	61
Milk Production—Nutrients Per kg Milk of Different Fat Percentages								
Fat %								
2.5	0.59	0.99	1.15	0.260	72	2.40	1.65	
3.0	0.64	1.07	1.24	0.282	77	2.50	1.70	
3.5	0.69	1.16	1.34	0.304	82	2.60	1.75	
4.0	0.74	1.24	1.44	0.326	87	2.70	1.80	
4.5	0.78	1.31	1.52	0.344	92	2.80	1.85	
5.0	0.83	1.39	1.61	0.365	98	2.90	1.90	
5.5	0.88	1.48	1.71	0.387	103	3.00	2.00	
6.0	0.93	1.56	1.81	0.410	108	3.10	2.05	
Body Weight Change During Lactation—Nutrients Per kg Weight Change								
Weight loss	−4.92	−8.25	−9.55	−2.17	−320			
Weight gain	5.12	8.55	9.96	2.26	500			

[a]To allow for growth of young lactating cows, increase the maintenance allowances for all nutrients except vitamin A by 20% during the first lactation and 10% during the second lactation.

APPENDIX TABLE 30 Recommended nutrients content of rations for dairy cattle. (From NRC Publication #3 on Dairy Cattle)

	LACTATING COW RATIONS				NONLACTATING CATTLE RATIONS					MAXIMUM CONCENTRATIONS (ALL CLASSES)
NUTRIENTS (CONCENTRATION IN THE FEED DRY MATTER)	COW WT, kg ≤400	500	600	≥700	DRY PREGNANT COWS	MATURE BULLS	GROWING HEIFERS AND BULLS	CALF STARTER CONCENTRATE MIX	CALF MILK REPLACER	
DAILY MILK YIELDS, KG	<8	<11	<14	<18						
	8–13	11–17	14–21	18–26						
	13–18	17–23	21–29	26–35						
	>18	>23	>29	>35						
RATION NO.	I	II	III	IV	V	VI	VII	VIII	IX	MAX.
Crude protein, %	13.0	14.0	15.0	16.0	11.0	8.5	12.0	16.0	22.0	—
Energy										
NE_l, Mcal/kg	1.42	1.52	1.62	1.72	1.35	—	—	—	—	—
NE_m, Mcal/kg	—	—	—	—	—	1.20	1.26	1.90	2.40	—
NE_g, Mcal/kg	—	—	—	—	—	—	0.60	1.20	1.55	—
ME, Mcal/kg	2.36	2.53	2.71	2.89	2.23	2.04	2.23	3.12	3.78	—
DE, Mcal/kg	2.78	2.95	3.13	3.31	2.65	2.47	2.65	3.53	4.19	—
TDN, %	63	67	71	75	60	56	60	80	95	—
Crude fiber, %	17	17	17	17[a]	17	15	15	—	—	—
Acid detergent fiber, %	21	21	21	21	21	19	19	—	—	—
Ether extract, %	2	2	2	2	2	2	2	2	10	—
Minerals[b]										
Calcium, %	0.43	0.48	0.54	0.60	0.37	0.24	0.40	0.60	0.70	—
Phosphorus, %	0.31	0.34	0.38	0.40	0.26	0.18	0.26	0.43	0.50	—
Magnesium, %[c]	0.20	0.20	0.20	0.20	0.16	0.16	0.16	0.07	0.07	—
Potassium, %	0.80	0.80	0.80	0.80	0.80	0.80	0.80	0.80	0.80	—
Sodium, %	0.18	0.18	0.18	0.18	0.10	0.10	0.10	0.10	0.10	—
Sodium chloride, %[d]	0.46	0.46	0.46	0.46	0.25	0.25	0.25	0.25	0.25	5
Sulfur, %[d]	0.20	0.20	0.20	0.20	0.17	0.11	0.16	0.21	0.29	0.35
Iron, ppm[d,e]	50	50	50	50	50	50	50	100	100	1,000
Cobalt, ppm	0.10	0.10	0.10	0.10	0.10	0.10	0.10	0.10	0.10	10
Copper, ppm[d,f]	10	10	10	10	10	10	10	10	10	80
Manganese, ppm[d]	40	40	40	40	40	40	40	40	40	1,000

APPENDIX TABLE 30 (Continued).

NUTRIENTS (CONCENTRATION IN THE FEED DRY MATTER)	LACTATING COW RATIONS — DAILY MILK YIELDS, KG (COW WT, kg: ≤400 / 500 / 600 / ≥700)				NONLACTATING CATTLE RATIONS					
	<8 / <11 / <14 / <18	8–13 / 11–17 / 14–21 / 18–26	13–18 / 17–23 / 21–29 / 26–35	>18 / >23 / >29 / >35	DRY PREGNANT COWS	MATURE BULLS	GROWING HEIFERS AND BULLS	CALF STARTER CONCENTRATE MIX	CALF MILK REPLACER	MAXIMUM CONCENTRATIONS (ALL CLASSES)
Zinc, ppm[d,g]	40	40	40	40	40	40	40	40	40	500
Iodine, ppm[h]	0.25	0.25	0.25	0.25	0.25	0.25	0.50	0.50	0.50	50
Molybdenum, ppm[i,j]	—	—	—	—	—	—	—	—	—	6
Selenium, ppm	0.10	0.10	0.10	0.10	0.10	0.10	0.10	0.10	0.10	5
Fluorine, ppm[j]	—	—	—	—	—	—	—	—	—	30
Vitamins[k]										
Vit. A, IU/kg	3,200	3,200	3,200	3,200	3,800	—	2,200	3,200	3,200	—
Vit. D, IU/kg	300	300	300	300	600	—	300	300	300	—
Vit. E, ppm	—	—	—	—	300	—	—	—	—	—

[a] It is difficult to formulate high-energy rations with a minimum of 17% crude fiber. However, fat percentage depression may occur when rations with less than 17% crude fiber or 21% ADF are fed to lactating cows.

[b] The mineral values presented in this table are intended as guidelines for use of professionals in ration formulation. Because of many factors affecting such values, they are not intended and should not be used as a legal or regulatory base.

[c] Under conditions conducive to grass tetany, should be increased to 0.25 or higher.

[d] The maximum safe levels for many of the mineral elements are not well defined; estimates given here, especially for sulfur, sodium chloride, iron, copper, zinc, and manganese, are based on very limited data; safe levels may be substantially affected by specific feeding conditions.

[e] The maximum safe level of supplemental iron in some forms is materially lower than 1,000 ppm. As little as 400 ppm added iron as ferrous sulfate has reduced weight gains.

[f] High copper may increase the susceptibility of milk to oxidized flavor.

[g] Maximum safe level of zinc for mature dairy cattle is 1,000 ppm.

[h] If diet contains as much as 25% strongly goitrogenic feed on dry basis, iodine provided should be increased two times or more.

[i] If diet contains sufficient copper, dairy cattle tolerate substantially more than 6 ppm molybdenum.

[j] Maximum safe level of fluorine for growing heifers and bulls is lower than for other dairy cattle. Somewhat higher levels are tolerated when the fluorine is from less-available sources such as phosphates. Minimum requirement for molybdenum and fluorine not yet established.

[k] The following minimum quantities of B-complex vitamins are suggested per unit of milk replacer: niacin, 2.6 ppm; pantothenic acid, 13 ppm; riboflavin, 6.5 ppm; pyridoxine, 6.5 ppm; thiamine, 6.5 ppm; folic acid, 0.5 ppm; biotin, 0.1 ppm; vitamin B_{12}, 0.07 ppm; choline, 0.26 percent. It appears that adequate amounts of these vitamins are furnished when calves have functional rumens (usually at 6 weeks of age) by a combination of rumen synthesis and natural feedstuffs.

APPENDIX TABLE 31 Nutrient requirements of Leghorn-type chickens as percentages or as milligrams or units per kilogram of diet. (From 1984 NRC Publication on Poultry)

| ENERGY BASE Kcal ME/kg diet[a] | → | GROWING | | | LAYING | | BREEDING |
		0–6 WEEKS 2,900	6–14 WEEKS 2,900	14–20 WEEKS 2,900	2,900	DAILY INTAKE PER HEN (mg)[b]	2,900
Protein	%	18	15	12	14.5	16,000	14.5
Arginine	%	1.00	0.83	0.67	0.68	750	0.68
Glycine and Serine	%	0.70	0.58	0.47	0.50	550	0.50
Histidine	%	0.26	0.22	0.17	0.16	180	0.16
Isoleucine	%	0.60	0.50	0.40	0.50	550	0.50
Leucine	%	1.00	0.83	0.67	0.73	800	0.73
Lysine	%	0.85	0.60	0.45	0.64	700	0.64
Methionine + cystine	%	0.60	0.50	0.40	0.55	600	0.55
Methionine	%	0.30	0.25	0.20	0.32	350	0.32
Phenylalanine + tyrosine	%	1.00	0.83	0.67	0.80	880	0.80
Phenylalanine	%	0.54	0.45	0.36	0.40	440	0.40
Threonine	%	0.68	0.57	0.37	0.45	500	0.45
Tryptophan	%	0.17	0.14	0.11	0.14	150	0.14
Valine	%	0.62	0.52	0.41	0.55	600	0.55
Linoleic acid	%	1.00	1.00	1.00	1.00	1,100	1.00
Calcium	%	0.80	0.70	0.60	3.40	3,750	3.40
Phosphorus, available	%	0.40	0.35	0.30	0.32	350	0.32
Potassium	%	0.40	0.30	0.25	0.15	165	0.15
Sodium	%	0.15	0.15	0.15	0.15	165	0.15
Chlorine	%	0.15	0.12	0.12	0.15	165	0.15
Magnesium	mg	600	500	400	500	55	500

APPENDIX TABLE 31 (*Continued*).

ENERGY BASE Kcal ME/kg diet[a]	→	GROWING			LAYING		BREEDING
		0–6 WEEKS 2,900	6–14 WEEKS 2,900	14–20 WEEKS 2,900	2,900	DAILY INTAKE PER HEN (mg)[b]	2,900
Manganese	mg	60	30	30	30	3.30	60
Zinc	mg	40	35	35	50	5.50	65
Iron	mg	80	60	60	50	5.50	60
Copper	mg	8	6	6	6	0.88	8
Iodine	mg	0.35	0.35	0.35	0.30	0.30	0.30
Selenium	mg	0.15	0.10	0.10	0.10	0.01	0.10
Vitamin A	IU	1,500	1,500	1,500	4,000	440	4,000
Vitamin D	ICU	200	200	200	500	55	500
Vitamin E	IU	10	5	5	5	0.55	10
Vitamin K	mg	0.50	0.50	0.50	0.50	0.055	0.50
Riboflavin	mg	3.60	1.80	1.80	2.20	0.242	3.80
Pantothenic acid	mg	10.0	10.0	10.0	2.20	2.242	10.0
Niacin	mg	27.0	11.0	11.0	10.0	1.10	10.0
Vitamin B_{12}	mg	0.009	0.003	0.003	0.004	0.00044	0.004
Choline	mg	1,300	900	500	?	?	?
Biotin	mg	0.15	0.10	0.10	0.10	0.011	0.15
Folacin	mg	0.55	0.25	0.25	0.25	0.0275	0.35
Thiamin	mg	1.8	1.3	1.3	0.80	0.088	0.80
Pyridoxine	mg	3.0	3.0	3.0	3.0	0.33	4.50

[a]These are typical dietary energy concentrations.
[b]Assumes an average daily intake of 110 g of feed/hen daily.

APPENDIX TABLE 32   Body weights and feed requirements of Leghorn-type pullets and hens. (From 1984 NRC Publication on Poultry)

AGE, WEEKS	BODY WEIGHT[a], g	FEED CONSUMPTION[b], g/week	TYPICAL EGG PRODUCTION, HEN-DAY %
0	35	45	—
2	135	90	—
4	270	180	—
6	450	260	—
8	620	325	—
10	790	385	—
12	950	430	—
14	1,060	460	—
16	1,160	460	—
18	1,260	460	—
20	1,360	460	—
22	1,425	525	10
24	1,500	595	38
26	1,575	665	64
30	1,725	770	88
40	1,815	770	80
50	1,870	765	74
60	1,900	755	68
70	1,900	740	62

[a]Pullets and hens of Leghorn-type strains are generally fed ad libitum but are occasionally control-fed to limit body weights. Values shown are typical but will vary with strain differences, season, and lighting. Specific breeder guidelines should be consulted for desired schedules of weights and feed consumption.
[b]Based on diets containing 2,900 ME Kcal/kg. Consumption will vary depending upon the caloric density of the diet, environmental temperature, and rate of production.

APPENDIX TABLE 33   Nutrient requirements of broilers as percentages or as milligrams or units per kilogram of diet. (From 1984 NRC Publication on Poultry)

ENERGY BASE Kcal ME/kg diet[a]	→	WEEKS 0–3 3,200	WEEKS 3–6 3,200	WEEKS 6–8 3,200
Protein	%	23.0	20.0	18.0
Arginine	%	1.44	1.20	1.00
Glycine + Serine	%	1.50	1.00	0.70
Histidine	%	0.35	0.30	0.26
Isoleucine	%	0.80	0.70	0.60
Leucine	%	1.35	1.18	1.00
Lysine	%	1.20	1.00	0.85
Methionine + Cystine	%	0.93	0.72	0.60
Methionine	%	0.50	0.38	0.32
Phenylalanine + Tyrosine	%	1.34	1.17	1.00
Phenylalanine	%	0.72	0.63	0.54
Threonine	%	0.80	0.74	0.68
Tryptophan	%	0.23	0.18	0.17
Valine	%	0.82	0.72	0.62
Linoleic acid	%	1.00	1.00	1.00
Calcium	%	1.00	0.90	0.80
Phosphorus, available	%	0.45	0.40	0.35
Potassium	%	0.40	0.35	0.30
Sodium	%	0.15	0.15	0.15
Chlorine	%	0.15	0.15	0.15
Magnesium	mg	600	600	600
Manganese	mg	60.0	60.0	60.0
Zinc	mg	40.0	40.0	40.0
Iron	mg	80.0	80.0	80.0
Copper	mg	8.0	8.0	8.0
Iodine	mg	0.35	0.35	0.35
Selenium	mg	0.15	0.15	0.15
Vitamin A	IU	1,500	1,500	1,500
Vitamin D	ICU	200	200	200
Vitamin E	IU	10	10	10
Vitamin K	mg	0.50	*0.50*	*0.50*
Riboflavin	mg	3.60	3.60	3.60
Pantothenic acid	mg	10.0	10.0	10.0
Niacin	mg	27.0	27.0	11.0
Vitamin B_{12}	mg	0.009	0.009	0.003
Choline	mg	1,300	*850*	*500*
Biotin	mg	0.15	0.15	*0.10*
Folacin	mg	0.55	0.55	*0.25*
Thiamin	mg	1.80	1.80	1.80
Pyridoxine	mg	3.0	3.0	*2.5*

[a]These are typical dietary energy concentrations.

APPENDIX TABLE 34   Body weights and feed requirements of broilers[a]. (From 1984 NRC Publication on Poultry)

AGE, WEEKS	BODY WEIGHTS, g		WEEKLY FEED CONSUMPTION, g		CUMULATIVE FEED CONSUMPTION, g		WEEKLY ENERGY CONSUMPTION, ME Kcal/BIRD		CUMULATIVE ENERGY CONSUMPTION, ME Kcal/BIRD	
	M	F	M	F	M	F	M	F	M	F
1	130	120	120	110	120	110	385	350	385	350
2	320	300	260	240	380	350	830	770	1,215	1,120
3	560	515	390	355	770	705	1,250	1,135	2,465	2,255
4	860	790	535	500	1,305	1,205	1,710	1,600	4,175	3,855
5	1,250	1,110	740	645	2,045	1,850	2,370	2,065	6,545	5,920
6	1,690	1,430	980	800	3,025	2,650	3,135	2,560	9,680	8,480
7	2,100	1,745	1,095	910	4,120	3,560	3,505	2,910	13,185	11,390
8	2,520	2,060	1,210	970	5,330	4,530	3,870	3,105	17,055	14,495
9	2,925	2,350	1,320	1,010	6,650	5,540	4,225	3,230	21,280	17,725

[a]Typical for broilers fed well-balanced diets containing 3,200 ME Kcal kg.

APPENDIX TABLE 35   Nutrient requirements of meat-type hens for breeding purposes[a].
(From 1984 NRC Publication on Poultry)

ENERGY BASE Kcal ME/kg diet	→	2,850[b]	DAILY INTAKE PER HEN (mg)
Protein	%	14.5	22,000
Arginine	%	0.74	1,110
Glycine + serine	%	0.62	932
Histidine	%	0.14	205
Isoleucine	%	0.57	850
Leucine	%	0.83	1,250
Lysine	%	0.51	765
Methionine + cystine	%	0.55	820
Methionine	%	0.35	520
Phenylalanine + tyrosine	%	0.75	1,112
Phenylalanine	%	0.41	610
Threonine	%	0.48	720
Tryptophan	%	0.13	190
Valine	%	0.63	950
Calcium	%	2.75	4,125
Phosphorus, available	%	0.25	375
Sodium	%	0.10	150

[a]Diets are generally fed on a limited intake basis to control body weight gains. Adjust quantity of feed offered based on desired body weights and egg production levels for specific breed or strain.
[b]Diets for laying hens generally are fed to provide daily energy intakes of 375 to 450 ME Kcal/day based on body weight, environmental temperature, and rate of egg production. Percentage of nutrients shown is typical of hens given 425 ME Kcal/day.

APPENDIX TABLE 36   Metabolizable energy required daily by chickens in relation to body weight and egg production.[a] (From 1984 NRC Publication on Poultry)

BODY WEIGHT kg	RATE OF EGG PRODUCTION (%)					
	0	50	60	70	80	90
	METABOLIZABLE ENERGY/HEN DAILY, Kcal[b]					
1.0	130	192	205	217	229	242
1.5	177	239	251	264	276	289
2.0	218	280	292	305	317	330
2.5	259	321	333	346	358	371
3.0	296	358	370	383	395	408
3.5	333	395	408	420	432	445

[a]A number of formulas have been suggested for prediction of the daily energy requirements of chickens. The formula used here was derived from that in *Effect of Environment on Nutrient Requirements of Domestic Animals* (NRC, 1981).

ME/hen daily = $W^{0.75} (173 - 1.95T) + 5.5\Delta W + 2.07EE$

where: W = body weight (kg),

T = ambient temperature (°C),

ΔW = change in body weight in g/day, and

EE = daily egg mass (g).

[b]Temperature of 22°, egg weight of 60 g, and no change in body weight were used in calculations.

APPENDIX TABLE 37 Nutrient requirements of turkeys as percentages or as milligrams or units per kilogram of feed. (From 1984 NRC Publication on Poultry)

		M: 0–4 / F: 0–4 / 2,800	4–8 / 4–8 / 2,900	8–12 / 8–11 / 3,000	12–16 / 11–14 / 3,100	16–20 / 14–17 / 3,200	20–24 / 17–20 / 3,300	HOLDING / 2,900	BREEDING HENS / 2,900
ENERGY BASE KCAL ME/KG DIET[b]	→			AGE (WEEKS)					
Protein	%	28	26	22	19	16.5	14	12	14
Arginine	%	1.6	1.5	1.25	1.1	0.95	0.8	0.6	0.6
Glycine + serine	%	1.0	0.9	0.8	0.7	0.6	0.5	0.4	0.5
Histidine	%	0.58	0.54	0.46	0.39	0.35	0.29	0.25	0.3
Isoleucine	%	1.1	1.0	0.85	0.75	0.65	0.55	0.45	0.5
Leucine	%	1.9	1.75	1.5	1.3	1.1	0.95	0.5	0.5
Lysine	%	1.6	1.5	1.3	1.0	0.8	0.65	0.5	0.6
Methionine + cystine	%	1.05	0.9	0.75	0.65	0.55	0.45	0.4	0.4
Methionine	%	0.53	0.45	0.38	0.33	0.28	0.23	0.2	0.2
Phenylalanine + tyrosine	%	1.8	1.65	1.4	1.2	1.05	0.9	0.8	1.0
Phenylalanine	%	1.0	0.9	0.8	0.7	0.6	0.5	0.4	0.55
Threonine	%	1.0	0.93	0.79	0.68	0.59	0.5	0.4	0.45
Tryptophan	%	0.26	0.24	0.2	0.18	0.15	0.13	0.1	0.13
Valine	%	1.2	1.1	0.94	0.8	0.7	0.6	0.5	0.58
Linoleic acid	%	1.0	1.0	0.8	0.8	0.8	0.8	0.8	1.0
Calcium	%	1.2	1.0	0.85	0.75	0.65	0.55	0.5	2.25
Phosphorus, available	%	0.6	0.5	0.42	0.38	0.32	0.28	0.25	0.35
Potassium	%	0.7	0.6	0.5	0.5	0.4	0.4	0.4	0.6
Sodium	%	0.17	0.15	0.12	0.12	0.12	0.12	0.12	0.15
Chlorine	%	0.15	0.14	0.14	0.12	0.12	0.12	0.12	0.12
Magnesium	mg	600	600	600	600	600	600	600	600

APPENDIX TABLE 37 (*Continued*).

					AGE (WEEKS)					
ENERGY BASE KCAL ME/KG DIET[b]	→	M: 0–4 F: 0–4 2,800	4–8 4–8 2,900	8–12 8–11 3,000	12–16 11–14 3,100	16–20 14–17 3,200	20–24 17–20 3,300	HOLDING 2,900	BREEDING HENS 2,900
Manganese	mg	60	60	60	60	60	60	60	60
Zinc	mg	75	65	50	40	40	40	40	65
Iron	mg	80	60	60	60	50	50	50	60
Copper	mg	8	8	6	6	6	6	6	8
Iodine	mg	0.4	0.4	0.4	0.4	0.4	0.4	0.4	0.4
Selenium	mg	0.2	0.2	0.2	0.2	0.2	0.2	0.2	0.2
Vitamin A	IU	4,000	4,000	4,000	4,000	4,000	4,000	4,000	4,000
Vitamin D[b]	ICU	900	900	900	900	900	900	900	900
Vitamin E	IU	12	12	10	10	10	10	10	25
Vitamin K	mg	1.0	1.0	0.8	0.8	0.8	0.8	0.8	1.0
Riboflavin	mg	3.6	3.6	3.0	3.0	2.5	2.5	2.5	4.0
Pantothenic acid	mg	11.0	11.0	9.0	9.0	9.0	9.0	9.0	16.0
Niacin	mg	70.0	70.0	50.0	50.0	40.0	40.0	40.0	30.0
Vitamin B$_{12}$	mg	0.003	0.003	0.003	0.003	0.003	0.003	0.003	0.003
Choline	mg	1,900	1,600	1,300	1,100	950	800	800	1,000
Biotin	mg	0.2	0.2	0.15	0.125	0.100	0.100	0.100	0.15
Folacin	mg	1.0	1.0	0.8	0.8	0.7	0.7	0.7	1.0
Thiamin	mg	2.0	2.0	2.0	2.00	2.0	2.0	2.0	2.0
Pyridoxine	mg	4.5	4.5	3.5	3.5	3.0	3.0	3.0	4.0

[a]These are typical ME concentrations for corn-soya diets. Different ME values may be appropriate if other ingredients predominate.
[b]These concentrations of vitamin D are satisfactory when the dietary concentration of calcium and available phosphorus conform with those in the table.

Glossary

A significant proportion of the terms defined in this glossary were taken directly from the glossary on pp. 499–510 of *Principles of Nutrition* by E. D. Wilson, K. H. Fisher, and M. E. Fuqua, 3rd ed., 1975, John Wiley and Sons, Inc., N.Y. In addition to the terms given, the reader interested in feed terms is directed to Appendix Glossary 1, Bulletin 479, Utah Agricultural Experiment Station, Utah State University, Logan, UT (1968) by L. E. Harris, J. M. Asplund, and E. W. Crampton, pp. 357–391.

ABOMASUM: fourth compartment of ruminant stomach; functions similarly to the true stomach of non-ruminant animals and is the most important compartment in the young ruminant.

ACETYLCHOLINE: an acetic acid ester of choline; normally present in many parts of the body; functions in the transmission of nerve impulses.

ACROLEIN: a volatile, irritating liquid—acrylic aldehyde, $CH_2{=}CH{\cdot}CHO$—that results from overheating fat; it is a decomposition product of glycerol.

ACTIVE TRANSPORT: the movement of substances (particularly electrolyte ions) across cell membranes, usually against a concentration gradient. Unlike diffusion or osmosis, active transport requires the expenditure of metabolic energy.

ADENINE: one of four nitrogenous bases found in DNA.

ADENOSINE TRIPHOSPHATASE (ATPASE): an enzyme in muscle that catalyzes the hydrolysis of the terminal phosphate group of adenine triphosphate.

ADENOSINE TRIPHOSPHATE (ATP): a compound that consists of one molecule each of adenine (a purine) and ribose (a 5-carbon atom sugar) and three molecules of phosphoric acid; it is required for energy transfer and the phosphorylation of compounds.

ADF: acid detergent fiber, the fraction of a feedstuff analyzed by the Van Soest scheme of detergent analysis used to divide carbohydrates in plant constituents into those highly available and poorly available to animals; ADF content of a feed reflects the amounts of carbohydrates not solubilized by acid detergent.

ADRENALINE: see epinephrine.

445

ALBUMIN: group of globular proteins; a major constituent of blood serum protein.

AMINE: a chemical compound formed from ammonia (NH_3) by replacement of one or more of the hydrogen atoms with hydrocarbon groups (—CH_3 or —C_2H_5 and others).

AMINO ACIDS: simplest organic structure of which proteins are formed; many different amino acids occur in nature of which about 10 (for most animals) are required in the diet; all have common property of containing a carboxyl group and an amino group on the adjacent C atom.

AMINO GROUP: a chemical structure, —NH_2; a constituent of all amino acids, attached to the C atom adjacent to the carboxy group.

ANEMIA: a deficiency in the blood of red cells, hemoglobin, or both.

HYPERCHROMIC ANEMIA: a decrease in hemoglobin that is proportionately much less than the decrease in the number of erythrocytes (where the color index is high).

HYPOCHROMIC ANEMIA: a decrease in hemoglobin that is proportionately much greater than the decrease in the number of erythrocytes (where the color index is low).

MACROCYTIC ANEMIA: a condition in which the erythrocytes are much larger than normal.

MEGALOBLASTIC ANEMIA: a condition in which there are megaloblasts in the bone marrow.

MICROCYTIC ANEMIA: an anemia in which the erythrocytes are smaller than normal.

NUTRITIONAL ANEMIA: hypochromic and microcytic anemia due to insufficient Fe, Cu, vitamin B_{12}, or other causes.

PERNICIOUS ANEMIA: macrocytic and hypochromic anemia due to lack of secretion of the intrinsic factor by the gastric mucous membrane (this factor is essential for the absorption of vitamin B_{12}.

ANTAGONIST: a substance that exerts a nullifying or opposing action to another substance.

ANTIBODY: a protein produced by the body in response to the presence of a foreign agent (antigen). Antibodies are part of the body's natural defense against invasion by foreign substances.

ANTIGEN: any substance not normally present in the body that produces an immune reaction upon introduction into the body.

ANTIOXIDANT: a substance that inhibits the oxidation of other compounds.

ANTIVITAMIN: a substance that interferes with the synthesis or metabolism of a vitamin.

ANUS: distal opening of the gastrointestinal tract through which undigested feed residues are excreted as feces.

APOFERRITIN: a protein in the mucosal cells of the small intestine; together with iron it forms the compound ferritin.

APPETITE: a desire for food or water; generally a long term phenomenon, in contrast to short term satiety.

ARACHIDONIC ACID: a 20-carbon atom fatty acid with four double bonds; in the body it is synthesized from the essential fatty acid linoleic acid.

ASCORBIC ACID (VITAMIN C): water soluble vitamin required in oxidation-reduction reactions (electron transport) and for normal tyrosine oxidation and collagen metabolism and in hydroxylation reactions (i.e., hydroxyproline from proline).

ASH: the residue remaining after complete combustion at 500 to 600°C of a feed or animal tissue or excreta during proximate analysis.

ATHEROSCLEROSIS: a condition in which the inner walls of the arteries have been thickened by deposits of plaques of lipid substances including cholesterol.

BASAL METABOLIC RATE: the basal metabolism expressed as kilocalories per unit of body size (square meter of body surface; weight to the three-fourths power ([$W^{3/4}$]).

BASAL METABOLISM: energy expenditure of the body at rest, under comfortable environmental conditions, and in the postabsorptive state (12 hours after the ingestion of food).

BERIBERI: a deficiency disease caused by an insufficient intake of thiamin and characterized by polyneuritis, edema (in some cases), emaciation, and cardiac disturbances (enlargement of the heart and an unusually rapid heartbeat).

BILE: secretion from the liver, containing metabolites such as cholesterol and important bile acid conjugates which aid in emulsification of fats for digestion and absorption.

BILE DUCT: tube carrying bile from liver to duodenal lumen.

BIOPSY: the removal and examination of tissue or other material from the living body, usually for diagnosis.

BIOTECHNOLOGY: any technique that uses living organisms or processes to make or modify products, to improve plants or animals, or to develop microorganisms for specific uses.

BIOTIN: water soluble vitamin required as a constituent of several enzymes related to energy and amino acid metabolism.

BMR: basal metabolic rate.

BOLUS: solid mass of ingesta regurgitated for remastication during rumination (secondary: a medicant or capsule administered orally in a discrete mass).

CALCITONIN (THYROCALCITONIN): a polypeptide secreted by the thyroid glands that lowers the level of calcium and phosphorus in the plasma.

CALCIUM (CA): mineral required as a structural component of the skeleton and for controlling excitability of nerve and muscle.

CALORIMETER: the equipment used to measure the heat generated in a system. In nutrition it is an instrument for measuring the amount of heat produced by a food on oxidation or by an individual.

CARBOXYL GROUP: a chemical structure —C—OH;

$$\begin{matrix} \\ \| \\ O \end{matrix}$$

a constituent of all amino acids and the characteristic group of all organic acids.

CARBOXYPEPTIDASE: a proteolytic digestive enzyme secreted by the pancreas; hydrolyzes peptides to amino acids.

CARTILAGE: a connective tissue characterized by nonvascularity (without blood vessels) and firm texture; consists of cells (chondrocytes), interstitial substance (matrix), and a ground substance (chondromucoid).

CASSAVA: a tropical plant of the spurge family with edible starchy roots.

CATALYST: a substance that either increases or decreases the rate of a particular chemical reaction without itself being consumed or permanently altered; enzymes are special chemical catalysts of biological origin.

CECUM: a blind pouch just distal to the small intestine and containing a large population of anerobic bacteria that ferment complex carbohydrates; appendix in humans corresponds loosely with a rudimentary cecum.

CELLULOSE: polymer of glucose in linkage resistant to hydrolysis by digestive enzymes.

CERULOPLASMIN: a copper-containing protein (an alpha-globulin) in blood plasma.

CHLORINE (CL): mineral required in regulation of extracellular osmotic pressure and in maintaining acid-base balance.

CHOLECYSTOKININ: hormone secreted by duodenal cells and perhaps by certain brain cells; release stimulated by fat in lumen of duodenum and perhaps by concentrations of metabolites in blood circulating in brain; causes gall bladder contraction and may exert short term effect on food intake.

CHOLIC ACID: a family of steroids comprising the bile acids; they are derived from cholesterol.

CHOLINE: water soluble vitamin required as a structural component of tissues (i.e., lecithin, sphingomyelin) and of acetylcholine and as a donor of labile methyl groups; there is no evidence for a role as a cofactor in enzymatic reactions.

CHROMIUM (CR): trace mineral required as trivalent ion for normal glucose metabolism.

CHYLOMICRON: a particle of emulsified fat present in lymph; they are especially numerous after a meal high in fat content.

CHYME: a semiliquid material produced by the action of gastric juice on ingested food; it is discharged from the stomach into the duodenum.

CHYMOTRYPSIN: a proteolytic digestive enzyme secreted by the pancreas.

CIRRHOSIS OF THE LIVER: a progressive destruction of the liver cells and an abnormal increase of connective tissue.

CITRIC ACID CYCLE: the major series of pathways through which carbohydrates are oxidized to produce energy in animal cells.

COBALT (CO): trace mineral required as a constituent of vitamin B_{12}.

COENZYME: an organic molecule that is required for the activation of an apoenzyme to an enzyme. The vitamin coenzymes are niacin, pyridoxine, thiamin, riboflavin, pantothenic acid, and folic acid.

COENZYME A: a complex molecule containing pantothenic acid; it is required for fatty acid oxidation and synthesis and for the synthesis of cholesterol and phospholipids; it combines with acetate to form acetyl coenzyme A (active acetate), which in turn combines with oxaloacetate to form citrate and enter the tricarboxylic acid cycle.

COLLAGEN: group of fibrous proteins: resistant to digestive enzymes, prevalent in muscle from aged animals; become gelatin on acid or alkaline hydrolysis.

COLON: large intestine, distal to cecum and small intestine; contains a large population of anaerobic bacteria that ferment complex carbohydrates which may represent a significant energy contribution in some animals.

CONVULSION: an involuntary spasm or contraction of muscles.

COPPER (CU): trace mineral required for normal red blood cell formation, apparently by allowing normal iron metabolism, and as a component of several oxidases involved in normal wool and hair growth.

CORNEA: the clear, transparent membrane covering of the anterior part of the eye.

CORONARY ARTERIES: the large arteries that supply blood to the heart muscle.

CORPUS LUTEUM: a yellow mass formed in the ovary at the site of the ruptured ovarian follicle; if impregnation takes place, the corpus luteum grows and persists for several months; if impregnation does not take place, the corpus luteum shrinks and degenerates.

CREATINE: a nonprotein nitrogenous substance in muscle; it combines with phosphate to form phosphocreatine, which serves as a storage form of high energy phosphate required for muscle contraction.

CREATININE: a nitrogenous compound that is formed as a metabolic end product of creatine; creatinine is produced in the muscle, passes into the blood, and is excreted in the urine.

CRUDE FIBER: the insoluble carbohydrates remaining in a feed after boiling in acid and alkali during proximate analysis; this fraction represents the poorly digested part of a feed by animals.

CRUDE PROTEIN: the content of nitrogen in a feed or animal tissue or excreta, multiplied by a factor (usually 6.25, since most proteins contain about 16% N) to provide an estimate of protein content; both non-protein N (amino acids, amines, ammonia, etc.) and true protein may be present.

CUD: the solid mass of ingesta regurgitated and masticated in the process of rumination.

CYANOCABALAMIN (B_{12}): water soluble vitamin required as a coenzyme in several enzymes including isomerases, dehydrases, and enzymes involved in methionine biosynthesis.

CYSTINE: a sulfur-containing, nonessential amino acid that occurs notably in keratin and insulin; in the diet, it exerts a sparing effect on methionine.

CYTOCHROMES: hemoproteins that contain iron in their structure; their principal biological function is electron and/or hydrogen transport.

CYTOSINE: one of four nitrogenous bases found in DNA.

DEAMINATION: removal of the amino group from a compound.

DEGRADATION: conversion of a chemical compound to one that is less complex.

DEHYDROGENASE: any of a class of enzymes found in plant and animal tissues that catalyze oxidation by the transference of hydrogen ions to hydrogen acceptors.

DEOXYRIBONUCLEIC ACID (DNA): a large complex molecule in the cell nucleus that carries the code of genetic information; it is composed of the (nitrogen-containing) bases: adenine, thymine, cytosine, and guanine, each of which is attached to a pentose (deoxyribose) and to a phosphate.

DIABETES MELLITUS: a disease characterized by elevated blood sugar (hyperglycemia), sugar in the urine (glycosuria), excessive urination (polyuria), increased appetite (polyphagia), and general weakness.

DIET: a regulated selection or mixture of feedstuffs or foodstuffs provided on a continuous or prescribed schedule; a balanced diet supplies all nutrients needed for normal health and productive functions.

DIGESTIBILITY, APPARENT: that percentage of a feed nutrient that is apparently digested and absorbed from the gastrointestinal tract as indicated by intake minus fecal output of the nutrient; differs from true digestibility in that feces contain endogenously derived as well as feed derived nutrients so that true digestibility must be estimated indirectly by feeding a diet devoid of the nutrient of concern.

DIGESTIBILITY, TRUE: see apparent digestibility.

DISACCHARIDE: dimer of simple sugars: sucrose (common cane or beet sugar) yields glucose and fructose.

DIURESIS: excretion of urine; commonly denotes production of unusually large volumes of urine.

DIURETIC: a substance that promotes the excretion of urine; diuretic drugs are used chiefly to rid the body of excess fluid.

DRY MATTER: that portion of a feed or tissue remaining after water is removed, usually expressed as a percent.

DUODENUM: upper part of small intestine into which emptys the secretions of the exocrine pancreas and liver bile.

EDEMA: an abnormal accumulation of fluid in the intercellular spaces of the body.

ELASTIN: group of fibrous proteins; similar to collagen but not converted to gelatin; a major constituent of tendons and cartilage.

ELECTROLYTE: any substance that, when in solution dissociates into charged particles (ions) capable of conducting an electrical current.

EMACIATION: excessive leanness; a wasted condition of the body.

ENDEMIC: a disease of low morbidity that persists over a long period of time in a certain region.

ENDOCRINE: pertains to internal secretions; endocrine glands are those that produce one or more internal secretions (hormones) that enter directly into the blood and affect metabolic processes.

ENDOGENOUS: produced within or caused by factors within the organism.

ENTEROCRININ: hormone secreted by jejunal cells; release perhaps stimulated by food digestion products; stimulates secretion of intestinal fluids and enzymes.

ENTEROGASTRONE: hormone secreted by duodenal cells; release stimulated by fat and fatty acids and bile in lumen of duodenum; inhibits gastric secretion and motility.

ENZYME: a protein formed in plant or animal cells that acts as an organic catalyst in initiating or speeding up specific chemical reactions.

EPINEPHRINE: adrenal medulla hormone that stimulates autonomic nerve action; increases heart rate, perspiration.

ERGOSTEROL: a sterol found chiefly in plant tissues; on exposure to ultraviolet irradiation, it becomes vitamin D.

ERUCTATION: belching of gas by ruminants as a normal means of expelling products of fermentation such as carbon dioxide and methane.

ERYTHROCYTE: red blood cell.

ERYTHROPOIESIS: formation of erythrocytes.

ESOPHAGEAL GROOVE: a muscular structure at the lower end of the esophagus which, when closed, forms a tube from the esophagus to the omasum; functions in suckling animals to allow milk to by-pass the reticulorumen and escape bacterial fermentation.

ESTROGENS: ovarian steroid hormones responsible for promoting estrus and the development and maintenance of secondary sex characteristics; estriol, $C_{18}H_{24}O_3$, and estrone, $C_{18}H_{22}O_2$, are two important estrogens.

ETHER EXTRACT: the fraction of a feed or animal tissue that is soluble in a fat solvent such as ethyl ether and removed by extraction during proximate analysis.

EXOGENOUS: originating outside or caused by factors outside the body.

FATTY ACIDS: organic acids, composed of carbon, hydrogen, and oxygen, which combine with glycerol to form fat.

FECES: excretory product of undigested feed residues plus endogenously produced digestive secretions, sloughed cells of the intestinal lining and metabolites reexcreted into the intestinal lumen in the bile from the liver.

FEED: food for animals.

FEEDSTUFF: any substance suitable for animal feed; several feedstuffs are normally combined to provide a balanced diet.

FERRITIN: form in which iron is stored in the body; it is an iron-protein complex made up of iron and the protein apoferritin.

FISTULA: an abnormal passage from an abscess, cavity, or hollow organ to the surface or from one abscess, cavity, or organ to another.

FLUORINE (F): trace mineral required for protection against dental caries.

FLUOROSIS (DENTAL): a mottled discoloration of the enamel of the teeth due to chronic ingestion of excessive amounts of fluorine.

FOLACIN (FOLIC ACID): water soluble vitamin required as a cofactor in a variety of metabolic reactions involving incorporation of single C units into large molecules.

FOLIC ACID: see folacin.

FOOD: any material, usually of plant or animal origin, containing essential nutrients.

FOODSTUFF: any substance suitable for food; several foodstuffs are normally combined to provide a balanced diet.

FORTIFICATION: the addition of one or more nutrients to a food in amounts so that the total amount will be larger than that contained in any natural (unprocessed) food of its class, for example, the fortification of fruit juices with vitamin C; the FDA has not established standards for fortification.

GALACTOSEMIA: the accumulation of galactose in the blood due to a genetic lack of the enzyme galactose-1-phosphate uridyl transferase, which is necessary for the conversion of galactose to glucose; it is characterized by vomiting and diarrhea, abdominal distension, enlargement of the liver, and mental retardation.

GASTRIN: hormone secreted by intestinal cells near pyloris; release stimulated by distension and movement of stomach; stimulates acid secretion by gastric glands in stomach.

GLOBULIN: group of globular proteins; alpha, beta, and gamma globulins are major constituents of blood serum protein.

GLOSSITIS: inflammation of the tongue.

GLUCAGON: a compound secreted by the alpha cells of the islets of Langerhans that is hyperglycemic (produces a rise in the blood glucose concentration), glycogenolytic (hydrolyzes glycogen to glucose), and stimulates gluconeogenesis.

GLUCONEOGENESIS (GLYCONEOGENESIS): the formation of glucose from noncarbohydrate sources, chiefly certain amino acids and the glycerol portion of the fat molecule.

GLUCOSE TOLERANCE TEST: a test indicating the efficiency of the body in its use of glucose; changes are noted in the concentration of glucose in the blood at determined intervals after ingestion of a standard amount of sugar.

GLUTELINS: group of globular proteins.

GLYCERIDE: a compound (ester) formed by the combination of glycerol and fatty acids and the loss of water (the ester linkage); according to the number of ester linkages, the compound is a mono-, di-, or triglyceride.

GLYCEROL (GLYCERIN): the 3-carbon atom alcohol derived from the hydrolysis of fat.

GLYCOGENESIS: the formation of glycogen from glucose.

GLYCOLYSIS: the conversion of glucose to lactic acid in various tissues, notably muscle; since molecular oxygen is not consumed in the process, it is referred to as "anaerobic glycolysis."

GOITRIN: the antithyroid, or goitrogenic, compound obtained from turnips and the seeds of cruciferous plants.

GRAM (G): a metric unit of weight that is equivalent to about 1/28 of an ounce (1 oz = 28.4 g), 1/1000 of a kilogram, or 1000 milligrams.

GROWTH HORMONE: see somatrotropin.

GUANINE: one of four nitrogenous bases found in DNA.

HEMATOCRIT: the volume percentage of erythrocytes in whole blood; it is determined by centrifuging a blood sample to separate the cellular elements from the plasma; the results of the test indicate the ratio of cell volume to plasma volume and are expressed as cubic millimeters of packed cells per 100 ml of blood.

HEMATOPOIESIS: the production of various types of blood cells and blood platelets.

HEME: the nonprotein, insoluble pigment portion of the hemoglobin molecule; the prosthetic group of the hemoglobin molecule.

HEMODILUTION: an increase in the fluid content of the blood, resulting in the diminution of the proportion of formed elements (red and white blood cells and platelets).

HIGH-ENERGY BONDS (ENERGY-RICH BONDS): the pyrophosphate bonds; on hydrolysis they yield a standard free energy near -8000 Kcal per molecule, whereas simple phosphate bonds on hydrolysis yield only -1000 to -4000 Kcal of standard free energy.

HISTONES: group of globular proteins.

HOMEOSTASIS: the tendency of the body to maintain uniformity or stability in its internal environment or fluid matrix.

HOMEOTHERMAL (HOMOTHERMAL): warm-blooded animals.

HORMONE: a secretion produced in the body (chiefly by the endocrine glands) that is carried in the bloodstream to other parts of the body; each hormone has a specific effect on cells, tissues, and organs.

HUNGER: desire for food; the antithesis of satiety.

HYDROGENATION: the addition of hydrogen to a compound, especially to an unsaturated fat or fatty acid, adding hydrogen at the double bond will solidify soft fats or oils.

HYDROLYSIS: a chemical process whereby a compound is broken down into simpler units with the uptake of water.

HYPOGLYCEMIA: a condition characterized by a lower than normal level of glucose in the blood.

HYPOMAGNESEMIA: an abnormally low magnesium content of the blood plasma.

HYPOTHALAMUS: a portion of the brain, lying beneath the thalamus at the base of the cerebrum, and forming the floor and part of the walls of the third ventricle; it contains centers for temperature regulation, appetite control, and others.

ILEUM: lower part of small intestine, distal to the jejunem and proximal to the large intestine; absorption of most nutrients occurs in jejunem and ileum.

IMMUNOGLOBULIN (IG): serum globulin having antibody activity; most of the antibody activity appears to be in the gamma fraction of globulin.

INORGANIC: compounds that do not contain carbon.

INSULIN: a hormone secreted by the beta cells of the islets of Langerhans of the pancreas; it facilitates glucose oxidation, as well as the synthesis of glycogen, fat, and protein.

INTERSTITIAL: relates to spaces in any structure, such as tissue.

INTESTINAL PEPTIDASE: a group of poly-, tri-, and dipeptide digestive enzymes secreted by epithelial cells in the small intestine.

INTOLERANCE: an allergy or sensitivity, for example, to certain foods or medicines.

INTRINSIC FACTOR: a transferase enzyme (mucoprotein) secreted by the mucosal cells of the stomach which is required for the absorption of vitamin B-12 through the intestinal wall; a lack of this factor will produce pernicious anemia.

IODINE (I): trace mineral required as a constituent of thyroxine.

IRON (FE): trace mineral required for hemoglobin and myoglobin formation as a constituent of several heme enzymes and of several nonheme metalloenzymes.

ISOMER: a compound having the same percentage composition and molecular weight as another compound but differing in chemical or physical properties; for example L (levorotary) amino acids are biologically active but D (dextrorotary) amino acids generally are not (see also racemic mixture).

ISOTOPE: one of two or more atoms, the nuclei of which have the same number of protons but different numbers of neutrons; for example ^{14}N and ^{15}N are both stable isotopes of nitrogen.

JEJUNEM: middle segment of small intestine, distal to the duodenum and proximal to the ileum; absorption of most nutrients occurs in jejunem and ileum.

JOULE (J): a unit of energy that is equal to 0.0002 Kcal.

KCAL: kilocalorie.

KERATIN: group of fibrous proteins; resistant to digestive enzyme; major constituent of skin, hooves, horns.

KREBS CYCLE: see citric acid cycle.

KETOGENIC: that which is conducive to the formation of ketone bodies, such as a high-fat, low-carbohydrate diet.

α-KETOGLUTARIC ACID: a compound that is common to the metabolic pathways of carbohydrates, fats, and certain amino acids.

KETONE: a chemical compound that contains the carbonyl group (CO); ketone bodies include beta-hydroxybutyric acid, acetoacetic acid, and acetone.

KILOCALORIE (KCAL): the quantity of heat required to raise the temperature of 1 kg of water 1°C (or, more precisely, from 15°C to 16°C).

KILOGRAM (KG): a metric unit of weight that is equivalent to 2.2 pounds, or 1000 grams.

KWASHIORKOR: a disease of infants and young children, due primarily to protein deficiency; it is characterized by edema, "pot belly," and pigmentation changes of skin and hair.

LACTIC ACID: a compound formed in the body during anaerobic glycolysis; it is also produced in milk by the bacterial fermentation of lactose.

LECITHIN: the traditional term for phosphatidyl choline.

LEUCINE: an essential amino acid.

LIGAMENT: a band or sheet of fibrous tissue connecting two or more bones, cartilages, or other structures, or serving as a support for muscles.

LIGNIN: biologically unavailable mixture of polymers of phenolic acids; it is a major structural component of mature plants and of trees; its presence affects the bioavailability of cellulose and hemicellulose in plants.

LINOLEIC ACID: the essential fatty acid; it is unsaturated; and occurs widely in plant glycerides.

LIPIDS: substances that are diverse in chemical nature but soluble in fat solvents (such as ethanol, ether, chloroform, benzene); lipids include fats and oils; phospholipids, glycolipids, and lipoproteins; fatty acids, alcohols (glycerol, sterols [including vitamin D and vitamin A], and carotenoids).

LIVER: a large internal organ of the body, which lies in the upper right section of the abdomen directly beneath the diaphragm. Among other things, it produces bile, glycogen, antibodies; interconverts proteins, carbohydrates, and fats; stores iron, copper, vitamins A and D; and detoxifies harmful substances.

LYMPH: a fluid that circulates within the lymphatic vessels and is eventually added to the venous blood circulation; it arises from tissue fluid and from intestinal absorption of fatty acids; it is colorless, odorless, slightly alkaline, and slightly opalescent.

LYMPHATIC SYSTEM: all of the vessels and structures that carry lymph from the tissues to the blood.

LYSINE: an essential amino acid.

MALNUTRITION: an over-all term for poor nourishment; it may be due to an inadequate diet or to some defect in metabolism that prevents the body from using the nutrients properly.

MAGNESIUM (MG): mineral required as a constituent of bone, for oxidative phosphorylation of mitochondria of cells, activation of numerous energy related enzymes.

MANGANESE (MN): trace mineral required for formation of chondroitin sulfate and as a component of metalloenzymes and as a cofactor in several enzymes.

MARASMUS: extreme emaciation due to insufficient food.

MEGALOBLAST: a large, nucleated, embryonic type of cell; it is found in the blood in cases of pernicious anemia, vitamin B-12 deficiency, and folacin deficiency.

METABOLIC POOL: the total amount of a specific substance in the body that is in a state of active turnover, such as the amino acid pool or vitamin D pool; subtractions from and additions to the pool are constantly being made.

METABOLIC SIZE: the body weight raised to the three-fourths power ($W^{3/4}$).

METABOLITE: any compound produced during metabolism.

METALLOENZYME: an enzyme containing a metal (ion) as an integral part of its active structure.

METHANE: a major product (CH_4) of anaerobic fermentation of carbohydrates in the rumen; its loss through eructation represents a significant reduction in available dietary energy to the ruminant.

METHIONINE: a sulfur-containing essential amino acid.

MICROGRAM (μG): a metric unit of weight that is equivalent to one-millionth of a gram or 1/1,000 milligram.

MICELLE: an aggregate of molecules of lipids and bile acids formed in the lumen of the gastro-intestinal tract during preparation of dietary lipids for absorption.

MILLIGRAM (MG): a metric unit of weight that is equivalent to 1/1,000 gram or 1000 micrograms.

MILLILITER (ML): a metric unit of liquid measure that is equivalent to 1/1,000 liter.

MILLIMETER (MM): a metric unit of length that is equivalent to 1/10 centimeter.

MISCARRIAGE: the spontaneous expulsion of the product of conception early in pregnancy.

MITOCHONDRIA: the largest organelles in the cytoplasm; the cell mitochondria contain important enzymatic, oxidative, and respiratory systems.

MOLECULAR WEIGHT: the weight of a molecule of a chemical compound as compared with the weight of an atom of hydrogen; it is equal to the sum of the weights of the constituent atoms.

MOLYBDENUM (MO): trace mineral required as a constituent of the metalloenzyme, xanthine oxidase.

MONOGASTRIC: simple stomach; the term often used for simple stomached (non-ruminant) animals; technically a misnomer, since ruminants have only one stomach with four compartments.

MONOSACCHARIDE: simple sugar of 5 (pentoses) or 6 (hexoses) C atoms; glucose is a prime example.

MUCIN: secretions containing mucopolysaccharides.

MUCOPOLYSACCHARIDE: a complex of protein and polysaccharides.

MUCOPROTEIN: a complex of protein and oligosaccharides (yield on hydrolysis: two to ten monosaccharides).

NDF: neutral detergent fiber, the fraction of a feedstuff analyzed by the Van Soest scheme of detergent analysis, containing mostly cell wall constituents of low biological availability.

NECROSIS: death of a cell or group of cells due to irreversible damage.

NEPHRITIS: inflammation of the glomeruli of the kidney causing impairment of the filtering process so that blood and albumin are excreted.

NEURITIS: inflammation of the peripheral nerves (which link the brain and spinal cord with the muscles, skin, organs, and other parts of the body).

NFE (NITROGEN FREE EXTRACT): consists primarily of readily available carbohydrates such as sugars and starches, but may contain hemicellulose and lignin; NFE is calculated by difference during proximate analysis by subtracting all measured components from 100.

NIACIN (NICOTINIC ACID): water soluble vitamin required as a constituent of coenzymes, nicotinamide adenine dinucleotide (NAD), and nicotinimide adenine dinucleotide phosphate (NADP); (another form of the vitamin is nicotinamide).

NICOTINAMIDE ADENINE DINUCLEOTIDE (NAD) (FORMERLY CALLED DIPHOSPHOPYRIDINE NUCLEOTIDE [DPN]): attached as a prosthetic group to a protein, it serves as a respiratory enzyme (part of an oxidative-reduction system, converting substrates to CO_2 and H_2O and the transfer of electrons removed to oxygen).

NICOTINAMIDE ADENINE DINUCLEOTIDE PHOSPHATE (NADP) (FORMERLY TRIPHOSPHOPYRIDINE NUCLEOTIDE [TPN]): a coenzyme that participates in oxidation-reduction processes.

NICOTINIC ACID: see niacin.

NITROGEN FREE EXTRACT: see NFE

NOREPINEPHRINE: hormone secreted by sympathetic nerve endings: it is a vasoconstrictor.

NUCLEIC ACID: complex, high molecular weight molecules that contain phosphate, ribose, and four bases—adenine, guanine, cytosine, and thymine; DNA and RNA, which are nucleic acids, are responsible for inherited characteristics.

NUCLEOPROTEIN: a complex of protein and nucleic acid.

NUCLEOTIDE: a combination of purine and pyrimidine bases, 5-carbon atom sugar, and phosphoric acid; a hydrolytic product of nucleic acid; a constituent of the coenzymes NAD and NADP.

NUCLEUS: typically the largest structure within cells; it contains DNA, RNA, and usually a distinct body—the nucleolus.

NUTRIENT: a chemical substance that nourishes, such as protein, carbohydrate, mineral, or vitamin.

OBESITY: the accumulation of body fat beyond the amount needed for good health.

OLEIC ACID: an 18-carbon fatty acid that contains one double bond; it is found in animal and vegetable fat.

OMASUM: third compartment of ruminant stomach; aids in reducing particle size of ingesta and is site of some nutrient absorption.

ORNITHINE CYCLE: see urea cycle.

OSMOSIS: the passage of a solvent through a membrane separating two solutions from the solution of lesser concentration to that of greater concentration.

OSTEOMALACIA: adult rickets; a softening of the bones caused by a vitamin D deficiency in adults.

OSTEOPOROSIS: a reduction in the normal quantity of bone.

OXIDATION: the increase of positive charges on an atom or loss of negative charges; oxidation is one of the changes that take place when fats become rancid.

OXYGEN (O): a gaseous element that combines with other elements to form oxides.

PALMITIC ACID: a saturated fatty acid with 16-carbon atoms; it is common in fats and oils.

PANCREAS: organ located in the abdominal cavity whose functions are both endocrine and exocrine; that is, its specialized cells produce the hormones insulin and glucagon for control of energy and protein metabolism and other cells produce several digestive enzymes for food digestion.

PANCREATIC DUCT: tube carrying pancreatic secretions, including lipases, amylase, chymotrypsin, and trypsin, from pancreas to duodenal lumen.

PANCREOZYMIN: hormone secreted by duodenal cells; release stimulated by acid and nutrients in lumen of duodenum; stimulates pancreatic secretion of enzymes.

PANTOTHENIC ACID: water soluble vitamin required as a constituent of coenzyme A, needed for acetylation of numerous compounds in energy metabolism.

PARTURITION: the birth of offspring.

PHENYLKETONURIA (PKU): an affliction characterized by mental retardation that is caused by the congenital lack of the enzyme required to convert phenylalanine to tyrosine; phenylpyruvic acid and other phenyl compounds are excreted in the urine.

PHOSPHORUS (P): mineral required as a structural component of the skeleton, as a component of phospholipids which are imortant in lipid metabolism and cell membrane structure and as a component of ATP, creatine phosphate and other essential compounds in energy metabolism.

PHOTOSYNTHESIS: process by which chlorophyll-containing cells in green plants convert sunlight to chemical energy and synthesize glucose from carbon-dioxide and water and release oxygen.

PHOSPHOCREATINE: a creatine-phosphoric acid compound that occurs in muscle; the energy source in muscle contraction.

PHOSPHOLIPIDS: fat-like substances consisting of glycerol, two fatty acids, a phosphate group, and a nitrogen-containing compound, such as choline (found in the phospholipid lechithin).

PHOSPHORYLATION: the addition of phosphate to an organic compound (such as glucose) to form glucose monophosphate.

PHYTIC ACID (INOSITOLHEXAPHOSPHORIC ACID): a phosphorus-containing organic acid; phytin is the mixed salt of phytic acid with calcium and magnesium.

PLACENTA: vascular specialized tissue associated with the uterus during pregnancy and through which the fetus is nourished.

PLAQUE: a patch or flat area; in atherosclerosis, a deposit of predominantly fatty material in the lining of the blood vessels.

PLASMA: the fluid portion of the blood in which corpuscles are suspended; serum is plasma from which the fibrinogen has been removed.

POLYNEURITIS: an inflammation encompassing many peripheral nerves.

POLYUNSATURATED FATTY ACIDS: fatty acids containing two or more double bonds, such as linoleic, linolenic,and arachidonic acids.

POLYURIA: excessive excretion of urine.

POTABLE WATER: water fit to drink.

POTASSIUM (K): mineral required for maintenance of acid-base balance, for activation of several enzymes, for normal tissue protein synthesis, integrity of heart and kidney muscle and for a normal electrocardiogram; it is located mostly within cells.

PROGESTERONE: ovarian steroid hormone produced by corpus luteum; required for maintenance of pregnancy.

PROLAMINS: a group of globular proteins.

PROTAMINES: group of globular proteins.

PROTEIN-BOUND IODINE (PBI): the binding of almost all thyroxine in the blood to protein (PBI); the measure of the amount of PBI is useful as an indicator of the quantity of circulating iodine.

PROXIMATE ANALYSIS: a combination of analytical procedures used to quantify the protein, lipid, dry matter, ash and carbohydrate (nitrogen free extract) content of feed, animal tissues or excreta.

PTH (PARATHYROID HORMONE): hormone secreted by the parathyroid gland; maintains blood plasma calcium homeostasis by promoting calcium resorption from bone in hypocalcemia.

PURINE: the parent substance of the purine bases; adenine and guanine are the major purine bases of nucleic acids; other important purines are xanthine and uric acid.

PYLORIS: muscular sphincter separating stomach from duodenum, which controls rate of movement of ingesta out of stomach.

PYRIDOXINE (B_6): water soluble vitamin required as a coenzyme in a large array of enzymes associated with protein and nitrogen metabolism (other forms of the vitamin are pyridoxamine and pyridoxal).

PYRIMIDINE: the parent substance of several nitrogenous compounds found in nucleic acids—uracil, thymine, and cytosine.

PYRUVIC ACID: a keto acid of 3-carbon atoms; it is formed of carbohydrate in aerobic metabolism; pyruvate is the salt or ester of pyruvic acid.

RADIOACTIVE: the emission of particles during the disintegration of the nuclei of radioactive elements; the emissions include alpha particles, beta particles, and gamma rays.

RADIOISOTOPE: a radioactive form of an element; the nucleus of a stable atom when charged by bombarding particles (in a nuclear reactor) becomes radioactive and is called "labeled" or "tagged."

REDUCTION: the gain of one or more electrons by an ion or compound; for example, ferric iron (Fe^{+++}), which is the common form that is found in food, is reduced to ferrous iron (Fe^{++}) in the acid medium of the stomach.

RACEMIC MIXTURE: pertaining to a chemical compound containing equal amounts of dextrorotary (D) and levorotary (L) isomers so that it does not rotate the plane of polarized light.

RATION: a fixed portion of feed, usually expressed as the amount of a diet allowed daily.

RECTUM: distal portion of gastro-intestinal tract, joined proximally to the colon and opening to the exterior via the anus.

RENNET (RENNIN): a partially purified milk-curdling enzyme that is obtained from the glandular layer of the stomach of the calf.

RETICULAR GROOVE: see esophageal groove.

RETICULUM: closely associated with the rumen of ruminant animals; functions in moving ingesta with the rumen or omasum and in regurgitation of ingesta during rumination.

RIBOFLAVIN (B_2): water soluble vitamin required as a constituent of coenzymes, flavin adenine dinucleotide (FAD) and falvin mononucleotide (FMN).

RIBONUCLEIC ACID (RNA): a nucleic acid found in all living cells; on hydrolysis it yields adenine, guanine, cytosine, uracil, ribose, and phosphoric acid; it takes part in protein synthesis.

RIBOSOME: a ribonucleic acid-containing particle in the cytoplasm of a cell; the site of protein synthesis.

RUMEN: largest compartment of a ruminant stomach, containing enormous populations of anaerobic microorganisms capable of degrading complex carbohydrates and synthesizing amino acids and vitamins from inorganic constituents to provide nutrients for the host animal.

RUMINATION: process in ruminants whereby semi-liquid ingesta is regurgitated into the esophagus, remasticated by the animal and reswallowed for further digestion.

SATIETY: the condition of being fully satisfied with food; the antithesis of hunger.

SECRETION: hormone secreted by duodenal cells; release stimulated by acid and nutrients in lumen of duodenum; stimulates pancreatic secretion of water and electrolytes.

SEDIMENTATION: the settling out of a precipitate.

ERYTHROCYTE SEDIMENTATION RATE (ESR): the rate at which erythrocytes settle out of un-clotted blood; inflammatory processes cause an aggregation (clumping together) of the red blood cells which makes them heavier and more likely to fall.

SELENIUM (SE): trace mineral required as a constituent of the enzyme glutathione peroxidase which destroys peroxides arising from tissue lipid oxidation.

SERUM: the clear portion of any fluid from an animal's body that remains after the solid elements have been separated out; blood serum is the clear, straw-colored liquid that remains after blood has clotted; the plasma from which fibrinogen has been removed.

SILICON (SI): trace mineral required for initiation of the mineralization process in bones.

SODIUM (NA): mineral required for maintenance of acid-base balance, transfer of nerve impulses and as an extracellular component of an energy dependent sodium "pump"; it is located mostly in extracellular fluids.

SOMATOTROPIN: anterior pituitary hormone active in promoting protein and mineral accretion in animals and stimulating animal growth.

SPHINGOMYELIN: a group of phospholipids found in the brain, spinal cord, and kidney; on hydrolysis it yields phosphoric acid, choline, sphingosine and a fatty acid.

SPLEEN: a large organ situated under the ribs in the upper left side of the abdomen; it functions in the normal destruction of old red blood cells.

SPRUE: a chronic disease caused by the imperfect absorption of nutrients (especially fats) from the small intestine.

STARCH: polymer of glucose readily hydrolyzed by digestive enzymes.

STEARIC ACID: a saturated fatty acid composed of 18-carbon atoms.

STEROL: an alcohol of high molecular weight, such as cholesterol and ergosterol.

STILLBIRTH: birth of a dead fetus.

STOMACH: the first portion of the gastro-intestinal tract on which chemical action occurs on ingested feeds in most animal species; in humans, pigs and many other species it is a single compartment (simple stomach); in ruminants such as cattle, sheep, goats, deer; it contains several compartments.

SULFUR (S): mineral required as a constituent of several organic metabolites, including methionine, cystine, thiamin, biotin, coenzyme A and mucopolysaccharides.

TASTE: to distinguish flavors between or among feed or water components.

TESTOSTERONE: testicular steroid hormone; stimulates sperm production and controls secondary sex characteristics and accessory reproductive organs; increases muscle protein accretion.

TETANY: a condition characterized by sharp bending (flexion) of the wrist and ankle joints, muscle twitchings, cramps, and convulsions; inadequate calcium in the blood causes irritability of the nerves and muscles so that they respond to a stimulus with greater sensitivity and force than normally.

TETRAIODOTHYRONINE: thyroid hormone active in regulation of basal metabolic rate (BMR); chemical formula is $C_{15}H_{11}I_4NO_4$.

THIAMIN (B_1): water soluble vitamin required as a constituent of the enzymes cocarboxylase and lipothiamide.

THYMINE: one of four nitrogenous bases found in DNA.

THREONINE: an essential amino acid.

THYMINE: one of the four nitrogenous bases in nucleic acid.

THYMUS GLAND: a two-lobed ductless gland located behind the upper part of the sternum and extending into the neck; it is fairly large in young animals but usually shrinks in adulthood; it is structured like a lymph node and contains lymphatic follicles; it may play a role in immune reactions.

THYROXINE: an iodine-containing hormone that is produced by the thyroid gland; it is a derivative of the amino acid tyrosine and has the chemical name tetraiodothyronine.

TRANSFERRIN (SIDEROPHILIN): an iron-binding protein in the blood that transports iron.

TRANSKETOLASE: an enzyme that uses thiamin pyrophosphate as a coenzyme; it brings about the transfer of a 2-carbon unit from one sugar (a 2-keto sugar) to aldoses (monosaccharides with the characteristic aldehydr group [—CHO]).

TRICARBOXYLIC ACID CYCLE (KREBS' CYCLE AND CITRIC ACID CYCLE): a series of biochemical reactions by which carbon chains of sugars, fatty acids, and amino acids are metabolized to yield carbon dioxide, water, and energy.

TRIGLYCERIDE (FAT): an ester composed of glycerol and three fatty acids.

TRISTEARIN: a triglyceride of stearic acid.

TRYPTOPHAN: an esssential amino acid; a precursor of niacin.

TRYPSIN: a proteolytic digestive enzyme secreted by the pancreas; its precursor trypsonogen is activated to trypsin by enterokinase.

TYROSINE: a nonessential amino acid; it spares the essential amino acid phenylalanine.

UNDERNUTRITION: a condition resulting from insufficient food.

UREA: the chief end product of protein metabolism in mammals and one of the chief nitrogenous constituents in the urine.

UREA CYCLE: major pathway of nitrogen excretion in mammals.

URIC ACID: a nitrogenous end product of purine metabolism; it is present in the blood and excreted in the urine.

VALINE: an essential amino acid.

VASOCONSTRICTOR: an agent (motor nerve or chemical compound) that acts to decrease the caliber of blood vessels.

VITAMIN A: fat soluble vitamin required for normal night vision, normal epithelial cells and normal bone growth and remodelling.

VITAMIN B_1: see thiamin.

VITAMIN B_2: see riboflavin.

VITAMIN B_6: see pyridoxine.

VITAMIN B_{12}: see cyanocobalamin.

VITAMIN D: fat soluble vitamin required for normal absorption of calcium from the intestinal tract as a precursor of 1,25 dihydroxy-cholecaliferol which acts in the control of mobilization of calcium from bone and stimulation of calcium absorption from the gastro-intestinal tract.

VITAMIN E: fat soluble vitamin required as an antioxidant in preventing a wide variety of diseases relating to maintaining integrity of cellular membranes.

VITAMIN K: fat soluble vitamin required for normal blood clotting, specifically for synthesis of prothrombin in liver.

XANTHURENIC ACID: a metabolite of tryptophan; it is found in normal urine, but appears in increased amounts in cases of vitamin B-6 deficiency.

XEROSIS: abnormal dryness, as of the conjunctiva (xerophthalmia) or skin (xeroderma).

ZINC (ZN): trace mineral required as a constituent of an array of enzyme systems in several body tissues, as an activator of several metalloenzymes and in binding reactants to the active site of enzymes.

Index

457